Financial Crises in Emerging Markets

Recent financial crises, beginning with Mexico in 1994–1995, the Asian crisis of 1997–1998, and the crises in Russia and Brazil in 1998–1999, illustrate the risks of financial volatility and macroeconomic instability during the process of economic growth and development. They also raise issues regarding the management of risks associated with liberalization and global integration, particularly in financial markets. Some have argued that emerging markets have been the innocent victims of mercurial global investors, whereas others have questioned the appropriateness of specific policies in the emerging markets themselves. The essays in this volume provide analysis and evidence on the determinants of these currency and banking crises in emerging markets, the specific roles of capital flows and the financial sector, and the appropriateness of various policy responses.

Reuven Glick is Vice President in charge of the International Studies Section of the Economic Research Department at the Federal Reserve Bank of San Francisco and Director of the Bank's Center for Pacific Basin Monetary and Economic Studies. Prior to joining the Bank staff, Dr. Glick was a professor in the departments of economics and international business in the Graduate School of Business at New York University. Dr. Glick is the author of journal articles and other professional writings. In addition, he edited *Managing Capital Flows and Exchange Rates: Perspectives from the Pacific Basin* (Cambridge University Press, 1998) and coedited (with Michael Hutchison) *Exchange Rate Policy and Interdependence: Perspectives from the Pacific Basin* (Cambridge University Press, 1994).

Ramon Moreno is Senior Economist, International Studies, and Associate Director of the Center for Pacific Monetary and Economic Studies at the Federal Reserve Bank of San Francisco. Prior to joining the Bank, he served with the United Nations Development Programme in New York and Latin America. Dr. Moreno is the author of academic and other professional articles in international economics.

Mark M. Spiegel is Research Officer, International Studies, Economic Research Department, Federal Reserve Bank of San Francisco. Dr. Spiegel was formerly an assistant professor in the department of economics of New York University. He is the author of academic and other professional articles in the field of international finance. He has also served as a consultant to the World Bank and visiting professor in the department of economics at the University of California, Berkeley.

Financial Crises in Emerging Markets

Edited by

REUVEN GLICK

Federal Reserve Bank of San Francisco

RAMON MORENO

Federal Reserve Bank of San Francisco

MARK M. SPIEGEL

Federal Reserve Bank of San Francisco

CAMBRIDGE
UNIVERSITY PRESS

CAMBRIDGE UNIVERSITY PRESS
Cambridge, New York, Melbourne, Madrid, Cape Town, Singapore,
São Paulo, Delhi, Dubai, Tokyo, Mexico City

Cambridge University Press
The Edinburgh Building, Cambridge CB2 8RU, UK

Published in the United States of America by Cambridge University Press, New York

www.cambridge.org
Information on this title: www.cambridge.org/9780521172189

First published 2001
First paperback edition 2010

A catalogue record for this publication is available from the British Library

Library of Congress Cataloguing in Publication data

Financial crises in emerging markets / edited by Reuven Glick,
Ramon Moreno, Mark M. Spiegel.
p. cm.
Essays originally prepared for a conference sponsored by the Center for
Pacific Basin Monetary and Economic Studies at the Federal Reserve Bank of
San Francisco on Sept. 23–24, 1999.
1. Financial crises – Case studies. 2. Business cycles – Case studies.
1. Glick, Reuven. 11. Moreno, Ramon. 111. Spiegel, Mark Maury, 1960– 1v.
Center for Pacific Basin Monetary and Economic Studies.
HB3722 .F544 2001 332 – dc21 00-58584

ISBN 978-0-521-80020-4 Hardback
ISBN 978-0-521-17218-9 Paperback

Contents

Preface

The essays in this volume provide a comprehensive analysis by distinguished economists of the theoretical and policy issues associated with recent financial crises in emerging markets. These essays are complemented by the comments of an equally distinguished set of discussants. The essays were originally prepared for a conference sponsored by the Center for Pacific Basin Monetary and Economic Studies at the Federal Reserve Bank of San Francisco on September 23–24, 1999. The conference brought together academics, central bankers, and other policymakers and researchers to review and compare the experiences of emerging market countries.

The conference was conceived with two purposes. First, it served as a natural sequel to a prior conference held at the Bank in September 1996, after the Mexican peso crisis of 1994–1995. The 1996 conference focused primarily on understanding the causes and policy responses to capital inflows and explaining why countries in Asia seemed different from Mexico and less vulnerable to currency and banking crises. At the time it appeared that East Asian countries had achieved a more successful approach to capital flow and exchange rate management. Since then, we have learned (or have been reminded) that all countries, even fast-growing Asian economies, can experience financial crises.

A second purpose of the conference was to carry on the Bank's Pacific Basin research program. Since 1974, the program has promoted cooperation among central banks in the Pacific Basin and sponsored research on major monetary and economic policy issues in the region. The Center for Pacific Basin Monetary and Economic Studies was established by the Bank in 1990 to open the program to greater participation by visiting scholars. The program was also augmented by the creation of a formal network of researchers in other central banks, universities, research institutes, and international organizations who share the Bank's recognition of the importance of Pacific Basin economic issues.

The Pacific Basin research agenda has been supported through the contributions of the Bank's own research staff as well as through international conferences. This work has been published in the Bank's *Economic Review*, academic journals, and conference volumes. Previously published conference volumes include: *Financial Policy and Reform in Pacific Basin Countries* (Lexington Books, 1986) and *Monetary Policy in Pacific Basin Countries* (Kluwer Press, 1988), both edited by Hang-Sheng Cheng; *Exchange Rate Policy and Interdependence: Perspectives from the Pacific Basin*, edited by Reuven Glick and Michael Hutchison (Cambridge University Press, 1994); and *Managing Capital Flows and Exchange Rates: Perspectives from the Pacific Basin*, edited by Reuven Glick (Cambridge University Press, 1998).

This book is the joint product of many people. Besides the contributing authors and discussants, special thanks are due to Regina Paleski and Robert Golden, for their work as production editor and copy editor, respectively; and Chrystie Nguyen, for her key role in organizing the conference, handling correspondence with the authors, and typing portions of the manuscript.

Finally, any opinions expressed in this volume are those of the respective contributors and do not necessarily reflect the views of the organizations with which they are associated. Nor do they reflect the views of the Federal Reserve Bank of San Francisco or of the Board of Governors of the Federal Reserve System.

Reuven Glick
Ramon Moreno
Mark M. Spiegel

Contributors

Pierre-Richard Agénor
World Bank

Joshua Aizenman
Dartmouth College and NBER

Henning Bohn
University of California, Santa Barbara

Roberto Chang
Federal Reserve Bank of Atlanta

Menzie D. Chinn
University of California, Santa Cruz

Stijn Claessens
World Bank

Robert Dekle
University of Southern California

Simeon Djankov
World Bank

Michael P. Dooley
University of California, Santa Cruz

Hali J. Edison
Board of Governors of the Federal Reserve System

ix

Kristin Forbes
Massachusetts Institute of Technology

Reuven Glick
Federal Reserve Bank of San Francisco

David Gould
Institute of International Finance

Cheng Hsiao
University of Southern California

Michael M. Hutchison
University of California, Santa Cruz

Steven Kamin
Board of Governors of the Federal Reserve System

Kenneth Kasa
Federal Reserve Bank of San Francisco

Kenneth M. Kletzer
University of California, Santa Cruz

Richard K. Lyons
University of California, Berkeley

Nancy Marion
Dartmouth College

Paul R. Masson
International Monetary Fund

Ramon Moreno
Federal Reserve Bank of San Francisco

Tatiana Nenova
Harvard University

Maurice Obstfeld
University of California, Berkeley

Paolo Pesenti
Federal Reserve Bank of New York and NBER

Assaf Razin
Stanford University and Tel-Aviv University

Carmen M. Reinhart
University of Maryland, College Park, and NBER

Andrew K. Rose
University of California, Berkeley, CEPR, and NBER

Efraim Sadka
Tel-Aviv University

Inseok Shin
Korea Development Institute

Mark M. Spiegel
Federal Reserve Bank of San Francisco

Siyan Wang
University of Southern California

Chi-Wa Yuen
University of Hong Kong

1

Financial Crises in Emerging Markets:

An Introductory Overview

Reuven Glick, Ramon Moreno, and Mark M. Spiegel

1.1 INTRODUCTION

Increasing openness and economic liberalization have been credited with fostering higher growth and record capital inflows in many emerging market countries. For many countries, especially in Asia but to some extent also in Latin America, the first part of the 1990s was characterized by considerable optimism and buoyant growth. However, this optimism has been tempered by recent financial crises, beginning with Mexico in 1994–1995, the Asian crisis of 1997–1998, and the crises in Russia, Brazil, and several other Latin American countries in 1998–1999. These crises have been costly to varying degrees – particularly where banking sector problems have been involved – both in terms of lost output and the fiscal expenditures to restore fragile financial sectors.

The recent crises illustrate the risks of financial volatility and macroeconomic instability during the process of economic growth and development. They also raise issues regarding the management of risks associated with liberalization and global integration, particularly in financial markets. Concerns about the implications of international capital flows for developing countries have grown with the sharply increased volume of these flows since the late 1980s. Some have argued that emerging markets have been the innocent victims of mercurial global investors, while others have questioned the appropriateness of specific polices in the emerging markets themselves.

The essays in this volume provide a comprehensive analysis of the theoretical and policy issues associated with recent financial crises in emerging markets. To provide a broad perspective, this chapter presents an overview of the common elements of these crises and the issues they have raised, as well as an analytical summary of the essays themselves.

1

1.2 COMMON ELEMENTS OF FINANCIAL CRISES

Recent financial crises in emerging markets share several features: (1) They occurred after extensive liberalization, particularly in financial markets, (2) they were preceded by significant capital inflow surges that subsequently ceased abruptly, (3) at the time of the crises, relatively rigid nominal exchange rate regimes tended to be in place, (4) unhedged foreign currency and interest rate exposure was high, and (5) the crises tended to be widespread, involving a number of countries simultaneously.

1.2.1 Liberalization and Global Integration

In recent years, economic reform, liberalization, and global integration have been key elements of the development strategy of almost all developing countries. During the late 1980s and early 1990s, most Latin America countries – particularly Mexico, Chile, and Argentina – undertook ambitious reforms aimed at modernizing their economies.[1] Although the details varied across countries, stabilization programs and fiscal consolidation were implemented to reduce inflation. Deregulation and privatization were undertaken to reduce the importance of the government in the economy, and product markets were generally opened to greater international competition. In addition, domestic financial markets were liberalized, with credit controls and lending restrictions removed, access to international financial markets improved, and the permissible activities of domestic financial institutions expanded. For example, over the period 1990–1992, Mexico privatized the 18 banks that had been nationalized in 1982–1983 during the debt crisis.

The Asian growth "miracle" over the past thirty years was largely the result of liberalization and opening of real sectors across the region. In contrast, Asian financial sectors were relatively less developed, with domestic credit often channeled through the banking sector to particular privileged domestic sectors and firms, though usually in accordance with export-promoting industrial policy. Beginning in the 1980s, financial markets were liberalized gradually across the region, first by allowing more market-oriented adjustment of interest rates and allocation of credit, and later by permitting domestic financial institutions greater freedom in asset and liability management. In Indonesia, for example, the number of private banks nearly tripled from 1988 to 1994. In

---

[1] Prior reform and liberalization efforts during the 1970s were largely aborted as a result of the 1982–83 debt crisis.

Thailand, credit expansion by commercial banks was limited by regulation, but financial liberalization in the 1990s led to the emergence of non-bank intermediaries that were largely unregulated.

At the beginning of the 1990s, policies towards international capital flows in East Asian emerging markets ranged from quite open (Hong Kong, Singapore) to significantly regulated (Korea). Measures adopted in the late 1980s and early 1990s to liberalize the capital account or develop offshore markets encouraged greater integration with global financial markets. However, existing restrictions or market conditions still limited foreign entry into onshore markets as well as direct access to domestic securities issuers or non-bank borrowers. This approach to financial market development ensured that domestic financial institutions would continue to play a significant intermediation role, and in some cases it encouraged the accumulation of short-term debt.

In Thailand, innovations fostering greater capital market integration included the establishment in 1993 of the Bangkok International Banking Facility (BIBF), which encouraged short-term borrowing and lending in foreign currencies, both onshore and offshore. Strong tax incentives were given to foreign banks, particularly from Japan, to lend at low rates to Thai institutions through the BIBF. Foreign banks participated actively in the BIBF, but restrictions to direct entry in the onshore market remained in place, so a significant amount of foreign borrowing was intermediated through domestic financial institutions. In Korea, regulations limiting corporate borrowing or bond issuance abroad also encouraged short-term international borrowing through the domestic financial system. The accession of Korea to the Organization for Economic Co-operation and Development (OECD) in 1996 made lending to Korean banks even more attractive, by lowering the perceived risk and providing regulatory advantages for some forms of credit. (The risk weights under the Basle accord fell to 20 percent from 100 percent for long-term loans, but were unchanged at 20 percent for loans up to one year maturity.)

Some efforts were at times made to contain short-term inflows, but these policies did not consistently reduce the vulnerability of domestic financial sectors to shocks. For example, in the early 1990s, Indonesia imposed ceilings on foreign borrowing (particularly on short-term inflows) by the banking sector. At the same time, however, Indonesian corporations were given greater freedom to borrow abroad for purposes of trade financing. In addition, the extent of foreign borrowing by these corporations was typically unhedged and apparently not effectively monitored; this borrowing was a major element in Indonesia's 1997 financial crisis.

1.2.2 Capital Inflows and Reversals

The Mexican and Asian crises were preceded by substantial capital inflows to developing countries. Total net private capital inflows to developing countries rose from an annual average of $9 billion over the period 1983–1989 to an average of $125 billion during 1990–1994 and peaked at $212 billion in 1996 (see Table 1.1). These capital inflows reflected a number of factors, including the search for higher yields on the part of international investors in an environment of low interest rates in industrial countries, strong macroeconomic and structural reform policies in many emerging markets, and capital account opening.

The bulk of net private capital flows to emerging markets went to Asia and Latin America. Capital flows to East Asia averaged $17 billion per year in the period 1983–1989, and rose to $95 billion in 1995 and $101 billion in 1996. In Latin America, resolution of the debt crisis of the early 1980s resulted in a shift from capital outflows averaging $17 billion a year during 1983–1989 to net inflows of $41 billion annually over 1990–1994. The inflows subsided to $38 billion in 1995, and then rebounded to $87 billion in 1997. The composition of the flows to these two regions differed, however. Inflows into Mexico and other Latin American countries were dominated by portfolio flows. In contrast, flows to Asia were dominated by bank lending flows.

When the crises broke out, sharp cutbacks in short-term financing occurred and access to international capital markets by many emerging countries was sharply curtailed. Capital flows to Latin America were abruptly reversed during the peso crisis in 1994–95. In Mexico portfolio flows fell from a peak inflow of $23 billion in 1993 to a net outflow of $14 billion in 1995 – a reversal of $37 billion. Flows to emerging Asia markets fell even more sharply as a result of crises in that region in 1997. For the most affected Asian countries – Thailand, Malaysia, the Philippines, Indonesia, and Korea – net inflows of $73 billion in 1996 were replaced by net outflows of $11 billion in 1997, largely as a result of a reversal of bank lending. Net capital inflows to emerging markets fell further in 1998, with much of the contraction occurring after Russia's forced debt restructuring, virtual default, and devaluation of August 1998.

1.2.3 Nominal Exchange Rate Rigidity and Unhedged Exposure

Nominal exchange rate pegs of one form or another were in place in almost every country that experienced financial difficulties. In the late 1980s a number of Latin American countries adopted exchange rate-based inflation stabilization programs, relying on the exchange rate as a

Table 1.1. Net Private Capital Flows to Emerging Markets

	1977–1982	1983–1989	1990–1994	1995	1996	1997	1998
			Annual Averages (US$ billion)				
By Asset:							
Total private capital flows	30.5	8.8	125.1	193.3	212.1	149.2	64.3
Net FDI	11.2	13.3	44.9	96.7	115.0	140.0	131.0
Net portfolio investment	–10.5	6.5	64.9	41.2	80.8	66.8	36.7
Bank loans and other	29.8	–11.0	15.2	55.4	16.3	–57.6	–103.5
By Region and Asset:							
Asia							
Total private capital flows	15.8	16.7	39.1	95.1	100.5	3.2	–55.1
Net FDI	2.7	5.2	23.4	49.8	55.1	62.6	50.0
Net portfolio investment	0.6	1.4	7.4	10.9	12.6	0.9	–15.4
Bank loans and other	12.5	10.1	8.3	34.4	32.8	–60.3	–89.7
Latin America							
Total private capital flows	26.3	–16.6	40.8	38.3	82.0	87.3	69.0
Net FDI	5.3	4.4	13.8	26.0	39.3	50.6	54.0
Net portfolio investment	1.6	–1.2	36.9	1.7	40.0	39.7	33.0
Bank loans and other	19.4	–19.8	–9.9	10.6	2.7	–3.1	–18.1
Other							
Total private capital flows	–11.6	8.7	45.2	59.9	29.7	58.7	50.4
Net FDI	3.2	3.7	7.8	20.9	20.6	26.7	27.2
Net portfolio investment	–12.7	6.3	20.6	28.7	28.3	26.2	19.1
Bank loans and other	–2.1	–1.3	16.8	10.3	–19.2	5.8	4.2

Sources: IMF *International Capital Markets,* 1995 for 1977–1989 data; IMF *International Capital Markets,* 1999 for 1990s data.

5

nominal anchor. Mexico's Pacto Plan involved initially fixing the peso against the dollar in October 1988, followed by a (gradual) preannounced depreciation within a band. Argentina's Convertibility Plan fixed its exchange rate to the dollar in April 1991. Brazil's Real Plan set a ceiling on the exchange rate relative to the dollar beginning in July 1994. Chile adopted a crawling peg regime in the mid-1980s. Although the stated exchange rate regimes of East Asian economies varied widely, ranging from unilateral pegs to the U.S. dollar (Hong Kong since 1983), to fixed or adjustable pegs to a currency basket (Indonesia, Malaysia, and Singapore; Korea until 1990; and Thailand since 1984), to managed floats (Korea since 1990), policymakers in almost all of these economies have tended to limit adjustment of their currencies against the U.S. dollar.

Investor confidence in the stability of these exchange rate pegs encouraged borrowers in emerging markets to take advantage of lower foreign interest rates through foreign borrowing without hedging foreign currency or interest rate risk. For example, in 1994 to refinance their domestic government debt cheaply and signal a commitment to their exchange rate policy, the Mexican authorities shifted from issuing peso-denominated debt to U.S.-dollar indexed short-term securities, known as *tesobonos*. The result was a massive increase in the government's foreign currency exposure. Foreign exchange risk exposure also played a key role in the Asian crisis, as both Asian banks and firms borrowed extensively in foreign currency.

Exposure to exchange rate risk was particularly troubling for commercial banks. As a legacy of financial liberalization, banks were particularly able to capitalize on interest rate differentials through foreign borrowing and domestic lending. However, the degree of exchange risk stemming from foreign borrowing by banks was commonly exacerbated by "maturity mismatching" – that is, financing long-term investment with short-term foreign liabilities. This exposed banks to the risk of having to refinance their short-term liabilities in the event of declines in the value of underlying assets.

1.2.4 Spillovers and Contagion

Recent crises were also accompanied by widespread spillover and contagion effects across countries. In the aftermath of the Mexican peso crisis that began in December 1994, the larger Latin American countries experienced varying degrees of volatility in their foreign exchange markets and declines in their equity markets. Argentina, though it successfully maintained its currency peg, suffered substantial costs in its defending its currency by keeping interest rates high. Asian currencies came under attack in mid-January 1995, and securities markets in some countries experienced sharp declines. After the floating of the Thai baht in July 1997 and the (unsuccessful) attack on the Hong Kong dollar in October 1997, financial disturbances spread elsewhere in East Asia. While the effects of the Asia crisis were felt mainly in the region, the Russian default in August 1998 was accompanied by even more widespread turbulence.[2] Bond spreads rose globally, and the access to foreign capital of emerging markets in all regions was severely curtailed.

1.3 DEBATE ABOUT WHAT WENT WRONG

Emerging market crises have spawned several controversies about their origin and spread as well as the appropriate policy response. Much of the current debate about the origin and spread of recent crises concerns whether they were caused by weak domestic economic fundamentals or by financial panic unrelated to economic conditions. While the two views are not mutually exclusive, their policy implications vary greatly. If a panic unrelated to fundamentals was the main impulse for the financial crises in emerging markets, reforms in macroeconomic or financial sector policy are not necessary in planning recovery. If, however, policy mistakes or other fundamentals were the most important contributors to the crises, reforms are indeed essential.

1.3.1 Theoretical Explanations of Crises

Several theoretical explanations of financial crises have been offered. One set of explanations of currency crises, termed first-generation models (e.g., Krugman, 1979), directs attention to inconsistencies between government policy commitments and domestic economic fundamentals. For example, excessive monetary expansion to monetize fiscal deficits can deplete the central bank's foreign exchange reserves and weaken its ability to defend a peg. An alternative set of explanations of currency crises, termed second-generation models (e.g., Obstfeld, 1994), relies on the idea that governments weigh the benefits against the costs of defending the exchange rate, which in certain circumstances may imply more than one equilibrium for the exchange rate.

In Obstfeld's model, a government can maintain a stable exchange rate as long as it perceives that the benefits of devaluing are smaller than

---

[2] The impact of the Asia crisis on Eurobond spreads was greatest in Asia, with spreads rising in 1997 to as high as 1000 basis points in Indonesia and Korea. After the Russian default in 1998, interest rate spreads in some Latin American and Asian countries rose above 1500 basis points – a level not witnessed since the period during the Mexican crisis of 1994–95.

the costs. However, shifts in market expectations can alter the government's calculations, resulting in a devaluation. For example, if the market for some reason believes that the government is going to devalue the exchange rate, then market participants would expect higher inflation and higher wages demands. The competitiveness of the economy would fall, and unemployment would rise, which may prompt the government to devalue. Thus, a shift in expectations can lead to an exchange rate crisis and devaluation that otherwise might not have occurred. Countries can then be subject to "self-fulfilling" crises in which a loss of confidence without any change in economic fundamentals compels a shift in government policy that validates investors' pessimism. However, fundamentals can also enter the picture, although in a way that differs from first-generation models. As market speculators initiate attacks based on their beliefs about the willingness of policymakers to resist pressure on the exchange rate, conditions that compromise the central bank's willingness to defend a currency peg, such as high unemployment or a weak banking system, may trigger speculative attacks.

Domestic bank runs and debt crises can be viewed as analogous forms of self-fulfilling financial crises in the presence of multiple equilibria. Even well-managed banks or financial intermediaries are vulnerable to runs, because they traditionally engage in maturity transformation, accepting deposits with short maturities to finance loans with longer maturities (Diamond and Dybvig, 1983). Under normal conditions, banks have no problem managing their portfolios to meet expected withdrawals with liquid funds. However, if all depositors decided to withdraw their funds from a given bank at the same time, as in the case of a run, the bank would not have enough liquid assets to meet its obligations. In this manner, a bank which would be financially solvent in the absence of a run may experience illiquidity in the presence of a run, validating the expectations of the depositors who withdrew their funds. Analogously, a debt crisis can arise if foreign creditors spontaneously refuse to roll over the existing stock of debt and the borrower has insufficient international liquidity with which to pay off the debt.

Closer integration with world financial markets can increase an economy's vulnerability to liquidity-related bank and debt crises. First, the presence of short-term foreign borrowing makes the domestic financial sector more vulnerable to a decision by foreign lenders not to roll over the existing stock of debt. In that sense, short-term foreign debt increases financial sector fragility. Second, vulnerability is greater if the central bank seeks to peg the exchange rate, since simultaneously maintaining stability of the financial system and targeting the exchange rate can be incompatible policy objectives. On the one hand, if a central bank chooses to combat a domestic bank crisis by acting as lender of last resort and/or by lowering interest rates, the potential for a run on the domestic currency can be exacerbated if residents turn around and sell the injected domestic funds for foreign exchange reserves. On the other hand, the bank crisis may go on unabated if the central bank limits liquidity injections in order to maintain the pegged external value of the currency. This interrelation implies that it may be difficult to distinguish whether a financial crisis originates in a run on domestic banks or on the domestic currency. As a result, currency and bank crises can appear to occur simultaneously (Dooley, 2000; Chang and Velasco, 1998a). Third, closer integration may lead foreign investors to downgrade more rapidly their assessments of one country in the wake of adverse news about another.

1.3.2 Mexico, Asia, and Other Recent Crises

In the aftermath of the Mexican peso crisis of 1994–1995, observers debated whether Mexico experienced a "death foretold" by evident disequilibria phenomena such as an overvalued real exchange rate and an unsustainable current account, or a "sudden death" caused by an unforeseen speculative panic by international investors. This debate, which has extended to the East Asian currency crises, was motivated by the fact that these crises were not easily predictable by traditional first-generation crisis models.

Indeed, one striking feature of the crises of the 1990s is that the commonly monitored macroeconomic fundamentals were sound. Mexico's fiscal policy was conservative, inflation had been under control for several years, and market interest rates preceding the crisis of December 1994 did not appear to indicate an expected devaluation of the peso.[3] Neither was there any evidence of "bad" government behavior in various macroeconomic indicators for East Asian economies in 1997. Growth rates were far superior to those in other emerging markets, inflation rates were moderate, and government budgets were in balance or showed surpluses. Generally declining bond spreads and high credit ratings during 1995 to mid-1997 provided little evidence of market pessimism prior to the Asian crises. Thus, purely on the basis of macroeconomic factors, it is difficult to argue that the Mexican or Asian economies were poised for the kind of turmoil they respectively experienced in 1994–1995 and 1997–1998.

Based on this evidence, some observers have argued that the Mexican and East Asian crises were not the result of fundamentals, but were

---

[3] The interest rate differential between dollar-denominated *tesobonos* and U.S. Treasury bills was relatively constant before the crisis, indicating no increase in market risk premium for holding Mexican assets.

largely unexpected and reflected self-fulfilling panics by foreign investors. (Sachs, Tornell, and Velasco [1996a, 1996c] make the case for Mexico, while Radelet and Sachs [1998] and Chang and Velasco [1998b] argue the case for East Asia.) In this view, these crises need not have occurred: If foreign lenders had not panicked, financial systems would not have experienced credit interruptions, and the resulting costly economic disruptions, justifying the pessimistic expectations, would have been avoided.[4]

In contrast, other observers attribute Mexico's and East Asia's "fall from grace" as largely the result of their own policy mistakes. In Mexico's case, some point to excessive private spending and overvaluation of the real exchange rate (Dornbusch and Werner, 1994), while others argue that the crisis was foretold by an inappropriate policy response to a decline in demand for Mexican assets following upward U.S. interest rate movements and adverse Mexican political developments in 1994 (Calvo and Mendoza, 1996). To avoid raising domestic interest rates while also limiting depreciation of the peso, Mexican authorities sought to sterilize the foreign exchange losses following the asset demand decline by increasing domestic credit. This policy stance was unsustainable and spawned the crisis.

Why did Mexico adopt such a stance? One possible reason, apart from a sluggish economy, was a weak banking system, which made the crawling peg exchange rate regime too costly to defend. Mexican banks suffered from poor asset quality and insufficient liquidity, and they had already experienced a sharp increase in past-due loans prior to 1994. This spurred efforts by the Mexican government to maintain domestic interest rates at relatively low levels, in part by the expansion of domestic credit, but also by the issuance of increasingly large amounts of dollar-indexed securities (*tesobonos*) to finance government debt.

In Asia, as in Mexico, there were some indications of increasing vulnerability in the period prior to the 1997–1998 crises provided by the large and growing current account deficits, slowing exports, and real appreciation of currencies in the region. Nevertheless, to most observers these indicators, though suggestive of needed policy corrections, were not regarded as signs of the depth of the crisis that eventually affected Asia. To explain the magnitude of the Asian crisis in the absence of obvious imbalances in conventional macroeconomic fundamentals, others have

---

[4] It cannot be ruled out that domestic residents as well as foreign residents participated in such runs. For example, there is evidence that domestic Asian residents, rather than foreign creditors, put the most selling pressure on Asian currencies in 1997 (Cooper, 1999).

emphasized the weaknesses and distortions in financial systems in the region (McKinnon and Pill, 1998; Corsetti, Pesenti, and Roubini, 1998, 1999a).

From this perspective, the Asian financial crisis was the legacy of bad lending and investment practices that were fostered by an environment of relationship lending, disincentives to fully monitor risk, and inadequate supervision and regulation of domestic financial institutions during the lending boom of the 1990s. Credit tended to flow to borrowers with relationships to government or private bank owners and to favored sectors, rather than on the basis of projected cash flows and risk assessment. Implicit and explicit guarantees exacerbated risk-taking incentives.[5] These financial distortions in turn led to a buildup of domestic debt and foreign borrowing and increasingly fragile East Asian financial systems. While some improvements in prudential supervision and regulation were undertaken in Asian economies in the first half of the 1990s, in most countries supervisory systems were limited in their ability to monitor effectively the quality of bank portfolios and the extent to which banks would abide by existing rules and regulations. Consequently, weakening balance sheets of both financial institutions and firms, which had been masked by the high growth rates of earlier years, became more exposed to movements in interest rates, exchange rates, and other asset values.[6] Rising interest rates and declining real estate and equity prices prior to the crisis put further stress on banking systems. When the currency pegs collapsed and foreign capital withdrew, the large stock of unhedged foreign-denominated borrowing made the crisis more severe than it would otherwise have been.

There has been much less debate about the underlying determinants of the August 1998 crisis in Russia and January 1999 crisis in Brazil. With large fiscal deficits, rigid nominal exchange rates, and overvalued exchange rates, both countries were obvious candidates for attacks. A key factor in Russia's case has been the chronic inability of the tax system to provide an essential minimum level of government revenue. Russia also had significant shortcomings in its banking and financial markets, as well as in its system of corporate governance. Nevertheless, the timing of these attacks suggests some contribution of investor panic, coming as they did on the heels of Asian difficulties.

---

[5] Corsetti, Pesenti, and Roubini (1999b) and Burnside, Eichenbaum, and Rebelo (1998) attribute collapsing East Asian currencies to the prospective monetization of expected fiscal deficits stemming from implicit government guarantees to bail out the financial sector.

[6] The role of financial sector balance sheets in explaining vulnerability to currency crises was first emphasized by Calvo (1998).

Ultimately, the two alternative views of the causes of the crisis – fundamentals versus investor panic – are not inconsistent with each other. On the one hand, weak macro and/or financial fundamentals contribute to vulnerability to liquidity and/or speculative crises. On the other hand, a crisis triggered by fundamentals may eventually lead to market over-reaction and conditions similar to a panic that magnify the overall severity of the crisis.

1.3.3 Contagion and Spillovers

Another interesting characteristic of recent international crises has been their rapid spread from one country to another. There are a variety of explanations for this "contagion" phenomenon. First, contagion can be the result of common external shocks, with simultaneous crises triggered by a change in the external environment, such as a rise in international interest rates. Second, crises can spread through trade and financial linkages. For example, in the presence of nominal rigidities, countries which devalue may gain at the expense of their trading competitors (Gerlach and Smets, 1995; Glick and Rose, 1999a, 1999b). These competitors are therefore less likely to resist attacks and thus more likely to be attacked themselves. Portfolio rebalancing by investors or common bank lenders in response to developments in one country may affect other countries' access to funds (Van Rijckeghem and Weder, 1999). For example, investors that have suffered losses on leveraged portfolios may have to sell other assets to meet collateral requirements and/or other portfolio targets.

Within Asia, for example, the impairment of Korean bank claims on Southeast Asian emerging markets after the Thai crisis contributed to a weakening of the liquidity position of Korean financial institutions and their ability to cope with credit withdrawals by international banks. Financial linkages also help explain the emergence of pressures in Brazil and Russia following the spread of the crisis to Korea in late October 1997, because Korean banks sold some of their holdings of Brazilian Brady bonds and Russian debt. In the case of the Russia crisis, some highly leveraged financial institutions and hedge funds that had been important investors in Russian instruments suffered large losses as a result of the Russian debt default. Margin calls sharply increased the liquidity needs of these institutional investors, which they attempted to meet, in part, through a broad sell-off of emerging market securities. This created another channel of contagion from Russia to other emerging markets, particularly Brazil.

Another possibility is that attacks spread to other countries where macroeconomic and financial conditions are broadly similar, so that there is reason to suspect that the same underlying problems exist. In this view, developments in Thailand caused investors to look more critically at countries with "similar" fundamentals and financial weaknesses they had previously ignored, including appreciated real exchange rates, banking systems potentially exposed to nonperforming loan problems, and interest rate and currency risk (Sachs, Tornell, and Velasco, 1996b; Tornell, 1999). In the process, they discovered new information that amplified their concerns, especially about the health of the financial system and the magnitude of short-term foreign debt. Market doubts were compounded by the lack of transparency about the financial and corporate sectors and, thus, about the magnitude of contingent liabilities.

Finally, crises may spread for reasons that cannot be accounted for by fundamentals. Such "pure" contagion is usually attributed to "herd behavior" by investors. If investors lack complete information about the economic environment in which they invest, including the way borrowers use their funds and what their financial situations actually are, they may pay attention to the actions of other investors. Such herding behavior is most likely to occur if the behavior of individual investors is viewed as revealing important information about borrowers' creditworthiness (Calvo and Mendoza, 1999). Calvo (1999) interprets the extent of the global turbulence during the Russian crisis in this light. In particular, the severest capital losses on Russian bonds were experienced by foreign banks that were more leveraged and were also perceived to be more informed than other investors. The resulting margin calls from these losses created the need to sell off assets in other regions, including Latin America and Asia. These sales governed concern by others about the general wisdom of investing in individual countries in these regions, resulting in a global transmission of the crisis.

The widespread nature of crises may also reflect a general reassessment of the desirability of investing in certain markets. For example, Russia's decision to devalue and default on its debt (as well as the subsequent imposition of capital controls by Malaysia) shook international investors' confidence and increased their concern that other emerging markets might follow similar policies. This may have led to a sharp increase in international investors' aversion to risk – that is, a general decline in taste for risk without any necessary change in perceived default probabilities.

1.4 PLAN OF THE BOOK

The chapters in this volume provide a comprehensive analysis of the theoretical and policy issues associated with financial crises in emerging markets. They address four broad issues.

First, how prevalent have financial crises been in emerging markets and what have been their general determinants? Were the currency and banking problems driven by panicky foreign creditors? How vulnerable are countries to contagion effects from other emerging market countries? Three chapters in the volume look at this issue. Glick and Hutchison (Chapter 2) analyze the incidence and underlying causes of banking and currency crises in a data set of industrial and developing countries over the 1975–1997 period. The chapter by Paul Masson (Chapter 3) discusses the usefulness of multiple equilibria models for understanding volatility, crises, and contagion in international capital markets. Kristin Forbes (Chapter 4) analyzes the empirical significance of various channels of contagion during the Asian and Russian crises.

Second, what are the specific roles of capital flows and the financial sector in the occurrence of financial crises? What explains the volatile pattern of capital movements – a surge in capital flows, followed by abrupt capital flow reversals? Three chapters address this issue. Joshua Aizenman and Nancy Marion (Chapter 5) focus on how market uncertainty about the magnitude of foreign debt obligations explains the abrupt decrease in the supply of credit to Asian countries during the crisis period. Menzie Chinn and Kenneth Kletzer (Chapter 6) present a model of domestic bank lending and foreign borrowing and government guarantees to explain financial crises; they also present empirical evidence on capital flows and bank lending behavior in Asia. Michael Dooley and Inseok Shin (Chapter 7) interpret the experience of Korea in terms of a government guarantee (insurance) model of crises.

Third, how might financial, legal, and other structural characteristics have affected the long-run vulnerability of countries to crises? Two essays address this question from different perspectives. These chapters illustrate that looking at policy issues from a long-term standpoint can not only clarify short-term policy issues, but actually overturn some conclusions that might be made from observations of a short-term nature. Assaf Razin, Efraim Sadka, and Chi-Wa Yuen (Chapter 8) question whether the persistence of foreign direct investment flows (FDI) into emerging economies may represent overinvestment attributable to informational distortions distinct to FDI. Stijn Claessens, Simeon Djankov, and Tatiana Nenova (Chapter 9) look at the long-term relationship between a destination-country's legal and institutional environment and the financing patterns of corporations operating there. They provide evidence that firms in countries with less legal protection of shareholders rights display more risky financing behavior and lower rates of profitability.

Fourth, what are the appropriate policies to reduce the occurrence and severity of financial crises? During the Asian crisis, the relationship between exchange rates and interest rates had been a topic of substantial controversy. What is the appropriate response of monetary policy to a rapid exchange rate depreciation? One (conventional) view advocated by the IMF is that higher interest rates are necessary to appreciate or stabilize the exchange rate. An opposing view argues that during periods of crisis, high interest rates may cause a currency to depreciate further by weakening the economy and the banking system and hence raising the risk premium or the probability of default on credit.

Two chapters seek to resolve this issue empirically. The chapters by Robert Dekle, Cheng Hsiao, and Siyan Wang (Chapter 10) and David Gould and Steven Kamin (Chapter 11) both analyze whether high interest rates had the desired effect of appreciating the nominal exchange rates in the Asian crisis countries. The latter, after controlling for the role of perceived country creditworthiness, seek to identify the independent impact of changes in interest rates on the exchange rate. The former chapter also assesses whether there has been contagion, as measured by excess co-movement across countries in asset returns during crisis periods. Lastly, the chapter by Hali Edison and Carmen Reinhart (Chapter 12) examines the role of capital controls as a policy instrument during currency crises.

The following sections present an analytical discussion of the individual essays and related literature.

1.4.1 Part I: Determinants and Propagation of Financial Crises

The coincidence of banking and currency crises associated with the recent economic turmoil in Asia has drawn renewed attention to the interrelationship between these two phenomena. Banking and currency crises appeared to arise virtually at the same time in Thailand, Indonesia, Malaysia, and Korea in 1997–1998. In fact, the incidence of "twin" crises has been relatively widespread, occurring in such diverse parts of the world as Latin America in the early and mid-1980s and Scandinavia in the early 1990s.

Kaminsky and Reinhart (1999) provide evidence of the strong link between bank and currency crises for a small sample of emerging markets. Glick and Hutchison in "Banking and Currency Crises: How Common Are Twins?" (Chapter 2) pursue their analysis for a broader set of countries including industrial and developing countries. They begin with a review of various theoretical explanations for possible linkages between currency and banking crises, including the impact of banking sector weakness on monetary and exchange rate policy, the impact of foreign exchange speculation on bank balance sheets, and the simultaneous effects of common factors (e.g., liquidity bank runs or boom–bust lending cycles) on the domestic and foreign asset positions of financial institutions.

The bulk of the chapter is devoted to an empirical analysis of the incidence and underlying causes of banking and currency crises in a data set consisting of 90 industrial and developing countries over the 1975–97 period. They define banking crises as situations in which actual or potential bank runs or failures induce banks to suspend the convertibility of their liabilities or which compel the government to intervene. Currency crises are constructed from "large" (i.e., two standard deviation) changes in an index of currency pressure, defined as a weighted average of real exchange rate changes and reserve losses. The frequency of currency crises is found to be relatively constant over time, while the frequency of individual banking and twin crises each has increased. Developing and emerging market countries suffered both banking and currency crises more often than industrial countries.

Glick and Hutchison find that the twin crisis phenomenon is primarily concentrated in financially liberalized emerging-market economies. This strong linkage between currency and bank crises in emerging markets is robust to the use of various modeling techniques, including bivariate, multivariate, and simultaneous equation probit specifications, as well as the inclusion of macroeconomic and financial structure control variables. Their empirical analysis reveals that the probability of a currency crisis generally rises with greater real overvaluation, a lower ratio of foreign exchange reserves to monetary liabilities, and lower export growth. A decline in output growth and greater financial liberalization or inflation are each highly correlated with the onset of banking sector distress.

The chapter also finds that the occurrence of banking crises provides a good leading indicator of currency crises in emerging markets. The converse does not hold, however, because currency crises are not a useful leading indicator of the onset of future banking crises. Glick and Hutchison conjecture that emerging market's openness to international capital flows and their liberalized financial systems combine to make them particularly vulnerable to twin crises. Domestic financial liberalization permitted greater maturity mismatching between assets and liabilities and increased the potential for illiquidity problems. The finding of a strong link between banking and currency crises in these economies implies that measures to limit the exposure of balance sheets and enhance confidence in the banking sector may reduce the incentives for capital flight and currency runs.

The chapter by Paul Masson, "Multiple Equilibria, Contagion, and the Emerging Market Crises" (Chapter 3), discusses how models with multiple equilibria can explain some of the stylized facts associated with recent events in international financial markets, including the "excessive" volatility of financial markets prices relative to that of macroeconomic fundamentals and the contemporaneous nature of financial crises across countries. Masson's chapter surveys three types of models that imply the possibility of multiple equilibria in financial markets. In so-called macroeconomic feedback models, increased fears of a devaluation can compel policymakers to defend the peg by raising domestic interest rates, which in turn feed back on the economy adversely by raising unemployment or hurting the financial sector, making the likelihood of a self-fulfilling devaluation more probable. In liquidity and bank run models, crises can occur if individual lenders and other creditors fear that they will be left "holding the bag" because they think other depositors are with drawing their money. In asymmetric information models in which observing the actions of others gives some clues as to what they might know, herding behavior may occur as individual investors choose to imitate and follow each other. In all of these models, jumps from a "good" to a "bad" equilibrium can be triggered by changes in investor confidence, which may be unrelated to economic fundamentals.

Masson also argues that the tendency of financial crises in emerging markets to occur simultaneously does not appear explainable by some common cause (e.g., a change in U.S. interest rates) affecting all developing countries, nor to macroeconomic linkages among developing countries themselves (e.g., trade flows). He also doubts any significant role for (a) "wake-up call" effects, whereby a crisis in one country prompts reevaluation of the potential seriousness of problem fundamentals elsewhere, and (b) portfolio rebalancing effects by creditors, who, facing losses in one market, sell off assets in other markets in order to realize liquidity. Rather, he prefers to interpret contagion within the context of multiple equilibria models as jumps between equilibria triggered by an attack elsewhere.

The chapter summarizes evidence supportive of the multiple equilibria view, including the nonlinear relation between financial asset prices and macro fundamentals, the apparent role of changing political sentiment during successive phases of speculative attacks on the European Exchange Rate Mechanism (ERM) in 1992–1993, and the abrupt reversal of capital flows to emerging market countries.

Masson concludes with some implications of the multiple equilibria view for the prediction and prevention of crises: (1) Crises are difficult to predict, though it might still be possible to gauge a country's vulnerability by assessing the extent to which the relevant economic fundamentals are beyond certain norms; (2) if capital flows are unduly influenced by apparently arbitrary shifts in market expectations, then greater regulation and control of capital flows may be justified; (3)

correspondingly, as international capital flows diverge to a greater extent from their market fundamentals, slower capital account liberalization might be warranted; and (4) the appropriate response of international financial institutions depends on whether crises are motivated by liquidity runs, macro feedbacks, or herding behavior; though there may be no consensus on the cause of recent crises, the international monetary system needs to find ways to enhance the confidence of international creditors without exacerbating moral hazard.

The recent crises in emerging markets have focused attention not just on the determinants of speculative attacks but also on how and why these attacks have been so widespread. An assessment of the possible channels of transmission of financial crises is ultimately an empirical question. The Forbes chapter, "How Are Shocks Propagated Internationally? Firm-Level Evidence from the Russian and East Asian Crises" (Chapter 4), analyzes the empirical magnitude of various channels through which shocks to one country can be transmitted to the financial markets of other countries. The empirical analysis takes a unique approach to evaluating how shocks are propagated internationally. Rather than rely on aggregate, macroeconomic country-level data, it utilizes firm-level information from the Worldscope data set to evaluate the impact of the East Asian and Russian crises on individual companies' stock market returns in other countries. The data set consists of stock return and other detailed characteristics for over 12,000 companies in 46 countries.

Forbes considers five mechanisms by which a country-specific shock could be propagated to firms around the globe. These mechanisms include (a) declining competitiveness for firms exporting similar products (product competitiveness effect), (b) falling demand for foreign firms selling in the crisis countries (income effect), (c) increasing cost of credit for firms relying more heavily on short-term debt (credit crunch effect), (d) increased sales of high-liquidity corporate stocks in order to meet portfolio rebalancing needs of investors who suffered losses elsewhere (liquidity effect), and (e) the tendency for investors to reevaluate firms in the same region (wake-up call channel). To analyze the importance of these various propagation mechanisms during the Asian and Russian crises, Forbes uses an event-study methodology to compare stock market returns in the period after each crisis. Firms are differentiated according to their degree of product competitiveness with crisis countries, direct exposure to the crisis zone, dependence on short-term debt, stock trading liquidity, and geographic proximity to the crisis region.

Her empirical analysis suggests that the income effect, liquidity effect, and wake-up call effect were all important propagation mechanisms during the Russian crisis. Each of these effects, as well as the product competitiveness effect, was also significant during the East Asian crisis. Thus contagion appears to spread through a number of channels simultaneously. However, Forbes finds that the economic magnitudes of these different effects vary greatly. The wake-up call effect is found generally to have the largest impact. The product competitiveness effect during the Asian crisis, as well as the income effect during the Russian crisis, is also large in magnitude. Although the liquidity effect is consistently significant during both crises, the magnitude of this channel appears to be relatively small. The credit crunch appears to have played a relatively minor role in the international propagation of shocks during both crises. An important implication of these results is that the relative strength of the various transmission mechanisms varies across crises. As a result, it is unlikely that a single model can capture how shocks are propagated during all crises.

1.4.2 Part II: Capital Flows and Reversals

The Asian financial crisis has raised questions about the factors underlying the large surges in capital flows to emerging markets and the reasons for their abrupt reversals. "Uncertainty and the Disappearance of International Credit" (Chapter 5), by Joshua Aizenman and Nancy Marion, provides one explanation for the abrupt decrease in the supply of credit to Asian countries during the crisis period by focusing on the uncertainty about the magnitude of outstanding foreign debt obligations of these nations. The authors describe the dramatic buildup of foreign debt in Thailand and South Korea, and they note that at critical junctures both countries announced significant upward revisions in the magnitude of their external debts. For example, outstanding external debt as reported by the Bank of Thailand grew from $25 billion in 1990 to $80 billion by the end of 1996. The latter figure was subsequently revised upwards 26 percent to $91 billion. The pattern of buildup in South Korea was similar.

Aizenman and Marion present two theoretical models for understanding how increases in the level of a borrowing nation's outstanding debt could lead to sharp decreases in the supply of credit. They first examine the implications of changes in uncertainty about the magnitude of existing debt for the level of new lending to a debtor nation. They derive a two-period model of international lending, in which in the event of default the debtor pays a penalty equal to a constant fraction of (stochastic) second-period output, as is commonly assumed in the sovereign debt literature. The authors demonstrate that in this framework increased uncertainty about the magnitude of outstanding debt decreases the probability of debt repayment which in turn reduces the supply of credit to the debtor country. Moreover, they show that this relationship is nonlinear; that is, the reduction in debt supply resulting from a given increase in uncertainty is itself increasing in the level of uncertainty.

A collapse in foreign lending may be seen alternatively as analogous to the occurrence of extreme home bias by international lenders toward holding home assets rather than foreign assets in their portfolios. To explore this interpretation, Aizenman and Marion examine conditions which would escalate home bias. For this purpose they present a portfolio-balance model in which a representative investor, with a generalized expected utility function that assigns a higher weight to bad outcomes than good ones, demands a risk premium to induce him to invest abroad. This form of preferences has been shown in the literature to lead to home bias and potentially preclude diversification of a portfolio across all countries (Aizenman, 1999).

Using this model, the authors then demonstrate that if the risk-adjusted return on foreign assets is sufficiently low, then international diversification is undesirable. This contrasts with the result from a standard utility function that implies that an investor generally chooses to hold positive amounts of both domestic and foreign assets. They conclude that it is possible that increased uncertainty about investment prospects in Asia, perhaps due to an increase in expected debt obligations of these countries, may have reduced the expected return on assets in Asia, contributing to the observed collapse in foreign investment in the region.

The central role of the banking sector in recent crisis episodes is highlighted in Chinn and Kletzer's chapter, "International Capital Inflows, Domestic Financial Intermediation, and Financial Crises under Imperfect Information" (Chapter 6). Chinn and Kletzer introduce a dynamic model of lending under uncertainty in which bank lending patterns interact with foreign investment and changes in the credibility of government guarantees to create "twin crises" in financial and currency markets.

In the model, government bailout guarantees raise risk-taking and lending by banks. These increased lending levels are financed by increased capital inflows from abroad. However, the bailout guarantees offered by the government are only credible up to a finite level. When net liabilities of the banking system exhaust the maximum credible level of government bailout funds, the system is attacked by creditors, who remove their assets from the banking system. These banks are then bailed out by the government.

The timing of such a crisis is uncertain in the Chinn and Kletzer model. A crisis can occur at any time after the buildup of lending levels has reached a sufficient magnitude to make the crisis feasible. As a result, the model could be characterized as a so-called third-generation model, in which the capacity for a crisis is based on fundamentals, but the ultimate triggering of the crisis may be based on panic or contagion. The government's bailout of the banking system in the event of a banking crisis has implications for its budget position and, as a result, for its ability to defend an exchange rate peg. Thus, in addition to causing a run on the domestic banking system, the exhaustion of funds needed for the service of government liabilities also leads to a currency crisis, as in Burnside, Eichenbaum, and Rebelo (1998) and Dooley (2000).

Empirical evaluation of the model is impeded by the difficulty of acquiring data on several of the model's key variables, such as implicit government liabilities and loan quality. Still, an informal empirical analysis provides some qualitative support for the model. In particular, as the model would predict, it is shown that the countries that were hit hardest by the Asian crisis were also the countries that experienced the greatest rise in foreign borrowing prior to the crisis. The chapter also provides evidence that in most countries loan quality deteriorated prior to the crisis.

A key element of the model of Chinn and Kletzer is that financial crises are precipitated by government guarantees to the private sector. As such guarantees have been long in place in many emerging markets, the question arises as to what precipitated the occurrence of crises in the 1990s. Dooley (2000) emphasizes the role of recent financial liberalization programs as the trigger for the sequence of capital inflows and crises observed.[7] These programs lessened restrictions on domestic financial institutions, opened access to foreign lenders, and prompted foreign capital to flow into emerging markets to take advantage of guaranteed ("insured") investment opportunities.

The chapter by Michael Dooley and Inseok Shin, "Private Inflows when Crises Are Anticipated: A Case Study of Korea" (Chapter 7), interprets the recent crisis in Korea in the context of Dooley's model. The authors argue that financial liberalization in Korea initiated in the late 1980s was the fundamental factor behind the country's 1997–1998 crisis. In their view, Korea's liberalization reduced the franchise value of the domestic banking system, and exposed already very weak balance sheets to competitive pressures that promoted risk seeking. As a result, Korean banks became the major intermediaries of massive private capital inflows that totaled about $120 billion from 1992 through mid-1997, before the reversal of these flows in the second half of 1997 and throughout 1998.

---

[7] This point is supported by Glick and Hutchison's finding (Chapter 2, this volume) that bank crises are more prevalent in emerging markets with liberalized financial systems.

The empirical part of the chapter examines the behavior of banks, creditors, and the government in Korea following its financial liberalization. The authors provide evidence of increasingly risky behavior by Korean commercial banks in the mid-1990s, including greater holdings of variable-price securities relative to cash, loans, and deposits on their balance sheets (implying more price risk), more lending to smaller firms and borrowers without collateral (implying more credit risk), and more short-term foreign liabilities (implying more liquidity risk). In addition, Dooley and Shin contend that foreign creditors failed to monitor the individual creditworthiness of Korean banks, inasmuch as the relatively weak private commercial banks in Korea were not precluded from borrowing large amounts from abroad. This failure to monitor is interpreted as evidence that foreign banks expected to have preferred creditor status when the crisis occurred; that is, they expected to be bailed out. The fact that foreign banks were able to withdraw about $30 billion from Korean banks in 1998 suggests that this expectation was well founded, in the opinion of the authors. Lastly, Dooley and Shin argue that Korean regulatory authorities failed to manage adequately the risky behavior of commercial banks, since the regulatory staff were more accustomed to applying direct quantity controls than to evaluating microeconomic financial risk and monitoring individual banks. More critically they failed to monitor the consolidated balance sheets of commercial banks, allowing the foreign branches of Korean banks to take on uncontrolled levels of foreign debt and enhance the opportunities to exploit government insurance.

The analysis of Dooley and Shin suggests that countries should consider eliminating deposit insurance and other explicit government guarantees that attract capital inflows. However, they argue that most such guarantees are usually not explicit, and developing (as well as industrial) country policymakers will always face *ex post* pressures to bail out depositors. Another possible implication is that capital inflows involving domestic financial intermediaries should be restricted. However, they point out, the government would still face pressure to bail out nonfinancial firms who borrow from domestic banks. This suggests, in their view, that it may be difficult to remove a key ingredient in the occurrence of financial crises in emerging markets.

1.4.3 Part III: Institutional Factors and Financial Structure

Most of the analysis in this volume deals with short-term problems and solutions associated with currency and financial crises. The chapters by Razin, Sadka, and Yuen (Chapter 8) and by Claessens, Djankov, and Nenova (Chapter 9) take a relatively longer-term perspective about potential problems for emerging markets, arising from financial, legal, and other structural factors. These chapters illustrate that looking at policy issues from a long-term standpoint can not only clarify short-term policy issues, but can actually overturn some conclusions that might be made from observations of a short-term nature.

In "Excessive FDI Flows under Asymmetric Information" (Chapter 8), Assaf Razin, Efraim Sadka, and Chi-Wa Yuen directly confront one of the conventional wisdoms of global financial crises. It is commonly believed that some forms of foreign investment are more desirable to destination countries than others. In particular, foreign direct investments are sometimes characterized as "cold" capital flows, which prove resilient during financial crises, while foreign portfolio investments are characterized as "hot" capital flows, ready to turn tail and flee at the first sign of difficulty. While the empirical foundation for this stylized fact has been questioned (see Claessens, Dooley, and Warner, 1995), the policy implication usually derived from belief in this stylized fact is that "cold" capital flows should be actively encouraged by recipient-country governments. Limits on the movements of "hot" capital flows may also be in order.

While acknowledging the resilience of foreign direct investment (FDI) in recent financial crises, Razin et al. ask whether this resilience is necessarily desirable. They question whether the surge of FDI inflows into emerging economies during tranquil periods and their persistence during crises may represent overinvestment attributable to distortions distinct to FDI. In particular, they concentrate on the potential for a "lemons" situation to arise when information asymmetries between domestic and foreign investors are present, similar to those in Gordon and Bovenberg's (1996) analysis of portfolio investment.

While Gordon and Bovenberg argued for an information asymmetry favoring domestic investors, Razin et al. argue that foreign operators of a multinational subsidiary possess an inside-information advantage over potential domestic investors. As a result of this asymmetry, owners of multinational subsidiaries with above-average valuations are unwilling to sell off equity at prices offered by uninformed potential domestic buyers. The authors demonstrate that the resulting adverse selection problem can lead to overinvestment by foreign direct investors. Essentially, this information advantage enjoyed by multinational subsidiaries acts as a subsidy to foreign investment. The apparently desirable property of FDI flow resilience during crises, then, may in fact reflect a distortion in the secondary market for equity assets.

There is a widespread perception that capital flows to emerging markets in the 1990s financed excessively risky projects and encouraged greater corporate exposure to interest and exchange rate risk

(McKinnon and Pill, 1998; Corsetti, Pesenti, and Roubini, 1998, 1999a). This perception has generated considerable interest in the factors that influence corporations' exposure to risk, the structure of their financing, and the profitability of their investments. Stijn Claessens, Simeon Djankov, and Tatiana Nenova, in "Corporate Growth and Risk around the World" (Chapter 9), look at the long-term nature of international finance, focusing on how the pattern of corporate finance and risk is affected by institutional factors, such as the legal system and degree of protection of creditors' rights. They explore this issue using a sample of over 11,000 firms in 46 countries from the Worldscope dataset (the same data used by Kristen Forbes in Chapter 4).

Following the work of La Porta, Lopez-de-Silanes, Shleifer, and Vishny (1997, 1998), Claessens et al. distinguish between two types of legal systems: common law (which prevails in the United States, the United Kingdom, and its ex-colonies) and civil law (which prevails in continental Europe and their ex-colonies). They posit that corporations operating in civil law countries will exhibit more risky financing patterns. Civil law systems tend to provide weaker protection of property rights than do common law systems, and thereby lessen the ability of investors to limit risk taking by corporations. The authors also hypothesize that firms in countries with greater creditor rights will exhibit greater leverage, as they will enjoy easier debt terms.

Differences in legal system and property rights may also influence the importance of bank financing relative to other forms of financing. Bank-based systems are more likely to emerge in environments with less-developed property rights and laws, with bank-firm relationships in effect serving as substitutes for poorly developed capital markets by overcoming information problems associated with arms-length market transactions (Rajan and Zingales, 1999). In such economies, debt is used more extensively, leverage is likely to be higher, and higher measures of overall corporate risk should be observed. Accordingly, Claessens et al. hypothesize that the share of bank financing will be greater in firms from countries with less-developed property rights.

The authors' empirical results confirm that firms in countries with civil law and less creditor rights display more risky financing patterns and lower profitability. Specifically, they find that firms in countries with civil law and weak creditor rights display higher cash-flow variability, higher operating and financial leverage ratios, lower liquidity levels, and greater use of short-term finance, as well as lower rates of return on assets and equity. They also find that corporations in more bank-dominated financial systems display more risky financing patterns and lower profitability.

1.4.4 Part IV: Policy Responses

Currency crises in emerging markets have typically been accompanied by a sharp contraction in output. Economists offer at least three possible explanations for the close timing of depreciations and recessions. First, depreciations can reduce aggregate demand or aggregate supply (for example, by raising the price of imported inputs), thus reducing output (Agénor and Montiel, 1996). Second, depreciations may reflect external shocks, such as an increase in global interest rates that reduces the flow of capital to emerging markets (Calvo, Leiderman, and Reinhart, 1996) that have contractionary effects. Third, depreciations may be associated with domestic conditions, such as a weak financial sector or foreign currency exposure of the kind discussed earlier, that make an economy more vulnerable to adverse shocks. The contraction associated with depreciations may be particularly severe if panics or the sudden withdrawal of financing disrupt economic activity, and if there is a significant amount of foreign currency borrowing that bankrupts domestic residents by raising the value of their external debts.

The fact that currency collapses are often associated with sharp contractions in spending and economic activity highlights the dilemma facing policymakers in responding to financial and currency crises. On the one hand, economic recovery may be imperiled if the currency does not stabilize. Greater depreciation may cause capital losses to investors, discouraging their return, and cause further bankruptcies of domestic firms with foreign currency exposure, thus increasing the extent of economic disruption. These considerations account for standard policy prescriptions calling for a relatively firm monetary policy stance that raises interest rates in the aftermath of currency crises in order to stabilize the exchange rate. On the other hand, the costs of keeping domestic interest rates high after a currency collapse may also be very large. Some economists have argued that raising interest rates under crisis conditions may so weaken the economy that it may destabilize the exchange rate, even causing it to depreciate further, by raising the risk premium or the probability of default on credit (Furman and Stiglitz, 1998; Radelet and Sachs, 1998).

Because either view of the effects of interest rates on the exchange rate during crisis periods can be supported theoretically, the disagreement can only be resolved by empirical analysis, a task undertaken by two chapters in this volume. In "Interest Rate Stabilization of Exchange Rates and Contagion in the Asian Crisis Countries" (Chapter 10), Robert Dekle, Cheng Hsiao, and Siyan Wang focus on two questions.

First, did high interest rates adopted in the wake of massive depreciations in East Asia in 1997 have the desired effect of supporting exchange
rates in the crisis countries? Second, was there contagion, or excess co-
movement across countries in asset returns?

The authors address these questions by estimating vector autoregres-
sion (VAR) models of the spot exchange rate, the interest rate differential, and the inflation rate differential with respect to the United States,
with weekly data for Korea, Malaysia, and Thailand over the period June
1997 through August 1998 (Indonesia is excluded because political instability appears to have been a primary determinant of exchange rate
behavior in that country).

The authors find that, in the short run, a rise in the domestic interest
rate (relative to the U.S. rate) in a country that is experiencing a
currency crisis does appreciate the nominal exchange rate. However,
their point estimates imply that such an interest rate defense against
speculative attacks requires extremely high interest rate levels. To
counter a 40 percent depreciation of the exchange rate, the authorities
would have needed to increase the interest rate differentials by about
300 percent in Korea, 150 percent in Malaysia, and 800 percent in Thailand. The long-run impact of interest rate increases is similar if purchasing power parity (PPP) is not assumed to hold. Specifically, if long-run
PPP holds, the direct impact of the interest rate change on the exchange
rate is offset by the indirect impact through the price differential. Specifically, if long-run PPP holds, the tendency for the real exchange rate to
appreciate in response to the rise in interest rates is offset by the fact
that PPP will tend to restore the nominal exchange rate back to its long-
run equilibrium level.

To address the issue of contagion effects, the authors augment the
individual-country VAR models by adding the lagged exchange rates and
contemporaneous and lagged "news" conditions in neighboring countries. For all three countries, the authors find that good, but not bad, news
from neighboring countries has a significant effect on its exchange rate;
however, only Korean won movements appear to have a contagion effect
on other currencies. Overall, these results provide some evidence of contagion effects in the region.

In "The Impact of Monetary Policy on Exchange Rates during Financial Crises" (Chapter 11), David Gould and Steven Kamin also test
whether interest rate increases are associated with currency appreciation. In their analysis, they directly address a problem in interpreting
the relationship between interest rates and exchange rates that arises
because domestic interest rates may be endogenous. Specifically, the
same factors that may cause an exchange rate to depreciate – expectations of future depreciation or default on debt – will also cause the

market interest rate to rise. However, a higher interest rate caused by tighter monetary policy may be found to lead to exchange rate appreciation once the effects of expectations of future depreciation or default on debt are taken into account. To control for these expectational effects in their error correction models of the exchange rate and interest rate, Gould and Kamin use various proxies for the country risk premium or default risk: (a) credit spreads of dollar-denominated government bonds over similar maturity U.S. treasuries, (b) aggregate stock returns, and (c) banking sector stock returns. They implement their empirical analysis using weekly data for the Asian crisis countries – Indonesia, Korea, Malaysia, the Philippines, and Thailand – from mid-1997 to mid-1998, as well as for Mexico after the peso crash of December 1994.

Gould and Kamin find that their country risk premium and default risk measures exert a significant impact on exchange rates for nearly all the countries in the sample. This is consistent with the hypothesis that during financial crises perceptions of country and credit risk become major determinants of currency values. They also find little consistent evidence of any effect (appreciation or depreciation) of interest rate increases on the exchange rate, even after controlling for credit spreads or stock returns. Gould and Kamin find that including stock market variables does little to change the minimal effect of interest rates on exchange rates. This suggests that monetary tightening neither undercuts nor supports the value of the exchange rate. The authors explain this result by suggesting that the impact of monetary policy on exchange rates may be apparent only very slowly and over relatively long time horizons and is therefore not detectable in the short sample used in their analysis.

Gould and Kamin's main findings differ qualitatively from Dekle, Hsiao, and Wang's, possibly because of differences in modeling strategies and in the choice of samples. However, the policy implication of these two papers is actually quite similar: policymakers need to exercise great caution in using an interest rate defense of the exchange rate during a crisis. Gould and Kamin's results suggests that caution is indicated because the interest rate defense would have no significant effect on the exchange rate in the short run. Dekle et al.'s results suggest that even if an interest rate defense has a significant effect, it is economically very small, so the high interest rates needed to restore exchange rate stability are potentially very disruptive. Taken together, the chapters give some limited empirical support to critics of the standard response to exchange rate crises.

However, such support is necessarily tentative and may have to be qualified. First, the qualitative differences in the results of the two chapters suggest that further research is needed, perhaps with larger datasets, to establish conclusively whether an interest rate defense of the currency during a crisis is indeed ineffective or weak. The need for further research is underscored by the fact that evidence from other studies is also mixed. Second, the recoveries from the Mexican and East Asian currency crises of the 1990s do not unambiguously support the argument that the policy responses were inappropriate. Output growth in the most severely affected economies rebounded relatively sharply in the aftermath of the crises, and these countries have been broadly successful in containing inflation. This impressive performance is in stark contrast to the 1980s, when, in the wake of an external debt crisis, Latin American countries experienced a "lost decade" in which per capita incomes in many countries stagnated or declined, and there were occasional bouts of hyperinflation.

Capital controls provide an alternative policy response to capital flow reversals. Proponents argue that curbs on capital outflows, particularly during crisis periods, could prevent the sudden withdrawal of capital and allow policymakers to avoid the uncomfortable choice of raising domestic interest rates or allowing the currency to depreciate sharply, both of which can be very costly.

The jury is still out on the value and effectiveness of such controls. In particular, innovations in financial technology appear to have made it easier to circumvent them. In addition, in the 1990s, controls on outflows have typically been imposed in response to crises, when the incentives to circumvent them are presumably very high. To shed light on these questions, in "Capital Controls during Financial Crises: The Cases of Malaysia and Thailand" (Chapter 12), Hali Edison and Carmen Reinhart assess the experiences with controls in Thailand and Malaysia during the recent Asia crisis. Both countries experienced downward currency pressure from investors in offshore markets taking positions against the domestic currency as well as from capital flight in the onshore domestic market. Each country enacted specific measures to combat these pressures.

Thailand took steps to segment the onshore and offshore markets in response to depreciation pressures on the baht in the early stages of the 1997 attack on the baht. In May 1997, access to baht funds in the offshore market was restricted, in order to curb short-selling of the currency, and a two-tier exchange rate regime was introduced in July 1997. In particular, the government prohibited spot and forward sales or lending via swaps by Thai banks to nonresidents. In addition, the government restricted repatriation (by foreigners) of proceeds from asset sales in baht, and it required that the conversion of the baht be done at the (less favorable) onshore exchange rate. These policies remained largely in place until January 1998.

Malaysia took action in September 1998, in the aftermath of the Russian crisis which triggered a flight to quality and put renewed pressure on emerging market currencies (as well as private U.S. debt markets). It effectively dismantled the offshore ringgit market, by closing all channels for the transfer of ringgit abroad and requiring the repatriation of all ringgit assets held abroad. The government also imposed a 12-month moratorium on the repatriation of portfolio capital in Malaysia held by nonresidents, and it restricted capital transfers by residents. In February 1999, the moratorium was replaced by a declining scale of exit levies. In both countries, current account and foreign direct investment transactions were exempt from these controls.

In order to assess the impact of these measures, Edison and Reinhart compare mean values of selected monthly macroeconomic and daily financial variables before and after controls were imposed. In Malaysia, they find evidence that after controls were imposed capital outflows fell, foreign reserves rose, interest rates fell (below precrisis levels), the exchange rate stabilized, and industrial production growth accelerated. In general, the opposite occurred in Thailand, implying that the controls were less effective.

In both countries, interest rates became less variable, while bid–ask spreads in the foreign exchange market widened compared to precrisis levels, as might be expected due to declining market liquidity. At the same time, stock prices became more variable, as capital controls forced the adjustment in portfolio allocations to shift to prices rather than quantities. Edison and Reinhart also estimate a generalized autoregressive conditional heteroskedasticity (GARCH)-model of nominal interest rates and of stock returns, and they find mixed evidence that controls may have reduced the volatility of interest rates in Malaysia and increased the volatility of stock returns in Thailand. However, a comparison with countries that did not impose capital controls suggests it is the timing of the controls, rather than the controls themselves, that may account for the increased volatility in Thailand.

Thus, controls on outflows appear to have been more effective in Malaysia than in Thailand. One reason is that the controls adopted in Malaysia were more restrictive than those in Thailand, as they eliminated the offshore ringgit market and prohibited certain capital outflows. Another reason is that Thailand imposed its controls as the crisis was unfolding, while Malaysia imposed them much later, just before a general recovery in the region. Further research is needed to assess the relative importance of these factors in explaining the different outcomes.

REFERENCES

Agénor, Pierre Richard and Peter Montiel (1996). *Development Macroeconomics*. Princeton, NJ: Princeton University Press.

Aizenman, Joshua (1999). "International Portfolio Diversification with Generalized Expected Utility Preferences," *Canadian Journal of Economics* **32**(4): 1010–1023.

Burnside, Craig, Martin Eichenbaum, and Sergio Rebelo (1998). "Prospective Deficits and the Asian Currency Crisis." NBER Working Paper No. 6758. Cambridge, MA.

Calvo, Guillermo (1998). "Varieties of Capital-Market Crises." In Guillermo Calvo and Mervyn King, eds., *The Debt Burden and Its Consequences for Monetary Policy*. London: Macmillan, pp. 181–202.

———(1999). "Contagion in Emerging Markets: When *Wall Street* Is a Carrier." Mimeo, University of Maryland, Department of Economics.

Calvo, Guillermo, Leonardo Leiderman, and Carmen Reinhart (1996). "Inflows of Capital to Developing Countries in the 1990s: Causes and Effects," *Journal of Economic Perspectives* **10**(Spring):123–139.

Calvo, Guillermo and Enrique Mendoza (1996). "Mexico's Balance-of-Payments Crisis: A Chronicle of a Death Foretold," *Journal of International Economics* **41**(November):235–264.

———(1999). "Rational Herd Behavior and the Globalization of Securities Markets." NBER Working Paper No. 7153. Cambridge, MA.

Chang, Roberto and Andrés Velasco (1998a). "Financial Crisis in Emerging Markets: A Canonical Model," NBER Working Paper No. 6606. Cambridge, MA.

———(1998b). "The Asian Liquidity Crisis." NBER Working Paper No. 6796. Cambridge, MA.

Claessens, Stijn, Michael Dooley, and Andrew Warner (1995). "Portfolio Capital Flows: Hot or Cold?" *World Bank Economic Review* **9**(1):153–174.

Cooper, Richard (1999). "The Asia Crisis: Causes and Consequences." In Alison Harwood, Robert Litan, and Michael Pomerleano, eds., *Financial Markets and Development: The Crisis in Emerging Markets*. Washington, D.C.: Brookings Institution Press, pp. 17–28.

Corsetti, Giancarlo, Paolo Pesenti, and Nouriel Roubini (1998). "Fundamental Determinants of the Asian Crisis: A Preliminary Empirical Assessment." Mimeo, Yale University, Department of Economics.

———(1999a). "The Asian Crisis: An Overview of the Empirical Evidence and Policy Debate." In Pierre-Richard Agénor, Marcus Miller, David Vines, and Axel Weber, eds., *The Asian Financial Crises: Causes, Contagion, and Consequences*. Cambridge, U.K.: Cambridge University Press, pp. 127–166.

———(1999b). "Paper Tigers? A Model of the Asian Crisis," *European Economic Review* **43**(7):1211–1236, June. Also issued as NBER Working Paper No. 6783.

Diamond, Douglas and Philip Dybvig (1983). "Banks Runs, Deposit Insurance, and Liquidity," *Journal of Political Economy* **91**:401–419.

Dooley, Michael P. (2000). "A Model of Crises in Emerging Markets," *Economic Journal* **110**(460):256–272. Previously issued as NBER Working Paper No. 6300.

Dornbusch, Rudiger and Alejandro Werner (1994). "Mexico: Stabilization, Reform, and No Growth," *Brookings Papers on Economic Activity*, No. 1:253–297.

Furman, Jason and Joseph E. Stiglitz (1998). "Economic Crises: Evidence and Insights from East Asia," *Brookings Papers on Economic Activity*, No. 2:1–114.

Gerlach, Stephan and Frank Smets (1995). "Contagious Speculative Attacks," *European Journal of Political Economy* **11**(1):45–63.

Glick, Reuven and Andrew Rose (1999a). "Contagion and Trade: Why Are Currency Crises Regional," *Journal of International Money and Finance* **18**(4):603–618.

———(1999b). "Contagion and Trade: Explaining the Incidence and Intensity of Currency Crises." In Pierre-Richard Agénor, Marcus Miller, David Vines, and Axel Weber, eds., *The Asian Financial Crises: Causes, Contagion, and Consequences.* Cambridge, U.K.: Cambridge University Press, pp. 284–311.

Gordon, Roger H. and A. Lans Bovenberg (1996). "Why Is Capital So Immobile Internationally?: Possible Explanations and Implications for Capital Income Taxation," *American Economic Review* **86**:1057–1075.

Kaminsky, Graciela and Carmen Reinhart (1999). "The Twin Crises: The Causes of Banking and Balance of Payments Problems," *American Economic Review* **89**(3):473–500. Previously issued as International Finance Discussion Paper No. 544. Washington, D.C.: Board of Governors of the Federal Reserve System.

Krugman, Paul (1979). "A Model of Balance of Payments Crises," *Journal of Money, Credit, and Banking* **11**:311–325.

La Porta, Rafael, Florencio Lopez-de-Silanes, Andrei Shleifer, and Robert Vishny (1997). "Legal Determinants of External Finance," *Journal of Finance* **52**:1131–1150.

———(1998). "Law and Finance," *Journal of Political Economy* **106**:1113–1155.

McKinnon, Ronald and Huw Pill (1998). "The Overborrowing Syndrome: Are East Asian Economies Different?" In Reuven Glick, ed., *Managing Capital Flows and Exchange Rates: Perspectives from the Pacific Basin.* Cambridge, U.K.: Cambridge University Press, pp. 322–355.

Obstfeld, Maurice (1994). "The Logic of Currency Crises," *Cahiers Economiques et Monetaires*, Banque de France **43**:189–213.

Radelet, Steven and Jeffrey Sachs (1998). "The East Asian Financial Crisis: Diagnosis, Remedies, and Prospects," *Brookings Papers on Economic Activity*, No. 1:1–74.

Rajan, Raghuram and Luigi Zingales (1999). "The Politics of Financial Development." Mimeo, University of Chicago and NBER.

Sachs, Jeffrey, Aaron Tornell, and Andrés Velasco (1996a). "The Collapse of the Mexican Peso: What Have We Learned?" *Economic Policy* **22**:13–56.

———(1996b). "Financial Crises in Emerging Markets: The Lessons from 1995," *Brookings Papers on Economic Activity*, No. 1:147–198.

————(1996c). " The Mexican Peso Crisis: Sudden Death or Death Foretold?" *Journal of International Economics* **41**(November):265–283.

Tornell, Aaron (1999). "Common Fundamentals in the Tequila and Asian Crises." NBER Working Paper No. 7139. Cambridge, MA.

Van Rijckeghem, Caroline and Beatrice Weder (1999). "Sources of Contagion: Finance or Trade?" IMF Working Paper No. 99/146. Washington, D.C.

PART I

DETERMINANTS AND PROPAGATION OF FINANCIAL CRISES

2

Banking and Currency Crises: How Common Are Twins?

Reuven Glick and Michael M. Hutchison

2.1 INTRODUCTION

The joint occurrence of banking and currency crises associated with the recent Asian financial turmoil has drawn renewed attention to the inter-relationship between these two phenomena. Banking and currency crises appeared to arise virtually at the same time in Thailand, Indonesia, Malaysia, and Korea in 1997–1998. In fact, the incidence of "twin" crises has been relatively widespread, occurring in such diverse parts of the world as Latin America in the early and mid-1980s and Scandinavia in the early 1990s.

There are good theoretical reasons to expect connections between currency and banking crises, especially because foreign assets and liabilities are a component in commercial banks' balance sheets. In principle, the causality between bank and currency crises may run in either direction. As we discuss in Section 2.2, bank crises may lead to currency crises under some circumstances, while under other conditions currency crises may cause bank crises. Moreover, some recent literature does not distinguish between the two phenomena and regards them as simultaneous manifestations of underlying common factors (Chang and Velasco, 1999).

Most of the empirical literature on currency and banking crises has involved analyzing the determinants of each type of crisis independently of the other. Little empirical work to date has systematically

We thank Mark Peralta, Rasmus Fatum, and Kathleen McDill for research assistance. The views presented in this chapter are those of the authors alone and do not necessarily reflect those of the Federal Reserve Bank of San Francisco or the Board of Governors of the Federal Reserve System. Hutchison's research was supported by The International Centre for the Study of East Asian Development (ICSEAD), the University of California Pacific Rim Research Program, and the Center for Pacific Basin Monetary and Economic Studies at the Federal Reserve Bank of San Francisco.

investigated the association of bank and currency crises. The few exceptions (e.g., Kaminsky and Reinhart, 1999; Rossi, 1999) typically restrict their data sets to a limited number of countries experiencing crises.[1]

In this chapter we empirically investigate the causal linkages between bank and currency crises using a broad country and time-series dataset. Using a broad control group of countries and periods that includes observations with and without crises allows us to draw more general conclusions about the conditions that distinguish crisis from tranquil periods both across countries and across time.

In our empirical analysis, we first provide a detailed statistical overview of the individual and joint ("twin") occurrence of bank and currency crises for 90 industrial and developing countries over the 1975–1997 period. We examine the frequency, regional concentration, association, and relative timing of the onsets of both bank and currency crises. In addition, we assess the value of banking crises in helping to predict future currency crises, and vice versa, using signal-to-noise ratio methodology. We also examine the contemporaneous and lagged relationship of currency and banking crises more formally by estimating the probabilities of the onset of currency and banking crises with probit regressions, using bivariate, multivariate, and simultaneous equation specifications.

We find that the twin crisis phenomenon is concentrated in financially liberalized emerging market economies and is not a general characteristic of either bank or currency crises in a broader set of countries. The linkage between the onset of currency and bank crises in emerging markets is strong, indicating that foreign exchange crises feed into the onset of banking problems and vice versa. This result is robust to model specification and estimation technique. Moreover, only in emerging market economies are banking crises a significant leading indicator of future currency crises. Currency crises do not appear to be a particularly good signal of future banking problems.

The organization of this chapter is as follows: Section 2.2 describes the relevant literature on the possible links between bank and currency crises. Section 2.3 discusses the data used in our empirical analysis. Section 2.4 presents the summary statistical features of the data and signal-to-noise ratio results. Section 2.5 presents the results of probability model (probit) estimates. Section 2.6 concludes the chapter.

[1] An exception is Eichengreen and Rose (1998), who examine the impact of exchange rate regimes and variability on the probability of bank crises in a large sample of developing countries.

2.2 LINKAGES BETWEEN CURRENCY AND BANKING CRISES

The association of bank and currency crises and the occurrence of "twin" crises may be attributable to a number of channels of causation: a bank crisis leading to a currency crisis, a currency crisis leading to a bank crisis, or joint causality. In this section we provide a brief survey of the existing literature concerning the linkages between the onset of bank and currency crises.

2.2.1 Causality from Banking Sector Distress to Currency Crises

A number of papers discuss the possibility of causality running from banking problems to currency crises. Obstfeld (1994), for example, argues that a weak banking sector may precipitate a currency crisis if rational speculators anticipate that policymakers will choose inflation over exchange rate stability in order to avoid bankruptcies and further strains on the banking sector rather than endure the costs of defending the domestic currency. Velasco (1987) and Calvo (1997) argue that a bank run can cause a currency attack if the increased liquidity associated with a government bailout of the banking system is inconsistent with a stable exchange rate. Miller (1999) explicitly considers currency devaluation as one of the logical policy options for a government confronted by a bank run in a fixed exchange rate regime. Gonzalez-Hermosillo (1996) shows that a bank crisis may lead to a currency crisis in a poorly developed financial system where agents may substitute foreign assets for domestic assets.

If banking sector unsoundness can contribute to a currency crisis, what causes a banking crisis? Leading candidate explanations include (a) the well-known "moral hazard" problems in banking associated with financial liberalization and government deposit insurance and (b) large macroeconomic shocks such as a sharp fall in underlying asset values (e.g., "bubble" crash in asset prices). An alternative, "nonfundamentals," explanation is that "bank runs" may occur because of the expectations of individual depositors and creditors (see Diamond and Dybvig, 1983).

2.2.2 Causality from Currency Crises to Banking Sector Distress

A possible reverse chain of causality, from currency crises to the onset of banking crises, is also well-recognized. Miller (1996), for example, shows that a speculative attack on a currency can lead to a bank crisis if deposit money is used to speculate in the foreign exchange market and banks are "loaned up." Rojas-Suarez and Weisbrod (1995) and Obstfeld (1994) argue that a currency crisis may lead to problems in a vulnerable banking sector if policymakers respond to the pressure on the exchange rate by sharply raising interest rates. A common feature of these mechanisms is that banks are already "vulnerable" because of (a) large unhedged foreign liabilities and/or a maturity mismatch between asset and liabilities and (b) a shock arising from the currency market pushes them "over the edge." A currency crisis shock can adversely alter the banking sector directly by causing a deterioration of bank balance sheets if the currency depreciates, or indirectly by causing the central bank to raise interest rates to defend the currency.

If currency crises lead to bank crises, what causes currency crises? Candidate explanations based on fundamentals, usually termed first-generation models of the collapse of fixed exchange rates, include over-valued real exchange rates and other macroeconomic factors such as inflation, budget deficits, and rapid credit expansion (Krugman, 1979). The main alternative explanations allow a role for nonfundamentals, and are frequently termed second-generation models of exchange rate regime collapse (Obstfeld, 1994). This literature focuses on the existence of multiple equilibria and self-fulfilling speculative attacks that can arise from the willingness of policymakers to give up a pegged exchange rate if output, unemployment, or other relevent costs exceed a certain threshold.

2.2.3 Joint Causality

The joint occurrence of "twin crises" may also reflect a response to a common factor. Chang and Velasco (1999), for example, emphasize the role of international illiquidity, defined as a situation in which a country's consolidated financial system has potential short-term obligations that exceed the amount of foreign currency to which it can have access on short notice. They argue that an international liquidity shortfall may be a sufficient, though not necessary, condition to trigger a crisis: "The options left after creditors lose confidence and stop rolling over and demand immediate payment on existing loans – whether to the private sector in Asia or to the government in Mexico and Brazil – are painfully few. The collapse of the currency, of the financial system, or perhaps both is the likely outcome."

Another common factor emphasized in this literature is financial liberalization combined with moral hazard incentives that induce banks to take on particularly risky portfolios, including unhedged foreign currency liabilities. McKinnon and Pill (1996, 1998), for example, emphasize the role of financial liberalization in generating dynamics leading to a twin crisis. Financial liberalization and deposit insurance may fuel a lending boom involving both foreign and domestic credit expansion that eventually leads to a banking and currency crisis.

More generally, Kaminsky and Reinhart (1999) point out that it is possible that "because the seeds of the problems are sown at the same time, which event occurs first is a matter of circumstance." An example they employ to illustrate a twin crisis, jointly caused by common factors, is the "perverse" dynamics of an exchange rate-based inflation stabilization plan, such as that of Mexico in 1987 and the Southern Cone countries in the late 1970s. Reinhart and Vegh (1995) provide empirical evidence that these types of plans have similar dynamics: An early consumption boom is financed by expansion of bank credit and foreign borrowing. The boom is accompanied by real exchange rate appreciation because domestic inflation only converges gradually to the international inflation rate due to inertial effects in wage contracting and price expectations. At some point, the high level of foreign borrowing, reflected in a current account deficit, may be perceived as unsustainable and trigger an attack on the currency. As capital inflows turn to outflows and asset markets crash, the banking sector is affected as well.

2.3 DATA

2.3.1 Defining Currency Crises

Currency crises are typically defined as "large" changes in some indicator of actual or potential currency value. Some studies focus on episodes of large depreciation alone (e.g., Frankel and Rose, 1996), while others include episodes of speculative pressure in which the exchange rate did not always adjust because the authorities successfully defended the currency by intervening in the foreign exchange market or raising domestic interest rates (e.g., Eichengreen, Rose, and Wyplosz, 1995; Moreno, 1995; Kaminsky and Reinhart, 1999). Alternative criteria have been employed in the literature for identifying "large" changes in currency value or pressure relative to what is considered "normal." Some studies employ an exogenous threshold rate of depreciation common to all countries in the analysis (e.g., Frankel and Rose, 1996; Kumar, Moorthy, and Perraudin, 1998), while others define the threshold in terms of country-specific moments (e.g., Kaminsky and Reinhart, 1999; Kaminsky, Lizondo, and Reinhart, 1998; IMF, 1998; Esquivel and Larrain, 1998; Glick and Moreno, 1998; Moreno, 1999).[2]

In this study our indicator of currency crises is constructed from "large" changes in an index of currency pressure, defined as a weighted average of monthly real exchange rate changes and monthly (percent)

---

[2] Furman and Stiglitz (1998) and Berg and Patillo (1999) evaluate the predictive power of a range of model methodologies and definitions for the 1997 Asia crisis.

reserve losses.[3] The weights are inversely related to the variance of changes of each component over the sample for each country. Our measure presumes that any nominal currency changes associated with exchange rate pressure should affect the purchasing power of the domestic currency – that is, result in a change in the real exchange rate (at least in the short run). This condition excludes some large depreciations that occur during high inflation episodes, but it avoids screening out sizable depreciation events in more moderate inflation periods for countries that have occasionally experienced periods of hyperinflation and extreme devaluation.[4] Large changes in exchange rate pressure are defined as changes in our pressure index that exceed the mean plus two times the country-specific standard deviation, provided it also exceeds five percent.[5,6]

2.3.2 Defining Bank Crises

Banking problems are usually difficult to identify empirically because of data limitations. The potential for a bank run is not directly observable and, once either a bank run or large-scale government intervention has occurred, the situation most likely will have been preceded by a protracted deterioration in the quality of assets held by banks. Identifying banking sector distress by the deterioration of bank asset quality is also difficult because direct market indicators of asset value are usually lacking. This is an important limitation because most banking problems in recent years are not associated with bank runs by depositors (affect-

---

[3] Our currency pressure measure of crises does not include episodes of defense involving sharp rises in interest rates. Data for market-determined interest rates are not available for much of the sample period in many of the developing countries in our dataset.

[4] This approach differs from that of Kaminsky and Reinhart (1999), for example, who deal with episodes of hyperinflation by separating the nominal exchange rate depreciation observations for each country according to whether or not inflation in the previous 6 months was greater than 150 percent, and they calculate for each subsample separate standard deviation and mean estimates with which to define exchange rate crisis episodes.

[5] Kaminsky and Reinhart (1999) use a three-standard-deviation cutoff. While the choice of cutoff point is somewhat arbitrary, Frankel and Rose (1996) and Kumar, Moorthy, and Perraudin (1998) suggest that the results are not very sensitive to the precise cutoff chosen in selecting crisis episodes.

[6] We have also constructed an alternative measure of currency crises following Esquivel and Larrain (1998) that employs a hybrid condition: The monthly depreciation in the (real) exchange rate either (i) exceeds 15 percent, provided that the depreciation rate is also higher than that in the previous month, or (ii) exceeds the country-specific mean plus 2 standard deviations of the real exchange rate monthly growth rate, provided that it also exceeds 5 percent. The first condition ensures that any large (real) depreciation is counted as a currency crisis, while the second condition attempts to capture changes that are sufficiently large relative to the country-specific monthly change of the (real) exchange rate. The results of our analysis are unaffected by use of this alternative measure.

ing the liability side of the bank balance sheet) but with deterioration in asset quality and subsequent government intervention. Moreover, it is often laxity in government analysis of banking fragility, and slow follow-up action once a problem is recognized, that allows the situation to deteriorate to the point of a major bank crisis involving large-scale government intervention.

Given these conceptual and data limitations, most studies have employed a combination of events to identify and date the occurrence of a bank crisis. Institutional events usually include forced closure, merger, or government intervention in the operations of financial institutions, runs on banks, or the extension of large-scale government assistance. Other indicators frequently include measures of nonperforming assets, problem loans, and so on. We have identified and dated episodes of banking sector distress following the criteria of Caprio and Klingebiel (1996, and updated on the World Bank WebPage) and Demirgüç-Kunt and Detragiache (1998a). If an episode of banking distress is identified in either study, it is included in our sample. If there is ambiguity over the timing of the episode, we use the dating scheme of Demirgüç-Kunt and Detragiache (1998a) because it tends to be more specific about the precise start and end of each episode.[7]

2.3.3 Determinants of Currency and Banking Crises

The theoretical and empirical literature has identified a vast array of variables potentially associated with currency and banking crises (see Kaminsky, Lizondo, and Reinhart, 1998; Demirgüç-Kunt and Detragiache, 1998a; and Hutchison and McDill, 1999). The choice of explanatory variables in our analysis was determined by the questions we posed earlier, the availability of data, and previous results found in the literature. Our objective is to postulate a "canonical" model of currency and banking crises in order to form a basic starting point to investigate the linkages between currency and banking crises. We postulate quite simple basic models with few explanatory variables. The main source of the macro data is the International Monetary Fund's *International Financial Statistics* (CD-ROM). The data series and sources are described in Appendix 2B.

---

[7] Demirgüç-Kunt and Detragiache (1998a, 1998b) identify banking sector distress as a situation where one of the following conditions hold: Ratio of nonperforming assets to total assets is greater than 2 percent of GDP; cost of the rescue operation was at least 2 percent of GDP; banking sector problems resulted in a large-scale nationalization of banks; and extensive bank runs took place or emergency measures such as deposit freezes, prolonged bank holidays, or generalized deposit guarantees were enacted by the government in response to the crisis.

The key explanatory variables used in our analysis of currency crises are the degree of real currency overvaluation, export revenue growth, and the M2/foreign reserves ratio. Prior to episodes of sharp depreciation, we expect the real trade-weighted exchange rate to be overvalued. We define overvaluation as deviations from the fitted trend in the real trade-weighted exchange rate, created by taking the trade-weighted sum of the bilateral real exchange rates (defined in terms of CPI indices) against the U.S. dollar, the deutsche mark, and the yen, where the trade weights are based on the average bilateral trade shares in 1980 and 1990 with the United States, Europe, and Japan.

We also expect export growth (in U.S. dollars) to be sluggish, and the growth rate of M2/foreign reserves to be higher, prior to a currency crisis. A slowdown in export growth indicates a decline in foreign exchange earnings that in turn may set up the expectation of – and speculative pressure for – a currency decline. A rise in the M2/foreign reserves ratio implies a decline in the foreign currency backing of the short-term domestic currency liabilities of the banking system. This would make it difficult to stabilize the currency if sentiment shifts against it.

Several other variables were considered in this study but were not included in the reported regressions (for brevity) because they did not increase explanatory power: the current account/GDP ratio, nominal and real M2 growth, nominal and real domestic credit (net of claims on the public sector), the M2/reserve money multiplier (often used as an indicator of the effects of financial liberalization, as in Calvo and Mendoza, 1996), the budget surplus/GDP ratio, and so on.[8]

The determinants of bank crises that we considered in the basic canonical model are real GDP growth, inflation, and financial liberalization. These are found to be significant determinants (or associations) of banking crises by Demirgüç-Kunt and Detragiache (1998a) and Hutchison and McDill (1999). The financial liberalization data is from Demirgüç-Kunt and Detragiache (1998b), supplemented by national and international sources. It is constructed on the basis of the beginning of observed policy changes to liberalize interest rates, taking on a value of unity during the liberalized period of market-determined rates and zero otherwise.

Several other possible determinants of bank crises were considered but were not reported because they did not contribute significantly to the explanatory power of the model. These variables are real credit growth, nominal (and real) interest rate changes, the budget position of

---

[8] We also do not consider possible contagion effects during currency crises. See Glick and Rose (1999).

the general government, and explicit deposit insurance.[9] An index of stock prices was also considered and this entered significantly in determining the onset of banking crises (see Hutchison and McDill, 1999). However, stock price data was only available for a small sample of countries and was therefore not included in the base regressions.[10]

2.3.4 Data Sample and Windows

Our data sample is determined by the availability of data on currency market movements and banking sector health, as well as on the determinants of currency and bank crises, discussed above. We do not confine our analysis to countries experiencing banking or currency crises. We also include developed and developing countries that did not experience either a severe banking problem or currency crisis/speculative attack during the 1975–1997 sample period. Using such a broad control group allows us to make general statements about the conditions distinguishing between countries encountering crises and others managing to avoid crises.

The minimum data requirements to be included in our study are that GDP are available for a minimum of 10 consecutive years over the period 1975–1997. This requirement results in a sample of 90 countries. We group the countries into three categories: industrial countries (21), emerging economies with relatively open capital markets (32), and other developing and transition economies (37).[11] The particular countries included in our dataset are listed in Appendix 2A. For each country-year in our sample, we construct binary measures of currency and bank crises, as defined in Sections 2.3.1 and 2.3.2 (1 = crisis, 0 = no crisis); a currency crisis is deemed to have occurred for a given year if the change in currency pressure for any month in that year satisfies our criterion (i.e., two standard deviations above the mean). The dates of currency and bank crises are reported in Appendix 2B.

---

[9] Data on the existence of explicit deposit insurance come from the survey by Kyei (1995). We constructed a dummy variable that took on a value of unity if the country, at the time in question, had a formal system of deposit guarantee arrangements in place, and zero otherwise. In the Kyei study, 47 explicit arrangements were identified, as against 55 arrangements implicitly guaranteeing government support for deposits.

[10] External conditions may also matter, but they were not considered in our analysis. Eichengreen and Rose (1998) find evidence that higher interest rates and slower growth in industrial countries contribute to bank crises in emerging markets.

[11] Our emerging economy sample accords roughly with Furman and Stiglitz's variant (1998) of that used by Sachs, Tornell, and Velasco (1996), augmented to include Hong Kong and Uruguay but excluding China, Israel, the Ivory Coast, and Taiwan. The full developing country sample excludes major oil-exporting countries. The United States is excluded from the sample as well.

Of the 90 countries in our sample, 72 countries had banking problems, and 79 countries experienced at least one currency crisis at some point during the sample period. Several countries had multiple occurrences of banking crisis and most had multiple currency crises.

In most of our analysis we are concerned with predicting the onset of currency and banking crises and their relative timing. To reduce the chances of capturing the continuation of the same currency or banking episode, we impose windows on our data. In the case of currency crises, after identifying each "large" monthly change in currency pressure, we treat any large changes in the following 24-month window as a part of the same currency episode and omit the year of that change before continuing the identification of new crises. In the case of multiyear banking crises, we use only the first year in a spell of banking distress – that is, the year of the banking crisis "onset." The duration of banking sector distress was greater than one year in most episodes.

We use annual crisis observations in our study. Attempting to date banking crises by month (as in Kaminsky and Reinhart, 1999) or by quarter seems arbitrary. We employ monthly data for our (real) exchange rate pressure index to identify currency crises and date each by the year in which it occurs. Of course, annual data may obscure or limit some insights about the relative timing of the onset of currency and banking crises, because it does not enable us to distinguish the lead and lag timing of crises to the extent that crises occur at different points of the same year. However, we do not believe that it is possible to date banking crises with such precision as monthly data presumes. Moreover, using annual data enables inclusion of a relatively large number of countries in the analysis (Kaminsky and Reinhart focus on a sample of only 20 countries).

2.4 THE INCIDENCE OF BANKING AND CURRENCY CRISES

Table 2.1 summarizes the number and frequency of bank and currency crises according to our definitions and disaggregates them by 5-year time intervals and country development categories.[12] The table also reports the incidence of "twin" crises, defined as instances in which a bank crisis is accompanied by a currency crisis in either the previous, current, or following year.[13] The data for the developing countries are also disaggregated by geographic region.

---

[12] These figures refer to observations for which data for both bank and currency crises are available; that is, we exclude observations where banking crisis data are available while currency crisis data are not, and vice versa.

[13] A larger window would obviously increase the number of "twins" identified. For example, Kaminsky and Reinhart (1999), who define twin crises as bank crises followed by a currency crisis within four years, identify 19 twin crises over the period 1970–95

Table 2.1. Bank and Currency Crises

	Time Distribution					
	1975–1997	1975–1979	1980–1984	1985–1989	1990–1994	1995–1997
Bank crises						
Number	90	6	16	21	30	17
Frequency[a]	5.0	1.6	4.2	5.3	7.2	6.8
Currency crises						
Number	202	39	45	50	48	20
Frequency[a]	11.3	11.0	12.0	12.6	11.6	8.0
"Twin" crises						
Number	37	3	5	8	11	10
Frequency[a]	2.1	0.8	1.3	2.0	2.6	4.0

Developmental and Geographic Distribution

			Developing				
	Industrial	Developing	Emerging	Africa	Asia	Latin America	Other[b]
Bank crises							
Number	19	71	46	21	15	26	9
Frequency[a]	4.4	5.2	6.6	5.8	5.0	5.1	4.8
Currency crises							
Number	42	160	78	59	29	53	19
Frequency[a]	9.6	11.8	11.2	16.5	9.6	10.4	10.2
"Twin" crises							
Number	7	30	23	11	7	8	4
Frequency[a]	1.6	2.2	3.3	3.1	2.3	1.6	2.2

Note: "Twin" crises are defined as banking crises accompanied by a currency crisis in previous, current, or following year.
[a] Number of crises divided by sum of country-years with and without crises during time interval, in percent.
[b] Includes Eastern Europe and the Middle East.

	Currency crisis$_t$	No currency crisis$_t$
Bank crisis$_t$	$A_{t,\,t}$	$B_{t,\,t}$
No bank crisis$_t$	$C_{t,\,t}$	$D_{t,\,t}$

Figure 2.1. Bank and currency crises matrix. *Note*: $A_{t,t}(B_{t,t})$ denotes the number of instances in which a bank crisis occurs in a particular year t, and it is (or is not) accompanied by a currency crisis in year t. $C_{t,t}(D_{t,t})$ denotes the number of instances in which there was no bank crisis in a particular year t, but it is (or is not) accompanied by a currency crisis in year t.

Our sample includes 90 banking crisis episodes and 202 currency crises; thus currency crises have been twice as common as bank crises.[14] Of the 90 bank crises, 37, (i.e., 41 percent) have been twins.

Observe that (the onset of) banking crises has increased over time: Bank crises have risen steadily both in number and frequency over our sample period and were four times as frequent in the 1990s as in the 1970s. However, the incidence of currency crises has been relatively constant. In fact, the number and frequency of currency crises were higher in the 1980s than in the 1990s. The frequency of twin crises appears to have risen in step with that of bank crises: In comparison to the 1975–1979 period, they were more than three times as frequent in 1990–1994 and were more than four times as frequent in 1995–1997.

Table 2.1 also indicates that individual banking and currency crises as well as twin crises have been more frequent in developing and emerging markets than in industrial countries. Banking and twin crises have been particularly evident in emerging markets. Among developing countries, the frequency of individual and twin crises has been highest in Africa.

Tables 2.2 and 2.3 present summary nonparametric indicators of the extent to which the onset of banking and currency crises are correlated with each other, using frequency statistics and signal-to-noise measures. Following the methodology of Kaminsky and Reinhart (1999) and Berg and Patillo (1999), consider the association of bank and currency crises in terms of Figure 2.1.

with their sample of 20 countries; we identify 37 such crises – less than twice as many – in a sample roughly four times as large. We implicitly consider a larger window for classifying twin crises when exploring lag relationships up to two years in length between bank and currency crises in the probit analysis in Section 2.5.

[14] With our alternative definition of currency crises [see footnote 6], we identify 94 banking crises and 210 currency crises.

Table 2.2a. Bank Crises and Frequency of Currency Crises (in percent)

	Number of Bank Crises	Frequency of Accompanying Currency Crisis[a]			Cumulative Frequency of Accompanying Currency Crisis[b]
		$t-1$	t	$t+1$	
All countries	90	11	16	15	41
Developing countries	71	10	18	15	42
Emerging markets	46	9	24	20	50

[a] Frequency with which onset of bank crisis in year t is accompanied by currency crisis in year $t-1$, t, or $t+1$.
[b] Total of currency crises in years $t-1$, t, and $t+1$ divided by banking crises in year t.

Table 2.2b. Currency Crises and Frequency of Bank Crises (in percent)

	Number of Currency Crises	Frequency of Accompanying Bank Crisis[a]			Cumulative Frequency of Accompanying Bank Crisis[b]
		$t-1$	t	$t+1$	
All countries	202	7	7	5	18
Developing countries	160	7	8	5	19
Emerging markets	78	11	14	6	29

[a] Frequency with which currency crisis in year t is accompanied by onset of bank crisis in year $t-1$, t, or $t+1$.
[b] Total of bank crisis onsets in years $t-1$, t, and $t+1$ divided by currency crises in year t.

The cell $A_{t,t}$ represents the number of instances in which a bank crisis occurring in a particular year t was accompanied by a currency crisis in year t (i.e., a bank crisis provides a "good signal" about the occurrence of currency crises); $B_{t,t}$ is the number of instances in which a banking crisis was not accompanied by currency crisis (i.e., a bank crisis provides a "bad signal" or "noise" about the occurrence of currency crises); $C_{t,t}$ is the number of instances in which banking performance failed to provide a good signal about a currency crisis that occurred; and $D_{t,t}$ is the number of instances in which neither a banking or currency crisis occurred. An analogous matrix can be constructed indicating the number of instances in which a banking crisis in year t was preceded (followed) by a currency crisis in year $t-1$ ($t+1$), denoted by $A_{t,t-1}$ ($A_{t,t+1}$), etc.

Table 2.2 presents information about the association of the onset of banking and currency crises contemporaneously, one period before, and one period ahead for our sample. Table 2.2a shows the frequency with which the onset of a bank crisis in year t was accompanied by a currency crisis in either year $t, t-1$, or $t+1$ – that is, $A_{t,t-1} / (A_{t,t-1} + B_{t,t-1})$, $A_{t,t} / (A_{t,t} + B_{t,t})$, $A_{t,t+1} / (A_{t,t+1} + B_{t,t+1})$. The last column shows the *cumulative* frequency with which a bank crisis onset in year t is accompanied by currency crises in years $t-1$, t, or $t+1$ – that is, $(A_{t,t-1} + A_{t,t} + A_{t,t+1}) / (A_{t,t} + B_{t,t})$. Table 2.2b shows the analogous measures of the frequency with which a currency crisis at time t was accompanied by the onset of a bank crisis at either $t-1$, t, or $t+1$.

We calculate these frequencies for three different country data samples – all available industrial and developing countries (90 countries), developing countries (79 countries), and emerging markets only (32 countries). We are concerned here with the onset of either a banking or currency crisis. We do not use windows in this exercise to exclude observations immediately following or preceding the onset of a crisis; that is, the onset of a crisis is coded as unity and all other observations are coded as zero.

Comparing Tables 2.2a and 2.2b, observe that the frequency of banking crises associated with currency crises is higher than the frequency of currency crises associated with banking crises. The cumulative frequency with which the onset of a banking crisis is accompanied by a currency crisis within one year before or after is 40 percent or higher. Correspondingly, the onset of a currency crisis is accompanied by a banking crisis within one year by less than 20 percent of the time for the full and developing country samples, though the frequency rises to 29 percent for the emerging market sample.

Comparing the figures for the frequency of banking crises accompanied by currency crises in years $t-1$ and $t+1$ in Table 2.2a provides weak evidence that the frequency of currency crises accompanying banking crises is higher in year $t+1$ than in year $t-1$. This suggests that currency crises tend to lag banking crises or, equivalently, that banking crises tend to lead currency crises. This result is strongest for emerging market countries, where 20 percent of banking crises in year t are accompanied by a currency crisis in year $t+1$, but only 9 percent at $t-1$.

Table 2.3 calculates the signal-to-noise association of banking and currency crises. Table 2.3a reports the signal-to-noise performance of banking crises as a lagging $(t-1)$, contemporaneous (t), and leading $(t+1)$ indicator of currency crises. For the contemporaneous indicator, this is defined as the number of times a banking crisis is accompanied by a currency crisis (i.e., banking crises are good signals of currency crises) as a share of total currency crises (i.e., $A_{t,t} / (A_{t,t} + C_{t,t})$), all divided by the number of times a banking crisis is *not* accompanied by a currency crisis (i.e., banking crises are "noise" or bad signals of currency crises) as a share of all bank crises (i.e., $B_{t,t} / (A_{t,t} + B_{t,t})$). A signal-to-noise greater

Table 2.3a. Performance of Bank Crises as a Signal
of Currency Crises

	Good Signal/Noise Ratio of Currency Crises[a]		
	$t-1$	t	$t+1$
All countries	0.98	1.44	1.42
Developing countries	0.82	1.66	1.35
Emerging markets	0.77	2.46	1.96

[a] Number of years in which the onset of a bank crisis in year
t is accompanied by a currency crisis in year $t-1$, t, or $t+1$
(i.e., bank crises are good signals) as a proportion of possible instances in which a currency crisis could have occurred,
divided by the number of years a bank crisis in year t is *not*
accompanied by a currency crisis in year $t-1$, t, or $t+1$ (i.e.,
banking crises are "bad" signals) as a proportion of all bank
crises.

Table 2.3b. Performance of Currency Crises as a
Signal of Bank Crises

	Good Signal/Noise Ratio of Bank Crises[a]		
	$t-1$	t	$t+1$
All countries	1.38	1.40	0.98
Developing countries	1.32	1.59	0.82
Emerging markets	1.87	2.30	0.78

[a] Number of years a currency crisis in year t is accompanied
by a bank crisis onset in year $t-1$, t, or $t+1$ (i.e., currency
crises are good signals) as a proportion of possible instances
in which a bank crisis could have occurred, divided by the
number of years a currency crisis in year t is *not* accompanied by a bank crisis in year $t-1$, t, or $t+1$ (i.e., currency
crises are "bad" signals) as a proportion of all currency crises.

than 1 implies that when banking crises occur, currency crises are more
likely than not. Table 2.3b reports the corresponding signal-to-noise measures for currency crises as an indicator of banking crises.

Observe that for the full sample the signal-to-noise ratio of banking
crises is higher for currency crises at time t and $t+1$ than at time $t-1$. This
is more pronounced for our developing country and emerging market
samples. This suggests that banking crises tend to be contemporaneous
and/or leading, rather than lagging, indicators of currency crises.

2.5 PROBIT EQUATION RESULTS

This section presents probit estimates involving currency and banking crises alone as well as with various macroeconomic and institutional determinants of currency and banking crises. Our use of probit models allows us to go beyond the bivariate relationship to focus on the joint contribution of macroeconomic and institutional variables to currency and banking crises.

We estimate the probability of either currency or banking sector crises using a multivariate probit model on an unbalanced panel dataset for both developing and developed countries over the 1975–1997 period (or years available). We observe that either a country at a particular time (observation t) is experiencing the onset of a crisis (i.e., the binary dependent variable, say y_t, takes on a value of unity) or it is not ($y_t = 0$). The probability that a crisis will occur, $\Pr(y_t = 1)$, is hypothesized to be a function of a vector of characteristics associated with observation t, x_t, and the parameter vector β. The likelihood function of the probit model is constructed across the n observations (the number of countries times the number of observations for each country), and the log of the function is then maximized with respect to the unknown parameters using nonlinear maximum likelihood

$$\ln L = \sum_{t=1}^{n} [y_t \ln F(\beta' x_t) + (1 - y_t)\ln(1 - F(\beta' x_t))].$$

The function $F(\cdot)$ is the standardized normal distribution.

In these equations we employ windows following the onset of either a currency or a banking crisis, as discussed in Section 2.3.4. In the currency crisis equation, a 24-month window following the onset of a crisis (or episode of exchange rate pressure) was employed and we eliminated from the dataset these observations. Banking crises are not as frequent as currency crises, so overlapping observations are not a major problem, but the duration of banking crises is often quite long. We employ a window in these cases such that every year of a continuing banking crisis, except the initial or onset year, was eliminated from the dataset.

2.5.1 Bivariate Probits

We start with a discussion of the probit estimates for the currency and banking crisis onsets alone – that is, without controlling for macroeconomic variables. These results are reported in Tables 2.4a and 2.4b. Tables 2.5a and 2.5b report results with macroeconomic and other control variables included.[15]

---

[15] All probit equations are estimated by maximum likelihood using LIMDEP Windows version 7.0.

Table 2.4a. Probit Regression Estimates for Currency Crises

Variable	All Countries			Developing Countries			Emerging Markets		
Bank crisis$_t$	4.89	5.38	5.60	6.64*	7.00*	7.16*	11.35***	12.26***	12.98***
	(1.38)	(1.51)	(1.56)	(1.67)	(1.77)	(1.81)	(2.52)	(2.78)	(2.96)
Bank crisis$_{t-1}$		4.71			4.58			10.58**	
		(1.29)			(1.06)			(2.14)	
Bank crisis$_{t-1}$ or $_{t-2}$			4.48			3.86			11.03***
			(1.63)			(1.19)			(2.98)
Summary Statistics									
Number of crises	202	193	193	160	152	152	78	73	73
Number of observations	1,587	1,520	1,520	1,196	1,147	1,147	615	589	589
Log likelihood	−604.0	−576.7	−576.2	−469.3	−446.7	−446.6	−230.9	−215.3	−213.3
Pseudo-R^2	0.28	0.28	0.28	0.29	0.29	0.29	0.29	0.29	0.30
Quadratic probability score	0.22	0.22	0.22	0.23	0.23	0.23	0.22	0.21	0.21
Log probability score	0.38	0.38	0.38	0.39	0.39	0.39	0.38	0.37	0.36
Goodness-of-Fit (25% Cutoff)[a]									
Percentage of observations correctly called	87	87	87	87	87	87	84	84	84
Percentage of crises correctly called	0	0	0	0	0	0	14	15	15
Percentage of noncrises correctly called	100	100	100	100	100	100	94	94	94
Goodness-of-Fit (10% Cutoff)[a]									
Percentage of observations correctly called	13	13	13	13	13	13	13	12	78
Percentage of crises correctly called	100	100	100	100	100	100	100	100	36
Percentage of noncrises correctly called	0	0	0	0	0	0	0	0	84

Note: The table reports the change in the probability of a crisis in response to a 1 unit change in the variable evaluated at the mean of all variables (×100, to convert into percentages) with associated z-statistic (for hypothesis of no effect) in parentheses below. Significance at 10 percent level is denoted by *; at the 5 percent level by **; at the 1 percent level by ***. Constant included, but not reported.

[a] Goodness-of-fit statistics defined respectively as $(A + D) / (A + B + C + D)$, $A / (A + C)$, and $D / (B + D)$, where A (C) denote number of crises with predictions of crises above (below) probability cutoff and B (D) denote number of corresponding noncrises with predictions of crises above (below) the cutoff.

51

Table 2.4b. Probit Regression Estimates for Bank Crises Onsets

Variable	All Countries			Developing Countries			Emerging Markets		
Currency crisis$_t$	2.70	2.85	3.21*	3.80*	3.88*	4.31*	9.72***	10.97***	11.26***
	(1.54)	(1.52)	(1.78)	(1.94)	(1.82)	(2.10)	(3.15)	(3.29)	(3.40)
Currency crisis$_{t-1}$		1.06			0.28			1.44	
		(0.53)			(0.11)			(0.34)	
Currency crisis$_{t-1}$ or $_{t-2}$			2.16			1.61			2.71
			(1.49)			(0.92)			(0.89)

Summary Statistics

Number of crises	90	87	89	71	69	71	46	46	46
Number of observations	1,537	1,443	1,470	1,152	1,079	1,103	562	530	536
Log likelihood	−341.6	−327.5	−333.5	−264.8	−254.9	−261.1	−154.5	−151.3	−151.4
Pseudo-R^2	0.20	0.20	0.21	0.21	0.21	0.21	0.25	0.26	0.26
Quadratic probability score	0.11	0.11	0.11	0.12	0.12	0.12	0.15	0.15	0.15
Log probability score	0.22	0.23	0.23	0.23	0.24	0.24	0.27	0.29	0.28

Goodness-of-Fit (25% Cutoff)[a]

Percentage of observations correctly called	94	94	94	94	94	94	92	91	92
Percentage of crises correctly called	0	0	0	0	0	0	0	0	0
Percentage of noncrises correctly called	100	100	100	100	100	100	100	100	100

Goodness-of-Fit (10% Cutoff)[a]

Percentage of observations correctly called	94	94	93	85	85	85	86	86	87
Percentage of crises correctly called	0	0	2	18	17	18	24	24	24
Percentage of noncrises correctly called	100	100	99	89	90	90	92	92	92

Note: See Table 2.4a.

Table 2.5a. Probit Regression Estimates for Currency Crises

Variable	All Countries			Developing Countries			Emerging Markets		
Overvaluation$_{t-1}$	0.26***	0.25***	0.24***	0.23***	0.22***	0.21***	0.22***	0.21***	0.18***
	(6.83)	(6.76)	(6.26)	(5.81)	(5.74)	(5.31)	(4.23)	(4.08)	(3.54)
Ln (M2/reserves)$_{t-1}$	0.96	0.96	1.11	1.58*	1.59*	1.62*	3.19***	3.19***	3.11***
	(1.23)	(1.26)	(1.42)	(1.80)	(1.81)	(1.82)	(2.64)	(2.68)	(2.61)
Export growth$_{t-1}$	-0.05	-0.05	-0.05	-0.05	-0.05	-0.06	-0.16**	-0.16**	-0.17**
	(1.16)	(1.20)	(1.06)	(1.14)	(1.19)	(1.22)	(2.03)	(2.00)	(2.11)
Bank crisis onset$_t$		4.26	4.76		5.01	5.72		8.82**	10.51**
		(1.22)	(1.35)		(1.30)	(1.48)		(2.10)	(2.54)
Bank crisis onset$_{t-1}$ or $_{t-2}$			2.60			3.65			8.69**
			(0.92)			(1.16)			(2.40)

Summary Statistics

	All Countries			Developing Countries			Emerging Markets		
Number of crises	183	183	174	151	151	143	78	78	73
Number of observations	1,471	1,471	1,408	1,145	1,145	1,097	601	601	575
Log likelihood	-522.5	-521.8	-499.0	-421.3	-420.5	-400.8	-213.1	-211.0	-196.9
Pseudo-R^2	0.32	0.32	0.31	0.32	0.32	0.32	0.34	0.35	0.35
Quadratic probability score	0.21	0.21	0.21	0.22	0.22	0.22	0.21	0.21	0.20
Log probability score	0.36	0.35	0.35	0.37	0.37	0.37	0.35	0.35	0.34

Goodness-of-Fit (25% Cutoff)[a]

	All Countries			Developing Countries			Emerging Markets		
Percentage of observations correctly called	87	86	86	86	86	85	86	86	86
Percentage of crises correctly called	13	12	11	15	15	13	21	23	30
Percentage of noncrises correctly called	97	97	97	96	96	96	96	95	94

Goodness-of-Fit (10% Cutoff)[a]

	All Countries			Developing Countries			Emerging Markets		
Percentage of observations correctly called	46	47	47	44	45	47	53	56	58
Percentage of crises correctly called	79	79	79	79	78	79	82	82	81
Percentage of noncrises correctly called	41	43	42	39	40	42	48	52	55

Note: See Table 2.4a.

Table 2.5b. Probit Regression Estimates for Bank Crisis Onsets

Variable	All Countries			Developing Countries			Emerging Markets		
Inflation$_t$	0.02*	0.02*	0.02*	0.01	0.01	0.01	0.01	0.00	0.01
	(1.88)	(1.68)	(1.74)	(0.61)	(0.41)	(0.56)	(0.23)	(0.07)	(0.26)
Output growth$_t$	−0.56***	−0.54***	−0.58***	−0.65***	−0.60***	−0.68***	−1.42***	−1.20***	−1.43***
	(3.64)	(3.30)	(3.40)	(3.56)	(3.22)	(3.40)	(4.08)	(3.53)	(3.80)
Financial liberalization$_t$	7.74***	7.96***	7.99***	9.82***	9.82***	10.11***	6.13*	6.96**	5.68
	(5.28)	(5.26)	(4.91)	(5.18)	(5.18)	(4.97)	(1.84)	(2.16)	(1.63)
Currency crisis$_t$		4.26**	4.41**		6.04**	6.09**		11.26***	11.03***
		(2.26)	(2.21)		(2.53)	(2.38)		(3.06)	(2.77)
Currency crisis$_{t-1}$ or $_{t-2}$			0.08			−1.12			−2.22
			(0.04)			(0.47)			(0.54)
Summary Statistics									
Number of crises	60	58	57	43	42	42	33	33	33
Number of observations	960	903	862	560	545	521	336	335	320
Log likelihood	−200.8	−190.4	−186.3	−131.1	−124.4	−123.2	−92.9	−87.9	−85.7
Pseudo-R^2	0.32	0.33	0.33	0.36	0.37	0.38	0.35	0.38	0.39
Quadratic probability score	0.11	0.11	0.11	0.13	0.12	0.13	0.16	0.15	0.15
Log probability score	0.21	0.21	0.22	0.23	0.23	0.24	0.28	0.26	0.27
Goodness-of-Fit (25% Cutoff)[a]									
Percentage of observations correctly called	94	94	94	92	90	90	89	89	88
Percentage of crises correctly called	7	12	12	14	19	19	21	33	33
Percentage of noncrises correctly called	99	99	99	98	96	96	96	95	94
Goodness-of-Fit (10% Cutoff)[a]									
Percentage of observations correctly called	85	85	85	72	78	77	74	76	76
Percentage of crises correctly called	50	48	49	77	76	74	70	76	79
Percentage of noncrises correctly called	87	87	87	71	78	77	75	76	75

Note: See Table 2.4a.

54

In each table we report the effect of a one-unit change in each regressor on the probability of a crisis (expressed in percentage points so that $0.01 = 1\%$), evaluated at the mean of the data. We include the associated z-statistics in parentheses; these test the null of no effect. Note that the sample size of the multivariate probit analysis varies depending on the set of variables considered.

We also report various diagnostic measures. The in-sample probability forecasts are evaluated with "pseudo" R^2 statistics and analogs of a mean squared error measure, the quadratic probability score (QPS), and the log probability score (LPS), which evaluate the accuracy of probability forecasts. The QPS ranges from zero to 2, and the LPS ranges from zero to infinity, with a score of zero corresponding to perfect accuracy for both.[16] For dependent binary variables, it is natural to ask what fraction of the observations are "correctly called," where, for example, a crisis episode is correctly called when the estimated probability of crisis is above a given cutoff level and a crisis occurs. Such "goodness-of-fit" statistics are shown for two probability cutoffs: 25 percent and 10 percent.

Table 2.4a shows the simple bivariate link between the onset of currency and banking crises. In addition to contemporaneous links, we consider a simple one-year lagged effect of bank crisis onsets as well as a composite lag if a bank crisis began in either of the two previous years. It is apparent from these tables that currency crises are contemporaneously and significantly correlated with bank crises for the emerging market and developing country samples, but not for the full sample of countries. Lagged banking crises, occurring within the past two years, also help to predict the onset of currency crises in emerging markets. Past banking crises, however, do not help predict the onset of currency crises in either the developing country sample or the full set of countries.

Table 2.4b reports the corresponding bivariate results for probit regressions of currency crises on the onset of banking crises. Contemporaneous, but not lagged, currency crises help explain bank crises in the developing and emerging market samples. The contemporaneous link is

---

[16] For each of the methods we can generate n probability forecasts where P_t is the probability of a crisis in the period t, $0 \leq P_t \leq 1$. R_t is the actual times series of observations; $R_t = 1$ if a crisis occurs at time t and equals zero otherwise. The analog to the mean squared error for probability forecasts is the QPS:

$$\text{QPS} = \frac{1}{n}\sum_{t=1}^{n} 2(P_t - R_t)^2$$

Large errors are penalized more heavily under the LPS, given by

$$\text{LPS} = \frac{1}{n}\sum_{t=1}^{n}[(1 - R_t)\ln(1 - P_t) + R_t \ln(P_t)]$$

weaker for the full sample of countries; that is, it is statistically significant at the 10 percent level in only one formulation of the model. Thus lagged banking crises help predict currency crises in the emerging markets sample, but not vice versa. This asymmetric result, albeit for a different and smaller sample of countries, is consistent with the findings of Kaminsky and Reinhart (1999).[17]

2.5.2 Multivariate Probits

Table 2.5a reports the results where the onset of currency crises are explained by both the onset of banking crises and a parsimonious set of (lagged) macroeconomic variables – that is, our canonical model. These results are generally consistent with our priors. That is, the probability of a currency crisis generally rises with greater real overvaluation, higher ratio of the log of M2-reserves ratio, and lower export growth. Overvaluation and the M2-reserves are generally significant for all of our three country samples; export growth is significant only for the emerging country sample.

The bank crisis variable, as an additional explanatory factor, is only significant for the emerging country sample. As with the bivariate results, lagged as well as contemporaneous bank crises help to predict future currency crises.[18]

Analogous probit equations for the onset of bank crises with contemporaneous macro and institutional control variables are reported in Table 2.5b.[19] A decline in output growth and greater financial liberalization, as measured by a "liberalized" interest rate structure, are each highly correlated with the onset of banking sector distress. Inflation is only correlated with the onset of banking sector distress in the full sample, apparently proxying for the developing economies (developing economies have a higher probability of having a banking crisis and also tend to have higher inflation than industrialized economies). It is noteworthy that the macroeconomic variables do not generally help predict the onset of a future banking crisis; that is, results (unreported) with lagged values of the macroeconomic variables are insignificant.

It is apparent that the onset of banking sector distress is highly correlated with currency crises, as indicated by the contemporaneous association reported in Table 2.5b. In contrast with the results in the previous table, the significance levels for the contemporaneous correla-

[17] In contrast, Eichengreen and Rose (1998) find that neither contemporaneous nor lagged currency "crashes" are significant in explaining bank crises for a large sample of developing countries.

[18] These results are robust to excluding all 1997 observations, including the recent Asia crisis episodes, from the dataset.

[19] Fewer observations are available for the bank crisis equations than for the currency crisis equations, primarily because of limited availability of financial liberalization data.

tion between the onset of banking crises and currency crises range from 1 to 5 percent in all three groups of countries; that is, the correlation holds not just in the emerging market sample, but also in the developing country and full country samples. Once again we find no future predictive power associated with currency crises: Lagged currency crises are not significant in explaining the onset of bank crises onsets in any of our samples. Lagged banking crises help predict currency crises in the emerging markets sample, but not vice versa.

2.5.3 Simultaneous Equation Probits

We have found significant contemporaneous correlation between banking and currency crises with single equation probit estimation procedures. Table 2.6 shows the model estimates based on simultaneous equation estimates of both the banking sector onset and currency crisis equations.[20] As the table indicates, the basic results for the emerging markets sample are robust. There is clear joint causality between the onset of currency and banking crises in the emerging markets sample. However, no contemporaneous association is seen in the developing country sample (in contrast with Tables 2.4a, 2.4b, and 2.5b) or in the full group of countries (in contrast with Tables 2.4b and 2.5b).

In summary, these results suggest a very strong and robust contemporaneous correlation among the onset of banking and currency crises in emerging market countries, even when controlling for simultaneity bias and a multitude of other explanatory factors such as financial liberalization, export growth, real GDP growth, and so on. There is weaker evidence of this contemporaneous link with a broader sample of developing countries and for the full sample of countries. The other strong result that emerges is that banking crises are a statistically significant leading indicator of currency crises in emerging markets.

2.5.4 Predicted Crisis Probabilities

To further illustrate the magnitude of the links between currency and bank crises, we examine how this association affects predicted crisis probabilities. Figure 2.2 reports crisis probabilities implied by the single-

---

[20] Our simultaneous equation methodology follows Maddala (1983, pp. 246–247), which describes the procedure for estimating the structural coefficients and standard errors in a two-equation system where both dependent binary variables (in a probit context) are endogenous. The two-step procedure involves first estimating the reduced forms for each endogenous crisis variable as a function of all exogenous and predetermined variables by probit, then calculating the fitted values of the endogenous variables implied by the reduced forms, and lastly using these fitted values as independent variables in the structural probit equations. The covariance matrices are calculated as in Maddala (1983, p. 247). We do not use lags of our endogenously determined crisis variables in these calculations. We assume that all other explanatory variables are exogenous.

Table 2.6. Simultaneous Probit Regression Estimates

Variable	All Countries		Developing Countries		Emerging Markets	
	Currency Crisis	Bank Crisis	Currency Crisis	Bank Crisis	Currency Crisis	Bank Crisis
Overvaluation$_{t-1}$	0.24***		0.16***		0.16*	
	(4.46)		(2.58)		(1.84)	
Ln (M2/reserves)$_{t-1}$	1.88		4.11**		4.08*	
	(1.51)		(2.28)		(1.84)	
Export growth$_{t-1}$	-0.05		-0.06		-0.18	
	(0.68)		(0.76)		(1.52)	
Bank crisis onset$_t$	1.82		4.16		7.44***	
	(0.74)		(1.53)		(2.64)	
Inflation$_t$		0.02		0.00		-0.00
		(1.44)		(0.14)		(0.18)
Output growth$_t$		-0.38**		-0.48**		-0.74*
		(2.09)		(2.02)		(1.66)
Fin. liberalization$_t$		7.98***		11.18***		9.61**
		(3.54)		(4.00)		(2.18)
Currency crisis$_t$		3.48		5.04		8.43**
		(1.26)		(1.44)		(2.30)
Summary Statistics						
Number of crises	83	47	58	39	35	32
Number of observations	730	730	463	463	303	303
Log likelihood	-242.3	-158.0	-160.4	-116.4	-92.6	-84.8

58

Pseudo-R^2	0.31	0.30	0.34	0.36	0.38	0.40
Quadratic probability score	0.18	0.20	0.20	0.21	0.18	0.19
Log probability score	0.32	0.38	0.34	0.41	0.31	0.33

Goodness-of-Fit (25% Cutoff)

Percentage of observations correctly called	88	94	87	91	86	87
Percentage of crises correctly called	12	13	19	18	34	34
Percentage of noncrises correctly called	98	99	97	98	93	94

Goodness-of-Fit (10% Cutoff)

Percentage of observations correctly called	55	85	55	68	66	70
Percentage of crises correctly called	80	45	83	74	77	72
Percentage of noncrises correctly called	52	88	51	68	64	69

Note: See Table 4.2a.

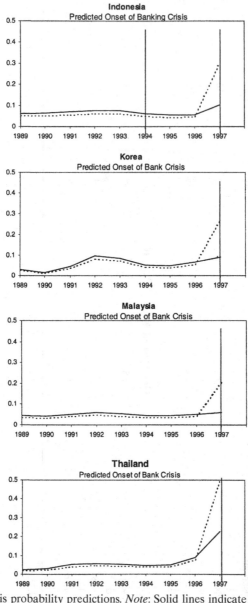

Figure 2.2. Crisis probability predictions. *Note*: Solid lines indicate currency (bank) crisis probabilities implied by benchmark probit equations. Dashed lines indicate currency (bank) crisis probabilities implied by probit equations augmented to include the contemporaneous and composite lagged occurrence of bank (currency) crises. Vertical lines denote the actual occurrence of a crisis.

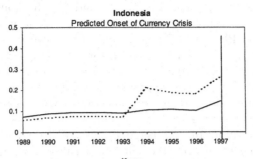

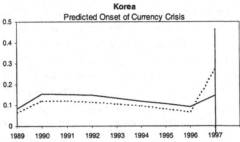

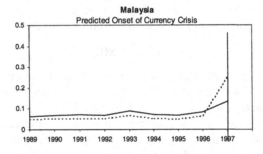

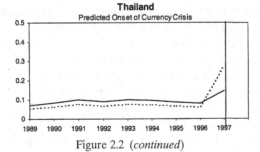

Figure 2.2 (*continued*)

equation probit estimates in Tables 2.5a and 2.5b for four East Asian emerging market economies – Korea, Malaysia, Indonesia, and Thailand – for the period 1989 to 1997. Two graphs are shown for each country: One depicts the probability predictions for the onset of banking sector distress, while the second depicts the onset of currency crises. Two prediction lines are plotted in each graph: The solid line plots the predicted crisis probabilities implied by the benchmark "canonical" probit estimates based only on macroeconomic and institutional variables, while the dashed line plots the predicted probabilities for currency (bank) crises implied by augmenting the benchmark canonical model to include the occurrence of contemporaneous and lagged bank (currency) crises. Vertical lines indicate the actual occurrence of a crisis.

Observe that the predicted probabilities of both currency and bank crises based on the benchmark model increase in all four countries at the time of the 1997 Asian crisis. Including information about the occurrence of other crises causes the predicted probabilities to increase even more sharply. (The occurrence of a banking crisis in Korea in 1994 causes the predicted probability of a currency crisis to rise even earlier.)

It should be emphasized that these plots are intended not to show the predictive power of our model, but rather to illustrate the statistical importance of linkages between banking and currency crises.[21]

2.6 CONCLUSIONS

This chapter investigates the relative timing of the occurrence of banking and currency crises over the 1975–1997 period. For our sample of 90 countries, 72 had at least one case of a serious banking problem and 79 experienced at least one currency crisis at some point during the sample period. Several countries experienced multiple occurrences of banking crisis, and most had multiple currency crises. A total of 90 banking crisis episodes, 202 currency crises, and 37 twin crises were identified. While the relative frequency of individual banking and twin crises has increased over time, the frequency of currency crises has been relatively constant. Developing and emerging market countries suffered both banking and currency crises more often than industrial countries.

The twin crisis phenomenon, however, is mainly concentrated in a limited set of countries, namely, financially liberalized emerging-market economies. Summary statistics indicate an association between crises in broader country groupings (including lesser developed and industrial countries), but we find a robust link only in emerging markets. In emerging markets, banking crises (currency crises) have been associated with

---

[21] It should be noted that these are in-sample probability predictions. An alternative approach is to generate out-of-sample probabilities for 1997 based on estimates generated from data through 1996.

currency crises (banking crises) almost 50 percent (30 percent) of the time. This result holds up to a variety of tests: signal-to-noise ratios, bivariate probit regressions, multivariate probit equations, and simultaneous probit estimates. A strong causal, joint feedback, link between banking and currency crises appears only in this group of countries.

This result implies that, at least in financially liberalized emerging-market economies, policy measures taken to help avoid a banking crisis (currency crisis) have the additional benefit of lowering the probability of a currency (banking) crisis. Thus, measures to limit the exposure of balance sheets and enhance confidence in the banking sector may reduce the incentives for capital flight and currency runs. Similarly, policies designed to promote exchange rate stability appear capable of fostering broader stability in domestic banking institutions.

Our analysis also provides evidence that banking crises provide some leading information about the possibility of future foreign exchange instability, though again only for our emerging markets group. Currency crises, by contrast, were not a good leading indicator of impending banking problems. The power of banking crises to predict future currency instability does not appear to be due to a common experience with financial liberalization (or other factors) because this is explicitly taken into account by other variables in our estimation procedure. Instead, it might reflect the footloose nature of capital flows into emerging markets, where the onset of banking problems can quickly lead to capital flight and both current and future currency crises.

APPENDIXES

Appendix 2A. Countries Included in Dataset

Industrial Countries	Emerging Markets	Other Developing Countries
Austria	Argentina	Belize
Belgium	Bangladesh	Bolivia
Canada	Botswana	Burundi
Denmark	Brazil	Cameroon
Finland	Chile	Costa Rica
France	Colombia	Cyprus
Germany	Ecuador	Dominican Republic
Greece	Egypt	El Salvador
Iceland	Hong Kong	Equatorial Guinea
Ireland	Ghana	Ethiopia
Italy	India	Fiji
Japan	Indonesia	Grenada
Luxembourg	Jordan	Guatemala

(continued)

Appendix 2A (*continued*)

Industrial Countries	Emerging Markets	Other Developing Countries
Netherlands	Kenya	Guinea-Bissau
New Zealand	Korea	Guyana
Norway	Malaysia	Haiti
Portugal	Mauritius	Honduras
Spain	Mexico	Hungary
Sweden	Morocco	Jamaica
Switzerland	Pakistan	Lao P.D. Republic
United Kingdom	Peru	Madagascar
	Philippines	Malawi
	Singapore	Mali
	South Africa	Malta
	Sri Lanka	Mozambique
	Thailand	Myanmar
	Trinidad and Tobago	Nepal
	Tunisia	Nicaragua
	Turkey	Nigeria
	Uruguay	Panama
	Venezuela	Paraguay
	Zimbabwe	Romania
		Sierra Leone
		Swaziland
		Syrian Arab Republic
		Uganda
		Zambia

Note: The "All Country" sample includes "Industrial Countries," "Emerging Markets," and "Other Developing Countries"; the "Developing Country" sample includes "Emerging Markets" and "Other Developing Countries."

Appendix 2B. Occurrences of Banking and Currency Crises

	Banking Crises[a]	Currency Crises[b]	Financial Liberalization[c]
United Kingdom	1975–1976, 1984	1976, 1979, 1982, 1986, 1992	1975–1997
Austria			1975–1997
Belgium		1982	1986–1997
Denmark	1987–1992		1981–1997
France	1994–1995	1982	1975–1997
Germany	1978–1979		1975–1997
Italy	1990–1995	1976, 1992, 1995	1975–1997
Luxembourg			NA
Netherlands			1975–1997

	Banking Crises[a]	Currency Crises[b]	Financial Liberalization[c]
Norway	1987–1993	1978, 1986, 1992	1984–1997
Sweden	1990–1993	1977, 1981, 1992	1980–1997
Switzerland		1978	1989–1997
Canada	1983–1985	1976, 1992	1975–1997
Japan	1992–1997	1979, 1989	1985–1997
Finland	1991–1994	1977, 1982, 1991	1986–1997
Greece	1991–1995	1980, 1982, 1985	1975–1997
Iceland	1985–1986, 1993	1983, 1988, 1992	NA
Ireland			1985–1997
Malta		1992, 1997	NA
Portugal	1986–1989	1976, 1978, 1982, 1993	1984–1997
Spain	1977–1985	1976, 1983, 1992	1975–1997
Turkey	1982–1985, 1991, 1994–1995	1978, 1994	1980–1982, 1984–1997
New Zealand	1987–1990	1975, 1983, 1988, 1991	1980, 1984–1997
South Africa	1977, 1985, 1989	1975, 1978, 1984, 1996	NA
Argentina	1980–1982, 1989–1990, 1995–1997	1975, 1982, 1989	1977–1997
Bolivia	1986–1987, 1994–1997	1981, 1983, 1988, 1991	1985–1997
Brazil	1990, 1994–1997	1982, 1987, 1990, 1995	1975–1997
Chile	1976, 1981–1983	1985	1975–1997
Colombia	1982–1987	1985	1980–1997
Costa Rica	1987, 1994–1997	1981	NA
Dominican Republic		1985, 1987, 1990	NA
Ecuador	1980–1982, 1996–1997	1982, 1985, 1988	1986–1987, 1992–1997
El Salvador	1989	1986, 1990	1991–1997
Guatemala	1991–1992	1986, 1989	1989–1997
Haiti		1977, 1991	NA
Honduras		1990	1990–1997
Mexico	1981–1991, 1995–1997	1976, 1982, 1985, 1994	1989–1997
Nicaragua	1988–1996	1993	NA
Panama	1988–1989		NA
Paraguay	1995–1997	1984, 1986, 1988, 1992	1990–1997

(continued)

Appendix 2B (*continued*)

	Banking Crises[a]	Currency Crises[b]	Financial Liberalization[c]
Peru	1983–1990	1976, 1979, 1987	1980–1984, 1990–1997
Uruguay	1981–1984	1982	1976–1997
Venezuela	1978–1986, 1994–1997	1984, 1986, 1989, 1994	1981–1983, 1989–1997
Grenada		1978	NA
Guyana	1993–1995	1978, 1989	1991–1997
Belize			NA
Jamaica	1994–1997	1978, 1983, 1990	1991–1997
Trinidad & Tobago	1982–1993	1985, 1988, 1993	NA
Cyprus			NA
Jordan	1989–1990	1983, 1987, 1989, 1992	1988–1997
Syrian Arab Republic		1977, 1982, 1988	No liberalization
Egypt	1980–1985, 1991–1995	1979, 1989	1991–1997
Bangladesh	1987–1996	1975	NA
Myanmar	1996–1997	1975, 1977	NA
Sri Lanka	1989–1993	1977	1980–1997
China, P.R.: Hong Kong	1982–1986		NA
India	1993–1997	1976, 1991, 1995	1991–1997
Indonesia	1994, 1997	1978, 1983, 1986, 1997	1983–1997
Korea	1997	1980, 1997	1984–1997
Lao People's D. R.	1991–1994, 1997	1995	NA
Malaysia	1985–1988, 1997	1986, 1997	1978–1997
Nepal	1988–1994	1975, 1981, 1984, 1991, 1995	NA
Pakistan			NA
Philippines	1981–1987, 1997	1983, 1986, 1997	1981–1997
Singapore	1982	1975	NA
Thailand	1983–1987, 1997	1981, 1984, 1997	1989–1997
Botswana	1994–1995	1984, 1996	NA
Burundi	1994–1997	1976, 1983, 1986, 1989, 1997	NA
Cameroon	1987–1993, 1995–1997	1982, 1984, 1994	NA
Equatorial Guinea	1983–1985	1991, 1994	NA
Ethiopia	1994–1995	1992	NA
Ghana	1982–1989, 1997	1978, 1983, 1986	NA

	Banking Crises[a]	Currency Crises[b]	Financial Liberalization[c]
Guinea-Bissau	1995–1997	1991, 1996	NA
Kenya	1985–1989, 1992–1997	1975, 1981, 1985, 1993, 1995, 1997	1991–1997
Madagascar	1988	1984, 1986, 1991, 1994	NA
Malawi		1982, 1985, 1992, 1994	NA
Mali	1987–1989	1993	No liberalization
Mauritius	1996	1979	NA
Morocco		1983, 1990	NA
Mozambique	1987–1997	1993, 1995	NA
Nigeria	1993–1997	1986, 1989, 1992	1990–1993
Zimbabwe	1995–1997	1982, 1991,1994, 1997	NA
Sierra Leone	1990–1997	1988, 1990, 1997	NA
Swaziland	1995	1975, 1979, 1982, 1984	NA
Tunisia	1991–1995	1993	NA
Uganda	1994–1997	1981, 1987, 1989	1991–1997
Zambia	1995	1985, 1994	1992–1997
Fiji		1986	NA
Hungary	1991–1995	1989, 1994	NA
Romania	1990–1997	1990	NA

[a] Banking crisis onsets defined as first year of period of bank distress.
[b] Currency crisis defined by criteria described in text, with 24-month exclusion windows between crisis imposed.
[c] Years in sample with liberalized domestic interest rates. NA denotes information not available.

REFERENCES

Berg, Andrew and Catherine Patillo (1999). "Are Currency Crises Predictable? A Test," *IMF Staff Papers* **46**(June):107–138.

Calvo, Guillermo (1997). "Varieties of Capital-Market Crises." In Guillermo Calvo and Mervyn King, eds., *The Debt Burden and Its Consequences for Monetary Policy*. London: Macmillan.

Calvo, Guillermo and Enrique Mendoza (1996). "Mexico's Balance of Payments Crises. A Chronicle of a Death Foretold," *Journal of International Economics* **41**:235–264.

Caprio, Gerard and Daniela Klingebiel (1996). "Bank Insolvencies: Cross-Country Experiences." World Bank Policy Research Paper No. 1620.

Chang, Roberto and Andres Velasco (1999). "Liquidity Crises in Emerging Markets: Theory and Policy." NBER Working Paper No. 7272. Cambridge, MA.

Demirgüç-Kunt, Asli and Enrica Detragiache (1998a). "Financial Liberalization and Financial Fragility." IMF Working Paper No. 98/83.

———(1998b). "The Determinants of Banking Crises in Developing and Developed Countries." *IMF Staff Papers* **45**(March):81–109.

Diamond, Douglas and Phillip Dybvig (1983). "Bank Runs, Deposit Insurance, and Liquidity." *Journal of Political Economy* **91**:401–419.

Eichengreen, Barry and Andrew Rose (1998). "Staying Afloat when the Wind Shifts: External Factors and Emerging-Market Banking Crises," NBER Working Paper No. 6370. Cambridge, MA.

Eichengreen, Barry, Andrew Rose, and Charles Wyplosz (1995). "Exchange Market Mayhem: The Antecedents and Aftermath of Speculative Attacks," *Economic Policy* **21**(October):249–312.

Esquivel, Gerardo and Felipe Larrain (1998). "Explaining Currency Crises." Mimeo, Harvard Institute for International Development.

Frankel, Jeffrey and Andrew Rose (1996). "Currency Crashes in Emerging Markets: An Empirical Treatment," *Journal of International Economics* **41**(November):351–366.

Furman, Jason and Joseph Stiglitz (1998). "Economic Crises: Evidence and Insights from East Asia," *Brookings Papers on Economic Activity*, No. 2:1–119.

Glick, Reuven and Ramon Moreno (1998), "Money and Credit, Competitiveness, and Currency Crises in Asia and Latin America." Paper prepared for the 13th Pacific Basin Central Bank Conference on "Monetary Policy and the Structure of the Capital Account" held in Los Cabos, Mexico, November 7–11, 1998, and issued as Federal Reserve Bank of San Francisco, Center for Pacific Basin Studies Working Paper No. PB98-07.

Glick, Reuven and Andrew Rose (1999). "Contagion and Trade: Why Are Currency Crises Regional?" *Journal of International Money and Finance* **18**(August):603–618. Earlier versions issued as CEPR Discussion Paper No. 1947 and NBER Working Paper No. 6806.

Gonzalez-Hermosillo, Brend (1996). "Banking Sector Fragility and Systemic Sources of Fragility." IMF Working Paper No. 96/12.

Hutchison, Michael M. and Kathleen McDill (1999). "Are All Banking Crises Alike? The Japanese Experience in International Comparison." Federal Reserve Bank of San Francisco, Center for Pacific Basin Studies Working Paper No. PB99-02.

IMF (1998). *World Economic Outlook*, May. Chapter 4: "Financial Crises: Characteristics and Indicators of Vulnerability."

Kaminsky, Graciela, Saul Lizondo, and Carmen Reinhart (1998). "Leading Indicators of Currency Crises," *IMF Staff Papers* **45**(March):1–48.

Kaminsky, Graciela and Carmen Reinhart (1999). "The Twin Crises. The Causes of Banking and Balance-of-Payments Problems," *American Economic Review* **89**(June):473–500. Earlier version issued as Board of Governors International Finance Discussion Paper No. 544.

Krugman, Paul (1979). "A Model of Balance of Payments Crises," *Journal of Money, Credit, and Banking* **11**:311–325.

Kumar, Manmohan, Uma Moorthy, and William Perraudin (1998). "Determinants of Emerging Market Currency Crises and Contagion Effects." Paper presented at CEPR/World Bank conference "Financial Crises: Contagion and Market Volatility," London, May 8–9.

Kyei, Alexander (1995). "Deposit Protection Arrangements: A Survey." International Monetary Fund Working Paper No. 95/134.

Maddala, G.S. (1983). *Limited-Dependent and Qualitative Variables in Econometrics.* Cambridge, U.K.: Cambridge University Press.

McKinnon, Ronald and Huw Pill (1996). "Credible Liberalizations and International Capital Flows: The Overborrowing Syndrome." In Takatoshi Ito and Anne Krueger, eds., *Financial Deregulation and Integration in East Asia.* Chicago: University of Chicago Press, pp. 7–12.

———(1998). "The Overborrowing Syndrome: Are East Asian Economies Different?" In Reuven Glick, ed., *Managing Capital Flows and Exchange Rates" Perspectives from the Pacific Basin,* Cambridge, U.K.: Cambridge University Press, pp. 322–355.

Miller, Victoria (1996). "Speculative Currency Attacks with Endogenously Induced Commercial Bank Crises," *Journal of International Money and Finance* **15**(June):385–403.

———(1999). "The Timing and Size of Bank-Financed Speculative Attacks," *Journal of International Money and Finance* **18**(June):459–470.

Moreno, Ramon (1995). "Macroeconomic Behavior during Periods of Speculative Pressure or Realignment: Evidence from Pacific Basin Economies," Federal Reserve Bank of San Francisco *Economic Review*, No. 3:3–16.

———(1999). "Was There a Boom in Money and Credit Prior to East Asia's Recent Currency Crisis?" Federal Reserve Bank of San Francisco *Economic Review*, No. 1:23–41.

Obstfeld, Maurice (1994). "The Logic of Currency Crises." NBER Working Paper No. 4640. Cambridge, MA.

Reinhart, Carmen and Carlos Vegh (1995). "Nominal Interest Rates, Consumption Booms, and Lack of Credibility – A Quantitative Examination," *Journal of Development Economics* **46**(April):357–378.

Rojas-Suarez, Liliana and Steven Weisbrod (1995). "Financial Fragilities in Latin America: The 1980s and 1990s." International Monetary Fund Occasional Paper No. 132.

Rossi, Marco (1999). "Financial Fragility and Economic Performance in Developing Countries." IMF Working Paper No. 99/66.

Sachs, Jeffrey, Aaron Tornell, and Andres Velasco (1996). "Financial Crises in Emerging Markets: The Lessons from 1995," *Brookings Papers on Economic Activity*, No. 1:147–215.

Velasco, Andres (1987). "Financial Crises and Balance of Payments Crises: A Simple Model of the Southern Cone Experience," *Journal of Development Economics* **27**(October):263–283.

Discussion

Banking and Currency Crises: How Common are Twins?

Andrew K. Rose

In my opinion there are four broad objectives for the emerging quantitative work on currency crises. The goals of this research program can be summarized in a series of questions:

1. What are the *determinants* of crises?
2. Can one *predict* crises or construct "early warning systems"?
3. Is there joint causality across countries – that is, *contagion*? What are the channels?
4. Is there *joint causality* between banking and currency crises?

In this fine chapter, Glick and Hutchison focus on the last issue, the problem of joint causality. This is an important issue, and the stakes are high for their work. A finding of joint causality between banking and currency crises has strong implications for our understanding of the causes of both, and, more importantly, for policy actions to prevent future crises. They also ask an important question which has thus far not been directly addressed in the literature, namely, "does country aggregation matter?" The extant literature disaggregates by time and sometimes the degree of capital mobility, but most papers use either OECD or emerging market data, but not both. Glick and Hutchison emerge from their extensive empirical analysis with two key conclusions. First, there is in fact joint causality; more specifically, banking crises tend to cause currency crises. Second, emerging markets are different. Both of their findings are plausible and sensible. This adds to the appeal of their chapter, though it makes the job of the discussant a bit more demanding.

One important methodological issue rears its head at the outset. Can one do an investigation of the fourth issue without taking a strong stand on the first three issues? Glick and Hutchison are clear about their assumptions vis-à-vis the rest of the research program. In particular, they assume that (a) they know the determinants of banking and currency crises, (b) crises are predictable, and (c) contagion is irrelevant. Fair enough. But one immediately asks, How sensitive are the results to these assumptions? If one disagrees with the assumptions, does it make suspect the conclusions that follow?

It is worth exploring this issue a little more deeply, since there is no consensus in the area at large. There is much disagreement about the determinants of crises; few "fundamentals" such as loose monetary or fiscal policy are present in most crises. There is even more dispute about the efficacy of early warning systems. My view is that mechanistic systems do not have a good *ex ante* track record. That conclusion is consistent with the evidence presented here: The predictions of crises have very low power in Glick and Hutchison. But there is certainly much dispute. Finally, no one disagrees that there are clusters of crises in 1982, 1993, 1995, and 1997. But the interpretation of this clustering is far from clear. Personally, I believe that there is contagion, and it is simply not the case that common external shocks cause whole regions to plunge into crisis simultaneously for the same reason. Thus, I think of it as a mistake to ignore foreign effects in general. But even if one believes that what looks like contagion is actually a series of common external shocks (such as U.S. or German interest rates and/or OECD growth), can one really discuss crises without analyzing these external phenomena?

I have a number of smaller issues that I fully imagine the authors will handle in future research. The authors place a good deal of emphasis on their country disaggregation scheme, appropriately so in my view. Still, it would be interesting to add more economic meat to the scheme itself, which currently seems somewhat arbitrary. One could imagine disaggregating countries in many different ways: Why is this appropriate? In particular, distinguishing between "emerging markets" and "developing countries" on well-specified economic criteria seems like a goal for future work. There may be better ways to disaggregate groups of countries, and establishing the sensitivity of the aggregation scheme is also a worthwhile objective.

Another issue is that their currency crisis construction scheme is based on multilateral (real) exchange rates. This is a novel approach. Most crises affect countries in fixed bilateral rate regimes; one thinks of the ERM crisis of 1992–1993, which is essentially a crisis which centered on Germany. Similarly the Mexican and Asian crises also centered on exchange rates which were formally or informally pegged to the U.S. dollar. In this regard, it is also interesting to note that the multilateral scheme leads a number of countries (e.g., Cameroon, Equatorial Guinea, Grenada, Guinea-Bissau, and Swaziland) to register currency crises while they were within currency unions.

A related issue is that the definition of currency crises measures outliers vis-à-vis *country-specific* distribution parameters. Doing so implies that each country should have approximately the same number of crises? Do we really believe this? The alternative approach of pooling across countries allows one to give Argentina a disproportionate share of crises, while allowing stable countries like the Netherlands to register long periods of tranquility.

Glick and Hutchison may also want to relax other aspects their methodology. For instance, they may want to focus on predictions other than one year in advance. I also recommend that they shy away from focusing on the real exchange rate as a determinant of currency crises. It is inherently difficult to measure; and because their definition of a currency crisis almost always entails depreciation, overvaluation is likely to precede crises.

Still, these are small issues. Essentially, they point to the enormous potential for future research. Glick and Hutchison have advanced the research program in the area, and I look forward to more of their work in the future.

3

Multiple Equilibria, Contagion and the Emerging Market Crises

Paul R. Masson

The dominant theme that emerges is that there is more than one plausible explanation for any slightly mysterious phenomenon (such as the arrival and spread of cholera or yellow fever), that these contending plausible explanations often have radically different implications for public action, and that societies are reluctant to undertake costly or even inconvenient actions on the basis of contending theories of uncertain merit.

(Cooper, 1989, pp. 180–181).

3.1 INTRODUCTION

It is not surprising that the increasing turmoil in global financial markets has stimulated interest in models with multiple equilibria, where the jumps between equilibria are triggered by extraneous events. What has seemed most striking about the crises in the mid- to late 1990s is that their timing and virulence seem quite unrelated to the fundamental problems facing the countries and markets concerned. For instance, though the crisis in Mexico in 1994–1995 seems to have among its causes an overvalued exchange rate and a large current account deficit, the devaluation of December 1994, which should have served to help solve these problems, instead led to a loss of confidence, a free-fall of the

Earlier versions of this chapter were presented at the Allied Social Sciences Association annual meeting in New York, January 3–5, 1999, and at a conference on "Financial Crises in Emerging Markets" at the Federal Reserve Bank of San Francisco, September 23–24, 1999. I am grateful to Olivier Jeanne and Marcus Miller for very useful discussions of the issues treated here, as well as to Joshua Aizenman, Roberto Chang, Enrica Detragiache, Ilan Goldfajn, Caroline Van Rijckeghem, and Tony Richards for helpful comments. Freyan Panthaki and Haiyan Shi provided research assistance, and Manny Sriram helped in obtaining the data. The views expressed are my own, however, and in particular do not represent those of the International Monetary Fund or its member countries.

exchange rate, and the prospect of a massive default on exchange-rate-linked foreign debt, the *tesobonos*.[1]

In addition, crises have triggered severe attacks on other currencies, where the trade and capital flow linkages between countries have been weak. This includes the contagion from Mexico to Argentina and Brazil, the contemporaneous crises in many East Asian countries in 1997, and the rippling effects of the Russian default in August 1998 on many emerging markets and even on U.S. corporate debt and mortgage backed securities spreads, resulting in a severe liquidity crisis that nearly brought down the hedge fund Long-Term Capital Management (LTCM). The puzzle is why a crisis in a relatively small market should have global effects. Though there may be subtle reasons why linkages through "wake-up calls," portfolio rebalancing, or "common creditor effects" may be sufficiently important to explain the above events, these explanations are not completely satisfying because they rely on assumptions of market imperfections, irrationality, or inability to exploit profit opportunities. Another possibility is that the emerging market crises were the result of moral hazard; an example is the "insurance model" of crises in Dooley (1997). These issues are explored more fully below. It is argued that models with multiple equilibria (in which investors also recognize the possibility of jumps between equilibria, so that they form their expectations rationally) can introduce volatility into financial markets that substantially exceeds that of the macroeconomic fundamentals, and as a result they square better with the stylized facts of global financial markets.

Such models in particular allow investors' expectations to be self-fulfilling. This gives a prominent role to what is commonly called "market sentiment" in the determination of asset prices, or, in the economic literature, "sunspots," – that is, irrelevant variables that nevertheless coordinate investors' expectations. For many economists this is troubling, since it introduces indeterminacy in contrast to mainstream models that generally lead to precise predictions. For instance, the contribution of first-generation speculative attack models (Krugman, 1979) was to show how the timing of a speculative attack, which seemed to be random, could in fact be predicted when the fundamentals were deteriorating at a predictable rate. Clearly, multiple-equilibria models acknowledge that asset prices are less predictable than implied by models with a unique equilibrium, but recent experience suggests that this feature corresponds well to reality rather than being an inconvenient property of a theoretical model. The resistance to second-generation crisis models (Obstfeld, 1986, 1994), where the authorities' decision to devalue is endogenous and can be provoked by a sufficiently strong speculative

---

[1] For a discussion of this episode and the resulting loss of confidence in the Mexican authorities, see Agénor and Masson (1999).

attack, was no doubt in part related to this concern (an example is Krugman, 1996).

Another objection is based on political economy; governments are always keen to deny that it is their policies which are out of line, and multiple-equilibria models allow them to blame attacks on wicked speculators rather than putting the blame where it belongs. It is not true, however, that multiple-equilibria models completely absolve policymakers, since a clear implication of most of such models is that only for a certain range of the economic fundamentals are multiple equilibria possible (Jeanne, 1997). It is therefore up to the policymaker to avoid the "crisis zone" – for instance, by limiting indebtedness, particularly short-term foreign currency borrowing (Cole and Kehoe, 1996).

A related point is that the models with unique and multiple equilibria may in some cases be observationally equivalent. If we observe a change in monetary policies after a devaluation, we cannot distinguish between two hypotheses – one that the change was anticipated, and hence that the single (devaluation) equilibrium was the only one, and another that the attack triggered the change in monetary policy, so that a no-attack equilibrium would have been validated by a tighter monetary policy (Garber, 1996). In such circumstances, one may have to be guided by the plausibility of each of the two models rather than a statistical test of one against the other.

This chapter, rather than attempting to provide new theories or econometric evidence, discusses in an informal way the plausibility of multiple equilibria models and their usefulness as a modeling technique. Section 3.2 gives a nonrigorous survey of some of the models that permit multiple equilibria in financial markets, with a distinction made between those that emphasize macroeconomic factors, bank runs, or the evaluation of imperfect information. Section 3.3 discusses issues of contagion of crises, arguing that multiple equilibria models allow a rich way of modeling contemporaneous crises even when macroeconomic linkages are not strong enough to explain them. In Section 3.4, stylized facts concerning international capital markets are presented and are used to evaluate existing theories of contagion. Finally, Section 3.5 gives some preliminary thoughts on the implications of multiple equilibria models for crisis prediction and prevention, and Section 3.6 concludes the chapter.

3.2 WHAT SORTS OF FINANCIAL MODELS PRODUCE JUMPS BETWEEN MULTIPLE EQUILIBRIA?

Without trying to present a formal taxonomy or an exhaustive survey, this section presents three different types of models that produce multiple equilibria for financial asset prices. These include: (1) macroeconomic feedback models, where adverse expectations of a particular event (typically a devaluation) make that event more likely (typically by raising borrowing costs or wages); (2) liquidity, or bank run models; and (3) models of fads and herding where the process of inferring information that feeds into expectations leads to an arbitrariness in the relationship between observed fundamentals and the prevailing equilibrium.

There is also an earlier literature on multiple equilibria in macro models that focused not on financial markets but on real investment, overlapping generations models, and seigniorage and the demand for money (Azariadis, 1981; Boldrin and Woodford, 1990; Chiappori and Guesnerie, 1991; Durlauf, 1991). Rather than explaining high-frequency fluctuations, the motivation for some of these models was to explain how the economy could be persistently stuck in a situation of low investment and animal spirits, or higher-than-optimal inflation. However, the focus here is on financial markets, and, as argued above, the notion that jumps between equilibria add volatility to asset prices has its own appeal. Hence, no further mention is made of this earlier literature.

3.2.1 Macroeconomic Feedback Models

In these sorts of models, a higher domestic interest rate, triggered by fears of devaluation or default, feeds back in an adverse way on the economy's prospects, making a devaluation or default more likely. The linkages producing this positive feedback between expectations of devaluation and the possibility of its occurrence are various. In so-called first-generation models, the decision to devalue is triggered when a particular variable, normally foreign exchange reserves, falls below a certain threshold. Higher interest rates can make reaching this threshold more likely because they increase the economy's foreign debt servicing (as in Masson, 1999b) or because higher interest rates trigger a run on the banking system, an expansion of domestic liquidity, and an outflow of reserves (Chang and Velasco, 1998).

In second-generation speculative attack models, the government's decision to devalue is endogenous, which widens the set of relevant macro fundamentals that are affected by investors' devaluation expectations and that can positively affect the devaluation probability. In Obstfeld (1994), two examples are given, one in which exchange rate expectations worsen the unemployment–inflation tradeoff, another where inflation expectations increase the burden of servicing government debt. In the former, the expectation of devaluation raises inflation expectations and wage demands, making it more likely that the authorities will give in to those demands and devalue in order to avoid unemployment. In the latter, higher interest rates reflect increased fears that the authorities will inflate away outstanding debt, raising the burden of that debt and hence the likelihood that the inflation option will be chosen. In both cases, therefore, shifts in expectations are to some extent self-fulfilling, and there are several rational expectations equilibria.

A general equilibrium model with optimizing private sector agents has been developed by Cole and Kehoe (1996). In this model, the key variable influencing vulnerability to self-fulfilling attacks is the amount of short-term government debt. The authors argue that Mexico's exposure put it into a crisis zone of multiple equilibria, and the crisis of 1994–1995 corresponded to such a self-fulfilling attack.

An objection that can be made to the interpretation of crises as jumps between multiple equilibria in macroeconomic feedback models is that the linkages involved typically take time to operate. Thus, a defense of a currency through high interest rates will only make a dent in the fiscal budget or the balance of payments if it is sustained for an extended period of time; the existence of multiperiod debt further reduces vulnerability. In the meantime, expectations need to be coordinated on the "bad" equilibrium; how expectations are coordinated is usually not modeled. Indeed, models of self-fulfilling attacks fit most comfortably in a world with a large speculator (a possibility considered by Krugman, 1996), not atomistic agents. When there are many agents, it needs to be explained why they all shift at the same time between equilibria.

Indeed, introducing heterogeneity among agents may in fact remove the possibility of multiple equilibria in such macroeconomic feedback models (Herrendorf et al., 1998). The intuition is that a continuum of values for preference parameters or technology may remove the discontinuity embodied in multiple equilibria. This is an area deserving greater theoretical and empirical attention.

3.2.2 Models of Liquidity and Bank Runs

In this type of model, lenders/depositors need to form expectations of what other depositors are doing: If others run, then it is optimal for a given individual to run too, if the amount of liquid assets available to the bank is less than demand deposits outstanding. In the formalization of Diamond and Dybvig (1983), it is a realization of a shock that determines whether each individual wants to consume now rather than later. However, even those wanting to consume later may want to withdraw their money if they think a bank run will occur; and if they do, the bank run exhausts the bank's liquid assets. Depending on whether depositors coordinate on the run or no-run equilibrium, a crisis does or does not occur.

This model has led to a number of variants and applications. In the area of international lending, an early paper by Sachs (1984) shows that if international indebtedness to a large number of domestic bank creditors is within a certain range relative to a country's income, then panics can occur; that is, ". . . if each bank believes that all other banks will stop lending, *all* banks will stop lending . . . It is precisely because panics occur only at high levels of debt that they are so difficult to distinguish from other forms of default. In every true liquidity crisis, it will seem to some observers that the problem really lies with the risk of debt repudiation or insolvency rather than with the supply of credit" (Sachs, 1984, p. 32). This raises the problem of collective action, because typically it will be in the creditors' interest to coordinate on a no-crisis equilibrium, but they may not be able to commit credibly not to run, even if the country's problem is one of liquidity, not solvency, an issue discussed in Detragiache (1996). Sachs, Tornell, and Velasco (1996) model the Mexican crisis as a self-fulfilling panic, while Radelet and Sachs (1998) argue that a run by international creditors played a role in the Asian crisis. Chang and Velasco (1998) develop a model where domestic bank runs and international crises are linked.

Interestingly enough, such liquidity models rely crucially on the existence of many uncoordinated agents, in direct contrast to macroeconomic feedback models. However, a criticism of the Diamond–Dybvig model of liquidity is that it depends on sequential servicing of withdrawals, making it desirable to run before others do so. In this context, it would therefore be easy to eliminate runs by altering the "first-come, first-served" assumption, by suspending convertibility when a run starts (Rogoff, 1999).

Another objection to the simple Diamond–Dybvig model is that runs do not occur out of the blue; they come when the banking system is under severe stress. Allen and Gale (1998) argue that the evidence rejects "sunspot" models in favor of "business cycle" models of bank runs, since bank failures typically occur when the economy experiences a cyclical downturn. More general models, however, do not involve such a false dichotomy. For instance, in the Sachs version of the model, macroeconomic fundamentals do matter in influencing the possibility of multiple equilibria. Clearly, to be realistic a model of bank runs should allow the state of the cycle to influence the vulnerability to a jump from a no-run to a run equilibrium. However, in general it is hard to distinguish between fundamental-based runs and self-fulfilling causes, as the above quote from Sachs highlights.

3.2.3 Models of Information Acquisition and Expectations Formation

A quite different reason for the absence of a unique relationship between macroeconomic fundamentals and equilibrium is provided by models of expectations formation with imperfect and asymmetric information.[2] These models explain how herding behavior among investors and fads can be rational (Banerjee, 1992; Bikchandani et al., 1992; Caplin and Leahy, 1994; Lee, 1997; Chari and Kehoe, 1998). If each individual investor has some private information (and knows that others do too), then observing the actions of others gives some clues as to what they know (assuming that they cannot credibly share their information), making it rational to imitate them. Depending on the sequence of "signals" received, the equilibrium asset price can take one of several values. Moreover, a new signal that tips the balance of sentiment from optimism to pessimism can provoke a "cascade" or "avalanche" of sell orders and a large change in price. Thus, such models provide some justification for the apparent coordination, in the macroeconomic feedback models discussed in Section 3.2.1, on one or another equilibrium.[3] Calvo and Mendoza (1996) present a model of herding behavior by international investors that is applied to the Mexican crisis; Calvo (1998) uses a model with informed and uninformed investors to try to understand contagion from Russia.

Morris and Shin (1998) show that models that do not depend on a sequence of actions by individual investors may be very sensitive to the information structure, though in a counterintuitive way. In particular, if agents do not share common knowledge about the distribution of the shock received, but still face some noise in their individual signals about fundamentals, then the possibility of multiple equilibria disappears, and it is rational for all agents to attack. However, the generality of this particular result is unclear.

3.3 MODELING CONTAGION AS JUMPS BETWEEN MULTIPLE EQUILIBRIA

In another paper (Masson 1999a) I propose a taxonomy of reasons why crises in developing countries might be contemporaneous in time. They include: a common cause affecting all developing countries – for instance, because of a change in U.S. monetary policy (monsoonal effects); macro-economic linkages among developing countries themselves, mainly through trade flows (spillovers); and other causes, not related to the

---

[2] Strictly speaking, these models yield a unique set of expectations, but they are sensitive to initial conditions. Thus, this class of models can be seen as providing explanations for the seemingly arbitrary formation of expectations. These expectations in turn may be consistent with one or another of the macroeconomic equilibria described in Sections 3.2.1 or 3.2.2, and hence be self-fulfilling.

[3] Arifovic and Masson (1999) consider boundedly rational agents who imitate others as well as experimenting in forming their expectations. Simulations replicate boom and bust cycles in lending to emerging market countries and associated currency crises.

country's macroeconomic fundamentals (pure contagion). I go on to argue that the first two channels do not seem sufficient to explain the tequila and Asian crises, and that the third type of contagion therefore is relevant. Moreover, it is desirable to allow for the possibility of contagion by building macroeconomic models that permit multiple equilibria – that is, depart from a unique mapping of the macroeconomic fundamentals onto financial asset prices. In such a framework, contagion might occur because a jump between equilibria was triggered by an attack elsewhere.

3.3.1 Other Models of Pure Contagion

There are at least three other explanations for contagion unrelated to a change in a country's macroeconomic fundamentals that deserve mention. One of them is that a crisis elsewhere provides new information about the seriousness of problems in the home country; this is the "wake-up call" hypothesis (Goldstein, 1998). As applied to Asia, problems with banks and other financial intermediaries and the evils of crony capitalism in Thailand made investors recognize that the "Asian miracle" was an "Asian mirage," leading to a reevaluation of the desirability of investing in Indonesia, Korea, and Malaysia, not to mention Hong Kong and Singapore. While there is some plausibility to this explanation in the case of Asia, it does not provide a convincing general explanation of "pure" contagion. It is true that we as economists and investors are now much more sensitive to banking sector problems and skeptical of the Asian model of development. Nevertheless, it seems likely that to some extent the change in beliefs was overdone, perhaps for reasons related to the models of "fads" mentioned above. Already, one sees a shift in sentiment toward investing in Asia, though many of the problems originally identified are still there. So that rather than a wake-up call, it seems more plausible to suppose that there are shifts in sentiment, some of which are not related to learning about a country's true fundamentals. Moreover, when applied to the Mexican crisis and the tequila effect on other countries of Latin America, it is not clear what similarities among the countries investors "woke up" to (since the Mexican economy was very different from that of Argentina or Brazil, for instance), or why, by 1996, they had fallen asleep again and were investing record amounts in emerging markets in Latin America and Asia.

A second explanation is that of portfolio rebalancing – that is, the existence of a common creditor or cross-market hedging (Kaminsky and Reinhart, 1998; Kodres and Pritsker, 1999). Major global financial institutions facing a loss in one market turn to other markets in order to realize liquidity, so that a crisis in one emerging market triggers crises in others (Valdés 1996). Mutual funds that are specialized in a region, which face redemptions as a result, say, of a crisis in Thailand, may be forced to liquidate in a number of countries in the region to meet those redemptions. Hedge funds may be highly leveraged, so that losses in one market lead to a write down of capital that requires shrinking the portfolio size, for a given leverage ratio, and this leads to liquidation of their holdings in a number of markets. In addition, a crisis may provoke a reexamination of the riskiness of investing in emerging markets and bring about a voluntary decline in the leverage ratio. Both effects may have operated after the Russian default in August 1998, because some investment banks and hedge funds suffered important losses on their investment in Russian bonds. Though this is a plausible story concerning short-run pressures on asset prices, the persistence of such effects either (a) denies the importance of other investors who, seeing the fundamentals unchanged, take advantage of the buying opportunity created by a few institutions in trouble or (b) requires that herding behavior be so pervasive that all investors are similarly affected. Either way, it seems that one needs to appeal to the types of phenomena described above that permit multiple equilibria and self-fulfilling expectations.

A third explanation for contagion links the boom in lending to (and investment in) emerging markets and the subsequent occurrence of crises to government guarantees and moral hazard. Dooley (1997) adapts the first-generation, Henderson-Salant/Krugman/Flood-Garber speculative attack model to an attack on the resources available to the emerging market government to provide guarantees of various kinds – for example, deposit insurance or the commitment to bailout banks.[4] Dooley argues that the boom in lending to emerging market countries in the early 1990s corresponded to an exogenous rise in their net worth due to lower world (i.e., U.S.) interest rates and debt write-downs. Clever investors found ways to appropriate this net worth through capital inflows; when they judged that those resources had been depleted, they pulled their money out, triggering a crisis. On the face of it, such a model seems not to explain contemporaneous crises, since countries' net worths are unlikely to begin at the same level and are unlikely to be depleted at the same time. Dooley argues, however, that investors' perceptions of the amount of *international* resources available for any given country would be reduced by a bailout elsewhere, making a crisis more likely in the former and leading to apparent contagion.

---

[4] Corsetti, Pesenti, and Roubini (1998) and Irwin and Vines (1999) offer models that similarly stress the role of government incentives and guarantees in leading to unprofitable investment. See Marion (1999) for an interesting discussion of the Dooley model.

This model is based on a simple view of the *solvency* of a country – based on a stock of assets rather than, for instance, the power of a government to raise future resources through taxation. It also gives no role to *liquidity*, which for many observers was key to understanding the vulnerability to attack of Mexico and Korea, with their large short-term, foreign currency liabilities. Finally, it requires a great deal of foresight by investors, who are assumed to have anticipated the possibility of international bailouts in Asia and also to have estimated the point when net worth went to zero.

3.3.2 How Are Crises Transmitted in Multiple-Equilibria Models?

There are several ways in which crises may be transmitted in models with multiple equilibria; these are detailed in Masson (1999b). In a single country model, jumps between equilibria are typically modeled using a Markov transition matrix, with constant transition probabilities; moreover, there is a particular region for the fundamentals where multiple equilibria can occur. Contagion could occur for the following reasons: (1) The transition probabilities could depend on the occurrence of a crisis elsewhere, so that the probability of moving from a noncrisis to a crisis state in country *a* would be greater if there was a crisis in country *b*. (2) Expectations of a crisis in country *b* could raise expectations of a crisis in *a*, because, for instance, a devaluation in *b*, if it occurred, would worsen the competitiveness of *a* (i.e., appreciate its real exchange rate). Here it is not spillovers, but expected spillovers, that would explain why interest rate spreads might increase in several emerging market countries, because they would each reflect expected devaluation. (3) A devaluation in *b* might worsen the fundamentals of *a* enough to put it into the "crisis" (i.e., multiple equilibrium) region, even if before it was not in the region. Then, though not for certain, a crisis might occur in *a* if triggered by a random event, or sunspot.

The regime-switching estimation techniques of Hamilton (1988, 1994) provide a useful framework for the estimation of multiple-equilibria models. As shown in Jeanne and Masson (2000), a canonical second-generation speculative attack model can be written in a form that can be estimated as a two-regime model, where the two regimes differ only in their intercept terms. Such a model does a good job in capturing fluctuations in French franc/deutsche mark exchange rate expectations over 1987–1993.

Applications to currency crises in Latin America and Asia are less straightforward. When such a model is applied separately to monthly data on interest rates for Argentina and Brazil over 1994–1998, using the real exchange rate, the trade balance, the output gap, and time as the set of fundamental variables, jumps between regimes are estimated to be relatively infrequent, and countries remain in each state for extended periods. Therefore, testing whether the occurrence of a crisis state (i.e., high interest rates) in one country is associated with the occurrence of a similar state in the other (or with a crisis in Mexico, for instance) is difficult. Cerra and Saxena (1998) actually estimate a regime switching model for the Asian crisis countries in which the transition probabilities depend on variables in another country, but they find no statistically significant effects. Thus, this idea, though promising, does not deliver any insights here. The problem seems to be that the significant variation in the data is across countries rather than over time, making cross-section or panel estimation techniques most useful. Most countries face few or no crises, so that pooling of countries is needed. An alternative may be to use higher-frequency data and to examine not crises per se, but just large asset price movements; for instance, both Kaminsky and Schmukler (1999) and Baig and Goldfajn (1999) use daily data on financial asset prices, along with actual announcements of economic news. It may be easier with such data to test hypotheses concerning contagion, even if the relevant macroeconomic data are only available monthly or quarterly and there are still few crises.

3.4 IS THERE EVIDENCE OF SELF-FULFILLING ATTACKS AND MULTIPLE EQUILIBRIA?

The case for formulating financial models with multiple equilibria would seem to rest in large part on the observation that the macroeconomic fundamentals do not exhibit enough volatility to explain the volatility in financial asset prices. There is a long literature, pioneered by Robert Shiller (e.g., Shiller, 1989), that examines the volatility of various asset prices in relation to the volatility of their underlying value – for instance, equity prices relative to dividends or earnings. Though there are difficult conceptual issues in such tests, including how to measure the discount factor used to value future earnings (which may itself be quite variable, introducing volatility into the fundamental valuation), this literature generally does support the idea that financial markets are excessively volatile in some sense.

It is interesting to consider the cross-country correlation of stock market price indices and each country's economic fundamentals, for a set of emerging market countries for which reasonably long time series are available (Table 3.1). Except for Turkey, the rates of change of equity prices (in real terms) are more highly correlated than either real dividend or GDP growth rates. It is interesting to note that Mexico's share prices are positively correlated with those of other countries, though

Table 3.1. Selected Emerging-Market Economies: Cross-Country Correlations, 1988–1999

	Hong Kong	Korea	Malaysia	Mexico	Philippines	Singapore	South Africa	Taiwan, China	Thailand	Turkey
					Real Equity Price Index Growth					
Hong Kong	1	0.60	0.84	0.54	0.58	0.78	0.40	0.38	0.58	−0.01
Korea		1	0.72	0.25	0.65	0.90	0.32	0.54	0.61	−0.01
Malaysia			1	0.54	0.77	0.88	0.39	0.25	0.87	0.09
Mexico				1	0.54	0.40	0.61	0.38	0.39	−0.27
Philippines					1	0.78	0.52	0.46	0.72	−0.24
Singapore						1	0.52	0.42	0.65	−0.01
South Africa							1	0.65	0.05	0.14
Taiwan, China								1	0.07	−0.11
Thailand									1	0.25
Turkey										1
					Real Dividend Growth					
Hong Kong	1	0.09	0.75	−0.46	0.48	0.15	−0.07	0.09	0.76	0.21
Korea		1	0.22	−0.05	0.15	0.14	0.18	0.36	0.14	0.30
Malaysia			1	−0.67	0.65	0.51	0.20	−0.15	0.76	0.23
Mexico				1	−0.80	−0.21	0.01	−0.10	−0.14	0.011
Philippines					1	0.46	−0.16	0.03	0.43	0.10

	Singapore	South Africa	Taiwan, China	Thailand	Turkey
Singapore	1	0.09	−0.05	0.59	−0.10
South Africa		1	0.48	−0.05	0.45
Taiwan, China			1	−0.16	−0.20
Thailand				1	0.25
Turkey					1

Real GDP Growth

	Hong Kong	Korea	Malaysia	Mexico	Philippines	Singapore	South Africa	Taiwan, China	Thailand	Turkey
Hong Kong	1	0.86	0.90	−0.09	0.42	0.83	0.24	0.66	0.76	0.10
Korea		1	0.94	−0.24	0.53	0.81	0.36	0.55	0.89	0.04
Malaysia			1	−0.15	0.53	0.84	0.28	0.60	0.87	0.12
Mexico				1	−0.13	−0.13	−0.35	0.06	−0.28	−0.19
Philippines					1	0.60	0.87	0.34	0.44	0.04
Singapore						1	0.49	0.72	0.79	0.03
South Africa							1	0.21	0.24	−0.09
Taiwan, China								1	0.59	−0.26
Thailand									1	−0.04
Turkey										1

Note: All data are in local currency.

Sources: Primark Datastream and International Monetary Fund, *World Economic Outlook*.

85

dividends and GDP are generally not. The efficient markets model would imply that dividends are the relevant fundamental; the first principal component explains 55 percent of equity price growth, but only 38 percent of dividend growth.[5]

The table thus provides suggestive evidence of excessive correlation of stock market prices relative to the fundamentals underlying a country's stock market.[6] Other asset prices give similar evidence either of excessive volatility or excessive co-movement, and this suggests that it may be necessary to introduce additional noise into asset valuation models. However, simply adding a normally distributed error does not do the job, since shocks to financial asset prices also seem to be characterized by occasional very large changes – that is, to be drawn from a distribution with fat tails. Moreover, observations do not seem to be clustered around a single point but rather correspond to discrete regimes. Jumps between multiple equilibria, between "euphoria" and "gloom," seem to be a useful way to capture that phenomenon. An interesting alternative approach is to assume that the distribution of shocks is bimodal (for whatever reason) and to try to estimate its parameters from the data (Lim and Martin, 1998). Both alternatives seem to characterize the data better than a single linear relationship with an additive error term drawn from a unimodal distribution, fat-tailed or not.

Another relevant stylized fact is that the fundamentals suggested by economic theory do not seem to explain asset price movements. For instance, Flood and Rose (1995) find no evidence that there is a linear relationship between exchange rates and a set of plausible macroeconomic fundamentals. This finding is destructive of our usual linear (or nearly linear) econometric models with unique equilibria, but not necessarily of models with substantial nonlinearity in some form or another. One way of introducing a large amount of nonlinearity is through jumps between equilibria.

Indeed, Jeanne and Masson (2000) find that the relationship between macro variables and exchange rate expectations (captured as the interest differential between short-term French franc and deutsche mark assets) comes through much more significantly when a two-state model is estimated than when only a single linear relationship is imposed on the data. In particular, the statistical significance of the coefficients with

[5] Discounted dividends, not contemporaneous dividends, should explain equity prices, but lack of observations precluded doing this calculation. In any case, at an annual frequency, dividends are already fairly smooth. See Shiller (1989, Chapter 10), who finds excess co-movement between United States and United Kingdom stock price indices.

[6] All indices are in local currency, so the comovement of exchange rates (relative, for instance, to the dollar) in emerging market crises are not the source of the excess correlation of stock prices.

respect to the macro fundamentals (the French trade balance, real effective exchange rate, and the unemployment rate) and time is much stronger when the relationship is allowed to include a different constant term (but the same slope coefficients) in two regimes than it is in a single-regime model. The two-regime model successfully captures several periods of turbulence, while the single-regime model yields a smooth, though somewhat curved, downward trend in the interest differential. Moreover, though testing the null hypothesis of a single regime versus the alternative of two regimes is not straightforward (since some of the parameters are not defined under the null), even an overly conservative criterion (allowing fully for the number of additional parameters in the degrees of freedom calculation) suggests that the increase in likelihood is significantly greater for the two-state model: 106.58 compared to a $\chi^2(4)$, whose 1 percent critical value is 13.28.

As mentioned above, it does not seem possible in general to distinguish conclusively multiple-equilibria models from unique-equilibrium models, since the former depend on unobserved expectations which may legitimately be assumed to depend on other considerations than the macroeconomic fundamentals. This is the tack taken by Krugman (1996), who argues that political fundamentals were shifting in the 1992–1993 period in France. This would explain why the speculative attack on the franc's ERM parity, repulsed in September–November 1992, revived in the spring of 1993 (as unemployment rose), culminating in widespread loss of confidence and flight from the franc (and other non-German currencies) in July and forcing a widening of the ERM bands. However, as argued in Jeanne and Masson (1997), this explanation raises as many questions as it provides answers. In particular, the June–July 1993 crisis immediately followed the sharp *narrowing* of differentials and appreciation of the franc in May, when in fact French rates went below German rates and there was talk of the franc taking over leadership of the ERM from the deutsche mark. The proximate political event triggering the crisis was not domestic concerns (the new government had received a large majority of seats in the National Assembly) but rather a tiff between the French and German finance ministers, and the notion that a relatively minor event could trigger a large crisis is, if anything, suggestive of shifts in self-fulfilling expectations rather than fundamental causes.

Another stylized fact that is supportive of the idea of multiple equilibria is the alternation of periods of overlending and capital outflow in emerging market countries, the latter precipitating major crises. As documented by many studies (see, for instance, Schadler et al., 1993), an initial period of euphoria brings about a narrowing of spreads and lack of concern for credit quality, as capital flows indiscriminately to many emerging markets. This is often followed by a sudden withdrawal of confidence and the occurrence of crises in a number of countries at the same time. Rather than stable capital flows that reflect a sober assessment of the economic reality of emerging market countries, we see periods of overoptimism and overpessimism suggestive of arbitrary swings in market sentiment.

Wolf (1999) emphasizes two other stylized facts relative to the contemporaneous occurrence of crisis, or contagion: (1) emerging market asset price co-movements increase dramatically in a crisis, and (2) the increased co-movement is particularly pronounced within regions. However, these stylized facts do not go unchallenged. First, Forbes and Rigobon (1999) correct correlation coefficients for bias introduced by focusing on periods when *variances* of asset prices are high: They conclude that corrected for this bias, the co-movements of stock prices during the 1987 stock market crash, the 1994 Tequila crisis, and the 1997 East Asian crises were no greater than in normal times. Second, the regional aspect of crises, which emerged strongly in Latin America after Mexico 1994 and in Asia after Thailand 1997, and which has been studied by, among others, Glick and Rose (1999), has been thrown into question by the Russian default of August 1998, which did not strongly affect neighboring countries, but rather had global repercussions extending even to U.S. mortgage-backed securities and junk bonds.

Table 3.2 presents the stylized facts discussed above and some of the theories that have been advanced to explain them.[7] The table first highlights the failure of first-generation speculative attack models to provide insights into the identified phenomena. The assessments made of the success of the various other theories to account for the stylized facts are admittedly subjective; their proponents would in some cases no doubt argue that a minor extension would allow them to explain more. What I think is hard to disagree with is the following: (1) There are many puzzles related to capital flows to emerging markets; and (2) no single theory does a fully convincing job of explaining all, or even most, of them.

The explanation that seems to come closest presumes institutional constraints and portfolio rebalancing, but this is not so much a theory as an assumption that a market imperfection (regional limits on portfolios of selected financial institutions, for instance) is empirically important relative to other investors that are not so constrained and can trade on the basis of economic fundamentals; moreover, this assumption does not

---

[7] This is a modified version of a table I used to focus discussion of a paper by Holger Wolf (1999), at a conference at the World Bank on "Capital Flows, Financial Crisis and Policies," April 15–16, 1999. Rather than providing another survey of the relevant theories, the interested reader is referred to Wolf (1999).

Table 3.2. International Capital Markets: Theories and Stylized Facts

Theories	Contemporaneous Booms of Capital Inflows	Contemporaneous Busts (Crises)	"Excessive" Co-movement of Asset Prices in Crises (Relative to Fundamentals)	Crises Tend to Be Regional	Home Bias	More Frequent and Global Crises in 1990s
			Stylized Facts			
1. First-generation speculative attack models	N	N	N	N	N	N
2. Multicountry transmission:						
(a) Spillovers through trade and economic activity	N	Y	N	Y	N	P
(b) Monsoons (U.S. monetary policy $/yen, oil price)	Y	Y	N	N	N	N
(c) Correlated jumps between equilibria	Y	Y	Y	N	N	N
3. Models of incomplete and asymmetric information:						
(a) Demonstration effects ("wake-up calls")	P	Y	P	P	Y	N
(b) Rational fads and herding due to private information	Y	Y	P	P	Y	N
(c) Fundamentalists vs. noise traders	P	P	Y	N	N	N
4. Institutional constraints and portfolio rebalancing	Y	Y	P	P	P	P
5. Insurance crises and moral hazard	Y	Y	P	N	N	P
6. Capital account liberalization and technological advances	N	N	N	N	N	Y

Note: N, no; Y, yes; P, possibly.

square well with some other evidence.[8] Though there is some support for
the hypothesis that institutional constraints may be important at some
points in time (Van Rijckeghem and Weder, 1999, who look at common
bank creditors as explanations of crises hitting several emerging market
countries), clearly much more empirical work needs to be done to establish the plausibility of this particular channel. What is striking from the
data on bank lending to emerging-market countries is that banks in the
mature-market countries are so diversified, arguing against the regional
contagion story (Table 3.3). European banks have roughly equal exposures to Asia, Latin America, and the rest of the emerging markets; while
North American banks are more concentrated in Latin America, and
Japanese banks are more concentrated in Asia, both have substantial
exposures in other parts of the world.

I would further suggest that there is a potentially useful role for
explanations based on multiple equilibria, bank runs, and herding (Table
3.2, Theories 2c and 3b), though here again more empirical work is
needed. In addition, an interesting avenue for theoretical research would
be to link the asymmetric information models of fads and herding, which
provide microeconomic explanations for sharp shifts in expectations, to
the jumps between macroeconomic equilibria.

3.5 IMPLICATIONS FOR CRISIS PREDICTION
AND PREVENTION

Existing unique-equilibrium models suggest that a fairly benign view of
capital flows and asset price volatility is appropriate. Models with multiple equilibria in financial markets are consistent with a more nuanced
view of the benefits of capital account liberalization, and they have been
used by some as an argument for limiting capital flows and regulating
markets. In this section, I will take a fairly agnostic stance on these issues,
but will attempt to marshall the arguments and try to make sense of
them.

If we believe that financial market valuations fluctuate around their
equilibrium levels, even if occasionally with large swings, we will probably look more favorably on financial markets than if we think that there
are arbitrary regime changes that are not dictated by fundamental economic factors but rather are the result of self-fulfilling expectations
driven by "sunspots." Of course, there is not necessarily a clear welfare
ranking between the two views of financial volatility: If there is a single
equilibrium but large variance around it, this could be worse than mul-

---

[8] For instance, the Investment Company Institute (1998) estimated that at the end of 1996,
   U.S. open-end emerging market equity mutual funds that invested primarily in Asia con-
   stituted only 0.8 percent of the value of these stock markets.

Table 3.3. Regional Distribution of Bank Lending to Emerging Markets, December 1998

Region of Borrowers	All Banks	European Banks	North American Banks	Japanese Banks	Other Banks
In Billions of U.S. Dollars					
Asia	299	150	26	86	37
Latin America	288	180	74	14	20
Middle East	63	40	6	4	13
Africa	57	45	5	2	5
Central and Eastern Europe	122	103	7	4	8
TOTAL	829	518	118	110	83
As a Percentage of Bank Exposure					
Asia	36.1	29.0	22.0	78.2	44.6
Latin America	34.7	34.7	62.7	12.7	24.1
Middle East	7.6	7.7	5.1	3.6	15.7
Africa	6.9	8.7	4.2	1.8	6.0
Central and Eastern Europe	14.7	19.9	5.9	3.6	9.6
TOTAL	100	100	100	100	100
As a Percentage of Lending to the Region					
Asia	100	50.2	8.7	28.8	12.4
Latin America	100	62.5	25.7	4.9	6.9
Middle East	100	63.5	9.5	6.3	20.6
Africa	100	78.9	8.8	3.5	8.8
Central and Eastern Europe	100	84.4	5.7	3.3	6.6

Source: Bank for International Settlements, *Statistics on External Indebtedness*.

tiple equilibria that are close together and possibly yield a higher level of per capita consumption. Another possibility is that the range of fundamentals where multiple equilibria occur is quite narrow and seldom is reached. But one suspects that the proponents of self-fulfilling crises have a presumption that the equilibria are very different, fundamentals are frequently in the multiple equilibria region, and a crisis involves large welfare costs.

The first implication of the multiple equilibria view is clearly that crises may be difficult to predict. This makes it less likely that we can correctly anticipate when crises will occur, though it may still be possible to gauge the relative *vulnerability* of countries to crises (see discussion of early warning indicators of crises in Berg and Pattillo, 1998). Vulnerability in such models, as described above, depends on the relevant fundamentals being in certain ranges, so that only certain countries are likely to be affected.

A second implication drawn by some economists (e.g., Wyplosz, 1998) is that capital flows should be subject to international regulation. One possible form this might take is Tobin taxes, and Bensaïd and Jeanne (1996) explicitly analyze their effect on multiple equilibria; they show that an appropriate level of the tax can eliminate the possibility of multiple equilibria, and therefore eliminate this form of financial market volatility. Of course, Tobin taxes and capital controls generally are open to the criticism that they may be difficult to enforce, lose effectiveness over time as ways around them are found, and impair economic efficiency.

A third implication, related to the second, is that arguments in favor of capital account liberalization that emphasize the disciplining effects on governments of being open to capital flows are somewhat less compelling. If valuations solely reflect economic fundamentals, then governments are well-advised to respect the signals of the market. However, if attacks on the market reflect the whims of investors, then rather than bowing to them, governments may well prefer to insulate themselves from them. Again, this dichotomy is not a clean one; economic fundamentals (in particular, the stance of economic policies) have their role even in models with multiple equilibria. In addition, the *effectiveness* of capital controls also needs to be considered. Calvo and Reinhart (1999), for instance, conclude that capital controls may be able to influence the composition of flows, but are unlikely to be the solution to the recurring problem of capital flow reversal.

Fourth, the view taken on multiple equilibria in global financial markets – and of the source of multiple equilibria – may well influence views on reform of the international monetary system. By analogy with the analysis of domestic financial markets (Diamond and Dybvig, 1983), certain institutions may prevent the occurrence of welfare-deteriorating bank runs or creditor panics, but this analysis addresses only one type of multiple equilibria – those related to liquidity and runs. Also, the analogy with domestic banks, which have a clear role in providing liquidity by maturity transformation, is not obvious for international lending, suggesting that measures to discourage short-term borrowing may be a solution that would have little cost. If the source of multiple equilibria is one of the other two – macroeconomic feedbacks or herding behavior – then the solutions are different. For the former, it will be important to reduce macroeconomic vulnerability, avoid foreign currency exposure, and build up reserves. Problems of herding and asymmetric information are best addressed by (a) increasing the transparency of government policies and data and (b) increasing disclosure requirements on financial institutions.

The literature has focused on four types of institutions that may help to prevent international crises or mitigate their effects: (1) a lender of last resort; (2) deposit insurance (more generally, guaranteed repayment of debts); (3) suspension of convertibility (or a stay of creditor action) in a crisis; and (4) modifications to the terms of loan contracts (including sharing agreements or majority voting) or the way bonds are auctioned (to limit unsustainable borrowing). The literature on this issue is too vast to be surveyed here, but various authors have shown that these institutional features may help eliminate multiple equilibria and achieve a good equilibrium.

However, proposals for international monetary reform are necessarily strongly influenced by what might be feasible as well as desirable. For instance, Sachs (1995) has called for an international lender of last resort, but in the current "architecture" there is no institution playing the same role as a national central bank, which can create money in the national currency. The recent creation of the Contingent Credit Line is intended to preapprove the availability of IMF resources to countries with strong economic fundamentals but that may be the object of contagion, and in this way ward off a crisis. However, the resources of the IMF are relatively small compared to the size of international claims and potential capital movements. In contrast, central banks can create an unlimited amount of liquidity to counter domestic panics and bank runs. Furthermore, there is no international regulator of financial institutions or private and public borrowers that parallels domestic regulators, which have the job of preventing reckless lending in the first place.[9]

Another proposal for reform concerns insuring international claims by charging a small insurance premium on all borrowers (Soros, 1998). Again, such a proposal would require for its implementation a quite different legal and regulatory framework than that which exists today. Without a treaty binding all countries, there would be no way to oblige borrowers to comply, and instead there might be some self-selection of debtors that might signal to lenders their desire to cash in on the insurance – that is, to default.

Rather than attempting to eliminate multiple equilibria entirely, a more realistic lesson for the international monetary system might be that

[9] Rogoff (1999) also notes that even the domestic case for a lender of last resort is less than completely convincing, since it neglects the moral hazard problem and could be made unnecessary by other institutional changes, such as allowing banks to suspend redemption of deposits temporarily.

ways need to be found to coordinate on the "good" (noncrisis) equilibrium by establishing the confidence of creditors without exacerbating moral hazard, and ways found to minimize the damage done by crises when they occur. Confidence-enhancing measures would include a track record of consistent and sustainable policies, increased "transparency," and making available adequate data and other information on government policies. Involving private creditors in sharing the cost of crises could lead to their quicker resolution and help to limit excessive lending in the first place. Whether because of a belief in multiple equilibria or just a generalized concern for volatility, these avenues are already being actively explored in various fora – for instance, the meetings of G-10 and the G-22 countries – and by various authors such as Sachs (1995), Minton-Beddoes (1995), Eichengreen and Portes (1995), and Eichengreen (1998). In any case, further research on the fundamental reasons for multiple equilibria (some of which were sketched above) and the causes of jumps between equilibria will help to make progress in these areas.

3.6 CONCLUSIONS

There is still no consensus on the causes of the recent emerging market crises. It seems likely in fact that there was no single cause, but rather that a number of factors – related to both macroeconomic fundamentals and self-fulfilling expectations of investors – came into play. Reform of the international monetary system to decrease the likelihood of crises and their economic costs needs to be directed at the most relevant factors, since the reforms that are appropriate differ depending on the causes. As the quote from Richard Cooper's study of cooperation in the health field that began this chapter suggests, more study of the sources of contagion will be needed before definitive and all-encompassing solutions can be agreed upon. Nevertheless, this lack of consensus should not be allowed to impede more modest steps that can be taken in the interim to improve the functioning of the international monetary system.

REFERENCES

Agénor, Pierre-Richard and Paul Masson (1999). "Credibility, Reputation and The Mexican Peso Crisis," *Journal of Money, Credit and Banking* **31**(February):70–84.

Allen, Franklin and Douglas Gale (1998). "Optimal Financial Crises," *Journal of Finance* **53**(August):1245–1284.

Arifovic, Jasmina and Paul Masson (1999). "Heterogeneity and Evolution of Expectations in a Model of Currency Crisis." Mimeo, IMF.

Azariadis, C. (1981). "Self-Fulfilling Prophecies," *Journal of Economic Theory* **25**:380–396.

Baig, Taimur and Ilan Goldfajn (1999). "Financial Market Contagion in the Asian Crisis," *IMF Staff Papers* **46**(June):167–195.

Banerjee, Ajiz (1992). "A Simple Model of Herd Behavior," *Quarterly Journal of Economics* **107**(August):797–817.

Bensaïd, Bernard and Olivier Jeanne (1996). "Fragilité des Systèmes de Change Fixe et Contrôle des Capitaux," *Economie et Prévision*, No. 123–124, pp. 163–174.

Berg, Andrew and Catherine Pattillo (1998). "Are Currency Crises Predictable? A Test." IMF Working Paper No. 98/154 (November).

Bikchandani, Sushil, David Hirshleifer, and Ivo Welch (1992). "A Theory of Fads, Fashion, Custom, and Cultural Change as Informational Cascades," *Journal of Political Economy* **100**(5):992–1026.

Boldrin, M. and M. Woodford (1990). "Equilibrium Models Displaying Endogenous Fluctuations and Chaos," *Journal of Monetary Economics* **25**(March): 189–222.

Calvo, Guillermo (1998). "Understanding the Russian Virus (with special reference to Latin America)." Paper presented at the Deutsche Bank's conference on "Emerging Markets: Can They Be Crisis Free?" Washington D.C., October 3.

Calvo, Guillermo and Enrique Mendoza (1996). "Mexico's Balance-of-Payments Crisis: A Chronicle of a Death Foretold," *Journal of International Economics* **41**:235–264.

Calvo, Guillermo and Carmen Reinhart (1999). "When Capital Inflows Come to a Sudden Stop: Consequences and Policy Options." Mimeo, University of Maryland.

Caplin, Andrew and John Leahy (1994). "Business as Usual, Market Crashes, and Wisdom after the Fact," *American Economic Review* **84**(June):548–565.

Cerra, Valerie and Sweta Saxena (1998). "Contagion, Monsoons, and Domestic Turmoil in Indonesia: A Case Study in the Asian Currency Crisis." Mimeo, IMF and University of Washington.

Chang, Roberto and Andrés Velasco (1998). "The Asian Liquidity Crisis." NBER Working Paper No. 6796. Cambridge, MA.

Chari, V.V. and Patrick Kehoe (1998). "Hot Money." Mimeo, Research Department, Federal Reserve Bank of Minneapolis, April.

Chiappori, P.-A. and R. Guesnerie (1991). "Sunspot Equilibria in Sequential Markets Models." In Werner Hildenbrand and Hugo Sonnenschein, eds., *Handbook of Mathematical Economics*, Vol. IV. Amsterdam: North-Holland, pp. 1683–1762.

Cole, Harold and Timothy J. Kehoe (1996). "A Self-Fulfilling Model of Mexico's 1994–95 Debt Crisis," *Journal of International Economics* **41**:309–330.

Cooper, Richard N. (1989). "International Cooperation in Public Health." In R.N. Cooper, Barry Eichengreen, C. Randall Henning, Gerald Holtham, and Robert D. Putnam, eds., *Can Nations Agree? Issues in International Economic Cooperation*, Washington, D.C.: Brookings Institute, pp. 178–254.

Corsetti, Giancarlo, Paolo Pesenti, and Nouriel Roubini (1998). "Paper Tigers? A Model of the Asian Crisis." NBER Working Paper No. 6783. Cambridge, MA.

Detragiache, Enrica (1996). "Rational Liquidity Crises in the Sovereign Debt Market: In Search of a Theory," IMF *Staff Papers* **43**(September):545–570.

Diamond, Douglas and Philip Dybvig (1983). "Bank Runs, Deposit Insurance, and Liquidity," *Journal of Political Economy* **91**:401–419.

Dooley, Michael (1997). "A Model of Crises in Emerging Markets." NBER Working Paper No. 6300. Cambridge, MA.

Durlauf, S.N. (1991). "Multiple Equilibria and Persistence in Aggregate Fluctuations," NBER Working Paper No. 3629. Cambridge, MA.

Eichengreen, Barry (1998). *Toward A New International Financial Architecture: A Practical Post-Asia Agenda.* Washington, D.C.: Institute for International Economics.

Eichengreen, Barry and Richard Portes, eds. (1995). *Crisis? What Crisis? Orderly Workout for Sovereign Debtors.* London: Centre for Economic Policy Research.

Flood, Robert and Andrew Rose (1995). "Fixing Exchange Rates: A Virtual Quest for Fundamentals." *Journal of Monetary Economics* **36**(August):3–37.

Forbes, Kristin and Roberto Rigobon (1999). "No Contagion, only Interdependence: Measuring Stock Market Co-movements." NBER Working Paper No. 7267. Cambridge, MA.

Garber, Peter (1996). "Comment on Krugman." *NBER Macroeconomics Annual 1996.* Cambridge, MA: MIT Press.

Glick, Reuven and Andrew Rose (1999). "Contagion and Trade: Why are Currency Crises Regional," *Journal of International Money and Finance* **18**(4):603–618.

Goldstein, Morris (1998). *The Asian Financial Crises: Causes, Cures, and Systemic Implications*, Policy Analyses in International Economics 55. Washington, D.C.: Institute for International Economics.

Hamilton, J.D. (1988). "Rational-Expectations Econometric Analysis of Changes in Regime: An Investigation of the Term Structure of Interest Rates," *Journal of Economic Dynamics and Control* **12**:385–423.

———(1994). *Time Series Analysis.* Princeton, NJ: Princeton University Press.

Herrendorf, B., A. Valentinyi, and R. Waldmann (1998). "Ruling Out Indeterminacy: The Role of Heterogeneity." University of Southampton, Department of Economics, Working Paper No. 9803.

Investment Company Institute (1998). *Perspective* (Washington, D.C.) **4**(June): 1–11.

Irwin, Gregor and David Vines (1999). "A Krugman–Dooley–Sachs Third Generation Model of the Asian Financial Crisis." Mimeo, Oxford University.

Jeanne, Olivier (1997). "Are Currency Crises Self-Fulfilling? A Test," *Journal of International Economics* **43**(3/4):263–286.

Jeanne, Olivier and Paul Masson (1997). "Was the French Franc Crisis a Sunspot Equilibrium?" University of California, Berkeley, Center for International and Development Economics Research Working Paper No. C97–045.

———(2000). "Currency Crises, Sunspots and Markov-Switching Regimes," *Journal of International Economics* **50**(2):327–350.

Kaminsky, Graciela and Carmen Reinhart (1998). "On Crisis, Contagion, and Confusion." Paper presented at the Duke University conference "Globalization, Capital Market Crises, and Economic Reform," November.

Kaminsky, Graciela and Sergio Schmukler (1999). "What Triggers Market Jitters? A Chronicle of the Asian Crises," *Journal of International Money and Finance* **18**(4):537–560.

Kodres, Laura and Matthew Pritsker (1999). "A Rational Expectations Model of Financial Contagion." Mimeo, IMF and Board of Governors of the Federal Reserve System.

Krugman, Paul (1979). "A Model of Balance of Payments Crises," *Journal of Money, Credit, and Banking* **11**:311–325.

———(1996). "Are Currency Crises Self-Fulfilling?" *NBER Macroeconomics Annual*. Cambridge, MA: MIT Press.

Lee, In Ho (1997). "Market Crashes and Informational Avalanches." Paper presented at a CEPR/ESRC/GEI conference on "The Origins and Management of Financial Crises," Cambridge, U.K., July 11–12.

Lim, G.C. and Vance Martin (1998). "Forecasting Exchange Rate Crises with an Application to the Asian Currency Meltdown." Mimeo, University of Melbourne.

Marion, Nancy (1999). "Some Parallels between Currency and Banking Crises." Mimeo, IMF.

Masson, Paul (1999a). "Contagion: Monsoonal Effects, Spillovers, and Jumps between Multiple Equilibria." In P.R. Agénor, M. Miller, D. Vines, and A. Weber, eds., *The Asian Financial Crisis: Causes, Contagion and Consequences*. Cambridge, U.K.: Cambridge University Press.

———(1999b). "Contagion: Macroeconomic Models with Multiple Equilibria," *Journal of International Money and Finance* **18**(4):587–602.

Minton-Beddoes, Zanny (1995). "Why the IMF Needs Reform," *Foreign Affairs* **74**(May/June):123–133.

Morris, Stephen and Hyun Song Shin (1998). "Unique Equilibrium in a Model of Self-Fulfilling Attacks," *American Economic Review* **88**(June):587–597.

Obstfeld, Maurice (1986). "Rational and Self-Fulfilling Balance of Payments Crises," *American Economic Review* **76**:72–81.

———(1994). "The Logic of Currency Crises," *Cahiers Economiques et Monétaires*, No. 43:189–213. Paris: Banque de France.

Radelet, Steven and Jeffrey Sachs (1998). "The East Asian Financial Crisis: Diagnosis, Remedies, Prospects," *Brookings Papers on Economic Activity*, No. 1:1–90.

Rogoff, Kenneth (1999). "International Institutions for Reducing Global Financial Instability." NBER Working Paper No. 7265. Cambridge, MA.

Sachs, Jeffrey (1984). "Theoretical Issues in International Borrowing," Princeton Studies in International Finance, No. 54 (July).

———(1995). "Do We Need an International Lender of Last Resort?" Frank D. Graham Lecture, Princeton University, April 20.

Sachs, Jeffrey, Aaron Tornell, and Andrés Velasco (1996). "The Mexican Peso Crisis: Sudden Death or Death Foretold?" *Journal of International Economics* **41**:265–283.

Schadler, Susan, Maria Carkovic, Adam Bennett, and Robert Kahn (1993). "Recent Experiences with Surges in Capital Inflows." IMF Occasional Paper No. 108.

Shiller, Robert (1989). *Market Volatility.* Cambridge MA: MIT Press.

Soros, George (1998). *The Crisis of Global Capitalism: Open Society Endangered.* New York: PABS/Public Affairs.

Valdés, Rodrigo (1996). "Emerging Market Contagion: Evidence and Theory." Mimeo, MIT.

Van Rijckeghem, Caroline and Beatrice Weder (1999). "Sources of Contagion: Finance or Trade?" IMF Working Paper No. 99/146. Washington, D.C.

Wolf, Holger (1999). "International Asset Price and Capital Flow Co-movements during Crisis: The Role of Contagion, Demonstration Effects, and Fundamentals." Mimeo, Georgetown University.

Wyplosz, Charles (1998). "Speculative Controls and Capital Mobility." Paper presented to the Fourth Dubrovnik Conference on Transition Economics, June 24–26.

Discussion

Multiple Equilibria, Contagion, and the Emerging Market Crises

Paolo Pesenti

This is the last, but certainly not the least, in a series of contributions on currency crises and contagion by Paul Masson. Making order – at least, *some* order – in what is currently the most chaotic and Byzantine niche of international macroeconomic literature is a burdensome but priceless task. In this and other recent essays, Masson contributes coherently and intelligently to an overdue process of intellectual housecleaning within the field, presenting reasonable taxonomies and shedding light on the implications of a vast array of models and theories for policy analysis. Specifically, this chapter provides a neat, extensive overview of "multiple-equilibria" models of speculative attacks and currency crises. It is an easy guess that this survey will frequently appear on the reading lists of courses in international capital markets, and I am confident it will have a long shelf life among researchers and policy analysts.

Masson is an earnest advocate of the relevance of multiple equilibria as a modeling device to understand complex issues such as the determinants and implications of the international currency and financial crises of the 1990s. But proselytizing need not mean being blind or unfair. While the strengths of the multiple-equilibria approach are emphasized, as we expect, its weaknesses are not hidden or dismissed. Rather, they are generally treated as open issues left to future investigations and analyses.

In my comments, I will try to emulate the standards of impartiality and objectivity of the analysis, although with a twist. In my view, what needs to be emphasized are not the strengths of the multiple-equilibria approach, but rather its weaknesses. This is not to deny or overlook its accomplishments. Simply, I think the time has now come to build on these past accomplishments and move over to a new paradigm for the analysis and assessment of international crises. Masson's study – and I quote directly – "rather than attempting to provide new theories or econometric evidence, discusses in an informal way the *plausibility* of multiple equilibria models and their *usefulness* as a modeling technique" (my italics). It is on these two italicized words that most of my comments will be focused.

Is "plausibility" a well-defined concept in the context of the multiple-equilibria literature? I am not sure. Sudden shifts in private agents expectations are consistent, almost by definition, with any episode of speculative attack and crisis. From this vantage point, to "explain" a crisis in terms of an arbitrary selection of a particular equilibrium is not much different from stating that a crisis occurs when a crisis occurs. Truisms are not falsifiable, and multiple-equilibria models are not testable. In both cases, one may be excused for regarding their empirical content – and their contribution to positive and normative analyses – with some degree of skepticism. Certainly it is not correct from an epistemological viewpoint to use the shortcomings and empirical failures of models based on fundamental explanations as evidence in favor of multiple equilibria models. And I haven't seen any convincing way of testing directly one approach against another, since the so-called first- and second-generation models are in practice observationally equivalent.

To give an example, consider the textbook first-generation model of balance of payments crises à la Krugman. A common misconception is the idea that what determines a crisis in this setting is the observed acceleration in domestic credit leading to a fall in the stock of reserves. Actually, the key factor triggering a crisis in this model is the deterioration in fundamentals – such as domestic credit expansion – that is expected to occur in the future, not the one that has occurred in the past. So, even if the record shows no deficit monetization in the past, even if the record shows an increasing stock of international reserves, a Krugman-style speculative attack can still occur in anticipation of future problems. In the end, both a model of this kind and a model based on jumps between multiple equilibria suggest that, on the basis of *observed* fundamentals, a crisis is unpredictable. Which model is more "plausible"? The answer is in the eye of the beholder, a matter of tastes more than econometrics.

In general, the rule is that for any "plausible" multiple equilibria-based story, one can tell there is an alternative interpretation that is just as plausible – that is to say, the debate between "fundamentalists" and "nonfundamentalists" is bound to be finely balanced for a long, long time. For instance, Masson argues that a multiple equilibria approach is plausible when applied to the analysis of speculative crises in France in 1993. He observes that in the late spring of 1993, French short-term rates were below German rates, and still there were attacks on the franc triggered not by deteriorating fundamentals but by "relatively minor events." He may be right. But there is at least one other plausible story. In retrospect, many have interpreted the behavior of French interest rates in 1993 as the result of a rather deliberate effort to promote the franc as a co-anchor of a new European Monetary System, an effort perceived at the time as unsustainable. The attacks against the franc were perhaps nothing but a way to test such effort – and, somebody would add, to call the bluff. Speculative tensions in Europe stopped only when the basis for political cooperation regarding the Maastricht project were reestablished, basically in the summer of 1993. In general, once we take into account political developments in Europe during 1992 and 1993 – and their implications for the credibility of the Exchange Rate Mechanism – we have absolutely no need to invoke jumps among multiple equilibria to make sense of the speculative attacks against the European Monetary System.[1]

I wholeheartedly agree with Masson as regards the "usefulness" of multiple equilibria as a modeling device. There is no doubt that this approach has had a huge impact on the academic literature. Some of the most innovative and thought-provoking currency crisis models of the last fifteen years have built upon the notion of multiple equilibria. To mention but one example, Maury Obstfeld's analysis of the destabilizing effects of escape clauses (Obstfeld, 1997) has supplied an important general argument against a less than fully credible commitment to the defense of an exchange rate parity. This argument has greatly reduced the appeal of disinflation strategies based on exchange rate targeting, and it is still used in favor of extreme forms of exchange rate regimes (such as free floats or currency boards) over intermediate forms such as adjustable pegs.

I would only like to point out that multiple equilibria models are, by the standards of year 2000, so much part of the typical conceptual apparatus of any self-respected international economist that any further advocacy on their behalf sounds, so to speak, *passé*, like preaching to the converted. The key question nowadays is, What next? In the past few years, and especially since the Asian crisis, my feeling is that both the academic and the policy environments have felt an urgent need to go beyond the traditional interpretive frameworks.

One of the outcomes of this quest for nontraditional crisis theories has been the development of a new approach in modeling confidence crises (see, for instance, Morris and Shin, 1998). This approach promises to take care of one of the most obvious problems with the multiple-equilibria models, namely, their oft-mentioned agnosticism on what causes the expectation shifts underlying currency and financial crises. Masson's chapter is perhaps a bit dismissive as regards these recent developments, and the reason – one suspects – is that the new research

---

[1] An interpretation along these lines appears in Buiter, Corsetti, and Pesenti (1998).

		Agent II	
		A	N
Agent I	A	X-1, X-1	-1, 0
	N	0, -1	0, 0

Figure 3.1. Payoff matrix to attack (A) or no attack (N).

agenda threatens to curtail the relevance and generality of the concept of multiple equilibria. In what follows, I will attempt to provide a non-technical comparison between the different approaches with the help of the apparatus presented in Corsetti (2000).

Let me start by considering a simple case of multiple equilibria at work. Here is the setup. A country pursues a unilateral peg. Its monetary authorities can only commit a given amount of resources (say, official reserves) to the defense of such peg. There are two agents in this economy (I and II) who can attack the peg by selling domestic currency to the central bank in exchange for foreign currency. No agent is large enough to deplete the entire stock of official international reserves and force the abandonment of the peg. If both agent attack simultaneously, however, their combined attack forces the central bank to capitulate.

Each agent can attack (strategy A) or not (strategy N), and he/she chooses to do so on the basis of the expected payoff. No coordination between agents is feasible. A speculative attack – no matter whether successful or not – involves a cost, here normalized to 1. So, if the attack is unsuccessful, the agent loses 1. If no attack occurs, the agent gets nothing and loses nothing. If a joint – and successful – run materializes, each agent's gains depend on the size of the post-attack exchange rate devaluation. Realistically, the size of such devaluation is a function of underlying fundamental weaknesses in the economy. We will denote the exchange rate gains by X. The higher X is, the weaker the fundamentals at the time of the attack. Figure 3.1 shows the matrix of the net payoffs described above.

We immediately observe that if agent I does not attack, agent II has no incentive to attack, and if agent II does not attack, agent I chooses not to attack either. So there is an equilibrium in which no attack occurs. Now suppose that X is a random variable whose realization is known to both agents. In other words, both agents face no uncertainty regarding the state of the economy. Clearly, if $X < 1$ no agent attacks (the payoff from an attack is negative, and each player can guarantee a zero payoff to herself by not attacking). If $X \geq 1$, there are multiple equilibria: one in which no one attacks, as seen above, and one in which both agents attack. If one agent chooses a specific strategy, A or N, the other agent is better off by following suit.

The model is highly stylized, yet it includes many key features of more sophisticated multiple-equilibria settings. Three considerations stand out. First, if fundamentals are sound enough, no speculative attacks occur. Second, when fundamentals are sufficiently weak, there are multiple equilibria. Third, provided that we are in the weak-fundamentals region, a speculative crisis occurs when agents shift from the no-attack equilibrium to the attack equilibrium. Why this happens and when does this happen, we don't know. The theory is silent on what determines such deterioration in confidence.

Now assume that X is a random variable whose realization is unknown to the agents. Rather than observing X directly, each agent receives some private information about the state of fundamentals in the form of a signal Z, which is distributed uniformly and symmetrically around the true value of X. In other words, from the vantage point of each agent, the true value of X lies somewhere between $Z - \varepsilon$ and $Z + \varepsilon$ – where ε is some positive, arbitrarily small number – with equal probability. So, Z is the best estimate of X.

Both the distributions of X and Z are common knowledge. Each agent's expected payoff if she attacks is given by $Z - 1$ when the other agent attacks as well, or -1 if the other agent does not attack. Thus, each agent's expected payoff if she attacks is

Prob{other agent attacks}*$(Z - 1) + (1 - $Prob{other agent attacks}$)*(-1)$
= Prob{other agent attacks}*$Z - 1$.

For this expected payoff to be positive, we need two elements. First, the signal Z received by the agent must be sufficiently high: If $Z < 1$, the expected payoff is negative regardless of what the other agent does. Second, the probability that the other agent attacks must be sufficiently high. If one agent receives a signal Z equal to, say, $1 + \eta$, with η very small, she will attack only if she believes that the other agent will attack with probability close to 100 percent.

The problem is that if agent I receives a signal $1 + \eta$, she cannot consider it highly likely that agent II will attack. The reasoning is as follows. Agent I's estimate of X is $1 + \eta$, so she must think that her opponent will receive a signal below $1 + \eta$ with probability 50 percent. This implies that agent I thinks that agent II is receiving a signal below 1 with probability close to 50 percent, and we have established above that no agent with a signal below 1 will ever attack the currency. So when $Z = 1 + \eta$, agent I's expected payoff cannot be positive, and she will decide not to attack.

We can iterate this argument: A slightly larger signal, say $1 + 2\eta$, will not be enough to generate a positive expected return from attacking because there is a probability close to 50 percent that her opponent will get a signal below $1 + \eta$, and so on. At some point we will find a cutoff point, say $Z = Z'$, at which agent I will rationally switch from a "no attack" to an "attack" strategy since her signal is now high enough to make her sufficiently confident that the other agent will also attack. In equilibrium, agents will find it optimal to follow a simple rule based on this cutoff point: Attack if and only if $Z > Z'$, do not attack otherwise. It can be shown that, in our case, such a cutoff point is $Z' = 2$ for both agents. Because agents can estimate the state of fundamentals with arbitrarily high precision, relatively weak fundamentals ($X > 2$) will be associated with currency collapses, relatively strong fundamentals ($X \leq 2$) with the absence of speculative attacks.

The message of this model is rather explicit. First, the realistic introduction of some uncertainty (incomplete information) on the state of fundamentals rules out multiple equilibria: An attack occurs if fundamentals are sufficiently weak, and no attack occurs when fundamentals are strong. Second, to "kill" the multiplicity of equilibria, we only need an arbitrarily small degree of uncertainty. Third, there are no longer self-fulfilling crises triggered by arbitrary shifts in expectations. Fundamentals – and fundamentals only – determine whether a currency crisis occurs or not. Fourth, multiple equilibria occur only in a very special case of the model in which there is no uncertainty whatsoever on the state of fundamentals (or, alternatively, in which all signals are common knowledge).

At this stage, it is still much too early to predict whether and when the new approach will produce a body of crisis literature able to supplant the traditional apparatus. But we cannot afford to overlook that models of speculation with incomplete information represent today the building blocks of a promising new and far-reaching theory of the determinants of market confidence and its swings. If this theory delivers on its promises, I look forward to reading a survey of its development as lucid and informative as the one Paul Masson has written for the multiple-equilibria literature.

REFERENCES

Buiter, Willem, Giancarlo Corsetti, and Paolo Pesenti (1998). *Financial Markets and European Monetary Cooperation: The Lessons of the 1992–93 Exchange Rate Mechanism Crisis.* New York: Cambridge University Press.

Corsetti, Giancarlo (2000). "Interpreting the Asian Financial Crisis: Open Issues in Theory and Policy," *Asian Development Review* 16(2):18–64.

Morris, Stephen and Hyun Song Shin (1998). "Unique Equilibrium in a Model of Self-Fulfilling Crises," *American Economic Review* 88:587–597.

Obstfeld, Maurice (1997). "Destabilizing Effects of Exchange-Rate Escape Clauses," *Journal of International Economics* 43(August):61–77.

4

How Are Shocks Propagated Internationally?

Firm-Level Evidence from the Russian and East Asian Crises

Kristin Forbes

4.1 INTRODUCTION

The 1990s were punctuated by a series of currency crises. A striking characteristic of many of these crises is how an initial country-specific shock was rapidly propagated to markets of very different sizes and structures around the globe. A number of studies have developed theories attempting to explain these patterns, and several others have used macroeconomic data to test their validity.

This chapter, however, takes a very different approach to evaluating how shocks are propagated internationally. It utilizes firm-level information, instead of aggregate macro-level data, to evaluate the impact of the East Asian and Russian crises on individual companies' stock market returns. It constructs a new dataset of financial statistics, product information, geographic data, and stock returns for over 14,000 companies in 46 countries. It uses this information to test if firm vulnerability to the East Asian and Russian crises is affected by factors such as: sector of production, global pattern of sales and profitability, debt quantity and structure, trading liquidity, and/or geographic location. Identifying which types of companies were (and were not) most vulnerable to these shocks is not only interesting in and of itself, but also helps assess how these financial crises were transmitted internationally.

The analysis presented in this chapter has many useful implications (in addition to addressing the academic question of how shocks are propagated internationally). For investors seeking to maintain a diversified portfolio, it shows what types of companies are more vulnerable to crises in other regions or markets. For management teams seeking to maximize company performance, it suggests what risks are involved from certain strategies and what practices could reduce exposure to financial crises. For a multilateral institution seeking to stop the spread of country-specific shocks, this chapter will show how crises tend to spread and therefore indicate where multilateral institutions need to focus their efforts.

The remainder of this chapter is divided into six sections. Section 4.2 surveys the theoretical literature on the international propagation of shocks and reinterprets much of this literature in the context of how individual firms could be affected by shocks to other countries. It also discusses the aggregate empirical work testing these theories and the limitations of this macroeconomic approach. Section 4.3 describes the extensive firm-level dataset that was compiled for the empirical analysis. Next, Section 4.4 outlines an event-study methodology and presents a graphical analysis of stock returns for various portfolios after the East Asian and Russian crises. Section 4.5 extends this analysis to a multivariate framework by estimating how firm characteristics affect a company's vulnerability to these crises.

Section 4.6 concludes that product competitiveness was an important propagation mechanism during the East Asian crisis, and an income effect was significant during the Russian and Asian crises. A credit crunch appears to have played a relatively minor role in the international transmission of shocks during both crises. Although other channels are more difficult to test, there is evidence supporting a forced-portfolio recomposition and "wake-up call" effect during both periods. Moreover, although less conclusive, results also provide preliminary evidence of the relative importance of these various propagation mechanisms during each crisis. Country-specific effects, which could reflect some sort of wake-up call, can have a larger impact than all of the other propagation mechanisms combined. The product competitiveness effect during the Asian crisis, as well as the income effect during the Russian crisis, are also large in magnitude. An important implication of this set of results is that the relative strength of the various transmission mechanisms varies across crises, so that it is unlikely that any single model can capture how shocks are propagated during all crises. This section concludes with a number of caveats.

4.2 THEORY AND PREVIOUS EVIDENCE: HOW ARE SHOCKS PROPAGATED INTERNATIONALLY?

Over the past few years, an extensive literature has explored how shocks are propagated internationally. Recent surveys of the literature have used a variety of different approaches toward coherently organizing this research and classifying potential transmission mechanisms.[1] This chapter will draw on these approaches but use a slightly different frame-

---

[1] For recent surveys of this literature, see Claessens, Dornbusch, and Park (1999) and Forbes and Rigobon (1999a).

work and terminology in order to focus on the company-specific impact of shocks. More specifically, this section explains that a shock to one country could be transmitted to firms in other countries through five different channels: a product competitiveness effect; an income effect, a credit crunch, a forced-portfolio recomposition, or a wake-up call. After discussing the theoretical underpinnings of each of these transmission mechanisms, this section will survey the macroeconomic empirical work testing each mechanism's relative importance. It will conclude by pointing out several limitations with this aggregate approach toward testing how shocks are propagated internationally.

4.2.1 Theory: How Are Shocks Propagated Internationally?

The first channel by which a shock to one country could be transmitted to firms in other countries is through product competitiveness. Gerlach and Smets (1995) and Corsetti, Pesenti, Roubini, and Tille (1998) formalize these ideas on the country level, but the general implications of their models can be extended to individual companies.[2] Basically, if one country devalues its currency, then that country's exports will be relatively cheaper in international markets. Similar products from firms in other countries which are sold in the same markets (including the country that initially devalued) will be relatively less competitive. Moreover, if exports from the initial country are a large enough share of global production in a given industry, then industry prices could fall worldwide. Therefore, even if a company does not directly compete with firms from the initial country in any specific markets, the company's competitiveness could be damaged by the currency crisis.[3]

A second mechanism by which a shock to one country could be propagated internationally is through an income effect that lowers demand for a firm's product. When a country undergoes a financial crisis or negative shock of any type, economic growth generally slows, often to the point of a severe economic contraction. Incomes in the country will fall, and any firm that exports to that country will face reduced demand (as long as the firm's product is not an inferior good). This income effect will be magnified if the country's currency is devalued, since a devaluation would further reduce purchasing power and real income levels. Moreover, if the initial crisis spreads to other countries (for whatever reason),

---

[2] Gerlach and Smets (1995) develop the first formal model of these effects. They focus on how the collapse of a currency affects the competitiveness of economies whose currencies remain pegged. Corsetti, Pesenti, Roubini, and Tille (1998) provide a recent extension of these ideas based on micro-foundations.

[3] There could be "secondary-product competitiveness" effects if exports from the country that devalued are used as inputs in the production of goods in other countries. In this case, the currency crisis could improve the competitiveness of these other products.

this income effect could reduce demand for a firm's product outside of the country initially subject to the shock.

A third channel by which firms can be affected by shocks in other countries is through a credit crunch. There are several different variants of this theory, but underlying them all is the idea that a crisis in one country can lead to a sharp reduction in the supply of credit, reducing financial liquidity and generating an excess demand for credit at the prevailing interest rates. In one model of this mechanism, Goldfajn and Valdés (1997) focus on financial intermediaries that supply liquid assets to foreigners. A financial shock to one country causes investors in that country to withdraw their deposits, reducing the liquidity of financial intermediaries and forcing them to liquidate loans to firms in other countries and/or be unable to renew their financing in the future. Chang and Velasco (1998) develop another model that focuses on the maturity mismatch of a financial system's international assets and liabilities. Kaminsky and Reinhart (1998) show how commercial banks with lending concentrated in a crisis-stricken region could be forced to withdraw lending in other regions in order to maintain solvency. Although these models aim to explain macroeconomic phenomena such as the spread of banking crises or speculative attacks, the implications for individual companies are straightforward. A shock to one country could lead to a credit crunch for firms in other countries, making it difficult for the firms to obtain new financing and/or renew old loans.

A fourth, and closely related, channel by which shocks could be transmitted internationally is through a forced-portfolio recomposition. More specifically, a shock to one country could reduce the liquidity of market participants and force them to sell assets in other markets in order to meet certain requirements. A number of studies model different variants of this forced-portfolio recomposition. For example, Frankel and Schmukler (1998) focus on closed-end country funds where a drop in the price of one market forces the funds to raise cash by selling assets in other markets. Valdés (1996) focuses on individual investors after a shock to one market. In order to continue operating in the market, to satisfy margin calls, or to meet regulatory requirements, the investors may be forced to sell assets in other countries. An implication of each of these theories is that stocks that are more liquid or more widely traded in global markets are more likely to be sold in this forced-portfolio recomposition.

A final channel by which country-specific shocks can be transmitted to firms in other countries is through a wake-up call effect. The basic idea behind this channel is that a crisis in one country (or investor behavior in one country) can provide information about other countries (or how investors will behave in other countries). One group of theories in this category focuses on the reassessment of macroeconomic fundamentals. If a country with certain macroeconomic characteristics (such as a weak banking sector) is discovered to be susceptible to a currency crisis, then investors will reassess the risk of other countries with similar macroeconomic fundamentals. A related group of theories focuses on investor behavior and information asymmetries, which can lead to herding or informational cascades.[4] These theories are often referred to as "contagion" and most predict multiple equilibria.[5] Tornell (1999) develops a model that combines both groups of wake-up call theories. In his model, a currency crisis in one emerging market will act as a coordinating device and cause money managers to expect attacks on "more vulnerable" countries. Country vulnerability is measured by the likelihood of a country depreciating its currency if it is attacked, which is directly related to macroeconomic fundamentals. Although each of these wake-up call theories focuses on how a shock to one country is transmitted to other countries, the impact on individual firms is straightforward. If a shock is transmitted to a second country through this channel, then all firms in the second market should be affected, and firm characteristics should not be significant.

It is worth noting that the potential transmission channels discussed above are not mutually exclusive and could overlap in important ways. For example, a crisis in one country could lead to a wake-up call and cause investors to withdraw from markets in a second country which has similar fundamentals. This attack could force the government in the second country to raise interest rates to defend its currency, which could in turn cause a credit crunch. It is also worth noting that this discussion of transmission mechanisms is somewhat limited and ignores several equally important, albeit related, topics. For example, it does not explore the timing or cause of the initial crisis. It also ignores the possibility that a "monsoonal" or global shock occurred which affected several countries simultaneously.[6] In order to focus on how shocks are transmitted to firms around the world, these subjects are left for future work. The following analysis takes the initial shock as given and focuses only on episodes where this initial shock is clearly country- or region-specific.

[4] For examples, see Banerjee (1992), Shiller (1995), Agénor and Aizenman (1997), Masson (1997), Calvo and Mendoza (1999), and Chari and Kehoe (1999). This includes "political contagion" such as that modeled in Drazen (1999).

[5] Although the term "contagion" is widely used, there is little agreement on what exactly it means. See Forbes and Rigobon (1999a) for a lengthy discussion of how the term is interpreted and a proposition for how it should be defined.

[6] Masson (1997) introduces the term "monsoonal" to describe global shocks.

4.2.2 Previous Evidence: How Are Shocks Propagated Internationally?

Several papers have used macroeconomic statistics to attempt to measure the empirical importance of one (or more) of the five propagation mechanisms discussed above. These papers have examined a variety of different crisis periods, included an assortment of countries, and used a range of statistical techniques. Not surprisingly, the results have been mixed.

Tests of the first two transmission mechanisms – product competitiveness and income effects – are often lumped together as tests of "trade" as a propagation channel. Two papers find evidence supporting the role of trade. Eichengreen, Rose, and Wyplosz (1996) use a panel of quarterly data from 1959–1993 to evaluate how speculative attacks on currencies spread across countries. They use two weighting mechanisms in order to compare the relative importance of trade and wake-up calls based on macro-similarities (which they call country reevaluation). In the first scheme, they weight crises in other countries by the importance of trade with those countries. In the second scheme, they weight crises by the similarity of macro policies and outcomes. Results suggest that currency crises are spread across countries mainly through international trade linkages and not through a revision of expectations based on macroeconomic similarities. Glick and Rose (1999) also test for the relative importance of trade and country reevaluation in the international propagation of shocks. They examine five currency crises in the 1970s and 1990s and estimate the probability of a currency crisis occurring and the magnitude of currency market pressures. They measure trade linkages by the degree to which countries compete in third markets (i.e., product competitiveness effects) as well as by the extent of direct trade between two countries (i.e., income effects). Results suggest that currency crises spread through both types of trade linkages, while macroeconomic variables have no significant impact. Therefore, the results of both of these papers suggest that shocks are propagated through product competitiveness and income effects and not through wake-up calls based on macroeconomic fundamentals.

Several other papers, however, argue that trade linkages were not significant propagation mechanisms during recent crises. Masson (1997) claims that trade was not important during the East Asian and Mexican crises because linkages (both direct and in third markets) are small between Thailand and the other East Asian economies and between Mexico and the largest Latin American economies. Baig and Goldfajn (1998) analyze the trade matrix of East Asian countries and also conclude that trade linkages among these countries are weak and therefore not important in spreading the East Asian crisis.

Tests of the third propagation channel – a credit crunch – also yield mixed results. Peek and Rosengreen (1997) examine if Japanese bank lending within the United States decreased after the 1990 Japanese stock market crash. They find that risk-based capital requirements were binding for many Japanese banks, which led to significant reductions in lending within the United States. Several other papers focus on the East Asian crisis. Ding, Domac, and Ferri (1998) find a sharp increase in the spread between bank lending rates and corporate bond yields during this period. They conclude that this tightening of the bank loan market provides evidence of a credit crunch. Kim (1999) estimates a disequilibrium model of the bank loan market and finds that loan demand exceeded supply by a significant margin in Korea after the East Asian crisis. On the other hand, Ghosh and Ghosh (1999) estimate a similar disequilibrium model of bank loans, but fail to find an excess demand for credit during most of the Asian crisis period in either Indonesia, Korea, or Thailand. They therefore argue that there is little evidence of quantity rationing causing a credit crunch.

Several papers have also attempted to test the importance of the fourth propagation mechanism – a forced-portfolio recomposition. Kaminsky, Lyons, and Schmukler (1999) use data on the portfolios of international mutual funds during the Mexican, East Asian, and Russian crises. They find that these funds systematically sell assets from one country when a crisis hits another. Valdés (1996) examines the impact of the Mexican peso crisis on the secondary market prices of sovereign debt. After controlling for macroeconomic fundamentals and "big news" events, he finds strong cross-country correlations in prices for debt in developing-country markets but not in medium- and large-sized OECD markets. He interprets this as evidence that investors were forced to recompose their portfolios after the crisis. Frankel and Schmukler (1998) examine closed-end fund data during the Mexican debt crisis of 1982 as well as during the peso crisis of 1994. They show that investors needed to raise cash during both crises, which forced them to sell-off assets in other markets. They find a direct impact of these sell-offs on other Latin American countries and on the United States, and an indirect effect (through the United States) on Asia. Other papers, however, argue that crises do not spread through this channel, since net redemptions and capital outflows by mutual fund investors were small during the Mexican and East Asian crises.[7]

---

[7] For example, see Rea (1996) and Froot, O'Connell, and Seasholes (1998). Note that Froot et al. examine all types of institutional investors (including mutual funds).

Most empirical tests of the fifth propagation mechanism – wake-up calls – have focused on the importance of country reevaluation based on macro fundamentals rather than on "contagion" through herding and/or information cascades. Sachs, Tornell, and Velasco (1996) examine data for twenty developing countries in 1994 and 1995 and find that three country fundamentals (real exchange rate overvaluation, banking system fragility, and low international reserves) explain about one-half of the variation in their crisis index. Tornell (1999) examines both the Mexican and Asian crises and finds that the same three fundamentals explain a significant amount of the variation in the severity of the crises. Baig and Goldfajn (1998) use daily data from five Asian countries between 1995 and 1998 to test for changes in the cross-country correlations of currency markets, stock markets, interest rates, and sovereign spreads. They use dummies constructed from daily news and show that after controlling for own-country news and other fundamentals, cross-country correlations in currency and equity markets remain large and significant. They interpret this as evidence of country reevaluation and/or herding effects. While this set of papers suggests that wake-up calls are an important propagation mechanism, Eichengreen, Rose, and Wyplosz (1996) and Glick and Rose (1999) argue that macroeconomic similarities do not play a significant role. As discussed above, they argue that trade is far more important than country reevaluation in the international transmission of crises.

A final series of tests on how shocks are propagated internationally uses a very different approach and does not easily fit into the five classifications utilized in this chapter. This approach categorizes transmission channels as crisis-contingent or noncrisis contingent, based on whether the propagation mechanism changes significantly after a shock. Crisis-contingent channels include credit crunches, portfolio recomposition, and some types of wake-up calls (such as herding), while noncrisis-contingent channels include product competitiveness, income effects, and wake-up calls (such as country reevaluation). Papers based on this approach test if correlations in cross-market returns increase significantly after a crisis. Calvo and Reinhart (1996) examine weekly returns for equities and Brady bonds and find a significant increase in market co-movements after the Mexican peso crisis. Baig and Goldfajn (1998) use daily data for East Asian countries during that region's crisis and find a significant increase in cross-market correlations for currencies and sovereign spreads, but not for stock markets and interest rates. Therefore both of these papers find evidence of the transmission of shocks through a crisis-contingent channel – at least in some markets. Forbes and Rigobon (1999b), however, show that the correlation coefficient utilized in these papers is biased. When they adjust for this bias, they find that cross-market correlations in stock returns do not increase significantly for most countries after the 1987 U.S. stock market crash, Mexican peso crisis, and East Asian crisis. Rigobon (1999) extends this analysis to address the problem of endogeneity and reports similar results for the Mexican, East Asian, and Brazilian crises. Therefore, both of these papers conclude that shocks are not transmitted through crisis-contingent channels. Instead, high cross-market correlations between many countries in all states of the world suggest that the financial shocks of the late 1980s and 1990s have been transmitted primarily through noncrisis-contingent channels.

4.2.3 Limitations of Macro-Tests of the International Propagation of Shocks

This literature review has shown that a range of samples, time periods, and econometric techniques have been used to test how shocks are propagated internationally. While the various macroeconomic tests provide an extremely useful set of results evaluating the importance of the different transmission mechanisms discussed above, the strategy of using aggregate country-level data to test how shocks are propagated has several limitations.

One limitation of aggregate empirical tests is that data availability makes it extremely difficult (if not impossible) to differentiate between many of the propagation channels. There are numerous examples of this problem. Most analyses of trade as a transmission mechanism focus on bilateral trade. However, tests based on this statistic are not only unable to distinguish between product competitiveness and income effects, but they also ignore competitive effects in third markets. Glick and Rose (1999) create several more complicated measures of trade in order to differentiate between these various effects, but they even admit that due to the aggregate nature of their data, some of the calculated strong competitors during currency crises are "not intuitive" and "are probably not direct trade competitors." Tests for the importance of wake-up call effects, and especially herding and/or informational cascades, are even more difficult to construct without investor-level data, and even with this data, it is difficult to differentiate between these sorts of wake-up calls and a forced-portfolio recomposition. In addition, Forbes and Rigobon (1999a) show that endogeneity and omitted variable bias make it virtually impossible to use aggregate tests to identify transmission mechanisms directly. Undoubtedly for this reason some empirical papers do not even try to differentiate between specific propagation mechanisms and instead focus on broad categories of linkages, such as crisis- or noncrisis-contingent channels.

A second limitation of the series of tests based on aggregate statistics is that the literature is far from reaching any sort of consensus. Granted, several transmission mechanisms may be important in the propagation of recent financial crises, and since many analyses only focus on a single transmission channel, the results from one paper do not necessarily contradict work on other channels. However, as the literature review in Section 4.2.2 showed, several papers that do compare the relative importance of more than one channel are in sharp disagreement. For example, Eichengreen, Rose, and Wyplosz (1996) and Glick and Rose (1999) argue that trade is an important propagation mechanism while macroeconomic similarities are generally not significant. On the other hand, Sachs, Tornell, and Velasco (1996) argue that macroeconomic similarities have a large and significant effect while trade is not important. Tests of the credit crunch channel by Kim (1999) and Ghosh and Ghosh (1999) use the same basic strategy for estimating loan supply and demand during the East Asian crisis, but one paper concludes that a credit crunch existed while the other concludes the opposite. Several papers argue that mutual funds were important in transmitting recent financial crises (through some sort of forced-portfolio recomposition or country reevaluation), while others argue that net redemptions and capital outflows by mutual fund investors were so small during recent crises that they could not have had a major impact. Even the more general tests of crisis- versus noncrisis-contingent propagation mechanisms, such as those performed by Calvo and Reinhart (1996) and Forbes and Rigobon (1999b), reach opposite conclusions on whether some sort of "contagion" occurred after recent financial crises.

A final limitation of tests based on macroeconomic data is that they ignore a tremendous wealth of information that is lost in the aggregation used to create the macroeconomic statistics. Within each country, there is a large variation in how different companies are affected by various shocks. For example, if a devaluation in one country increases the competitiveness of its exports, firms in other countries should only be directly affected by the devaluation if they sell products that compete with those exports. Companies that produce nontraded goods should be less affected by the devaluation. Similarly, if a crisis in one country leads to a global credit crunch, firms that are more dependent on short-term loans to finance current operations should be more affected by the increased cost of credit. Empirical studies that simply look at a country's aggregate trade statistics, balance of payments, or total market returns will ignore these important differential effects across firms. Utilizing firm-level information could be extremely useful in identifying how shocks are propagated internationally.

4.3 THE FIRM-LEVEL DATASET

The obvious difficulty with utilizing firm-level information to identify how shocks are propagated internationally is that these micro-level tests require a larger dataset composed of much less readily available statistics. To construct this firm-level dataset, I began by compiling balance sheet, income statement, cash flow, and general company information from the Worldscope database.[8] Worldscope contains information on approximately 16,000 companies from 51 countries, representing about 90 percent of global market capitalization (according to their literature). Records begin as early as 1980 for many companies, and they include historical information on firms that became inactive due to a merger, bankruptcy, or any other reason. Worldscope reports both (a) the original data as reported by each company and (b) templated figures that have been adjusted to account for cross-country variations in accounting practices. The templated figures are designed to be directly comparable across national boundaries. I compiled Worldscope information on all available companies for the one-year period preceding the 1997 East Asian crisis and the 1998 Russian crisis. Then I matched this information with data on daily stock returns from Datastream[9] and excluded the five countries that had information on fewer than 10 firms.[10]

The resulting data set includes information from 46 countries for 14,154 companies before the East Asian crisis and 12,570 companies before the Russian crisis. Table 4.1 lists the number of companies in each country and region for each of the crisis periods. As the table shows, there is extensive coverage of companies in the Americas, Asia, Australasia, and Europe, and more limited coverage of Africa and the Middle East. Table 4.2 lists median market capitalization, assets, and net income, as well as the total number of companies by industry group.[11] Appendix 4A presents detailed information on how all firm-level statistics are defined and/or calculated.

Several limitations of this firm-level dataset should be noted. First, because Worldscope only reports information which is publicly available,

---

[8] The Worldscope database is produced by Disclosure, which is part of the Primark Global Information Services Group. For further information, see the website: http://www.primark.com.

[9] Returns are calculated as the difference in logs and are not adjusted for inflation. Returns were also adjusted for weekends, with no significant impact on the results.

[10] Countries excluded are: Liechtenstein, Russian Federation, Slovakia, Sri Lanka, and Zimbabwe.

[11] I focus on median statistics because means tend to be skewed by several extreme outliers. These outliers undoubtedly represent reporting and/or measurement error and are adjusted for in the empirical analysis.

Table 4.1. Number of Companies by Country and
Region

	Asian Crisis	Russian Crisis
Asia	*4,656*	*3,954*
China	93	18
Hong Kong	390	344
India	209	167
Indonesia	133	95
Japan	2,308	2,240
Korea	257	225
Malaysia	424	304
Pakistan	44	19
Philippines	111	91
Singapore	219	191
Taiwan	204	64
Thailand	264	196
Australasia	*263*	*205*
Australia	216	159
New Zealand	47	46
Europe	*4,232*	*3,840*
Austria	77	74
Belgium	111	96
Czech Republic	50	48
Denmark	162	154
Finland	86	85
France	506	465
Germany	476	456
Greece	112	68
Hungary	26	24
Ireland	59	53
Italy	171	155
Luxembourg	16	16
Netherlands	162	159
Norway	112	110
Poland	46	20
Portugal	62	52
Spain	130	124
Sweden	157	147
Switzerland	153	147
United Kingdom	1,558	1,387

(*continued*)

Table 4.1 (*continued*)

	Asian Crisis	Russian Crisis
Latin America	*357*	*325*
Argentina	32	31
Brazil	135	118
Chile	69	67
Colombia	25	20
Mexico	66	62
Peru	18	16
Venezuela	12	11
North America	*4,400*	*4,036*
Canada	460	415
United States	3,940	3,621
Other Emerging Markets	*246*	*210*
Israel	20	19
South Africa	165	137
Turkey	61	54
Total Sample	*14,154*	*12,570*

Source: Calculated based on information from the Worldscope database.

Table 4.2. Sample Statistics

	Asian Crisis[a]	Russian Crisis[a]
Median Firm Market Capitalization (in $000)		
Asia	$216,154	$118,104
Australasia	306,295	291,104
Europe	154,399	184,213
Latin America	292,901	336,381
North America	385,628	480,730
Other emerging markets	267,581	295,645
Entire sample	*$245,963*	*$234,116*
Median Firm Assets (in $000)		
Asia	$372,440	$377,506
Australasia	388,881	405,763
Europe	233,470	258,020
Latin America	606,854	726,708
North America	372,929	464,204
Other emerging markets	281,328	318,449
Entire sample	*$335,532*	*$367,885*

Table 4.2 (*continued*)

	Asian Crisis[a]	Russian Crisis[a]
Median Firm Net Income (in $000)		
Asia	$7,458	$3,938
Australasia	17,124	18,286
Europe	7,756	9,950
Latin America	22,064	26,843
North America	14,692	17,230
Other emerging markets	19,095	20,571
Entire sample	*$9,845*	*$9,472*
Percent of Firms by Industry[b]		
Petroleum	2.3%	2.2%
Finance/real estate	18.6	18.6
Consumer durables	15.6	15.8
Basic industry	12.2	12.0
Food/tobacco	6.2	6.1
Construction	6.7	6.6
Capital goods	9.9	10.1
Transportation	3.4	3.3
Utilities	4.8	4.9
Textiles/trade	8.3	8.1
Services	7.6	7.7
Leisure	4.4	4.4
Public administration	0.1	0.1

[a] Data from the annual report in the one-year period preceding the relevant crisis. Asian crisis defined as starting on 6/25/97. Russian crisis defined as starting on 8/17/98.

[b] Based on firm's primary SIC code. Industry definitions largely based on two-digit SIC groups defined in Campbell (1996). The only changes are: the addition of a group for Public administration, and the addition of several two-digit codes (which were not included anywhere by Campbell) to prespecified groups. More specifically, SIC codes for each group are: Petroleum (13, 29); Finance/real estate (60–69); Consumer durables (25, 30, 36–37, 39, 50, 55, 57); Basic industry (8, 10, 12, 14, 24, 26, 28, 33); Food/tobacco (1, 2, 7, 9, 20, 21, 54); Construction (15–17, 32, 52); Capital goods (34, 35, 38); Transportation (40–42, 44, 45, 47); Utilities (46, 48, 49); Textiles/trade (22, 23, 31, 51, 53, 56, 59); Services (72, 73, 75, 76, 80–82, 87, 89); Leisure (27, 58, 70, 78, 79, 83–86, 88); and Public administration (43, 91–97).

Source: Calculated based on information from the Worldscope database.

virtually all of the sample consists of publicly traded companies. Most private and government-owned companies are not included. As a result, countries where many firms tend to be majority-owned by the state (such as China) tend to be underrepresented. Also, smaller firms, which are more likely to be privately owned, are underrepresented. A second problem is that although Worldscope attempts to correct for major differences in cross-country accounting standards, significant differences may still exist for certain variables. The analysis in the following section addresses this problem by using a number of different statistics to test each hypothesis and by examining the impact of country-specific effects on the results. A third problem is that there are a number of extreme outliers that undoubtedly represent reporting errors. The analysis below addresses this problem not only by utilizing estimation techniques that minimize outliers, but also by performing an extensive set of sensitivity tests.

4.4 METHODOLOGY AND UNIVARIATE TEST RESULTS

In order to test how a shock to one country is transmitted to firms in other countries, this chapter uses an event study methodology. It closely follows the framework laid out in Chapter 4 of Campbell, Lo, and MacKinlay (1997). The first part of this section explains the basic methodology and estimates a constant-mean-return model of normal stock returns before the East Asian and Russian crises. It then uses these estimated coefficients to calculate abnormal returns and cumulative abnormal returns for each stock after each crisis. The second part of this section aggregates these abnormal returns into different stock portfolios to test the strength of the various propagation mechanisms discussed above. Graphs of these various portfolios provide preliminary evidence of which groups of companies were more vulnerable to the East Asian and Russian crises, and therefore how these shocks were propagated internationally.

4.4.1 Methodology

To calculate normal returns for the sample of stocks discussed in Section 4.3, I utilize a constant-mean-return model. More specifically, for the precrisis period of length P, I estimate

$$\mathbf{r}_i = \mu_i \mathbf{I} + \boldsymbol{\varepsilon}_i \tag{1}$$

where $\mathbf{r}_i$ is the $(P \times 1)$ vector of daily returns for stock i over the precrisis period; μ_i is the estimated mean return for stock i; $\mathbf{I}$ is a $(P \times 1)$ vector of ones; and $\boldsymbol{\varepsilon}_i$ is the $(P \times 1)$ vector of disturbance terms. Campbell et al.

(1997) show that under general assumptions, OLS estimates of equation (1) are consistent and efficient.[12]

Although this constant-mean-return model may appear simplistic, and including additional variables (such as market returns) could minimize the variance of the abnormal return, I focus on this model for two reasons.[13] First, several of the tests performed below will estimate the impact of financial crises on aggregate market and industry returns for different countries and sectors. If I utilize a model of normal returns which controls for these market or industry returns, then it would be impossible to perform these tests. Second, Campbell et al. report that this constant-mean-return model yields results similar to those of much more sophisticated models and that: "This lack of sensitivity to the model choice can be attributed to the fact that the variance of the abnormal return is frequently not reduced much by choosing a more sophisticated model."[14]

To estimate equation (1), I define the precrisis period (of length P) as the one-year period before the "events" of the Russian and East Asian crises. I define the Russian crisis as starting on August 17, 1998 because this is the date that the government devalued the ruble and imposed a forced restructuring of its government debt.[15] I define the Asian crisis as starting on June 25, 1997, because this is date that the Thai government removed support from a major finance company (implying that creditors could incur losses) and reported that the government's stock of international reserves was grossly overstated.[16] These events prompted a massive speculative attack on Thailand which forced the government to float the baht on July 2nd. Admittedly, the Asian crisis had several different phases and it is possible to define other event windows for the various phases of the crisis. Section 4.5.2 will test for the sensitivity of the results to different windows, such as defining the East Asian crisis as

---

[12] Specifically, Campbell et al. (1997) show that it is necessary to assume the joint normality of asset returns. This implies that if $\mathbf{r}_t$ is an $(N \times 1)$ vector of stock returns over the time period t, then $\mathbf{r}_t$ is independently multivariate normally distributed with mean μ and covariance matrix Ω for all t. Under the constant-mean-return model, $\sigma_{\varepsilon_i}^2$ is the (i,i) element of Ω, $E[\varepsilon_{it}] = 0$, and $\text{Var}[\varepsilon_{it}] = \sigma_{\varepsilon_i}^2$.

[13] Moreover, Forbes (2000) performs a similar analysis using a market model (instead of a constant-mean-return model). Results do not change significantly.

[14] Campbell et al. (1997), p. 154.

[15] More specifically, on August 17th, the Russian government widened the band for the ruble exchange rate, defaulted on its treasury bills, and declared a ninety-day moratorium on foreign debt payments. The currency did not officially float until August 27th.

[16] As recently as May 1997, the Thai government had pledged public commitment to support Finance One. Reneging on this promise threatened the extensive system of government backing (both implicit and explicit). See Corsetti, Pesenti, and Roubini (1998) or Radelet and Sachs (1998) for a detailed record of key events in the Asian crisis.

starting in October when the Hong Kong peg was attacked. The central analysis, however, will focus on an event window starting on June 25, 1997, since this is the earliest phase of the East Asian crisis and should therefore capture the full impact of the entire crisis on firms around the world.

Next, I utilize the parameter estimates from equation (1) during the precrisis period to calculate abnormal returns for each stock after the crisis. I define the Asian crisis as lasting for seven months (ending on January 24, 1998), in order to include the Korean debt restructuring of mid-January 1998, which is generally considered the last major phase of the crisis. I define the Russian crisis as lasting for one month (ending on September 16, 1998), since the bailout of Long-Term Capital Management in the United States was announced on September 23rd and I do not want to include the impact of this announcement. Once again, it is possible to define each of these crises as ending on different dates, and the sensitivity analysis tests for the impact of changing the length of the event window. The resulting vector of abnormal returns ($\hat{\varepsilon}_i^*$) for firm i during the defined crisis period (i.e., event window) of length C is therefore

$$\hat{\varepsilon}_i^* = \mathbf{r}_i^* - \hat{\mu}_i \mathbf{I} \tag{2}$$

where $\mathbf{r}_i^*$ is the $(C \times 1)$ vector of returns during the crisis, $\hat{\mu}_i$ is the estimated parameter from equation 1 for stock i, and $\mathbf{I}$ is a $(C \times 1)$ vector of ones. Then, I add the abnormal returns for each stock to calculate the cumulative abnormal returns (CARs) over the full crisis period C:

$$\text{CAR}_{i,C} = \sum_{t=1}^{C} \hat{\varepsilon}_{i,t}^* \tag{3}$$

These CARs are utilized in the graphs and regression analysis for the remainder of the chapter.

4.4.2 Graphical Results

Once the CARs have been calculated for each stock, it is possible to construct portfolios to test if different types of stocks were more vulnerable to the shocks of the East Asian and Russian crises. As discussed in Section 4.2, there are five channels by which each crisis could have been transmitted to firms in other countries: product competitiveness, an income effect, a credit crunch, a forced-portfolio recomposition, and a wake-up call. Although data limitations make it difficult to construct definitive tests of the strength of each of these channels, testing if certain types of companies are more vulnerable to these two crises can provide strong evidence for or against each of the propagation mechanisms.

The first propagation channel, product competitiveness, argues that firms that produce the same goods as those exported by the crisis country

Table 4.3. Major Industries in the Crisis Zone[a]

Asian Crisis[b]	Russian Crisis
(8) Forestry	(10) Metal mining
(16) Heavy construction, excluding building	
(22) Textile mill products	
(23) Apparel and other textile products	
(31) Leather and leather products	
(32) Stone, clay, and glass products	
(33) Primary metal industries	
(36) Electronic and other electric equipment	
(44) Water transportation	
(45) Transportation by air	
(50) Wholesale trade-durable goods	
(55) Automotive dealers and service stations	
(56) Apparel and accessory stores	

[a] "Major industries" defined as two-digit SIC groups (in parentheses) for which net sales from companies based in the crisis zone are 5 percent or more of net sales for the entire sample. Sales are measured in US$ and taken from annual reports in the one-year period prior to the defined start of the crisis. Industries that are nontraded and are not directly competitive across countries are excluded. More specifically, the excluded industries are: utilities; services; leisure; finance/real estate; and public administration. SIC codes for the excluded industries are defined in Table 4.2.

[b] Asian-crisis countries defined as: Hong Kong, Indonesia, Korea, Malaysia, Philippines, Singapore, Taiwan, and Thailand.

will become less competitive (given that the crisis-country's currency loses value). Therefore, companies that produce in the same major industries as the crisis country should experience lower returns than companies that do not compete in those sectors. To test this channel, I define "major industries" for the crisis zone as the two-digit SIC groups for which net sales by companies from the crisis zone are five percent or more of net sales for the entire sample of companies.[17] I do not include industries which are nontraded and would not be expected to have competitive effects across countries.[18] Table 4.3 lists these SIC groups that are major industries for the crisis zone – that is, industries that could experience a

[17] The Asian-crisis zone is defined as: Hong Kong, Indonesia, Korea, Malaysia, Philippines, Singapore, Taiwan, and Thailand. The Russian-crisis zone is simply Russia. Total sales are measured in US$ and are taken from the companies annual report for the one year preceding the crisis.

[18] More specifically, the excluded industries are: utilities, services, leisure, finance/real estate, and public administration. SIC codes for the excluded industries are defined in Table 4.2.

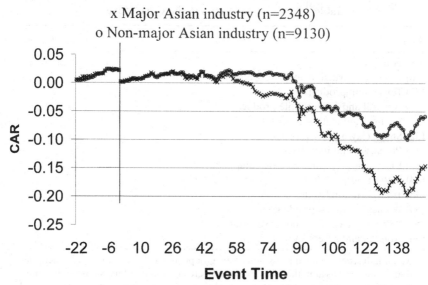

x Major Asian industry (n=2348)
o Non-major Asian industry (n=9130)

Figure 4.1. Product competitiveness: Asian crisis.

competitiveness effect from the Asian and Russian crises. Granted, this classification procedure is not a precise measure of competitiveness and has a number of problems,[19] but it does provide a rough approximation of what industries are most likely to be affected by the two crises. Moreover, the sensitivity analysis in Section 4.5.2 shows that modifications to this competitiveness indicator have no significant impact on results.

Next, I use the two-digit SIC codes listed in Table 4.3 to divide the firms in the data set into two portfolios for each crisis: companies whose primary output competes with output from the crisis zone (i.e., is in the same 2-digit SIC group) and companies whose primary output does not compete.[20] Figures 4.1 and 4.2 graph the CARs of each portfolio over time for the Asian and Russian crises, as well as for the one-month period before each crisis (which is calculated as a separate CAR). The horizon-

---

[19] One problem is that different countries could produce goods of varying quality within the same SIC category and therefore not compete directly. Another problem is that all firm sales are included under the firm's primary SIC code, although firms could have branches that produce in other sectors.

[20] Throughout this section, reported results are based on equally weighted portfolios. Estimates based on market-weighted portfolios are not significantly different. Also, I do not include firms from the relevant crisis area in either portfolio for two reasons. First, these firms are not relevant to this chapter's investigation of how shocks to one country affect firms in other countries. Second, crises could affect local firms differently, such as increasing the competitiveness of their exports instead of decreasing it.

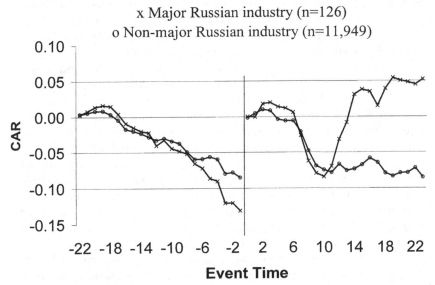

Figure 4.2. Product competitiveness: Russian crisis.

tal axes are labeled in event time, with zero equal to the date of the relevant crisis. Figure 4.1 shows that for the first two months of the Asian crisis, CARs were virtually identical for firms producing in the major industries of the Asian crisis countries and those not producing in these SIC groups. After about two months, however, firms whose primary output was in the major industries experienced significantly lower returns. This difference increases over time, suggesting not only that there was a product competitiveness effect during the Asian crisis, but that this effect was more important in the later phases of the crisis. This is not surprising because the countries that devalued in the earlier stages of the crisis (i.e., Thailand and Indonesia) produced smaller shares of global output than countries that devalued in the later stages of the crisis (i.e., Korea).

Figure 4.2 shows that the product-competitiveness effect during the Russian crisis was significantly different than that during the Asian crisis. During the first two weeks of the Russian crisis, CARs were virtually identical for firms producing in Russia's major industry and those not producing in this SIC group. After about two weeks, however, firms that produced in this major industry experienced significantly higher, instead of lower, returns. It appears that companies that competed with Russia's products actually gained from Russia's crisis. This could reflect the turmoil in Russia and the breakdown of the payments mechanism, which may have counteracted the competitive advantage of the ruble devaluation. Finally, because Asian output is a much larger share of global production than

Russian output, it is not surprising that there was a stronger product competitiveness effect during the Asian crisis than during the Russian crisis.

The second channel through which shocks could be propagated internationally is an income effect. A country (or region) suffering from a
crisis generally experiences a contraction of aggregate demand, which
reduces the profitability of firms that sell in that country (or region). To
test this channel, I calculate the percent of sales, operating income, and
assets in Russia and the Asian-crisis countries for each firm during the
one year preceding the relevant crisis. This classification procedure is not
precise, since many companies report sales, income, and assets by region
instead of by country, but it does provide a useful proxy of a firm's direct
exposure to the crisis zone.[21] Then, for each variable, I divide the sample
into two portfolios: firms that have direct exposure to the crisis zone
(defined as at least five percent of assets, sales, or net income in the
region) and firms that do not have direct exposure. I continue to exclude
firms that are based within the relevant crisis zone.

The CARs for each portfolio are graphed in Figures 4.3 and 4.4. Figure
4.4 shows evidence of a strong income effect during the Russian crisis.
Although the sample of companies with direct exposure to Russia is
small, these firms experienced significantly lower CARs than did firms
in the rest of the sample. On the other hand, Figure 4.3 shows that in the
early stages of the Asian crisis, companies with direct exposure to the
Asian-crisis countries actually outperformed companies with no direct
exposure. This could indicate that firms with direct exposure to Asia
share other characteristics that generate higher CARs during this period
(such as being larger or more internationally diversified). This could also
indicate that the Asian countries affected during the early phases of the
crisis were relatively small markets. This interpretation is supported by
the fact that midway through the Asian crisis, firms with direct exposure
to Asia experienced a significant drop in their CARs. This later phase
is when the largest Asian-crisis markets experienced the most severe
phases of their country-specific crises. It is therefore not surprising that
any income effect from reduced demand in the entire Asian-crisis region
is larger during the later phase of the crisis.

The third channel by which a shock to one country could be transmitted to firms in other countries is a credit crunch. As discussed in
Section 4.2, there are several different variants of this theory, but under-

---

[21] Russia is often grouped with Europe, and individual Asian countries are often grouped
together as Asia. In order to be consistent, I only include exposure that is specifically
linked to the relevant country. For example, for the Russian crisis, I only include
sales, income, or assets in Russia or the former USSR. For the Asian crisis, I only include
sales, income, or assets in Hong Kong, Indonesia, Korea, Malaysia, Philippines,
Singapore, Taiwan, or Thailand. The sensitivity analysis tests for the impact of using
broader definitions of these variables (i.e., including sales to all of Asia).

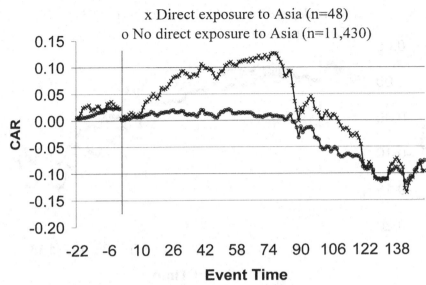

Figure 4.3. Income effect: Asian crisis.

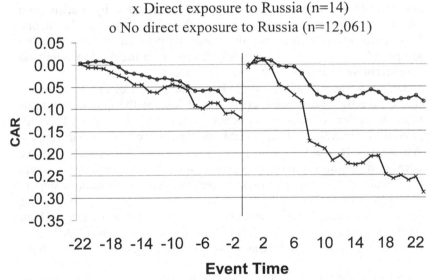

Figure 4.4. Income effect: Russian crisis.

lying them all is the idea that a crisis in one country leads to a sharp reduction in the international supply of credit, raising the cost of credit to firms in other countries. A direct implication of this theory is that companies that rely more heavily on short-term debt to finance inventories

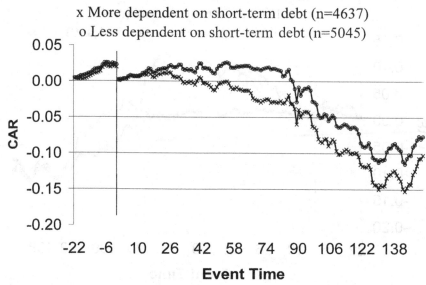

Figure 4.5. Credit crunch: Asian crisis.

and provide working capital would be more affected by a crisis (and experience relatively lower abnormal stock returns).[22] To test this theory, I use each firm's ratio of net short-term debt to equity to divide the sample of firms into two portfolios: those more highly dependent on short-term financing and those less dependent.[23]

Figures 4.5 and 4.6 graph the CARs for the two crises. Figure 4.5 shows that during the entire Asian-crisis period (except the first week), firms more dependent on short-term debt experienced lower CARs. This supports the hypothesis that there was some type of credit-crunch during the Asian crisis. It is worth noting, however, that this test is not definitive because firms more reliant on short-term debt could experience lower returns during the crisis for other reasons. For example, firms more dependent on short-term debt financing could be smaller or riskier companies. During the Russian crisis, however, firms that are more reliant on short-term debt financing do not have significantly lower CARs than the rest of the sample. In fact, as shown in Figure 4.6, midway through the

[22] For theoretical and empirical information on this balance sheet channel, see Bernanke and Gertler (1995) or Bernanke and Lown (1991).

[23] The sensitivity analysis uses a number of other measures of short-term debt dependence to construct these portfolios. Results do not change significantly. For each crisis, I use the sample median as the division between more-dependent and less-dependent firms. The sample median of net short-term debt to equity is 1.31 percent during the East Asian crisis and 0.97 percent during the Russian crisis.

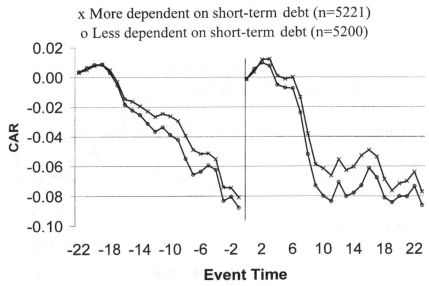

x More dependent on short-term debt (n=5221)
o Less dependent on short-term debt (n=5200)

Figure 4.6. Credit crunch: Russian crisis.

crisis these more-dependent firms experience slightly higher, instead of lower, CARs. Therefore, these graphs provide support for some sort of credit crunch during the Asian crisis, but not during the Russian crisis.

A forced-portfolio recomposition, the fourth propagation channel, suggests that after a crisis investors may need to sell assets in markets not directly affected by the crisis in order to meet certain requirements. It is impossible to test this propagation mechanism directly using this paper's firm-level dataset. One implication of this set of theories, however, is that a company would be more vulnerable to a forced sell-off if a larger percent of its shares is held by financial institutions (such as mutual funds) that could be subject to the regulatory requirements that cause this type of portfolio recomposition. Moreover, Falkenstein (1996) shows that mutual funds tend to bias their investment toward more liquid stocks. Therefore, since more liquid stocks tend to have a higher share of institutional ownership, they may be more susceptible to a forced-portfolio recomposition. To test this channel, I calculate each firm's stock liquidity as the percent of trading days for which stock returns are nonzero (in the precrisis period). Then, I define high-liquidity stocks as those for which returns are nonzero in at least 75 percent of the precrisis trading days.[24] All other stocks are classified as low-liquidity.

---

[24] The sensitivity analysis uses other measures of stock liquidity. Results do not change significantly.

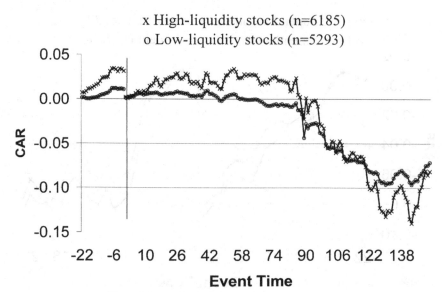

Figure 4.7. Portfolio recomposition: Asian crisis.

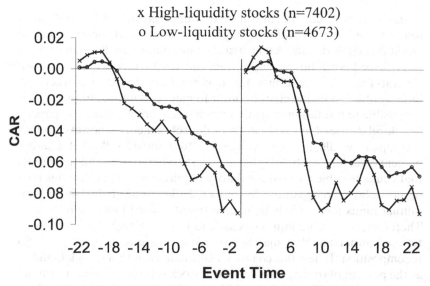

Figure 4.8. Portfolio recomposition: Russian crisis.

Figures 4.7 and 4.8 graph the CARs for portfolios of high-liquidity and low-liquidity stocks for the Asian and Russian crises. During the first half of the Asian crisis, high-liquidity stocks slightly outperform low-liquidity stocks, while during the second half of the crisis, high-liquidity stocks underperform low-liquidity stocks. This suggests that any forced portfolio recomposition caused by the Asian crisis occurred during the later stages of the crisis. As discussed above, this is not surprising given that the largest Asian countries experienced the most severe phases of their country-specific crises during this later stage. On the other hand, Figure 4.8 shows that during the entire Russian crisis (excluding the first five days), high-liquidity stocks experienced lower CARs than low-liquidity stocks. Therefore, although stock liquidity is a very rough proxy for capturing any sort of forced-portfolio recomposition, these results do suggest that this transmission mechanism could have been important during the Russian crisis and the later half of the Asian crisis.

The final channel by which a shock to one country could be transmitted to firms in other countries is a wake-up call or country reevaluation. This transmission channel incorporates a number of different theories. Once again, it is difficult to test this transmission channel directly using this paper's firm-level data. Each variant of this theory, however, has one important implication: A crisis in one country causes investors to pull out of all firms in another country or region. As a result, most of the movement in individual stock prices should be driven by movement in the aggregate country index. Firm characteristics should have no significant effect.[25] As a rough test of this channel, I divide the sample into different portfolios based on the country and region where each firm is based. This is a very imprecise test of the wake-up call channel, because any number of country-specific effects could cause fluctuations in aggregate market indices. If country-specific or region-specific effects do not exist, however, this suggests that the wake-up call effect was not an important transmission mechanism.

Figures 4.9 though 4.18 show a sample of the CARs for these different portfolios. The differences between the Asian and Russian crises are striking. During the Asian crisis, OECD and North American firms perform significantly better than those in the rest of the world, while during the Russian crisis, OECD and North American firms perform significantly worse. During the Asian crisis, Asian firms (excluding those in the crisis countries) perform significantly worse than those in the rest of the world, while during the Russian crisis, Asian firms perform significantly better.[26] Latin American performance is similar to that of the rest of the world during the Asian crisis (although it diverges at the end of the period), but significantly worse during the Russian crisis. Finally, the odd group of firms from Israel, South Africa, and Turkey (labeled "other

[25] One caveat, however, is that if this wake-up call and the resultant sell-off occurs quickly, more liquid stocks would be more affected. In this case, it would be difficult to differentiate between a "wake-up call" effect and a "forced-portfolio recomposition."

[26] This is undoubtedly due to the fact that the "normal" returns for Asian countries are calculated during late 1997 and early 1998.

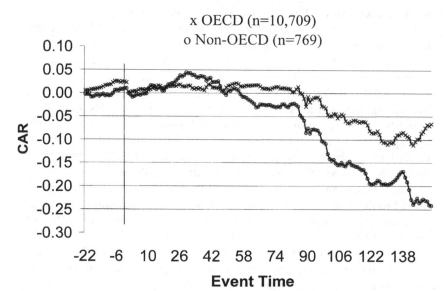

Figure 4.9. Wake-up call: Asian crisis.

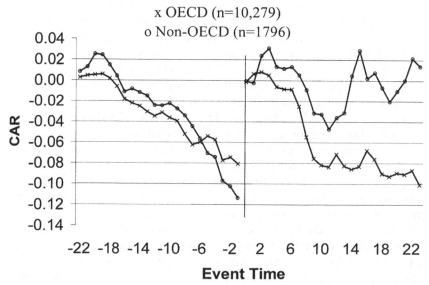

Figure 4.10. Wake-up call: Russian crisis.

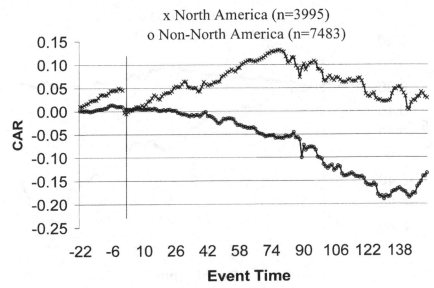

Figure 4.11. Wake-up call: Asian crisis.

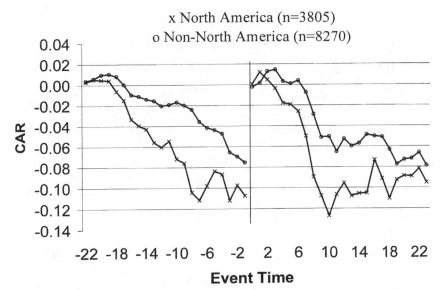

Figure 4.12. Wake-up call: Russian crisis.

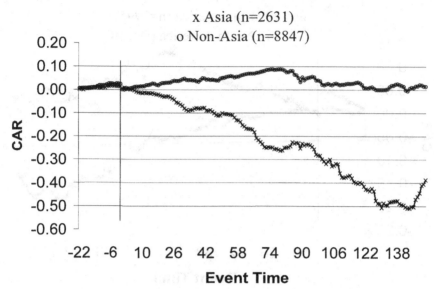

Figure 4.13. Wake-up call: Asian crisis.

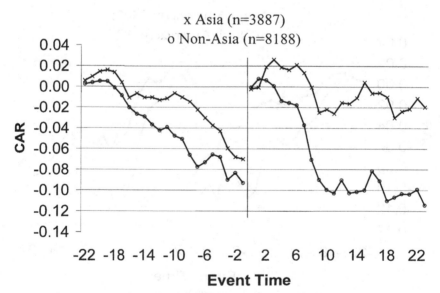

Figure 4.14. Wake-up call: Russian crisis.

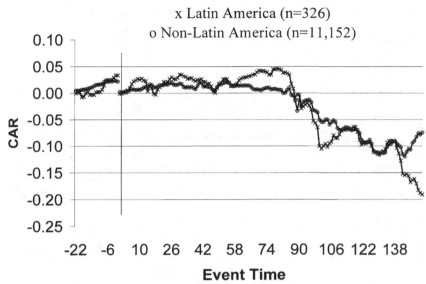

Figure 4.15. Wake-up call: Asian crisis.

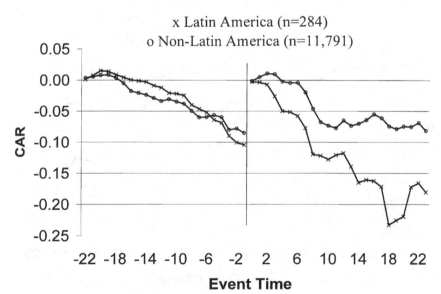

Figure 4.16. Wake-up call: Russian crisis.

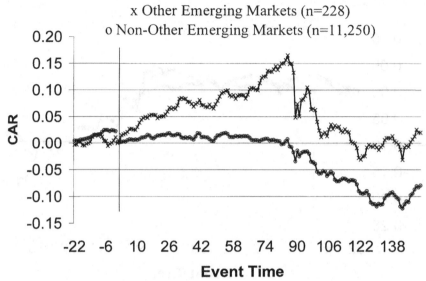

Figure 4.17. Wake-up call: Asian crisis.

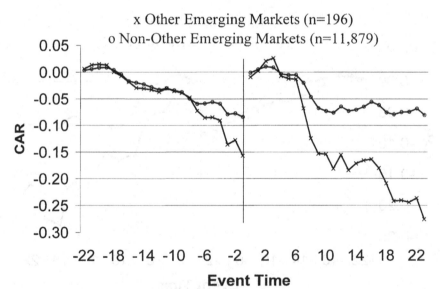

Figure 4.18. Wake-up call: Russian crisis.

emerging markets") significantly outperform the rest of the world during the Asian crisis, but underperform during the Russian crisis. These graphs clearly show that regional and country effects are important during both crises. They also suggest that the Asian crisis did not cause investors to "wake-up" and pull out of the Americas or other small emerging markets. On the other hand, the Russian crisis did appear to cause a significant reevaluation of both North and South America, as well as small (non-Asian) emerging markets.

To summarize, the graphical results presented in this section provide mixed support for the five international propagation mechanisms. There is strong support for a product competitiveness effect during the later stages of the Asian crisis, but none during the Russian crisis. There is strong evidence of an income effect during the Russian crisis, some evidence during the later phases of the Asian crisis, but no evidence during the initial phases of the Asian crisis (and actually evidence of the opposite). There is support for a credit crunch during the Asian crisis, but not during the Russian crisis. There is evidence of a forced-portfolio recomposition during the Russian crisis and later half of the Asian crisis, but not during the early phases. Moreover, during each crisis there are strong country and regional effects which could reflect some sort of wake-up call. This reevaluation affects a broader range of countries during the Russian crisis than the Asian crisis. Finally, and perhaps most important, these graphs suggest that different transmission mechanisms played relatively different roles in the international propagation of shocks during the Asian and Russian crises.

4.5 MULTIVARIATE TESTS

Although these graphical results are suggestive, it is difficult to draw any strong conclusions from this type of univariate approach. If two (or more) firm characteristics are highly correlated, then it may be difficult to isolate the impact of a specific characteristic on stock returns. For example, as mentioned above, larger firms are more likely to have direct sales exposure to the Asian crisis region, and larger firms may be less vulnerable to global crises (if investors switch to larger, more stable companies after a shock). In this case, a portfolio of firms with direct exposure to the Asian crisis region may outperform firms with no exposure to the region, although this difference in performance has no direct relationship to the variable under consideration (exposure to Asia). In other words, an international shock could simultaneously have several different effects on a firm, and it is difficult to identify these effects by focusing on only one variable. This section will address this problem by estimating a number of cross-section, multivariate regressions and attempt to isolate and quantify the relative importance of the five propagation mechanisms during the Asian and Russian crises. The section begins by explaining the basic methodology and presenting a set of preliminary results. The next part of the section reports a number of sensitivity tests and extensions to the base model. The section concludes by discussing a potential econometric problem with this analysis and how this problem could affect results.

4.5.1 Methodology and Central Results

To begin, define **y** as the $(N \times 1)$ vector of cumulative returns during the full crisis period (of length C as defined above) for the entire sample of N stocks.[27] Then if X is a $(N \times K)$ matrix of firm characteristics (with the first column a vector of ones), it is possible to estimate

$$\mathbf{y} = X\boldsymbol{\theta} + \boldsymbol{\eta} \qquad (4)$$

where $\boldsymbol{\theta}$ is a $(K \times 1)$ vector of coefficients and $\boldsymbol{\eta}$ is a $(N \times 1)$ vector of disturbances. For consistency with the graphical analysis I include five firm characteristics in X, each of which is designed to test one of the propagation mechanisms discussed above. These variables and their definitions are listed in Table 4.4.

Table 4.5 presents the base estimates of equation (4) for the Asian and Russian crises. Countries from the crisis zone continue to be excluded from the relevant analysis. Columns 1 and 3 present OLS estimates with standard errors White-adjusted for heteroscedasticity. As discussed above, however, one problem with the Worldscope data is that there are a number of extreme outliers. Many are undoubtedly reporting errors, but it is difficult to judge which outliers are mistakes and which represent unusual corporate practices (such as the extremely high debt to equity ratios of several Asian firms). Therefore, instead of trying to evaluate which outliers should be dropped, I use an estimation technique which reduces the weight given to outliers. First, I calculate Cook's distance statistic for each firm and eliminate gross outliers. Then, I use an iterative estimation technique that places less weight on observations with larger residuals.[28] Columns 2 and 4 present these results and show that several coefficient estimates change significantly when outliers are given less weight. Moreover, results in columns 2 and 4 are virtually identical to those obtained by simply dropping extreme outliers (based on a graphical analysis). Therefore, outliers appear to be a problem;

---

[27] Specification continues to be based on Campbell et al. (1997).

[28] More specifically, in the first stage I eliminate gross outliers for which Cook's distance statistic is greater than one. Then I estimate the base regression and calculate Huber weights based on the absolute value of these residuals. I use these weights to re-estimate the regression, reiterating until convergence, and then use this result and biweights to further reiterate until convergence. For further information on this procedure, see Hamilton (1998).

Table 4.4. Base Regression Specification

Independent Variable	Propagation Channel	Relevant Statistic[a]
Sector competition	Product competitiveness	Dummy = 1 if firm produces in the same SIC group as a "major industry" of the crisis zone (see Table 4.3)
Direct exposure	Income effect	Dummy = 1 if firm has over 5 percent of sales, assets, or net income in the crisis zone
Debt liquidity	Credit crunch	Ratio of net short-term debt to equity
Trading liquidity	Forced-portfolio recomposition	Dummy = 1 if stock return ≠ 0 in at least 75 percent of the trading days in the one-year precrisis period
Country dummies	Wake-up call	Dummy variable equal to one if firm is based in a given country; United States is excluded country

[a] For more information, see Section 4.4 and/or Appendix 4A.

Table 4.5. Regression Results[a]

	Asian Crisis[b]		Russian Crisis[c]	
	Base Results (1)	Outliers Underweight[d] (2)	Base Results (3)	Outliers Underweight[d] (4)
Constant	0.073**	0.089**	−0.064**	−0.042**
	(0.008)	(0.006)	(0.005)	(0.003)
Sector competition	−0.063**	−0.063**	0.139**	0.105**
	(0.007)	(0.006)	(0.024)	(0.014)
Direct exposure	−0.061	−0.082*	−0.134**	−0.133**
	(0.045)	(0.040)	(0.054)	(0.035)
Debt liquidity	−0.004**	−0.046	−0.025	−0.018
	(0.000)	(0.057)	(0.015)	(0.014)
Trading liquidity	−0.027**	−0.023**	−0.023**	−0.031**
	(0.007)	(0.006)	(0.004)	(0.003)
Country dummies[e]	Yes**	Yes**	Yes**	Yes**
Number of observations	*9,692*	*9,691*	*10,464*	*10,464*
R^2	*0.30*		*0.27*	
F-statistic	*209.7*	*153.9*	*46.1*	*117.0*

[a] Standard errors in parentheses. All errors are White-adjusted for heteroscedasticity. See Table 4.4 for variable definitions. * is significant at the 5 percent level; ** is significant at the 1 percent level.

[b] Dependent variable is CAR from 6/25/97 through 1/24/98. Asian crisis firms excluded from the regression.

[c] Dependent variable is CAR from 8/17/98 through 9/16/98. Russian firms excluded from the regression.

[d] Estimated following Hamilton (1998). See text for details.

[e] Country dummies reported in Table 4.6. Asterisks indicate joint significance of dummy variables. United States is excluded country.

and in the discussion that follows, I focus on the estimates in columns 2 and 4.

Most of the estimates reported in Table 4.5 support the results and discussion from the graphical analysis. The coefficient on sector competition is negative and highly significant during the Asian crisis, but positive and significant in the Russian period. This supports the claim that product competitiveness was an important propagation mechanism during the former period, but not during the latter one. Moreover, the coefficient on sector competition in column 2 suggests that the magnitude of this impact could be large. Firms that competed in the same sectors as major industries from the Asian-crisis zone had CARs 6.3 percent lower than those of noncompetitive firms (over the entire seven-month Asian-crisis period).

The coefficient on the second variable, direct exposure, is negative and just significant (at the 5 percent level) during the Asian period, but is negative and highly significant during the Russian crisis. This borderline significance during the Asian crisis is not surprising given the graphical result that there was no income effect during the first half of the period. Overall, however, these results suggest that an income effect was important during these crises and that the magnitude of this effect was significant. Firms with direct exposure to the Asian-crisis countries had CARs 8.2 percent lower than the rest of the sample, and firms with direct exposure to Russia had returns 13.3 percent lower.

The coefficient on debt liquidity is negative (although insignificant) during both crisis periods. This weak evidence of a credit crunch agrees with the graphical evidence during the Asian crisis, and it suggests that the graphical evidence against a credit crunch during the Russian period is spurious. Finally, the coefficient on trading liquidity is negative and highly significant during both crises. Although this is a rough proxy for a forced-portfolio recomposition, these estimates suggest that this channel could have been important during both crises (even though this effect did not begin during the Asian crisis until midway through the event horizon). The coefficient values, however, suggest that the magnitude of this effect may have been smaller than that for the product competitiveness or income effects. More-liquid stocks had CARs 2.3 percent lower than the rest of the sample during the Asian crisis and 3.1 percent lower than the rest of the sample during the Russian crisis.

Coefficient estimates for the country dummy variables included in these regressions are reported in Table 4.6.[29] For each crisis, a majority of the coefficients are individually significant (with the United States as

---

[29] Due to space constraints, I only report coefficient estimates based on columns 2 and 4 of Table 4.5. Estimates based on columns 1 and 3 are not significantly different.

Table 4.6. Country Dummy Variables[a]

		Asian Crisis		Russian Crisis	
		Coefficient	Std. Error	Coefficient	Std. Error
Asia	China	−0.405**	(0.027)	0.227**	(0.031)
	Hong Kong	—	—	0.135**	(0.007)
	India	−0.345**	(0.019)	0.120**	(0.010)
	Indonesia	—	—	−0.114**	(0.014)
	Japan	−0.455**	(0.007)	−0.010**	(0.004)
	Korea	—	—	0.147**	(0.009)
	Malaysia	—	—	0.384**	(0.008)
	Pakistan	−0.161**	(0.039)	0.106**	(0.031)
	Philippines	—	—	0.038**	(0.014)
	Singapore	—	—	0.139**	(0.010)
	Taiwan	—	—	0.055**	(0.016)
	Thailand	—	—	−0.015	(0.010)
Australasia	Australia	−0.118**	(0.020)	0.053**	(0.012)
	New Zealand	−0.143**	(0.040)	0.049*	(0.021)
Europe	Austria	−0.068*	(0.032)	−0.011	(0.016)
	Belgium	−0.008	(0.026)	−0.004	(0.013)
	Czech Republic	−0.113**	(0.041)	−0.069**	(0.019)
	Denmark	−0.052**	(0.021)	0.009	(0.011)
	Finland	0.002	(0.028)	−0.092**	(0.014)
	France	−0.031**	(0.013)	−0.030**	(0.006)
	Germany	−0.108**	(0.014)	−0.008	(0.007)
	Greece	−0.067**	(0.027)	−0.093**	(0.016)
	Hungary	0.030	(0.052)	−0.433**	(0.026)
	Ireland	0.099**	(0.035)	−0.098**	(0.018)
	Italy	0.218**	(0.021)	−0.125**	(0.011)
	Luxembourg	−0.027	(0.075)	0.017	(0.037)
	Netherlands	−0.072**	(0.021)	−0.043**	(0.011)
	Norway	−0.035	(0.027)	−0.075**	(0.014)
	Poland	−0.287**	(0.054)	−0.127**	(0.039)
	Portugal	0.005	(0.034)	−0.039*	(0.019)
	Spain	0.061**	(0.024)	−0.093**	(0.012)
	Sweden	−0.043	(0.025)	−0.083**	(0.011)
	Switzerland	−0.030	(0.022)	−0.089**	(0.011)
	United Kingdom	−0.038**	(0.009)	−0.047**	(0.005)
Latin America	Argentina	−0.279**	(0.046)	−0.243**	(0.023)
	Brazil	−0.347**	(0.025)	−0.080**	(0.013)
	Chile	−0.289**	(0.032)	−0.088**	(0.016)
	Colombia	−0.100*	(0.050)	−0.065*	(0.028)
	Mexico	−0.046	(0.034)	−0.012	(0.017)

(*continued*)

Table 4.6 (*continued*)

		Asian Crisis		Russian Crisis	
		Coefficient	Std. Error	Coefficient	Std. Error
	Peru	−0.346**	(0.062)	−0.137**	(0.033)
	Venezuela	−0.456**	(0.072)	−0.028	(0.037)
North	Canada	−0.040**	(0.015)	0.006	(0.008)
America	United States	Omitted	Omitted	Omitted	Omitted
Other	Israel	−0.173*	(0.083)	−0.054	(0.041)
Emerging	South Africa	−0.245**	(0.024)	−0.047**	(0.012)
Markets	Turkey	0.527**	(0.037)	−0.400**	(0.019)
F-test[b]		*164.1***		*124.11***	

[a] All standard errors are White-adjusted for heteroscedasticity. Results based on regressions reported in columns 2 and 4 of Table 4.5. See Table 4.4 for variable definitions. * is significant at the 5 percent level; ** is significant at the 1 percent level.
[b] Statistic is an *F*-test for joint significance of the country dummy variables.

the omitted country) and an *F*-test indicates that the coefficients are jointly, highly significant. Once again, many of the results support the graphical analysis presented above. For example, noncrisis Asian countries have significant negative coefficients during the Asian crisis, but many have significant positive coefficients during the Russian crisis. This undoubtedly results from the fact that the "normal" returns for the Asian countries during the Russian crisis were based on the preceding one-year period that included the Asian crisis. Most other emerging markets also have negative (and usually significant) coefficients during both crisis periods. Moreover, the magnitude of these country-specific coefficients can be large, ranging from −0.456 for Venezuela to 0.527 for Turkey (both during the Asian crisis). Granted, these coefficients only capture returns relative to the U.S. average (the omitted country), but the magnitude and range of the coefficients suggests that country-specific effects can overshadow the effects of the other transmission mechanisms.

To summarize, this set of results suggests that an income effect was an important propagation mechanism during the Russian crisis, and an income effect and product competitiveness were significant during the East Asian crisis. A credit crunch appears to have played a relatively minor role in the propagation of shocks during both crises. Although it is difficult to test for the importance of a forced-portfolio recomposition or wake-up call effect, some rough tests indicate that both of these channels could have been important during both crises. Moreover, the magnitude of these propagation channels varies significantly. The country-specific effects have the largest impact on CARs over the two crisis periods. Product competitiveness and income effects are smaller, although still large in terms of the relative influence on firm performance. Any liquidity effect, which could reflect a forced-portfolio recomposition, is significantly smaller.

4.5.2 Sensitivity Tests and Model Extensions

The estimates reported in Section 4.5.1 are based on a number of strong assumptions and simplifications. Therefore, this section will perform a number of sensitivity tests. More specifically, it will test for the impact of: redefining key variables, including additional explanatory variables; utilizing stricter inclusion criteria and sample selection; and reclassifying period definitions. Due to space constraints, I do not show the univariate graphs or report all of the multivariate regression results. Any results that differ significantly from the base estimates reported above, however, are discussed in detail.[30]

4.5.2.1 Sensitivity Tests 1: Redefining Key Variables

As a first set of sensitivity tests, I examine the impact of redefining each of the variables used in the base analysis. The first variable, sector competition, was measured by a dummy variable equal to one if a firm produced in the same sector as a "major industry" from the crisis zone. Major industry was defined as any two-digit SIC group for which sales by firms in the crisis zone were at least 5 percent of global sales (and nontraded sectors were excluded). I begin by slightly tweaking this definition, by raising the criteria to be a major industry to 10 percent of global sales and/or including nontraded goods. Results do not change significantly for the Asian crisis, although when the 10 percent division is utilized, Russia no longer has any major industry. Moreover, including firms in oil and gas extraction (SIC code 13) as a major industry for Russia (since Russia has almost 5 percent of global production) does not change the significant, positive coefficient on sector competition for this period.

Next, I make a more significant adjustment to the definition of sector competition. Instead of using sample information to calculate major industries for each crisis zone, I use the *Country Profile* published by the Economist Intelligence Unit to construct a list of major exports (ranked by f.o.b. price) for Russia and the Asian-crisis countries.[31] Table 4.7 lists these general export categories and their closest relevant two-digit SIC codes. Granted, this classification procedure is imprecise and does not

---

[30] Full results are available from the author.

[31] I define major exports as the five largest exports (ranked by f.o.b. price) for each country. Exports for the Asian countries are taken from 1996 and for Russia from 1997. Specific exports are generally reclassified by broader industry group. (For example, rice is listed as food.)

Table 4.7. Primary Exports from the Crisis Zone[a]

Asian Crisis[b]	Russian Crisis[c]
Food	Timber, cellulose, and paper
(01, 02)	(08, 26)
Crude materials and crude petroleum	Fuel, minerals, metals, and
(13)	precious stones
Manufactured goods and miscellaneous	(10, 12, 13, 14)
manufacturers includes: textiles, apparel,	Chemicals and rubber
processed food products; Chemicals,	(28, 30)
petroleum and coal products; metal industries	Machinery and equipment
and products; machinery; electronic and other	(35)
electric equipment; transportation equipment	
(20–39)	
Transportation, travel, and trade-related services	
(37, 44, 47)	
Communications products	
(48)	

[a] SIC Codes (in parentheses) are an approximation given the information available.
[b] Data for 1996.
[c] Data for 1997.

Source: Compiled based on the Economist Intelligence Unit, *Country Profile*, 1999 edition for each country. Exports taken from Reference Tables in the Appendix. The five most important exports for each country (ranked by f.o.b price) are included. Specific exports are generally reclassified by broader industry group (for example, rice is categorized as food).

adjust for the relative share of each export industry in global production, but it is a useful complement to the measure utilized above. Column 2 of Table 4.8 shows the results for the Asian crisis. The coefficient on product competitiveness is still negative and significant. The slight reduction in magnitude is not surprising given the greater imprecision in this new definition of sector competition. Column 2 of Table 4.9 shows the results for the Russian crisis. The coefficient on sector competition is now equal to zero and insignificant. This is not surprising given that Russian exports in the stated industries are a small share of global production.

The second variable in the base specification, direct exposure, is a dummy variable equal to one if a company has over 5 percent of sales, assets, or income in the crisis region. Once again, I begin by tweaking this definition, and utilize 10 percent or 20 percent as the cutoff for direct exposure. The number of companies with direct exposure falls significantly, and the coefficient on direct exposure remains significant and

Table 4.8. Sensitivity Tests 1 & 2: Asian Crisis[a]

	Base Results (1)	Redefine Sector Competition[b] (2)	Redefine Debt Liquidity[c] (3)	Redefine Trading Liquidity[d] (4)	Add Regional Dummies (5)	Add control for Firm Size[e] (6)	Add control for Leverage[f] (7)	Add Industry Dummies[g] (8)
Constant	0.089**	0.098**	0.073**	0.111**	0.085**	0.087**	0.084**	-0.160
	(0.006)	(0.007)	(0.007)	(0.006)	(0.006)	(0.006)	(0.006)	(0.172)
Sector competition	-0.063**	-0.048**	-0.040**	-0.057**	-0.060**	-0.062**	-0.060**	-0.037**
	(0.006)	(0.005)	(0.006)	(0.011)	(0.006)	(0.006)	(0.006)	(0.007)
Direct exposure	-0.082*	-0.073	-0.069	-0.037	-0.081*	-0.083*	-0.085*	-0.065
	(0.040)	(0.040)	(0.042)	(0.067)	(0.041)	(0.040)	(0.039)	(0.040)
Debt liquidity	-0.046	-0.073	-0.129	-0.088	-0.084	-0.047		-0.110*
	(0.057)	(0.057)	(0.094)	(0.184)	(0.058)	(0.057)		(0.056)
Trading liquidity	-0.023**	-0.019**	-0.024**	-0.041**	-0.026**	-0.026**	-0.019**	-0.019**
	(0.006)	(0.006)	(0.006)	(0.003)	(0.005)	(0.006)	(0.005)	(0.005)
Country dummies	Yes**	Yes**	Yes**	Yes**	No	Yes**	Yes**	Yes**
Number of observations	*9,691*	*9,691*	*9,424*	*3,143*	*9,691*	*9,691*	*10,427*	*9,691*
F-statistic	*153.9*	*154.8*	*130.5*	*24.5*	*577.7*	*150.0*	*161.8*	*125.4*

[a] Standard errors in parentheses. All errors are White-adjusted for heteroscedasticity. Estimated using the technique outlined in Hamilton (1998) and described in the text. Dependent variable is CAR from 6/25/97 through 1/24/98. Asian crisis firms excluded from the regression. All variables defined in Table 4.4 except as noted. * is significant at the 5 percent level; ** is significant at the 1 percent level.
[b] Sector competition is redefined by major exports as listed in the EIU *Country Profile*. See Table 4.7 for details.
[c] Debt liquidity defined by the current ratio (ratio of current assets to current liabilities).
[d] Trading liquidity defined as the percent of shares traded to shares outstanding.
[e] Firm size measured by total market capitalization (in US$).
[f] Leverage measured by ratio of total debt to total capital.
[g] Industry dummies based on divisions specified in Table 4.2.

145

Table 4.9. Sensitivity Tests 1 & 2: Russian Crisis[a]

	Base Results (1)	Redefine Sector Competition[b] (2)	Redefine Debt Liquidity[c] (3)	Redefine Trading Liquidity[d] (4)	Add Regional Dummies (5)	Add Control for Firm Size[e] (6)	Add Control for Leverage[f] (7)	Add Industry Dummies[g] (8)
Constant	-0.042**	-0.043**	-0.050**	-0.062**	-0.039**	-0.043**	-0.042**	-0.139
	(0.003)	(0.004)	(0.004)	(0.003)	(0.003)	(0.003)	(0.003)	(0.121)
Sector competition	0.105**	0.000	0.108**	0.252**	0.119**	0.105**	0.111**	0.110**
	(0.014)	(0.003)	(0.012)	(0.023)	(0.014)	(0.014)	(0.013)	(0.014)
Direct exposure	-0.133**	-0.134**	-0.144**	-0.200**	-0.158**	-0.133**	-0.131**	-0.132**
	(0.035)	(0.035)	(0.035)	(0.053)	(0.037)	(0.035)	(0.035)	(0.034)
Debt liquidity	-0.018	-0.018	-0.003	-0.124	-0.023	-0.018		-0.020
	(0.014)	(0.014)	(0.004)	(0.087)	(0.015)	(0.013)		(0.013)
Trading liquidity	-0.031**	-0.030**	-0.028**	-0.010**	-0.035**	-0.033**	-0.031**	-0.032**
	(0.003)	(0.003)	(0.003)	(0.002)	(0.003)	(0.003)	(0.003)	(0.003)
Country dummies	Yes**	Yes**	Yes**	Yes**	No	Yes**	Yes**	Yes**
Number of observations	10,464	10,464	9,925	3,137	10,464	10,422	11,153	10,464
F-statistic	117.0	115.3	83.4	20.8	116.4	115.2	118.9	97.7

[a] Standard errors in parentheses. All errors are White-adjusted for heteroscedasticity. Estimated using the technique outlined in Hamilton (1998) and described in the text. Dependent variable is CAR from 8/17/98 through 9/16/98. All variables defined in Table 4.4 except as noted. * is significant at the 5 percent level; ** is significant at the 1 percent level.

[b] Sector competition is redefined by major exports as listed in the EIU *Country Profile*. See Table 4.7 for details.

[c] Debt liquidity defined by the current ratio (ratio of current assets to current liabilities).

[d] Trading liquidity defined as the percent of shares traded to shares outstanding.

[e] Firm size measured by total market capitalization (in US$).

[f] Leverage measured by ratio of total debt to total capital.

[g] Industry dummies based on divisions specified in Table 4.2.

146

increases. Next, I make a more significant adjustment to the variable definition. As discussed above, this measure is imprecise because many of the companies only list sales by broad geographic region (i.e., Asia or Europe) and not by specific country. Now I broaden the definition of direct exposure to include sales, assets, or income in all of Asia (for the Asian crisis) or all of Europe (for the Russian crisis). This is clearly a rough measure, since a majority of the direct exposure is now with non-crisis countries (such as Japan for the Asian crisis, or Germany for the Russian crisis). Not surprisingly, the coefficient on direct exposure is insignificant in each case. The other coefficient values, however, do not change significantly.

The third variable in the base specification, debt liquidity, is measured by the ratio of net short-term debt to equity. There are a number of different ratios that could also capture a firm's dependence on short-term financing and its vulnerability to a credit crunch. Therefore, I try eight different definitions of this variable: net short-term debt to working capital, net short-term debt to total assets, net short-term debt to total capital, coverage ratio, current ratio, quick ratio, share of short-term debt in total debt, and the ratio of working capital to assets. Each of these variables is defined in detail in Appendix 4A. Then I reestimate the base regression using each of these definitions. Column 3 of Tables 4.8 and 4.9 reports the results using the current ratio; these results are typical of the results based on the other measures. The coefficient on debt liquidity is generally not only insignificant at the 5 percent level (in 7 of the 8 cases during the Asian crisis and 6 cases during the Russian crisis), but often has the wrong sign. The other coefficients and signs, however, are highly robust. The only noteworthy change is that the coefficient on direct exposure during the Asian crisis occasionally becomes insignificant (although it always remains negative).

The fourth variable in the base regression, trading liquidity, is measured by a dummy variable equal to one if the stock had nonzero returns in at least 75 percent of the precrisis trading days. Once again, I tweak the definition and use the less stringent criteria that stocks are highly liquid if they have nonzero returns in at least 50 percent of the precrisis trading days. Results do not change significantly, although the magnitude of the trading liquidity coefficient decreases during the Asian crisis and increases during the Russian crisis. Next, I make a more substantial change to this variable definition. I redefine trading liquidity as the percent of shares traded to shares outstanding. Because this measure is not available for a majority of firms, the sample size shrinks significantly, but column 4 in Tables 4.8 and 4.9 shows that the central results are unchanged. In both cases the coefficient on trading liquidity remains negative and significant.

Finally, I modify the variables that are designed to capture any sort of wake-up call effect. Because any reevaluation or wake-up call is just as likely to take place along regional as country-specific borders, I replace the country dummy variables with regional dummy variables (using the regions defined in Table 4.1). Results are reported in column 5 of Tables 4.8 and 4.9 and do not change significantly. In each case, the regional dummies are jointly significant, and each is even individually significant. Moreover, when I repeat the analysis with both country and regional dummies, both sets of dummy variables are jointly significant (and the other coefficient estimates do not change significantly).

4.5.2.2 Sensitivity Tests 2: Including Additional Explanatory Variables

As a second set of sensitivity tests, I add a number of new explanatory variables to the base specification. First, as mentioned above, company size could interact with the propagation of shocks if, for example, small firms have more difficulty raising capital and are therefore more vulnerable to a credit crunch. To control for the impact of firm size, I add several variables to the base regression: total market capitalization, total equity, total assets, total sales, or net income (all expressed in US$). Column 6 of Tables 4.8 and 4.9 reports the results based on total market capitalization, which are virtually identical to those based on the other measures, as well as virtually identical to the base results in column 1. In most cases, the coefficient on the measure of firm size is positive and highly significant.

Several analyses of the Asian crisis have focused on the importance of overborrowing (and crony capitalism) in causing this crisis and/or making firms in Asia more vulnerable to an initial shock. Although this chapter does not address the initial cause of crises, it is possible that these concerns led to a "reevaluation" of firms which were highly leveraged and/or had unusually low levels of profitability. To test for this effect, I add a number of controls for leverage and profitability to the base regression: total debt to equity, net long-term debt to equity, total debt to total capital, total debt to assets, return on equity, return on assets, and return on invested capital. Column 7 of Tables 4.8 and 4.9 reports the results based on the ratio of total debt to total capital; these results are typical. The coefficients on the leverage statistics are usually negative and occasionally significant, even if the measure of debt liquidity is dropped from the regression. The coefficients on the profitability measures are always positive and significant during the Asian crisis, but negative and significant during the Russian crisis (except for return on equity which is insignificant). None of the other coefficient estimates change significantly.

As a final addition to the base model, I include a set of dummy variables for the industry groups specified in Table 4.2. The results are reported in column 8 of Tables 4.8 and 4.9, and an F-test indicates that the industry dummy variables are jointly significant. Most coefficient estimates do not change significantly, except during the Asian crisis when the coefficient on debt liquidity becomes significant and the coefficient on direct exposure becomes insignificant. It is worth noting that the coefficient on sector competition remains negative and significant during the Asian crisis, despite the fact that the industry dummy variables undoubtedly capture some of the product-competitiveness effect.

4.5.2.3 Sensitivity Tests 3: Stricter Inclusion Criteria and Sample Selection

As a third set of sensitivity tests, I use stricter criteria for inclusion in the sample and examine the impact of dropping various countries and groups of stocks from the analysis. First, because some stocks in the sample are not heavily traded, I exclude stocks that have nonzero returns in over half of the precrisis trading days. The sample for the Asian-crisis period shrinks by 1960 companies, and the sample for the Russian crisis shrinks by 194. Results are reported in column 2 of Tables 4.10 and 4.11. Coefficient estimates do not change significantly, and in fact, the magnitude of most estimates increases. This suggests that all of the results reported above would actually be strengthened by excluding less liquid stocks from the sample. It is also worth noting that the coefficient on stock liquidity remains negative and significant, despite the fact that many of the less liquid stocks have been excluded.

Next, because different industries may have different reporting standards (such as financial companies or public-sector institutions), I repeat the base analysis but exclude one industry group at a time (using the industry groups specified in Table 4.2). Column 3 in Tables 4.10 and 4.11 reports the estimates from dropping the "finance/real estate" sector, which is the only test that yields results significantly different from the base analysis. During the Russian crisis, coefficient estimates are unchanged, but during the Asian crisis the coefficient on direct exposure becomes (barely) insignificant, while the coefficient on debt liquidity becomes significant.

Finally, as mentioned previously, different countries have different reporting standards and the templated statistics reported in the Worldscope database may not sufficiently correct for these differences. Therefore, to ensure that any remaining differences in reporting standards do not have a significant impact on results, I exclude one country at a time from the base analysis. In each case, the central results do not change significantly (except during the Asian crisis, the coefficient on direct exposure occasionally becomes insignificant).

Table 4.10. Sensitivity Tests 3 & 4: Asian Crisis[a]

	Base Results (1)	Exclude Illiquid Stocks[b] (2)	Exclude Finance Sector[c] (3)	Crisis Ends on 3/24/98 (4)	Crisis Ends on 9/24/97 (5)	Crisis Starts on 10/01/97 (6)
Constant	0.089**	0.089**	0.073**	0.161**	0.105**	-0.032**
	(0.006)	(0.007)	(0.007)	(0.007)	(0.004)	(0.005)
Sector competition	-0.063**	-0.069**	-0.045**	-0.060**	-0.006	-0.045**
	(0.006)	(0.007)	(0.006)	(0.007)	(0.004)	(0.004)
Direct exposure	-0.082*	-0.094*	-0.070	-0.111**	0.050*	-0.122**
	(0.040)	(0.046)	(0.044)	(0.044)	(0.025)	(0.030)
Debt liquidity	-0.046	-0.163	-0.192**	-0.075	-0.018	-0.044
	(0.057)	(0.087)	(0.039)	(0.062)	(0.030)	(0.041)
Trading liquidity	-0.023**	-0.024**	-0.029**	0.005	-0.001	-0.012**
	(0.006)	(0.006)	(0.006)	(0.006)	(0.003)	(0.004)
Country dummies	Yes**	Yes**	Yes**	Yes**	Yes**	Yes**
Number of observations	*9,691*	*7,731*	*8,233*	*9,629*	*9,846*	*9,691*
F-statistic	*153.9*	*131.4*	*124.8*	*156.4*	*131.3*	*39.7*

[a] Standard errors in parentheses. All errors are White-adjusted for heteroscedasticity. Estimated using the technique outlined in Hamilton (1998) and described in the text. Dependent variable is CAR from 6/25/97 through 1/24/98. Asian crisis firms excluded from the regression. All variables defined in Table 4.4 except as noted. * is significant at the 5 percent level; ** is significant at the 1 percent level.
[b] Illiquid stocks defined as stocks for which returns are nonzero in over 50 percent of the precrisis trading days.
[c] Finance (and real estate) sector defined as firms whose main sector of production is two-digit SIC code 60–69.

Table 4.11. Sensitivity Tests 3 & 4: Russian Crisis[a]

	Base Results (1)	Exclude Illiquid Stocks[b] (2)	Exclude Finance Stocks[c] (3)	Crisis Ends on 8/31/98 (4)
Constant	−0.042**	−0.044**	−0.047**	−0.084**
	(0.003)	(0.004)	(0.004)	(0.002)
Sector competition	0.105**	0.108**	0.110**	−0.001
	(0.014)	(0.014)	(0.014)	(0.009)
Direct exposure	−0.133**	−0.148**	−0.146**	−0.054**
	(0.035)	(0.038)	(0.037)	(0.023)
Debt liquidity	−0.018	−0.019	−0.009	0.000
	(0.014)	(0.013)	(0.014)	(0.000)
Trading liquidity	−0.031**	−0.031**	−0.029**	−0.029**
	(0.003)	(0.003)	(0.003)	(0.002)
Country dummies	Yes**	Yes**	Yes**	Yes**
Number of observations	*10,464*	*10,270*	*8,746*	*10,477*
F-statistic	*117.0*	*117.3*	*83.4*	*82.5*

[a] Standard errors in parentheses. All errors are White-adjusted for heteroscedasticity. Estimated using the technique outlined in Hamilton (1998) and described in the text. Dependent variable is CAR from 8/17/98 through 9/16/98. All variables defined in Table 4.4 except as noted. * is significant at the 5 percent level; ** is significant at the 1 percent level.

[b] Illiquid stocks defined as stocks for which returns are nonzero in over 50 percent of the precrisis trading days.

[c] Finance (and real estate) sector defined as firms whose main sector of production is two-digit SIC code 60–69.

4.5.2.4 Sensitivity Tests 4: Reclassifying Period Definitions

As a final set of sensitivity tests, I reclassify the period definitions used in the base analysis. I begin with the Asian crisis. First, I extend the length of the crisis period by two months (ending on March 24, 1998) in order to capture some of the continuing pressure on the Asian markets during late February and early March. Results are reported in column 4 of Table 4.10 and show several significant differences from the base analysis. The coefficient on direct exposure has increased in magnitude and is now highly significant. This could indicate that the full income effect from the Asian crisis took several months to be fully reflected in stock prices. The other significant change is that (for the first time in all the results reported above) the coefficient on trading liquidity is insignificant. This could indicate that over longer time periods, liquidity and any forced-portfolio recomposition become less important.

Next, because the graphical results in Section 4.3 showed important differences between the earlier and later phases of the Asian crisis, I analyze these two subperiods separately. I shorten the crisis period to only three months (ending on September 24th) so as to focus on the initial phase of the crisis when only the lower-income Asian countries (Indonesia, Malaysia, the Philippines, and Thailand) were under speculative attack. Then I focus on only the later part of the crisis, when the higher-income Asian economies began to be attacked. I define this "crisis" as starting on October 1, 1997 (in order to include the mid-October speculative attack on Hong Kong and crash of that economy's stock market).[32] Results from these two tests are reported in columns 5 and 6 of Table 4.10 and support the graphical analysis reported above. Most of the coefficients are not significant during the early phase of the Asian crisis, but all are highly significant (except debt liquidity) during the later phase of the crisis. As discussed above, given the larger market size of the countries attacked during the later phase of the crisis, it is not surprising that any product competitiveness, income, or forced-portfolio recomposition effect is larger during this later stage.

Finally, although the period classifications for the Russian crisis are more straightforward than for the Asian crisis, I repeat the base tests for the Russian period, but end the crisis after one week, two weeks, or three weeks, instead of after one month. (I do not extend the length of the crisis window because I do not want to include the collapse of Long-Term Capital Management.) Results for the two-week crisis period are reported in column 4 of Table 4.11 and are similar to those based on the other periods. One significant change from the base analysis is that the coefficient on product competitiveness is now negative (and insignificant) instead of positive and significant.

4.5.3 Econometric Caveat: Cross-Correlation in Returns

Although the multivariate regression results reported in this section are an improvement over the univariate, graphical analysis presented in Section 4.4, they are still only preliminary. This estimation is based on a number of strong identifying assumptions, such as the independence of the error terms across firms. More specifically, for two firms i and j during any time period t, if $E(\varepsilon'_{it}\varepsilon_{jt}) \neq 0$ for each i and j in equation 1 then the disturbances are cross-correlated across firms. This problem is likely to occur in the model estimated above because all firms in the sample

---

[32] Even though the period from June 25th to October 18th is no longer technically part of the event window, I continue to exclude it from the precrisis calculation of normal returns.

are affected by the crisis at the same time (as opposed to most event studies where the event, such as a stock split, occurs in different firms at different dates). The resulting cross-correlation in disturbances causes coefficient estimates and standard errors to be biased and inconsistent.

One technique for adjusting for this problem is to use a GLS estimator that utilizes the covariance matrix of returns for firms in the precrisis period. This technique is not feasible, however, for a large number of firms, and it generally requires that the number of time periods is greater than the number of firms (i.e., that $T > N$).[33] This requirement is clearly not satisfied in the dataset described in Section 4.3.

A second approach for adjusting for this problem is to use a technique developed by Sefcik and Thompson (1986). They utilize a weighting matrix to divide the sample of firms into different portfolios and then use these portfolios to estimate the impact of firm characteristics on stock returns. By dividing the sample into a smaller dimension (K portfolios instead of N companies), it is possible to correct for the cross-correlation in returns. Coefficient estimates are unbiased and consistent, and standard errors are unbiased, consistent, and efficient. This technique, however, is more complicated than the analysis presented above and is beyond the realm of this chapter. Forbes (2000) explains this methodology in more detail and shows that correcting for the cross-correlation in returns can significantly increase standard errors and reduce the significance of coefficient estimates. Although her analysis uses a different model specification, time period delineation, and sample, her results support the central conclusions reported above.[34]

4.6 CAVEATS AND CONCLUSIONS

This chapter began by reinterpreting previous theoretical work on the transmission of crises as describing five mechanisms by which a country-specific shock could be propagated to firms around the globe. These five transmission mechanisms are: product competitiveness, an income effect, a credit crunch, a forced-portfolio recomposition, and a wake-up call. After briefly reviewing the macroeconomic empirical work testing these various channels, the paper constructs a new firm-level dataset of financial statistics, product information, geographic data, and stock returns for over 14,000 companies in 46 countries.

---

[33] For an example and proof of these claims, see Collins and Dent (1984).

[34] There are only two noteworthy changes. First, the income effect is consistently negative and significant during the Asian crisis. Second, the portfolio-recomposition effect is no longer consistently significant during the Russian crisis.

The remainder of the chapter uses this firm-level data and an event-study methodology to test if firm vulnerability to the Asian and Russian crises is affected by factors such as: sector competitiveness, direct exposure to the crisis zone, debt liquidity, trading liquidity, and geographic location. These tests suggest that an income effect was an important propagation mechanism during the Russian crisis, and an income effect and product competitiveness were important during the East Asian crisis. A credit crunch appears to have played a relatively minor role in the international propagation of shocks during both crises. Although it is difficult to test for the importance of a forced-portfolio recomposition or wake-up call effect, some rough tests indicate that both of these channels could have been important during both crises. An extensive set of robustness tests examines the impact of redefining variable definitions, including additional explanatory variables, using different sample selection criteria, and reclassifying period definitions. Results are highly robust (except that the income effect occasionally becomes insignificant during the Asian crisis).

Although less conclusive, results also provide preliminary evidence of the relative importance of these various propagation channels during each crisis. The country-specific effects, which could reflect some sort of wake-up call, have the largest impact on stock returns over the two crisis periods. The product competitiveness effect during the Asian crisis, as well as the income effect during the Russian crisis, is also large in magnitude. Any trading liquidity effect, which could indicate a forced-portfolio recomposition, is consistently significant during both crises, but the magnitude of this channel appears to be relatively small. An important implication of this set of results is that the relative strength of the various transmission mechanisms varies across crises. As a result, it is unlikely that a single model can capture how shocks are propagated during all crises.

These results, however, are only a first step. Several statistics are imprecisely measured (such as sector competition and direct exposure). Other variables are only rough proxies for the propagation mechanism being tested (such as using trading liquidity to capture the impact of a forced-portfolio recomposition). Reporting errors in the Worldscope database could still affect results (despite the use of an estimation technique which minimizes outliers). Econometric issues, such as the cross-correlation in returns across firms, could affect estimates and bias standard errors. Therefore, this chapter's results should be interpreted as a useful (and hopefully edifying) complement to the macroeconomic, empirical evidence on how shocks are propagated internationally.

Appendix 4A. Variable Definitions[a]

Common equity	Common shareholder's investment in a company. Includes common stock value, retained earnings, capital surplus, capital stock premium, cumulative gain or loss of foreign currency translations, discretionary reserves, and negative goodwill.
Coverage ratio*	Ratio of earnings before interest and taxes to interest expense on debt.
Common shares traded to common shares outstanding*	Common shares outstanding are the number of shares outstanding at the company's year end and is the difference between issued shares and treasury shares. For companies with more than one type of common/ordinary shares, common shares outstanding represents the combined shares adjusted to reflect the par value of the share type. Common shares traded is the number of shares of the company traded during the year.
Current assets	Cash and other assets that are reasonably expected to be realized in cash, sold or consumed within one year or one operating cycle.
Current liabilities	Debt or other obligations that the company expects to satisfy within one year.
Current ratio	Percent of current assets to current liabilities.
Days return is nonzero*	Dummy variable equal to one if the stock return is not equal to zero in at least three-quarters of the nonweekend days in the precrisis period.
Market capitalization	Product of shares outstanding and market price at fiscal year end. For companies with more than one type of common/ordinary shares, market capitalization represents total market value of the company.
Net income	Income after all operating and nonoperating income, expenses, reserves, income taxes, minority interest, and extraordinary items. Represents income before preferred dividends.
Net long-term debt*	Any interest bearing financial obligations (excluding amounts due within one year and net of premium or discount) minus cash and cash equivalents.
Net sales	Gross sales and other operating revenue less discounts, returns and allowances. For financial companies, sales represents total operating revenue.
Net short-term debt*	Any debt payable within one year (including the current portion of long-term debt and sinking

(continued)

	fund requirements of preferred stock or debentures) minus cash and cash equivalents.
Percent assets by region*	Ratio of assets in a given region to total assets.
Percent operating income by region*	Ratio of operating income in a given region to total operating income, where operating income is the difference between sales and total operating expenses.
Percent sales by region*	Ratio of sales in a region to net sales.
Quick ratio	Ratio of (cash and equivalents + net receivables) to current liabilities.
Return on assets	100* (Net income before preferred dividends + ((interest expense on debt – interest capitalized)* (1 – Tax rate))) / Last year's total assets. Calculated differently for financial companies.
Return on equity	100* (Net income before preferred dividends – preferred dividend requirements) / Last year's common equity.
Return on invested capital	100* (Net income before preferred dividends + ((Interest expense on debt – interest capitalized)* (1 – Tax rate))) / (Last year's total capital + last year's short-term debt and current portion of long-term debt).
Share of short-term debt in total debt*	Ratio of net short-term debt to total debt.
Total assets	For industrials: the sum of total current assets, long-term receivables, investment in unconsolidated subsidiaries, other investments, net property, plant and equipment, and other assets. For banks: the sum of cash held and due from other banks, total investments, net loans, customer liability on acceptances, investment in unconsolidated subsidiaries, real estate assets, net property, plant and equipment, and other assets. For insurance companies: sum of cash, total investments, premium balance receivables, investments in unconsolidated subsidiaries, net property, plant and equipment, and other assets.
Total capital	Total investment in the company. The sum of common equity, preferred stock, minority interest, long-term debt, nonequity reserves and deferred tax liability in untaxed reserves.
Working capital	Difference between current assets and current liabilities.

[a] Variables are either taken directly from the Worldscope database or calculated based on information provided by Worldscope and/or price information from Datastream. Statistics marked with an * are not directly available from Worldscope and are calculated as stated. For more information on specific statistics, see Worldscope database.

REFERENCES

Agénor, Pierre-Richard and Joshua Aizenman (1997). "Contagion and Volatility with Imperfect Credit Markets." NBER Working Paper No. 6080. Cambridge, MA.

Baig, Taimur and Ilan Goldfajn (1998). "Financial Market Contagion in the Asian Crisis." IMF Working Paper No. 98/155. Washington, D.C.

Banerjee, Abhijit (1992). "A Simple Model of Herd Behavior," *Quarterly Journal of Economics* **107**(3):797–817.

Bernanke, Ben and Mark Gertler (1995). "Inside the Black Box: The Credit Channel of Monetary Policy Transmission," *Journal of Economic Perspectives* **9**(4):27–48.

——and Cara Lown (1991). "The Credit Crunch," *Brookings Papers on Economic Activity*, No. 2:205–247.

Calvo, Guillermo and Enrique Mendoza (1999). "Rational Herd Behaviour and the Globalization of Securities Markets." NBER Working Paper No. 7153. Cambridge, MA.

Calvo, Sarah and Carmen Reinhart (1996). "Capital Flows to Latin America: Is There Evidence of Contagion Effects?" In G. Calvo, M. Goldstein, and E. Hochreiter, eds., *Private Capital Flows to Emerging Markets after the Mexican Crisis.* Washington, D.C.: Institute for International Economics.

Campbell, John (1996). "Understanding Risk and Return," *Journal of Political Economy* **104**(2):298–345.

——, Andrew Lo, and A. Craig MacKinlay (1997). *The Econometrics of Financial Markets.* Princeton, NJ: Princeton University Press.

Chang, Roberto and Andrés Velasco (1998). "Financial Crises in Emerging Markets: A Canonical Model." NBER Working Paper No. 6606. Cambridge, MA.

Chari V.V. and Patrick Kehoe (1999). "Herds of Hot Money." Mimeo, Federal Reserve Bank of Minneapolis.

Claessens, Stijn, Rudiger Dornbusch, and Young Chul Park (1999). "Financial Contagion: How it Spreads, How it Can Be Stopped." Paper prepared for IMF/World Bank/Asian Development Bank project on Financial Contagion.

Collins, Daniel and Warren Dent (1984). "A Comparison of Alternative Testing Methodologies Used in Capital Market Research, "*Journal of Accounting Research* **22**(1):48–84.

Corsetti, Giancarlos, Paulo Pesenti, and Nouriel Roubini (1998). "What Caused the Asian Currency and Financial Crisis?" NBER Working Papers Nos. 6833 and 6834. Cambridge, MA.

——, ——, ——, and Cedric Tille (1998). "Trade and Contagious Devaluations: A Welfare-Based Approach." Mimeo.

Ding, Wei, Ilker Domac, and Giovanni Ferri (1998). "Is There a Credit Crunch in East Asia?" World Bank Policy Research Working Paper No. 1959. Washington, D.C.

Drazen, Allen (1999). "Political Contagion in Currency Crises." NBER Working Paper No. 7211. Cambridge, MA.

Economist Intelligence Unit (1999). *Country Profile.* For select countries.

Eichengreen, Barry, Andrew Rose, and Charles Wyplosz (1996). "Contagious Currency Crises." NBER Working Paper No. 5681. Cambridge, MA.

Falkenstein, Eric (1996). "Preferences for Stock Characteristics as Revealed by Mutual Fund Portfolio Holdings, " *Journal of Finance* **51**(1):111–135.

Forbes, Kristin (2000). "The Asian Flu and Russian Virus: Firm-Level Evidence on How Crises are Transmitted Internationally." NBER Working Paper No. 7807. Cambridge, MA.

——and Roberto Rigobon (1999a). "Measuring Contagion: Conceptual and Empirical Issues." Mimeo, MIT-Sloan School of Management. Paper prepared for IMF/World Bank/Asian Development Bank Project on Financial Contagion.

——and ——(1999b). "No Contagion, Only Interdependence: Measuring Stock Market Co-Movements." NBER Working Paper No. 7267. Cambridge, MA.

Frankel, Jeffrey and Sergio Schmukler (1998). "Crisis, Contagion and Country Funds: Effects on East Asia and Latin America." In R. Glick, ed., *Managing Capital Flows and Exchange Rates: Perspectives from the Pacific Basin.* New York: Cambridge University Press.

Froot, Kenneth, Paul O'Connell, and Mark Seasholes (1998). "The Portfolio Flows of International Investors I." NBER Working Paper No. 6687. Cambridge, MA.

Gerlach, Stephan and Frank Smets (1995). "Contagious Speculative Attacks," *European Journal of Political Economy* **11**(1):45–63.

Ghosh, Swati and Atish Ghosh (1999). "East Asia in the Aftermath: Was There a Crunch?" IMF Working Paper No. 99/38. Washington, D.C.

Glick, Reuven and Andrew Rose (1999). "Contagion and Trade: Why Are Currency Crises Regional?" *Journal of International Money and Finance* **18**(4):603–617.

Goldfajn, Ilan and Rodrigo Valdés (1997). "Capital Flows and Twin Crises: The Role of Liquidity." IMF Working Paper No. 97/87. Washington, D.C.

Hamilton, L. (1998). *Statistics with Stata.* Pacific Grove, CA: Brooks/Cole Publishing Company.

Kaminsky, Graciela, Richard Lyons, and Sergio Schmukler (1999). "Managers, Investors, and Crises: Mutual Fund Strategies in Emerging Markets." Mimeo, World Bank.

——and Carmen Reinhart (1998). "On Crises, Contagion, and Confusion." Mimeo, George Washington University.

Kim, Hyun (1999). "Was the Credit Channel A Key Monetary Transmission Mechanism Following the Recent Financial Crisis in the Republic of Korea." World Bank Policy Research Working Paper No. 2103. Washington, D.C.

Masson, Paul (1997). "Monsoonal Effects, Spillovers, and Contagion." Mimeo, International Monetary Fund.

Peek, Joe and Eric Rosengreen (1997). "The International Transmission of Financial Shocks: The Case of Japan," *American Economic Review* **87**(4):495–505.

Radelet, Steven and Jeffrey Sachs (1998). "The Onset of the East Asian Financial Crisis."NBER Working Paper No. 6680. Cambridge, MA.

Rea, James (1996). "U.S. Emerging Market Funds: Hot Money or Stable Source of Investment Capital?" *Perspective* **2**(6):1–14.

Rigobon, Roberto (1999). "On the Measurement of Contagion." Mimeo, MIT-Sloan School of Management.

Sachs, Jeffrey, Aaron Tornell, and Andrés Velasco (1996). "Financial Crises in Emerging Markets: The Lessons from 1995," *Brookings Papers on Economic Activity*, No. 1:147–198.

Sefcik, Stephan and Rex Thompson (1986). "An Approach to Statistical Inference in Cross-Sectional Models with Security Abnormal Returns as Dependent Variable," *Journal of Accounting Research* **24**(2):316–334.

Shiller, Robert (1995). "Conversation, Information, and Herd Behavior," *American Economic Review Papers and Proceedings* **85**(2):181–185.

Tornell, Aaron (1999). "Common Fundamentals in the Tequila and Asian Crises." NBER Working Paper No. 7139. Cambridge, MA.

Valdés, R. (1996). "Emerging Market Contagion: Evidence and Theory." Mimeo, MIT.

Discussion

How Are Shocks Propagated Internationally? Firm-Level Evidence from the Russian and East Asian Crises

Kenneth Kasa

By definition, currency crises are high-frequency events. They happen suddenly, within a matter of days or even hours. To date, most empirical studies of currency crises use low-frequency data, usually monthly or quarterly. For some questions, this timing mismatch is not important. However, for other questions it could be crucial. For example, crisis theories are typically divided into fundamentals-driven first-generation models and sunspot-driven second-generation models. Distinguishing these theories requires an answer to the following question: Do policies cause crises, or do crises cause policies? Clearly, it is impossible to answer this question using data sampled at a frequency coarser than the interval between government policy choices.[1]

An analogous problem arises in distinguishing theories of "contagion" – that is, the transmission of crises across countries. Is contagion driven by fundamentals, like trade flows, or do crises spread through their effects on expectations, with trade flows being merely an ex post response to an exogenous exchange rate change? Once again, if we are to distinguish between "real" and "financial" theories of contagion, then it would seem to be essential to use high-frequency data. This is exactly what Kristin Forbes does in her analysis of the recent financial crises in Asia and Russia. To my knowledge, this is one of the first essays that is even capable of empirically distinguishing first- and second-generation theories of contagion.

Forbes employs a standard event-study methodology, using daily data on the stock returns of more than 10,000 firms in 46 countries. The chapter examines five, not necessarily mutually exclusive, crisis propa-

---

[1] As noted by Burnside, Eichenbaum, and Rebelo (1998), "cause" does not necessarily mean temporally prior. That is, it is expectations about *future* fundamentals that matter in first-generation crisis models. The potential importance of news about future fundamentals reinforces the desirability of using high-frequency data.

gation mechanisms: (1) export competitiveness, (2) an income effect, (3) a credit crunch, (4) a portfolio rebalancing effect, and (5) a wake-up call effect. The first two are real-side theories of contagion, while the last three are financial theories. For each propagation mechanism, Forbes identifies a single variable that presumably captures a firm's exposure to that propagation mechanism. For example, firms with high leverage ratios are assumed to be more exposed to a crisis-induced credit crunch.

It turns out that for the Asian crisis, four of the five propagation mechanisms appear to have been at work; that is, only the credit crunch variable fails to enter the returns regressions significantly. For the Russian crisis, three of the five propagation mechanisms enter significantly. Once again, the credit crunch variable is insignificant, while the export competitiveness variable enters significantly but with the wrong sign. Given the apparent significance of several propagation mechanisms, the chapter comes to the eminently reasonable conclusion that no single theory of contagion is likely to be able to account for the spread of currency crises across countries.

Overall, I think this is an excellent essay. The use of high-frequency financial market data to measure exposure to various channels of crisis propagation is a strategy that is likely to be emulated in many subsequent papers. My only substantive comments concern a few details of the empirical methodology. This methodology consists of the following three steps: (1) Define a crisis period and measure "abnormal returns" during this period, (2) identify accounting and other variables that are presumably correlated with exposure to one of the crisis propagation mechanisms, and (3) compute a cross-sectional multiple regression of the cumulative abnormal returns on the exposure variables, and then draw inferences about the propagation of crises based on the coefficient estimates. The following comments address each of these three steps.

DEFINING A CRISIS AND MEASURING ABNORMAL RETURNS

The first step in the analysis is to identify a crisis date. It might seem obvious that a crisis occurs when the exchange rate experiences a sharp devaluation. Can't we just plot the exchange rate and define the crisis date to be the point at which the exchange rate jumps (with a surrounding window possibly omitted to allow for a lag between the initial attack and the eventual collapse)? Unfortunately, this strategy could be highly misleading in a study of crisis propagation. For example, did the Asian crisis begin for Korean firms in November 1997, when the won first began to depreciate sharply, or did it really start in July, when the baht was devalued?

Forbes handles this ambiguity by omitting crisis country firms from the cross-sectional regression (of course, this is not an issue for the case of the Russian crisis). That is, only the stock prices of firms located in countries that were *not* hit by the crisis are used to measure crisis propagation. In my opinion, this potentially throws out the baby with the bath water. Omitting firms from fellow crisis countries likely understates the importance of crisis propagation (unless the crisis was caused by a common external shock). In a sense, the "event window" is too wide. I suspect that a finer resolution would magnify the importance of propagation.

Event studies have been a staple of empirical finance for years now, and this literature has devised several ways to handle event date uncertainty. The most common approach is to simply try various surrounding dates and see whether the results change. This is what Forbes does, and she finds that indeed the results don't change much for minor changes in the event date. However, this doesn't mean that the effects are not robustly biased! A more systematic way of handling event date uncertainty was proposed by Ball and Torous (1988). They use a latent variable approach that jointly estimates the event date and the magnitude of its effect. I think that this kind of approach would provide more information on the temporal propagation of crises across industries and regions.

Once a crisis date is defined, the next step is to measure "abnormal returns" following the crisis. Doing this of course requires some notion of what a normal return is. Forbes defines normality by firm-specific mean returns, estimated over a period prior to the crisis. That is, equilibrium expected returns are assumed to be constant over time. Any significant change in the level of a stock price during the event window will then show up as a significant cumulative abnormal return.

Whether this is reasonable depends on the question you are asking. As a theory of capital asset pricing, it is clearly unreasonable. Financial economists have been statistically rejecting this model for decades. At the same time, however, the finance literature has found that often the results of event studies do not change significantly when time-varying risk factors are incorporated into the definition of normal returns. The responses to firm- or industry-specific events are typically so large that they dominate movements in macroeconomic risk factors. Forbes appeals to these prior findings to support her definition of abnormal returns.

Unfortunately, studying the response to a macroeconomic event, like a currency crisis, is quite different from studying the response to idiosyncratic events like dividend or merger announcements. For a given crisis, there is really only one event, although the responses of firms can of course differ by industry or country. Omitting common time-varying macroeconomic risk factors induces a sort of cross-sectional dependence in the regression disturbances, which reduces effective degrees of freedom. At a minimum, this causes size distortions. At worst, it can produce biased estimates if these omitted risk factors are correlated with the included exposure variables.

Forbes bases her inferences on the assumption that she has over 10,000 independent observations. This just doesn't seem plausible to me. Instead, I think the analysis here suffers from the same kind of problem that plagued early panel tests of purchasing power parity (see O'Connell, 1998). One way to account for cross-sectional dependence would be to use a GLS estimator. Alternatively, time dummies could be added when computing cumulative abnormal returns.

LINKING ACCOUNTING VARIABLES TO CRISIS PROPAGATION MECHANISMS

There are several issues involved with linking firm-specific accounting variables to crisis exposure. First, there is the basic issue of measurement error. How accurately do these accounting variables measure their economic counterparts? Given the widely varying accounting conventions used in different countries, how comparable are these measures across countries? Unfortunately, I am not sufficiently knowledgeable of the Worldscope database to pass judgment on these questions. Forbes does use a version that supposedly corrects for different accounting rules; and without a better alternative, we'll just have to hope that this does a reasonable job of making the numbers comparable. My only comment along these lines is that the accuracy of the numbers themselves may not be as important as the comparability of regulatory regimes across countries. A given set of accounting numbers can mean quite different things, depending on the specifics of bankruptcy and forbearance policies.

Once we are satisfied that we have accurate and comparable accounting information, we still face the problem of linking these variables to crisis propagation. Ideally, of course, this would be done within the context of a fully specified theoretical model. Unfortunately, these models are still too stylized to be taken directly to the data, so I am sympathetic to Forbes' informal and intuitive approach. For example, the proxies for the trade channels seem quite reasonable. The leverage variable also seems reasonable, although it is probably related to several of the propagation mechanisms. Also, there is a marginal/average distinction that could be important. My main concern relates to the wake-up call channel. It seems rather heroic to assume that country dummies are accurate measures of a wake-up call effect. These dummies are all defined relative to the United States; and since the vast majority of the estimates are negative, an equally plausible interpretation of these dummies is that they are picking up a "safe haven" effect. Maybe this is the same thing as a "wake-up call." I don't know. But it would be interesting to normalize with respect to a different country and see whether the results change.

REGRESSING ABNORMAL RETURNS ON THE EXPOSURE VARIABLES

The final step in the analysis is to run a cross-sectional multiple regression of the cumulative abnormal returns on the exposure variables (with a lot of pooling imposed). I have only one comment here. As far as I can tell, the estimates and inferences are based on an assumption of (temporal) homoskedasticity that is probably violated rather strongly in the data. To the extent that return variances increase during a crisis, the estimates of the (conditional) mean effects are likely overstated.

REFERENCES

Ball, Clifford A. and Walter N. Torous (1988). "Investigating Security-Price Performance in the Presence of Event-Date Uncertainty," *Journal of Financial Economics* **22**:123–153.

Burnside, Craig, Martin Eichenbaum, and Sergio Rebelo (1998). "Prospective Deficits and the Asian Currency Crisis." NBER Working Paper No. 6758. Cambridge, MA.

O'Connell, Paul G.J. (1998). "The Overvaluation of Purchasing Power Parity," *Journal of International Economics* **44**:1–19.

PART II

CAPITAL FLOWS AND REVERSALS

5

Uncertainty and the Disappearance of International Credit

Joshua Aizenman and Nancy Marion

5.1 INTRODUCTION

In this chapter we examine how increased uncertainty about an emerging market's debt overhang might affect the willingness of foreign investors to supply new international credit. We show that increased uncertainty about the debt overhang has a nonlinear and potentially large adverse effect on the supply of international credit. As a result, it can contribute to the liquidity shortage often experienced by emerging markets during a crisis. We also show that if international creditors have preferences characterized by first-order risk aversion, a moderate increase in uncertainty about debt overhang – or about other relevant factors affecting repayment prospects – can cause the supply of credit to dry up completely. We therefore offer one possible explanation for why emerging markets may find themselves suddenly cut off from international capital markets.

We begin by describing events that contributed to increased uncertainty about the debt overhang in two of the Asian economies hit hard by the financial crisis in 1997 – Thailand and South Korea. We then compare reported external debt levels before the crisis with higher figures uncovered once the crisis began. We suggest that external debt levels for these two countries turned out to be much higher than what was reasonably foreseen. Surprised by the size of the upward adjustments, investors likely attached greater uncertainty to the size of the debt as well.

This chapter was presented at the conference on "Financial Crises in Emerging Markets" sponsored by the Center for Pacific Basin Monetary and Economic Studies at the Federal Reserve Bank of San Francisco, September 23–24, 1999. We wish to thank Mark Spiegel, our discussant, and other participants at the conference for their comments. We wish to thank Changyong Rhee and officials at the Ministry of Finance and Economy of Korea for help in obtaining data. Any errors are ours.

Previous investigations of debt overhang have generally focused on the *level* of outstanding debt and its impact on the economy. We use a modified model of sovereign risk to analyze the impact of greater *uncertainty* about the debt level. We show that more uncertainty reduces the supply of international credit when there is a chance of default. More uncertainty also magnifies the effect of news about the level of outstanding debt. We also observe that if we abandon the capital asset pricing model as a way of explaining portfolio choice and instead rely on a specification where agents attach more weight to utility from "bad' outcomes than from "good" outcomes, investors will require a substantial risk premium to diversify internationally. Furthermore, a moderate increase in the perceived risk of lending can induce investors to shift out of emerging-market assets completely. We do not claim that greater uncertainty about external debt levels triggered the Asian crisis. Rather, the crisis revealed that uncertainty about external debt levels was higher than previously thought and that increased uncertainty magnified the crisis.[1]

The chapter is organized as follows. Section 5.2 illustrates the buildup of external debt levels in Thailand and South Korea and makes a case for increased uncertainty about the debt. Section 5.3 formulates a model to analyze the effects of increased uncertainty about debt overhang on the supply of international credit offered emerging markets. Section 5.4 examines how greater uncertainty may lead risk-averse investors to shift out of emerging-market assets entirely, even if those assets offer a risk premium. Section 5.5 concludes the chapter.

5.2 EXTERNAL DEBT LEVELS IN THAILAND AND SOUTH KOREA

Figure 5.1 shows the growth of Thailand's external debt over the 1990s. In 1990, the Bank of Thailand reported an external debt of US$ 25.1 billion. By the end of 1995, this figure had grown 172 percent to $68.1 billion. At the end of 1996, this figure was $79.8 billion, 17 percent higher than the previous year. Once the financial crisis for Thailand began on July 2, 1997, the Bank of Thailand reported revised debt figures for 1995 and 1996. Both the original and revised 1995 and 1996 debt figures captured the foreign borrowing of banks in the Bangkok International Banking Facility, the primary offshore center for Thai banks to

---

[1] While we focus on uncertainty about external debt, there was also enormous uncertainty during this period about other factors affecting the repayment prospects of the Asian economies. These factors included the size and availability of international reserves for possible bailouts, the extent of currency depreciation and its impact on real debt burdens, and the impact of declining property values on balance sheets.

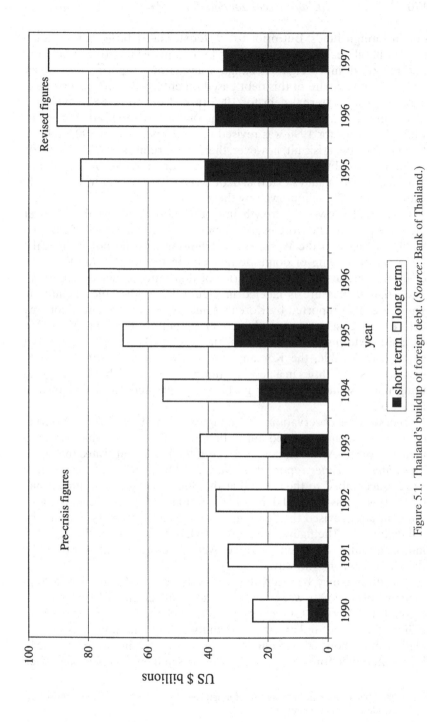

Figure 5.1. Thailand's buildup of foreign debt. (*Source:* Bank of Thailand.)

obtain foreign funds. But prior to 1997, external debt figures excluded foreign liabilities contracted directly by nonfinancial entities that were not recorded in foreign exchange transactions reported by banks, although an estimate of this debt based on enterprise surveys had been included. Total external debt for 1995 turned out to be $82.6 billion, a 21 percent upward adjustment over the previously reported 1995 value, while the figure for 1996 was revised up by 13 percent, to $90.5 billion. Even before the crisis hit, however, there were rumors and press reports about higher debt figures. On May 17, 1997, for example, *The Economist* reported that Thailand's external debt was probably closer to $90 billion, with perhaps $70 billion owed by the private sector.

Figure 5.2 shows the growth in South Korea's external debt over the same period. The Korean government's original measure of external liabilities followed the World Bank definition and did not include the off-shore borrowing of domestic financial institutions or the liabilities of foreign branches and subsidiaries of domestic financial institutions. The original measure is labeled in Figure 5.2 as the "old" definition. These are data reported by Korea's Ministry of Finance and Economy before the crisis engulfed the country (before October 25, 1997). Because external liabilities from the excluded entities turned out to be considerable, the Korean government and the IMF agreed to include these liabilities in a new definition of external debt.[2] Debt figures using the new definition now go back to 1995 and are also shown in Figure 5.2.

The striking observation about Figure 5.2 is that Korea's external debt, like Thailand's, turned out to be much higher than what was originally reported. An examination of the 1996 figures illustrates the point. The *Financial Times* reported on May 7, 1997, just five months before Korea succumbed to the crisis, that the South Korean government had put its 1996 gross external debt (old definition) at $104.5 billion. The government later revised the figure upward to $113.6 billion (still using the old definition). The figure jumped to $164.37 billion under the new definition, about a 60 percent increase over what was initially reported by the *Financial Times* in May.

The discrepancy between the originally reported and revised September 1997 estimate was equally dramatic. In December 1997, investors learned that Korea's total external debt for September was about $170 billion when measured by the new definition. More alarming was the revelation that about 60 percent of it was short-term in nature. The IMF later stated that "In December, . . . investors and lenders panicked when

---

[2] The liabilities of foreign branches and foreign subsidiaries of domestic enterprises are not included in either definition.

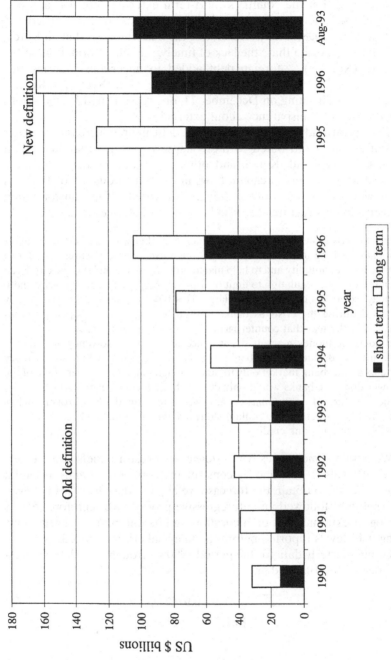

Figure 5.2. Korea's buildup of foreign debt. (*Source:* Ministry of Finance and Economy, Korea.)

they learned that the country's short-term external debt was approximately $104 billion – rather than the $66 billion originally reported . . ." (Adams et al., 1998, p. 155).[3] Describing the financial crisis that hit Korea, the OECD reported that "the lack of timely, reliable information on the state of (Korea's) . . . foreign debt added to uncertainty" during this period (OECD, 1998, p. 31). When Standard and Poor's lowered Korea's sovereign credit rating on December 11, one reason cited for its actions was the lack of transparency about external debt.

The upward adjustments in external debt figures increased investor pessimism and contributed to the collapse of the international credit market for Thailand, Korea, and other emerging markets. The large reversal of international capital flows in the fourth quarter of 1997 has been widely documented (e.g., Adams et al., 1998). The transformation in institutional structures has also been noted (Mathieson, 2000):

> Before the crisis, the typical foreign exchange market was an interbank market with banks willing to take on intraday foreign exchange exposures in order to provide market liquidity and to help match order flows throughout the day. Even when required by regulation to limit overnight foreign exchange exposure, these intraday exposures could be quite large. This type of interbank market totally collapsed during the crisis as banks refused to take intraday open positions (because of the fear that counterparties would not deliver). . . .
>
> In domestic money markets, . . . as concerns about the solvency of domestic banks increased, many foreign banks would make loans in the domestic currency in the local interbank market only to other foreign banks. Moreover, some of the stronger domestic banks would only deal with the local foreign banks.
>
> The structure of equity markets also was transformed when broker dealers that acted as market makers could no longer serve that function because of their inability to obtain bank credit.

We obtain some suggestive evidence on investor beliefs about external debt levels in Thailand by constructing confidence bands around a debt forecast. To obtain the forecast, we assume that investors believed external debt followed an autoregressive process. We therefore regress the log of external debt on a constant and its one-period lagged value, using debt levels reported before the financial crisis occurred.

Using quarterly data for the period 1990:4 through 1995:3, the regression results for Thailand are:

$$\overline{D}_t = 0.2969 + 0.9767\overline{D}_{t-1} \qquad (1)$$
$$(0.2271)\ (0.0215)$$

---

[3] Park and Rhee (1998) argue that the Korean government made the market more speculative by not confirming or officially announcing these figures.

where $\overline{D}$ is the logarithm of (US\$ million) total external debt and standard errors of the estimated coefficients are reported in parentheses. The adjusted R^2 is 0.99, and the standard error of the regression is 0.0262. The Durbin's h-statistic of 0.12 suggests that serial correlation is not a problem.[4]

Figure 5.3 illustrates the data on Thailand's external debt reported prior to the crisis as well as the revised figures from 1996:3 onwards.[5] In addition, the figure shows the predicted values of Thai external debt for the estimation period based on the autoregressive process and the 95 percent confidence band surrounding that prediction. For the period 1995:4 and after, we assume that investors continue to use equation (1) to predict quarterly debt. However, the confidence bands around the future predictions widen over time to reflect the growing uncertainty about the true value of Thailand's debt. Note that by the second half of 1996, the revised external debt figure is considerably above the upper confidence band.

We repeat the exercise using the initially reported data over 1990:4–1996:4 to estimate equation (1). As we see in Figure 5.4, the revised debt figure is once again above the upper confidence band from at least 1996:3 onwards. Thus Thailand's external debt turned out to be much higher than any reasonable forecast.

For Korea, we do not have quarterly debt data using the old definition, and a forecasting equation that relies on annual data over the 1990–1995 period of financial liberalization gives an unreliable forecast with very wide confidence bands. So we consider instead the inference problem of investors who try to evaluate the magnitude of the surprise generated by the revision of the reported debt data. We suggest that the greater the debt surprise relative to the standard deviation of the debt process, the greater the reevaluation of the uncertainty about the size of the total debt. Using the conventional yardstick, if the revision in the reported data is greater than two standard deviations of the debt process, we conclude that the size of the revision is more than what could reasonably have been expected if one maintained the old assumption about the volatility of the underlying debt process. These circumstances would lead investors to increase their assessment of the uncertainty regarding the debt.

For example, consider the case where investors learn in late 1997 that the 1996 external debt is higher than previously reported. In order to

---

[4] For small samples, one cannot reject the hypothesis that log external debt in Thailand follows a random walk. Both the autoregressive process and the random walk formulation have similar implications for our topic of interest.

[5] We have not been able to obtain revised quarterly data for 1995:1–1996:2, although we have revised annual estimates.

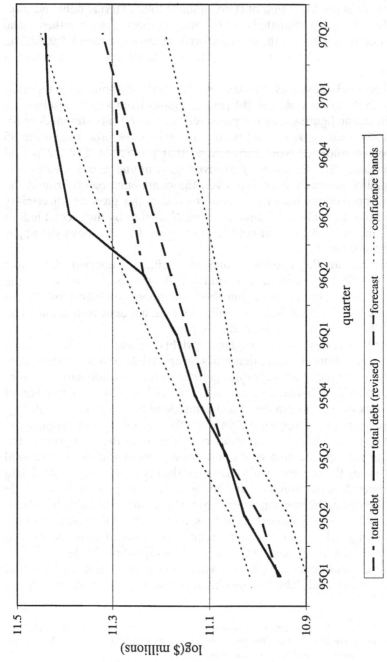

Figure 5.3. Thailand's external debt: actual and forecast from estimates over 1990:4–1995:3.

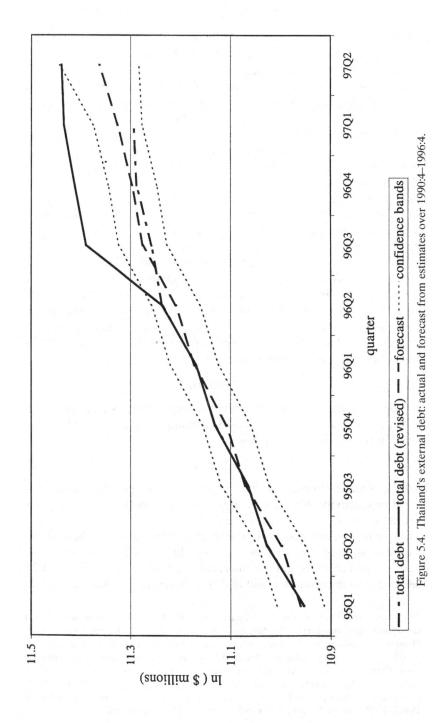

Figure 5.4. Thailand's external debt: actual and forecast from estimates over 1990:4–1996:4.

total debt — total debt (revised) — forecast ······ confidence bands

evaluate the surprise, the investors compare the percentage size of the revision of the 1996 debt figure to the standard deviation of the debt process. To obtain the latter, investors use a first-order autoregressive process (AR-1) to describe the path of the log of the debt in the years 1989–1995 and calculate the standard deviation of the residuals. (The investor takes 1989 as the starting point of the time series of the debt process because a regime switch toward more financial liberalization occurred in the early 1990s.) Investors repeat the procedure for the years 1989–1996 to evaluate the magnitude of the surprise about the revised debt figure for 1997:3.

Figure 5.5 illustrates the results of this exercise for Korea's total debt and short-term debt. The magnitude of the surprise about the upward revisions in debt figures is substantial. The upward revision in the 1996 total external debt figure exceeds four standard deviations, and the revision in the 1997:3 figure is in excess of three standard deviations. The upward revisions in the 1996 and 1997:3 estimates for short-term debt are each about three standard deviations. The upward revisions were thus much greater than what could have been reasonably predicted.[6]

We now develop a model that can show how increased uncertainty about the size of an emerging market's external debt can affect the willingness of foreign investors to supply credit.

5.3 THE MODEL

Consider a global economy with high-income countries and emerging-market economies and a two-period planning horizon. Second period output in the emerging markets is

$$Y_2^* = Y^* (1+\varepsilon) \tag{2}$$

Its value is uncertain because emerging markets are subject to a second-period productivity shock ε whose probability density function $f(\varepsilon)$ lies over the range $-\varepsilon_0 \leq \varepsilon \leq \varepsilon_0$, with $\varepsilon_0 \geq 0$.

Emerging markets may borrow internationally. However, their ability to borrow is constrained by two factors: the limited enforceability of international contracts and the uncertainty about the size of their debt overhang. The uncertainty about debt overhang can be characterized in

---

[6] The upward revision in Korea's debt figures overestimates the surprise to investors to the extent they anticipated the foreign liabilities of domestic financial institutions. However, the upward revision underestimates the surprise to investors to the extent they attached less credibility to the announced revisions and anticipated further upward revisions. There is no way to sort out the net bias of these two factors. When we calculate the debt surprise relative to the standard deviation of the debt process for Thailand's total and short-term external debts, the upward revisions in the quarterly estimates for 1996:3–1997:1 are each on the order of 5.5 to 6.5 standard deviations.

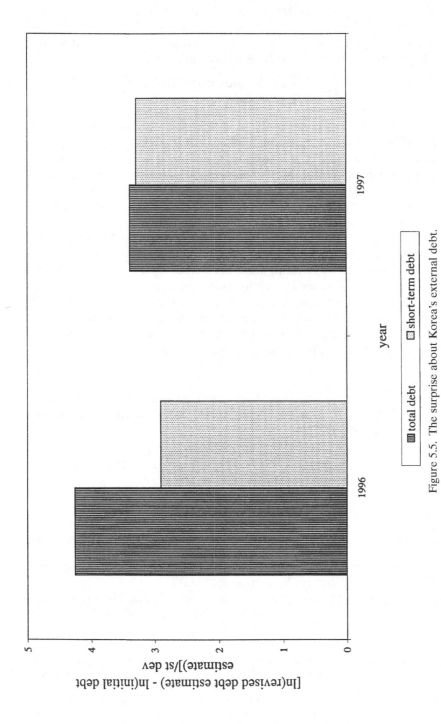

Figure 5.5. The surprise about Korea's external debt.

a simple way. Suppose the outstanding debt due to be repaid next period can be either high or low with equal probability[7]:

$$D_2 = \begin{cases} \overline{D}(1+\lambda) & \text{with probability} \quad 0.5 \\ \overline{D}(1-\lambda) & \text{with probability} \quad 0.5 \end{cases} \qquad (3)$$

Creditor-country banks must decide on how much new lending they are willing to provide emerging markets. Let B_1^* represent the aggregate amount of new short-term loans offered emerging markets in period one at a contractual interest rate of r. In period two, emerging markets must repay these loans plus the debt overhang. Emerging markets may end up defaulting, however, if their period two output turns out to be too low or their repayments too high.

Let S_2 denote the total debt repayment to foreign creditors in period two. In the event of a default, suppose creditors can penalize the borrowing countries by reducing their net output by an amount χY_2^*. The parameter χ reflects the bargaining power of foreign lenders, where up to a fraction χ of output can be "confiscated" by lenders through retaliatory trade measures or other actions.[8] Consequently, the effective ceiling on net resource transfers to creditors is the lesser of either the contractual repayments or the confiscated output:

$$S_2 = \min\left[(1+r)\,B_1^* + D_2;\ \chi Y_2^*\right] \qquad (4)$$

The size of the productivity shock that makes emerging markets indifferent between repaying their loans or defaulting and facing the output penalty is ε^*, where

$$\varepsilon^* = \begin{cases} \varepsilon_+^* = \max\left[\dfrac{(1+r)B_1^* + \overline{D}(1+\lambda)}{\chi Y^*} - 1;\ -\varepsilon_0\right] \\ \text{if the initial debt is high} \\ \varepsilon_-^* = \max\left[\dfrac{(1+r)B_1^* + \overline{D}(1-\lambda)}{\chi Y^*} - 1;\ -\varepsilon_0\right] \\ \text{if the initial debt is low} \end{cases} \qquad (5)$$

Because the size of the debt overhang is uncertain, the value of ε^* is contingent on the realized debt overhang.

The intertemporal pattern of net lending and consumption is determined by price-taking agents who maximize their discounted expected

---

[7] The specification in equation (3) is the simplest way to model uncertainty about debt overhang. The key results of the model hold for other distributions of λ, such as the uniform or truncated normal.

[8] The term χ is influenced by a host of factors that relate to the integration of markets. See Bulow and Rogoff (1989) for details.

utility. Agents in the high-income countries are risk neutral, so their preferences over a two-period planning horizon are characterized by

$$V \equiv C_1 + \frac{C_2}{1+\rho} \tag{6}$$

where ρ is the rate of time preference and coincides with the risk-free interest rate.

Agents in the emerging-market economies have preferences represented by

$$V^* \equiv u(C_1^*) + \frac{u(C_2^*)}{1+\rho^*}; \qquad u' > 0; \qquad u'' \le 0 \tag{7}$$

We assume that $\rho^* > \rho$ because the real interest rate in emerging markets is substantially above the rate in the high-income group.

The international credit market is characterized by competition among creditor banks. A default by emerging markets requires creditor banks to spend real resources μ in order to verify the productivity shock and the size of the debt overhang and to enforce the transfer of resources from emerging markets according to equation (4).[9]

The risk neutrality of lenders implies that they offer an elastic supply of new credit at an expected yield equal to their rate of time preference. In the event of default, confiscated output first goes to cover repayment of the old debt, which is considered senior. To simplify exposition, we focus on the case where confiscated output can fully cover the required repayment of old debt. Thus r, the interest rate on new credit to emerging markets, is determined by an arbitrage condition that equates the expected yield on new loans to emerging markets to the risk-free return:

$$0 = (1+\rho)B_1^* - \begin{cases} 0.5\left[\{(1+r)B_1^* + \overline{D}(1+\lambda)\} \int\limits_{\varepsilon_+^*}^{\varepsilon_0} f(\varepsilon)\,d\varepsilon \right. \\ \left. + \int\limits_{-\varepsilon_0}^{\varepsilon_+^*} \{\chi Y^*(1+\varepsilon) - \mu\} f(\varepsilon)\,d\varepsilon - \overline{D}(1+\lambda) \right] \\ + 0.5\left[\{(1+r)B_1^* + \overline{D}(1-\lambda)\} \int\limits_{\varepsilon_-^*}^{\varepsilon_0} f(\varepsilon)\,d\varepsilon \right. \\ \left. + \int\limits_{-\varepsilon_0}^{\varepsilon_-^*} \{\chi Y^*(1+\varepsilon) - \mu\} f(\varepsilon)\,d\varepsilon - \overline{D}(1-\lambda) \right] \end{cases} \tag{8}$$

[9] To simplify, we lump together monitoring and enforcement costs and we ignore the possibility of randomized monitoring. Boyd and Smith (1994) show that random monitoring makes the financial contract more complex without altering first-order welfare effects. See Townsend (1979) for a model where a debt contract with state verification costs is optimal. See Bernanke and Gertler (1989) for a related analysis.

The second term on the right-hand side of equation (8) evaluates the expected repayment on new loans when there is an equal chance that the debt overhang will turn out to be high or low. For a given realization of debt overhang, the expected repayment is the sum of three components: (i) the return on new loans and repayment of the debt overhang in the absence of default; (ii) the confiscated output in the case of default, less enforcement costs; and (iii) minus the repayment of the debt overhang whether or not there is a default.

Using equation (5), we can rewrite equation (8) as

$$(r - \rho)B_1^* = 0.5 \left[\int_{-\varepsilon_0}^{\varepsilon_+^*} \{ \chi Y^* (\varepsilon_+^* - \varepsilon) + \mu \} f(\varepsilon)\, d\varepsilon \right]$$

$$+ 0.5 \left[\int_{-\varepsilon_0}^{\varepsilon_-^*} \{ \chi Y^* (\varepsilon_-^* - \varepsilon) + \mu \} f(\varepsilon)\, d\varepsilon \right] \tag{9}$$

Note that monitoring and enforcement costs are passed on to borrowers by way of higher borrowing rates.

We now examine how uncertainty about debt overhang affects the supply of new loans that foreign creditors are willing to offer.[10] Equation (8) defines the supply of international credit facing emerging markets (along with the definitions of $\varepsilon_+^*; \varepsilon_-^*$). We denote the right-hand side of equation (8) by H. Applying the implicit function theorem to equation (8), the slope of the supply curve is

$$\frac{dB_1^*}{dr} = \frac{-H_r'}{H_{B_1^*}'} \tag{10}$$

where

$$-H_r' = 0.5 B_1^* \left\{ \left[\int_{\varepsilon_+^*}^{\varepsilon_0} f(\varepsilon)\, d\varepsilon - \frac{\mu}{\chi Y^*} f(\varepsilon_+^*) \right] \right.$$

$$\left. + \left[\int_{\varepsilon_-^*}^{\varepsilon_0} f(\varepsilon)\, d\varepsilon - \frac{\mu}{\chi Y^*} f(\varepsilon_-^*) \right] \right\}$$

$$H_{B_1^*}' = 1 + \rho - 0.5(1 + r) \left[\int_{\varepsilon_+^*}^{\varepsilon_0} f(\varepsilon)\, d\varepsilon + \int_{\varepsilon_-^*}^{\varepsilon_0} f(\varepsilon)\, d\varepsilon \right.$$

$$\left. - \frac{\mu}{\chi Y^*} \{ f(\varepsilon_+^*) + f(\varepsilon_-^*) \} \right] \tag{11}$$

[10] We ignore the possibility of a bailout in case of default. See Aizenman and Marion (1999b) for a model where emerging-market governments are willing to bail out international creditors. In that case, uncertainty about the size of international reserves held by emerging markets for a possible bailout can also affect the supply of new loans.

We assume that the emerging-market economies operate along the upward-sloping portion of the supply of international credit.[11] Such would be the case if $-H'_r > 0$ and $H_{B_1^*}' > 0$.[12]

> **Proposition 1:** Greater uncertainty about debt overhang in emerging markets reduces the supply of international credit. Moreover, the supply of credit shifts in a nonlinear manner.

Applying equation (8), we find that for a given amount of new credit, B_1^*, increased uncertainty about the debt overhang shifts the supply of credit curve upwards by the amount

$$\frac{dr}{d\lambda}\bigg|_{B_1^*} = \frac{\overline{D}\left[\int_{\varepsilon_*^*}^{\varepsilon_+^*} f(\varepsilon)\,d\varepsilon - \frac{\mu}{\chi Y^*}\{f(\varepsilon_+^*) - f(\varepsilon_-^*)\}\right]}{B_1^*\left\{\left[\int_{\varepsilon_+^*}^{\varepsilon_0} f(\varepsilon)\,d\varepsilon - \frac{\mu}{\chi Y^*}f(\varepsilon_+^*)\right] + \left[\int_{\bar{\varepsilon}}^{\varepsilon_-^*} f(\varepsilon)\,d\varepsilon - \frac{\mu}{\chi Y^*}f(\varepsilon_-^*)\right]\right\}}$$

$$(12)$$

An important implication of equation (12) is that greater uncertainty about the debt overhang (a larger λ) has a nonlinear effect on the supply of international credit. Greater uncertainty does not affect the supply of credit when the probability of default is zero.[13] If the default probability is positive, however, greater uncertainty about the debt overhang reduces the supply of credit.

> **Proposition 2:** The greater the uncertainty about debt overhang, the more a given increase in uncertainty reduces the supply of credit. The greater the expected debt overhang, the more a given

---

[11] For a sufficiently low level of emerging-market debt, $\varepsilon^* = -\varepsilon_0$. In these circumstances, the critical condition for $dB_1^*/dr > 0$ reduces to $\mu f(-\varepsilon_0)/\chi Y^* < 1$, a condition that is satisfied for a low enough but positive enforcement cost, μ. If $\mu f(-\varepsilon_0)/\chi Y^* > 1$, the supply of credit is backward bending at interest rates marginally above the risk-free rate. In these circumstances it would be in the interest of emerging markets to prohibit borrowing. Consequently, we assume $\mu f(-\varepsilon_0)/\chi Y^* < 1$, so that the supply-of-credit curve is upward sloping at relatively low interest rates. In general, the supply curve may contain a backward-bending section at high interest rates and external debt levels. In these circumstances, it would be in the interest of the borrowers to adopt policies that prevent them from reaching the backward-bending section of the supply curve because such a point entails lower welfare than the point where external borrowing is maximized. See Aizenman (1989) for further discussion.

[12] The supply of international credit (defined implicitly by equation (8)) and the demand for international credit jointly determine the equilibrium interest rate and level of credit. We focus our attention on the supply side.

[13] In this case $\varepsilon_+^* = \varepsilon_-^* = -\varepsilon_0$ and $\dfrac{dr}{d\lambda}\bigg|_{B_1^*} = 0$.

increase in uncertainty about debt overhang reduces the supply of credit.

We can rewrite equation (12) as

$$\frac{dr}{d\lambda}\bigg|_{B_1^*} = \frac{2\lambda(\overline{D})^2}{\chi Y^* B_1^*}$$

$$\frac{f(\tilde{\varepsilon}) - f'(\tilde{\varepsilon})\dfrac{\mu}{\chi Y^*}}{\left[\displaystyle\int_{\varepsilon_+^*}^{\varepsilon_0} f(\varepsilon)\, d\varepsilon - \dfrac{\mu}{\chi Y^*} f(\varepsilon_+^*)\right] + \left[\displaystyle\int_{\varepsilon_-^*}^{\varepsilon_0} f(\varepsilon)\, d\varepsilon - \dfrac{\mu}{\chi Y^*} f(\varepsilon_-^*)\right]} \tag{13}$$

where $\hat{\varepsilon}$ and $\tilde{\varepsilon}$ are defined by the midpoints in the segment $[\varepsilon_-^*, \varepsilon_+^*]$, with

$$f(\tilde{\varepsilon}) = \frac{\displaystyle\int_{\varepsilon_-^*}^{\varepsilon_+^*} f(\varepsilon)\, d\varepsilon}{\varepsilon_+^* - \varepsilon_-^*}, \qquad f'(\hat{\varepsilon}) = \frac{f(\varepsilon_+^*) - f(\varepsilon_-^*)}{\varepsilon_+^* - \varepsilon_-^*}$$

We maintain the assumption that the monitoring and enforcement cost (μ) is relatively small, so that

$$f(\tilde{\varepsilon}) - f'(\hat{\varepsilon})\mu/\chi Y^* > 0.$$

Equation (13) reveals that when there is a chance of default, increased uncertainty about the debt overhang reduces the supply of credit in proportion to the product of the expected debt overhang ($\overline{D}$) and the initial degree of uncertainty (λ). Consequently, the greater the expected debt overhang or the initial degree of uncertainty, the greater the impact additional uncertainty has on the supply of credit.[14]

One can also verify that bad news about the expected *level* of outstanding debt ($d\overline{D} > 0$) reduces the supply of new credit ($dr/d\overline{D}|_{B_1^*} > 0$). Figures 5.1–5.5 suggest that the financial crisis increased both the expected *level* of outstanding debt and the *uncertainty* about its actual size. Our model shows that uncertainty magnifies the reduction in credit induced by the level effect and does so in a nonlinear way.

5.4 THE DISAPPEARANCE OF MARKETS

At the onset of the Asian financial crisis, the international credit market for these emerging markets collapsed. Countries that presumed they

---

[14] We can obtain the same results by modeling investment in period one that provides a random return in period two, since a low return is analogous to low productivity.

could access the international credit market learned the hard way that when credit is desperately needed, the market may go dry. This phenomenon can be explained in several ways.[15] In terms of our model, if the crisis increases uncertainty about the debt overhang – or about other relevant factors affecting repayment – the shift in the supply of funds may be abrupt enough to dry up the market. Such will be the case, for example, if the expected debt overhang or the uncertainty about its level is larger than the one anticipated by the *a priori* distribution, so that the revised supply of funds is backward bending at $B_1^* = 0$.

There is an alternative and more general explanation, however. It is well known that agents exhibit home bias in their asset holdings.[16] Their unwillingness to supply new credit to emerging markets during a crisis may be viewed as a strengthening of the home-bias phenomenon. If one uses the capital asset-pricing model (CAPM) as the benchmark for explaining portfolio choice, then the complete shift to home assets during a crisis is a puzzle because the CAPM predicts continued diversification. However, if portfolio choice is derived from a generalized expected utility framework with first-order risk aversion, then the risk premium needed to maintain international diversification is much larger. A small increase in uncertainty can eliminate the desire to diversify internationally, making investors unwilling to supply new international credits or roll over existing credits. Consequently, the disappearance of the market during a crisis may be the rule, rather than the exception. If this is the case, the potential benefits of liquidity and the proper maturity structure on debt are much larger than those predicted using the conventional CAPM framework.

We can formalize the argument by using a generalized expected utility (GEU) framework to describe preferences. We focus on a simple version of GEU that is a one-parameter extension of the standard (Savage, 1954) neoclassical expected utility model. In this version, agents attach greater weight to utility derived from "bad" outcomes than to utility derived

[15] Radelet and Sachs (1998) and Chang and Velasco (1998a, 1998b) attribute the phenomenon to an investor panic, but without addressing the origin of the panic. Caballero and Krishnamurthy (1998) suggest it may be due to the real or perceived inadequacy of international collateral stemming from microeconomic contractual problems. Calvo (1999) hypothesizes that poorly informed investors may misread a shift out of emerging-market assets by liquidity-constrained informed traders as signaling low returns, and this confusion may lead to a market collapse.

[16] For example, French and Poterba (1991) and Tesar and Werner (1995) note that 94 percent of U.S. investor wealth is held in domestic equity, much more than the optimal share predicted by the conventional capital asset-pricing model (CAPM). See Lewis (1995) and Obstfeld and Rogoff (1996) for comprehensive overviews of the home-bias puzzle and existing interpretations within the context of the CAPM.

from "good" outcomes. A consequence of this weighting pattern is that agents exhibit downside risk aversion and require a substantial risk premium to diversify internationally.[17]

Preferences are summarized by $[u(x), \gamma]$, where u is a conventional utility function describing the utility of consuming x, $(u' > 0, u'' < 0)$, and $1 \geq \gamma \geq 0$ is a parameter that measures the weighting of a high-ranked outcome relative to a low-ranked one. This weighting is obtained by replacing the probability weight p_i attached to utility $u(x_i)$ in the standard expected utility framework with a modified weight, defined by a proper transformation of p^γ.

Suppose that with probability α the agent receives income x_1, and with probability $(1 - \alpha)$ income x_2, where $x_1 > x_2$. The generalized expected utility $V(\gamma)$ is defined by[18]

$$V(\gamma) = \left[1 - (1-\alpha)^\gamma\right] u(x_1) + (1-\alpha)^\gamma u(x_2) \qquad (14)$$

Alternatively,

$$V(\gamma) = \alpha \left[1 - \frac{1-\alpha}{\alpha} \omega\right] u(x_1) + (1-\alpha)[1+\omega]u(x_2)$$

where $\omega = (1 - \alpha)^{\gamma-1} - 1$.

For $\gamma = 1$, V is identical to the conventional expected utility. In this case, good and bad states of nature are treated symmetrically when $u(x_i)$ is weighted by the probability of its occurrence. For values of γ less than one, the agent attaches an extra weight of $(1 - \alpha)\omega$ to the "bad" outcome and attaches a lesser weight of $(1 - \alpha)\omega$ to the "good" outcome.

---

[17] We examine whether the GEU approach can help explain the significant unwillingness of investors to supply loanable funds when there is increased volatility in their expected returns. Researchers have previously turned to the GEU framework to help explain the excess volatility of stock prices and the equity risk premium puzzle because these anomalies are difficult to rationalize using the standard expected utility approach. While the appropriateness of the standard versus generalized utility paradigm continues to be debated, the GEU approach deserves further theoretical and empirical work. Instead of GEU preferences, the asymmetric evaluation of gains and losses may also be the result of the incentives facing portfolio managers who understand that their loss from underperforming the market is more costly than their gain from outperforming it.

[18] The formulation in equation (14) is based on Yaari (1987). Our results are applicable to other generalized expected utility approaches sharing the property of "first-order" risk aversion as defined by Segal and Spivak (1990). See Epstein (1992) for a review of these approaches.

We focus now on a simple, partial equilibrium example of allocating initial wealth among three assets: a risk-free asset and risky domestic and foreign assets. The safe asset offers a real yield of r_0. The risky domestic and foreign assets offer random yields of r and r^*, respectively. The realized yield for each risky asset may be high or low, depending on the state of nature. We denote the corresponding states of nature by h and l for the home asset and by h^* and l^* for the foreign one. The realized returns are given by

$$r = \begin{cases} r_0 + e + \sigma & \text{in state of nature} \quad h \\ r_0 + e - \sigma & \text{in state of nature} \quad l \end{cases};$$

$$r^* = \begin{cases} r_0 + e^* + \sigma^* & \text{in state of nature} \quad h^* \\ r_0 + e^* - \sigma^* & \text{in state of nature} \quad l^* \end{cases}$$

where e and e^* denote the expected excess yields attached to the risky domestic and foreign assets, respectively, relative to the yield of the safe asset, and σ and σ^* denote the standard deviations of the yields. The probabilities of these states are given by

$$\begin{rcases} (h, h^*) \\ (l, l^*) \\ (l, h^*) \\ (h, l^*) \end{rcases} = \begin{cases} p \\ p \\ q \\ q \end{cases}, \qquad \text{with } p + q = 0.5$$

The correlation between the returns of the two risky assets is $\rho = 4p - 1$.

The agent allocates fractions x and x^* of his initial wealth to the risky domestic and foreign asset, respectively. In financial autarky, $x^* = 0$. International diversification is beneficial if, in the autarky equilibrium, $\frac{\partial V}{\partial x^*}|_{x=\tilde{x}} > 0$, where $\tilde{x}$ denotes the optimal share of the risky domestic asset in financial autarky. It can be shown that with financial openness, the demand for the foreign asset is positive if

$$\tau^* > \frac{(2p)^\gamma - (p)^\gamma + (1-p)^\gamma - 1}{1 - (0.5)^\gamma} + \tau \frac{(2p)^\gamma \left[1 - (0.5)^\gamma\right] + (0.5)^\gamma - (1-p)^\gamma}{1 - (0.5)^\gamma}$$

$$\tau = \frac{e}{\sigma}, \qquad \tau^* = \frac{e^*}{\sigma^*} \tag{15}$$

In equation (15), τ and τ^* are the normalized premiums on the risky domestic and foreign assets, respectively, where the normalization is obtained by dividing the premium by the standard deviation of the yield.[19]

With the standard expected utility framework, $\gamma = 1$ and equation (15) is reduced to $\tau^*/\tau > \rho$. Hence, the risky foreign asset is demanded if its normalized premium exceeds the product of the correlation between returns and the normalized premium of the risky domestic asset. This condition is met trivially if the correlation is zero (or negative). For a positive correlation, an agent maximizing a conventional expected utility tends to diversify as long as the correlation among yields is not too close to one.

This result does not hold for an agent that demands a first-order risk premium, however. As long as the correlation between returns is positive, first-order risk aversion increases the normalized foreign premium needed for diversification. This result follows from the observation that the right-hand side of equation (15) depends negatively on γ.

Figure 5.6 plots the dependency of the foreign premium [the right-hand side of equation (15)] on γ for the case where the normalized premium on the risky domestic asset is one-half [i.e., $\tau = e/\sigma = 0.5$] and the correlation between returns on the two risky assets can be either zero or 0.5. Points above the curve [area D] define the range where the demand for the foreign asset is positive. Notice that if the correlation among returns is zero, the CAPM (with $\gamma = 1$) predicts that the agent will always demand a foreign asset offering a positive return.

---

[19] In order to obtain equation (15), we use the specification for generalized utility in equation (14) and our assumptions about the properties of asset returns to infer that expected utility is

$$V = \begin{cases} \begin{bmatrix} \left(1-[2q+p]^\gamma\right)u(h,h^*)+\left([2q+p]^\gamma-[q+p]^\gamma\right)u(h,l^*) \\ +\left([q+p]^\gamma-[p]^\gamma\right)u(l,h^*)+[p]^\gamma u(l,l^*) \end{bmatrix} & \text{if } x\sigma > x^*\sigma^* \\[2em] \begin{bmatrix} \left(1-[2q+p]^\gamma\right)u(h,h^*)+\left([2q+p]^\gamma-[q+p]^\gamma\right)u(l,h^*) \\ +\left([q+p]^\gamma-[p]^\gamma\right)u(h,l^*)+[p]^\gamma u(l,l^*) \end{bmatrix} & \text{if } x\sigma \leq x^*\sigma^* \end{cases} \quad (A)$$

where

$$u(h,h^*) = u[1+r_0+x(e+\sigma)+x^*(e^*+\sigma^*)], \quad u(l,l^*) = u[1+r_0+x(e-\sigma)+x^*(e^*-\sigma^*)]$$
$$u(h,l^*) = u[1+r_0+x(e+\sigma)+x^*(e^*-\sigma^*)], \quad u(l,h^*) = u[1+r_0+x(e-\sigma)+x^*(e^*+\sigma^*)]$$

We then use (A) and the first-order condition for the optimal portfolio in autarky to obtain equation (15), writing the condition in terms of normalized returns. Aizenman (1999) and Aizenman and Marion (1999a) use a generalized utility framework that relies on a second-order approximation to derive results. Here we find the *exact* analytical condition leading to a positive demand for foreign assets in autarky.

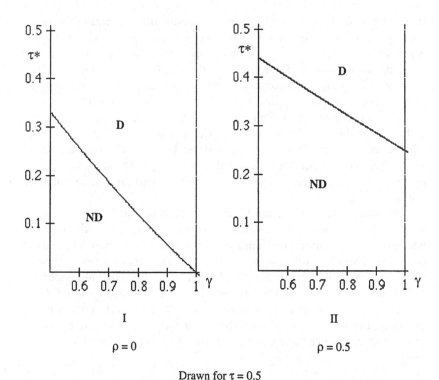

Drawn for $\tau = 0.5$

Figure 5.6. The foreign premium required for diversification. *Note*: $\tau(\tau^*)$ is the normalized premium on risky domestic (foreign) assets, ρ is the correlation of returns, and γ is a risk-weighting parameter. D(ND) denotes region of asset (no asset) diversification.

The case for diversification is much weaker if the agent exhibits first-order risk aversion, with $\gamma < 1$.[20] Similar results hold if the correlation is positive, although with positive correlation the foreign normalized excess return must be positive to induce diversification even in the CAPM model.

The implication of this analysis is that a moderate increase in the risk of the foreign asset will terminate diversification if agents are first-order risk averse. Using Figure 5.6, suppose that $\rho = 0.5$ and $\gamma = 0.75$ and that initially the normalized excess return of the foreign assets is $\tau^* = 0.4$. In

---

[20] In the generalized expected utility specified by equation (14), the term $\omega = (0.5^{\gamma-1} - 1)$ measures the first-order risk aversion exhibited by agents. Loss aversion, defined as the ratio of the marginal utility of a loss to the marginal utility of a gain, is $[1 + \omega]/[1 - \omega]$. Empirical estimates of loss aversion are typically in the neighborhood of two, suggesting that $\gamma \cong 0.74$ if preferences conform to the generalized utility framework. See Tversky and Kahneman (1991) and Kahneman, Knetsch, and Thaler (1990).

these circumstances, we will observe diversification, because the point corresponding to the initial equilibrium is in the D range above the zero-diversification curve. An exogenous drop of τ^* from 0.4 to 0.3 will end diversification, causing the market for the foreign assets to dry up. The drop in τ^* may be the outcome of many combinations of changing e^* and σ^*. For example, suppose that initially $e = 0.05$, $\sigma = 0.10$, $e^* = 0.06$ and $\sigma^* = 0.15$ (so that $\tau = 0.5$ and $\tau^* = 0.4$). A rise in σ^* to 0.20 will reduce τ^* to 0.3, terminating diversification. Alternatively, a drop in e^* to 0.045 will induce the same change in τ^* and eliminate diversification. If instead agents behave according to the CAPM (where $\gamma = 1$), the same decline in the normalized foreign excess return will not end diversification, only reduce it.

Our analysis is partial equilibrium in nature in that it focuses on the supply of loanable funds by investors with downside risk aversion and ignores the demand for funds by borrowers in the emerging market economy. Even so, we can make the general observation that first-order risk aversion magnifies the increase in the expected yield on foreign investment needed to prevent the market from drying up. Consequently, downside risk aversion magnifies the credit crunch facing the emerging market economy when there is a drop in its expected productivity or greater uncertainty about the expected returns on its borrowed funds.

5.5 CONCLUSION

We have shown how a collapse of the international credit market can occur when the perceived risk of lending to emerging markets increases, even moderately. Any number of factors can alter risk perceptions. We focus on one factor that was important for Thailand, Korea, and other emerging markets in late 1997. This factor was a growing awareness on the part of investors that the uncertainty about emerging-market external debt was greater than previously thought. Once the market updated its risk assessment, the reduction of international credit to these countries – or even the collapse of the market altogether – can be explained by models of sovereign risk or models that reveal the "home bias" investment patterns of agents with first-order risk aversion.

For expositional simplicity, we have illustrated the reduction and collapse of international credit in two separate models. The first model is one of sovereign risk, extended to account for uncertainty about debt overhang. There we maintain the conventional assumptions about risk preferences, such as the risk-neutrality of foreign lenders. The second model describes the portfolio diversification patterns of agents who are first-order risk averse. We use it to derive the exact analytical condition that terminates international diversification, causing a market collapse. We have left for future work the ambitious task of integrating these two models in order to study sovereign risk when all agents are first-order risk averse.

While we have focused on the role of debt overhang in altering risk perceptions about some of the Asian economies, we believe that other factors also could have played a role. For example, if the market changed its perception about the growth prospects of the Far East from the upbeat view of the "East Asian Miracle" to the more somber assessment of Young (1992) and Krugman (1994), this revision in perceived risk could have contributed to the collapse of the international credit market.

REFERENCES

Adams, Charles, D. Mathieson, G. Schinasi, and B. Chadha (1998). *International Capital Markets: Developments, Prospects, and Key Policy Issues.* International Monetary Fund, September. Washington, D.C.

Aizenman, Joshua (1989). "Country Risk, Incomplete Information and Taxes on International Borrowing," *Economic Journal* **99**:147–161.

———(1999). "International Portfolio Diversification with Generalized Expected Utility Preferences," *Canadian Journal of Economics* **32**(4): 1010–1023.

Aizenman, Joshua and N. Marion (1999a). "Volatility and Investment: Interpreting Evidence from Developing Countries," *Economica* **66**:157–179.

———(1999b). "Reserve Uncertainty and the Supply of International Credit." NBER Working Paper No. 7202 (July). Cambridge, MA.

Bernanke, Ben and M. Gertler (1989). "Agency Costs, Net Worth, and Business Fluctuations," *American Economic Review* **79**:14–31.

Boyd, J.H. and B.D. Smith (1994). "How Good are Standard Debt Contracts? Stochastic versus Nonstochastic Monitoring in a Costly State Verification Environment," *Journal of Business* **67**:539–561.

Bulow, Jeremy and K. Rogoff (1989). "A Constant Recontracting Model of Sovereign Debt," *Journal of Political Economy* **97**(1):155–178.

Caballero, Ricardo and Arvind Krishnamurthy (1998). "Emerging Market Crises: an Asset Markets Perspective." NBER Working Paper No. 6843, December. Cambridge, MA.

Calvo, Guillermo (1999). "Contagion in Emerging Markets: When Wall Street Is a Carrier." Paper presented at World Bank/Universidat Torcuato Di Tella Conference on Integration and Contagion, June 17–18, 1999.

Chang, Roberto and Andrés Velasco (1998a). "Financial Crises in Emerging Markets: A Canonical Model." NBER Working Paper No. 6606 (June). Cambridge, MA.

———(1998b). "The Asian Liquidity Crisis." NBER Working Paper No. 6796 (November). Cambridge, MA.

Economist (1997). "Feeling the Heat," May 17, p. 82.

Epstein, L.G. (1992). "Behavior under Risk: Recent Developments in Theory and Applications." In Jean-Jacques Laffont, ed., *Advances in Economic Theory: Sixth World Congress*, Volume 1. New York: Cambridge University Press, Chapter 1, pp. 1–63.

French, K. and J. Poterba (1991). "International Diversification and International Equity Markets," *American Economic Review* **81**(2):222–226.

Harless, D.W. and C. Camerer (1994). "The Predictive Utility of Generalized Expected Utility Theories," *Econometrica* **62**(6):1251–1289.

Kahneman, D., J. Knetsch, and R. Thaler (1990). "Experimental Tests of the Endowment Effect and the Coase Theorem," *Journal of Political Economy* **98**:1325–1348.

Krugman, Paul (1994). "The Myth of Asia's Miracle, a Cautionary Fable," *Foreign Affairs* **73**(November/December):62–78.

Lewis, Karen (1995). "Puzzles in International Financial Markets." In G. Grossman and K. Rogoff, eds., *Handbook of International Economics*, Volume 3, Chapter 37. Amsterdam: North Holland, pp. 1913–1971.

Mathieson, Don (2000). "Comment." In Peter Isard, Assaf Razin, and Andrew Rose, eds., *International Finance in Turmoil: Essays in Honor of Robert F. Flood*. Washington, D.C. and Boston: IMF and Kluwer Academic Publishers.

Obstfeld, M. and K. Rogoff (1996). *Foundations of International Macroeconomics*. Cambridge, MA: MIT Press.

Organization for Economic Co-Operation and Development (1998). *Economic Survey: Korea*. Paris: OECD Publications.

Park, Daekeun and C. Rhee (1998). "Currency Crisis in Korea: How Has It Been Aggravated?" Mimeo, Seoul National University, December.

Radelet, Steven and Jeff Sachs (1998). "The East Asian Financial Crisis: Diagnosis, Remedies, Prospects," *Brookings Papers on Economic Activity*, No. 1:1–74.

Savage, L.J. (1954). *Foundations of Statistics*. New York: John Wiley.

Segal, U. and A. Spivak (1990). "First-Order Versus Second-Order Risk Aversion," *Journal of Economic Theory* **51**:111–125.

Tesar, L.L. and I.M. Warner (1995). "Home Bias and High Turnover," *Journal of International Money and Finance* **14**(4):467–492.

Townsend, R.M. (1979). "Optimal Contracts and Competitive Markets with Costly State Verification," *Journal of Economic Theory* **21**:265–293.

Tversky, A. and D. Kahneman (1991). "Loss Aversion and Riskless Choice: A Reference Dependence Model," *Quarterly Journal of Economics* **106**:1039–1061.

Yaari, M.E. (1987). "The Dual Theory of Choice under Risk," *Econometrica* **55**:95–115.

Young, A. (1992). "A Tale of Two Cities: Factor Accumulation and Technical Change in Hong Kong and Singapore." In O. Blanchard and S. Fischer, eds., *NBER Macroeconomics Annual 1992*. Cambridge, MA: MIT Press, pp. 13–54.

Discussion

Uncertainty and the Disappearance of
International Credit

Mark M. Spiegel

Once again, Joshua Aizenman and Nancy Marion have provided us with an interesting and well-executed paper. The authors examine the role that uncertainty concerning the level of outstanding debt obligations in Asia may have played in promoting that region's financial crisis. The analysis is organized in three fairly self-contained sections: The first section reviews the buildup of debt levels in Thailand and South Korea. The second section introduces a sovereign debt model in which increases in uncertainty about a nation's debt overhang can result in reduced lending towards that country. The third section looks at the optimal response of an individual foreign investor with first-order risk aversion to an increase in uncertainty about returns in investment in a foreign nation. The authors demonstrate that a sufficient increase in uncertainty can induce the investor to completely stop investing in that country. I will discuss each section individually.

EXTERNAL DEBT BUILDUPS IN THAILAND AND
SOUTH KOREA

The external debt buildups described by the authors were indeed large. I am somewhat less convinced, however, that all of the increase could be characterized as surprising. Both of the reported increases resulted partly from revisions in the manner in which debt burdens were calculated by the government. In particular, the South Korean revision resulted from the inclusion of off-shore liabilities of commercial banks. While the market did not have a good idea of the magnitude of these off-shore obligations prior to the revision announcements, it is implausible that their expected value was zero, given the large buildup in the reported portion of outstanding debt obligations. Consequently, using the estimated autoregressive coefficients from the old series to characterize the surprise associated with debt levels after the revision would overestimate the surprise to investors.

In the end, however, I am less concerned about the merits of this exercise than I am about the relevance of buildups of stocks of debt in general. To elaborate on this point, I turn first to a brief review of Aizenman and Marion's debt overhang model.

THE DEBT OVERHANG MODEL

The authors specify a two-period model of international lending. As is common in the sovereign debt literature, institutional enforcement of repayment is infeasible. Instead, default occurs when a debtor perceives it in his or her interest not to repay.

The mechanism inducing repayment is that the debtor pays a default penalty equal to a constant fraction of stochastic second-period output in the event of default. Under these models, the expected value to the debtor of default is increasing in the stock of outstanding debt, while the expected value of debt service (the default penalty) is invariant with respect to the size of outstanding debt. The stock of lending is therefore restricted such that the expected return on lending is profitable.

Aizenman and Marion introduce uncertainty about the magnitude of outstanding debt into this standard framework. They demonstrate that the introduction of uncertainty reduces the supply of credit to the debtor country. The reason for this is that when we hold the contractual rate of interest constant, increased uncertainty about the magnitude of outstanding debt reduces the probability of debt service. Because of the fixed contractual payment in a debt contract, increased uncertainty raises downside risk faced by creditors, but has no impact on the upside risk, as in the case of a "put" option. To bring the expected return on lending to the debtor nation back to a competitive level, therefore, the contractual rate of interest must be increased. However, this increase in the interest rate reduces the magnitude of debt necessary to avoid default, holding all else equal.

Moreover, the authors demonstrate that this relationship is nonlinear. The sensitivity of the supply of credit to an increase in uncertainty about the magnitude of outstanding debt is increasing in its magnitude. Loosely, the intuition behind the nonlinearity is that the possibility of default provides the channel through which increased uncertainty affects the supply of credit. An increase in the magnitude of outstanding credit, again holding all else equal, raises the probability of default and increases the importance of this channel.

I have two main comments on the debt overhang model. First, there is no investment in the model. An increase in borrowing therefore invariably raises the probability of default. However, if the increased debt were profitably invested, the real bills doctrine would suggest that the default implications of an increase in the stock of debt are unclear. Default risk would then be a function of shocks to the quality of investments undertaken rather than the stock of debt. This would bring the model much closer to those in the previous literature.

My second comment concerns the relevance of the empirical evidence offered by the authors concerning the buildup of debt stocks by Thailand and South Korea. Their model predicts that the effective ceiling on net resource transfers to creditors will be the lesser of contractual repayments or the magnitude of the default penalty. However, the default penalty is proportionately increasing in debtor nation output. This implies that the relevant ceiling will be on the ratio of contractual debt obligations to output, rather than the stock of outstanding debt.

This distinction is nontrivial, since output was growing rapidly in both Thailand and South Korea during the period of debt buildup studied by the authors. See Figure 5.7.

Figure 5.7 plots the ratio of total Thai debt service as a percentage of GDP over the buildup period. Two features stand out: First, debt-service-to-GDP ratios did not markedly increase over this period of debt buildup, because output growth matched increases in borrowing. Second, this ratio seems to be relatively stable over this period, suggesting that uncertainty over the magnitude of this ratio would not be a great issue.

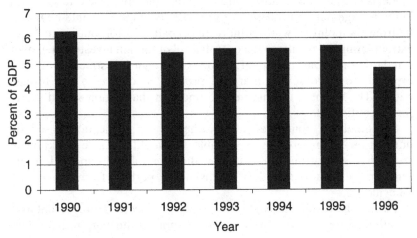

Figure 5.7. Thailand Total Debt Service as a Percent of GDP (*Source:* World Bank, *World Development Indicators, 1998*).

PORTFOLIO BALANCE MODEL

The analysis closes with a simple model of international investment by a representative first-order risk-averse investor. The authors note that a collapse in foreign lending is analogous to an outbreak of extreme home bias. They suggest looking toward conditions that could escalate home bias as potential sources of lending collapses. In particular, the authors introduce an agent with a generalized expected utility function that weighs bad outcomes more severely than good ones. Under this assumption, investors demand a risk premium to induce them to invest abroad.

The authors then to derive the conditions under which international diversification is desirable under autarky. They introduce a model in which the agent chooses its portfolio allocation from three assets: a risk-free domestic asset, a risky domestic asset, and a risky foreign asset. The authors demonstrate that a sufficient reduction in the normalized interest rate premium (the excess return on foreign assets divided by the uncertainty of that return, as measured by the variance) on foreign assets can make international diversification undesirable. In contrast, a standard utility function would imply that agents would always hold a positive amount of each asset in its optimal portfolio.

They conclude that it is possible that increased uncertainty about investment prospects in Asia, resulting in a reduction in the normalized expected return on assets in that region, led to the observed collapse in foreign investment toward that region.

I have three comments on the portfolio balance model. First, the model is partial equilibrium in the sense that the domestic rate of return in the foreign nation is taken as given. This assumption would be realistic from the point view of an individual small investor, but it precludes extrapolating the results to the overall level of foreign investment. Under standard conditions, a general pullout of foreign investment would be expected to increase the marginal product of capital in the foreign nation. The ultimate decline in investment in that nation would therefore be mitigated.

Second, I am concerned about whether a specification based on differences in preferences is testable. It would be nice to know if there was supporting evidence for the generalized expected utility function the authors introduce in this model, perhaps from experimental evidence.

Finally, the results derived in the analysis concern the representative agent's decision to invest in the foreign nation on the margin, given zero initial exposure. I am not sure how this would correspond to developments in Asia, where investors began from exposed positions. It is not obvious to me that the discrete zero investment results derived in the chapter for initially unexposed investors would also apply to investors with stocks of positive foreign exposure.

CONCLUSION

Aizenman and Marion have provided a compelling argument that increased uncertainty about foreign debt obligations may have played a role in the reversal of capital flows into Asia during its financial crisis. However, there is good reason to doubt that the channels they discuss are sufficiently powerful to tell the entire story. In terms of the debt over-hang model, the empirical evidence reviewed here suggests that the relevant criteria, the ratio of debt service to GDP, failed to increase markedly prior to the crisis. The portfolio balance model ignores general equilibrium responses, which may mitigate the decision of an individual investor to cut off investments toward a foreign country. In fairness to the authors, the spirit of their analysis is only that uncertainty about debt contributed to the crisis. They do not claim this to be the only cause of the crisis, or even the most important one.

6

International Capital Inflows, Domestic Financial Intermediation, and Financial Crises under Imperfect Information

Menzie D. Chinn and Kenneth M. Kletzer

6.1 INTRODUCTION

Recent financial crises in emerging markets have been preceded by periods of large capital inflows and expansions of the domestic banking sector. In the aftermath of these crises, economic growth has fallen sharply and, in some cases, has been slow to recover. Many of the recent crises have been associated with implicit guarantees by sovereign governments of foreign currency debts accumulated by the private sector. Recently several economists, notably Calvo (1998a), have observed that these crises evolve through complicated interactions between domestic financial sectors, international lenders, and national governments. Financial crises have often been characterized by concurrent banking and currency crises.[1] Recent experience suggests that banking crises are not necessarily just an outcome of a collapsing exchange rate regime. Instead, the source of a financial crisis may be found in the interaction between the microeconomics of private financial intermediation and government macroeconomic policies.

In this chapter we propose a theoretical model of the dynamics of bank lending, domestic production, and the accumulation of foreign currency liabilities by domestic financial intermediaries that ultimately leads to a financial crisis. These dynamics derive from the introduction of an agency problem in domestic financial intermediation that originates in an informational advantage for domestic banks in domestic lending and government provision of insurance to private financial activities. The equilibrium for the model economy predicts twin banking and currency crises that end a period of high gross domestic output growth and inflows

---

[1] The empirical relationship between these "twin crises" is the subject of Kaminsky and Reinhart (1998, 1999), Hutchison and McDill (1998), and Glick and Hutchison (Chapter 2, this volume).

of foreign capital. Before the crisis occurs, capital inflows rise with domestic production while private foreign debt grows more rapidly than output. Output declines at the time of the crisis, as capital suddenly flows outward, and has a lower trend growth rate post-crisis than pre-crisis. These predictions are compared with the data for the East Asian crisis countries in the second part of the chapter.

In our model, the loan porfolio choices of banks are subject to adverse selection in the presence of government deposit insurance for domestic savers and government guarantees of foreign currency loans for foreign creditors with insufficient monitoring. The economy is represented by a simple endogenous growth model in which the productivity for each firm is stochastic. Banks intermediate lending to firms. The banking system becomes progressively more indebted through foreign borrowing until it is ultimately insolvent. This process ends in a government bailout of foreign creditors and domestic depositors. The anticipation of the bailout induces the trend debt accumulation that ultimately triggers the crisis and the bailout.

As argued by Calvo (1998a), following the literature on sovereign debt, a sovereign government has an incentive to subsidize foreign capital inflows to overcome the problem of its own moral hazard in setting trade, fiscal and monetary policies. We observe that government guarantees of foreign currency obligations incurred by the private sector are typically associated with the abandonment of an exchange rate peg. Government insurance that at least partially indemnifies foreign investors in the event of devaluation appears to be an implicit part of a pegged exchange rate regime, as noted by Mishkin (1996) and Obstfeld (1998). Our model links a banking crisis with a currency crisis by adopting this form of contingent government subsidization of foreign lending.[2]

When a currency crisis occurs, the government realizes a sudden increase in its outstanding liabilities. The exchange rate regime collapses because the ultimate monetization of these liabilities is anticipated by market participants. The contingent liabilities of the government are endogenously accumulated through the foreign capital inflows induced by the public sector guarantees of private foreign currency debt. Because the size of the government liabilities is endogenous, the timing of the collapse is indeterminant in this model. The role of contingent public sector liabilities for generating currency crises has been emphasized by Calvo (1998a, 1998b), Burnside, Eichenbaum and Rebelo (1999), and Dooley

---

[2] This link between contingent government liabilities and currency crises is also used by Calvo (1998a), Burnside, Eichenbaum, and Rebelo (1999), Chinn, Dooley, and Shrestha (1999), and Dooley (2000).

(2000). Our model adds the role of agency in domestic intermediation to generate the endogenous dynamics of output growth, capital inflows, banking sector insolvency, and currency crisis. In our economy, banking crises and currency crises are the inevitable consequence of financial and capital account liberalization in the presence of debt guarantees and an exchange rate peg.

Many authors have offered various explanations for the financial crises in East Asia in 1997.[3] Our approach emphasizes the relationship between large foreign capital inflows and high output growth and the ultimate collapse of the domestic financial sector along with the exchange rate regime. The currency crisis and realization of losses by the domestic financial intermediaries coincide, but the timing of this event is indeterminate. This leaves room for the simultaneity of crises across countries to be explained by panic or contagion models.[4] The source of the financial crises generated by our model are fundamentals and contrast with the liquidity crisis view presented by Chang and Velasco (1999), Goldfajn and Valdes (1997), and others.

Section 6.2 presents the theoretical model and its implications. Our model of bank intermediation with limited liability firms is distantly related to that of Kiyotaki and Moore (1997) but contrasts with their model sharply in that loans can and will be renegotiated in our economy. The empirical implications of the model are summarized at the end of the section. Section 6.3 compares the predictions of the model to the data for the Asian crisis countries with broad success. The last section concludes.

6.2 A THEORETICAL MODEL OF FINANCIAL CRISES

We model international capital flows and domestic banking in an infinitely lived small open economy. Households and firms are represented by entrepreneurs who establish firms, save, and consume. A fixed number of these entrepreneurs operate banks. These banks intermediate between domestic and foreign savers and domestic investors. We set up the behavior of each of these agents and of the equilibrium dynamics for the economy in sequence.

---

[3] Examples responsive to the Asian crisis of 1997 include Caballero and Krishnamurthy (1998), Chang and Velasco (1999), Dooley (2000), Eichengreen and Rose (1998), Furman and Stiglitz (1998), Goldfajn and Valdes (1997), Kumhof (1998), Krugman (1998), McKinnon and Pill (1999), and Miller and Stiglitz (1999). Other recent papers on international capital flows to emerging markets include Edwards and Vegh (1997), Frankel and Rose (1996), and Sachs, Tornell, and Velasco (1996).

[4] We do not pursue any such explanations of the timing of a crisis once one is viable.

6.2.1 The Economy

There is a single good that can be consumed, invested, or traded internationally. It can be produced using entrepreneurial labor and capital. Capital in this model should be thought of as working capital; it is exhausted in the production process. Output is stochastic, and production takes one period.

All residents have identical preferences over infinite-horizon consumption plans and are endowed with a single unit of labor each period. Each person is a potential entrepreneur who can invest in a project each period. The investment opportunities available to different people need not be the same, allowing entrepreneurs to be heterogeneous with respect to skills or knowledge. For example, a subset of entrepreneurs are able to operate banks. The services provided by banks will be defined below. The technique of production available to each entrepreneur does not change over time.

Each firm uses one unit of entrepreneurial labor and is identified with a particular entrepreneur. Goods production displays constant returns to capital and increasing returns to entrepreneurial effort. Production is risky. The projects available to different entrepreneurs vary with respect to the distribution of output produced across states of nature. For example, the output distribution per unit of capital for one entrepreneur's project may have higher variance and mean than that for another entrepreneur.

The output realized in any period by an individual firm is private information that can be observed by others at a fixed cost per observation. Banks operate a technology that allows them to observe project outcomes at a lower cost than others. This inhibits direct equity investment by individuals in the projects undertaken by other entrepreneurs and encourages lending using conventional debt contracts by banks. The optimality of conventional loan contracts under costly observability is demonstrated by Diamond (1984). Because the cost of observing actual outcomes for individual firms are fixed, there is a cost advantage to having a single bank make loans to a particular entrepreneur. Therefore, the role of banks in this model is to diversify income risk for individual savers in the presence of moral hazard in reporting firm earnings.

Individuals are risk averse and smooth consumption over time. A household seeks to maximize utility,

$$U_t = E_t \sum_{s=t}^{\infty} \beta^{s-t} u(c_s) \tag{1}$$

where $u(c)$ is strictly concave and $0 < \beta < 1$, with respect to their consumption plans given the intertemporal budget identity,

$$w_{s+1} - w_s = i_s^d w_s + \pi_s - c_s \tag{2}$$

solvency condition,

$$\lim_{s \to \infty} w_s \prod_{v=t}^{s-1} \left(\frac{1}{1+i_v^d} \right) \geq 0 \tag{3}$$

and initial financial wealth, w_t. Here, w indicates deposits held in banks, π represents entrepreneurial income from production, and i^d is the deposit rate of interest. We assume that money is required to make consumption purchases and that domestic transactions are denominated in units of domestic currency. Demand deposits pay a positive rate of return so that money is held only as deposits in equilibrium. In this economy, the government provides deposit insurance so that the domestic currency value of household claims against banks is fully insured.[5]

Entrepreneurs can finance investment by borrowing from banks or using their own savings. Entrepreneurial income is the residual of the stochastic gross returns to investment after the firm's current debt obligation is satisfied. When the returns to investment are insufficient to meet the debt repayment obligation, the firm reports this to the bank, which, in turn, expends the fixed cost, c, to verify actual returns. In this event, the firm and the bank can agree to rollover the unpaid debt or to declare the firm bankrupt. Bankruptcy is assumed to be costly for the entrepreneur. She cannot simply abandon her debt and return to the loan market. The bank and the firm will rollover loans under these circumstances.

The production function for firm j is given by

$$y_t^j = r_t^j k_t^j \tag{4}$$

where k_t^j is the investment undertaken by firm j in period $t - 1$. Capital depreciates fully. r_t^j is the stochastic (marginal and average) productivity of capital. r_t^j is nonnegative and distributed identically and independently across time.

The firm's debt, d^j, evolves as

$$d_{t+1}^j = \left(1 + i_{t+1}^j\right)\left(d_t^j + \ell_t^j - \rho_t^j\right) \tag{5}$$

---

[5] For simplicity, we have left out elements of a model that would make this a welfare-improving policy. If the model were extended to incorporate time-to-build into the production process and market incompleteness as in Diamond and Dybvig (1983), then deposit insurance could be justified on welfare grounds.

where i_{t+1}^j is the borrowing rate of interest for firm j and ℓ_{t+1}^j is the amount of new funds lent by the bank in period t. $\rho_t^j = \max\{d_t^j, r_t^j k_t^j\}$. Therefore, d^j is always nonnegative; entrepreneurs lend to banks through household deposits. The terms of the new loan made at time t, ℓ_t^j and i_t^j, are determined after ρ_t^j is known. Competition between banks will determine the rate of interest charged a firm with no existing debt overhang. The specifics of loan rollovers are discussed below.

Entrepreneurial income is given by

$$\pi_t^j = \max\{r_t^j k_t^j - d_t^j, r_t^j(k_t^j - \ell_t^j)\} \tag{6}$$

where $k_t^j - \ell_t^j$ is the share of the investment undertaken by the firm in period $t - 1$ that was self-financed. Firms are modeled as corporations in that owners' assets held outside the firm cannot be claimed by the firm's creditors. Limited liability for firm owners is displayed by equation (6). The consequence of costly observability and limited firm liability is that entrepreneurs cannot purchase insurance against income risk. They share risk by borrowing from banks using conventional loan contracts with bankruptcy [as demonstrated by Diamond (1984)].

International financial capital inflows equal the current account deficit plus the increase in central bank reserve holdings through the balance of payments identity. Private foreign borrowing is intermediated by domestic banks. The current account surplus is given by

$$b_{t+1} - b_t = i_t^* b_t + y_t - c_t - k_{t+1} \tag{7}$$

The current account equation is written in units of foreign currency. Nominal prices are perfectly flexible, and purchasing power parity holds. Uncovered interest parity also holds, so that if the exchange rate is fixed, i_t^* and i_t^d will be equal.

We consider fiscal policy only in its role for generating a currency crisis under a pegged exchange rate regime. Therefore, there are no public expenditures and all government revenues are collected through money creation. Any transfers are fully monetized, leading to a one-for-one increase in domestic credit. Any transfers will be contingent and paid as government guarantees to creditors.

6.2.2 Dynamics of Bank Lending

In this section we consider the dynamics of domestic bank lending and firm debt, taking the nominal rate of interest on deposits as constant. That is, the exchange rate is fixed.

Bankers have the incentive to roll over debts that client firms are not able to repay in any current period. If the bank ever desires to make a loan to firm j, we obtain

$$E_t[(r^j - (1+i^*))u'(c_{t+1})] \geq 0 \qquad (8)$$

when the bank is solvent with certainty, where c_{t+1} is the bank entrepreneur's consumption in period $t + 1$. The inequality is strict unless the interest rate charged is high enough to exhaust the firm's revenues with probability one. When the probability that the bank becomes bankrupt is positive, the expectation is conditional on the event that bankruptcy does not occur. If a bank receives $r^j k_t^j < d_t^j$ from firm j in period t, then the bank can add the difference, $d_t^j - r^j k_t^j$, to new loans it makes in period t, ℓ_t^j. For events such that $r_{t+1}^j k_{t+1}^j > (1 + i_{t+1}^j)\ell_t^j$, the bank receives repayment of part of the rolled over debt from period t. This additional return is possible because the bank can declare the firm bankrupt and bankruptcy is costly for the firm. To limit the market power of the bank, we impose the institutional assumption that the bank can only charge the same initial rate of interest in a rollover. Making this arbitrary assumption simplifies the model. The opportunity cost of the new loan is $(1 + i^*)\ell_t^j$.

Figure 6.1 depicts the bank's return per unit of new funds, ℓ^j, when its client's debt rollover equals d^j and the lending rate of interest is i^j, as a function of the marginal productivity of capital, r^j (superscripts are omitted from the figure). The expected return for the bank is given by $\ell^j E(r^b)$, where

$$r^b = \min\left\{r^j, (1+i^j)\left(1+\frac{d^j}{\ell^j}\right)\right\} - (1+i^*) \qquad (9)$$

when the probability that the bank becomes insolvent in the period is zero. Here, $k^j = \ell^j$ for simplicity (we impose this condition because it makes no difference for the dynamics of interest below).[6] For any given size investment, ℓ^j, this expression is increasing in d^j. The bank also incurs a cost, c, in the event that

$$r^j < (1+i^j)\left(1+\frac{d^j}{\ell^j}\right) \qquad (10)$$

Suppose that $d_t^i = 0$ for each client firm i of the bank and that the bank's loan portfolio is optimally allocated at the beginning of period t. The bank's portfolio at the beginning of period $t + 1$ satisfies the Euler conditions given by

$$E_t\left[u'(c_{t+1})\left(\min\left\{r_{t+1}^i, (1+i^i)\left(1+\frac{d_{t+1}^i}{\ell_{t+1}^i}\right)\right\} - (1+i^*) - c_{t+1}^i\right)\right] = 0 \qquad (11)$$

---

[6] The portfolio dynamics of the banks demonstrated here imply that bank portfolios will become dominated by lending firms that are no longer self-financing in any part.

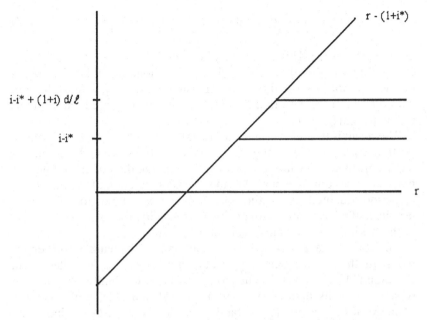

Figure 6.1. Bank return for loan rollovers. *Note:* r represents the marginal product of capital, i and i^* denote domestic and foreign interest rates, and d/ℓ represents the ratio of outstanding debt to new lending.

for each client firm i (equality holds for an interior solution), where c_{t+1}^i is the random variable that equals c when $r_{t+1}^i < (1 + i^i)(1 + d_{t+1}^i/\ell_{t+1}^i)$ but equals zero otherwise. Consider the case that the productivity of capital for firm j in period t, r_t^j, falls below $(1 + i^j)$, but $r_t^i \geq (1 + i^i)$ for each $i \neq j$. By equation (5), $d_t^j > 0$ while $d_t^i = 0$ for $i \neq j$. The Euler conditions in equation (11) imply that the bank's choice of ℓ_{t+1}^j will rise relative to loans to other firms, ℓ_{t+1}^i, in comparison to the portfolio held in period t. For example, if the total size of the bank's loan portfolio remains constant between periods t and $t + 1$, $\ell_{t+1}^j > \ell_t^j$ and $\ell_{t+1}^i < \ell_t^i$ for $i \neq j$.

The extent to which the bank's portfolio shifts toward loans to firm j depends on the magnitude of d_{t+1}^j, the joint distribution of all the r^i, and the degree of risk aversion of the bank entrepreneur. If the r^i are perfectly correlated for the bank's clients, then the bank shifts its entire portfolio to the borrower that first realizes revenues less than current debt service. If the r^i are imperfectly correlated, the relative increase in ℓ_{t+1}^j declines with the bank entrepreneur's relative risk aversion (the bank's portfolio allocation problem is just the consumption-based capital asset pricing model).

The probability that d_{t+2}^j exceeds d_{t+1}^j is given by

$$\Pr\{d_{t+2}^j \geq d_{t+1}^j\} = \Pr\left\{r^j \leq (1+i^j)\left(1+\frac{d_{t+1}^j}{\ell_{t+1}^j}\right)\right\} \tag{12}$$

using equation (5). This probability is rising in the ratio d_{t+1}^j/ℓ_{t+1}^j. There-fore, the probability that firm j's share in the loan portfolio rises again between periods $t+1$ and $t+2$ is increasing in firm j's portfolio share in period $t+1$. In the case that the total amount lent by the bank remains constant, $E_{t+1}(\ell_{t+2}^j) > \ell_{t+1}^j$.

The result is that the variance of the rate of return to the bank's entire portfolio rises over time, in expectation, when the r^j are i.i.d. and imper-fectly correlated. Because the probability that the debt of any individual borrower rises during a period is an increasing function of the beginning of period indebtedness of the borrower, the bank's portfolio becomes less diversified over time with positive probability. The expected increase in the riskiness of the bank's portfolio rises with time.

Thus far, we have imposed the restriction that the bank entrepreneur bears all the risk of bank's portfolio allocation. This is reflected in equation (11). However, in our model the bank has limited liability for repayment of its debts. The conditions (11) and (12) imply that the variance of the returns to the bank's loan portfolio rises stochastically over time. The deposit liabilities of the bank, b_t, follow

$$b_{t+1} = (1+i^*)(b_t + \ell_t - \omega_t) \tag{13}$$

where ℓ_t is the total amount of new loans made and ω_t is the total with-drawal of deposits in total debt of the bank's clients and r^b is the return to the bank's loan portfolio net of costs of monitoring firm incomes and gross of debt repayments. The bank realizes the positive income,

$$\pi^b = \ell\left[\min\left\{r,(1+i)\left(1+\frac{d}{\ell}\right)\right\} - (1+i^*)\left(1+\frac{b}{\ell}\right)\right] \tag{14}$$

for

$$r > (1+i^*)\left(1+\frac{b}{\ell}\right)$$

and zero otherwise.

Figure 6.2 illustrates how the bank's income depends on its deposit liabilities. An increase in b will induce the bank entrepreneur to choose a riskier portfolio among portfolios offering the same mean return. This is a consequence of conditions (11) and (12). An increase in b leads to adverse selection in the choice of the bank's portfolio from the per-spective of the government (as the bank's creditor). This follows from the analysis of Stiglitz and Weiss (1981) of an increase in the interest rate

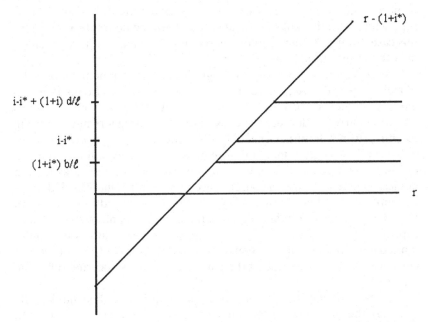

Figure 6.2. Bank return with foreign lending. *Note*: b/ℓ denotes the ratio of deposit liabilities to new lending. See Figure 6.1 for other variable definitions.

charged to a risk neutral agent. Although our bank entrepreneur is risk averse and makes a more complex choice, the analysis clearly still applies.

The end result of these intermediate results is that the variance of a bank's income rises stochastically; it follows a submartingale as bank portfolios become more concentrated. The unconditional probability of individual firm illiquidity rises over time as firm indebtedness is self-reinforcing (the probability of a debt increase rises with existing indebtedness). If the support of the distribution of r^i for each firm i is bounded from above, then firms eventually become insolvent in this economy. This carries through to banks. Eventually, the probability of insolvency for each bank rises toward one in this economy.

6.2.3 Foreign Lending and Domestic Financial Intermediation

We next consider this banking sector in the open economy. Domestic banks intermediate between foreign and domestic creditors and domestic firms. The banks have a cost advantage over foreign lenders in observing the realized outputs of domestic firms. This advantage is assumed to be large enough to preclude any direct foreign portfolio lending to domestic entrepreneurs. However, foreign lenders face the risk of bank-ruptcy by domestic banks in the absence of government intervention. In this case, foreign lenders should charge domestic banks a risk premium over the international rate of interest.

Foreign creditors also face sovereign risk; the government chooses the monetary growth rate, hence the rate of depreciation. Loans denomi-nated in domestic currency are proportionately reduced in real terms when the currency depreciates or is devalued. Foreigners have a strong incentive to not hold net claims in domestic currency. If foreign credi-tors write loans denominated in foreign currency, they still face the risk of losses due to exchange rate changes because domestic banks lend in domestic currency. This is a consequence of the limited liability of domes-tic banks. A devaluation that is not fully anticipated reduces the return to banks in terms of foreign currency. If a domestic bank becomes bank-rupt as a result, then its foreign creditors realize real losses. Under limited liability, the domestic banker will not desire to fully hedge against currency risk because some of the gains from doing so accrue to foreign creditors.

As a consequence of sovereign risk, capital inflows will be inefficiently low and the government has an incentive to intervene. One way to address this problem is to peg the nominal exchange rate and guarantee repayment of foreign currency loans contingent on devaluation. We adopt this policy regime not because it is optimal (it surely is not in general), but because it is the kind of policy adopted by East Asian countries before the crisis. Under a fixed exchange rate with contingent foreign currency liability guarantees, Burnside, Eichenbaum, and Rebelo (1999) demonstrate that foreign currency loans are not hedged. In this policy regime, foreign lenders still face the risk of debtor insolvencies when lending to domestic banks. They are not insured by the govern-ment against bank insolvencies that do not occur simultaneously with devaluation.

We will assume that the return to foreign lenders in the event of a bailout by government following a currency crisis is i^*, the international rate of interest. This assumption can be relaxed to allow losses to foreign lenders in a financial crisis at the cost of complicating the analysis. In our model economy, foreign creditors will have an incentive to keep banks going until the moment of a crisis. At the time of a crisis, foreign lenders will be better off becoming creditors of the government and not of domestic banks.

To see this, consider the decision of a foreign lender. If a bank is illiq-uid at date t and has foreign debt, f_t, then its foreign creditors can assure themselves an eventual rate of return equal to i^* on any loans they make by lending more to the bank if an eventual currency crisis is assured. Because banks become illiquid eventually with probability one in our model, bank foreign debt will rise over time. Bankers will demand additional foreign capital inflows every time one of their client firms realizes a poor investment outcome. This follows from the Euler condition for the individual bank, equation (11), as depicted in Figure 6.1. As total bank notional assets, d, rise, so does the bank's demand for foreign inflows. Forcing an idiosyncratic bank failure yields a loss for foreign creditors, while continuing to lend does not because devaluation is inevitable.

Foreign lending to domestic banks covers the difference,

$$-\pi^b = \ell\left[(1+i^*)\left(1+\frac{b+f}{\ell}\right) - \min\left\{r,(1+i)\left(1+\frac{d}{\ell}\right)\right\}\right] \qquad (15)$$

when positive, and increases in the size of its loan portfolio induced by rises in the debts of the bank's client firms, d^i. In equation (15), b denotes the face value of domestic deposits and f the foreign debt of the bank.

Because firm debt is an increasing random variable, capital inflows must be rising, stochastically, over time. Output is rising proportionately with inflows that fund investment in this endogenous growth model ($y = rk$). Each time a firm's output is less than its debt, inflows and investment rise in equilibrium. Consumption is also rising along with income [although not proportionately for the general concave utility function, $u(c)$].[7] In addition, the probability that a bank cannot meet the net demands of domestic depositors is rising over time as its portfolio becomes riskier. Whenever banks borrow from abroad to meet net domestic deposit withdrawals, the loans are financing consumption not investment. Because this occurs with positive (and increasing) probability, the foreign debt of each bank as a ratio of its lending, f/ℓ, is an increasing random variable (a submartingale). Therefore, foreign debt is rising (stochastically) as a ratio of gross domestic product. Also, because f/ℓ is monotonically increasing in expectation for the individual bank, individual banks become insolvent eventually with probability one.

6.2.4 Currency and Banking Crises

The arguments for these dynamics are conditional on an eventual government bailout of foreign lenders. This is conditional on devaluation. To ensure that such a bailout occurs, we need to add the assumption that the government has finite resources available to repay foreign lenders and that foreign lenders know this. There is an upper bound on

---

[7] The income risk facing households is not the same as in a basic stochastic AK model. Therefore, we do not state that isoelastic utility is a sufficient condition for consumption growth to equal investment and output growth, although this may turn out to be true.

the amount of foreign bank debt that will be guaranteed ex post by the government. This will include the residual resources of the debtor banks and central bank reserves. In this model economy, this upper bound is reached in finite time with probability one as a consequence of the bank debt dynamics in the previous subsection.

The mechanics of a crisis are as follows. Let the maximum amount of the government bailout of foreign currency debts equal $\overline{D} > 0$. Eventually, the foreign debt of the banking sector will exceed the value of the banking sector plus central bank reserves minus domestic deposits.[8] This excess claim at time t is denoted by D_t. D_t is stochastic. If a run occurs in period t, the resources to pay D_t in present value will be raised through monetization. With a conventional first-generation model of currency crises (Krugman, 1979; Flood and Garber, 1984), the timing of a crisis (given a subsequent rate of monetization) depends upon the initial level of reserves.

The timing of the crisis in this model depends upon the share of reserves attacked by other parties than the foreign creditors. In the event of an attack, foreign creditors claim the remainder of the reserves plus D_t. The drop in money demand equals that part of central bank reserves purchased during the attack by others. The domestic money supply equals the domestic currency deposits of households in this economy. In the period of an attack, domestic households seek to convert all their domestic currency deposits to foreign currency. The fall in money demand exactly equals domestic savers' demand for reserves. Foreign creditors' claims exceed the rest of reserves, so the attack is viable. The attack occurs at the moment that foreign debt equals the maximum that foreign creditors can expect to get. If they receive the international interest rate on foreign currency loans from the government (as we assumed), the attack can happen at any time that $0 < D_t$. D_t simply has to be large enough to generate an ex post inflation rate inconsistent with the existing exchange rate peg. Because D_t is endogenous, the timing of the attack is indeterminant once D_t is positive.[9]

---

[8] We do not preclude banks lending to each other. Because they can do so, what matters is the aggregate solvency of the banking sector and not the solvency of the individual banks.

[9] The determinacy of the timing of the attack because D_t is endogenous can be seen by adding a Cagan-style money demand equation. In that case, the difference between household deposits at the beginning of period t and the reserves demanded by households in the attack during period t will equal their demand for money, given the rate of devaluation implied by D_t. At the time of an attack on the currency peg,

$$b_t - m^d(D_t) + f_t = R_t + D_t$$

where R_t represents reserves.

This model does not have equilibria in which lending and ultimate financial crises do not occur under a simple condition on the productivity of capital. If foreign lenders did not anticipate an attack and bailout, they would lend if

$$E[\max\{1+i,r\}] - c^f \Pr\{r < 1+i\} = 1 + i^* \tag{16}$$

This has a solution for i when d is zero. This condition ensures that a profitable loan can be made when the lender commits to take what she can after one period, where c^f is the foreign lender's cost of observing a domestic bank's portfolio return, r. If the foreign lender rolls over unpaid debt service, then her ex ante return increases. Therefore, foreign loans will be made. Eventually, the crisis occurs.

6.2.5 Crisis Aftermath

When the financial crisis occurs, there is a sudden reversal of capital inflows as foreign lending halts and domestic savers seek foreign assets. Domestic lending and output contract sharply in the model economy. Lending will resume under the floating regime if the banks are left to operate. The government implicitly partially bails out the private domestic financial sector in the equilibrium of the model because it takes over the foreign debt. It can also forgive any deposit insurance indemnity payments during the crisis. The banks will be able to borrow from domestic households and foreign lenders. The return to domestic residents for holding domestic or foreign assets is the same under uncovered interest parity if the government continues to provide deposit insurance.

Foreign lenders, however, have exhausted (partly or in whole) the resources that the government can commit to an eventual bailout $(\overline{D})$. The government cannot offer the same guarantee. Foreign creditors still offer loans to domestic banks given condition (16). Without the implicit subsidy from the government, foreign financial capital inflows will be less than before at any level of bank claims against domestic firms, d. Output must contract and grow more slowly than before the crisis as foreign capital inflows are no longer subsidized.

If the government does not bail out the domestic financial sector, the growth rate of output in recovery can be lower as a consequence of the loss of bank intermediation. The loss of domestic banking would force the use of alternative, higher cost means of intermediation. If banks operate with an overhang of debt to the government, then, as shown by the conditions for a bank's optimal portfolio choice, domestic loan portfolios will be riskier. Calvo (1998a) makes the general point that the loss of bank services can result in a further output contraction by disrupting the payments mechanism. Lastly, we have assumed full nominal price flexibility. If this fails, the output effects could be exacerbated by the consequent real exchange rate movements.

6.2.6 Empirical Implications of the Model and Extensions

Our theoretical model implies that banking and currency crises coincide and occur with probability one in the absence of effective prudential regulation. Before the crisis, private foreign debt rises as a ratio of gross domestic production. Foreign financial capital inflows will be a constant fraction of trend output in the case that consumption growth equals income growth. Otherwise, the ratio of inflows to output can rise or fall in trend. The shadow value of domestic banks should be declining before the crisis. This could be measured by comparing the stock market value of domestic banks to the stock market value of the domestic sector. Bank capital should be decreasing over time.

After a financial crisis, the model implies that output declines and that the growth rate of output is lower in recovery than it was before the crisis. This is because the contingent government bailout has been exercised so that the resources that previously subsidized foreign capital inflows are no longer available to subsidize new inflows at the same level. The currency crisis should also lead to a contraction in money demand and an increase in the rate of monetary growth. The latter effect is consistent with the monetization of the sudden increase in government liabilities. This is the mechanism by which a currency crisis occurs in our model, so we need to check if it arises in the empirical record.

The riskiness of the loan portfolio of domestic intermediaries is rising in this model. An increasing share of bank loans goes to firms that have realized low capital productivities in the past, while a decreasing share goes to firms that have realized high productivities of capital. In the endogenous growth model used, the productivity of capital is an i.i.d. random variable. If we allow for a small degree of serial correlation in the productivity of inputs for individual firms, then the marginal productivity of capital in the aggregate will be decreasing in trend.

Possible extensions of the basic model could allow firms to choose riskier projects as they become more heavily indebted. Banks would then face adverse project selection by firms. Following Bernanke and Gertler (1989, 1990), banks would require firms to partially self-finance investments. However, in our framework, banks would relax self-financing requirements and the projects selected by individual firms would become riskier as individual firm debt rises. That is, banks would choose a riskier portfolio both by concentrating lending more on firms rolling over unpaid past debts and by allowing firms to choose riskier projects. In such a more complicated, two-tier agency model, the investments chosen by firms could become riskier simultaneously with bank portfolios as part of the same optimal portfolio behavior under limited liability for banks. This is another reason that capital to output ratios might rise before financial crises. In addition to the strict implications of the model as written, we also investigate the data for this possibility.

6.3 EMPIRICAL EVIDENCE FOR THE MODEL

6.3.1 A First Pass at the Data

Formal testing of the model is hampered by the unavailability of data for many of the variables of interest. Indeed some of the key variables in the model are not directly observable. These are the riskiness of investment, the size of the contingent liabilities, and the share of bank capital (as opposed to foreign capital) in domestic investment.

The model, however, can be examined along a number of dimensions using indirect measures of the factors of interest. In this informal examination, we discuss the patterns that can be observed, and whether they conform to the model. The model incorporates a number of important assumptions and implies several relationships. The key condition is that increases in capital inflows are intermediated through the banking system and result in increases in lending to the private sector. This is the case to the extent that capital inflows to the domestic banking sector are not sterilized, resulting in reserve accumulations rather than financing debits on the current account.

The patterns we expect to observe for economies subject to these agency problems include the following:

1. An increasing ratio of foreign and domestic lending as a share of output.
2. Capital inflows rising with GDP for crisis countries; the ratio of inflows to GDP can be rising.
3. Increasing riskiness of domestic investment; this may be reflected in falling capital productivity.
4. Deterioration of bank portfolios as the share of nonperforming assets rises.
5. Postcrisis increases in money supply growth rates.

Each of these factors is examined in turn.

6.3.1.1 Capital Inflows and Domestic Lending

The model requires that capital inflows are manifested in lending by banks and other financial intermediaries. We do not present a detailed

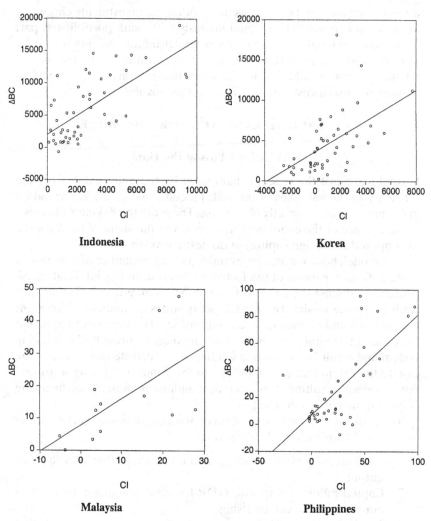

Figure 6.3. Change in bank credit (ΔBC) against capital inflows (CI), in billions of local currency. Quarterly data (1985:1–1997:1) except for Malaysia and Singapore, which are annual (1985–1997). Bank credit data for Indonesia and Korea is for deposit banks only.

discussion of how effective these countries have been in sterilizing capital inflows; such accounts are provided by Spiegel (1995) and Moreno (1996). Rather we focus on the broad relations between capital inflows and lending over the precrisis period. We measure capital flows using the financial account data reported by the IMF (in US$ converted to domestic currency), while deposit bank lending to the domestic

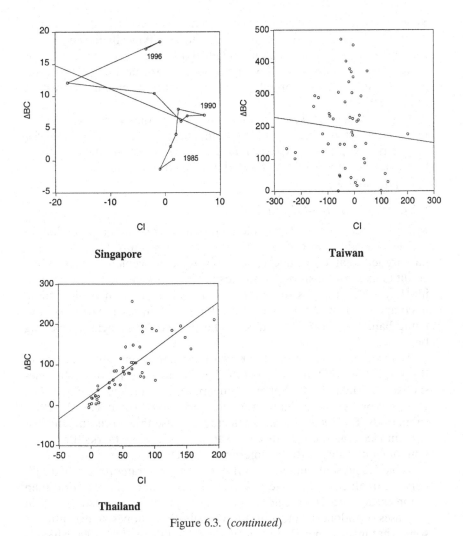

Singapore

Taiwan

Thailand

Figure 6.3. (*continued*)

private sector is measured by domestic credit (IFS, line 32d). For certain countries, additional lending is provided by non-deposit-taking banks and nonbank financial institutions; we will refer to the sum of deposit bank lending and these additional categories as total lending (as opposed to bank lending). In Figure 6.3, scatterplots of the relationship between changes in bank lending and capital inflows (in billions of units of domestic currency) are presented for Indonesia, Korea, Malaysia, Philippines, Singapore, Taiwan, and Thailand for the 1985:1–1997:1 period (annual data are plotted for Malaysia and Singapore). In all cases, except for

Singapore and Taiwan, the slope coefficient is positive in a simple regression of bank lending changes and capital inflows. Typically the coefficient is above 0.5 but below 1.00. One might think that some of the effect is omitted because we only allow for contemporaneous effects; however, most of the impact of capital inflows appears to be manifested within one quarter.

Singapore and Taiwan are interesting exceptions. These two economies ran substantial and persistent current account surpluses; and for certain periods, Taiwan exports financial capital. Whatever increase there is in financial intermediation through the banking system, it is not driven by capital inflows.

6.3.1.2 Surges in Bank Lending

Much has been made of the role of rapidly increasing bank lending in the years leading up to the 1997 crises. More recently, Moreno (1999) has argued that only in certain cases were movements in domestic credit in excess of historical averages in the period immediately preceding July 1997. Analysis of whether there was a surge in bank lending is complicated by the fact that developing countries typically exhibit rising bank loan to GDP ratios, as the process of financial deepening proceeds.

To examine whether the 1990s were anomalous in their behavior in this respect, we plot in Figure 6.4 the lending-to-GDP ratios for Indonesia, Korea, Malaysia, Philippines, Singapore, Taiwan, and Thailand. The graphs show the trend lines[10] for the 1985:1–1989:1 and 1989:2–1997:2 subperiods. The 1989:2 break is selected because this represents the last peak in U.S. real interest rates. The subsequent decline marks the beginning of capital surges to the emerging markets.

Table 6.1 presents lending-to-GDP ratio growth rates for the two subperiods. In all cases, the rate of growth is faster in the later period than in the earlier one. The acceleration in credit growth is marked, except in the cases of Indonesia and Taiwan. Actually, the Indonesian exception is somewhat misleading: There is a surge of lending in 1989–1990 which is not completely captured in the estimated trends. Hence, the one clear exception to the pattern of accelerating growth in the credit-to-GDP ratio is Taiwan.

Figure 6.5 depicts the various credit ratios and four quarter growth rates of GDP (in log difference terms). There is not a clear pattern in the

---

[10] The trend lines are estimated by regressing the first difference of the credit-to-GDP ratio on a constant and a dummy variable taking on a value of one beginning in 1989:2, and then dynamically forecasting from the beginning of the sample using the estimated equation.

Table 6.1. Lending-to-GDP Ratio Growth Rates (in percent)

Sample	Indonesia	Korea	Malaysia	Philippines	Singapore	Taiwan	Thailand
Deposit Bank Lending							
1985:1–1989:1	2.29	−0.89	0.34	0.56	−1.53	1.33	0.99
1982:2–1997:2	4.20	4.04	4.36	4.27	2.73	1.52	5.91
Total Lending							
1985:1–1989:1	—	−0.57	3.84	0.63	−1.06	—	0.82
1989:2–1997:2	—	3.09	13.68	4.75	6.17	—	6.93

Notes: Percentage point changes in the lending-to-GDP ratios calculated by regressing the first difference of the ratios on a constant and a dummy variable. Implied trends are depicted in Figure 6.4.

data. However, lending rises as ratio of GDP for Korea even as the GDP growth rate falls. As output growth declines from 9 percent to 6 percent in 1995–1996, the lending ratios rise at an accelerating rate. At the other end of the spectrum, Taiwan does not evidence rising lending ratios during the drop in growth rates in 1995–1996. The rest of the cases are indefinite.

6.3.1.3 The Quality of Investment Projects

Adverse selection under limited liability in financial intermediation implies that bank portfolios become progressively riskier in our model. In the aggregate, lending and investment are increasingly allocated over time to firms that have experienced low productivities in the past, rather than to firms that have had high productivity experiences. If productivity has a small serial correlation, then the aggregate productivity of investment will be decreasing over time. A commonly used aggregate statistic to measure the return to investment is the incremental capital-to-output ratio (ICOR). This measures the increase in the capital stock needed to produce a unit increase in output. Higher values of the ICOR suggest that the productivity of capital being put into use is low. Figure 6.6 presents a series of ICORs calculated from national income accounting data, taking account of business cycle factors. What is clear is that Korea, Thailand, and Malaysia all exhibit high and rising ICORs, while the ratio for Indonesia is declining from very high levels to match the ICORs of Korea and Thailand. On the other hand, Taiwan once again stands out with by far the lowest ICOR. Singapore's ICOR

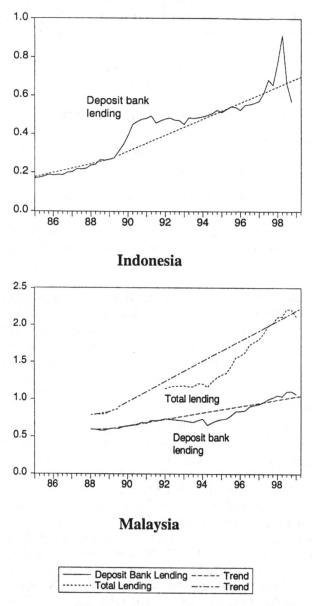

Figure 6.4. Deposit bank and lending-to-GDP ratios, along with segmented trends.

is comparatively high, but then its emplaced capital stock per worker exceeds that of the other countries, so Singapore's values are not too surprising.

The aggregate numbers are not terribly illuminating because they con-

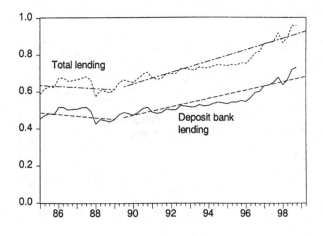

Korea

Philippines

Figure 6.4. (*continued*)

found many other factors that are not held constant in the calculations (ICORs are of the nature of total differentials). To get a less aggregate view of the situation, we also look at firm level data, drawn from two recent World Bank studies (Claessens, Djankov, and Lang, 1998; Pomerleano, 1998). The series we examine are the return on assets (ROA) and the pre-tax return on capital employed (ROCE) for nonfinancial firms in the seven East Asian countries. These data are depicted in Figure 6.7.

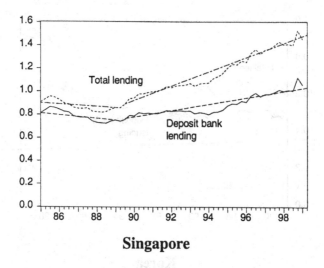

Singapore

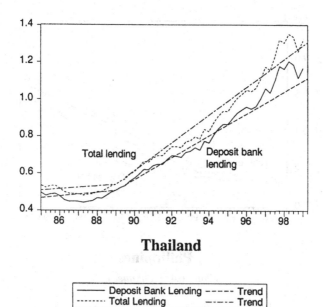

Thailand

| —— Deposit Bank Lending | ----- Trend |
| ------- Total Lending | ----- Trend |

Figure 6.4. (*continued*)

The median ROA is calculated on the basis of samples ranging from 66 corporations in Korea in 1988 to 3567 corporations in Malaysia in 1996. In the case of sales-weighted mean ROCE, panel data ranging from 16 firms in Taiwan to 211 in Malaysia are used.

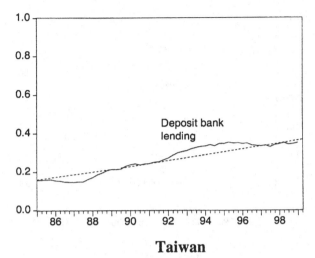

Taiwan

Figure 6.4. (*continued*)

Table 6.2. Return on Assets (in percent)

	Indonesia	Korea	Malaysia	Philippines	Singapore	Taiwan	Thailand
1988	NA	4.40	5.40	NA	4.90	NA	10.80
1989	NA	3.90	5.60	NA	4.50	NA	11.00
1990	**9.40**	**4.10**	**5.40**	NA	**4.20**	NA	**11.70**
1991	9.10	4.00	6.20	**7.10**	3.90	**5.10**	11.20
1992	8.60	3.90	6.00	6.40	5.20	6.20	10.20
1993	7.90	3.60	6.50	8.10	4.60	6.50	9.80
1994	7.40	3.40	6.30	8.50	4.50	6.80	9.30
1995	6.20	3.60	6.10	6.80	3.90	6.50	7.80
1996	**6.50**	**3.10**	**5.60**	**8.40**	**4.00**	**6.60**	**7.40**
Change	−2.90	−1.00	0.20	1.30	0.20	1.50	−4.30

Notes: "Change" is the change in ROA (in percentage points) between figures in **bold**.
Source: Claessens, Djankov, and Lang (1998) and authors' calculations.

The standard caveats apply. The financial institutions and environments differ substantially across the countries, as do the levels of capital per worker. Therefore, cross-country comparisons of the levels of return on assets and return on capital must be viewed with great caution. In contrast, the within-country time series patterns may be very informative with respect to the evolution of firm (and hence investment) profitability.

Indonesia and Thailand, two of the countries that encountered the most severe banking problems, experienced pronounced downward

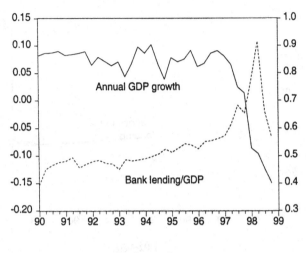

Indonesia

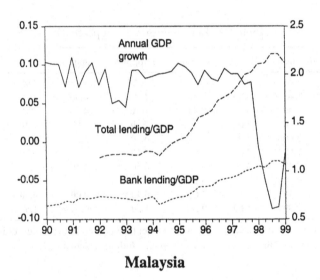

Malaysia

Figure 6.5. Annual GDP growth rate (ΔGDP, left scale) and deposit bank and total lending-to-GDP ratios (DB/GDP and TL/GDP, respectively, right scale).

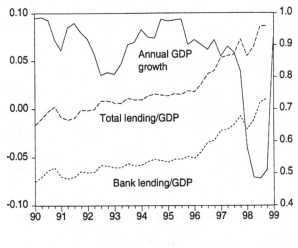

Korea

Philippines

Figure 6.5 *(continued)*

trends in both ROA and ROCE. As shown in Table 6.2, over the 1990s the ROA declined 2.9 percentage points in Indonesia and declined 4.3 percentage points in Thailand. In contrast, the countries that did not experience substantial banking problems also exhibited stable or rising

[11] The Korean ROCE actually rose up to 1995 (the last year for which data are available). However, these ROCE statistics are based on a particularly small panel of only 66 corporations; hence we rely more upon the longer ROA series for inference.

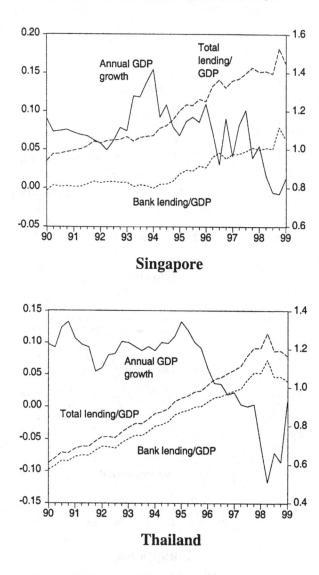

Singapore

Thailand

| —— ΔGDP | ...... DB/GDP | ---- TL/GDP |

Figure 6.5 (*continued*)

ROAs: Taiwan's ROA rose 1.5 percentage points, while Singapore's was essentially unchanged.

In the case of Korea the ROA only declined one percentage point over the 1990s.[11] However, what is unique about Korea is that its ROA

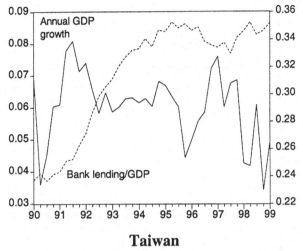

Taiwan

Figure 6.5 (*continued*)

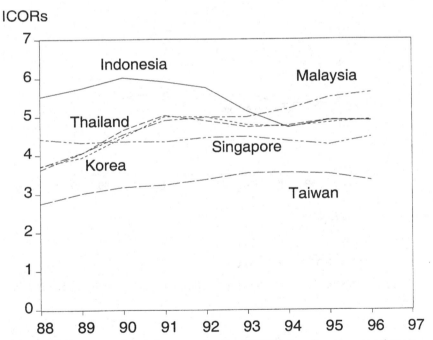

Figure 6.6. Incremental capital-to-output ratios (ICORs), based on two-year changes and detrended GDP data.

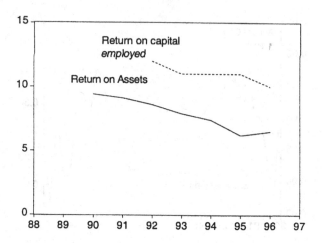

Indonesia

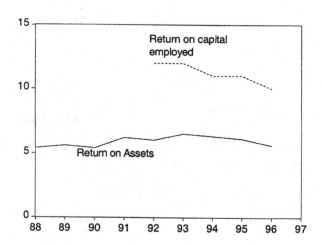

Malaysia

Figure 6.7. Return on assets (ROA) and return on capital employed (ROCE), in percent.

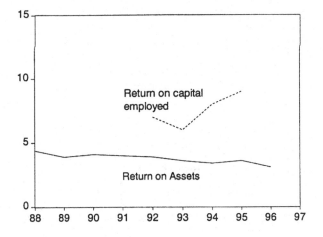

Korea

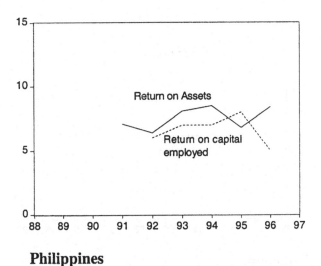

Philippines

Figure 6.7 (*continued*)

is uniformly low over the entire 1988–1996 period. The Korean ROA is even below the U.S. ROA. If we compare Korea to Taiwan, a country of comparable GDP per capita, we find that the gap between the two ROAs widens from about 1 percentage point to 3.5 percentage points over the 1990s. Hence, these statistics validate the anecdotal evidence, suggesting that Korean investment expenditures deteriorated markedly in the run-up to the crisis.

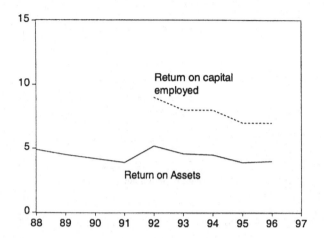

Singapore

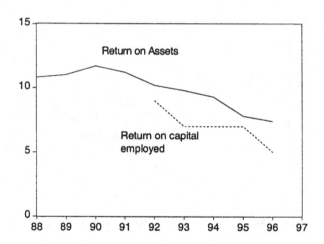

Thailand

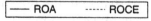

Figure 6.7 (*continued*)

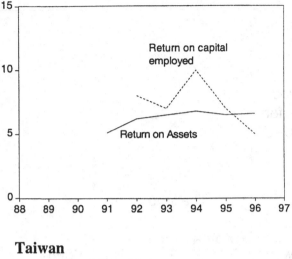

Taiwan

Figure 6.7 *(continued)*

6.3.1.4 Bank Capital

Little time-series evidence on bank capital is available on a consistent basis. The evidence does suggest that the amount of bank capital divided by assets (the capital-to-asset ratio, or CAR) is inversely related to the severity of financial crisis in East Asia. In Hong Kong, the Philippines, and Singapore, the capital-to-asset ratios were 15–20, 15–18, and 18–22 percent, respectively. In contrast, these ratios were 8–10, 6–10, and 6–10 for Indonesia, Korea, and Thailand, respectively.

These CAR data are based on accounting conventions; in principle, we need to have the ratio calculated after taking into account the assets that have gone to zero value. In this case, the CARs for the first group are slightly reduced, while those for the last three countries fall to −17, −10, and −11, respectively (Morgan Guaranty Trust Company, 1998, p. 6).

6.3.1.5 Contingent Liabilities

The model predicts that, in the presence of government guarantees, lending to GDP will rise; moreover, the size of contingent liabilities will also rise. These contingent liabilities represent the costs of bailing out the banking system. In theory, the share of nonperforming loans (NPLs) gives a measure of the proportion of total loans that will have to be assumed by the government. In several studies, the share of NPL multiplied by the loans-to-GDP ratio has been used as a measure of the cost

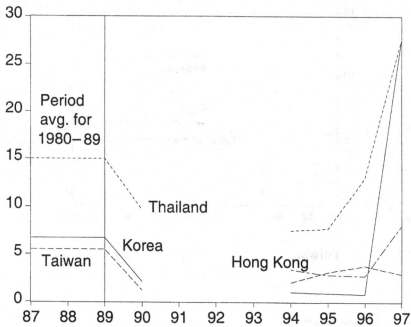

Figure 6.8. Nonperforming loan ratios (in percent). No data available for years 1991–1993. Averages for 1980–1989 demonstrate that nonperforming loan ratios in 1994 were low relative to historic benchmarks.

of bailing out the banking sector, expressed as a percentage of GDP (Corsetti, Pesenti, and Roubini, 1998a, 1998b; Burnside, Eichenbaum, and Rebelo, 1999). Therefore, we anticipate observing a rising NPL share as the economy approaches the onset of a financial crisis. However, as pointed out by many observers, there are numerous ways in which to circumvent these accounting and regulatory definitions of nonperforming bank assets.[12]

Consequently, as illustrated in Figure 6.8, NPL ratios provide only approximate estimates of the magnitudes of contingent liabilities, both over time and across countries. In the figure, the Thai NPL does rise in the year before the crisis. However, the Korean NPL ratio is both low and declining in the mid-1990s; the end-of-year 1996 value of NPL is 0.8 percent!

---

[12] See Morgan Guaranty Trust Company (1998, p. 8) for a table describing the accounting and prudential standards for Indonesia, Japan, Malaysia, Korea, and Thailand.

Table 6.3. Determinants of Capital Inflows and Lending in Noncrisis and
Crisis Countries

Dependent Variable	CI/GDP	CI/GDP	Δ(BC/GDP)	Δ(BC/GDP)	Δ(DC/GDP)	Δ(DC/GDP)
Constant	0.028***	0.008***	0.019***	0.033***	0.028***	0.047***
	(0.003)	(0.003)	(0.003)	(0.007)	(0.007)	(0.008)
CriCtr	0.036***	0.055***	0.019***	0.018*	0.016**	0.031***
	(0.003)	(0.003)	(0.007)	(0.011)	(0.008)	(0.011)
Adjusted R^2	0.11	0.15	0.01	−0.01	0.00	0.00
Number of observations	133	91	133	91	123	91
Sample	89:2–93:4	94:1–97:1	89:2–93:4	94:1–97:1	89:2–93:4	94:1–97:1

Notes:
Estimates from seemingly unrelated regression (SUR) estimation of the dependent variable (expressed in decimal form) on a constant and a dummy variable (with standard errors in parentheses). CI/GDP denotes capital inflow-to-GDP ratio. BC/GDP and DC/GDP denote total bank credit and deposit bank credit-to-GDP ratios, respectively. Δ is the (annualized) first difference operator. Countries included are Indonesia, Korea, Malaysia, Philippines, Singapore, Taiwan, and Thailand. The dummy variable CriCtr takes on a value of unity for Indonesia, Korea, Malaysia, and Thailand. * (**) [***] denotes significance at the 10 percent (5 percent) [1 percent] marginal significance level. Capital inflow-to-GDP ratios for Malaysia and Singapore are annual averages.

6.3.2 Statistical Tests

We report in column 1 of Table 6.3 the results of a regression of the capital flow-to-GDP ratio against a constant and a dummy variable over the 1989:2–1993:4 period. The dummy variable takes a value of unity for those East Asian countries that experienced a financial crisis in 1997 – Indonesia, Korea, Malaysia, and Thailand. [We define a country to have suffered a financial crisis if the implied postbailout capital-to-asset ratio is negative, according to Morgan Guaranty Trust Company (1998) estimates.]

The noncrisis countries averaged capital inflows of 2.8 percent of GDP over this period, while the crisis countries averaged 6.4 percent. In the two years leading up to the crisis, as inflows decreased to the noncrisis countries, those to the crisis countries remained roughly the same. In other words, the gap between inflow rates widened in the run-up to July 1997. These differences are statistically significant between the two groups, in both periods.

Lending ratios exhibit similar behavior. In both sets of countries, bank lending accelerates from the 1982:1–1993:4 period to the 1994:1–1997:1

Table 6.4. Determinants of Financial Crises

	(1)	(2)	(3)	(4)	(5)	(6)
ROA	−0.120	—	−0.407*	−0.193	−0.204***	−0.538**
	(0.097)		(0.249)	(0.126)	(0.103)	(0.243)
NPL_{t-4}		0.041	0.136	—	—	0.152*
		(0.057)	(0.088)			(0.086)
$\Delta(BC/GDP)_{t-4}$				18.033***	—	—
				(5.633)		
$\Delta(BC/GDP)_{t-8}$					10.075**	10.281**
					(4.809)	(4.951)
Adjusted R^2	0.02	0.32	0.09	0.23	0.10	0.17
Number of observations	96	70	70	96	90	67

Notes:
Dependent variable is a binary indicator of financial crisis defined as taking a value of 1 for 1997:3 in Indonesia, Korea, Malaysia, and Thailand, and a value of zero otherwise. Estimates from probit estimation of the dependent variable (Huber–White robust standard errors in parentheses). Sample period is 1995:1–1997:4. Countries included are Hong Kong, Indonesia, Korea, Malaysia, Philippines, Singapore, Taiwan, and Thailand. ROA is the return on assets from Claessens et al. (1998) interpolated. NPL is the nonperforming loan ratio (in percent) from BIS (1997) and other sources. $\Delta(BC/GDP)_{t-k}$ is the k quarter change in the bank lending-to-GDP ratio. * (**) [***] denotes significance at the 10 percent (5 percent) [1 percent] marginal significance level.

period. If total lending (deposit bank, other bank and nonfinancial institution lending) is considered, then the acceleration in lending is even more marked. While the growth rate in lending to GDP ratios rises from 2.8 percentage points per year to 4.7 percentage points per year in the noncrisis countries, it rises from 4.4 percentage points per year to 7.8 percentage points per year in the crisis countries.

Next we conduct an econometric investigation of the determinants of the timing and location of financial crises. We relate the onset of financial crises in the East Asian countries to corporate returns on assets (ROA) in percentages, the lagged nonperforming loan (NPL) ratios (in percentages) and changes in the bank lending-to-GDP ratios (in decimal form), over the 1995–1997 period (estimating it over a period spanning 1998 only strengthens the results, since the ROA and NPL indicators move very strongly in the expected direction with the continuation of the crisis). The results of various specifications are reported in Table 6.4; The dependent variable is a binary indicator defined as taking a value of zero, except for 1997:3 – in Indonesia, Korea, Malaysia, and Thailand – when it is unity; the estimation technique is probit.

If project quality declines, one should expect that bank liabilities will be increasing relative to assets, and the banks will find the bankruptcy option more and more attractive. A simple regression involving only ROA yields the correct sign on the variable, but not any statistical significance. Similarly, a regression on only NPL lagged a year also yields correctly signed but statistically insignificant coefficients. Only when the two variables are included does one obtain a significant estimate for ROA.

In many recent studies, the rate of growth of bank lending has been found to be an important determinant of a currency crisis (Kaminsky and Reinhart, 1999; Corsetti, Pesenti, and Roubini, 1998a; Chinn, Dooley, and Shrestha, 1999). We replace NPL with the change in the bank lending-to-GDP ratio to see if it proxies for the share of nonperforming loans. This variable has the anticipated (positive) sign when entered contemporaneously into the regression (column 4) or lagged two years (column 5). However, it appears that NPL has independent informational content above what is provided by lagged lending growth, as shown in column 6. In this specification, lower ROA significantly increases the probability of a financial crisis, as does a higher NPL ratio. Lagged bank lending growth has an independent effect above and beyond the NPL variable. This effect is consistent with the model's implication that increasing lending-to-GDP ratios will occur in economies where the public sector guarantees make bankruptcy an increasingly attractive option.

6.3.3 Postcrisis Events

A consequence of financial intermediation with agency is that the model implies that output falls in the wake of the financial crisis. This is a prediction shared by many other models, so it does not differentiate this view of crises from others. The model also predicts that the output growth rate will be lower after the crisis (during recovery) than before. This pattern is evident in the data. Currency crises in our equilibrium under fixed exchange rates arise because the sudden increase in public sector budget deficit is monetized in the wake of a financial crisis, as the government realizes the contingent obligations associated with the bank bailout. Figure 6.9 shows that this pattern of results is more or less evident in the data. The Korean M2-to-GDP ratio grows rapidly in the second and third quarters of 1998; so too does the Thai ratio. In both cases, some of this growth is due to the contraction in the economies. However, even if money stocks alone were examined, a similar pattern would emerge. In contrast, the Taiwanese M2-to-GDP ratio remains fairly constant.

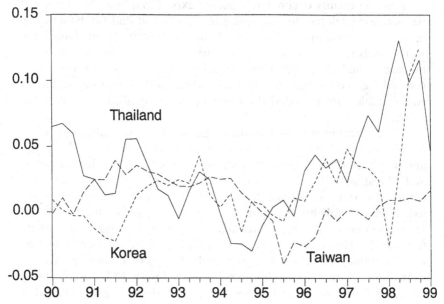

Figure 6.9. Annual growth rates of the money supply to GDP ratios (M2/GDP) for Thailand, Korea, and Taiwan.

6.4 CONCLUSION

The theoretical model generates the endogenous accumulation of foreign debt by domestic financial sectors that ultimately becomes unsustainable, leading to a banking crisis. During this process, the domestic output growth is high while foreign debt is rising in proportion to GDP. Capital inflows rise with GDP, but allocation of these resources by the banking sector becomes progressively more concentrated and risky. The banking crises portrayed by this simple agency model of financial intermediation are solvency crises and are inevitable under the policies assumed. The dynamics of twin crises in this approach are generated by anticipation of government guarantees of foreign loans or bailouts of the domestic banking industry (or both). It is also essential that these guarantees are offered, explicitly or implicitly, to the domestic financial sector without regulation of lending behavior or monitoring of market values of outstanding bank loans. The link between currency and banking crises is created by government guarantees of foreign currency debts in the event that the government abandons a pegged exchange rate. The timing of crises is indeterminate in our model (this is not a novel feature), allowing a role for contagion or panics to explain the timing or coincidence of crises. However, crises in this approach are due to fundamentals and are not due to financial panics that bring on liquidity crises.

The empirical analysis provides support for the implications of the model, although formal hypothesis testing was not possible. In particular, countries that underwent a crisis appear to experience higher rates of international capital inflows and domestic bank intermediation. External debt has played a key role in crises in countries that have been experiencing historically high rates of economic growth before the crisis. An important feature of this model is that domestic output and investment growth is high before the crisis. Countries that undergo crises tend to experience declining aggregate investment productivites before the crisis. Postcrisis events are consistent with the role of contingent government liabilities for generating financial crises.

APPENDIX

Appendix 6A. Data Appendix

Most of the data for Chapter 6 are from IMF, *International Financial Statistics*, March 1999 CD-ROM, except for data for Taiwan, Bank of China website.

Q	$= \log(X*CPI/CPIUS)$
INTLQ	$= INTLQ\backslash\$ / XR$
INTLQ\$	Foreign exchange reserves, IFS line 1l.d.
X	Exchange rates, IFS line ae, in U.S. dollars/national currency unit, monthly, end of period.
XR	Exchange rates, IFS line rf, in U.S. dollars/national currency unit, monthly, end of period.
M1	Narrow money, IFS line 34.
M2	Broad money, M1 plus quasi-money (IFS line 35).
BC	Domestic credit extended to private sector by deposit banks, IFS line 32d.
DC	Domestic credit extended to private sector by all banks and/or nonbank financial institutions. For Malaysia, Philippines, and Thailand, DC is the sum of IFS lines 32d and 42d. For Japan, Korea, and Singapore, DC is sum of 32d, 42d, and other categories of credit extended to nonfinancial private sector.
CPI	Consumer price index, IFS line 64, 1990 = 100.
PPI	Producer price index, IFS line 63, 1990 = 100.
CA$	Current account, IFS line 78ald, quarterly rates in U.S. dollars.

CF$ Financial account, IFS line 78bjd, quarterly rates in U.S. dollars.

ERR$ Net errors and omissions, IFS line 78cad, quarterly rates in U.S. dollars.

I Interest rates are short-term, interbank interest rates, IFS line 60b, in decimal form (average of daily rates). Data for Hong Kong is from J.P. Morgan up until 1993:4. The Taiwanese 3-month interest rate is from the Federal Reserve Board.

IL Bank lending rates, from IFS line 60p.

GDP Income is real GDP, IFS line 99b.r, in 1990 national currency units. The GDP series are seasonally adjusted over the 1975Q1–1999Q1 periods, using the X-11 seasonal adjustment additive procedure (except for Japan, in which case the data are adjusted by Japanese statistical agencies). Taiwanese GDP is originally in 1991 New Taiwan dollars, but is rebased to 1990 units. Indonesian data are from the IMF's Indonesia country desk (provided by Ilan Goldfajn). Thai GDP is estimated using the annual relationship between GDP, exports, imports, the real exchange rate and time, and quarterly data on these variables to generate a quarterly GDP series. For post-1992 data, GDP data are actual quarterly GDP obtained from the Bank of Thailand website, in 1988 baht, rescaled to 1990 baht.

ICOR $= (INV_t + INV_{t-1})/(GDP_t - GDP_{t-2})$, where INV is IFS line 93e and GDP is IFS line 99b.r (annual data). (Indonesia INV is IFS line 93.)

ICORHP2 $= (INV_t + INV_{t-1})/(GDPHP_t - GDPHP_{t-2})$, where HP superscript denotes Hodrik–Prescott filtering over 1970–1997 period, using the default smoothing parameter for annual data.

ROA Returns to assets, annual data from Claessens, Djankov, and Lang (1998), Table 1. In regressions using quarterly data, annual ROAs are interpolated using a moving average.

OPM Operating margin, annual data from Claessens, Djankov, and Lang (1998), Table 3.

ROCE Return on capital employed, annual data from Pomerleano (1998), Table 10.

NPL Nonperforming loan ratios from Bank for International Settlements (1997), Table VI.5. Data for 1997 from Morgan Guaranty Trust Company (1998) *Asian Financial Markets*, 1998Q2, p. 6, except for Taiwan, from Morgan Guaranty Trust Company (1999) *Asian Financial Markets*, 1999Q1,

p. 39; 1996 observation for Singapore and Thailand from Jardine Fleming, as reported in Corsetti, Pesenti, and Roubini (1998b), Table 21. In regressions using quarterly data, annual NPLs are arithmetically interpolated by assuming that the reported NPLs apply to loan portfolios at year-end. For 1997, end-of-1996 values are assumed for 1997:1–1997:2.

REFERENCES

Bank for International Settlements (1997). Annual Report. Basel, Switzerland: Bank for International Settlements.

Bernanke, Benjamin and Mark Gertler (1990). "Financial Fragility and Economic Performance," *Quarterly Journal of Economics* **105**(February):87–114.

———(1989). "Agency Costs, Net Worth and Business Fluctuations," *American Economic Review* **79**(March):14–31.

Burnside, Craig, Martin Eichenbaum, and Sergio Rebelo (1999). "Hedging and Financial Fragility in Fixed Exchange Rate Regimes." NBER Working Paper No. 7143, May. Cambridge, MA.

Caballero, Ricardo and Arvind Krishnamurthy (1998). "Emerging Markets Crises: An Assets Markets Perspective." Mimeo, MIT.

Calvo, Guillermo (1998a). "Balance of Payments Crises in Emerging Markets: Large Capital Inflows and Sovereign Governments." Paper presented at NBER Conference on Currency Crises, Cambridge, MA, February.

———(1998b). "Varieties of Capital-Market Crises." In Guillermo Calvo and Mervyn King, eds., *The Debt Burden and its Consequences for Monetary Policy.* London: Macmillan, pp. 181–202.

Chang, Roberto and Andrés Velasco (1999). "Liquidity Crises in Emerging Markets: Theory and Policy." NBER Working Paper No. 7272. Cambridge, MA.

Chinn, Menzie D., Michael P. Dooley, and Sona Shrestha (1999). "Latin America and East Asia in the Context of an Insurance Model of Currency Crises," *Journal of International Money and Finance* **18**:659–681.

Claessens, Stijn, Simeon Djankov, and Larry Lang (1998). "East Asian Corporates: Growth, Financing and Risks over the Last Decade." World Bank Policy Research Working Paper No. 2017. Washington, D.C.: World Bank.

Corsetti, Giancarlo, Paolo Pesenti, and Nouriel Roubini (1998a). "Paper Tigers? A Preliminary Assessment of the Asian Crisis." NBER Working Paper No. 6783. Cambridge, MA.

———(1998b). "What Caused the Asian Currency and Financial Crisis? Part I: A Macroeconomic Overview." NBER Working Paper No. 6833. Cambridge, MA.

———(1998c). "What Caused the Asian Currency and Financial Crisis? Part II: Theory and Policy Responses." NBER Working Paper No. 6834. Cambridge, MA.

Diamond, Douglas (1984). "Financial Intermediation and Delegated Monitoring," *Review of Economic Studies* **51**:393–414.

Diamond, Douglas and Phillip Dybvig (1983). "Bank Runs, Deposit Insurance and Liquidity," *Journal of Political Economy* **91**(June):401–419.

Dooley, Michael P. (2000). "A Model of Crises in Emerging Markets," *Economic Journal* **110**(460):256–272.

Edwards, Sebastian and Carlos Vegh (1997). "Banks and Macroeconomic Disturbances under Predetermined Exchange Rates," *Journal of Macroeconomics* **40**:239–278.

Eichengreen, Barry and Andrew Rose (1998). "Staying Afloat when the Wind Shifts: External Factors and Emerging-Market Banking Crises." NBER Working Paper No. 6370. Cambridge, MA.

Flood, Robert and Peter Garber (1984). "Collapsing Exchange Rate Regimes: Some Linear Examples," *Journal of International Economics* **17**(August):1–13.

Frankel, Jeffrey and Andrew Rose (1996). "Currency Crashes in Emerging Markets: An Empirical Treatment," *Journal of International Economics* **41**:351–368.

Furman, Jason and Joseph Stiglitz (1998). "Economic Crises: Evidence and Insights from East Asia," *Brookings Papers on Economic Activity*, No. 2:1–115.

Glick, Reuven and Michael Hutchison (Chapter 2, this volume). "Banking and Currency Crises: How Common Are Twins?"

Goldfajn, Ilan and Rodrigo Valdes (1997). "Capital Flows and the Twin Crises: The Role of Liquidity." IMF Working Paper No. 97/87. Washington, D.C.

Hutchison, Michael and Kathleen McDill (1998). "Determinants, Costs and Duration of Banking Sector Distress: The Japanese Experience in International Comparison." Paper presented at the NBER-TCER Japan Project Meeting, Tokyo, October.

Kaminsky, Graciela and Carmen Reinhart (1998). "Currency and Banking Crises: The Early Warnings of Distress." International Finance Discussion Paper No. 629. Washington, D.C.: Board of Governors of the Federal Reserve System.

———(1999). "The Twin Crises: The Causes of Banking and Balance-of-Payments Problems," *American Economic Review* **89**(June):473–500.

Kiyotaki, Nobuhiro and John Moore (1997). "Credit Cycles," *Journal of Political Economy* **105**:211–248.

Krugman, Paul (1979). "A Model of Balance-of-Payments Crises," *Journal of Money Credit and Banking* **11**(August):311–325.

———(1998). "Bubble, Boom, Crash: Theoretical Notes on Asia's Crisis." Mimeo, MIT.

Kumhof, Michael (1998). "Balance of Payments Crises: The Role of Short-Term Debt." Mimeo, Stanford University.

McKinnon, Ronald and Huw Pill (1999). "Credible Liberalizations and International Capital Flows: The Overborrowing Syndrome." In Ito, T. and A.O. Krueger, eds., *Financial Deregulation and Integration in East Asia*. Chicago: University of Chicago Press.

Miller, Marcus and Joseph Stiglitz (1999). "Bankruptcy Protection against Macroeconomics Shocks: The Case for a 'Super Chapter 11.'" Mimeo, Centre for the Study of Globalisation and Regionalisation, University of Warwick.

Mishkin, Frederic (1996). "Understanding Financial Crises: A Developing Country Perspective." In Michael Bruno and Boris Pleskovic, eds., *Annual World Bank Conference on Development Economics, 1996.* Washington, D.C.: World Bank, pp. 29–62.

Moreno, Ramon (1996). "Intervention, Sterilization, and Monetary Control in Korea and Taiwan," Federal Reserve Bank of San Francisco *Economic Review* **1996**(3):23–33.

———(1999). "Depreciation and Recessions in East Asia," Federal Reserve Bank of San Francisco *Economic Review*, No. 3:27–40.

Morgan Guaranty Trust Company (1998). *Asian Financial Markets*, 2nd quarter, New York: J.P. Morgan.

———(1999). *Asian Financial Markets*, 1st quarter, New York: J.P. Morgan.

Obstfeld, Maurice (1998). "The Global Capital Market: Benefactor or Menace?" *Journal of Economic Perspectives* **12**:9–30.

Pomerleano, M. (1998). "The East Asian Crisis and Corporate Finances: The Untold Micro Story." World Bank Policy Research Working Paper No. 1990. Washington, D.C.: World Bank.

Sachs, Jeffrey, Aaron Tornell, and Andrés Velasco (1996). "Financial Crises in Emerging Markets: The Lessons from 1995," *Brookings Papers on Economic Activity*, No. 2:147–215.

Spiegel, Mark M. (1995). "Sterilization of Capital Inflows through the Banking Sector: Evidence from Asia." Federal Reserve Bank of San Francisco *Economic Review*, No. 3:11–34.

Stiglitz, Joseph and Andrew Weiss (1981). "Credit Rationing in Markets with Imperfect Information," *American Economic Review* **71**:393–410.

Discussion

International Capital Inflows, Domestic Financial Intermediation, and Financial Crises under Imperfect Information

Roberto Chang

While the recent literature on financial crises in emerging markets is enormous, two clearly distinct positions have emerged. The first one, which I have called the bad policy view elsewhere (Chang, 1999), holds that observed crises have been the inevitable consequence of misguided government policies. In particular, according to this view, implicit or explicit government guarantees to private borrowing from abroad induced private agents to borrow too much and/or to take too much risk. The accumulation of hidden liabilities resulting from this process led, ultimately, to the collapse of the policy regime and to economic crisis (see McKinnon and Pill, 1996; Dooley, 2000; and Krugman, 1998).

An alternative view stresses not policy mistakes but financial panics. Proponents of this view argue that the chief force behind recent crises was a sudden loss of confidence by holders of short-term liabilities of developing countries. Such a confidence loss resulted in the bankruptcy of those financial systems whose potential short-term liabilities in hard currency exceeded the liquidation value of their assets, a condition that Velasco and I have called *international illiquidity*. [Chang and Velasco (1999a); see also Cole and Kehoe (1996) and Radelet and Sachs (1998)]. Notably, this view stresses that crises may have occurred in countries that were illiquid but essentially solvent.

Given this context, it is natural to start the study of Menzie Chinn and Ken Kletzer's essay by assigning it to one of the two camps just described. To some extent, the essay is an attempt to integrate the bad policy and the financial panic views. However, I found it fruitful to think of the essay as providing ammunition to the bad policy camp. This is because the specification of government policy is, as will be clear shortly, the key aspect of the analysis.

The opinions expressed here are mine and not necessarily those of the Federal Reserve Bank of Atlanta or the Federal Reserve System. In particular, any errors are solely mine.

Given its authors' previous accomplishments, I approached the essay wondering if it could successfully address some of my concerns about the bad policy view. This was because, while that view is theoretically plausible, I believe that its proponents have to deal with a number of serious issues. First, its key hypothesis, the existence of inappropriate government guarantees to private borrowing, is not sufficient by itself to explain a *crisis*, as opposed to a *growth slowdown*. While one should expect such guarantees to result in less socially profitable investment and, consequently, in slower growth, it does not follow that one should observe those dramatic collapses of economic activity and financial intermediation that we associate with the word "crisis." To remedy this shortcoming, models of bad policy rely on auxiliary assumptions, such as the existence of an exogenous limit to implicit government accumulated losses. But these auxiliary assumptions, which then become crucial to the argument, are often unnatural and rarely justified in a convincing manner.

To the extent that the bad policy view is based on strong assumptions about government policy, a second issue emerges: Why do governments pursue those bad policies? In particular, many models of bad policy assume that, in a crisis, domestic governments end up bailing out foreign creditors at a substantial cost for the domestic population. I find that description of policy hard to defend, unless one is willing to attach some explanation of what incentives and constraints might lead a government to act in such a way. In addition, such an explanation is also needed if one is to identify the policy implications of the bad policy view.

A third problem with the bad policy view is that compelling evidence in its favor is yet to be found. Many papers have been content with observing that crises occurred in countries whose governments did in fact guarantee private borrowing. But, is there any government that does not provide such guarantees? And, was the existence of guarantees sufficient for a crisis to occur? The answer to both questions is probably negative, which means that guarantees to private borrowing do not help in discriminating between countries that had crises and those that did not.[1] The corollary is that advocates of the bad policy view need to come up with stronger empirical, perhaps more direct, evidence in order not to lose the intellectual debate.

It turns out that Chinn and Kletzer's essay provides some, but not complete, answers to the challenges just posed. Let me turn to justifying this assertion in some detail, which will hopefully be instructive.

---

[1] In contrast, measures of international illiquidity have been much more successful in predicting which countries had crises. See Radelet and Sachs (1998).

The theoretical framework proposed by Chinn and Kletzer focuses on a small open economy with some special features. Domestic banks have an informational advantage over foreign lenders in providing credit to domestic agents. As a consequence, domestic banks borrow from abroad to finance risky domestic investments, and the domestic financial system plays a crucial role.

As I emphasized at the beginning, Chinn and Kletzer follow the bad policy camp in assuming that the government of the economy under analysis guarantees foreign loans. However, they depart from most other analyses in an interesting way: Guarantees are assumed to cover only aggregate failures, not individual cases. This is a very realistic departure. It may be credible for a government not to bail out creditors in the case of an isolated bank run, but the political pressure for a bailout in the case of a generalized financial panic may be impossible to resist. In this regard, I find this way of modeling bad policy more appealing than what was described in previous papers.[2]

Chinn and Kletzer argue that these assumptions imply several consequences that are consistent with actual crises. Some are straightforward. There is too much foreign borrowing; this is an obvious consequence of the existence of government guarantees. Capital inflows are channeled through domestic banks, which follows from the assumed informational asymmetries.

In my view, the most novel and interesting implication is that individual foreign creditors have an incentive to keep lending to banks in trouble and wait (or hope) for everyone else to be in the same boat. This is because the government will compensate foreign lenders only when a sufficient number of them face default; as long as this is not the case, each individual lender's return to roll over his loans is abnormally high because of the probability of an aggregate failure in the future. As a consequence, a generalized crisis occurs after a period of progressive deterioration in bank portfolios, at which point it becomes apparent that foreign lenders should have exited much earlier.

Hence, the essay is partly successful in responding to my theoretical concerns about the bad policy view. In particular, it does have the potential to explain how a growth slowdown may become a crisis. Clearly, the key assumption is that government bailouts happen only in response to aggregate failures, which implies that bankruptcies will tend to happen at the same time. Hence that assumption is not only realistic but consequential and deserves closer study.

On the other hand, it is still hard to see why the government would be willing to bail out foreigners at the expense of its domestic popula-

---

[2] The same assumption has been exploited recently by Schneider and Tornell (1999).

tion. The idea that political pressure may force the government to intervene in a crisis is appealing, but why would that intervention help only foreigners? Finding some kind of justification for these modeling choices, while not impossible, is not a trivial task and it is crucial to develop the policy implications of the theory.

At this point, it must be mentioned that the version of the essay that I had access to did not include a fully worked out formal model. Hence I could not check the mathematical validity of Chinn and Kletzer's theoretical claims. I mention this issue to warn the reader, and also because I cannot be convinced of the truth of all of the claims until I see their proofs. In particular, the essay argues that there is a unique equilibrium in their theory. But there is a lot of complementarity in individual decisions, so I suspect that multiple equilibria must emerge. In particular, I suspect that there are (a) equilibria where foreigners lend to domestic banks because they correctly expect repayment and (b) equilibria in which they refuse to lend because each individual lender expects a crisis, which itself is brought about by the lack of lending.

Finally, and perhaps due to all these considerations, Chinn and Kletzer do not obtain clear policy lessons from their theory. This is obviously a considerable shortcoming, and I would encourage them to spend some time thinking about policy. This may be useful, I believe, not only for practical purposes but also to understand better the theory.

Let me turn to the empirical work in the analysis. Chinn and Kletzer do present convincing evidence that crises countries experienced rising capital inflows-to-GDP ratios, and that capital inflows were channeled mostly via domestic financial institutions. Along these dimensions, their theory is consistent with the data. It must be noted, though, that these pieces of evidence are only mildly supportive of their arguments, because they are also consistent with other, quite different theories.[3]

Other aspects of the evidence are not as sanguine to Chinn and Kletzer's views. The evidence on diminishing investment quality (Figure 6.7) is inconclusive: The return on capital seems to have indeed fallen before the crisis in some countries, but increased in others. I should reemphasize that, in order to make a convincing case that government policy did induce overinvestment and too much risk taking, one should look at the data not only from countries that experienced crises but also from those that did *not* succumb to crises. Data for some of the latter may also show diminishing investment quality. If that were the case, which I suspect it is, this kind of evidence would be of little use.

[3] For a specific example, see the section on financial liberalization in Chang and Velasco (1999b).

I was not convinced, either, that the empirical results establish that measures of return on assets and nonperforming loan ratios are good predictors of crises. The basis for the argument is a regression analysis summarized in Table 6.4. One can see that the strongest predictor of crises is the increase in the bank lending-to-GDP ratio; see the last three columns of the table. The ROA and NPL ratios are not significant unless such increases are lagged two years. In that case, however, the overall fit of the regression, as measured by the adjusted R-squared, deteriorates. Given these problems, one must be uncomfortable with the claim that ROA and NPL are important determinants of crises.

It is time to summarize. I believe that Chinn and Kletzer have written a useful essay, one that responds to some of my concerns about the bad policy view of crises. In particular, they have convinced me that modeling how a growth slowdown may become a crisis may be easier than I first thought. But a lot remains to be done, both on the theory and the empirical front. After studying the essay, my priors about the most fruitful ways to approach crises have changed in favor of the bad policy view, but not by a lot.

REFERENCES

Chang, Roberto (1999). "Understanding Recent Crises in Emerging Markets," *Federal Reserve Bank of Atlanta Economic Review* (second quarter):6–17.

Chang, Roberto and Andrés Velasco (1999a). "Liquidity Crises in Emerging Markets: Theory and Policy." In B. Bernanke and J. Rotemberg, eds., *NBER Macroeconomic Annual 1999.* Cambridge, MA: MIT Press.

———(1999b). "A Model of Liquidity Crises in Emerging Markets." Mimeo, Federal Reserve Bank of Atlanta.

Cole, Harold L. and Timothy J. Kehoe (1996). "A Self Fulfilling Model of Mexico's 1994–95 Debt Crisis," *Journal of International Economics* **41**(3–4):309–330.

Dooley, Michael (2000). "A Model of Crises in Emerging Markets," *Economic Journal* **110**:256–272.

Krugman, Paul (1998). "What Happened to Asia?" Mimeo, MIT.

McKinnon, Ronald and Huw Pill (1996). "Credible Liberalizations and International Capital Flows: The Overborrowing Syndrome." In T. Ito and A. Krueger, eds., *Financial Deregulation and Integration in East Asia.* Chicago: University of Chicago Press.

Radelet, Steven and Jeffrey D. Sachs (1998). "The East Asian Financial Crisis: Diagnosis, Remedies, Prospects," *Brookings Papers on Economic Activity*, No. 1:1–74.

Schneider, Martin and Aaron Tornell (1999). "Lending Booms and Speculative Crises." Mimeo, Harvard University.

7

Private Inflows when Crises Are Anticipated:

A Case Study of Korea

Michael P. Dooley and Inseok Shin

7.1 INTRODUCTION

The economic costs of recent financial crises in emerging markets have been enormous. The predictable response has been calls to reform the system, and there is no shortage of official and academic suggestions as to how architecture of the international monetary system could be improved. The problem with evaluating these proposals is that they are based on very different views about why crises have become so frequent and severe in recent years.

We do not think this very basic question can be answered by examining economic developments in the months or days just before and after a crisis occurs. The unfortunate fact is that regardless of the cause of a crisis, its effects on asset values and economic activity are likely to be observationally equivalent. Fischer (1999) makes the point that a poorly managed liquidity crisis will generate permanent declines in the asset values that are identical to losses that are generated by distorted investment decisions. In our opinion, this seems to be correct and is a reasonable basis for government intervention once a crisis has occurred. But in considering how to improve the international monetary system's performance, it is crucial to know whether recent crises were caused by distorted private credit markets or by runs on otherwise healthy markets. If distortions were the fundamental problem, it would be prudent to reduce the scale of IMF assistance packages and focus on capital controls and prudential regulation in developing countries. If runs were fundamental, it would be prudent to expand the scale and flexibility of fund programs and to focus on debt management policies in developing countries.

The purpose of this chapter is to take a careful look at the $120 billion private capital inflow to Korea from 1992 through the crisis in mid-1997. We will interpret this data within the analytical framework developed in

Dooley (2000). The basic idea of the insurance model is that the micro-economics of financial intermediation and the government's role in financial intermediation are the primary sources of crises. Crises in this framework are not related to changes in private expectations or to inconsistencies in macro regimes. Instead, the policy inconsistency arises from the desire of governments to accumulate financial assets in order to smooth national consumption and the desire to insure the domestic financial system.

The insurance model is particularly appealing when placed in the context of the Korean crisis. In Korea, banks were the major intermediaries of capital inflows before the crisis and, indeed, the foreign creditors' run from Korean banks triggered the crisis in November 1997 (see Shin, 1998). Thus, in the following pages we will attempt to interpret the recent crisis in Korea in the context of this model. The analysis suggests that financial liberalization in Korea was the fundamental factor behind the crisis. Liberalization reduced the franchise value of the banking system and exposed very weak balance sheets to competitive pressures that promoted risk-seeking by banks. The second problem was the failure to regulate the consolidated balance sheet of commercial banks. The failure to control foreign branches of Korean banks created an ideal vehicle for exploiting insurance. The important role played by interbank flows suggests that foreign banks expected to have preferred creditor status when the crisis occurred. The fact that foreign banks were able to withdraw about $30 billion from Korean banks in 1998 suggests that this expectation was well-founded.

The chapter is structured as follows. In Section 7.2 we provide background information on capital flows in the 1990s up to and during the crisis. In Section 7.3 we discuss three analytic frameworks for crises and identify the insurance model as the most suitable alternative for the Korean case. In Section 7.4 we analyze how actual developments in Korea fit the general case. Then, in Section 7.5 we raise and discuss an interesting question revealed by the Korean crisis: whether it was just coincidence that capital inflows and a crisis followed liberalization. Lessons will be drawn to conclude the chapter.

7.2 NATURE OF THE KOREAN CRISIS: BANK RUN PRECEDED BY PRIVATE CAPITAL INFLOWS

7.2.1 Capital Inflows to Korea in the 1990s

7.2.1.1 Background: Policy Stance and Capital Flows in the 1980s

Prior to the 1990s, Korea's policies on capital account liberalization were pursued in a passive manner and largely in reaction to the developments in the external current account (Figure 7.1). The exchange rate was rigidly managed and not allowed to respond to capital flows. As a result, the burden of financing current account deficits (surplus) was assigned to direct quantitative controls over flows. For example, in the first half of the 1980s when the current account showed chronic deficits, various liberalization measures were taken to induce capital inflows. In particular, the Korean government guided domestic banks to borrow from abroad. As a result, Korea saw significant net capital inflows, most of which consisted of bank borrowings (Figure 7.2).

In the late 1980s, the policy stance toward capital flows changed dramatically as the current account balance began to show a large surplus. Instead of allowing the domestic currency to appreciate, the government resorted to quantitative capital controls in an effort to manage the overall external balance. External borrowing by domestic firms, with the exception of public enterprises, was prohibited. The overseas issuance of bonds and depository receipts by residents was also restricted. In addition, banks were advised to reduce their exposure to external debt.

7.2.1.2 Capital Account Liberalization in the 1990s

In the early 1990s, the benefits of capital account liberalization were considered in their own right for the first time. Market reform and globalization became key words in the policy agenda. In fact, the Y. S. Kim administration declared "se-gye-wha" (globalization) as the top policy priority. Roughly balanced current accounts during the years were thought to be favorable conditions for pursuing liberalization.

Given the changed policy environment, the government began capital account liberalization. Overseas issuance by domestic firms of foreign-currency-denominated bonds was deregulated in 1991. In January 1992 the Korean stock market was opened to foreign investors for the first time. Commercial loans by domestic firms, which had been prohibited since 1986, were allowed in 1995.

However, for portfolio flows the Korean government remained cautious and preferred gradual liberalization. Thus, both explicit quantity restrictions and discretionary controls remained prevalent. For stock investment, a 10 percent aggregate ceiling on the foreign ownership of listed firms was imposed. This ceiling continued to exist until the crisis of 1997, although it was relaxed to 12 percent in December 1994 and further to 15 percent in July 1995. Regarding commercial loans by firms, restrictions on the uses of funds existed and government approval was required. Likewise, the overseas issuance by domestic firms of foreign-currency denominated bonds was subject to discretionary quantity control.

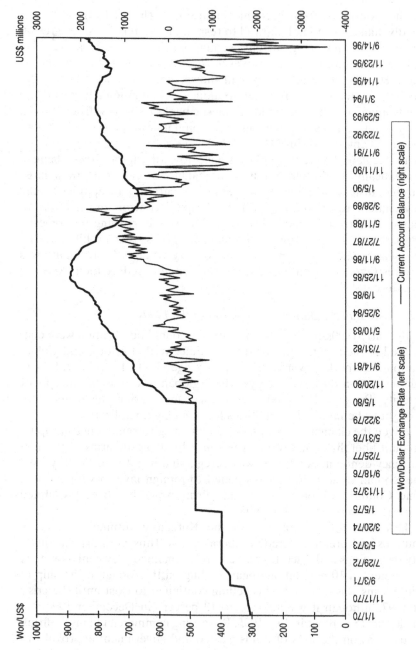

Figure 7.1. Won/dollar exchange rate and Korean current account balance. (*Source:* Bank of Korea on-line service.)

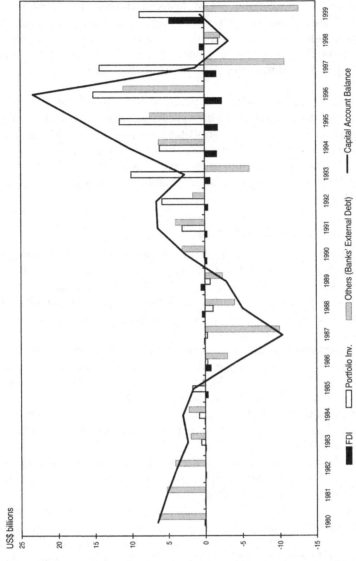

US$ billions

Figure 7.2. Trends and composition of net capital inflows to Korea. (*Source:* Bank of Korea on-line service.)

■ FDI   ☐ Portfolio Inv.   ▨ Others (Banks' External Debt)   — Capital Account Balance

Thus, most capital flows led by firms or through the stock market were not free from explicit or implicit quantitative controls. The only exception was trade-related short-term financing. Various restrictions on deferred import payments and the receipt of advance payments for exports were lifted step by step throughout the 1990s.[1]

In contrast, the government allowed banks to enjoy relatively greater freedom in borrowing from foreign creditors. No explicit quantity regulations existed on long-term or short-term borrowings of banks in foreign currencies. Though the government exerted discretionary control over banks, it has not been binding or restrictive (at least) since the mid-1990s judging from the rapid increase in capital inflows channeled through banks.

7.2.1.3 Capital Inflows in the 1990s

Korea began experiencing net capital inflows in 1990. The magnitude of inflows remained small in the first four years at 1.2 percent of GDP on average. But for the three years from 1994 to 1996, the size of inflows more than doubled to 3.5 percent of GDP on average (Figure 7.2). The increased capital inflows for these three years displayed two salient features.

First, debt instruments were the dominant vehicle for capital transactions. Debt instruments accounted for the bulk of total foreign portfolio investment (Figures 7.2 and 7.3). Stock investment by foreigners explains only a limited portion of the capital inflows, which seems to be a reflection of the quantity restrictions mentioned above. Consequently, the surge in net capital inflows was tantamount to a sharp increase in Korea's external debt (Figure 7.4).

Second, the major portion of the increase in external debt involved the financial sector, particularly banks (Table 7.1). Out of the total increase in external debt during the 1994–1996 period, the financial sector explains about 70 percent. The remaining 30 percent reflects growth of the corporate sector's external debt related to trade financing. In addition, the total foreign currency liabilities of banks were much larger than their external debt. As part of liberalization measures, banks were allowed to open and expand operations of overseas branches. Banks exploited this opportunity aggressively so that the value of foreign currency liabilities of overseas branches was comparable to the external debt of domestic branches (Table 7.2).

---

[1] Shin (1998) provides detailed liberalization measures in this area.

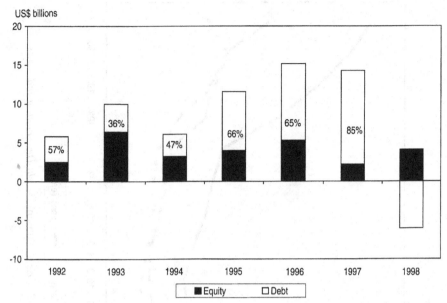

Figure 7.3. Composition of portfolio investment in Korea. (*Source*: Bank of Korea, *Economic Statistics Yearbook.*)

Table 7.1. Korean External Debt by Sector (in US$ billion)

	1992	1993	1994	1995	1996	1997
Public sector	5.6	3.8	3.6	3.0	2.4	22.3
Long term	5.6	3.8	3.6	3.0	2.4	22.3
Short term	0.0	0.0	0.0	0.0	0.0	0.0
Corporate sector	13.7	15.6	20.0	26.1	35.6	46.2
Long term	6.5	7.8	9.0	10.5	13.6	25.3
Short term	7.2	7.8	11.0	15.6	22.0	20.9
Financial sector	23.5	24.4	33.3	49.3	66.7	58.4
Long term	12.2	13.0	13.9	19.6	27.7	31.0
Short term	11.3	11.4	19.4	29.7	39.0	27.4
Total debt	42.8	43.9	56.8	78.4	104.7	126.8
Long term	24.3	24.7	26.5	33.1	43.7	78.6
Short term	18.5	19.2	30.4	45.3	61.0	48.2
Total debt/GNP (in percent)	14.0	13.3	15.1	17.3	21.8	28.6

Data Source: Korea Ministry of Finance.

US$ billions

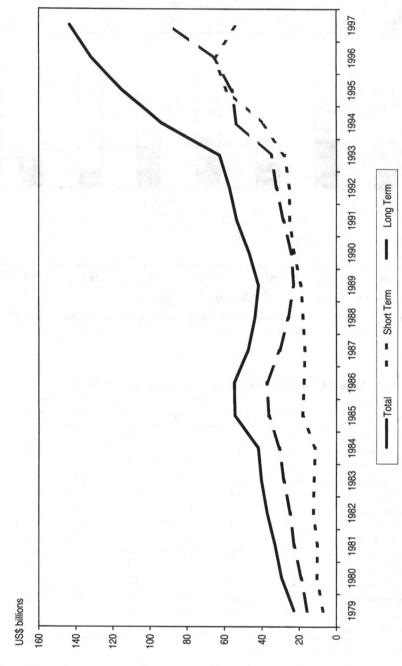

Figure 7.4. Trend and composition of Korean external debt. (*Source:* world Bank, *World Development Indicators.*)

Total · ■ · Short Term ▬ Long Term

Table 7.2. Foreign Currency Liabilities of Korean Banks (in US$ billion)

	1992	1993	1994	1995	1996	1997
Domestic branches	15.7	16.3	22.6	36.3	50.7	38.8
Foreign branches	20.1	23.1	31.7	41.3	52.9	31.2
Total	35.8	39.4	54.3	77.6	103.6	70.0

Data Source: Korea Ministry of Finance.

7.2.2 Nature of the Korean Crisis: Pattern of Capital Outflows in 1997

7.2.2.1 Creditors' Run in November

Accumulation of foreign currency liabilities in banks and associated risks culminated in a crisis late in 1997. As shown in Figure 7.5, foreign creditors ran the Korean banks in November. Though foreign capital invested in stocks also flowed out at the same time, in terms of magnitude its role remained minor.

Based on the capital account balance, the amount of foreign currency borrowing that creditors refused to refinance in November may appear too small to justify the word "run." However, the actual magnitude of the creditors' run in November was much larger than suggested by the capital account balance for two reasons. First, banks repaid some of their debt by selling external assets, which reduced the stock of deposits to be rolled over. Second and more important, the larger portion of the run was targeted at overseas branches of the Korean banks, a run not captured in the capital account balance because the Bank of Korea (BOK) replaced these deposits.

Although official data on the creditors' run in November are not available, it is possible to estimate the magnitude of private withdrawals. As the run occurred, the Bank of Korea acted as the lender of last resort and provided foreign currency liquidity to troubled banks by increasing the Bank of Korea's foreign currency deposits in those banks. Taking the increase in the Bank of Korea's deposits as an indicator for the size of run, we note that it reached an astounding US$15 billion in November. About $9 billion of this was deposited directly in foreign branches of Korean banks. This bailout exhausted the foreign exchange reserves of the BOK (Table 7.3).

7.2.2.2 Banking Panic in December

The Korean government announced its plan to resort to IMF rescue loans on the 21st of November. Apparently it failed to calm foreign creditors and the severity of the run intensified. According to unofficial data

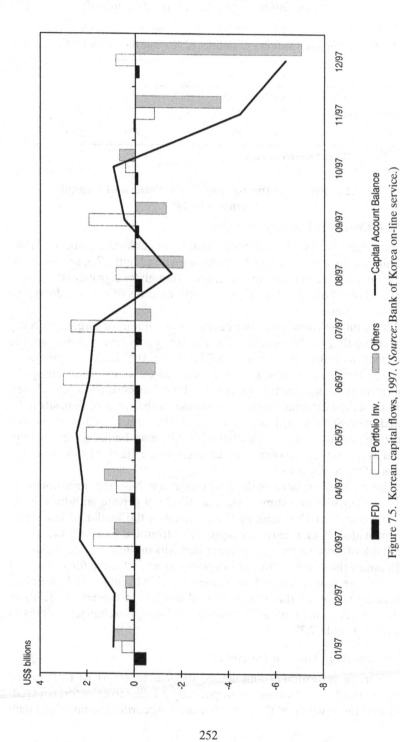

Figure 7.5. Korean capital flows, 1997. (*Source:* Bank of Korea on-line service.)

Table 7.3. BOK's Foreign Currency Deposits in Korean Banks, 1997
(in US$ billion)

	11/3–11/7	11/10–11/14	11/17–11/21	11/24–11/28	Sum
Domestic branches	−9.9	−10.6	35.0	41.2	55.7
Foreign branches	0.5	7.9	19.4	61.3	89.1
Sum	−9.4	−2.7	54.4	102.5	144.8

Data Source: Bank of Korea, unpublished data.

Table 7.4. Rollover of Foreign Credit to Seven Largest Korean Banks, 1997[a]
(in percent)

Week	July	Aug	Sept	Oct	Nov	Dec
1	157.3	64.1	82.2	83.7	70.0	23.7
2	95.5	84.8	82.8	83.9	67.2	26.8
3	83.6	86.9	84.1	80.5	55.9	26.2
4	76.1	76.2	89.8	84.9	48.7	31.9
5	87.5		127.3			53.3
Average	89.1	79.2	85.5	86.5	58.8	32.2

[a] Percent of outstanding foreign credit rolled over.
Data Source: Bank of Korea, unpublished data.

of the Bank of Korea, rollover of credits by foreign banks for the seven largest Korean banks continued to decline in December (Table 7.4). This was probably related to a cascade of bad information on the size of the short-term external debt of Korea relative to foreign exchange reserves, as well as Moody's and S&P's downward adjustment of the sovereign credit of Korea.[2] The run that began in November was followed by a typical banking system panic.[3]

7.3 A GENERAL FRAMEWORK FOR THE KOREAN CRISIS

7.3.1 Deficiency of Currency Attack Models

The description of the Korean crisis in the previous section is a familiar sequence of private capital inflows and crises. There are several

[2] Both Moody's and S&P downgraded the sovereign credit of Korea three times for the one-month period of 11/26 to 12/25 in 1997.
[3] It is interesting to note that, unlike bank borrowing, equity investment showed positive inflows in December.

different analytic frameworks that might help us understand the mechanics underlying this sequence.

Macro-fundamental, or first-generation, models of speculative attacks on currencies developed by Krugman (1979) assume that the driving force is a conflict between the government's exchange rate commitment and its fiscal/monetary policy. As long as the fixed exchange rate regime survives, a deficit is financed by gradual reductions in the government's reserves. On the day the attack occurs, the government's reserves fall discreetly to zero and the exchange rate is allowed to float.

Confidence in these models as complete explanations of crises has been eroded by the observation that, in many cases, the underlying policy conflict seems to be missing.[4] The ERM crisis in 1992 and the Mexican crisis of 1994 have been cited as examples of crises not preceded by policy conflicts. Moreover, an important empirical regularity associated with recent crises in emerging markets is that speculative attacks are preceded by very large private capital inflows into the country. The lack of policy conflicts and prior capital inflows are repeated in the Korean case as well, which suggests the irrelevancy of first-generation models for the Korean crisis.[5]

Second-generation models explain crises in terms of the fundamentals identified in first-generation models, but the fundamentals are themselves sensitive to shifts in private expectations about the future. This is a radical departure in that it implies that a consistent macro regime is vulnerable to speculative attacks and crises.

Several papers have examined crises in emerging markets and concluded that shifts in private expectations are important elements in an attack sequence in some cases.[6] But, they do not seem to provide a convincing story for the events in Asia including the Korean crisis. As with first-generation models, they do not explain why there were capital inflows in the first place. Moreover, a foreign creditors' run from foreign branches of the Korean banks is not easy to understand in this framework, since creditors were free from foreign exchange risk.

In some sense, the deficiency of conventional first- and second-generation models in explaining the Korean crisis is destined by their nature. They are designed to explain speculative attacks on currencies.

---

[4] See Frankel and Rose (1996) for general evidence that fundamental conflicts emphasized in first generation models are not apparent preceding recent crises.

[5] For a detailed discussion on lack of policy conflict before the crisis in Korea, see Shin and Hahm (1998).

[6] Eichengreen and Wyplosz (1993) argue that self-fulfilling models offer a better interpretation of the ERM crisis in 1992 compared to first generation models. For the Mexican crisis of 1994, Calvo and Mendoza (1995), Cole and Kehoe (1996) and Sachs et al. (1996) argue for the role of shift in expectations.

In other words, they are able to explain capital outflows based on agents' arbitrage based on expected price (exchange rate) changes. Therefore, understanding massive capital inflows and speculative attacks to financial intermediaries that may not be related to exchange rate risk are simply beyond their focus.

7.3.2 Alternative Framework: Insurance Attacks

Dooley (2000) develops an alternative first-generation model that seems to be consistent both with private capital inflows preceding a crisis and the absence of devaluation expectations. The policy conflict in the background in the model is between the desire of a credit-constrained government to hold reserve assets as a form of self-insurance and the government's desire to insure financial liabilities of residents. The first objective is met by the accumulation of foreign exchange reserves. The second objective generates incentives for investors to acquire the government's reserves when yield differentials make this optimal.

The insurance model predicts that three fundamentals must be present in order to generate a private capital inflow followed by a speculative attack. The first is that the government must have positive net international reserves. Net reserves in this model are defined to include contingent assets and liabilities. Second, the government's commitment to exhaust these net reserves to pay off an implicit or explicit insurance contract must be credible. That is, it must be consistent with the government's incentives and ability to mobilize and exhaust its net worth after the attack begins. Third, private investors must have access to transactions that produce insured losses. As long as one ingredient is missing, there will be no capital inflow and no crisis. Therefore, crisis episodes are associated with the relaxation of a *binding* constraint.

These ingredients provide a plausible capital inflow-crisis sequence. The availability of free insurance raises the market yield on a set of liabilities issued by residents for a predictable time period. This yield differential generates a private gross capital inflow (a sale of domestic liabilities to nonresidents) that continues until the day of attack. The private inflow is necessarily associated with some combination of an increase in the government's international reserve assets, a current account deficit, and a gross private capital outflow. But the distribution among these offsetting transactions is unimportant.

As long as the "foreign" investors earn above market yields, there is a disincentive for an attack on the government's assets. Investors will prefer to hold the growing stock of high-yield insured liabilities of residents and allow the government to hold reserves that earn the risk-free rate. Private profits are realized before the attack.

The attack itself is generated by competition to avoid losses. When the contingent liabilities of the government are just equal to the government's assets, competition among investors will insure that all will call the insurance option. The incentive to do so is that, given plausible assumptions about asset markets, from that date forward, yields on insured deposits will fall below market rates.

Following an attack, the regime returns to its initial equilibrium in which the government's net international reserves have returned to zero. The loss of reserves might force the government to abandon its commitment to manage the exchange rate. An observer determined to apply a currency attack model will have to appeal to multiple equilibria. In fact, there is no shift in expectations.

7.3.3 Banking Crises Associated with Insurance Attacks

The empirical association between banking and currency crises itself is well established. Gavin and Hausmann (1995) document the relationship between lending booms and financial crises in Latin America. Kaminsky and Reinhart (1996) show, in a sample of 76 balance-of-payments crises and 26 banking crises in 20 developing countries from 1970 to 1995, that about one-quarter of the banking crises occur within one year of a balance of payments crisis. Their interpretation of the evidence is that balance of payments crises were unrelated to banking crises during the 1970s when financial markets within these countries were highly regulated. Following liberalization of domestic financial markets in the 1980s, banking and balance-of-payments crises were closely linked and banking crises preceded balance of payments crises. Glick and Hutchison (this volume) find similar links for a broader set of countries, particularly emerging markets.

Goldfajn and Valdés (1997) examine four recent examples of banking/balance of payments crises in Finland, Mexico, Sweden, and Chile. In each case, capital inflows preceded the crises by three to six years, and lending booms occurred in domestic banking markets over the same intervals. The crises were followed, except in the case of Sweden, by substantial capital outflows and in all cases by a sharp reduction in bank credit. Their model suggests that intermediation involving maturity transformation is likely to increase capital inflows relative to equilibria in which there is no intermediation, but at the cost of increasing the probability of a run on the banking system. Because the run on the banking system depletes reserves, it also increases the chances that a fixed exchange rate regime is abandoned.

This literature has clarified two important points. First, the government's net reserves support two policy regimes: the banking/financial system and the exchange rate regime. An attack on either regime that exhausts reserves will necessarily have important implications for the other regime. This will make identification of the causes of a crisis difficult.[7] Second, rapid growth in the stock of bank credit may be an early warning that potential losses in the financial system and the associated contingent government insurance liability are approaching a crisis level.

7.4 PRIVATE INFLOWS MOTIVATED BY AN INSURANCE FUND: THE CASE OF KOREA

7.4.1 Specifying Preconditions for Insurance Attack in Korea

The model set out in Dooley (2000) is a very stylized model of bank behavior. To confront the Korean data we first must develop a more realistic model. We interpret Dooley's insurance model as a banking crisis model in an open economy where claims on banks are guaranteed by the government. Given the interpretation, we may relate it to the rich literature on banks' behavior in the presence of deposit insurance in a closed economy. In this line of literature, insured banks seek to maximize the value of their deposit insurance options by selecting the riskiest available asset portfolio (Merton, 1977). An immediate implication of this is the following: In the presence of insurance, *without other checking mechanisms*, banking failures and crises should be prevalent. Checking mechanisms include: the franchise values of banks, capital regulation and monitoring by supervisory authorities (Merton, 1978; Buser, Chen, and Kane, 1981; Marcus, 1984).

It follows that there are three conditions under which dangerous capital inflows through banks might occur: (1) lack of self-monitoring (risk management) by banks due to declines in franchise values, (2) lack of adequate supervisory monitoring, and (3) lack of foreign creditors' monitoring due to government guarantee which is validated by sufficient insurance funds. We will examine whether and how these conditions were satisfied in Korea before the crisis.

7.4.2 Declines in Franchise Values of Korean Banks in 1990s

Throughout the 1980s and until 1992 stocks of banks in Korea had been market performers. But since 1994 they have become underperformers,

---

[7] The two-objective/one-policy tool problem is well known. Wigmore (1987), for example, argues that the choice of the new Federal Reserve system to protect its gold reserves in order to maintain the fixed exchange rate forced them to accept the bank failures that may have triggered the 1930s' depression. For a discussion of the conflict in the context of currency boards see Caprio et al. (1996).

Table 7.5. Mismatch Gap Ratios of Seven Largest Korean Banks,[a] March 1997
(in percent)

A Bank	B Bank	C Bank	D Bank	E Bank	F Bank	G Bank	Average
21.9	27.5	22.4	23.3	20.2	16.8	11.3	20.3

[a] Difference between one-month assets and liabilities as a percent of assets.
Data Source: Bank of Korea, unpublished data.

in stark contrast with the merchant banking industry (Figure 7.6). This stock market performance suggests that the franchise value of commercial banks was declining, perhaps because of expectations that the financial markets would become more competitive as they were liberalized.

The decline in franchise values was associated with changes in the asset structure of banks. Namely, judging from the aggregate balance sheet of banks, the Korean banks were increasingly taking larger risks. As Figure 7.7 shows, banks were replacing cash, call loans, and deposits with securities in their asset portfolios. Because securities are exposed to price changes, this led to larger market risk of the banks.

More importantly, credit risks of assets were also increasing. First of all, among the total credits provided by banks, the portion of credits without collateral was rising (Figure 7.8). Second, the portion of consumer loans was expanding in the composition of total loans by type (Figure 7.9). Third, in the case of loans to firms, lending to small and medium firms began to explain increasingly larger portions in comparison to lending to large firms (Figure 7.10). All of these three changes indicate that the asset structure was moving to exacerbate asymmetry problems between banks and borrowers, raising the associated credit risks.

Moreover, banks were taking large liquidity risks in their foreign currency positions. By regulation, Korean banks were not allowed to take net open currency positions exceeding certain limits and thus were protected from currency risk. But, maturity mismatches between assets and liabilities in foreign currencies were very large. Measuring the severity of the mismatch problem by a one-month mismatch gap, as of early 1997 the seven largest banks were taking large foreign currency liquidity risks (Table 7.5).[8] Hence, declines in the franchise values of banks and an increase in risk of asset structure was emerging as a characterizing feature of Korean banks in the 1990s.

[8] The mismatch gap is a ratio of the gap between liabilities and assets, both of which are due within a month. The Korean supervisory authority introduced a 10 percent standard for the gap as a guideline.

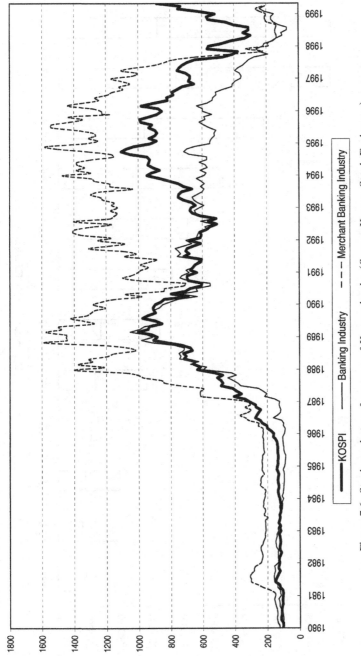

Figure 7.6. Stock market performance of Korean banks. (*Source:* Korean Stock Exchange.)

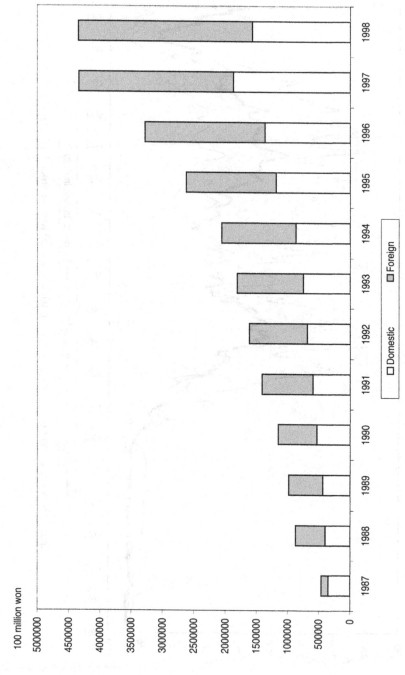

100 million won

Figure 7.7. Korean bank total assets: Composition by type. (*Source:* Bank of Korea, Bank Management Institute.)

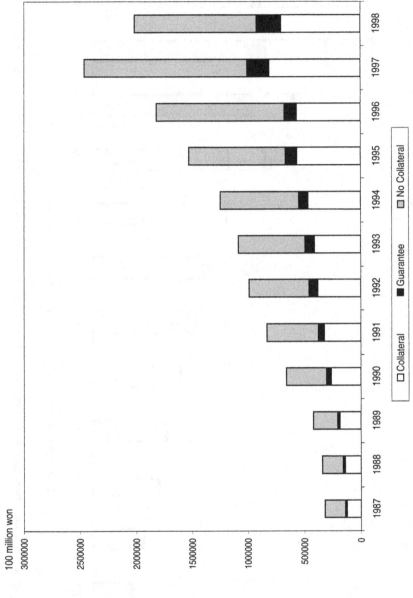

Figure 7.8. Korean bank total credit: Composition by type of collateral. (*Source:* Bank of Korea, Bank Management Institute.)

261

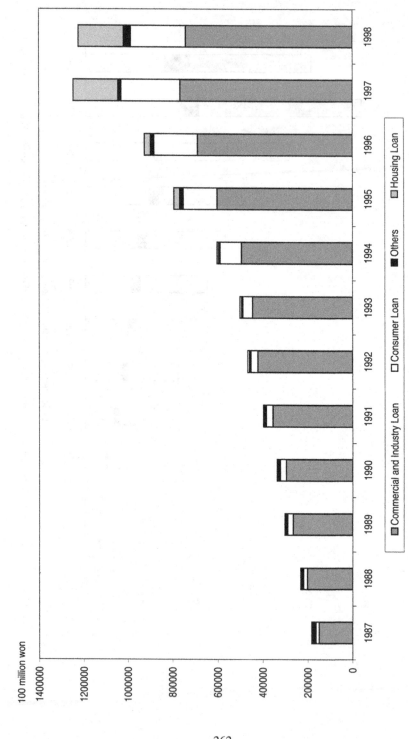

100 million won

Figure 7.9. Korean bank total loans: Composition by type. (*Source:* Bank of Korea, Bank Management Statistics.)

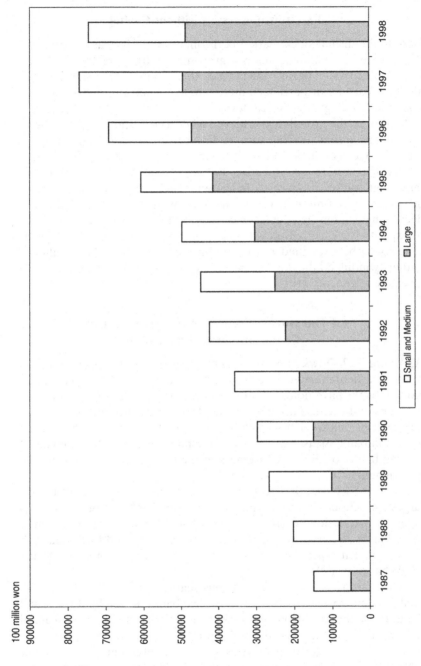

Figure 7.10. Korean bank industrial loans: Composition by firm size. (*Source:* Bank of Korea, Bank Management Statistics.)

7.4.3 Growth of Assets without Capital

Despite the dismal stock market performance and risky asset structure, the volume of banking assets was growing rapidly. Over the five years from 1992 to 1996, banks' assets more than doubled. Considering that annual inflation rates had been moderate at 5.3 percent on average, this was remarkable growth in real terms.

Moreover, the growth was achieved while a corresponding increase in capital was absent, leading to a decline of capital asset ratios (Figure 7.11). A vicious cycle of declines in franchise values and reaching for risk was evident well before the crisis. In the presence of the government's implicit guarantee, it is easy to understand that bank owners did not have incentives to self-monitor or manage risks while franchise values were decreasing. Under the circumstance their best strategies must have been to exploit insurance option values as discussed in Merton (1977). What remains to be explained is why foreign creditors and the regulatory authority indulged the adverse development? We will take up these two questions consecutively.

7.4.4 Did Foreign Creditors Lend on Individual Creditworthiness of Banks?

As Figure 7.12 shows, more than half of the assets of the Korean banks have been denominated in foreign currencies since 1988. Because the Korean banks have not been allowed to hold net open foreign currency positions and because nonbank residents' foreign currency deposits are negligible, it follows that foreign creditors funded more than half of the growth in bank assets. Did nonresident lenders evaluate the behavior of Korean banks, or did they assume that their loans were insured by the government?

Figure 7.13 shows the trends in foreign currency liabilities of the six largest private commercial banks and various bank performance variables. The expansion in foreign currency liabilities of banks for the three years before the crisis was quite remarkable. Compared to the sluggish growth pattern in previous years, it certainly suggests an important structural change in 1994.

While faster growth than in previous years is common to all of the six banks, we are particularly interested in two banks: Korea First Bank and Seoul Bank, the most troubled banks during the period of strong capital inflows. The capital of both banks was discovered to be completely eroded, and the government was forced to intervene in December 1997. Although both banks were industry underperformers even before the crisis, in terms of foreign currency liabilities they displayed quite

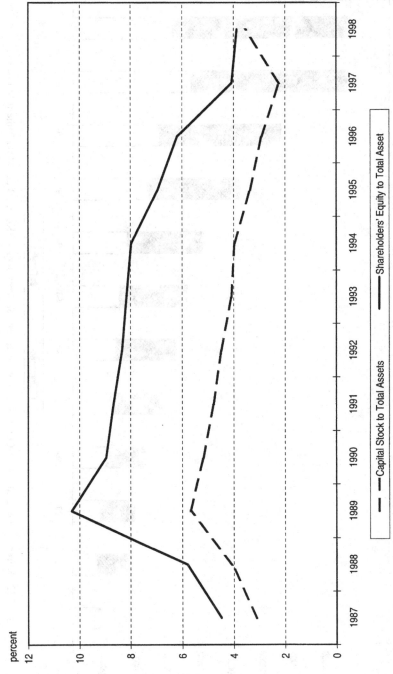

Figure 7.11. Capital asset and equity asset ratios of Korean banks. (*Source:* Bank of Korea, Bank Management Statistics.)

265

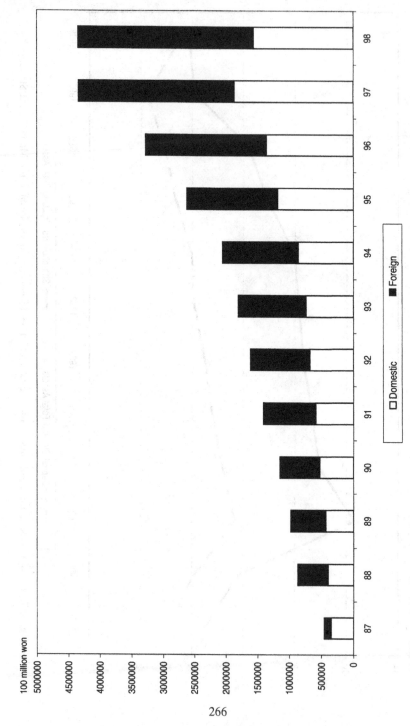

100 million won

Figure 7.12. Korean bank total assets: Composition by currency. (*Source:* Bank of Korea, Bank Management Statistics.)

□ Domestic   ■ Foreign

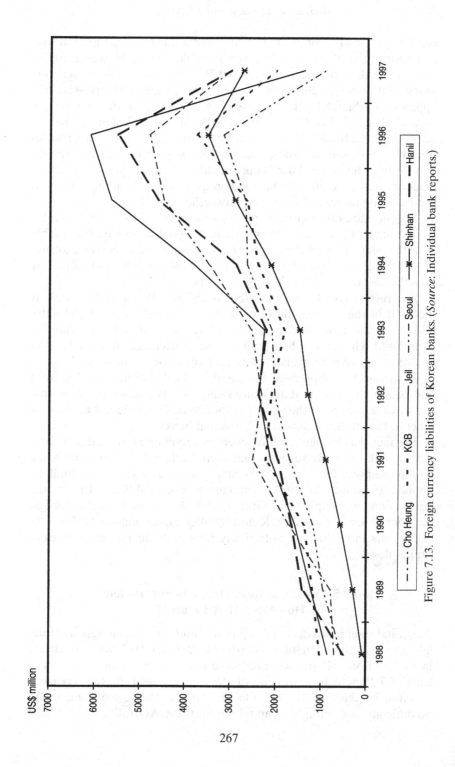

US$ million

Figure 7.13. Foreign currency liabilities of Korean banks. (*Source:* Individual bank reports.)

- - - - Cho Heung   — — KCB   —— Jeil   —*— Shinhan
—— Seoul   — — Hanil

267

contrasting trends. Korea First Bank recorded the highest growth rate and Seoul Bank the lowest by a considerable margin. However, we do not believe that the inability of Seoul Bank to expand its foreign currency operation was due to the screening of foreign creditors. Rather it appears that Seoul Bank's expansion was limited by the supervisory authority's restriction. Even in terms of the supervision standard before the crisis, Seoul Bank was considered in trouble and discretionary restrictions were imposed on its domestic and foreign operations. Therefore we believe that the Korea First Bank should be focused on as a valid test case for foreign creditors' behavior. Foreign creditors' lending policy was not based on individual bank's creditworthiness.

To generalize our argument, we compute correlations of growth rates of six banks with various performance and capital status variables (Table 7.6). In order to account for other characteristics of each bank, we use growth rates over the three years from 1994 to 1996 normalized by growth rates over the previous three years.

The results can be summarized as follows. When Seoul Bank is included in the sample, the growth rate of foreign currency liabilities does not show a statistically significant relationship with any variable considered. However, when Seoul Bank is excluded, foreign liability growth is negatively correlated with each of the performance and capital position variables; moreover, the negative relation with return on asset and equity measures is statistically significant. Hence we conclude that this evidence supports the view that foreign creditors did not monitor or react to the creditworthiness of individual banks.

The fact that foreign creditors were not looking at the status of individual banks strongly suggests that their lending decisions were based on the insurance fund, namely the ability of the government to fulfill its implicit guarantees of banks' foreign currency liabilities. To test the implication, we implement Granger-causality tests between foreign currency reserves of the BOK and liability capital inflows (Table 7.7). The results show that causality, if any, runs from changes in reserves to capital flows.

7.4.5 Caveats in Regulation and Supervision: How Were They Created?

As capital asset ratios declined, regulation and supervision were less than adequate. Capital regulation according to BIS standards was introduced in 1992 in Korea. Banks were required to maintain a capital ratio of at least of 7.25 percent at the end of 1993 and to meet the full 8 percent required by the end of 1995. On the surface, the Korean banks had no difficulty in meeting the capital requirement. According to published

Table 7.6. Relationship of Foreign Currency Liabilities of Korean Banks with Performance and Capital Position Variables

	Foreign Liability Growth Rate (%)	ROA (%)	ROE (%)	Stock Price (won)	Capital Ratio	Net Worth Ratio
Cho Heung	2.78	0.41	5.98	9,701	3.23	6.52
KCB	4.43	0.30	4.80	7,841	3.54	6.23
Je Il	5.77	0.18	2.85	8,588	3.03	6.86
Seoul	1.19	−0.14	−2.09	6,937	4.23	6.84
Shin Han	2.25	0.72	7.76	15,702	3.32	9.65
Han Il	5.98	0.33	4.80	9,067	3.36	7.33
Correlation coefficient		0.75	0.24	−0.22	−0.63	−0.26
OLS coefficient		0.13	0.52	−0.00	−2.96	−0.41
		(0.28)	(3.48)	(0.00)	(1.82)	(0.77)
Correlation coefficient ②		−0.82	−0.87	−0.70	−0.15	−0.47
OLS Coefficient ②		−6.91	−0.81	−0.00	−1.41	−0.58
		(2.73)	(0.27)	(0.00)	(5.19)	(0.63)

Notes:

1. Foreign liability growth rate $= \dfrac{1993\text{--}1996 \text{ growth rate of foreign currency liabilities}}{1990\text{--}1993 \text{ growth rate of foreign currency liabilities}}$

2. ROA and ROE denote return on assets and equity, respectively.

3. Capital ratio $= \dfrac{\text{Capital stock}}{\text{Total assets}}$, Net worth ratio $= \dfrac{\text{Shareholders' equity}}{\text{Total assets}}$

4. Correlation coefficient is cross-bank correlation of liability growth rates with each variable. OLS coefficient is estimated by regressing growth rates on each variable.

5. Correlation ② and OLS coefficient ② are estimated after excluding Seoul Bank.

6. Numbers in parentheses are standard deviations.

Data Source: Bank Management Statistics, BOK, 1995–1998; Korea Stock Exchange.

statistics by the Office of Supervision, the BIS capital ratios averaged across the city banks had been declining slightly but were always over 8 percent. However, Shin and Hahm (1998) explain why these numbers are misleading. In general, there can be two ways that regulatory authorities manipulate the BIS capital ratios. One is by applying "soft" accounting rules. The other is by allowing "flexibility" in enforcing the regulations. Shin and Hahm show that both of them were prevalent in Korea before the crisis.

Why did regulators let the sorry state continue and the banks expand? To better understand the failures of banking supervision in Korea, we must look first at the traditional modus operandi of the supervision, which was "direct quantity control." As is well known, Korea succeeded in keeping fiscal soundness and monetary stability throughout the 1980s

Table 7.7. Granger-Causality Test: Foreign Currency
Reserves of BOK and Liability Capital Flows

	F-Statistic	Probability
1990:1–1997:2		
Reserves → Capital Flows	1.74	0.19
Capital Flows → Reserves	0.31	0.87
1994:1–1997:2		
Reserves → Capital Flows	2.27	0.19
Capital Flows → Reserves	0.09	0.98

Notes:
Reserves are defined as change in foreign currency reserves.
Capital flows are defined as sum of debt portfolio net inflows
and other investment liability flows in the capital account. Four
lags are included. Data are quarterly.
Data Source: Bank of Korea on-line service.

and early 1990s until the crisis. The major tool at the aggregate level had
been monetary targeting based on aggregate quantities like M2 and
MCT. Given that the financial market was repressed, monetary targeting inevitably resulted in the government's heavy reliance on direct
quantity controls in many areas. Controlling the amount of financial
flows for the purpose of containing excessive monetary expansion thus
became a well-established policy in Korea. As a result, direct discretionary quantity controls at both aggregate and microeconomic levels
were bread and butter for policymakers in managing all financial risks.

This way of managing financial markets, however, made microeconomic risk management redundant. The government set the targets for
aggregate money growth rates, inflation rates, exchange rates, and interest rates, and then utilized all the available intervention tools to achieve
the targets. Within these constraints there was very little room to exploit
government insurance.

While the costs to efficiency were probably high, the policy mechanism worked well enough to attain macroeconomic and financial
stability for the Korean economy for decades. Therefore, it is not surprising that while the government pursued financial liberalization, it
did not completely relinquish direct controls on financial flows and was
confident that such controls would continue to maintain financial
stability.

One interesting example of the coexistence of liberalization and direct
controls was direct quantity control on equity issues of banks. In order

to "stabilize" the stock market the government kept control over new equity issues of banks and in 1995 permitted only 30 percent of the amount originally planned by banks.[9] Thus, the problem of capital shortage of banks was not only known to the government but was aggravated – a good example illustrating the government's belief that macroeconomic stability could be obtained through the old way of going about business.

It seems that just prior to the crisis in 1997 the government had succeeded in maintaining macroeconomic and financial stability. Inflation rates were lower than ever and the fiscal account was balanced. M2 growth rates seemed to be stable as well. What went wrong? Why and how did the government fail to detect increasing vulnerability of the economy? Our explanation is that capital account liberalization provided a loophole in the traditional management system through which banks could increase the risk of insurance attack or run. As pointed out in Section 7.2.1.3, about half of the foreign currency operations of the banking sector was handled by overseas branches. Because these transactions were not reflected in domestic monetary indicators, it was impossible for policymakers to detect this new development when watching traditional macroeconomic measures.

In sum, caveats in supervision were there simply because the traditional modus operandi of supervision left some areas not watched by the policymakers. These areas quickly became a new source of risk by enabling banks to exploit implicit insurance.

7.5 DISCUSSION AND LESSONS

In retrospect, one must wonder whether there was anything new in the Korean crisis. In the presence of implicit or explicit deposit insurance, there are numerous examples of crises generated by changes in banks' incentives to exploit insurance. The triggers for such episodes are changes in the environment following financial liberalization.

Following the debt crisis of 1982, free deposit insurance extended to banks in newly liberalized financial markets was widely cited as a source of instability in financial markets (McKinnon and Mathieson, 1981; Hanson and de Melo, 1985; Diaz Alejandro, 1985; Corbo, de Melo, and Tybout, 1986; Balino, 1991; McKinnon, 1991; Velasco, 1991). The argument familiar to similar discussions in the context of banking markets in industrial countries is that a deadly brew of free insurance, undercapitalized banks, unrestricted competition for deposits, and poor prudential regulation and supervision induces banks to reach for risk (Akerlof and Romer, 1993; Kane, 1996). Several authors identified the competition for

[9] Press Release of Ministry of Finance and Economy, January 30, 1995.

deposits to make high-risk loans as a partial explanation of apparently high real loan rates in reformed markets.

One can find dramatic examples of this process in both developed and developing countries. The combination of deposit insurance and a relaxation of controls over deposit rates and portfolio selection in the United States led to explosive growth in inflows into savings and loan institutions and to their eventual collapse. The problem, clear in retrospect, was that the contingent liability of the United States government provided the private investor with a virtual guarantee that high yields offered by savings and loan deposits would not be matched by depositors' losses. Depositors did not question the ability of some savings and loans to offer deposit rates 200–400 basis points over the market rate. As long as deposits were "probably" guaranteed, there was little downside risk.

7.5.1 Elimination of Deposit Insurance?

The fact that neither developing nor developed countries were immune to the trap of liberalization and crises raises a question of how solutions can be found. Because the existence of government insurance constitutes a fundamental condition for crises eruption, one may argue for the elimination of it. However, this is easier said than done. It should be noted that in many developing countries, including Korea, no explicit deposit insurance existed before crises, although it was taken for granted. It suggests that given policymakers' preferences, market agents should regard ex-post bailout of depositors as a time-consistent equilibrium. Therefore, unless one can figure out elaborate institutional settings that will support no bailout as a time-consistent solution, elimination of deposit insurance will not work.

7.5.2 Discretionary Capital Account Liberalization?

If insurance for banks or depositors cannot be denied credibly, one may argue that capital flows by insured domestic agents should be subject to restrictions. In particular, limiting the access of investors to domestic financial intermediaries or some class of domestic assets eliminates the market distortion. It follows that portfolio and direct investment that characterized inflows to emerging markets after 1990 is not guaranteed by the debtor government and so is more likely to be welfare improving.

However, the flaw in this line of reasoning is that governments have strong incentives to maintain the market value of nonfinancial firms' liabilities in the face of a change in the private sector's preferences for domestic assets. This is because such firms are heavily indebted to the domestic banking system. If nonresident creditors want out, these firms can be expected to ask for and receive credit from the domestic banks. To refuse to do so would depress the market value of the banks' existing claims on the domestic firms and call into question the solvency of the domestic banking system.

This does not mean that capital controls are necessarily ineffective. But it does mean that controls would have to be comprehensive. It is well accepted that control programs can change the structure of capital flows, but the evidence that controls can limit capital inflows in the face of incentives to exploit insurance is much less clear.

REFERENCES

Akerlof, George and Paul Romer (1993). "Looting: The Economic Underworld of Bankruptcy for Profit," *Brookings Papers on Economic Activity*, No. 2:1–60.

Balino, Tomas (1991). "The Argentine Banking Crisis of 1980." In V. Sundararajan and T. Balino, eds., *Banking Crisis: Cases and Issues*. Washington, D.C.: International Monetary Fund, pp. 58–112.

Buser, Stephen, Andrew Chen, and Edward Kane (1981). "Federal Deposit Insurance, Regulatory Policy, and Optimal Bank Capital," *Journal of Finance* **36**(1):51–60.

Calvo, G. and E. Mendoza (1995). "Reflections on Mexico's Balance-of-Payments Crisis: A Chronicle of Death Foretold." Mimeo, University of Maryland.

Caprio, G., M. Dooley, D. Leipziger, and C. Walsh (1996). "The Lender of Last Resort Function under a Currency Board: The Case of Argentina." *Open Economies Review* 7:625–650.

Cole, H. and T. Kehoe (1996). "A Self-Fulfilling Model of Mexico's 1994–5 Debt Crisis," *Journal of International Economics* **41**(3–4):309–330.

Corbo, Vittorio, Jaime de Melo, and James Tybout (1986). "What Went Wrong with the Recent Reforms in the Southern Cone," *Economic Development and Cultural Change* **34**(3):607–640.

Diaz-Alejandro, C. (1985). "Good-bye Financial Repression, Hello Financial Crash," *Journal of Development Economics*, **19**(September–October):1–24.

Dooley, Michael P. (2000). "A Model of Crises in Emerging Markets," *Economic Journal*, **110**(460):256–272.

Eichengreen, Barry and Charles Wyplosz (1993). "The Unstable EMS." *Brookings Papers on Economic Activity*, No. 1:51–143.

Fischer S. (1999). "On the Need for an International Lender of Last Resort." Mimeo, IMF.

Frankel, J. and A. Rose (1996). "Currency Crashes in Emerging Markets: An Empirical Treatment," *Journal of International Economics* **41**(3–4):351–366.

Gavin, M. and R. Hausman (1995). "The Roots of Banking Crises: The Macroeconomic Context." Mimeo, Interamerican Development Bank.

Glick, R. and M. Hutchison (Chapter 2, this volume). "Banking and Currency Crises: How Common Are Twins?"

Goldfajn, I. and R. Valdés (1997). "Balance of Payments Crises and Capital Flows: The Role of Liquidity." Mimeo, MIT.

Hanson, James and Jaime de Melo (1985). "External Shocks, Financial Reforms, and Stabilization Attempts in Uruguay during 1974–83," *World Development* **13**(8):917–939.

Kaminsky, G. and C. Reinhart (1996). "The Twin Crises: The Causes of Banking and Balance-of-Payments Problems." International Finance Discussion Paper No. 544, Board of Governors of the Federal Reserve System.

Kane, Edward (1996). "Difficulties in Making Implicit Government Risk-Bearing Partnerships Explicit," *Journal of Risk and Uncertainty* **12**(2–3):189–199.

Krugman, P. (1979). "A Model of Balance-of-Payments Crises," *Journal of Money, Credit, and Banking* **11**(3):311–325.

McKinnon, Ronald (1991). *The Order of Economic Liberalization: Financial Control in the Transition to a Market Economy.* Baltimore and London: John Hopkins University Press.

McKinnon, Ronald and Don Mathieson (1981). "How to Manage a Repressed Economy," Princeton Essays in International Finance No. 145. Princeton, NJ: Princeton University.

Marcus, Alan (1984). "Deregulation and Bank Financial Policy," *Journal of Banking and Finance* **8**(4):557–565.

Merton, Robert (1978). "On the Cost of Deposit Insurance When There Are Surveillance Costs", *Journal of Business* **51**(3):439–452.

Merton, Robert (1997). "An Analytic Derivation of the Cost of Deposit Insurance and Loan Guarantees: An Application of Modern Option Pricing Theory," *Journal of Banking and Finance* **1**(June):3–11.

Sachs, J., A. Tornell, and A. Velasco (1996). "Financial Crises in Emerging Markets: The Lessons from 1995." *Brookings Papers on Economic Activity*, No. 1:147–215.

Shin, Inseok (1998). "The Korean Crisis: On the Mechanics," *Korea Development Institute Policy Studies* **20**(3) (in Korean).

Shin, Inseok and Joon-Ho Hahm (1998). "The Korean Crisis – Causes and Resolution." Paper presented at the KDI-EWC Conference on the Korean Crisis, Honolulu, Hawaii, August 8.

Velasco, Andrés (1991). "Liberalization, Crisis, Intervention: The Chilean Financial System, 1975–85." In V. Sundararajan and Tomas Balino, eds., *Banking Crisis: Cases and Issues.* Washington, D.C.: International Monetary Fund, pp. 113–174.

Wigmore, Barrie (1987). "Was the Bank Holiday of 1933 Caused by a Run on the Dollar?" *Journal of Economic History* **47**(3):739–755.

Discussion

Private Inflows When Crises are Anticipated: A Case Study of Korea

Carmen M. Reinhart

This chapter makes a compelling case that the Korean financial crisis of 1997 was not the consequence of a misaligned exchange rate and external imbalance, nor was it the classic first-generation credit-financed fiscal deficit stressed by Krugman (1979). The authors also cast doubt on explanations of the Korean crisis that rely exclusively on a liquidity-crisis/banking panic story, as in Goldfajn and Valdés (1995), or on earlier models with self-fulfilling expectations (see, for instance, Obstfeld, 1994). Instead, they argue that the Korean banking and currency crises had their origins in the financial liberalization that took place in the earlier part of the 1990s. Financial liberalization, coupled with explicit or implicit government guarantees, fueled a surge in capital inflows that were largely intermediated through Korean banks. Owing to (in part) increased competition, the banks saw their franchise value erode, took on greater risk, and relied increasingly on foreign creditors.[1] A central theme of the chapter, as the title suggests, is that the financial liberalization/Dooley (2000) insurance explanations of the crisis offer testable predictions as to what the antecedents of the crisis should be – particularly as to the nature of capital flows and bank lending – and that these predictions accord well with the Korean stylized facts.

I will divide my remarks into three parts. First, I will elaborate on some of the points made in the chapter, as to why financial liberalization and moral hazard have played a very important role in explaining the antecedents of the twin crises – in Korea and elsewhere. I will also refer to a variety of "stylized facts" that, over and beyond the Korean episode, fit well with the insurance/capital inflow story. Second, I will focus on two types of macroeconomic policies that significantly influenced the volume and composition of Korean capital inflows prior to the crisis which are not discussed in the chapter. Lastly, I will argue that the authors dismiss

[1] Those foreign creditors were largely, although not exclusively, Japanese banks.

too lightly explanations of the Korean crisis that are offered by variants of the earlier first- and second-generation currency crises models. When confronting competing models with the data, serious observational equivalence problems arise, making it difficult to pin down "the model" – as the authors suggest.

In my earlier work on capital flow cycles, I once compared the surge in capital inflows to emerging markets that took place in the early 1990s with the flows of the late 1970s–early 1980s (see Calvo, Leiderman, and Reinhart, 1994). A striking difference between the two episodes appeared to be that in the 1990s it was the private sector who was borrowing from abroad, while in the 1980s it was the governments. Of course, the external debt data I was analyzing reflected the state of affairs *after* the debt crisis; when someone suggested that I look at the distribution of public and private external debt as it stood *before* the crisis, it became very evident that an important reason why governments held the lion's share of external debt *ex post* was that they had assumed much of what was private sector debt *ex ante*. Given such antecedents, and the scores of bailouts of collapsing banking systems around the globe, it is not difficult to see why implicit guarantees would give rise to indiscriminate borrowing by Korean banks and firms and equally reckless lending – this time, by the Japanese and European banks. In the case of Korea, at least, expectations of a government guarantee *expost* turned out to be well-justified. Korea, however, is not unique in this regard.

The insurance model predicts booming credit growth financed by capital inflows prior to the crisis. It also predicts that the maturity of those inflows would shorten as the crisis nears – not surprisingly, as the crisis is fully anticipated. Because there is insurance, the model also suggests that interest rates need not rise on the eve of the crisis. The initial trigger factor for the inflows of capital could be a financial liberalization, a decline in international interest rates, or both of these. Indeed, above and beyond the evidence presented in the analysis for the Korean case, there is much broader empirical evidence to support all these stylized facts – even the more surprising prediction about interest rates (see Kaminsky and Reinhart, 1999).

I also share the authors' assessment of the importance of the pullout of Japanese creditor banks in explaining the sudden and massive capital outflows from Korea toward the end of 1997. Indeed, in a recent chapter of mine with Graciela Kaminsky we present evidence that a powerful channel of contagion during the Asian crisis came from the behavior of Japanese banks after they suffered initial losses in Thailand, where they had their greatest exposure (see Kaminsky and Reinhart, 2000).

Above and beyond the motives discussed in the chapter, however, there are two key reasons why Korea experienced a surge in capital inflows and why an increasing share of those inflows were tilted toward very short maturities. The first of these reasons had to do with how the authorities responded to the initial surge in capital inflows. In Korea, as in many other emerging markets, there was a marked reluctance to allow the currency to appreciate during the capital inflow phase of the cycle. The authorities dealt with pressures on the currency by intervening in the foreign exchange market and accumulating foreign exchange reserves. The Korean monetary authorities were also concerned, however, that unsterilized intervention would lead to a rapid expansion in the monetary aggregates and fuel overheating and inflationary pressures. The solution they found to this dilemma was sterilized intervention. However, persistent sterilization policies kept domestic short-term interest rates well above international levels for a prolonged period of time. The banks responded to this differential in rates of return by borrowing offshore at short maturities. Indeed, this outcome was also not unique to Korea; Montiel and Reinhart (1999), who study a panel of fifteen emerging markets in the 1990s, show that sterilized intervention significantly increases the volume of capital inflows. Furthermore, this policy skews their maturities toward the short end of the spectrum. As the paper notes, all this short-term borrowing set the stage for the December banking panic, as Japanese and European creditors pulled out. This "policy inconsistency" is yet another complement to the insurance story/botched liberalization story.

The second reason why such a trivial share of the borrowing was long term had to do with how the liberalization proceeded. While some countries, such as Chile and Colombia, introduced impediments or disincentives to external short-term borrowing – even as they continued to liberalize – in Korea the opposite was true. Barriers to short-term offshore borrowing were significantly reduced, while impediments to equity investment and other types of long-term finance remained in place.

Lastly, however, I do not share the authors' assessment of the uselessness of first- and second-generation models of currency crises in providing useful insights into the Korean crisis. Consider, first, the Krugman (1979) explanation. Surely, a fiscal deficit was not a problem for Korea – that was not the source of the policy inconsistency. Yet, a very simple variation of Krugman's story fits Korea and some of the other recent twin crises rather well. It is not the government who needs credit from the central bank – it is the ailing financial institutions. The central bank's usual willingness to support the banks (as it did in Korea) creates the policy inconsistency. Being lender of last resort requires credit creation, which is, of course, incompatible with maintaining the exchange rate.

Turning to a second-generation setting, we can entertain a very plausible reinterpretation of the Obstfeld (1996) explanations for shifts in investor sentiment that are highly pertinent for Korea. In the Obstfeld stories, investors know that the authorities will be reluctant to raise interest rates to defend the currency for one reason or another. In his examples, the authorities are concerned about the consequences of high interest rates for unemployment or the implications for the burden of servicing the public sector debt. To fit Korea, only a moderate adjustment is needed. Although a high stock of public sector debt was not an issue, the private sector was highly leveraged. If, as this chapter suggests, private sector debt is a contingent liability of the government, then the Obstfeld debt story is still applicable – except in a slightly disguised form. Furthermore, even without considerations about debt, the authorities may feel constrained in hiking interest rates because of the weak state of the banks. If investors know this, then we have the prerequisites for a self-fulfilling speculative attack in place.

In the end, I am still compelled to conclude, Will the "real model" please stand up?

REFERENCES

Calvo, Guillermo A., Leonardo Leiderman, and Carmen M. Reinhart (1994). "Capital Inflows to Latin America: The 1970s and 1990s." In E. Bacha, ed., *Economics in a Changing World*, Vol. 4: *Development, Trade and the Environment*, Proceedings of the Tenth IEA World Congress. London: Macmillan.

Dooley, Michael P. (2000). "A Model of Crises in Emerging Markets," *Economic Journal* **110**(460):256–272.

Goldfajn, Ilan and Rodrigo Valdés (1995). "Balance-of-Payments Crises and Capital Flows: The Role of Liquidity." Mimeo, Massachusetts Institute of Technology.

Kaminsky, Graciela and Carmen M. Reinhart (1999). "The Twin Crises: The Causes of Banking and Balance of Payments Problems," *American Economic Review* **89**(3):473–500.

——— (2000). "Bank Lending and Contagion: Evidence from the Asian Crisis." In T. Ito and A. Krueger, eds., *Regional and Global Capital Flows: Macroeconomic Causes and Consequences*. Chicago: University of Chicago Press for the NBER.

Krugman, Paul (1979). "A Model of Balance-of-Payments Crises." *Journal of Money, Credit, and Banking* **11**(3):311–325.

Montiel, Peter and Carmen M. Reinhart (August 1999). "Do Capital Controls and Macroeconomic Policies Influence the Volume and Composition of

Capital Flows? Evidence from the 1990s," *Journal of International Money and Finance* **18**(4):619–635.

Obstfeld, Maurice (1994). "The Logic of Currency Crises." NBER Working Paper No. 4640. Cambridge, MA.

———(1996). "Models of Currency Crises with Self-fulfilling Features," *European Economic Review* **40**(1):1037–1047.

PART III

INSTITUTIONAL FACTORS AND FINANCIAL STRUCTURE

8

Excessive FDI Flows Under Asymmetric Information

Assaf Razin, Efraim Sadka, and Chi-Wa Yuen

8.1 INTRODUCTION

An important aspect of foreign direct investment (FDI) is that it has proven to be resilient during financial crises. In situations of international illiquidity, when the country's consolidated financial system has short-term obligations in foreign currency in excess of foreign currency that the country has access to on short notice, FDI flows provide the only direct link between the domestic capital market in the host country and the world capital market at large. For instance, FDI flows to the East Asian countries were remarkably stable during the global financial crises of 1997–1998. In sharp contrast, portfolio equity and debt flows, as well as bank loans, dried up almost completely during the same period. The resilience of FDI to financial crises was also evident in the Mexican crisis of 1994 and the Latin American debt crisis of the early 1980s. This may reflect a unique characteristic of FDI, which is determined by considerations of ownership and control by multinationals of domestic activities, which are more long-term in nature, rather than by short-term fluctuations in the value of domestic currency and the availability of credit and liquidity.[1] The Asian crisis, although it featured massive outflows of short-term capital and sales of foreign equity holdings, was also accompanied by a wave of inward direct foreign investment, when after the financial collapse Asian companies were sold to foreign control at fire-sale prices. As Paul Krugman puts it (Krugman, 1998): "Does the foreign purchase of Asian assets represent the transfer of control to efficient owners or does it represent sales to inefficient owners who happen to have cash?"

---

[1] During a crisis, though, foreign direct investors may contribute to capital withdrawals by accelerating profit remittances or reducing the liabilities of affiliates towards their mother companies. While these are not recorded as negative FDI flows, they result from decisions made by foreign investors.

In other words, could FDI persistency in the face of financial crisis, along with the abundance of FDI flows into emerging economies in a period of tranquility, be a reflection of foreign overinvestment? In this chapter we try to assess the flip side of the relatively abundant FDI flows from the viewpoint of the host country, especially when FDI is leveraged domestically. Although foreign direct investors are naturally able to reap their profits from the host country, their investment may at the same time exacerbate distortions in the domestic capital market. The distortions originate mainly from the lack of corporate transparency, which gives rise to the familiar problem of asymmetric information between "insiders" and "outsiders" of firms operating in the domestic economy, including firms owned and controlled by the foreign direct investors. The domestic capital market could be trapped in a "lemons" situation described by Akerlof (1970): At the price offered by uninformed equity-buyers, which reflects the average productivity of firms whose shares are sold in the market, owners of firms (including FDI-owned firms) which have experienced a higher-than-average value will pull out of the market. This adverse selection problem in the domestic equity market could be magnified by the introduction of FDI flows, resulting in excessive investment by the foreign direct investors. At the same time, the adverse-selection effect worsens misincentives for the domestic savers, caused by a wedge that is driven between the marginal productivity of capital, on the one hand, and the intertemporal marginal rate of substitution in consumption, on the other hand.[2]

Typically, also, the domestic investment undertaken by FDI establishments is heavily leveraged through the domestic credit market. As a result, the fraction of domestic investment actually financed by foreign savings through FDI flows may not be as big as it may seem, and the size of the traditional gains from FDI may thus be further limited by the very sizable quantity of domestic leverage relative to the quantity of capital inflow. Note, nevertheless, that the model is not intended to explain a sudden reversal of flows leading to a financial crisis.

International capital flows, which typically fall into three major categories – portfolio flows, loans, and FDI – perform a variety of functions in the world economy. Their common traditional role lies in the blending of foreign savings with domestic savings to finance domestic investment. FDI, distinct from all other types of capital flows, performs an important additional function. FDI is not only an exchange of the own-

---

[2] There is no direct evidence on the extent of undersaving resulting from these misincentives. A study by the World Bank (1999) shows, however, that the correlation between FDI flows and total factor productivity growth in developing countries with high saving rates is positive and significant, whereas in countries with low saving rates the correlation is negative and significant.

ership of domestic investment sites from domestic residents to foreign residents, but also a corporate governance mechanism in which the foreign investor exercises management and control over the host country firm. In so doing, the foreign direct investors gain crucial inside information about the productivity of the firm under their control – an obvious advantage over the uninformed domestic savers, who are offering to buy shares in the firm which do not entail control. Taking advantage of their superior information, the foreign direct investors will tend to retain the high-productivity firms under their ownership and control and sell the low-productivity firms to these uninformed savers. This adverse selection problem, which plagues the domestic stock market, leads to overinvestment by the foreign direct investors even up to a point that, although first best capital inflows through FDI are not warranted, they nevertheless take place.

This view of FDI, no doubt only one aspect of the complex FDI phenomenon[3] that we shall focus on in this chapter, is that, although these flows are the most persistent among the major types of capital flows, they may actually bring social losses to the host country (to be distinguished from private gains or losses). We model capital flows through FDI in a familiar asymmetric information framework. In the welfare assessment we attempt to disentangle the nontraditional gains/losses from FDI flows from the traditional gains that are attributed to capital inflows, in general.

The rest of the chapter is organized as follows. In Section 8.2 we start with a reminder of the traditional argument in favor of capital mobility. We then develop in Section 8.3 a stylized model of FDI interacting with the domestic credit and stock markets. It turns out that the model may have more than one equilibrium. Different equilibria are characterized by significantly different volumes of FDI flows, as well as savings rates and welfare levels. In Section 8.4 we employ numerical simulations to

---

[3] Evidently, there are important aspects of FDI not dealt with in this chapter. It is commonly believed that FDI is beneficial for growth in less developed countries. Among other things, direct investment by multinational corporations in developing countries is considered as a major channel for access to advanced technologies owned by the major industrial countries. In particular, technological diffusion can take place through the importation of new varieties of inputs. This is in addition to the usual role of FDI as a channel for bringing in foreign savings to augment the stock of domestic capital. Both the technology-transfer and the traditional capital-augmenting roles of FDI translate into greater income growth in the host country.

FDI can also improve efficiency by promoting competition. The advanced technology possessed by the large size of multinational enterprises often enable them to invest in industries in which barriers to entry (such as large capital requirements) limit the potential access of local competitors. See Borenzstein, De Gregorio, and Lee (1998).

compute two FDI-equilibria and a financial autarky equilibrium, in order to assess the benefits of FDI. Section 8.5 concludes.

8.2 FIRST-BEST GAINS FROM CAPITAL MOBILITY

Textbook economic setups suggest that factors of production, if not constrained, move from locations where their marginal product is low, to other locations where their marginal product is high. In these setups, perfect competition with complete information prevails and there are no distortions (created by taxation, increasing returns, externalities, etc.), so that private returns to the factor owners coincide with the social returns. Accordingly, factor mobility, induced by private factor return differentials, is beneficial both for the owners of the factors that actually move from one location to another and to the source and destination economy.

The welfare impact of capital mobility can be neatly presented with the aid of the familiar scissors diagram (Figure 8.1) in which the marginal product capital for two countries (home and foreign) that comprise the world economy are depicted originating at opposite ends. Following MacDougall (1960), suppose that originally the world allocation of capital is at A with the home country having a higher marginal product of capital than the foreign country. If capital flows from the foreign country to the home country until the marginal product of capital is the same in the two countries, bringing the world allocation of capital to point E, then the world output is at a maximum.

In a laissez-faire, competitive environment with complete information and no barriers to capital mobility, AE units of capital will indeed flow from the foreign country to the home country. This is because in the aforementioned classical setup the market return to capital is equal to its marginal product, so that it will pay the owners of capital in the foreign country to invest AE units of it in the home country. After such investment is made, the return to capital is equalized in the two countries. Furthermore, not only world output (namely, the sum of the home and foreign GNP) rises, but the GNP of each country rises as well: The GNP of the home country rises from O_HMKA to O_HMRQA[4] and the GNP of the foreign country rises from O_FNSA to O_FNRQA,[5] so that world output rises by KSR.

This textbook description, which underscores the benefits that are associated with capital mobility, serves in this chapter as background to

---

[4] The GNP of the home country consists of its GDP, which is O_HMRE minus the income accruing to foreign owners of capital that is $AQRE$.

[5] The GNP of the foreign country consists of its GDP, which is O_FNRE plus foreign-source income that is $AQRE$.

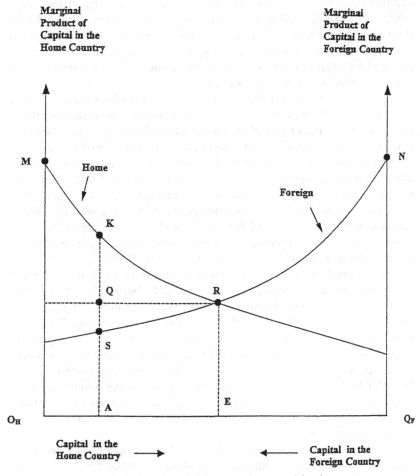

Figure 8.1. Allocation of capital between home and foreign country.

studying a sharply different setup that we develop here. FDI, a resilient type of capital flows, is introduced into an analytical framework in which domestic capital markets are characterized by imperfect information.

8.3 INTERACTIONS BETWEEN FDI FLOW AND THE DOMESTIC CREDIT MARKET

In the remainder of this chapter we examine an important feature of capital mobility which is not captured in the textbook analysis. This feature refers to imperfect information that leads to adverse selection in the capital market. This imperfection may turn around the flow of capital and thereby turn the welfare gain upside down. We assume a two-period model of a small, capital-importing country, referred to as the home country. It is assumed that capital imports are channelled solely through FDI. The economy is small enough so that, in the absence of any government intervention, it faces a perfectly elastic supply of external funds at a given risk-free world rate of interest, r^*.

We follow Gordon and Bovenberg (1996) and Razin, Sadka and Yuen (1998a, 1999a, 1999b) in modeling the risk in this economy. Suppose there is a very large number (N) of *ex-ante* identical domestic firms. Each firm employs capital input (K) in the first period in order to produce a single composite good in the second period. We assume that capital depreciates at the rate δ. Output in the second period is equal to $F(K)(1 + \varepsilon)$, where $F(\bullet)$ is a production function exhibiting diminishing marginal productivity of capital and ε is a random productivity factor with zero mean and is independent across all firms. (ε is bounded from below by -1, so that output is always nonnegative.) We assume that ε is purely idiosyncratic, so that there is no aggregate uncertainty. Through optimal portfolio decisions, consumer-savers will thus behave in a risk-neutral way.[6]

Investment decisions are made by the firms before the state of the world (i.e., ε) is known. Because all firms face the same probability distribution of ε, they all choose the same level of investment. They then seek funds to finance the investment. At this stage, the owner-managers of the firms are better informed than the outside fund-suppliers. There are many ways to specify the degree of this asymmetry in information. In order to facilitate the analysis, however, we simply assume that the owner-managers, being "close to the action," observe ε before they make their financing decisions, but the fund-providers, being "far away from the action," do not.

When investment is equity-financed, the original owner-managers observe ε while the new potential shareholders of the firm do not. The market will be trapped in the lemons situation described by Akerlof (1970). At the price offered by the new (uninformed) potential equity buyers, which reflects the average productivity of all firms (i.e., the average level of ε) in the market, the owner-manager of a firm experiencing a higher-than-average value of ε will not be willing to sell its shares and will pull out of the market completely. The equity market will fail to serve its investment-financing functions efficiently.

However, a domestic credit market can do the job of channeling domestic savings into domestic investment. Even FDI can utilize this

---

[6] Free trade in capital allows the spreading and sharing of risk and affects output growth (e.g., Obstfeld, 1994). By abstracting from aggregate risk in the chapter, we also abstract from the risk-sharing benefits that are potentially associated with FDI.

market. In fact, it is often observed that FDI is highly leveraged domestically. After gaining control of the domestic firm, a foreign direct investor usually resorts to the domestic credit market to finance new investments and possibly sell shares of the firm in the domestic equity market after flow profits from its original investment are realized.

8.3.1 FDI Equilibrium

In a formal sense, foreign acquisition of shares in domestic firms is classified as FDI when the shares acquired exceed a certain fraction of ownership (say, 10–20 percent). From an economic point of view, we look at FDI not just as ownership of a sizable share in a company but, more importantly, as an actual exercise of control and management and acquisition of inside information (the value of ε in our model). Indeed, it is the aspect of control which distinguishes FDI from other types of capital inflows, such as portfolio capital flows.

The sequencing of firm decisions is as follows. Before ε is revealed to anyone (i.e., under symmetric information), foreign investors bid up domestic firms from their original domestic owners, investment decisions are made, and full financing through domestic credit is secured. Then, ε is revealed to the owner-managers (who are all foreigners), but not also to domestic equity investors. At this stage, shares are offered in the domestic equity market, and the ownership in some of the firms is transferred to the domestic investors. In the initial stage (i.e., before ε is revealed to anyone), the foreign direct investors are able to outbid the domestic savers because the latter lack access to large amounts of funds necessary in order to seize control of the firms while the former, by assumption, are not liquidity-constrained.[7]

Because credit is extended *ex ante*, before ε is revealed, firms cannot sign default-free loan contracts with the lenders. We therefore consider loan contracts that allow for the possibility of default. We adopt the "costly state verification" framework *à la* Townsend (1979) in assuming that lenders make firm-specific loans, charging an interest rate of r^j to firm j ($j = 1, 2, \ldots, N$).[8] The interest and principal payment commitment will be honored when the firms encounter relatively good shocks, and

---

[7] The existence of wealthy individuals or families in the home country may possibly limit the scope of our analysis to the extent that they can compete with the foreign direct investors on control over these greenfield investment sites. Our analysis will carry over, however, if they form joint ventures with the foreign direct investors. On the other hand, the foreign direct investors need not be excessively resourceful. Even a small technological advantage they may enjoy above and beyond the domestic investors will enable them to bid up all these investment sites from the domestic investors and to gain control of these industries.

[8] See also Bernanke and Gertler (1989) and Stiglitz and Weiss (1981).

they will be defaulted when they encounter relatively bad shocks. The loan contract is characterized by a loan rate (r^j), with possible default, and a threshold value $(\bar{\varepsilon}^j)$ of the productivity parameter as follows:

$$F(K^j)(1+\bar{\varepsilon}^j)+(1-\delta)K^j = \left[K^j - (1-\delta)K_0^j\right](1+r^j) \qquad (1)$$

When the realized value of ε^j is larger than $\bar{\varepsilon}^j$, the firm is solvent and will thus pay the lenders the promised amount, consisting of the principal $K^j - (1 - \delta)K_0^j$ plus the interest $r^j[K' = (1 - \delta)K_0^j]$ as given by the right-hand side of equation (1). If, however, ε^j is smaller than $\bar{\varepsilon}^j$, the firm will default. In the case of default, the lenders can incur a cost in order to verify the true value of ε^j and to seize the residual value of the firm. This cost, interpretable as the cost of bankruptcy, is assumed to be proportional to the firm's realized gross return, $\mu[F(K^j)(1 + \varepsilon^j) + (1 - \delta)K^j]$, where $\mu < 1$ is the factor of proportionality. Net of this cost, the lenders will receive $(1 - \mu)[F(K^j)(1 + \varepsilon^j) + (1 - \delta)K^j]$.

Because there is no aggregate risk, the expected rate of return required by domestic consumer-savers, denoted by $\bar{r}$, can be secured by sufficient diversification. Therefore, the "default" rate of interest, r^j, must offer a premium over and above the default-free rate, $\bar{r}$, according to

$$[1-\Phi(\bar{\varepsilon}^j)]\left[K^j - (1-\delta)K_0^j\right](1+r^j)$$
$$+\Phi(\bar{\varepsilon})(1-\mu)\left\{F(K^j)[1+e^-(\bar{\varepsilon}^j)]+(1-\delta)K^j\right\}$$
$$=\left[K^j - (1-\delta)K_0^j\right](1+\dot{r}) \qquad (2')$$

where $\Phi(\bullet)$ is the cumulative probability distribution of ε, that is, $\Phi(\bar{\varepsilon}^j)$ = prob$(\varepsilon \leq \bar{\varepsilon}^j)$, and $e^-(\bar{\varepsilon}^j)$ is the mean value of ε realized by the low-productivity firms, that is, $e^-(\bar{\varepsilon}^j) \equiv E(\varepsilon|\varepsilon \leq \bar{\varepsilon}^j)$. For later use, we also denote by $e^+(\bar{\varepsilon}^j)$ the mean value of ε realized by the high-productivity firms, that is, $e^+(\bar{\varepsilon}^j) \equiv E(\varepsilon|\varepsilon \geq \bar{\varepsilon}^j)$.[9]

The first term on the left-hand-side of equation (2') is the contracted principal and interest payment, weighted by the no-default probability. The second term measures the net residual value of the firm, weighted by the default probability. The right-hand side is the no-default return required by the domestic lender. Observe that equations (1) and (2') together imply that

$$[1-\Phi(\bar{\varepsilon}^j)]+\frac{\Phi(\bar{\varepsilon}^j)(1-\mu)\left\{F(K^j)[1+e^-(\bar{\varepsilon}^j)]+(1-\delta)K^j\right\}}{F(K^j)(1+\bar{\varepsilon}^j)+(1-\delta)K^j}=\frac{1+\bar{r}}{1+r^j}$$

---

[9] The weighted average of $e^-(\bar{\varepsilon}^j)$ and $e^+(\bar{\varepsilon}^j)$ must yield the average value of ε, that is, $\Phi(\bar{\varepsilon}^j)$ $e^-(\bar{\varepsilon}^j) + [1 - \Phi(\bar{\varepsilon}^j)]e^+(\bar{\varepsilon}^j) = E(\varepsilon) = 0$. This, in turn, implies that $e^-(\bar{\varepsilon}^j) < 0$ while $e^+(\bar{\varepsilon}^j) > 0$ – that is, the expected value of ε for the "bad" ("good") firm j negative (positive).

Because $\varepsilon^-(\bar{\varepsilon}^j) < \bar{\varepsilon}^j$ and $0 \le \mu \le 1$, it follows that $r^j > \bar{r}$, the difference being a risk-premium (which depends, among other things, on K^j, $\bar{\varepsilon}^j$, and μ).

The firm in this setup is competitive (i.e., a price-taker) only with respect to $\bar{r}$, the market default-free rate of return. This $\bar{r}$ cannot be influenced by the firm's actions. However, r^j, K^j, and $\bar{\varepsilon}^j$ are firm-specific and must satisfy equations (1) and (2'). In making its investment [i.e., choosing $K^j - (1 - \delta)K_0^j$] and its financing (loan contract) decisions, the firm takes these constraints into account. Because these decisions are made before ε is known – that is, when all firms are (*ex ante*) identical – they all make the same decision. We henceforth drop the superscript *j*.

In the equity market that opens after ε is revealed to the (foreign) owner-managers, there is a cutoff level of ε, denoted by ε^0, such that all firms experiencing a value of ε above ε^0 will be retained by the foreign direct investors and all other firms (with ε below ε^0) will be sold to domestic savers. This cutoff level of ε is given by

$$\frac{[F(K)(1+\varepsilon^o)+(1-\delta)K]-[K-(1-\delta)K_0](1+r)}{1+r^*} = \left(\frac{\Phi(\bar{\varepsilon})}{\Phi(\varepsilon^o)}\right) \bullet 0$$

$$+\left(\frac{\Phi(\varepsilon^o)-\Phi(\bar{\varepsilon})}{\Phi(\varepsilon^o)}\right)$$

$$\bullet \left(\frac{\{F(K)[1+\hat{e}(\bar{\varepsilon},\varepsilon^o)]+(1-\delta)K\}-[K-(1-\delta)K_0](1+r)}{1+\bar{r}}\right) \qquad (3')$$

where $\hat{e}(\bar{\varepsilon}, \varepsilon^o) \equiv E(\varepsilon | \bar{\varepsilon} < \varepsilon < \varepsilon^o)$ is the conditional expectation of ε given ε lies between $\bar{\varepsilon}$ and ε^o.

Notice that firms that experience a value of ε below $\bar{\varepsilon}$ default and have zero value. These firms are not retained by the foreign direct investors; hence $\varepsilon^o \ge \bar{\varepsilon}$. All other firms generate in the second period a *net* cash flow of $\{F(K)(1 + \varepsilon) + (1 - \delta)K\} - [K - (1 - \delta)K_0](1 + r)$. The left-hand side of equation (3') represents the marginal (from the bottom of the distribution) firm retained by foreign investors. The right-hand side of equation (3') is the expected value of the firms that are purchased by domestic savers. With a conditional probability of $[\Phi(\varepsilon^o) - \Phi(\bar{\varepsilon})]/\Phi(\varepsilon^o)$, they generate a net expected cash flow of $\{F(K)[1 + \hat{e}(\bar{\varepsilon}, \varepsilon^o)] + (1 - \delta)K\} - [K - (1 - \delta)K_0](1 + r)$; and with a probability of $\Phi(\bar{\varepsilon})/\Phi(\varepsilon^o)$, they generate a zero net cash flow. This explains equation (3').

We can substitute equation (1) into (2') and (3') in order to eliminate r and then rearrange terms to obtain

$$[1-\Phi(\bar{\varepsilon})]F(K)(1+\bar{\varepsilon})+\Phi(\bar{\varepsilon})(1-\mu)F(K)[1+e^-(\bar{\varepsilon})]$$
$$+[1-\Phi(\bar{\varepsilon})\mu](1-\delta)K = [K-(1-\delta)K_0](1+\bar{r}) \qquad (2)$$

and

$$\frac{\varepsilon^o - \bar{\varepsilon}}{1 + r*} = \left(\frac{\Phi(\varepsilon^o) - \Phi(\bar{\varepsilon})}{\Phi(\varepsilon^o)}\right) \cdot \left(\frac{\hat{e}(\bar{\varepsilon}, \varepsilon^o) - \bar{\varepsilon}}{1 + \bar{r}}\right) \tag{3}$$

Consider now the capital investment decision of the firm that is made before ε becomes known, while it is still owned by foreign direct investors. With a probability of $\Phi(\varepsilon^o) - \Phi(\bar{\varepsilon})$, it will be sold to domestic savers who pay a positive price equalling

$$\{F(K)[1 + \hat{e}(\bar{\varepsilon}, \varepsilon^o)] + (1 - \delta)K - [K - (1 - \delta)K_0](1 + r)\}/(1 + \bar{r})$$
$$= F(K)[\hat{e}(\bar{\varepsilon}, \varepsilon^o) - \bar{\varepsilon}]/(1 + \bar{r})$$

by using equation (1). With a probability of $1 - \Phi(\varepsilon^o)$, it will be retained by the foreign investors for whom it is worth:

$$\{F(K)[1 + e^+(\varepsilon^o)] + (1 - \delta)K - [K - (1 - \delta)K_0](1 + r)\}/(1 + r*)$$
$$= F(K)[e^+(\varepsilon^o) - \bar{\varepsilon}]/(1 + r*)$$

by using (1). Hence, the firm seeks to maximize

$$V = [1 - \Phi(\varepsilon^o)] \cdot \left(\frac{F(K)[e^+(\varepsilon^o) - \bar{\varepsilon}]}{1 + r*}\right)$$
$$+ \Phi(\bar{\varepsilon}) \cdot 0 + [\Phi(\varepsilon^o) - \Phi(\bar{\varepsilon})] \cdot \left(\frac{F(K)[\hat{e}(\bar{\varepsilon}, \varepsilon^o) - \bar{\varepsilon}]}{1 + \bar{r}}\right) \tag{4}$$

subject to constraint (2), by choice of K and $\bar{\varepsilon}$, given ε^o.[10] The first-order conditions are spelled out in Appendix 8A.

The (maximized) value of V in equation (4) is the price paid by the foreign direct investors at the greenfield stage of investment. Because the value of ε is not known at this point, the same price is paid for all firms. The low ε firms are then (after ε is revealed to the foreign direct investors) resold to domestic savers, all at the same price, because ε is not observed by these savers. Net capital inflows through FDI are given by

$$FDI = N[1 - \Phi(\varepsilon^o)]F(K)[e^+(\varepsilon^o) - \bar{\varepsilon}]/(1 + r*) \tag{5}$$

[see equation (4)]. Unlike the case with no domestic credit (in which the foreign direct investors have to bring in their own capital to finance the domestic investment projects), all capital outlays are financed domestically and FDI consists only of the price paid for the ownership and control of the high ε firms.

---

[10] The ε^o condition, as given by equation (3), is determined by equilibrium in the equity market. As such, it will not be taken into account by the price-taking firms when choosing their investment levels.

The remainder of the equilibrium conditions is standard. The first-period resource constraint is given by

$$FDI = N[K - (1-\delta)K_0] - [NF(K_0) - c_1] \quad (6)$$

The second-period resource constraint is

$$c_2 = N[F(K) + (1-\delta)K] - FDI(1+r^*)$$
$$- N\mu\Phi(\bar{\varepsilon})\{F(K)[1 + e^-(\bar{\varepsilon})] + (1-\delta)K\} \quad (7)$$

Note that the last term on the left-hand side of equation (7) reflects the existence of real default costs. Finally, the consumer-savers do not have access to the world capital market and can only borrow/lend from the domestic market. As a result, in maximizing utility, they will equate their intertemporal marginal rate of substitution to the domestic risk-free rate of return:

$$\frac{u_1(c_1, c_2)}{u_2(c_1, c_2)} = 1 + \bar{r} \quad (8)$$

In this model, the eight equations [i.e., (2), (3), (5)–(8) together with the two first-order conditions associated with the choice of K and $\bar{\varepsilon}$] determine the eight endogenous variables, that is, K, $\bar{r}$, $\bar{\varepsilon}$, ε^o, c_1, c_2, FDI, and the Lagrange multiplier λ associated with the constraint (2).

8.4 GAINS FROM FDI

To flesh out in a simplified manner the kind of gains or losses brought about by FDI, we compare the laissez-faire allocation in the presence of FDI with the closed economy laissez-faire allocation. The latter economy is referred to as autarky.

In the autarky case, the "lemons" problem will drive the equity market out of existence. Firms will have to rely solely on the provision of domestic credit in financing their investment projects. The firm-specific debt contract for any firm j continues to be characterized by a default-risky interest rate (r^j) and a threshold productivity level ($\bar{\varepsilon}^j$) that satisfy the cutoff condition (3'). The default-free interest rate ($\bar{r}$) is still defined implicitly by (2'). Again, because all firms are *ex ante* identical, we can drop the superscript j. The firm's investment decision is to choose K, r, and $\bar{\varepsilon}$ to solve the following problem:

$$\underset{\{K, r, \bar{\varepsilon}\}}{Max} F(K) - \Phi(\bar{\varepsilon})\{F(K)[1 + e^-(\bar{\varepsilon})] + (1-\delta)K\}$$
$$- [1 - \Phi(\bar{\varepsilon})][K - (1-\delta)K_0](1+r) \quad (4')$$

subject to equations (1) and (2′). We can use equation (1) to substitute out the risky interest rate (r) in equation (2′) as well as in the objective function above. The first-order conditions with respect to K and $\bar{\varepsilon}$ for this reduced problem are laid out in Appendix 8A. Utility maximization by the consumer-savers continues to yield the same intertemporal condition (8). In the absence of capital flows, $FDI \equiv 0$ in the two resource constraints (6) and (7). The five equations (2), (6), (7), and the two first-order conditions for K and $\bar{\varepsilon}$ (laid out in Appendix 8A) determine the five endogenous variables K^A, $\bar{r}^A$, $\bar{\varepsilon}^A$, c_1^A, and c_2^A.

In the open economy case with domestic credit, FDI has conflicting effects on welfare. Its first role [discussed in detail in Razin, Sadka, and Yuen (1999b)] is to facilitate the channeling of domestic saving into domestic investment by getting around a "lemons" problem and sustaining a domestic equity market. This, by itself, is welfare-enhancing. But, as we have already indicated, FDI is driven also by distorted incentives; in their presence the channeling of foreign savings into domestic investment may generate an excessive stock of domestic capital (either when capital inflows are not needed at all or, when they are needed to start with, too much takes place). This foreign overinvestment (coupled with the possibility of domestic undersaving) tends to reduce welfare.

We use numerical examples to illustrate the effect of FDI on welfare. In these examples, we employ a logarithmic utility function [$u(c_1, c_2) = \ln(c_1) + \gamma \ln(c_2)$], with a subjective discount factor γ, a Cobb–Douglas production function ($F(K) = Ak^a$), and a uniform distribution of ε defined over the interval $[-\alpha, \alpha]$. The welfare gain (loss) is measured by the uniform percentage change (in c_1 and c_2) which is needed in order to lift the autarkic utility level to the FDI utility level. We set the parameter values as follows: $\gamma = 0.28$, $\alpha = 0.33$, $\delta = 0.56$, $N = 1$, $A = 0.9$, $K_0 = 0.03$, $\alpha = 0.84$, and $\mu = 0.05$. Because we think of each period as constituting half of the lifetime of a generation (i.e., about 25 years), the values of γ and δ are chosen in such a way as to reflect an annual time preference rate of about 3 percent and an annual depreciation rate of about 3 percent.

Unlike the case of no domestic credit market, where the domestic stock market fails to finance investment because of the "lemons" problem, an autarkic economy in this case can utilize domestic savings to debt-finance domestic investment. The beneficial role of FDI as a vehicle for sustaining a domestic stock market through which domestic savings are channeled into domestic investment is thus substantially diminished. Consequently, the negative effect of FDI associated with the distorted incentives emanating from the domestic equity market dominates, and altogether there may exist a net welfare loss from intertemporal trade.

We now focus our attention on the second effect of FDI. Figure 8.2 compares the utility of the representative consumer generated by free

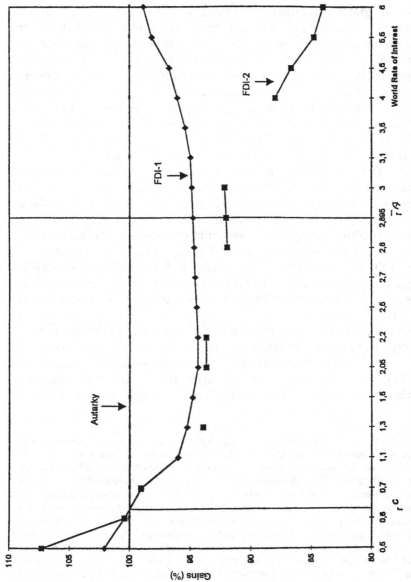

Figure 8.2. Welfare gains from FDI relative to financial autarky. *Note:* FDI-1 (diamonds) refers to low default rate equilibrium; FDI-2 (squares) refers to high default rate equilibrium.

295

flows of FDI for different world rates of interest ($r*$) with the utility entailed under autarky. Naturally, the autarky utility level does not depend on the world rate of interest ($r*$): The horizontal line describes the utility level under autarky. We measure the utility level by an index, where the level under autarky is set equal to 100. The utility index in the presence of FDI is measured against this base index by calculating the percentage change in lifetime consumption under autarky which will lift autarkic utility to the corresponding utility level in the presence of FDI.

It turns out that there are *two* FDI equilibria.[11] The first equilibrium (FDI −1), represented by the curve with diamonds in Figure 8.2, is characterized by a relatively low rate of default on credit (low $\bar{\varepsilon}$), while the second (FDI −2), indicated by squares, is characterized by a high default rate (high $\bar{\varepsilon}$). Evidently, a sudden shift from the bad equilibria to the good equilibria, triggered by a switch in expectations, can have significant effect on the economy. For example, as shown in Figures 8.2 and 8.3, at the world interest rate 5.5 percent, a shift from the good equilibrium to the bad equilibrium leads to a rise in FDI from a medium fraction of GDP (about 8 percent) to a large fraction (about 13 percent) of GDP.[12]

A critical value of the rate of interest, which implies that the inflows of capital are neither welfare improving nor welfare reducing, is denoted by r^c. If the world rate of interest is equal to this rate, the beneficial effect of FDI, being the flow of foreign saving that complements domestic saving in the financing of domestic investment (when the world rate of

---

[11] Notice that there is a strong element of *circularity* involved in two credit-market relationships, equations (1) and (2′). To see this, note that, on the one hand, a rise in the firm-specific rate of interest (including risk premium), r, implies that the cutoff productivity level (which determines the number of solvent firms and the number of insolvent firms in equilibrium), $\bar{\varepsilon}$, must rise. This is because more firms are expected to default with the rise in the rate of interest [see equation (1)]. On the other hand, when the cutoff productivity level, $\bar{\varepsilon}$, rises, the return on risky credit must rise, and therefore r should rise as well. The increase in r is needed in order to restore the balance between the risky return and the alternative return on the risk-free credit, governed by the risk-free rate of interest, $\bar{r}$ [see equation (2′)]. Interacting with the adverse-selection effect of FDI, the circularity property leads, under some parameter configurations, to a multiplicity of equilibria.

[12] At the same time, the capital stock rises from 0.05 to 0.75; the risk-free rate of interest falls from about 2.25 to 1; first-period consumption rises from 0.255 to 0.275, while second period consumption declines from 0.24 to 0.125; the solvency/insolvency cutoff productivity level, $\bar{\varepsilon}$, rises from −0.84 to −0.75; and the productivity cutoff level, ε^o, which determines the number of low-productivity firms that the FDI investors sell in the domestic stock market, declines from 0.65 to −0.65.

interest is still below the autarkic domestic rate of interest), is offset by the adverse-selection effect of FDI on the domestic stock market. The rate r^c is shown in Figure 8.2 by the intersection between the flat line, representing autarky equilibrium, and the two curves representing the FDI equilibria (overlapping, at this point).

Consider first the case where the world rate of interest (r^*) is above the critical rate of interest; that is, $r^* > r^c (<\bar{r}^A$, the autarkic rate of interest).[13] In this case, FDI is clearly welfare reducing. Among the two FDI-equilibria depicted in Figure 8.2, the equilibrium associated with the high FDI delivers low utility (the curve with squares) while the equilibrium associated with the low FDI generates relatively high level of utility (the curve with diamonds). However, the utility levels that are associated with low- and high-FDI equilibria fall short of the level of utility under financial autarky, in the absence of FDI. Therefore, the adverse-selection effect of FDI leads to *excessive* FDI flows under both low- and high-default rate equilibria.

The policy implication in the short run is nonorthodox: A quantity ceiling on FDI flows. Indeed, a total ban on FDI is desirable whenever the world rate of interest exceeds the critical rate of interest. An alternative is to not allow foreign control of industries in which the asymmetric information is severe. In the longer run, a regulatory reform that will enhance the balance sheet transparency of domestic corporations is, evidently, a more efficient cure.

Consider, next, the case where the world rate of interest (r^*) is below the critical rate of interest, r^c (which, in turn, is smaller than autarky rate of interest, $\bar{r}^A$). In this case we expect the positive (traditional) traditional welfare effect of FDI, which allows foreign-saving financing of domestic investment in addition to the domestic saving finance, to dominate the adverse-selection (negative) effect of FDI on the domestic stock market. In this case we again have multiplicity of equilibria. At least one of these equilibria delivers utility level above the autarkic level of utility (the curve with squares), in accordance with the traditional gains-from-trade theorem. It turns out that in this case also, the good

---

[13] Recall that in a distortion-free, perfectly competitive setup, the autarkic rate of interest is the benchmark rate for predicting the direction of capital movements. If the world rate of interest falls short of the benchmark rate, capital flows in; if the world rate of interest exceeds the benchmark rate, capital flows out. The larger the (absolute) difference between the rates, the larger the gains from capital mobility. See, however, Helpman and Razin (1983) for a different setup, with increasing returns to scale and imperfect competition, in which capital inflows are taking place even though they are not warranted under the first principle which compares the autarkic marginal productivity of capital to the world rate of interest.

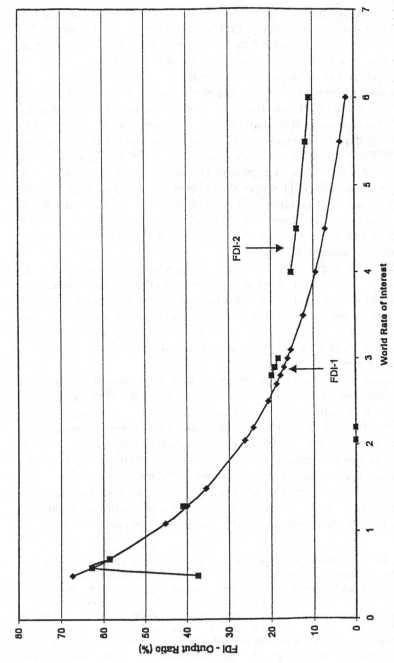

Figure 8.3. Intensity of FDI flows. *Note:* FDI-1 (diamonds) refers to low default rate equilibrium; FDI-2 (squares) refers to high default rate equilibrium.

equilibrium is associated with relatively low FDI flows (but it is now the high rate of default equilibrium, indicated by squares; see Figure 8.3). In order to sustain this low-FDI equilibrium (and thus avoid the trap of falling into a high-FDI equilibrium), policymakers may resort again to a ceiling on FDI. But, since FDI flows are now evidently warranted, in contrast to the first case in which $r^* \geqslant r^c$, the quantity ceiling does not at all mean a total ban on FDI inflows. The quantity ceiling's role, in the case $r^* \leqslant r^c$, is to eliminate one of the two equilibria – the one with relatively large FDI inflows.

8.5 CONCLUSION

Elsewhere, in Razin, Sadka, and Yuen (1998, 1999a), we explored the policy implications of the home bias in international portfolio investment as a result of asymmetric information problems in which domestic savers, being "close" to the domestic market, have an informational advantage over foreign portfolio investors, who are "far away" from the domestic market. However, FDI is different from foreign portfolio investment, concerning relevant information about domestic firms. Through the stationing of managers from the headquarters of multinational firms in the destination countries, FDI investors can monitor closely the operation of such establishments, thus circumventing these informational problems.

Furthermore, FDI investors not only have an informational advantage over foreign portfolio investors, but also are more informed than domestic savers, because FDI entails direct control on the acquired domestic firm, which the typical domestic savers with ownership position do not have. Being "insiders," the FDI investors can "overcharge" the uninformed domestic savers, the "outsiders," when multinational subsidiaries shares are traded in the domestic stockmarket. By anticipating future domestic stock market trade opportunities in advance, foreign investment becomes excessive. However, unlike the home-bias informational problem, which leads to inadequate foreign portfolio capital inflows, but may be correctable by Pigouvian taxes on nonresident income, tax interest income, or corporate income (see Razin, Sadka, and Yuen, 1998, 1999a), excessive FDI flows under the insider–outsider informational problem call for *nontax* corrective policy – first, because they are governed by unobservable variables; and second, because there exist self-fulfilling expectations equilibria which cannot be efficiently corrected by taxation. The corrective policy tool that is left available is then simply quantity restrictions on FDI.

Finally, note that excessive FDI stems from the asymmetry in information between FDI investors and outsiders. Persistence of this asymmetry requires that domestic savers cannot infer the productivity factor (ε) of FDI-owned firms from their price. This may happen if the firms are not traded.

APPENDIX

Appendix 8A. Derivation of First-order Conditions for the Firm's Investment Problem

In the presence of FDI, the maximization of the firm value V, as specified in equation (4), with respect to K and $\bar{\varepsilon}$ yields the following first-order conditions:

$$0 = \left\{\frac{[1-\Phi(\varepsilon^o)][e^+(\varepsilon^o)-\bar{\varepsilon}]}{1+r^*} + \frac{[\Phi(\varepsilon^o)-\Phi(\bar{\varepsilon})][\hat{e}(\bar{\varepsilon},\varepsilon^o)-\bar{\varepsilon}]}{1+\bar{r}}\right\}F'(K)$$
$$+\lambda\{[1-\Phi(\bar{\varepsilon})](1+\bar{\varepsilon})+\Phi(\bar{\varepsilon})(1-\mu)[1+e^-(\bar{\varepsilon})]\}F'(K)$$
$$-\lambda(\bar{r}+\delta)-\lambda\Phi(\bar{\varepsilon})\mu(1-\delta) \tag{8A.1}$$

and

$$0 = \frac{1-\Phi(\varepsilon^o)}{1+r^*} + \frac{\Phi'(\bar{\varepsilon})[\hat{e}(\bar{\varepsilon},\varepsilon^o)-\bar{\varepsilon}]}{1+\bar{r}}$$
$$+\frac{[\Phi(\varepsilon^o)-\Phi(\bar{\varepsilon})]\left[\dfrac{\partial\hat{e}}{\partial\bar{\varepsilon}}(\bar{\varepsilon},\varepsilon^o)-1\right]}{1+\bar{r}} - \lambda\Phi'(\bar{\varepsilon})(1+\bar{\varepsilon})$$
$$+\lambda[1-\Phi(\bar{\varepsilon})]+\lambda\Phi'(\bar{\varepsilon})(1-\mu)[1+e^-(\bar{\varepsilon})]$$
$$-\lambda\Phi(\bar{\varepsilon})(1-\mu)\frac{de^-(\bar{\varepsilon})}{d\bar{\varepsilon}}F(K)-\lambda\mu\Phi'(\bar{\varepsilon})(1-\delta)K \tag{8A.2}$$

where λ is a Lagrange multiplier. Our numerical simulations suggest that there will be domestic undersaving and foreign overinvestment, that is, $\bar{r} < F'(K) - \delta < r^*$.

In the absence of FDI, the first-order conditions for the maximization problem as stated in equation (4′) with respect to K and $\bar{\varepsilon}$ are

$$0 = F'(K)-\Phi(\bar{\varepsilon})\{F'(K)[1+e^-(\bar{\varepsilon})]+(1-\delta)\}$$
$$+[1-\Phi(\bar{\varepsilon})][F'(K)(1+\bar{\varepsilon})+(1-\delta)]$$
$$+\lambda[1-\Phi(\bar{\varepsilon})][F'(K)(1+\bar{\varepsilon})+(1-\delta)]$$
$$+\lambda\Phi(\bar{\varepsilon})(1-\mu)\{F'(K)[1+e^-(\bar{\varepsilon})]+(1-\delta)\}$$
$$-\lambda(1+\bar{r}) \tag{8A1.1′}$$

and

$$0 = -\Phi'(\bar{\varepsilon})\{F(K)[1 + e^-(\bar{\varepsilon})] + (1 - \delta)K\}$$
$$-\Phi(\bar{\varepsilon})F(K)[de^-(\bar{\varepsilon})/d\bar{\varepsilon}] - [1 - \Phi(\bar{\varepsilon})]F(K)$$
$$+\Phi(\bar{\varepsilon})[F(K)(1 + \bar{\varepsilon}) + (1 - \delta)K] + \lambda[1 - \Phi(\bar{\varepsilon})]F(K)$$
$$-\lambda\Phi'(\bar{\varepsilon})[F(K)(1 + \bar{\varepsilon}) + (1 - \delta)K]$$
$$+\lambda\Phi'(\bar{\varepsilon})(1 - \mu)\{F(K)[1 + e^-(\bar{\varepsilon})] + (1 - \delta)K\}$$
$$+\lambda\Phi(\bar{\varepsilon})(1 - \mu)\{F(K)[de^-(\bar{\varepsilon})/d\bar{\varepsilon}]\} \tag{8A1.2'}$$

REFERENCES

Akerlof, George (1970). "The Market for 'Lemons': Qualitative Uncertainty and the Market Mechanism," *Quarterly Journal of Economics* **89**:488–500.

Bernanke, Benjamin and Marc Gertler (1989). "Agency Costs, Net Worth, and Business Fluctuations," *American Economic Review* **79**:14–31.

Borensztein, Eduardo, Jose De Gregorio, and Jong-Wha Lee (1998). "How Does Foreign Direct Investment Affect Economic Growth?" *Journal of International Economics* **45**:115–135.

Gordon, Roger H. and A. Lans Bovenberg (1996). "Why Is Capital So Immobile Internationally?: Possible Explanations and Implications for Capital Income Taxation," *American Economic Review* **86**:1057–1075.

Helpman, Elhanan, and Assaf Razin (1983). "Increasing Returns, Monopolistic Competition and Factor Movements: A Welfare Analysis," *Journal of International Economics* **14**:263–276.

Krugman, Paul (1998). "Fire-Sale FDI." Mimeo, MIT (available at http://web.mit.edu/krugman/www/FIRESALE.html).

MacDougall, G.D. (1960). "The Benefits and Costs of Private Investment from Abroad: A Theoretical Approach," *Economic Record* **26**(1):13–35.

Obstfeld, Maurice (1994). "Risk-Taking, Global Diversification, and Growth," *American Economic Review* **84**(5):1310–1329.

Razin, Assaf, Efraim Sadka, and Chi-Wa Yuen (1998). "A Pecking Order of Capital Inflows and International Tax Principles," *Journal of International Economics* **44**:45–68.

——— (1999a). "Implications of the Home Bias: A Pecking Order of Capital Inflows and Corrective Taxation." In Assaf Razin and Efraim Sadka, eds., *The Economics of Globalization: Policy Perspectives from Public Economics*. New York: Cambridge University Press, Chapter 4, pp. 85–122.

——— (1999b). "An Information-Based Model of Foreign Direct Investment: The Gains from Trade Revisited," *International Tax and Public Finance* **4**(6):579–596.

Stiglitz, Joseph E., and Andrew Weiss (1981). "Credit Rationing in Markets with Imperfect Information," *American Economic Review* **71**:393–410.

Townsend, Robert M. (1979). "Optimal Contracts and Competitive Markets with Costly State Verification," *Journal of Economic Theory* **21**:265–293.

World Bank (1999). *Global Development Finance.*

Discussion

Excessive FDI Flows under Asymmetric Information

Maurice Obstfeld

The conventional wisdom holds that foreign direct investment (FDI) flows are less volatile, and therefore less dangerous, than short-term port-folio debt flows, especially for emerging markets. Econometrically detectable positive linkages to domestic investment seem clearest for FDI inflows. As a result, countries often woo foreign direct investors.

This analysis of Razin, Sadka, and Yuen turns the conventional wisdom on its head. It argues that under asymmetric information, FDI inflows can be excessive and produce multiple equilibria.

An important paper by Gordon and Bovenberg (1996) provides background for this one. In that paper, the setup is as follows:

- Domestic residents invest within their home country.
- They see a signal ε of productivity that is invisible to foreign equity investors.
- The domestic investors sell to foreigners, at an endogenous price, those of their investments for which ε is low enough that the return from selling, and buying a riskless domestic asset, exceeds the return from retaining the project.
- The result is a "lemons" problem; and because foreigners know about the adverse selection problem in equity sales, equity prices depends on the conditional expectation $E(\varepsilon \mid \varepsilon \leq \varepsilon^*)$, where ε^* is the cutoff productivity signal below which domestic residents wish to unload their investments onto foreign direct investors.

A key question in the Gordon–Bovenberg setup is, Why is there any equity trade at all? Why doesn't the home equity market simply collapse, as in Akerlof's basic lemons model?

The answer hinges on the international setting of the model. The reason for trade between domestic and foreign wealth owners is that rate of return differentials partially counteract the lemons effect. Specifically, the domestic risk-free interest rate, r, exceeds the world risk-free rate,

$r*$, due to restrictions on risk-free capital inflows. This interest-rate wedge lowers domestic equity prices compared to those of comparable world equities, making them attractive despite adverse selection. The model's implications include insufficient equity inflows and home bias in equity holdings. A consequence of the Gordon–Bovenberg setup's assumed international bond-market segmentation, however, is that it does not explain how arbitrage for riskless assets can coexist with Feldstein–Horioka-type saving-investment correlations and home bias.

The chapter by Razin, Sadka, and Yuen (RSY), in effect, "inverts" Gordon and Bovenberg's assumptions. In the RSY setup:

- Foreign FDI investors buy greenfield sites, financing by borrowing in the *domestic* (not world) credit market.
- They, and not the locals, see the private productivity signal ε.
- After observing ε, they sell to the locals all projects with ε below a cutoff $\varepsilon*$. (If ε is very low, there is default on loans.)
- Once more, a lemons problem arises. This time it *encourages* FDI inflows, since lemons can be pawned off on the natives.

A reader of Akerlof would want to know again why the equity market doesn't simply collapse. The reasoning is the inverse of that in Gordon and Bovenberg. RSY assume that the configuration of riskless interest rates entails $r < r*$, so the locals are getting equity at bargain prices, all else equal; see their equation (3). The immediate implication is that excessive FDI occurs, and, presumably, excessive international diversification. The model also implies the possibility of multiple equilibria. As foreign FDI investors encounter higher borrowing rates in the domestic credit market, the cutoff productivity signal $\varepsilon*$ is pushed higher, the expected return to investment rises, and FDI rises. The reasoning is reminiscent of that in the Stiglitz–Weiss model of credit rationing. The authors are led to favor quantitative restrictions over taxes on FDI due to the danger of multiple equilibrium situations.

The analysis provokes a number of reactions. Most obviously, the authors' theoretical point, valid given their assumptions, does not explain any striking empirical regularities. Indeed several assumptions and implications of the model seem decidedly counterfactual. Do multinationals really finance their projects in FDI target countries' credit markets? Do bond rates in such countries, which I tend to think of as emerging markets, really hover below rather than above industrial-country bond rates? Indeed, is it sensible to think of risk-free rates at all in this setting? Can anyone seriously contend that there is too much FDI relative to other forms of capital inflow?

The chapter would benefit in clarity from a more detailed description of which asset markets meet when, which capital controls are in effect, and so on. For example, domestic residents lend to FDI investors here; but then what do they use to buy equities from them? Do they use their prior loans, some of which are about to go sour?

The model contains big incentives for capital flight (because $r < r^*$); there could be overinvoicing of equity, for example. This raises another question about asset-market restrictions. Can FDI investors borrow at the domestic risk-free rate? If so, they could move funds abroad and invest at r^*.

Are there domestic financial intermediaries in the background, and does it matter? Why can't domestic residents borrow from domestic credit institutions and invest themselves? Their capital could serve as collateral. Do foreigners put up collateral? They would have a strong incentive to pronounce that they are investing, and instead spirit funds abroad secretly, as in the analysis of North–South lending by Gertler and Rogoff.

The multiplicity of equilibria is suggestive of crisis models, but this is not a plausible story of sudden shifts in capital flows. Here, in a "bad" equilibrium, FDI rises spectacularly. We do not observe this just prior to or during real-life crises.

In sum, the authors draw logically correct conclusions from implausible assumptions, with the result being implausible predictions, both positive and normative. A more detailed account of the foundations of the model would be useful, however, in helping readers to judge whether this version of the world or that depicted by Gordon and Bovenberg is more likely to govern FDI flows.

REFERENCE

Gordon, Roger H. and A. Lans Bovenberg (1996). "Why is Capital So Immobile Internationally? Possible Explanations and Implications for Capital Income Taxation," *American Economic Review* **86**:1057–1075.

9

Corporate Growth and Risk around the World

Stijn Claessens, Simeon Djankov, and Tatiana Nenova

9.1 INTRODUCTION

Firm financing patterns have long been the object of study of the corporate finance literature. Financing patterns have traditionally been analyzed in the Modigliani–Miller framework, expanded to incorporate taxes and bankruptcy costs. More recently, asymmetric information issues have drawn attention to agency costs and their impact on firm financing choices. An important literature also exists relating financing patterns to firm performance and governance.

The financial structure of the corporate sector has proven relevant in other areas of economic research as well. Several recent studies have focused on identifying systematic cross-country differences in firm financing patterns. Those studies have identified the effects of such differences on financial sector development and economic growth. They have also examined the causes of different financing patterns, particularly the role of countries' legal and institutional environments.[1] Finally, firm financing choices have emerged as an important factor in the literature on predicting and explaining financial instability.[2]

Corporate sector risk characteristics, however, have not been much examined in the literature, aside from leverage and debt maturity considerations. Even these measures have been the object of few empirical

We thank Ying Lin for excellent research support; Richard Lyons and participants in the conference on "Financial Crises in Emerging Markets," organized by the Federal Reserve Bank of San Francisco; seminar participants at Harvard University and George Washington University; Reuven Glick, Oliver Hart, Rafael La Porta, Randall Morck, Ramon Moreno, Andrei Shleifer, and the three reviewers for helpful comments.

[1] See Demirgüç-Kunt and Maksimovic (1998, 1999) on financing patterns and growth, and La Porta et al. (1999b) on legal and institutional environments and their impact on the corporate sector.

[2] Krugman (1999) draws attention to the possibility of a "transfer problem" arising if the corporate sector has large foreign exchange liabilities.

investigations, mainly due to a paucity of data on corporate sectors around the world. Building on data that have recently become available, we fill this gap in the literature and shed light on the risk characteristics of corporate sectors around the world. We use data for 11,000 firms from 46 countries over the period 1995–1996, and we calculate 12 indicators typically used by financial analysts to gauge a firm's risk. We also analyze three corporate accounting profitability characteristics. These measures show large cross-country differences in corporate risk and performance.

We examine whether differences in corporate financing patterns and risk-taking behavior across countries reflect the legal, regulatory, and financial environments in the respective countries. We document that there are a number of institutional features that are consistently associated with the degree of financial risk-taking behavior by corporations. In particular, corporations in common law countries and those in market-based financial systems appear less risky. Stronger protection of property rights is associated with lower measured financial risks. These institutional factors also appear to be related to cross-country profitability characteristics.

The rest of the chapter is organized as follows. Section 9.2 discusses the related literature. Section 9.3 provides motivation for our work. Section 9.4 describes the data. Section 9.5 shows some simple comparisons across different cross-sectional characteristics of our sample. Section 9.6 develops the regression analysis. Section 9.7 concludes the chapter.

9.2 RELATED LITERATURE

Our study relates to three different strands of literature. First we discuss the corporate finance literature that investigates firms' financing patterns (including leverage and debt maturity, and other measures of company risk-taking) and the relationship between financing patterns and firm performance and governance [see Harris and Raviv (1991), for a review]. The starting point for this literature has been the notion, as reflected in the Modigliani–Miller theory, that in "perfect" financial markets firm financing patterns should not affect a firm's valuation or a firm's real activities. More recent studies have drawn attention to the relationships between, on the one hand, the type of firm assets being financed, the risks of different types of business, and the role of taxes and bankruptcy costs and, on the other hand, firm financing patterns. It has been established that advantageous tax benefits associated with debt financing induce higher leverage. Bankruptcy costs, on the other hand, mitigate the benefits of an all debt-financed firms, leading to an internal, optimal leverage ratio. The type of assets financed also matter. Risky types of business will be financed in ways to so as to balance the (dead-weight) costs of bankruptcy with the possible investment returns. And fixed types of investments, such as plant and equipment, will more likely be financed with long-term debt, while working capital will more likely be financed with short-term liabilities.

The analysis of agency costs and informational asymmetries has furthermore highlighted the role a firm's financial structure plays in disciplining and monitoring its management and has highlighted the impact financing patterns can have on firm valuation and behavior. This literature has made clear that financing patterns are endogenous to the firm's characteristics, including the variability of its income stream, the degree of informational asymmetries in the type of businesses the firm is engaged in, ownership structures, and so on. For example, in firms with high profitability of existing operations but with limited new, profitable investment opportunities, debt financing may be a useful device to prevent managers from investing in a suboptimal manner. And businesses that exhibit a larger degree of monitoring costs may be financed with more equity to permit greater control by owners of business activities.

Studies so far, however, have largely analyzed these firm-specific determinants and effects of firm financing patterns in a single country context, mainly focusing on the United States. As such, this work neglects the effect of different institutional environments on financing patterns. A more recent strand of the literature, and the second research area that closely relates to this chapter, is the work that compares financial structures across countries, looking for systematic differences and underlying explanatory factors. In a series of papers, Andrei Shleifer and coauthors have drawn attention to the impact of corporate governance frameworks and legal environments on (aggregate and firm-specific) financial structure and corporate sector performance. They have found that financial markets are less well-developed, equity markets are used less frequently by firms to raise funds, and dividend payout policies are less generous when creditor and equity rights are less well-protected, thus suggesting relationships between financial structure at the aggregate level and countries' legal characteristics. La Porta et al. (1998), for example, show that common law countries – Anglo-Saxon countries and their ex-colonies – which have stronger protection of creditor and equity rights, are characterized by more developed equity and other capital markets and by higher firm valuation than civil law countries – essentially continental European countries and their ex-colonies. Cross-country comparisons of aggregate financial structure have been made by Ross Levine and his coauthors (see, for example, Demirgüç-Kunt and Levine, 1996). Papers using firm-specific data include Rajan and Zingales (1995, 1998) and La

Porta et al. (2000a, 2000b). The last two papers relate agency problems and dividend policies around the world and the expropriation of minority shareholders arising from the separation of ownership and control to the strength of countries' equity and creditor rights.

In addition to comparing financing patterns across countries, some papers have investigated the impact of different corporate financing patterns on economic growth. Demirgüç-Kunt and Maksimovic (1998), for example, find that the degree to which specific firms (or the corporate sector in general) use long-term external financing from either stock markets or banks affects their growth. Levine and Zervos (1998) stress the complementarity between banks and stock markets in facilitating economic growth. Stulz (1999) reviews these and other papers on the relationships between financial structure and economic growth.

The third strand of economic literature that bears relevance to this chapter is the evolving theory and empirical evidence on financial crises in emerging markets and developed countries. Two different waves (generations) can be distinguished in this literature: (a) those papers focused on fundamental weaknesses, whether related to macroeconomic policies, existence of moral hazard in the financial sectors, or weak institutional frameworks,[3] and (b) those pursuing the possibility of unstable (international) financial markets.[4] In this context, weaknesses in the corporate sector have been mentioned as important factors for either view. Corsetti et al. (1998), for example, mention weak corporate performance and risky financing patterns as important causal factors for the East Asian financial crisis. Krugman (1999) argues that corporate balance sheet problems may have played a role in causing the East Asian financial crisis, independent of macroeconomic or other weaknesses. In particular, Krugman suggests that a depreciation of the currency causes an increase in the domestic currency value of foreign-denominated firm debt. The resulting balance sheet problems (and reversal of capital flows) weaken the corporate sector and, in turn, weaken the financial system. This triggers a further currency depreciation with a current account surplus to accommodate the capital reversal and financial system weakness. Krugman ascertains that the risks of such an event occurring are

---

[3] There has been extensive theoretical and empirical literature building on the Krugman (1979) model – for example, Edwards and Santaella (1993), Eichengreen, Rose, and Wyplosz (1995), and Chang and Velasco (1998). The moral hazard view is theoretically and empirically explored by Akerlof and Romer (1993) and by Corsetti, Pesenti, and Roubini (1998).

[4] Based on the Diamond and Dybvig (1983) bank run model and the Obstfeld (1986) second-generation balance of payments model, Radelet and Sachs (1998) defend the view that in macroeconomic and otherwise sound countries a crisis can be provoked by a self-fulfilling panic.

higher when there is low profitability of firms relative to the cost of funds of financial institutions.

As mentioned above, empirical tests that include the role of the corporate sector in explaining financial crises are few so far.[5] Johnson et al. (1998) identify a channel where weak corporate governance results in more stealing by managers, which, in turn, leads to a large currency depreciation and recession in the economy. The stealing occurs in part through excessive leveraging of the firm. They show empirical support for their model in a sample of 25 developing countries.

In this chapter, we investigate the relationships between countries' regulatory and legal environment and firm financing characteristics, focusing on individual firms' degree of risk-taking, but also including some performance measures. As noted, recent papers highlight that institutional factors in a particular country are likely to greatly influence the performance and financing patterns of firms, including their risk-taking behavior. The body of available knowledge on financial crises further suggests that a detailed study of the impact of legal frameworks and other institutional characteristics on corporate risk-taking may have implications for the vulnerability of countries to financial crises, as well as be of interest for other reasons. So far, however, these studies have mainly concentrated on the degree to which firms use external financing and a few selected aspects of firm financing patterns which may constitute risks (such as firm leverage and the degree of short-term debt). Some of these studies have also used a limited sample of countries [Rajan and Zingales (1995), for example, focus on only seven developed countries].

---

[5] For one, predicting financial crises is a risky business, with mixed explanatory powers, especially when considering Type I versus Type II errors; also see Portes (1999) for a critical review of crisis prediction models. Furthermore, there are few theoretical models on the importance of corporate sector financing patterns and the risk of a financial crisis. In addition, systemic risks arising from the corporate sector likely are due not only to risky financial structures of individual corporations but also to cross-firm interactions within the corporate sector and across the corporate sector, the financial sector, and the rest of the economy. A robust analysis requires a well-specified model to investigate the role of the corporate sector in contributing to a financial crisis while avoiding the risks of an *ex post* data-mining exercise to find weaknesses that can "explain" the occurrence of crises. This becomes important because financing patterns often do not change much over short periods of time. Related work suggests that there were no obvious changes in measures of East Asian corporations' performance or financing patterns in the period before the Asia crisis. The classification of countries as "crisis" or "noncrisis" is not free of subjective judgment either. There are, for example, many countries with a systemic, long-drawn crisis which do not suffer from a financial crisis involving a currency collapse or open banking crisis. In general, the relationships between countries' financial crises and their corporate sector financing structures and performance is complex and requires rigorous modeling before any empirical conclusions are made.

We extend the literature in several directions. We use a large sample of countries and corporations to allow for broader cross-country comparisons as to the role of institutional factors. We also explore the relationships between various institutional factors – a country's legal origin, the regulatory and legal protection provided to creditors and equity holders, respectively, and the market- or bank-based characterization of the country – and the financial and operating risks taken by firms in that country. We further use a large set of risk measures to ensure complete and robust results.

9.3 HYPOTHESES

A sizable literature started by La Porta and others introduces country legal characteristics as determinants of the functioning of the financial and corporate sectors of the economy. Specifically, La Porta et al. (1998) divide countries into those with civil and common law origin.[6] They find that common law origin countries are characterized by higher efficiency of contract enforcement. Common law countries are also documented to offer stronger legal protection of outside investors' rights, for both shareholders and creditors. The process by which the system arrives at a legal decision is also more predictable in common law origin countries. Namely, common law systems can react faster to new developments, including those in the financial sector, and convey much less uncertainty as to the outcome of a given legal dispute resolution. This may be a result of the manner in which legal decisions are arrived at in the different

---

[6] Roman law was compiled under the direction of Byzantine Emperor Justinian in the sixth century. Over subsequent centuries, the law was interpreted and adapted to confront problems as they arose throughout Europe. Eventually, individual countries formalized individual legal codes. The French Civil Code was written in 1804 under the direction of Napoleon. He had the Code adopted in all conquered territories, including Italy, Poland, the low countries, and the Habsburg Empire. Through conquest and colonization, France extended her legal influence to parts of the Near East, Northern and Sub-Saharan Africa, Indochina, Oceania, French Guiana, and the French Caribbean islands during the colonial era. Furthermore, because the French Civil Code exerted a major influence on the Portuguese and Spanish legal systems, this helped spread the French legal tradition to Central and South America. Following the unification of Germany under Bismarck in 1871, the German Civil Code was completed in 1896. The German Code exerted a big influence on Austria and Switzerland, as well as China, Czechoslovakia, Greece, Hungary, Italy, and Yugoslavia. The German Civil Code also heavily influenced the Japanese Civil Code, which helped spread the German legal tradition to Korea. The Scandinavian countries developed their civil codes in the seventeenth and eighteenth centuries. These countries have remained relatively unaffected by the far-reaching influences of the English, German, and French legal traditions.

The common law tradition, prevalent in countries formerly part of the British Empire, is not characterized by laws that are heavily shaped by legal scholars. Instead, laws are influenced by judges trying to resolve particular cases.

systems. The legal process in civil law countries is based to a larger extent on the code of the law; whereas in the common law system, precedents are much more important. Thus, there are large differences in judicial systems between common and civil law countries which might affect firms' risk-taking patterns.

The Modigliani–Miller framework provides a convenient approach to thinking about a relationship between the countries' institutional and legal environment and company financing and risk choices. Using this framework, one could envision that worse protection of investor rights imposes a cost on corporate claim-holders, thus increasing their required return on investment. Thus in countries with better property rights, investors will be better able to limit risk-taking by corporations than in countries where investors are not sufficiently protected. The value of creditors' and equity-holders' claims depends importantly on the degree of risk-taking by the corporations. When claim-holders have stronger legal tools at their disposal, both creditors and shareholders will be able to mitigate the degree of risk-taking by managers to protect the value of their claims.[7] The effect on profitability, on the other hand, is much more direct: Better protection of investor rights will immediately translate into more discipline on company management. In other words, our first hypothesis is that civil law countries have higher overall risk than common law countries. This will reflect in more unstable cash flows, higher variability of the income stream in response to sales shocks, higher financial leverage, a mismatch between the maturity structure of assets and liabilities, low liquidity, and insufficient interest coverage. Corporations in civil law countries will also display lower profitability measures than those in common law countries.

Looking at the effects of creditor and shareholder rights on overall risk, we can hypothesize, by the above arguments, a negative partial relationship between risk and protection of the rights of both claim-holder groups. While overall risk is unambiguously negatively affected by stronger rights protection, debt levels determination is more complex due to considerations of risk transfer between the two groups of claim-

---

[7] In this context, the effect of investor rights protection on leverage is more complex, since higher leverage does not always signify higher risk. Higher debt, for example, may be optimal in a company with more stable cash flows, holding other factors constant. The relation between investor rights and leverage thus needs to be isolated by controlling for all company-specific leverage determinants, as per the Modigliani–Miller framework – for example, stability of the income stream and type of industry. After proper controls, however, we can conclude that higher-than-optimal leverage increases overall corporate risk, thus reducing corporate value to both creditors and shareholders. We would thus hypothesize that, all other factors constant, better investor rights protection is associated with lower leverage at the optimum.

holders. A proper analysis of this relationship requires an explicit theoretical framework and is not pursued here.

It is important to note that risk-sharing mechanisms can differ across countries. This may be a problem because it allows for the possibility of a particular economic group bearing excessive risk, even if overall risk in the economic system is not that high. For example, firms may have high leverage, even with high income variability in response to weak disciplining by creditors, which, in turn, may reflect the existence of implicit or explicit government guarantees. Or, more generally, firms with high leverage and high income variability may be able to share risks in alternative ways, including creditor forbearance, reduction in wages and employment, and sacrifices from suppliers. These risk-sharing mechanisms, while perhaps individually optimal, may or may not be socially optimal. Excessive risk-sharing with banks, for example, could increase the chance of a systemic crisis. It is therefore useful to consider several measures of risks.

We also explore the difference between market-based and bank-based (or relationship-based) financial systems, in part because that distinction relates to firm financing patterns, the nature of risk-sharing, and the strength of outside investors' rights. Almost by definition, bank-based systems will be characterized by higher leverage as debt financing is used more extensively. The distinction also relates to the nature of corporate sector risk-taking and the degree of implicit versus explicit risk-sharing [see also Allen and Gale (1999) and Stulz (1999)]. Allen and Gale (1995) highlight that in bank-based systems a lot of nondiversifiable risk is intertemporally smoothed through close relationships between banks and corporations. In an arm's length environment, risk-sharing happens more directly through markets and has a more intratemporal, cross-sectional nature (through price and other adjustments). While the operational risks of firms need not be different between the two systems, measures of financial risk (such as leverage) could be quite different because the forms of risk-sharing are different. Bank-based systems may thus exhibit higher measures of contemporaneous financial risk-taking, whereas in market-based systems, risk measures may be lower as risk-taking is directly disciplined through the required rate of return by the market. The distinction might be further accentuated when financial intermediaries have access to a government-supplied (and subsidized) safety net, which allows and induces them to take on more corporate risks.

The distinction also relates to the strength of legal rights. Banks can more easily overcome informational asymmetries than markets can, and relationship-based systems may therefore function better than arm's length systems in more opaque, legally less efficient environments with

large informational asymmetries. As Rajan and Zingales (1999a) emphasize, bank-based systems – with greater use of debt and concurrent higher
measures of financial risks – are more likely to emerge in environments
with less-developed property rights, laws, and institutions, with bank–firm
relationships in effect serving as substitutes for weak market structures.[8]
This would mean that corporations in systems with weaker property
rights exhibit riskier financing patterns than those in systems with
stronger rights. It is worth investigating whether the bank-based versus
market-based distinction has an independent influence on corporate
risk-taking, above and beyond that of the legal framework of the country.
Thus our final hypothesis is that corporations in bank-based financial
systems have higher debt and overall higher measures of corporate
risk; however, the relationship could possibly be indirect, with the legal
system being a common causal factor.

We explore a multitude of measures of firm financial risk, in addition
to the commonly used leverage and maturity structure of debt measures.
We do so because there exist different sources of risks and because not
all risk measures need move in the same direction. Much of a firm's risk
arises from the variability of its income. These risks are not captured by
leverage and maturity structure of debt measures, but rather by the
relative variation of income or sales over time. Financial measures such
as leverage, in contrast, capture only the exposure of firms to financial
shocks, such as changes in exchange rates or shocks to the supply of
funds, and do not control for the operational risks of the firm. Measures
such as the ability of a firm to cover interest payment from its operational income try to cover both financial and operational risks, but again
provide only a partial picture because the focus is on flow rather than
stock measures of risks.

9.4 DATA

We collect data from Worldscope, a database that has been used in a
number of recent papers. Worldscope covers publicly listed corporations
in 54 countries. The sample we use includes all companies except
financial firms (SIC codes 6000–6999) and regulated utilities (SIC
codes 4900–4999). We use a balanced sample of firms over the period

---

[8] Demirgüç-Kunt and Levine (1999) explore whether fundamental differences can explain
why some countries are characterized as bank-based while others are characterized as
market-based. They find that countries with common law tradition and strong investor
rights tend to be more market-based, and civil law countries tend to be more bank-based.
The fact that legal systems help in the taxonomy of financial systems does not resolve
the issue of causality because political economy might well result in the adoption of legal
and other institutional features that are consistent with either system (see Rajan and
Zingales, 1999b).

1995–1996, with the exception of five ratios that are computed over the period 1991–1996, because their calculation requires a longer time series.[9] We exclude 8 countries that have less than 10 firms with non-missing data for both years (Egypt, Jordan, Liechtenstein, Luxembourg, Morocco, Russian Federation, Slovakia, and Zimbabwe). We are left with 11,033 firms in 46 countries.

Table 9.1 presents the sample countries and shows the number of firms per country. The mean number of firms per country is 240, and the median is 94. The lowest number of firms per country is 11 for Venezuela, and the maximum number is 2715 for the United States. The data cover mainly large firms. This selection pattern arises because firms have to be listed on a stock exchange in order to enter the database, and listed companies tend to be among the largest firms in each country. Previous work for nine East Asian countries (Claessens et al., 2000) suggests that the Worldscope sample covers between 64 percent and 96 percent of the total market capitalization of firms listed on the stock market. We expect this to be the case for this larger sample of countries as well – especially for the developed countries, where reporting is generally better.

The table also provides the classification of countries along different dimensions (for detailed definitions, see Table 9.2). We use information from La Porta et al. (1998) on legal origin to classify countries as common or civil law origin countries, with the latter further classified as French, German, or Scandinavian. Using the same primary sources, we expand on their sample of legal origin by classifying China, the Czech Republic, Hungary, and Poland as Germanic civil law countries. We end up with 14 common law countries and 32 civil law counties, 18 of which were French, 10 Germanic, and 4 Scandinavian civil law countries.

We also report the strength of shareholder and creditor rights from La Porta et al. (1998). The shareholder index is the sum of five 0–1 indicators: (1) if the country allows shareholders to mail their proxy vote; (2) if shareholders are not required to deposit their shares prior to the General Shareholders' Meeting; (3) if cumulative voting is allowed; (4) if an oppressed minorities mechanism is in place; and (5) if the minimum percentage of share capital that entitles a shareholder to call an Extraordinary Shareholders' Meeting is less than or equal to 10 percent. The creditor index aggregates creditor rights by adding 1 if (1) the country imposes restrictions, such as creditors' consent, to file for reorganization as opposed to bankruptcy; (2) the incumbent management loses control of the company during reorganization or bankruptcy;

---

[9] Specifically, the sensitivity of changes in operating income and EBIT to sales, the variability of operating income and EBIT, and a measure for firm growth, the total assets growth rate.

Table 9.1. The Sample

Country	Sample Size	Legal Origin	Shareholder Rights	Creditor Rights	Bank-Oriented System
Argentina	25	Civil law (French)	4	1	1
Australia	189	Common law	4	1	0
Austria	57	Civil law (German)	2	3	1
Belgium	72	Civil law (French)	0	2	1
Brazil	119	Civil law (French)	3	1	0
Canada	403	Common law	5	1	0
Chile	48	Civil law (French)	5	2	0
China	76	Civil law (German)	1	0	1
Colombia	20	Civil law (French)	3	0	1
Czech Republic	14	Civil law (German)	2	2	1
Denmark	121	Civil law (Scandinavian)	2	3	0
Finland	79	Civil law (Scandinavian)	3	1	1
France	428	Civil law (French)	3	0	1
Germany	414	Civil law (German)	1	3	1
Greece	94	Civil law (French)	2	1	1
Hong Kong	182	Common law	5	4	0
Hungary	14	Civil law (German)	3	2	1
India	283	Common law	5	4	1
Indonesia	104	Civil law (French)	2	1	1
Ireland	46	Common law	4	1	1
Israel	28	Common law	3	4	1
Italy	125	Civil law (French)	1	2	1
Japan	2,116	Civil law (German)	4	2	1
Korea (South)	214	Civil law (German)	2	3	0
Malaysia	253	Common law	3	3	0
Mexico	68	Civil law (French)	1	0	0
Netherlands	152	Civil law (French)	2	2	0
New Zealand	37	Common law	4	3	1
Norway	85	Civil law (Scandinavian)	4	2	1
Pakistan	72	Common law	5	4	1
Peru	21	Civil law (French)	3	0	0
Philippines	64	Civil law (French)	3	0	0
Poland	36	Civil law (German)	3	2	1
Portugal	53	Civil law (French)	3	1	1
Singapore	158	Common law	4	4	0
South Africa	139	Common law	5	3	0
Spain	97	Civil law (French)	4	2	1
Sri Lanka	12	Common law	3	3	1
Sweden	143	Civil law (Scandinavian)	3	2	0
Switzerland	117	Civil law (German)	2	1	0
Taiwan	177	Civil law (German)	3	2	1
Thailand	190	Civil law (French)	2	3	0
Turkey	38	Civil law (French)	2	2	0
United Kingdom	1,124	Common law	5	4	0
United States	2,715	Common law	5	1	0
Venezuela	11	Civil law (French)	1	NA	1
Average	240		3.02	1.96	0.56

Source: La Porta, Lopez-de-Silanes, Shleifer, and Vishny (1998).

Table 9.2. Firm-Level Risk Measures and Control Variables

Variable	Definition
Cash flow risk: Operating income variability	St. dev. [OPINC(t) – OPINC(t – 1)] / abs (mean OPINC), over 91–96
Operating leverage: Sensitivity of changes in operating income to changes in sales	% Change operating income / % change sales, over 91–96
Operating leverage: Sensitivity of changes in EBIT to changes in sales	% Change EBIT / % change sales, over 91–96
Financial leverage: Total debt to equity	(ST debt + LT debt) / market (or book) value of common equity, average 95–96
Financial leverage: Long-term debt to the sum of long-term debt and equity	LT debt / (LT debt + market value of common equity), average 95–96
Liquidity: Current ratio	(Current assets / current liabilities), average 95–96
Liquidity: Quick ratio	(Current assets net of inventory / current liabilities), average 95–96
Liquidity: Short-term financing needs	Net working capital / total assets, average 95–96
Interest coverage	EBIT / interest expense, average 95–96
ST debt use: Debt maturity structure	ST debt / LT debt, average 95–96
ST debt use: Short-term financing structure	ST debt / working capital, average 95–96
Profitability: Net income margin	Net income before preferred dividends / net sales or revenues *100, average 95–96
Profitability: ROE	EBIAT(t) / book value of common equity(t – 1)* 100 – GDP deflator, average 95–96
Profitability: ROA	EBIAT(t) / total assets(t – 1) * 100 – GDP deflator, average 95–96
Control for firm characteristics: Availability of collateral	(Inventory + gross PPE) / total assets, average 95–96
Control for firm characteristics: Nondebt tax shields	Depreciation / total assets, average 95–96
Control for firm characteristics: Industry	12 large industry groups, as defined by Campbell (1996)
Control for firm characteristics: Operating income as a share of total assets	Operating income / total assets – GDP deflator, average 95–96
Control for firm characteristics: Volatility of earnings	St. dev. [EBIT(t) – EBIT(t – 1)] / abs (mean EBIT), over 91–96
Control for firm characteristics: Total asset growth	Average % change (TA – GDP deflator), over 91–96

Variable	Definition
Control for firm characteristics: Firm size	ln (market value), US$, average 95–96
Control for debt tax advantage	[1 – (1 – corporate tax)*(1 – dividend tax)/(1 – bond interest tax)]* ln(debt), US$, tax rates effective in 1996
Control for level of development	ln (GNP / capita), 1994, US$

Law and Corporate Governance Measures

Legal origin	Legal origin of the Company Law or Commercial Code of each country, as per classification of La Porta et al. (1998).
Shareholder rights	Index aggregating different shareholder rights. Ranges from 0 to 5, as per classification of La Porta et al. (1998).
Creditor rights	Index aggregating different creditor rights. Ranges from 0 to 4, as per classification of La Porta et al. (1998).

Financial System Characteristics

Bank-oriented system dummy	Equals 1 for countries whose financial system is bank-dominated as opposed to market-oriented, as per the classification of Demirgüç-Kunt and Levine (1999)

(3) creditors can take action against debtor assets during bankruptcy proceedings (no "automatic stay"); or (4) secured creditors have the first priority claims on the debtor's assets. We expand on these data by including these rights for the four transition economies in our sample. We do not have creditor rights data for Venezuela.

Shareholder rights (also known as "Antidirector rights") strongly relate to legal origin and vary from a low of 0 for Belgium to a high of 5 for common law countries such as Canada, Hong Kong, India, and the United States. Creditor rights vary between 0 for several French and Germanic civil law countries (for example, China, France, and the Philippines) to a high of 4 for some common law countries (for example, the United Kingdom, Pakistan, and Singapore).

For the classification of countries by the relative importance of banks versus capital markets in their financial system, we use Demirgüç-Kunt and Levine (1999). Using a number of indicators on the aggregate size, activity (turnover), and efficiency of a country's respective stock market and banking system, they classify countries as bank- or market-based. We expand on their classification for China and the transition economies in our sample. We have 26 countries in our sample that are bank-based (1) by these criteria and 20 which are market-based (0). Of the 14 common law countries, only 6 are bank-based – that is, most common law countries are market-based – whereas of the 32 civil law countries, 20 are bank-based.

For the measures of firms' financial risks, we use a number of ratios traditionally mentioned in corporate finance textbooks (see, for example, Brealey and Myers, 1998) and used by financial analysts to assess a firm's riskiness. We also study profitability indicators. Table 9.2 presents the definitions of the 15 specific firm-specific variables we study.

We classify these firm-level variables into seven groups. The first group measures cash-flow risk: the variability of operating income (OPINC), defined as the standard deviation of the change in operating income relative to mean operating income in absolute value over the period 1991–1996. Corporations with a higher volatility in operating income are more susceptible to shocks and have earnings that fall below debt service requirements, resulting in financial distress.

The second group includes two operating leverage variables: (1) the elasticity of operating income with respect to sales and (2) the elasticity of change in earnings before interest and taxes (EBIT) with respect to sales, both over the period 1991–1996. A higher sensitivity of operational income to sales can contribute to risk if external financial markets do not allow a perfect smoothing of cash-flow variations, which in turn may cause financial and operational distress. This imperfect smoothing may be due to financial markets imperfections and informational asymmetries, which can be more important in weaker institutional environments.

The third group covers three financial leverage variables: the ratio of total debt to the book (market) value of equity, and the ratio of long-term debt to the sum of long-term debt and equity. High financial leverage, along with associated large interest payments, will reduce the ability of a corporation to deal with financial shocks, especially interest rate increases and reductions in available financing.

The fourth group covers three liquidity measures: the current ratio, defined as the ratio of current assets (cash, inventory, other working capital and trade receivables) to current liabilities (short-term debt and trade payables); the quick ratio, defined as the ratio of current assets net of inventory to current liabilities; and a measure of the usage of short-term financing, defined as the ratio of net working capital (current assets minus current liabilities) to total assets. These ratios try to capture the corporation's ability to turn assets and earnings into liquidity quickly, which can be especially important if the company has relatively large amounts of short-term debt. Financial market imperfections can contribute to the inability of a corporation to transfer (some of) its assets quickly into cash, which, if faced at the same time with large amounts of debt service payments falling due, can cause financial distress. The current ratio captures the magnitude of assets that the company can transform into cash within a short period of time relative to what it owes in the short-term. The quick ratio recognizes that among current assets, inventories are the least liquid, and it compares only the most liquid short-term assets to all short-term liabilities. Finally, net working capital to total assets measures the short fall between current assets and current liabilities relative to total assets.

The fifth group includes one solvency measure: the interest coverage ratio, defined as the ratio of EBIT over interest expenses. This interest coverage ratio is a standard measure of credit risk: The higher the degree that cash flows are relative to interest payments for debt service, the less likely the company is at risk of default on its debt service.

The sixth group includes two measures of debt maturity structure: the relative use of short-term debt, defined as the ratio of short-term debt to long-term debt; and the ratio of short-term debt to working capital, indicating the use of short-term debt to finance different types of assets. The ratio of short-term debt to long-term debt provides a measure of rollover risks and risks of short-term liquidity crunches. The ratio of short-term debt to working capital tries to capture the risk of the firm running into financial distress when it cannot liquidate some of its investments. This risk is exacerbated in bad economic times when lenders would be more concerned with collecting their loans and less willing to roll over debt.

Lastly, we have three profitability measures: the net income margin, defined as the ratio of net income before preferred dividends to sales; the rate of return on equity (ROE), defined as the ratio of earnings before interest but after taxes (EBIAT) relative to the book value of common equity; and the rate of return on assets (ROA), defined as the ratio of earnings before interest but after taxes relative to total assets, with all ratios averaged for 1995–1996. The latter two are deflated with the average annual GDP deflator (obtained from the IMF's IFS), to obtain profitability measures in real terms. The three profitability measures are not influenced directly by financing patterns of the firm as they exclude interest payments. The net income margin is not influenced by inflation.

9.5 RESULTS

We start with a simple comparison of financing patterns for corporations in all countries with common law versus civil law origin. Table 9.3 compares the medians of our measures of firm risk and profitability, and provides z-tests for equality of the sample distributions, where we use all firms within our sample. We control for industry factors, however, on the logic that risk and performance measures of corporations differ across industries.[10] To avoid differences in industrial structure across countries driving our results, we calculate medians for each industry group in each country. For these 552 medians (46 countries times 12 industries, with 44 missing observations), we then conduct z-tests. This procedure controls for differences in sample sizes across countries. It avoids putting more weight on countries with a larger number of observations – for example, the United States and Japan. The table also presents the medians of these variables for the civil law origin countries broken down into French, German, and Scandinavian.

The comparison shows that firms in civil law countries generally display more risky financing patterns and have lower rates of return on assets and equity. Many differences are statistically significant, with p-values generally less than 1 percent.[11] Specifically, corporations in civil law countries have higher cash-flow variability and financial leverage ratios, have lower interest cover ratios, and use to a greater degree short-term debt to finance their operations. These differences are statistically significant. Civil law companies also have higher operating leverage and maintain higher liquidity, but the differences lack statistical significance. Corporations in civil law countries also exhibit statistically significant lower profitability on all three measures. The latter finding suggests that there is not necessarily a tradeoff between riskiness and performance: Instead, corporations in civil law countries have both higher risk measures and lower profitability measures. Disaggregating the sample of

---

[10] We control for country and industry differences in distribution by splitting the sample firms into 522 groups, which we form using all 12 industry groups in our 46 countries. We then take the median of each group, and we use the medians as observations whose distributions we compare. This methodology has the advantage that cross-country differences in firm size are not a concern, since medians have no obvious size bias. The median firm in the United States may be smaller or larger than a median firm in a developing country.

[11] We repeat the z-tests under the assumption of a common distribution (where the distribution is allowed to vary only along the two groups being compared in the z-test), and we obtain results consistent with the ones reported here, only much stronger.

Table 9.3. Civil Versus Common Law Origin

	Common	Civil	Z-Test	French	German	Scandinavian
					Civil by Origin	
Number of observations	162	346		191	105	50
Cash flow risk: Operating income variability	0.3803	0.5796	6.8030[a]	0.6161	0.4590	0.6124
Operating leverage: Sensitivity of changes in operating income to changes in sales	1.0654	1.1324	0.8700	1.0397	1.2296	1.4841
Operating leverage: Sensitivity of changes in EBIT to changes in sales	1.0050	1.0299	1.0950	0.9912	1.0299	1.6407
Financial leverage: Total debt to equity	0.2653	0.4009	4.0850[a]	0.4232	0.3846	0.3321
Financial leverage: LT debt to the sum of LT debt and equity	0.1187	0.1497	2.2600[b]	0.1441	0.1490	0.1799
Liquidity: Current ratio	1.4229	1.4443	0.4050	1.4159	1.4778	1.6451
Liquidity: Quick ratio	0.9915	1.0109	0.3390	0.9376	1.0567	1.1008
Liquidity: ST financing needs	0.1152	0.1360	0.8640	0.1181	0.1543	0.1729
Interest cover	5.0541	3.4225	4.4460[a]	3.1464	3.4686	4.5938
ST debt use: Debt maturity structure	0.5852	0.8497	3.7590[a]	0.9095	1.2466	0.3377
ST debt use: ST financing structure	0.1590	0.2607	1.5140	0.2913	0.2486	0.1904
Profitability: Net income margin	5.1017	4.0931	2.3440[b]	4.7193	3.2195	4.5072
Profitability: ROE	13.0454	10.4417	3.0980[a]	10.1014	6.8409	13.4739
Profitability: ROA	6.9891	5.9114	2.5760[a]	6.6475	4.3066	6.9159

Note: The z-tests are performed on medians for industry groups in each country.
[a] Significant at the 1 percent level.
[b] Significant at the 5 percent level.

corporations in civil law countries further, we find that corporations in Germanic law countries have lower profitability than corporations in other countries and seem to take on relatively high levels of risk. Corporations in Scandinavian law countries score quite high on the three profitability measures, similar to corporations in common law countries, but have higher measures of risk, to the order of one-and-a-half to two times larger than those of common law countries.

Table 9.4 presents all 15 risk and profitability measures, in terms of country medians (we do not report or use means to avoid large outliers influencing the results). The variation of the variables is considerable. Looking at cash flow risk (column 1), the values range from 1.39 for Brazil to 0.20 for New Zealand. In other words, the earnings of the median corporation in Brazil have a standard deviation that is almost one and a half times larger than the earnings themselves. Earnings in Brazil can thus be expected to fluctuate between less than a quarter and more than four times their value with a 95 percent probability, assuming a normal distribution. The earnings of the median company in New Zealand, on the other hand, are expected to move by at most 60 percent of their value 95 percent of the time.

Operating leverage is also very different across countries. The sensitivity of changes in EBIT to changes in sales ranges from 1.96 in Finland to 0.30 in Austria. In other words, a 1 percent fall in sales from one year to the next decreases EBIT by 2 percent in Finland, and by only 0.3 percent in Austria. Because operating leverage is very heavily dependent on the type of industry that the company is in, companies usually have little control over this risk factor.

Comparing leverage across countries, we see the highest leverage in Korea, where the median company has long-term debt and total debt equal to 49 percent and 249 percent of the equity value of the company, respectively. The lowest total debt is found for South Africa (7.5 percent of equity value), and the lowest long-term debt is found for Turkey (0.3 percent of equity value). Liquidity is the highest in Turkey and Peru and is the lowest in Pakistan. The median Pakistani company has a current ratio of 0.99 and a quick ratio of 0.51, which means that its current assets are only slightly smaller than its current liabilities, and half of those current assets are actually inventories, which are considered the least liquid of current assets. The median Pakistani company also has negative net working capital.

The median Malaysian company's earnings cover interest payments almost seven times, whereas the median Korean company's interest coverage is less than one and a half. New Zealand companies have short-term debt that is only 11 percent of long-term liabilities. In Hungary, in contrast, short-term debt is more than five times long-term debt. Comparing short-term debt to net working capital, which proxies a measure of immediate financing needs, we find that in Pakistan the median company's short-term debt is 4 percent of short-term financing needs. In Sri Lanka, short-term financing needs are 43 percent of short-term liabilities. Turkey's companies have the highest median profitability, while Korean and Japanese companies have the lowest profitability measures.

We next compare countries by the quality of the legal protection offered to creditors. Table 9.5 shows medians and corresponding z-tests, when we divide the sample into corporations in countries with good creditor protection (scores of 3 and 4 on the creditor rights index, denoted by "cred") and those with bad protection (scores of 0, 1, and 2). The table also presents firm risk and profitability characteristics by the individual creditor protection scores from 0 to 4. Again, we control for industry effects in the manner discussed above. The effects of creditor protection on firm risk and profitability characteristics are large, with firms in countries with less creditor protection generally displaying more risky financing patterns and lower rates of return on assets and equity. Fewer differences are statistically significant, however, compared to the distinction between civil and common law countries. Specifically, corporations in weak creditor rights countries have significantly higher cash-flow variability. Corporations in weak creditor rights countries also have significantly higher liquidity (quick ratio). In good creditor protection countries, operating and financial leverage are lower, and interest cover ratios are higher, though the differences are not significant. Corporations in weak creditor rights countries use, to a significantly lesser degree, short-term debt to finance their operations. Finally, corporations in weak creditor rights countries exhibit significantly lower profitability. Breaking down results by the specific creditor rights index value, we do not find any monotonic relationships.

We then divide the sample of corporations into those in countries with good minority protection (scores of 4 and 5 on the shareholder rights index denoted by "shr" rights) and those in countries with weak minority rights (scores of 0, 1, 2, and 3). Table 9.6 shows the medians and z-tests for firm risk and profitability characteristics of corporations divided in these two classes, controlling for industry effects. We find that corporations in weak minority rights countries have statistically significant higher cash-flow variability. Operating leverage results do not differ. All measures of financial leverage are significantly higher for corporations in weaker minority rights countries, and those for liquidity risks are lower (although not significant). Interest coverage is significantly higher in better protection countries. Both measures of short-term debt are higher among corporations in weaker minority rights countries, and again the difference is statistically significant. Finally, profitability appears to

Table 9.4. Firm-Level Risk Measures: Country Medians

Country	Number of Observations	CF Risk: Operating Income Variability	Operating Leverage: Sensitivity of Changes in Operating Income to Changes in Sales	Operating Leverage: Sensitivity of Changes in EBIT to Changes in Sales	Financial Leverage: Total Debt to Book Value of Equity	Financial Leverage: Total Debt to Market Value of Equity	Financial Leverage: Long-Term Debt to Sum of Long-term Debt and Market Value of Equity
Argentina	25	0.840	1.999	1.814	0.356	0.328	0.094
Australia	189	0.426	0.994	0.933	0.339	0.198	0.122
Austria	57	1.240	0.87	0.302	0.773	0.463	0.229
Belgium	72	1.057	1.000	0.770	0.784	0.423	0.176
Brazil	119	1.391	0.941	1.267	0.447	0.934	0.269
Canada	403	0.529	1.059	1.102	0.433	0.267	0.170
Chile	48	0.310	0.921	1.073	0.343	0.224	0.103
China	76	0.547	0.486	0.730	0.536	0.553	0.055
Colombia	20	0.945	1.266	0.771	0.196	0.467	0.202
Czech Republic	14	NA	NA	NA	0.398	0.234	0.157
Denmark	121	0.516	1.520	1.794	0.601	0.325	0.163
Finland	79	0.664	2.633	1.960	0.757	0.586	0.283
France	428	0.597	1.278	1.467	0.631	0.478	0.203
Germany	414	1.020	1.212	1.278	0.609	0.371	0.130
Greece	94	0.455	1.216	0.788	0.325	0.166	0.008
Hong Kong	182	0.398	0.985	0.990	0.471	0.420	0.136
Hungary	14	0.342	0.900	0.981	0.115	0.171	0.010
India	283	0.422	1.276	1.047	0.853	0.546	0.238
Indonesia	104	0.307	1.025	1.022	0.727	0.559	0.166
Ireland	46	0.320	1.881	1.084	0.517	0.281	0.170
Israel	28	0.386	0.879	1.007	0.416	0.296	0.093
Italy	125	0.812	0.499	0.977	0.619	0.718	0.223
Japan	2,116	0.357	1.926	1.372	0.707	0.432	0.157
Korea (South)	214	0.334	0.910	0.862	1.946	2.485	0.489
Malaysia	253	0.388	0.916	1.072	0.464	0.144	0.038
Mexico	68	0.500	1.200	0.961	0.534	0.342	0.150
Netherlands	152	0.352	1.040	0.900	0.495	0.247	0.111
New Zealand	37	0.195	0.943	0.531	0.535	0.265	0.189
Norway	85	0.819	0.643	1.582	0.783	0.574	0.314
Pakistan	72	0.382	1.284	1.123	1.134	0.999	0.244
Peru	21	0.680	1.734	0.822	0.197	0.100	0.048
Philippines	64	0.506	0.795	1.194	0.409	0.239	0.052
Poland	36	0.305	0.396	0.580	0.108	0.115	0.026
Portugal	53	0.872	1.429	1.090	0.667	0.591	0.222
Singapore	158	0.449	1.008	0.668	0.359	0.214	0.059
South Africa	139	0.269	0.899	0.976	0.190	0.079	0.043
Spain	97	0.771	1.571	0.910	0.317	0.293	0.103
Sri Lanka	12	0.202	0.459	0.730	0.395	0.277	0.057
Sweden	143	0.628	2.016	1.407	0.486	0.260	0.159
Switzerland	117	0.584	2.177	1.164	0.709	0.544	0.261
Taiwan	177	0.448	1.657	1.623	0.391	0.195	0.050
Thailand	190	0.435	1.002	0.979	1.046	0.915	0.220
Turkey	38	0.703	0.923	1.137	0.235	0.097	0.003
United Kingdom	1,124	0.363	1.178	1.022	0.374	0.182	0.068
United States	2,715	0.415	1.240	1.155	0.354	0.160	0.103
Venezuela	11	1.002	0.962	1.173	0.351	0.411	0.141

Liquidity				Short-Term Debt Use		Profitability (in percent)		
Current Ratio	Quick Ratio	Net Working Capital to Total Assets	Interest Coverage	Short-Term Debt to Long-Term Debt	Short-Term Debt to Net Working Capital	Net Income Margin (of Sales)	Return to Equity	Return to Assets
1.195	0.747	0.036	4.279	0.796	0.448	8.192	12.354	8.139
1.601	1.033	0.104	5.480	0.209	0.116	5.859	9.916	6.649
1.702	1.034	0.212	2.726	1.570	0.298	3.104	13.357	4.504
1.332	0.945	0.142	3.798	0.712	0.393	2.523	9.403	5.160
1.275	0.911	0.066	1.497	1.138	0.381	1.754	3.979	4.229
1.686	1.047	0.134	3.888	0.190	0.048	4.310	8.940	5.570
1.776	1.264	0.104	5.604	0.458	0.382	8.724	10.999	8.239
1.321	0.968	0.138	3.887	4.801	0.983	8.274	7.586	6.584
1.684	0.979	0.066	2.694	1.064	0.224	6.206	5.864	6.029
1.950	1.117	0.162	3.139	0.958	0.333	5.433	—	—
1.756	1.087	0.232	4.574	0.510	0.256	4.153	12.040	6.825
1.430	1.015	0.149	4.505	0.419	0.425	4.572	12.669	6.917
1.417	0.986	0.172	3.390	0.928	0.360	2.553	9.2464	4.251
1.756	1.026	0.229	3.175	0.982	0.189	1.509	8.814	3.499
1.516	1.086	0.176	4.702	3.083	0.186	—	—	—
1.352	0.947	0.092	3.789	1.380	0.457	6.862	8.870	5.830
1.784	1.056	0.173	4.437	5.685	0.108	—	—	—
1.438	0.904	0.145	3.025	0.710	0.723	8.699	21.727	12.08
1.612	1.127	0.176	2.915	1.013	0.564	8.219	12.327	8.597
1.576	1.143	0.185	4.420	0.274	0.186	5.396	13.554	6.603
1.813	1.165	0.234	5.189	0.912	0.298	4.865	6.685	4.555
1.454	1.096	0.170	2.891	1.405	0.256	2.269	5.659	3.179
1.319	1.025	0.138	3.594	1.201	0.241	1.182	3.675	2.005
1.078	0.773	0.035	1.240	1.429	0.331	0.843	3.640	5.168
1.296	0.913	0.086	6.773	2.351	0.127	9.256	14.306	8.571
1.303	0.890	0.058	2.354	0.455	0.244	7.857	17.155	11.948
1.414	0.899	0.178	5.711	0.666	0.327	3.369	16.369	7.389
1.504	0.925	0.062	6.652	0.111	0.124	7.611	14.439	9.499
1.705	1.277	0.167	3.641	0.132	0.127	5.359	13.761	6.703
0.993	0.510	0.012	1.795	1.909	0.036	2.306	9.366	8.103
2.396	0.975	0.199	4.233	0.950	0.085	7.174	17.892	10.738
1.370	0.961	0.078	3.898	0.926	0.144	11.305	8.023	5.591
2.132	1.284	0.227	3.521	1.008	0.141	5.396	11.574	10.794
1.220	0.837	0.048	2.108	1.057	0.090	2.390	5.050	4.215
1.474	1.122	0.145	5.360	1.377	0.302	4.744	6.209	4.164
1.441	0.937	0.156	7.377	0.745	0.110	2.244	13.777	6.114
1.302	0.951	0.123	3.053	1.676	0.185	3.114	9.809	5.154
1.555	1.087	0.137	3.662	4.187	1.379	7.528	9.988	6.366
1.705	1.116	0.193	4.581	0.244	0.061	4.523	14.606	7.606
1.640	1.148	0.200	3.591	0.512	0.296	3.072	7.887	4.582
1.587	1.037	0.159	4.521	1.680	0.427	6.936	9.706	6.878
1.143	0.697	0.047	2.675	1.464	0.193	5.180	9.400	6.827
1.925	1.388	0.285	5.687	1.986	0.282	9.036	55.581	41.258
1.370	0.921	0.146	5.950	0.740	0.125	4.079	13.804	7.314
2.097	1.385	0.263	4.917	0.165	0.043	4.124	13.349	7.239
1.559	0.964	0.112	2.464	0.756	0.760	8.263	18.086	16.048

Table 9.5. Creditor Protection and Risk Measures

	Poor (0,1,2)	Good (3,4)	z-Test	Cred = 0	Cred = 1	Cred = 2	Cred = 3	Cred = 4
Number of observations	329	172		60	128	141	102	70
Cash flow risk: Operating income variability	0.5281	0.4033	3.7680[a]	0.5662	0.5102	0.5269	0.4146	0.4013
Operating leverage: Sensitivity of changes in operating income to changes in sales	1.1639	0.9869	1.4450	1.0179	1.2278	1.1642	0.9135	1.0358
Operating leverage: Sensitivity of changes in EBIT to changes in sales	1.0514	0.9893	1.3390	0.9595	1.0388	1.0867	0.9834	0.9893
Financial leverage: Total debt to equity	0.3484	0.3355	0.3930	0.4164	0.3902	0.2806	0.3391	0.3296
Financial leverage: LT debt to sum of LT debt and equity	0.1421	0.1316	0.1060	0.1293	0.1874	0.1176	0.1381	0.1222
Liquidity: Current ratio	1.4471	1.4142	1.6300	1.3846	1.4443	1.4778	1.4025	1.4176
Liquidity: Quick ratio	1.0292	0.9543	1.9330[b]	0.9824	1.0095	1.0651	0.9543	0.9507
Liquidity: ST financing needs	0.1400	0.1152	0.8080	0.1103	0.1229	0.1531	0.1134	0.1304
Interest cover	3.9346	4.3828	1.5690	3.1217	3.6655	4.3949	3.9409	4.9727
ST debt use: Debt maturity structure	0.6689	0.9281	2.0600[c]	0.9861	0.4489	0.7583	0.8737	1.0174
ST debt use: ST financing structure	0.2017	0.2144	0.0460	0.3185	0.1843	0.2486	0.1658	0.2985
Profitability: Net income margin	4.2791	4.9401	1.4520	6.6505	4.0854	3.9151	4.8484	5.2102
Profitability: ROE	10.4959	12.2200	2.2800[c]	10.1014	10.0241	11.4899	12.0591	13.3793
Profitability: ROA	6.2623	6.5368	1.6750[b]	6.8631	5.9850	6.2674	6.1489	7.3327

Note: Using a sample that excludes the G-7 countries leads to results that differ from those reported here: Two measures of financial leverage are both statistically significantly lower for poor creditor protection countries, and the short- to long-term debt ratio are statistically significantly higher for poor creditor protection countries.

[a] Significant at the 1 percent level.
[b] Significant at the 5 percent level.
[c] Significant at the 10 percent level.

Table 9.6. Shareholder Protection and Risk Measures

	Poor (0–3)	Good (4,5)	z-Test	Shr = 0	Shr = 1	Shr = 2	Shr = 3	Shr = 4	Shr = 5
Number of observations	306	202		12	54	112	128	107	95
Cash flow risk: Operating income variability	0.5916	0.4035	5.6830[a]	1.0633	0.8201	0.4399	0.5849	0.4296	0.3821
Operating leverage: Sensitivity of changes in operating income to changes in sales	1.0555	1.1360	0.7730	1.3670	0.9817	1.0583	1.1280	1.1991	1.0784
Operating leverage: Sensitivity of changes in EBIT to changes in sales	1.0191	1.0163	0.1730	0.4545	1.0626	0.9904	1.0990	1.0059	1.0163
Financial leverage: Total debt to equity	0.4145	0.2878	4.1700[a]	0.4215	0.5201	0.4162	0.3426	0.2899	0.2687
Financial leverage: LT debt to sum of LT debt and equity	0.1509	0.1215	1.9970[b]	0.1733	0.1575	0.1637	0.1304	0.1231	0.1100
Liquidity: Current ratio	1.4720	1.4039	1.2600	1.3249	1.4317	1.5035	1.4742	1.3797	1.4209
Liquidity: Quick ratio	1.0130	0.9873	0.6910	0.8962	1.0133	0.9988	1.0225	1.0071	0.9756
Liquidity: ST financing needs	0.1419	0.1152	1.2560	0.1467	0.1155	0.1669	0.1364	0.1017	0.1344
Interest cover	3.3020	4.8620	4.6890[a]	4.0459	3.0458	3.3836	3.6054	5.2373	4.4888
ST debt use: Debt maturity structure	0.8657	0.5852	4.1480[a]	0.7892	1.0494	0.8766	0.8370	0.5802	0.5940
ST debt use: ST financing structure	0.2842	0.1703	2.1460[b]	0.4162	0.2488	0.2899	0.2744	0.1823	0.1547
Profitability: Net income margin	4.4264	4.8280	1.4240	2.2796	5.3920	4.4400	4.5072	4.7767	4.8280
Profitability: ROE	10.1589	12.6891	2.7460[a]	9.1521	9.8370	11.8390	8.9091	11.6722	13.5518
Profitability: ROA	5.8064	6.9146	2.1270[b]	4.1471	5.1457	6.6897	5.6976	6.3600	7.4575

Note: Using a sample that excludes the G-7 countries leads to results that differ from those reported here for only one variable: The sensitivity of changes in operating income to changes in sales is statistically significant higher in poor investor-protection countries.
[a] Significant at the 1 percent level.
[b] Significant at the 5 percent level.

328   *Stijn Claessens, Simeon Djankov, and Tatiana Nenova*

Table 9.7. Market Versus Bank-Centered Systems and Risk Measures

	Market	Bank	z-Test
Number of observations	232	276	
Cash flow risk: Operating income variability	0.4407	0.5352	2.9580[a]
Operating leverage: Sensitivity of changes in operating income to changes in sales	1.0502	1.1635	0.5630
Operating leverage: Sensitivity of changes in EBIT to changes in sales	1.0341	0.9975	0.1650
Financial leverage: Total debt to equity	0.2811	0.3919	3.0440[a]
Financial leverage: LT debt to sum of LT debt and equity	0.1255	0.1513	0.9330
Liquidity: Current ratio	1.4397	1.4418	0.5550
Liquidity: Quick ratio	0.9894	1.0120	0.3100
Liquidity: ST financing needs	0.1162	0.1345	0.9390
Interest cover	4.3078	3.6613	1.7390[c]
ST debt use: Debt maturity structure	0.6304	0.8759	3.0810[a]
ST debt use: ST financing structure	0.1776	0.2853	2.2720[b]
Profitability: Net income margin	4.8477	4.1387	1.8210[c]
Profitability: ROE	11.7499	10.2652	1.9630[b]
Profitability: ROA	6.8993	5.6154	3.2500[a]

[a] Significant at the 1 percent level.
[b] Significant at the 5 percent level.
[c] Significant at the 10 percent level.

be significantly lower among corporations in weaker minority rights countries.

Breaking down results by the specific minority rights index values, we do not find many monotonic relationships. For some variables we find a U-shaped pattern, for others we find an inverse U-shaped pattern, and for some we find no pattern at all. For profitability measures, for example, we find that profitability generally increases with the protection of equity rights; however, for the index value of 3, profitability is less than for equity rights values of 2 and 4. We expect that firm-specific characteristics play a role in explaining this particular effect, but we also venture that the relationship between firm financing patterns and minority rights is complex.

We next use the Demirgüç-Kunt and Levine (1999) classification of countries into bank-oriented and market-oriented systems to explore the relationship of the type of financial system with firm risk and profitability characteristics (Table 9.7). We find that corporations in bank-oriented systems have more risky financial structures and appear less profitable. These corporations have statistically significant higher cash-flow variability and higher financial leverage. Operating leverage and liquidity measures do not differ significantly. Interest coverage is significantly lower for corporations in bank-centered countries. Corporations in those countries also use significantly more short-term debt than their counterparts in market-based economies. Finally, firms in market-based financial systems have statistically higher profitability.

As a robustness check, we repeat all tests above on a sample excluding the G-7 countries. Because many common law countries display a high level of development, our results on legal origin could reflect development effects instead of legal framework effects. Excluding the G-7 does not change the results substantially, except that the level of statistical significance increases slightly. All results are maintained qualitatively.

In summary, the results suggest that legal origin, the degree of creditor and minority rights protection, and the characterization of the financial system are important in influencing the risk-taking behavior of corporations. Whether legal origin alone can explain corporate financing patterns has been recently countered by Rajan and Zingales (1999b). They argue that legal systems are not exogenous to political and other circumstances. If a particular legal system were proven to be effective, other countries would imitate valuable regulations including equity and creditor protection, and gradually differences in legal systems would disappear. Thus any causality from legal origin to financial characteristics is disputable. We find, however, that the legal origin is at least as discriminating a factor as the degree of creditor or shareholder protection. But, because these results do not control for other firm characteristics, we need to be careful in interpretation. We next turn to regression results to investigate firm financing patterns more carefully.

9.6 REGRESSION RESULTS

The results so far provide comparisons of median risk and profitability measures across countries without controlling for firm characteristics. As noted, the corporate finance literature has drawn attention to a number of firm-specific factors that can affect financing patterns (see Harris and Raviv, 1991, for a review). We next report regression results using firm-specific control variables.[12]

---

[12] In addition to the impact of the firm-specific characteristics that we control for, it is important to note that corporate risk may be affected by industry group affiliation of the company. In particular, it is possible that in countries where industrial groupings are common, there exists an intragroup risk-sharing mechanism. Such intragroup risk sharing will result in high measured company-level risk, even though risk at the group level is consistent with optimal behavior.

We use nine variables as control variables at the firm level (see Table 9.2). Those have been used in other studies trying to explain firm financing patterns [Titman and Wessels (1988), Demirgüç-Kunt and Maksimovic (1998, 2000), Rajan and Zingales (1995)]. We divide these variables into an expanded control set, used only for the leverage regressions, and a smaller control set, used for all other regressions. The smaller control set consists of four variables. The first variable is firm size as measured by market value (in log terms and expressed in U.S. dollars to allow comparability across countries), to control for the effects of size on financing patterns. The second variable is the growth of total assets, deflated using a GDP-price index, to control for the firm-specific growth opportunities which can influence financing patterns. The third variable is the industry classification, because financing patterns can be expected to depend on the type of activity financed including the volatility of the underlying income stream, the degree of informational asymmetries in the management of the particular type of business, and so on. We have the two-digit SITC groups for each firm, but this classification is too detailed for our purposes. Instead, we use Campbell (1996) to reclassify the two-digit SIC groups to 12 industry categories.[13] The fourth variable is the level of development as measured by GNP per capita (in log terms and expressed in U.S. dollars), to control for cross-country differences in the level of development. The latter could affect the amount of risk that the corporate sector is willing to assume.[14]

The expanded set of controls includes five additional firm-level characteristics. The first variable is the availability of collateral which can influence the degree to which a firm can obtain long-term financing. It is defined as the sum of inventory and gross plant and equipment, relative to total assets. The second variable controls for the presence of nondebt tax shields, which would influence the relative tax advantages of debt financing vis-à-vis other sources of tax savings. It is defined as the degree

---

[13] The sectors are defined as follows: petroleum industry (SIC 13 and 29); finance and real estate (SIC 60–69); consumer durables (SIC 25, 30, 36, 37, 50, 55, and 57); basic industry (SIC 10, 12, 14, 24, 26, 28, 33); food and tobacco (SIC 1, 20, 21, 54); construction (SIC 15–17, 32, 52); capital goods (SIC 34, 35, and 38); transportation (SIC 40–42, 44, 45, and 47); utilities (SIC 46, 48, and 49); textiles and trade (SIC 22–23, 31, 51, 53, 56, 59); services (SIC 72–73, 75, 80, 82, 89); and leisure (SIC 27, 58, 70, 78–79). We add a twelfth category: "other services," which includes SIC codes 43, 76, 83, 84, 86, 87, 92, 95, 96, 99.

[14] For example, according to standard convergence arguments, countries at a lower level of development grow faster. Therefore, the corporate sectors in such countries may be justified in pursuing riskier financing and operating policies, given the higher rates of return to investments in a faster-growing economy. That will introduce a bias because economies at a lower level of development also happen to be predominantly of civil legal origin. We control for this bias by including initial GNP per capita as a control variable.

of depreciation relative to total assets. The third control variable is operating income to total assets, deflated using the respective GDP price index, to control for the profitability of the particular firm. We expect more profitable firms to have higher cash flows available, and therefore use less debt and more internal financing. To further control for the instability of the corporate cash flow stream, we include as a fourth variable the volatility of earnings, defined as the standard deviation of changes in EBIT, scaled by average EBIT.[15] Finally, we control for the relative tax advantage of debt versus equity financing. The reason for a tax advantage of debt over equity financing is that an equal amount of debt and equity financing costs differ in their net of tax values, due to the different tax rates applied to interest payments as opposed to dividend payments (or capital gains).[16]

In all regressions, we reduce the importance of outliers in our estimates by capping observations at the 10 percent level (both tails). We use OLS regressions with dummies for each of the 12 industry groups in the sample.[17] To simplify the amount of information presented, we use in our regressions only one measure for each of the seven groups of risk or performance measures. The results for each measure within a class are very similar, however. Table 9.8 provides the regression results for the financial leverage ratio, while Table 9.9 provides all regression results in a summary form, where we report the sign of the coefficients if they are statistically significant, positive (+) or negative (−), 0 otherwise.[18]

---

[15] We argue that the optimal leverage would decrease with the volatility of a company's earnings, because management minimizes the probability of earnings falling below interest expenses; however, Titman and Wessels (1988) point out counterarguments.

[16] We control for the debt tax advantage using the classical formula for the gain from leverage from Miller (1977): $\left[1 - \dfrac{(1-\tau_C)(1-\tau_S)}{(1-\tau_B)}\right]D$, where τ_C is the corporate tax rate, τ_s is the tax rate applicable to income form stock (specifically, dividend tax), τ_B is the tax rate applicable to income from bonds (specifically, interest tax rate), and D is the value of outstanding firm debt (in US$, logs). Alternatively, some authors use the personal tax rate as the rate applicable to income from bonds, and they use the capital gains tax as the rate applicable to income from stock. Our analysis is unaffected by using these alternative measures. The tax data are drawn from withholding tax rates in 1996 collected by PriceWaterhouse.

[17] A random industry effects specification (not reported) leads to virtually the same results.

[18] We repeat all regressions using the 522 country-industry group medians, instead of all 11033 observations, to obtain results that are directly comparable to the z-tests above. The results are broadly consistent with those reported in Tables 9.8 and 9.9. The differences are as follows. The operating leverage and liquidity regressions show that the relationships between these variables and country regulatory frameworks are not robust, as none of the coefficients are significant. The relationship between the regulatory framework and cash flow risk, financial leverage, and interest coverage is robust to this more stringent regression specification. Debt maturity structure regressions show that only

Table 9.8. Regression Analysis for Financial Leverage (Total Debt over Book Value of Equity)

Explanatory Variable	I	II	III	IV	V
Civil legal origin	15.7176				27.5133
	(9.40)				(13.64)
Creditor rights		−1.2630			
		(2.03)			
Shareholder rights			−7.0136		
			(11.78)		
Bank-oriented system				−6.1892	−24.5224
				(3.13)	(10.33)
Availability of collateral	68.1912	64.4392	66.3859	61.5338	64.8671
	(15.38)	(14.45)	(15.09)	(13.80)	(14.68)
Nondebt tax shield	−93.2423	−81.2125	−93.9026	−75.6188	−87.6583
	(12.66)	(11.08)	(12.86)	(10.27)	(11.94)
Operating income as a	−166.9541	−205.4908	−158.2961	−213.4947	−171.7963
share of total assets	(12.48)	(16.02)	(11.88)	(16.31)	(12.91)
Market capitalization	−1.7712	−2.3708	−2.0897	−2.5510	−2.7506
	(3.21)	(4.25)	(3.81)	(5.54)	(4.94)
Total asset growth	37.0054	36.2118	33.7810	34.9390	34.5994
	(6.99)	(6.59)	(6.40)	(6.57)	(6.57)
Volatility of earnings	7.0081	5.4958	7.0487	5.3566	6.8096
	(9.07)	(7.18)	(9.20)	(6.97)	(8.87)
Tax advantage of debt	0.0674	0.0785	0.0777	0.0851	0.0863
	(23.75)	(30.07)	(30.07)	(25.04)	(25.66)
GNP per capita	−0.8918	−1.0413	−0.1224	−0.9490	−2.0742
	(1.06)	(1.21)	(0.15)	(1.21)	(2.46)
Industry dummies	Yes	Yes	Yes	Yes	Yes
Number of Observations	9,016	9,008	9,016	9,016	9,016
Overall R^2	0.1632	0.1555	0.1679	0.1559	0.1730

Notes: OLS regressions with industry fixed effects. Standard errors are in parentheses. The dependent variable is total debt over book value of common equity. The independent variables are: (1) civil legal origin dummy that equals one if the country is of civil legal origin; (2) creditor rights index, ranging from 0 to 4, where higher values signify stronger creditor protection; (3) shareholder rights index, ranging from 0 to 5, where higher values signify stronger minority shareholder protection; or (4) bank-market indicator that equals one if the country's financial system is bank-based. The control variables are (5) availability of collateral, (6) nondebt tax shields; (7) operating income as a share of total assets; (8) company market capitalization; (9) total asset growth; (10) volatility of earnings; (11) tax advantage of debt; (12) GNP per capita. For definitions of variables see Table 9.2. Observations are capped at the 10 percent level (both tails).

short-term debt usage is related to creditor rights protection in a robust way. Net income margin regressions maintain the significance of the relationship of profitability to the country legal origin and to shareholder rights, but not to creditor rights. In all regressions, the nature of the financial system – whether it is bank- or market-based – has weak explanatory power over and above the regulatory framework in the country.

Table 9.9. Summary Regression Results

Dependent Variable	Explanatory Variables	I	II	III	IV	V
Cash flow risk: Operating income variability	Civil legal origin	+				+
	Creditor rights	−				
	Shareholder rights			−		
	Bank-oriented system				+	−
Operating leverage: Sensitivity of EBIT to changes in sales	Civil legal origin	+				0
	Creditor rights		0			
	Shareholder rights			−		
	Bank-oriented system				+	0
Financial leverage: Total debt to equity (market value)	Civil legal origin	+				+
	Creditor rights	−				
	Shareholder rights			−		
	Bank-oriented system				+	0
ST debt use: Debt maturity structure	Civil legal origin	+				+
	Creditor rights		+			
	Shareholder rights			−		
	Bank-oriented system				+	+
Liquidity: Current ratio	Civil legal origin	−				−
	Creditor rights	−				
	Shareholder rights			+		
	Bank-oriented system				−	0
Interest coverage	Civil legal origin	−				−
	Creditor rights		+			
	Shareholder rights			+		
	Bank-oriented system				−	+
Profitability: Net income margin	Civil legal origin	−				−
	Creditor rights		+			
	Shareholder rights			+		
	Bank-oriented system				−	−

Notes: Signs of coefficients reported are statistically significant, positive (+) or negative (−), 0 otherwise. OLS regressions with industry fixed effects. The dependent variables are (1) operating income variability, (2) sensitivity of EBIT to changes in sales, (3) total debt to market value of common equity, (4) the current ratio, (5) interest coverage, and (6) net income margin. The independent variables are as in Table 9.8. The control set for total debt to market value of equity are as in Table 9.8. The control set for all other regressions is composed of market capitalization; total asset growth; GNP per capita. For definitions of variables see Table 9.2. Observations are capped at the 10 percent level (both tails).

Similarly to the z-tests, we check the results for robustness by repeating the regressions on a sample which excludes the G-7 countries. We obtain qualitatively identical results.

The financial leverage regressions use the total debt to book value of equity as the left-hand-side variable. Civil legal origin increases leverage in a statistically and economically significant way. Both better creditor rights and shareholder rights protection have a negative and significant impact on leverage. Bank-based financial systems are characterized by lower leverage. When both the bank-based financial system indicator and the civil legal origin indicator are included in the regression as explanatory variables, the legal origin has a positive impact and the type of financial system dummy has a negative impact on leverage, both being statistically significant.

The controls are of the expected signs and are statistically significant. More collateral increases leverage, whereas the availability of alternative sources of tax savings decreases debt usage. More profitable companies have less debt, possibly because they finance themselves to a larger extent out of retained earnings. Larger companies are less leveraged, possibly because they face a relatively lower cost of equity financing. Higher asset growth is associated with higher leverage, which is consistent with higher financing needs and unconstrained credit markets, but is inconsistent with the argument that high growth companies usually have poor collateral to borrow against. The volatility of earnings is positively related to leverage. A higher tax advantage of debt over equity increases leverage, and firms in more developed countries have less debt, possibly due to the presence of more developed stock markets. The industry dummies are jointly significant in all regressions.

In terms of legal origin, controlling for firm characteristics, the results are the same as for the simple z-test comparisons (regression I of Table 9.9). Corporations in civil countries have higher cash-flow variability, higher operating and financial leverage, and have lower interest coverage. They also use more short-term debt and are less profitable. Different from the z-test results, civil legal origin is significantly associated with lower liquidity. These findings correspond to those of others, most notably La Porta et al. (1998), that legal systems matter for the financing patterns of corporations.

Controlling for individual firm characteristics, the influence of creditor and shareholder rights on financing patterns is consistent with our hypotheses, and with the legal origin results mentioned above.[19] Stronger creditor rights are associated with lower firm risk characteristics, in particular, lower cash-flow risk, financial leverage and liquidity, and higher interest coverage (regression II). Further, stronger creditor rights are positively related to profitability. Creditor protection is not statistically significantly associated with operating leverage, and is significantly asso-

---

[19] Results are similar when we control in addition for the relative degree of enforcement of creditor and shareholder protection in each country, using an index of judicial efficiency.

ciated with more short-term debt use. The relationship of credit rights with debt maturity lacks significance in some of the alternative measures, however. The lack of explanatory power of creditor rights for debt maturity structure has been noted elsewhere in the literature (Demirgüç-Kunt and Maksimovic, 1999).

The effect of shareholder rights protection after controlling for firm characteristics is similar, but the results are stronger: Good shareholder protection is associated with lower firm risk, in particular, lower cash-flow risk, operating leverage, financial leverage, and short-term debt use (regression III). Good protection is also associated with higher interest coverage, liquidity, and profitability.[20]

The results for bank- versus market-based financial systems (regression IV) are that corporations in bank-based countries have higher cash flow risk, operating and financial leverage, and more short-term debt. Corporations in these countries also have lower liquidity, interest coverage, and profitability. These results confirm our priors. However, this link may not be causal; in particular, when controlling for legal origin, the statistical significance of the relationship disappears in some cases (for operating and financial leverage and for liquidity) (regression V). The relationship between legal systems and the type of financial system is complex and likely influences these results (Rajan and Zingales, 1999b).

9.7 CONCLUSIONS

In this chapter we show that corporations' financial and operating structures relate to the institutional environments in which they operate. A country's legal origin, the strength of its shareholder and creditor rights, and the nature of its financial system can account for the degree of corporate risk-taking. In particular, corporations in common law countries and market-based financial systems appear less risky. Greater protection of investor rights is associated with lower measured financial risks as

---

[20] An alternative measure that reflects the effectiveness of the country's regulatory framework is the quality of accounting standards and the transparency of corporate financial statements reporting. Accounting standards may be an important factor to control for further, since our risk measures are based on accounting data, as opposed to financial market-based figures. Thus one could envision that differences in reporting standards would impact our risk measures in a country-specific, systematic manner, thus necessitating a control for reporting-induced bias. We check the impact of accounting standards as a robustness check to our regression results, using the accounting standards variable constructed by La Porta et al. (1998). The results are maintained as reported above. In addition, the quality of corporate reporting has the expected impact on corporate risk. Specifically, better and more transparent reporting is negatively associated with cash-flow risk, financial leverage, and liquidity, and it is positively associated with interest coverage and profitability. There is no significant relationship between accounting standards quality and operating leverage or debt maturity structure.

well. This suggests that the financing patterns of the corporate sector across countries reflect countries' institutional environments.

Our work points to the importance of constructing useful and operational measures of corporate sector risk, at the micro level, in addition to monitoring sectoral and country-wide economic risks. The risk measures we propose constitute a step toward a system for measuring such risk. Further work is necessary to formulate well-specified models linking firm-level risk to corporate sector stability. Those models will also help test whether there exists a connection between corporate risk-taking behavior and financial crises. A further policy implication of the chapter is the importance of a country's institutional development in relation to its corporate sector stability, as well as that of the overall economy.

Research in this area needs to distinguish further between the influence of legal variables and the importance of the type of financial system. The insights gained in this study can also be utilized in future models of corporate behavior as regards the use of external financing. Finally, one important unanswered question is the exact causality or transmission mechanism that is responsible for the observed higher risk measures in civil law countries.

REFERENCES

Akerlof, George and Paul Romer (1993). "Looting: The Economic Underworld of Bankruptcy for Profit," *Brookings Papers on Economic Activity*, No. 2:1–60.

Allen, Franklin and Douglas Gale (1995). "Welfare Comparison of Intermediaries and Financial Markets in Germany and the US," *European Economic Review* **39**(2):179–209.

———(2000). *Comparing Financial Systems*. Cambridge, MA: MIT Press.

Brealey, Richard and Stewart Myers (1998). *Principles of Corporate Finance*. New York: McGraw-Hill.

Campbell, John (1996). "Understanding Risk and Return," *Journal of Political Economy* **104**:298–345.

Chang, Roberto and Andrés Velasco (1998). "Financial Crises in Emerging Markets: A Canonical Model." NBER Working Paper No. 6606, Cambridge, MA.

Claessens, Stijn, Simeon Djankov, and Larry Lang (2000). "The Separation of Ownership and Control in East Asian Corporations," *Journal of Financial Economics* **58**(1).

Corsetti, Giancarlo, Paolo Pesenti, and Nouriel Roubini (1998). "What Causes the Asian Currency and Financial Crises? A Macroeconomic Overview." NBER Working Paper No. 6833, Cambridge, MA.

Demirgüç-Kunt, Asli and Ross Levine (1996). "Stock Markets, Corporate Finance, and Economic Growth: An Overview," *World Bank Economic Review* **10**(2):223–239.

———(1999). "Bank-Based and Market-Based Financial Systems: Cross-Country Comparisons." World Bank Policy Research Working Paper No. 2146. Washington, D.C.

Demirgüç-Kunt, Asli and Maksimovic, Vojislav (1998). "Law, Finance, and Firm Growth," *Journal of Finance* 53(6):2107-2137.

———(1999). "Institutions, Financial Markets, and Firm Debt Matunity," *Journal of Financial Economics* 54(3):295–336.

Diamond, Douglas and Philip Dybvig (1983). "Bank Runs, Deposit Insurance, and Liquidity," *Journal of Political Economy* 91(3):401–419.

Edwards, Sebastian and Julio Santaella (1993). "Devaluation Controversies in the Developing Countries: Lessons from the Bretton Woods Era." In Michael Bordo and Barry Eichengreen, eds., *A Retrospective on the Bretton Woods System: Lessons for International Monetary Reform*. Chicago: University of Chicago Press, pp. 405–455.

Eichengreen, Barry, Andrew Rose, and Charles Wyplosz (1995). "Exchange Market Mayhem: The Antecedents and Aftermath of Speculative Attacks," *Economic Policy* 21:249–296.

Harris, Milton and Artur Raviv (1991). "The Theory of Capital Structure," *Journal of Finance* 46(1):297–355.

Johnson, Simon, Peter Boone, Alasdair Breach, and Eric Friedman (1998). "Corporate Governance in the Asian Financial Crisis, 1997–8." Mimeo, MIT.

Krugman, Paul (1979). "A Model of Balance-of-Payments Crises," *Journal of Money, Credit, and Banking* 11(3):311–325.

———(1999). "Balance Sheets, the Transfer Problem, and Financial Crises." Mimeo, MIT (available at http://www.mit.edu/krugman/).

La Porta, Rafael, Florencio Lopez-de-Silanes, Andrea Schliefer, and Robert Vishnay (1998). "Law and Finance," *Journal of Political Economy* 106(6):1113–1155.

———(2000a). "Agency Problems and Dividend Policies around the World," *Journal of Finance* 55(1):1–33.

———(2000b). "Investor Protection: Origins, Consequences, Reform." Mimeo, Harvard University.

Levine, Ross and Sara Zervos (1998). "Stock Markets, Banks, and Economic Growth," *American Economic Review* 88:537–558.

Miller, Merton (1977). "Debt and Taxes," *Journal of Finance* 32(2):261–275.

Obstfeld, Maurice (1986). "Rational and Self-Fulfilling Balance-of-Payments Crises." *American Economic Review* 76:72–81.

Portes, Richard (1999). "The Use and Misuse of Financial Crisis Prediction Models." In Pierre-Richard Agénor, Marcus Miller, David Vines, and Axel Weber, eds., *The Asian Financial Crisis*. Cambridge, MA. Cambridge University Press.

Radelet, Steven and Jeffrey Sachs (1998). "The East Asian Financial Crisis: Diagnosis, Remedies, Prospects," *Brookings Papers on Economic Activity*, No. 1:1–74.

Rajan, Raghuram and Luigi Zingales (1995). "What Do We Know About Capital Structure? Some Evidence from International Data," *Journal of Finance* 50(5):1421–1460.

————(1998). "Financial Dependence and Growth," *American Economic Review* **80**(3):559–586.

————(1999a). "Which Capitalism? Lessons from the East Asian Crisis," *Journal of Applied Corporate Finance* **2**:16–26.

————(1999b), "The Politics of Financial Development." Mimeo, University of Chicago.

Stulz, Rene (1999). "Financial Structure, Corporate Finance, and Economic Growth." Mimeo, Ohio State University.

Titman, Sheridan and Roberto Wessels (1988). "The Determinants of Capital Structure Choice," *Journal of Finance* **43**(1):1–19.

Discussion

Corporate Risk around the World

Richard K. Lyons

The authors of this chapter have done a fine job with a fascinating topic. The broad question they address is how country characteristics influence corporate risk taking. What is especially refreshing is that both pieces of this question – the country piece and the corporate piece – are not addressed in ways familiar to most macroeconomists. The country piece, for example, does not examine the macro-policy environment, but rather the micro-institutional environment (e.g., legal systems, regulatory systems, and financial systems). The corporate piece does not examine corporate risk from the asset-pricing perspective (e.g., covariance risk), but instead examines it from the perspective of corporate financial distress: leverage ratios, liquidity ratios, profit ratios, and so on.

Addressing countries and corporate risk from these less familiar (at least to the macroeconomist) perspectives is important for completing the picture of financial crises. Several authors have suggested that corporate risk taking – in particular foreign-currency debt financing – was important in aggravating East Asian crises. This chapter does not, in itself, complete this part of the crisis picture, but it does provide an excellent platform on which this type of analysis can build. The links to the underlying corporate finance literature are nicely surveyed and well-exposited.

The main message of the paper is that there is a consistent corporate response to institutional settings. This response accords, broadly, with predictions in the corporate-finance literature in that environments that provide greater incentives for risk taking do indeed produce more risk taking. (I will refrain from repeating the specifics of their results because the authors provide a clear summary.) Of course, there is a lot of *ceteris paribus* going on here. The authors do a good job, though, controlling for potentially confounding environmental factors (drawing from previous work). The chapter's distinguishing features relative to previous work are that it examines (1) many more countries, (2) a more comprehensive set of institutional factors, and (3) a more comprehensive set of corporate risk measures.

I divide the remainder of my comments into two parts. The first part addresses some issues that lie within the scope of the chapter. None of my concerns in this first part is particularly worrisome, and it's clear that the authors are aware of them, but they warrant note nonetheless. The second part steps out of the chapter and addresses possible next steps for researchers interested in this micro-institutional agenda.

ISSUES WITHIN CHAPTER'S SCOPE

I would like to address three sets of issues that relate directly to this chapter's analysis. The first set concerns controls. Specifically, in accounting for corporate risk taking, does the analysis control fully for country-, industry-, and firm-specific factors? The second set of issues concerns taxes and how they might distort results. The third set of issues concerns data.

Regarding controls, note at the outset that the authors have done much to account for potentially confounding factors. Naturally, though, some concerns remain. Let me touch on a few. In this version of the analysis, the regressions of Table 9.8 include no country dummy. In a previous version there was a country dummy. R^2 statistics in this version are about half as high as those in the previous version (17 percent versus 31 percent). How much of the change in explanatory power is due to the country dummy? More important, does the seeming significance of the country dummy indicate that there are country factors that have not been controlled, which may be correlated with variables in the regression, leading to omitted-variables bias? For example, some of the countries experienced hyperinflation in the ten years preceding the sample. Recent hyperinflation may severely restrict longer-maturity financing alternatives in local currency, thereby affecting capital structure. Another possible control is the extent to which firms in a given country are rated by an international ratings agency. This can, de facto, affect financing alternatives and capital structure. (I would add that a credit rating might also proxy for access to foreign-currency debt, an issue I return to below.) I do not intend these comments about controls to be a cheap shot. They are much easier to identify than to test. I simply offer them as issues worth considering.

Let me turn to the second set of issues – that concerning taxes. Tax avoidance plays a huge role in corporate decision-making. It also plays a huge role in the literature on optimal capital structure. Indeed, many capital-structure models predict that debt would never be chosen over equity if it were not tax-advantaged. I was therefore heartened to see that this final version of their analysis includes a control for whether debt is tax-advantaged. This control is extremely significant in their Table 9.8 regressions, a result that does not surprise me. I have a concern, however, about the way they introduce this control. From footnote 16 it appears that this tax-advantage variable includes as a component firm-specific debt. In a regression of firm-specific debt-equity ratios, it is not clear to me that this is capturing what the authors intend it to capture. Instead, I would have included only the country-specific portion of the tax-advantage variable (the first term in footnote 16). This would capture country-level variation in this factor, without introducing firm-specific debt to the regressor – an endogenous variable. Also, by taking a country-level approach to tax advantage, the implications for policy are clearer.

Continuing with tax issues, I also believe that tax has consequences for other parts of their analysis, and their interpretation of results. For example, the authors write that "the latter finding suggests there is not necessarily a tradeoff between riskiness and performance; rather, corporations in civil-law countries have both higher risk measures and lower profitability measures." Well, this statement is certainly consistent with their results. Let me offer a different interpretation. Among these civil-law countries, the authors find that this result is largely due to the Germanic-law subset, which has lower reported earnings. In Germany, though – and I suspect other Germanic-law countries as well – accounting principles are "tax-driven," meaning that there is no distinction between what accountants refer to as TAP and GAAP (see Choi and Levich, 1991). TAP is the set of accounting principles used for the calculation of taxes. GAAP is the set of accounting principles used for external reporting. Because a German firm knows that its external accounts also establish its tax basis, the firm has less incentive to inflate reported earnings. (I am presuming that external accounts are the accounts covered by Worldscope, the authors' data source.) Many other countries – including the United States – maintain important differences between TAP principles and GAAP principles. This leaves more room for inflating earnings on the external accounts without tax consequences.

The third set of issues in the chapter that I want to address concerns data. These are issues the authors have surely considered, though readers may not be aware of them. For example, in their regressions the authors exclude 10 percent of the dependent-variable observations (both tails) to control for outliers. Not unreasonable. Note, though, that these excluded observations are likely to concentrate on Korea, at least in Table 9.8, since Korean debt–equity ratios are much higher on average than those of other countries. One would like to have some sense of the country distribution of these outlier observations. (If the Korean mean debt–equity ratio is much higher than other countries, and Korean firms

are tightly distributed about that mean, should one think of these observations as noise, in the usual sense of the word "outlier"?) Another data
issue pertains to measures of risk that are performance-related. Per the
previous paragraph, reported earnings can be an unreliable measure of
performance. It would be interesting to know whether performance
measured from stock returns tells a similar story. Finally, one wonders
whether the firms that are included for each country are a "steady-state"
cross section, or whether we are looking at, for example, a set of relatively immature firms in developing countries. Firm age, measured as the
time it has been publicly held, is likely to correlate with capital structure.
(For example, a recently privatized state-run enterprise might still have
substantial government loans on its balance sheet.) To their credit, the
authors do exclude G7 countries from their sample and find qualitatively
similar results. It would be nice to examine the age of firms more fully.

ISSUES BEYOND CHAPTER'S SCOPE

Four directions for further work within this micro-institutional agenda
strike me as particularly interesting. These are as follows:

Foreign-Currency Debt

The story that initially sparked interest in the micro-institutional
approach to financial crises focuses on firms' exchange-rate risk – in particular, that arising from foreign-currency borrowing. Many firms became
insolvent when their home currency devalued. Why firms chose to take
on so much currency exposure remains unanswered (moral hazard of
some kind being a leading hypothesis). The approach of this chapter provides a nice means of addressing this key issue. In particular, specific
alternatives to moral hazard could be formulated and tested. The rub, of
course, is the data. There is certainly room for clever approaches to
proxying for firms' foreign-currency borrowing.

Financial Hedging of Operating Risk

Textbooks in international corporate finance cover the technique of
using the currency denomination of liabilities as a hedge for operating
exposure. For example, a firm might take on foreign-currency liabilities
so that exchange-rate effects on operating cash flows and financing cash
flows are offsetting. The tricky part is that exchange-rate effects on operating cash flows can be highly nonlinear, so that the hedge is only effective for smaller exchange rate changes. Considering Asia, small
devaluations are likely to be good for competitiveness – and operating
cash flows – even though dollar liabilities become more expensive to
service. Large devaluations, however, were often bad for operating cash

flows, at least in the short run (due to credit crunches, supply-chain disruption, increasing uncertainty, etc.). The relevant point here is that this type of "balancing" of operating and financial risks is completely overlooked within the approach of this chapter. There is room for empirical refinement here.

Two-Way Causality

The authors of this chapter are well aware that, in addition to firms responding to institutions, institutions also respond to firms. In Section 9.5, they present an argument by Rajan and Zingales (1999) that "if a particular legal system were proven effective, other countries would imitate valuable regulations, including equity and creditor protection, and *gradually* differences in legal systems would disappear" (italics mine). Sensible enough. I would like to add a twist, however, based on my reading of Asia's reform. The twist turns on the word *gradual*. In the spirit of Toynbee's challenge-response mechanism, I would suggest that the feedback from firm characteristics to institutions is punctuated, not gradual. Large shocks laid bare the ways in which Asia's legal/regulatory systems were deficient, ushering in a period of punctuated institutional reform.

Corporate Risk versus Equity Risk

The type of risk this chapter examines is firmly rooted in the corporate-finance concept of financial distress. That is, the measures of risk used here are leverage ratios, liquidity ratios, profit ratios, etc. The type of risk more familiar to asset-pricing researchers is covariance risk – covariance of returns with consumption growth (or market returns, or wealth, etc.). There is room to address the mapping from these micro corporate-risks to the more macro-covariance risks. Are the stock prices of firms that are more risky in the micro-sense of this chapter also the firms whose stock prices are more variable? How about the link between a firm's micro-risk and its covariance with the home or world market? Are these micro-risks diversifiable? Or are they systematic, as the Asian financial crises might suggest?

REFERENCES

Choi, Frederick, and Richard Levich (1991). "International Accounting Diversity: Does It Affect Market Participants?" *Financial Analysts Journal* July/August:73–82.
Rajan, Raghuram and Luigi Zingales (1999). "The Politics of Financial Development." Mimeo, University of Chicago.

PART IV

POLICY RESPONSES

10

Interest Rate Stabilization of Exchange Rates and Contagion in the Asian Crisis Countries

Robert Dekle, Cheng Hsiao, and Siyan Wang

10.1 INTRODUCTION

For the countries most affected by the Asia crisis – Thailand, Indonesia, Malaysia, and Korea – economic events have been dramatic and have defied expectations. Exchange rates that had enjoyed a sustained period of stability depreciated precipitously. Between June 1997 and July 1998, nominal exchange rates vis-à-vis the U.S. dollar in Thailand, Indonesia, Malaysia, and Korea depreciated by about 67 percent, 500 percent, 40 percent, and 88 percent, respectively.

In response to these massive depreciations, the monetary authorities in these countries adopted tight monetary policies; specifically, they raised their short-term interest rates. After the implementation of the tight monetary policies, overnight call rates were raised from 15 percent to 22 percent in Thailand; from 10 percent to 47 percent in Indonesia; from 6 percent to 11 percent in Malaysia; and from 15 percent to 32 percent in Korea.

This chapter tries to answer the following basic question: Have the high interest rates had the desired effect of appreciating the nominal exchange rates in the crisis countries? It is well known that, in general, there is no stable empirical short-run relationship between exchange rates and interest rates (Frankel and Rose, 1995). Nominal exchange rates move as if they are a random walk (Meese and Rogoff, 1983). However, many policymakers believe, and anecdotal evidence suggests, that historically high interest rates have succeeded in

Support from the National Science Foundation is gratefully acknowledged. We thank P.-R. Agenor, Menzie Chinn, Y.-W. Cheung, Reuven Glick, and Ramon Moreno, as well as participants in the Federal Reserve Bank of San Francisco conference, for helpful comments.

stabilizing nominal exchange rates in some crisis countries, especially in Latin America.[1]

During the recent Asian crisis, the relationship between exchange rates and interest rates has again been a topic of substantial controversy. The traditional view stresses that tight monetary policies are necessary to support the exchange rate: Higher interest rates raise the return that an investor obtains from investing in the country, reduce capital flight, and discourage speculation. However, several prominent economists have argued a revisionist view that a rise in interest rates has a negative effect on the exchange rate (Radelet and Sachs, 1998; Feldstein, 1998; Furman and Stiglitz, 1998).

The revisionist view is that under the unique conditions of a financial panic, tight monetary policies and high interest rates would result in capital outflows and exchange rate depreciation. That is, the high interest rates cause a financial implosion and raise default probabilities, thus weakening the currency. Radelet and Sachs (1998, p. 31) express this view strongly:

... It is entirely possible that in the unique conditions of the midst of a financial panic, raising interest rates could have the perverse effect of weakening the currency. ... Creditors understood that highly leveraged borrowers could quickly be pushed to insolvency as a result of several months of high interest rates. Moreover, many kinds of interest-sensitive market participants, such as bond traders, are simply not active in Asia's limited financial markets. The key participants were the existing holders of short term debt, and the important question was whether they would or not roll over their claims. High interest rates did not feed directly into these existing claims (which were generally floating interest rate notes based on a fixed premium over LIBOR). It is possible, however, that by undermining the profitability of their corporate customers, higher interest rates discouraged foreign investors from rolling over their loans.

While most of the work examining the relationship between tight monetary policies and exchange rates for the Asian crisis countries has been anecdotal, there have been recent papers that have empirically estimated this relationship. Goldfajn and Baig (1998), Kaminsky and Schmukler (1998), and Ghosh and Phillips (1998) use daily nominal interest rate and exchange rate data to attempt to calculate impulse response functions. Generally, because of the noise in daily data and possibly other specification issues, they are unable to find statistically significant coefficients in their vector autoregressive (VAR) models. Gould and Kamin (Chapter 11, this volume) use weekly data to examine the relationship between real exchange rates and real interest rates, but

---

[1] See the case studies in Goldfajn and Baig (1998) and Furman and Stiglitz (1998).

generally fail to find a stable relationship. Goldfajn and Gupta (1999), Furman and Stiglitz (1998) and Kraay (1998) examine episodes of currency crises using cross-country data. The results are mixed. While Goldfajn and Gupta find that high interest rates appreciate the nominal exchange rate, Furman and Stiglitz show that if the sample is restricted to low inflation countries – which includes East Asia – high interest rates lead to exchange rate depreciations. Kraay creates binary indicator variables for Thailand, Malaysia, and Korea for whether or not speculative attacks occur and applies probit analysis to a cross section of countries. He finds that a rise in the interest rate does not lower the probability of an attack.

In this chapter we use high-frequency (weekly) data during the crisis and its aftermath to examine the relationship between an increase in interest rates and the behavior of exchange rates.[2] In contrast to much earlier work, we find that the lead–lag relation between the exchange rate and the interest rate clearly indicates that raising the interest rate has had the traditional impact of appreciating the nominal exchange rate during the crisis period.

In addition, we also examine the role of "contagion" in the Asian currency crisis. Contagion is usually defined as an excessive co-movement across countries in asset returns, including exchange rates. The co-movement is said to be excessive if it persists even after common fundamentals have been controlled for. A burgeoning empirical literature has recently examined the role of contagion during the Asian crisis. Using daily data, Baig and Goldfajn (1998) find that during the crisis period, the Southeast Asian currencies were highly correlated with each other, but not with the won. However, Forbes and Rigobon (1998) find that correlation coefficients, when properly estimated, are not significantly higher during crisis periods. Kaminsky and Reinhart (1998) find significant evidence of contagion and that the larger the number of the countries that are "infected," the higher the probability of contagion.

In addition to the above studies that have examined the cross-correlation of assets returns, there are studies that have examined the impact of "news" elsewhere on domestic asset returns. Baig and Goldfajn (1998) and Kaminsky and Schmukler (1998) use dummy variables to quantify the impact of policy announcements and other news on the

---

[2] Unfortunately, for the noncrisis periods we do not have data at the weekly frequency. Thus, we cannot examine the relationship between interest rates and exchange rates for the noncrisis periods. We omit Indonesia because exchange rate movements there appear to be dominated by political factors rather than more fundamental economic ones.

respective markets. Generally, the research has found that news elsewhere has effects on asset prices, even after controlling for domestic fundamentals, and that there are large asymmetries: Good news affects
exchange rates far more than bad news.

Our results mostly corroborate the findings of earlier papers. We add
to our framework used to examine the relationship between interest
rates and exchange rates, lagged neighboring country exchange rates, and
lagged news. We find that lagged Korean exchange rates are positively
correlated with current Thai and Malaysian exchange rates, but that
lagged Thai and Malaysian rates do not affect current Korean exchange
rates, nor each other. With regard to the impact of news, we too find that
there are large asymmetries in the response of exchange rates to news:
Lagged bad news does not affect exchange rates, but lagged good
news does.

In Section 10.2 we review the theoretical and empirical literature on
the relationship between interest rates and exchange rates. In Section
10.3 we present two simple models that capture versions of the traditional and revisionist stories. We show that tight money can appreciate
or depreciate the nominal exchange rate, depending on how tight money
affects the long-run real exchange rate. In Section 10.4 we describe the
data and examine some charts relating nominal interest rates with
nominal exchange rates. In Section 10.5 we use Asian data during the
crisis period and its aftermath to see if the tight monetary policies have
appreciated or depreciated the nominal exchange rate. We find that the
Asian experience clearly indicates that high interest rates have had the
usual impact of appreciating the nominal exchange rate. We also examine
the possibility of contagion. Conclusions are in Section 10.6.

10.2 INTEREST RATES AND EXCHANGE RATES: THEORETICAL AND EMPIRICAL PERSPECTIVES

The starting point in the analysis of the relationship between interest
rates and exchange rates is the uncovered interest parity (UIP)
equation:

$$i_t - i_t^* = E_t(e_{t+1}) - e_t + \rho_t + \phi_t$$

where i_t is the domestic interest rate, i_t^* is the foreign interest rate, e_t is
the domestic exchange rate, ρ_t is the exchange rate risk premium, ϕ_t is
the default risk premium (on domestic bonds), and thus $E_t(e_{t+1}) - e_t$ is the
expected depreciation of the domestic currency.

If $E_t(e_{t+1})$, ρ_t, ϕ_t are assumed to be constant, then the UIP condition
says that a rise in domestic interest rates will lower e_t, that is, appreciate
the exchange rate. These assumptions provide the basis of the claim in

academic and policy circles that a rise in domestic interest rates will appreciate the exchange rate (Goldfajn and Baig, 1998; Goldfajn and Gupta, 1998). However, as noted by Furman and Stiglitz (1998), and Kraay (1998), these assumptions are far from innocuous. In times of economic crisis, expectations can be highly volatile, making the constancy of $E_t(e_{t+1})$ and ρ_t questionable. In addition, ϕ_t can be positively correlated with interest rates. If the correlation is high enough, then a rise in interest rates can perversely raise e_t, depreciating the exchange rate.

Furman and Stiglitz (1998), Radelet and Sachs (1998), Kraay (1998), and Min and McDonald (1999) stress that cross-border and international influences can make $E_t(e_{t+1})$ and ρ_t highly volatile in times of economic crisis. Namely, the thinness of foreign exchange markets in most emerging market currencies make currencies susceptible to the influences of speculators.[3] If the expectations of speculators are driven by "bandwagon" or "positive feedback"-type effects or are "irrational," then expectations can be destabilizing and $E_t(e_{t+1})$ and ρ_t can fluctuate wildly as these expectations shift (Frankel and Rose, 1995).[4] The existence of these types of expectations suggests that cross-country contagion may play an important role in the movements of emerging market currencies (Goldfajn and Baig, 1998). For example, the collapse of the Thai baht, say, can cause expectations of movements in the Korean won to shift in ways unrelated to Korean fundamentals, and cause the won to depreciate.

In addition to these international factors, Furman and Stiglitz (1998) and Radelet and Sachs (1998) stress domestic factors. These researchers argue that during times of economic crisis, ϕ_t is likely to be highly positively correlated with the level of interest rates. This is because high interest rates can severely impact the ability of firms to pay back their loans, both domestic and foreign. High rates can compromise the net worth of many firms, and the bankruptcy of these firms can have adverse effects on the net worth of the firms' creditors, especially that of domestic financial institutions. In turn, as these financial institutions go bankrupt and as banks cut lending, credit can become highly constrained. A credit crunch can set in, exacerbating the economic downturn, further hampering the ability of firms to pay back their borrowing.

---

[3] Min and McDonald (1999) show that for Indonesia, Malaysia, Korea, and Thailand, daily foreign exchange market turnover averages $9.1 billion, while for the OECD countries, foreign exchange market turnover averages $1.3 trillion.

[4] Expectations can be destabilizing when the effect of a depreciation can induce speculators to forecast more depreciation in the future. If speculators act on such expectations, they will seek to sell the currency, thereby exaggerating the original depreciation.

Thus, theory is ambiguous about whether a rise in domestic interest rates will appreciate the exchange rate, and the results of empirical research are similarly ambiguous. Using industrialized country data during the floating rate period, a large amount of econometric work has shown that a rise in domestic interest rates is perversely correlated with a *depreciation* of the domestic currency (see Lewis, 1995, for a review). However, recent VAR estimates using industrialized country data have found a more traditional impact: Positive innovations to interest rates lead to an *appreciation* of the domestic currency (Eichenbaum and Evans, 1995).

Recently, empirical work has been performed using data from emerging market economies during times of crisis. This work can be divided into studies using high-frequency (daily) time-series data and studies using cross-country or panel data. With regard to work using time-series data, the results have been mixed. Goldfajn and Baig (1998) and Ghosh and Phillips (1998) use daily nominal interest rate and exchange rate data for Korea, Indonesia, Malaysia, and Thailand to estimate VAR models. Generally, because of the noise in daily data and possibly other specification issues, they are unable to find statistically significant coefficients in their VAR models. Using their VAR results, these researchers have then calculated impulse response functions. Goldfajn and Baig (1998) and Ghosh and Phillips (1998) find that a shock to domestic interest rates tends to be associated with an appreciation of the domestic currency in most countries, while Kaminsky and Schmukler (1998) find the opposite.

With regard to work using cross-country or panel data, the results are again mixed. Goldfajn and Gupta (1998), Furman and Stiglitz (1998), and Kraay (1998) look at currency crisis episodes in the 1990s using cross-country data. Goldfajn and Gupta (1998) find that high interest rates appreciate the nominal exchange rate, but only in countries with strong banking sectors. Furman and Stiglitz (1998) find that if the sample is restricted to low inflation countries – which includes East Asia – high interest rates lead to exchange rate depreciations. Kraay (1998) controls for the endogeneity of interest rates using instrumental variables and finds no evidence that raising interest rates lowers the probability that a speculative attack succeeds.

10.3 A SIMPLE MODEL OF THE TRADITIONAL AND REVISIONIST VIEWS

To illustrate the traditional and revisionist views and to motivate the later empirical work, we present below a simple model of money supply and exchange rate determination.

10.3.1 The Model

We adapt the "workhorse" Dornbusch (1976) perfect foresight model, as modified by Obstfeld and Rogoff (1996, pp. 609–621).[5] The model consists of five equations involving domestic and foreign interest rates, i and i^*; real money demand, $m - p$; the real exchange rate, q; aggregate demand, y; and the domestic inflation rate, $p_{t+1} - p_t$. (All variables are in logs. Variables that are marked with a * are for the foreign country; those that are marked with an overbar are long-run steady-state values.):

1. Uncovered interest parity:

$$i_{t+1} = i^* + e_{t+1} - e_t \qquad (3.1)$$

2. Money demand:

$$m_t - p_t = -\eta i_{t+1} + \phi y_t \qquad (3.2)$$

3. Real exchange rate:

$$q_t = e_t + p^* - p_t \qquad (3.3)$$

4. Aggregate demand:

$$y_t = \bar{y} + \sigma(e_t + p^* - p_t - \bar{q}) \qquad (3.4)$$

5. Phillips curve:

$$p_{t+1} - p_t = \psi(y_t - \bar{y}) + e_{t+1} - e_t \qquad (3.5)$$

In addition, short-run prices are taken as fixed. That is, if the economy is shocked at time 0, then

$$\Delta p_0 = 0 \qquad (3.6)$$

Obstfeld and Rogoff (1996, p. 617) show that these equations yield (normalizing: $p^* = i^* = \bar{y} = 0$):

$$e_t = \frac{1}{(1+\eta)} \sum_{s=t}^{\infty} \left(\frac{\eta}{1+\eta}\right)^{s-t} m_s + \frac{(1-\phi\sigma)}{(1+\psi\sigma\eta)}(q_t - \bar{q}) \qquad (3.7)$$

where $\bar{q}$ is the long-run level of the real exchange rate, consistent with full employment.

10.3.2 Monetary Tightening – The Traditional View

Suppose that the economy starts at a long-run ("steady-state") level of $\bar{m}$, and $\bar{e} = \bar{m} + \bar{q}$. At time 0, an unanticipated permanent *decrease* in

---

[5] Recently, Lahiri and Vegh (1999) and Drazen (1999) have also developed models analyzing the relationship between interest rates and exchange rates in the crisis countries.

the money supply to $\overline{m}'$ occurs. It can be shown that the nominal exchange rate at time 0 will be (Obstfeld and Rogoff, 1996, p. 617):

$$e_0 = \overline{m} + \overline{q} + \frac{(1+\psi\sigma\eta)}{(\phi\sigma+\psi\sigma\eta)}(\overline{m}'-\overline{m}) < \overline{e} \qquad (3.8)$$

That is, a fall in the supply of money will appreciate the nominal exchange rate. Given (3.4) and (3.6), y_t falls. Then given (3.2) and (3.6), i_{t+1} will rise if $\sigma\phi < 1$. In short, in the traditional view, monetary tightening will appreciate the nominal exchange rate and raise nominal interest rates.

10.3.3 Monetary Tightening – The Revisionist View

Assume now that instead of being constant, the long-run real exchange rate, $\overline{q}'$, depends negatively on the change in the nominal money supplies at time 0:

$$\overline{q}' = \overline{q} - \theta(m_0' - m_0) \qquad (3.9)$$

Equation (3.9) captures the revisionist notion that tighter monetary policies during times of economic crisis increases bankruptcies, increases corporate defaults, and generally damages the long-run performance of the economy, if θ is positive.[6] Thus, a more depreciated real exchange rate is needed to achieve full employment.[7]

We assume that the long-run (irreversible) damage to the economy from tight money occurs entirely in the short-run, at time 0, when prices

---

[6] There is a macroeconomics literature starting from Bernanke (1983) that has argued that because markets for financial claims are incomplete, intermediation between some classes of borrowers and lenders requires nontrivial market-making and information-gathering sources. Tight money can reduce the effectiveness of the financial sector as a whole in performing these services, and thus cause a credit crunch. In fact, Bernanke (1983) has argued that such a credit crunch helped convert the U.S. downturn of 1929–1930 into a protracted depression.

Some commentators (Furman and Stiglitz, 1998) have pointed out that during the recent Asian crisis, these depression-like phenomena have been replicated by the tight monetary policies. High interest rates compromised the net worth of many Asian firms, and the bankruptcies of these firms had adverse effects on the net worth of the firms' creditors, especially that of domestic financial institutions. In turn, as these financial institutions went bankrupt and as banks cut lending, credit became highly constrained. A credit crunch set in, exacerbating the economic downturn.

[7] Most econometric studies cannot reject the null hypothesis that the real exchange rate is a random walk, suggesting that shocks to the real exchange rate are permanent (Froot and Rogoff, 1995). In fact, Obstfeld and Rogoff (1996) offer an optimizing model in which a monetary shock leads to long-lasting changes in the real exchange rate.

are sticky. Clearly, as prices adjust, real money supply is constant. Thus, we assume that the behavior of money from time 0 onward does not affect the long-run real exchange rate.

Because by assumption, nominal money supplies from time 1 to infinity (m_1 to m_∞) do not affect $\bar{q}'$, we can assume that the money supply changes are permanent and rewrite (3.9) as

$$\bar{q}' = \bar{q} - \theta(\bar{m}' - \bar{m}) \tag{3.10}$$

Equation (3.8) now becomes

$$e_0 = \bar{m} + \bar{q} - \theta(\bar{m}' - \bar{m}) + \frac{(1 + \psi\sigma\eta)}{(\phi\sigma + \psi\sigma\eta)}(\bar{m}' - \bar{m}) \tag{3.11}$$

For a monetary tightening to depreciate the nominal exchange rate, $e_0 > \bar{e}$, we require

$$\theta > \frac{(1 + \psi\sigma\eta)}{(\phi\sigma + \psi\sigma\eta)} \tag{3.12}$$

By inspection of (3.2) and (3.4), it can be seen that even with the modification (3.10), the fall in y_0 and the rise in i_1 are of the same magnitudes as in the traditional case above.

Equations (3.11) and (3.12) capture the revisionist notion that if the negative impact of the nominal money tightening on the long-run real economy is high enough, then the money tightening can perversely cause the nominal exchange rate to depreciate.

Given plausible parameter values, what must θ be for (3.12) to be satisfied? For example, for Korea, Tseng and Corker (1991) estimate that $\eta = 0.01$, $\phi = 1.0$, $\psi = 5$, and $\sigma = 1.0$. Given these parameter values, (3.12) can be satisfied by a value of θ greater than unity; if θ is greater than unity, the nominal exchange rate will *depreciate*.

Is a value of 1 for θ plausible? From money demand (3.2), it can be shown that for nominal interest rates to increase by 17 percentage points (as in December 1997 in Korea), nominal money would need to fall by about 10 percent.[8] Then from (3.9), given $\theta = 1$, the long-run real exchange rate should depreciate by about 10 percent. A fall in $\bar{q}$ of this magnitude certainly seems plausible. For example, Goldfajn and Baig (1998) show that in many Latin American countries, following a currency crisis, real exchange rate depreciations on the order of 20–25 percent were common. Thus, from a theoretical viewpoint, the revisionist position certainly seems justified.

[8] Assuming a projected 10 percent decline in y_t.

10.4 INTEREST RATES AND EXCHANGE RATES IN KOREA, MALAYSIA, AND THAILAND

To implement our empirical analysis, we collected daily interest rate data from Bloomberg for Korea, Malaysia, and Thailand spanning the period June 4, 1997 to August 5, 1998 (to June 24, 1998 for Malaysia). However, we conduct all of our analysis at the weekly frequency, using the data for each Wednesday. We begin by informally discussing developments in interest rate and exchange rate behavior in these economies, illustrated in Figures 10.1 to 10.3, and then report the results of our econometric analysis of the relationship between these two series.

Korea

Korea initially appeared relatively little affected by the crisis in the region, with the exchange rate remaining broadly stable through October 1997. While macroeconomic fundamentals were relatively favorable, concerns about the soundness of financial institutions increased significantly in the wake of several large corporate bankruptcies earlier in 1997. In late October 1997, external financing conditions deteriorated significantly and foreign exchange reserves plummeted. Monetary policy was tightened briefly, but was relaxed again in light of concerns about the impact of higher interest rates on the highly leveraged corporate sector. By early December, the won had depreciated by over 20 percent against the U.S. dollar and foreign exchange reserves had declined to about $6 billion. Unable to stem the declines in the won and in foreign exchange reserves, the Korean authorities in early December 1998 asked the IMF for assistance.

To establish conditions for an early return of market confidence, the underlying IMF adjustment program called for a fiscal tightening of 1.5 percent of GDP and a sharp rise in interest rates. The positive impact on the won of the initial rise in interest rates was short-lived. Within two weeks, by mid-December 1997, the won dropped sharply. Confidence was undermined by new information becoming available about the state of financial institutions, the level of reserves, and foreign short-term obligations falling due. To combat the plummeting won, structural aspects of the IMF program were strengthened, and interest rates were raised further.

By early January, 1998, signs of stability in the won emerged. Following a temporary arrangement with foreign private banks to maintain their short-term exposure to Korea, rollovers of short-term lending to Korea increased significantly and reserves started to increase, buoyed by a sharp improvement in the current account.

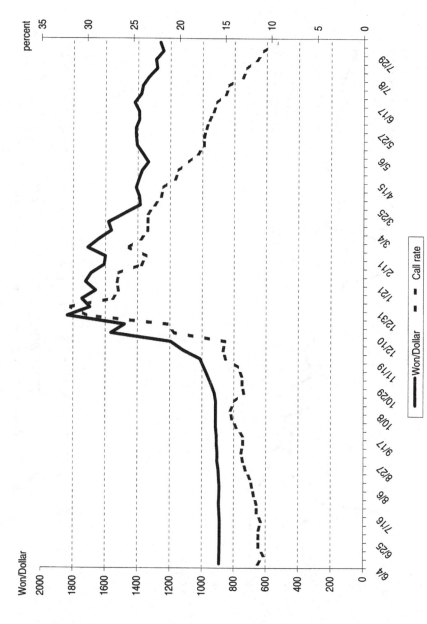

Figure 10.1. Korea: Exchange rate (left scale) and interest rate (right scale).

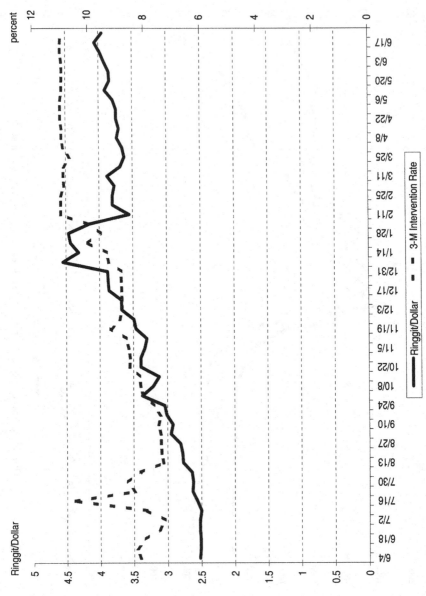

Figure 10.2. Malaysia: Exchange rate (left scale) and interest rate (right scale).

358

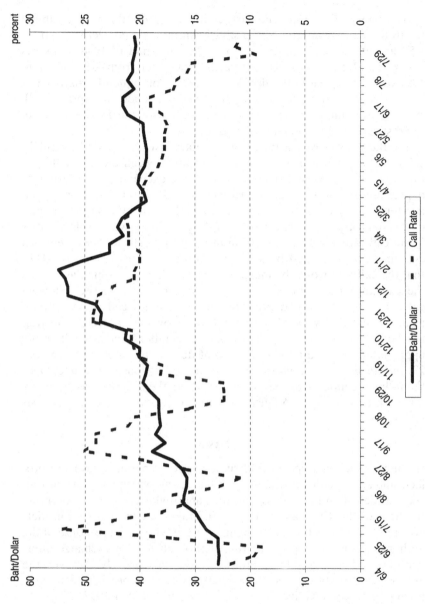

Figure 10.3. Thailand: Exchange rate (left scale) and interest rate (right scale).

359

Throughout the spring and early summer of 1998, the won continued to strengthen. Owing to a sharp slowdown in economic activity – from 5.5 percent in 1997 to –5.3 percent in the first half of 1998 – imports declined and the current account balance increased from –\$8.2 billion in 1997 to \$21.8 billion in the first half of 1998. Consequently, there was a further sharp increase in reserves and market confidence strengthened. As the won stabilized and, as agreed upon with the IMF, short-term interest rates were gradually brought down.

For the Bank of Korea, the main monetary instrument is the overnight call rate. Figure 10.1 depicts the relationship between the overnight call rate and the spot exchange rate. The spot exchange rate started to depreciate during the week of October 20 and the rates of depreciation accelerated during the week of November 17. After the announcement of the stand-by agreement with the IMF during the week of December 8, the call rate was increased from about 12 percent to 24 percent. An agreement was reached between the Korean authorities and the IMF that the call rate would be increased and would be kept high as long as the exchange rate remained at a depreciated level.[9] In the following week, however, the won depreciated further, and the call rate was raised again during the week of December 22 to over 32 percent. The won reached its low point during the week of December 1 and, while it briefly appreciated, reached another low point during the week of December 22. In late February 1998 the won started to steadily appreciate. Over the following months, as the won appreciated, the call rate was gradually lowered, and by early August the call rate was even below precrisis levels.

Malaysia

In the years leading up to the crisis, high-profile public investment projects and strong consumption growth had led to widening of the current account deficit and sharply rising stock and real estate prices. Following the float of the Thai baht in July 1997, Malaysia experienced considerable pressures in its foreign exchange market. The initial response of the authorities was to support the ringgit through foreign exchange interventions and a sharp hike in interest rates. Subsequently, however, the authorities quickly allowed the exchange rate to depreciate, tightening fiscal policy, and lowering interest rates in late October 1997.

In part reflecting interest rates lower than those of neighbors, short-term capital outflows from Malaysia accelerated toward the end of 1997,

---

[9] An understanding was reached between both parties that the won/dollar exchange rate above 1,500 was too weak (depreciated). The understanding was that as long as the won remained below 1,500, the call rate could gradually be brought down.

weakening the ringgit and reducing foreign exchange reserves from \$28 billion from the end of 1996 to \$22 billion at the end of 1997. However, because of its relatively healthy (compared to its neighbors) reserve position, Malaysia refused assistance from the IMF and therefore did not have to adopt a committed interest rate defense of its currency. In light of the continued weakness of the ringgit, which depreciated by over 44 percent in 1997, the authorities decided to raise interest rates again in stages starting in early December 1997.

The high interest rates and the tight fiscal policy stance severely depressed the domestic economy, as private consumption and aggregate private investment contracted sharply. Real GDP in the first half of 1998 contracted by about 5 percent. By early March 1998 the authorities came to believe that tight money was deleterious to Malaysia's short- and long-term economic prospects and that movements in exchange rates, rather than reflecting movements in interest rates, reflected external developments and irrational market behavior. Consequently, the authorities started lowering interest rates again in early March 1998. This lack of a committed interest rate defense, coupled with rhetoric against speculators and measures to restrict trading in the domestic stock and currency markets, possibly led to a sustained decline of the ringgit. The ringgit remained depreciated from February to June 1998.

For Bank Negara Malaysia (BNM), the main monetary control variable is the three-month intervention rate. BNM sharply raised the intervention rate in the middle of July 1997 (Figure 10.2). However, the ringgit continued to deteriorate. Around late October 1997, because of the perceived lack of success of the interest rate defense, the authorities decided to rely less on interest rate instruments to tackle exchange rate volatility. Subsequently, however, the intervention rate was raised again, from 9 to 11 percent, but not nearly to the extent that rates were raised in Korea and Thailand.

Thailand

Following episodes of speculative attack in 1996, the Thai baht came under strong pressure in early 1997. The main immediate concerns were the sustainability of the exchange rate peg in the face of the large current account deficit, rising short-term external debt, and collapsing stock and property prices.

The policy response to the pressures on the baht focused on spot and forward market intervention, and the introduction of controls on some capital account transactions. Following mounting speculative attacks and concerns about Thailand's foreign exchange position, the baht was floated in early July 1997. The accompanying policy package, however, failed to bolster market confidence and the baht depreciated by 20 percent in July 1997 against the dollar, while short-term interest rates were sharply brought down, after a temporary increase in early July.

Unable to stem the collapses in the baht and in foreign exchange reserves, the Thai authorities asked for assistance from the IMF in early August 1997. Key elements of the policy package included measures to restructure the financial sector (including closure of insolvent financial institutions), fiscal adjustment measures equivalent to 3 percent of GDP to bring the fiscal balance back into surplus, and indicative ranges for short-term interest rates. Although interest rates rose significantly, the baht continued to depreciate as rollover of short-term loans declined and the crisis in Asia spread.

To further stem the collapse of the baht, the IMF program was strengthened in December 1997. The program called for an acceleration of financial sector restructuring and a further substantial increase in interest rates. After falling to an all-time low against the dollar in early January 1998, the baht began to strengthen in early February as market confidence improved. The baht strengthened markedly between February and May of 1998 (some 35 percent vis-à-vis the dollar from the low in January), and short-term interest rates were cautiously reduced starting in late March.

For the Bank of Thailand, the main monetary instrument is the overnight call rate. Figure 10.3 depicts the relationship between the overnight call rate and the spot exchange rate. In response to pressures on the baht, the authorities first raised call rates in early July 1997, but fearing the impact of the high rates on the domestic economy, the rates were subsequently lowered. As was the case with Korea, an agreement was reached between the Thai authorities and the IMF that the call rate would be increased and kept high as long as the baht remained weak. The call rate was raised sharply again in early August and remained high until early 1998, when it was gradually brought down, as the baht stabilized.

As these country case studies show, to defend their currency, interest rates were raised in all three countries. However, the countries differed in their degrees of commitment to the interest rate defense. Korea was the most committed: Interest rates were raised almost immediately after the collapse of the won and were kept high until the won stabilized. Malaysia was the least committed: Interest rates were lowered even before the ringgit stabilized. Figures 10.1–10.3 appear to show that a rise in interest rates in Korea has tended to be associated with an appreciation of the won. For Malaysia and Thailand, the relationships between interest rates and the exchange rates are less clear.

10.5 EMPIRICAL RESULTS

Because of the controversy surrounding the role of tight monetary policies and high interest rates in stabilizing the exchange rate, in this section we hope to shed light on this dispute by examining high-frequency financial market data during the crisis in Korea, Malaysia, and Thailand. We also see whether there has been contagion among the countries hit most severely by the crisis. We examine the respective countries' weekly spot exchange rate, the policy interest rate, and the price level differential with respect to the United States from June 1997 to August 1998. We focus on this period because of the availability of data and because the monetary policy regime in these countries can most clearly be identified with stabilizing the exchange rate. Including later or earlier time periods may result in mixing different monetary policy regimes.

Because we are using policy interest rates, changes in interest rates clearly reflect changes in the monetary policy stance. Had we used market interest rates, changes in interest rates would be endogenous, say, affected by rising uncertainty. That we find a negative relationship between interest and exchange rates is support that we are using policy interest rates. If our interest rates were market determined, we should be biased toward finding a positive relationship between exchange and interest rates, since both are affected in the same direction by market uncertainty.

Given that the right model for the Asian crisis is unknown, structural estimation can lead to biased estimates. Therefore, instead of estimating model-based parameters, we take the approach of letting the data speak for themselves. However, because of the appeal of the long-run purchasing power parity relationship, we impose this restriction on one of our model specifications. Thus, our empirical specification is not directly derived from the theoretical model in Section 10.3, which implies shifting long-run real exchange rates. Rather, we use the theoretical model to informally guide what variables to include in our specification.

10.5.1 Interest Rates and Exchange Rates

The advantage of our vector autoregressive time-series approach is that it is an unrestricted reduced form specification, and thus it avoids the possibility of misleading inference due to incorrect model specification. In fact, the same reduced form can correspond to different structural models with the proper imposition of *a priori* restrictions (e.g., Hsiao, 1983, 1997, 1998; Hsiao and Fujiki, 1998). The disadvantage of a time-series specification is that it usually involves a large number of parameters.[10] This makes the selection of an appropriate time-series specification difficult, because the distribution theory on which tests are based is asymptotic. For many of the hypothesis tested, the degrees of freedom of the test statistics are of the same magnitude as the degrees of freedom left in the data after fitting the model.

To partially alleviate the problems associated with estimating a profligately specified time-series model, we shall combine the notion of Granger (1969) causality and cointegration (Engle and Granger, 1987) to reduce the number of parameters estimated, and to get around the issue of nonstandard test statistics with the presence of integrated variables. In addition, we also consider the interrelationships between our time-series model and some simple structural models (such as purchasing power parity) by placing the restrictions implied by the structural models on the corresponding time series model. Our goal is to obtain robust inferences of the relationship between the exchange rate and the policy interest rate.

As described in Section 10.4, even though the chief goal of monetary policy in Korea, Malaysia, and Thailand is to stabilize the exchange rate, countries differ substantially in their institutional arrangements. When the data-generating process is heterogeneous, pooling the data can yield misleading inference (e.g., Hsiao and Sun, 1999). Therefore, we shall fit time-series models for each of these countries separately.

We take the following steps to fit the time-series models:

First, because estimates based on stationary and nonstationary data have very different limiting distributions (e.g., Anderson, 1971; Johansen, 1988, p. 91; Phillips, 1986, 1987, 1991, 1998), we test for the presence of unit roots in the logarithmic transformation of the spot exchange rate, s_t, the policy interest rate, i_t, and the price level differential, p_t.[11] The monetary policy interest rates for Korea, Malaysia, and Thailand are the call rate, the three-month intervention rate, and the call rate, respectively. We use the Schwarz (1978) criterion to choose the optimal order of lags to conduct the ADF test (Dickey and Fuller, 1979). Table 10.1 gives the ADF test statistics for the level and the first difference of s_t, i_t, and p_t for each country. These results indicate that we should treat all these variables as integrated of order 1, $I(1)$, process for Korea and Malaysia. For

---

[10] For an unrestricted VAR model involving four variables with the order of lag equal to 5, we will have to estimate 80 coefficients and 10 variance–covariances. The shortages of degrees of freedom and multicollinearity can yield a large number of statistically insignificant coefficient estimates. This empirical phenomenon makes the interpretation of the significance tests difficult.

[11] That is, $p_t = p_t^u - p_t^A$, where p_t is the log price-level differential, p_t^u, is the log U.S. price level and p_t^A is the log price level for the Asian country.

Table 10.1. Unit Root Tests

Variables	Augmented Dickey–Fuller Test Statistics	P	95% Critical Values
K_S	−1.762	2	−2.914
K_I	−0.455	0	−2.906
K_P	−0.533	1	−2.889
M_S	−2.094	0	−2.920
M_I	−1.731	0	−2.910
M_P	0.680	0	−2.891
T_S	−2.396	0	−2.914
T_I	−3.471	1	−2.906
T_P	0.620	3	−2.889
ΔK_S	−2.955	1	−2.915
ΔK_I	−7.184	0	−2.906
ΔK_P	−4.768	0	−2.890
ΔM_S	−8.159	0	−2.922
ΔM_I	−9.186	0	−2.911
ΔM_P	−8.420	0	−2.891
ΔT_S	−6.931	0	−2.915
ΔT_I	−7.228	0	−2.907
ΔT_P	−5.097	2	−2.890

Notes:
1. P gives the order of lags selected by the SBC, Schwarz Bayesian Criterion. Δ denotes first difference operator.
2. K_S, M_S, and T_S are log of Korea spot exchange rate, Malaysia spot exchange rate, and Thailand spot exchange rate, respecitively.
   K_I, M_I, and T_I are Korea–U.S. interest rate differential, Malaysia–U.S. interest rate differential, and Thailand–U.S. interest rate differential, respecitvely.
   K_P, M_P and T_P are Korea–U.S. inflation rate differential, Malaysia–U.S. inflation rate differential, and Thailand–U.S. inflation rate differential, respectively.
3. Test statistics for K_S and ΔK_S are based on observations from 6/4/97 to 8/5/98.
   Test statistics for K_I and ΔK_I are based on observations from 3/26/97 to 8/5/98.
   Test statistics for K_P and ΔK_P are based on observations from 7/3/97 to 8/5/98.
   Test statistics for M_S and ΔM_S are based on observations from 6/4/97 to 6/24/98.
   Test statistics for M_I and ΔM_I are based on observations from 3/26/97 to 6/24/98.
   Test statistics for M_P and ΔM_P are based on observations from 7/3/97 to 6/24/98.
   Test statistics for T_S and ΔT_S are based on observations from 6/4/97 to 8/5/98.
   Test statistics for T_I and ΔT_I are based on observations from 4/2/97 to 8/5/98.
   Test statistics for T_P and ΔT_P are based on observations from 7/3/97 to 8/5/98.

Thailand, although both the exchange rate and inflation rate are $I(1)$ processes, the interest rate is stationary, $I(0)$.

Second, because the results of hypotheses testing are very sensitive to the order of the autoregressive process (e.g., Hsiao, 1979a, 1982a, 1982b), we use the Schwarz (1978) criterion to determine the order of the vector autoregressive process. Because we have only a limited number of obser-

Table 10.2. Cointegration Tests

	Order of VAR	Maximum Eigenvalue Test	Trace Test
Korea	2	12.98 (21.12)	17.02 (31.54)
Malaysia	1	17.75 (21.12)	29.43 (31.54)
Thailand	2	12.56 (14.88)	15.01 (17.86)

Notes:
Ninety-five percent critical values are in parentheses.
Test statistics for Korea and Thailand are based on observations from 6/4/97 to 8/5/98.
Test statistics for Malaysia are based on observations from 6/4/97 to 6/24/98.

vations, *a priori* we specify the highest order of lag to be five. The Schwarz criterion selects the optimal order of lag to be 2 for Korea, 1 for Malaysia, and 2 for Thailand.

Third, we test for the rank of cointegration using the Johansen likelihood ratio test (Table 10.2). The likelihood ratio test statistics of rank 0 against rank 1 based on the maximum eigenvalue of the stochastic matrix are 12.98, 17.75, and 12.56 for Korea, Malaysia, and Thailand, respectively. The 95 percent critical value is 21.12 for Korea and Malaysia and 14.88 for Thailand (because there are only two $I(1)$ variables). The likelihood ratio test statistics based on the trace of the stochastic matrix are 17.02, 29.43, and 15.01, respectively. The 95 percent critical value is 31.54 for Korea and Malaysia and is 17.86 for Thailand. They indicate that there is no cointegration relationship among s_t, i_t, and p_t for the period under consideration.

Fourth, because we are not able to find cointegrating relations among these three variables, we take the first difference of $I(1)$ variables to transform them into $I(0)$ variables. We then use Hsiao's (1979a, 1979b) method to select a parsimonious vector autoregressive specification that allows each variable to enter into each equation with different orders of lags. We use Zellner's (1962) seemingly unrelated regression method to estimate the final specifications for Korea and Thailand. However, since the contemporaneous interest rate appears in Malaysia's exchange rate equation, we use the three-stage least-squares method to estimate the final specification for Malaysia.

Fifth, the lack of a cointegration relation for the time period considered could be due to the rapid adjustment of the structural imbalance, especially in the overvaluation of the real exchange rate, which was in existence prior to the crisis. For instance, in 1990, the Thai baht/U.S. dollar exchange rate was 25.6. In 1996, it was 25.3, virtually unchanged. During the same period, the GDP deflator increased by 17 percent in the United States and 33 percent in Thailand. That is, the real exchange rate of the

Thai baht had appreciated by about 16 percent by 1996 relative to the real exchange rate in 1990. It is the same story for the Korean won and for the Malaysian ringgit. The real exchange rate for Korea and Malaysia appreciated by about 25 percent and about 5 percent, respectively, between 1990 and 1996 (e.g., Lau, 1999). If the devaluation of the currencies of these countries during the crisis period is in part a response to the overvaluation of their currencies prior to the crisis, then one would not expect to find a cointegrating relation between the nominal exchange rate movement and the price level differential movement for the time period considered. However, the short time horizon discrepancy between the nominal exchange rate movement and the price level differential movement does not necessarily preclude the existence of a cointegrating relation between them over a longer time horizon. We therefore impose the long-run purchasing power parity (PPP) restriction and reestimate our models. The results of the final specification without (Model 1) and with (Model 2) the imposition of the long-run purchasing power parity restrictions (but without "contagion" effects) are reported in Tables 10.3a, 10.4a, and 10.5a for Korea, Malaysia, and Thailand, respectively. (The results with contagion effects, reported in Tables 10.3b, 10.4b, and 10.5b, are discussed in Section 10.5.2.)

From the results of imposing the PPP assumption, the error-correction terms $v_{t-1} = s_{t-1} - p_{t-1}$ all have the expected sign of being negative in the exchange rate equations. The coefficient on v_{t-1} indicates that if the level of the exchange rate exceeds the price level differential ($v_{t-1} > 0$), then the nominal exchange rate would appreciate.

As Friedman and Schwarz (1991) have said, "the real proof of (the) pudding is whether the model produces a satisfactory explanation of the data not used in baking the model – data for subsequent or earlier years, for other countries, or for other variables." Thus, we compare the predictive performance of our models 1 and 2. We split the sample period in two. The first period consists of observations from the first week of June 1997 to the third week of June 1998 for Korea and Thailand, and to the first week of May for Malaysia. The second period consists of the fourth week of June to the first week of August for Korea and Thailand, and the second week of May to the fourth week of June for Malaysia. We use the first period data to reestimate the final specifications for each country, then use the estimated coefficients and the first period data to generate (a) deterministic forecasts for all seven observations in the second period and (b) the adapted forecasts for the one-period-ahead prediction.

Columns 1 and 2 (Panel A) of Tables 10.6 and 10.7 present the root-mean-square prediction errors of the one-period-ahead and

Table 10.3a. Parameter Estimates: Korea, Model without Contagion

	Model 1			Model 2		
	ΔK_S	ΔK_I	ΔK_P	ΔK_S	ΔK_I	ΔK_P
Intercept	−0.00377	−0.0159	0.000896	0.442	0.589	−0.00131
	(−0.61)	(−1.51)	(2.18)	(2.48)	(1.8)	(−0.1)
ΔK_S (−1)	−0.000244	0.0238	0.0244	0.0185	0.0398	0.0244
	(−0.00)	(0.12)	(2.23)	(0.13)	(0.2)	(2.2)
ΔK_S (−2)	0.426	0.453	—	0.421	0.472	—
	(3.46)	(2.33)		(3.59)	(2.48)	
ΔK_S (−3)	—	0.469	—	—	0.489	—
		(2.68)			(2.67)	
ΔK_I (−1)	−0.131	—	0.00463	−0.151	—	0.00455
	(−1.55)		(0.68)	(−1.8)		(0.66)
ΔK_I (−2)	—	—	0.0160	—	—	0.0159
			(3.25)			(3.19)
ΔK_I (−3)	—	—	−0.0126	—	—	−0.0126
			(−2.47)			(−2.45)
ΔK_P (−1)	4.064	6.086	—	3.974	6.080	—
	(2.30)	(2.01)		(2.39)	(2.05)	
ΔK_P (−2)	0.916	—	—	1.407	—	—
	(0.64)			(0.98)		
ΔK_P (−3)	1.804	—	—	2.562	—	—
	(1.26)			(1.77)		
K_PPP (−1)[a]	—	—	—	−0.0622	−0.0841	0.000306
				(−2.5)	(−1.85)	(0.16)

Note: See Table 10.1 for variable definitions. *t*-ratios are in parentheses.
[a] $K\_PPP = K\_S − K\_P$.

deterministic forecasts of the changes and the levels of the spot exchange rate, the policy interest rate, and the price-level differential. It is interesting to note that the predictions generated by imposing the long-run purchasing power parity restrictions are just as good as the predictions from the unrestricted time series models, if not better. More specifically, models imposing the PPP restriction generate more accurate one-period-ahead predictions than the unrestricted time-series models for the Korean exchange rate and interest rate, the Malaysian exchange rate, and the Thai exchange rate and the Thai–U.S. price-level differential.

Because of differences in institutional arrangements, the reactions of the exchange rate to interest rate changes differ among the countries, in magnitude and in lag time. However, the coefficients of the policy interest rate changes are all negative, indicating that raising the interest rate would have the traditional impact of appreciating the nominal exchange

Table 10.3b. Parameter Estimates: Korea, Model with Contagion

	Model 1			Model 2		
	ΔK_S	ΔK_I	ΔK_P	ΔK_S	ΔK_I	ΔK_P
Intercept	0.00901	−0.00453	0.00106	0.406	0.597	−0.00257
	(0.95)	(−0.35)	(1.98)	(1.98)	(1.63)	(−0.16)
ΔK_S (−1)	0.0121	−0.0699	0.0287	0.00979	−0.0481	0.0285
	(0.07)	(−0.31)	(2.18)	(0.06)	(−0.22)	(2.14)
ΔK_S (−2)	0.346	0.426	—	0.332	0.447	
	(2.38)	(2.01)		(2.35)	(2.14)	
ΔK_S (−3)	—	0.508	—	—	0.527	
		(2.65)			(2.63)	
ΔK_I (−1)	−0.154	—	0.00216	−0.156	—	0.00213
	(−1.55)		(0.26)	(−1.57)		(0.25)
ΔK_I (−2)	—	—	0.0159	—	—	0.0157
			(2.71)			(2.65)
ΔK_I (−3)	—	—	−0.0152	—	—	−0.0153
			(−2.50)			(−2.47)
ΔK_P (−1)	4.438	5.432	—	4.514	5.551	
	(2.29)	(1.67)		(2.43)	(1.73)	
ΔK_P (−2)	0.525	—	—	0.983	—	
	(0.34)			(0.63)		
ΔK_P (−3)	2.847	—	—	3.710	—	
	(1.58)			(1.99)		
K_NGN (−1)[a]	−0.0224	—	—	−0.0208	—	
	(−1.93)			(−1.75)		
K_PPP (−1)[b]	—	—	—	−0.0558	−0.0839	0.000507
				(−1.93)	(−1.64)	(0.23)

Note: See Table 10.1 for variable definitions. *t*-ratios are in parentheses.
[a] K_NGN = Neighboring country good news for Korea.
[b] $K\_PPP = K\_S - K\_P$.

rate in the short-run. On the other hand, because the policy interest rate appears in difference form in the Korean and Malaysian exchange rate equations, it would have a zero long-run elasticity in the conventional sense. However, the exchange rate is an $I(1)$ process. A shock to the exchange rate persists over time as long as the shock is not reversed. Therefore, we can still compute the eventual impact on the exchange rate due to a permanent change in interest rates. With the risk of abusing the terminology, we shall call this eventual impact on the exchange rate due to a permanent change in interest rate the *long-run exchange rate elasticity*.

The Malaysian exchange rate responds with a three-week lag. Its short-run elasticity is −0.176, assuming no PPP and −0.163 assuming PPP.

Table 10.4a. Parameter Estimates: Malaysia, Model without Contagion

	Model 1			Model 2		
	ΔM_S	ΔM_I	ΔM_P	ΔM_S	ΔM_I	ΔM_P
Intercept	0.0110	0.0102	0.000628	0.0847	−0.0457	−0.00124
	(1.76)	(1.13)	(1.18)	(1.84)	(−0.66)	(−0.30)
ΔM_S (−1)	−0.146	—	—	−0.134	—	—
	(−1.12)			(−1.04)		
ΔM_S (−2)	—	—	—	—	—	—
ΔM_S (−3)	—	—	—	—	—	—
ΔM_I (−1)	—	−0.222	−0.00265	—	−0.226	−0.00271
		(−1.64)	(−0.33)		(−1.65)	(−0.33)
ΔM_I (−2)	—	−0.232	0.0165	—	−0.240	0.0164
		(−1.73)	(2.07)		(−1.76)	(2.01)
ΔM_I (−3)	−0.176	—	0.0116	−0.163	—	0.0112
	(−1.96)		(1.41)	(−1.82)		(1.33)
ΔM_P (−1)	—	—	—	—	—	—
ΔM_P (−2)	—	—	—	—	—	—
ΔM_P (−3)	—	—	—	—	—	—
M_PPP (−1)[a]	—	—	—	−0.0642	0.0486	0.00163
				(−1.62)	(0.81)	(0.46)

Note: See Table 10.1 for variable definitions. *t*-ratios are in parentheses.
[a] $M\_PPP = M\_S - M\_P$.

The Korean exchange rate responds with a one-week lag. Its short-run elasticity is estimated to be −0.131 assuming no PPP and −0.151 assuming PPP. Thailand's exchange rate response to the interest rate change is the weakest; the short-run interest rate elasticity after five weeks of delay is estimated at −0.0538 assuming no PPP and −0.0315 assuming PPP.

The long-run exchange rate response to a shock to the interest rate is computed by solving the exchange rate equation from the system of the VAR models we estimated in terms of the interest rate only.

The long-run impact of a permanent change in the interest rate on the exchange rate depends critically on the model assumed. When there is no cointegration (no PPP restriction), a shock to the interest rate creates a permanent shock to the exchange rate as long as the shock is not reversed because the exchange rate is an $I(1)$ process. Under PPP, although a positive shock to the interest rate may have a desirable direct effect on appreciating the nominal exchange rate, its impact on the price-level differential may have an adverse effect of depreciating the nominal exchange through the long-run equilibrium relation between s_t and p_t. The eventual impact is the sum of these two offsetting forces.

Table 10.4b. Parameter Estimates: Malaysia, Model with Contagion

	Model 1			Model 2		
	ΔM_S	ΔM_I	ΔM_P	ΔM_S	ΔM_I	ΔM_P
Intercept	0.0275	0.0144	0.000698	0.0822	–0.0193	–0.00231
	(2.87)	(1.44)	(1.37)	(1.69)	(–0.25)	(–0.60)
ΔM_S (–1)	–0.211	—	—	–0.201	—	—
	(–1.66)			(–1.58)		
ΔM_S (–2)	—	—	—	—	—	—
ΔM_S (–3)	—	—	—	—	—	—
ΔM_I (–1)	—	–0.232	–0.00537	—	–0.232	–0.00574
		(–1.67)	(–0.74)		(–1.65)	(–0.78)
ΔM_I (–2)	—	–0.265	0.02	—	–0.270	0.0193
		(–1.92)	(2.78)		(–1.92)	(2.65)
ΔM_I (–3)	–0.203	—	0.0115	–0.186	—	0.0105
	(–2.34)		(1.57)	(–2.10)		(1.41)
ΔM_P (–1)	—	—	—	—	—	—
ΔM_P (–2)	—	—	—	—	—	—
ΔM_P (–3)	—	—	—	—	—	—
ΔK_S (–1)	0.170	—	—	0.167	—	—
	(1.69)			(1.65)		
ΔK_S (–2)	0.167	—	—	0.180	—	—
	(1.71)			(1.81)		
M_NGN (–1)[a]	–0.0316	—	—	–0.0274	—	—
	(–2.52)			(–2.08)		
M_PPP (–1)[b]	—	—	—	–0.0501	0.0295	0.00265
				(–1.14)	(0.45)	(0.79)

Note: See Table 10.1 for variable definitions. *t*-ratios are in parentheses.
[a] M_NGN = Neighboring country good news for Malaysia.
[b] $M\_PPP = M\_S - M\_P$.

For models without PPP, a permanent one percent change in the interest rate would have an eventual impact on the exchange rate of –0.1985 for Korea, –0.3667 for Malaysia, and –0.053776 for Thailand. For models under the PPP assumption, we estimate the long-run exchange rate elasticity by solving the exchange rate in terms of past (and present) changes in the policy interest rate. These elasticities are 0.0265, 0.014, and 0.002044, respectively for Korea, Malaysia, and Thailand.

Thus, we find that the rise in the policy interest rate has the traditional impact of appreciating the nominal exchange rate in the short-run. We have not found evidence supporting the revisionist view that a rise in the interest rate has a perversive effect on the exchange rate. However, the

Table 10.5a. Parameter Estimates: Thailand, Model without Contagion

	Model 1			Model 2		
	ΔT_S	T_I	ΔT_P	ΔT_S	T_I	ΔT_P
Intercept	0.0713	0.218	0.00174	0.291	−0.360	0.0168
	(2.66)	(2.18)	(3.19)	(2.01)	(−0.79)	(1.17)
ΔT_S (−1)	—	—	—	—	—	—
ΔT_S (−2)	—	—	—	—	—	—
ΔT_S (−3)	—	—	—	—	—	—
T_I (−1)	—	1.047	—	—	1.026	—
		(8.81)			(8.67)	
T_I (−2)	—	−0.239	—	—	−0.262	—
		(−1.92)			(−2.10)	
T_I (−5)	−0.0538	—	—	−0.0315	—	—
	(−2.45)			(−1.29)		
ΔT_P (−1)	—	—	−0.242	—	—	−0.254
			(−1.91)			(−1.97)
ΔT_P (−2)	—	—	—	—	—	—
ΔT_P (−3)	—	—	—	—	—	—
T_PPP (−1)[a]	—	—	—	−0.0671	0.172	−0.00409
				(−1.58)	(1.32)	(−1.05)

Note: See Table 10.1 for variable definitions. *t*-ratios are in parentheses.
[a] $T\_PPP = T\_S - T\_P$.

cost of the interest rate defense is quite high. To appreciate the nominal exchange rate by 40 percent, the authorities need to increase interest rates by about 300 percent for Korea, 152 percent for Malaysia, and 800 percent for Thailand. These increases may have a significant negative impact on the real economy.

However, the long-run impact of the interest rate change is less clear. If the long-run PPP relation does not hold, the long-run impact also supports the traditional view. If the PPP relation does hold in the long-run, then the direct impact of the interest rate change on the exchange rate is canceled by the indirect impact through the price-level differential. Under the assumption that long-run PPP does not hold, the authorities will need to permanently increase the policy interest rate about 200 percent for Korea, 94 percent for Malaysia, and 800 percent for Thailand to defend a 40 percent depreciation of the exchange rate. Balanced against this, however, is that the cost to the domestic economy of a freely falling exchange rate could be very high. Many of the East Asian countries have high dollar-denominated foreign liabilities, and the cost of servicing these liabilities could be prohibitively high when the exchange rate depreciates (Fischer, 1998).

Table 10.5b. Parameter Estimates: Thailand, Model with Contagion

	Model 1			Model 2		
	ΔT_S	T_I	ΔT_P	ΔT_S	T_I	ΔT_P
Intercept	0.0735	0.370	0.00227	0.185	−0.462	0.0175
	(2.82)	(3.74)	(3.35)	(1.13)	(−1.23)	(1.11)
ΔT_S (−1)	—	—	—	—	—	—
ΔT_S (−2)	—	—	—	—	—	—
ΔT_S (−3)	—	—	—	—	—	—
T_I (−1)	—	1.0980	—	—	1.060	—
		(9.61)			(9.58)	
T_I (−2)	—	−0.401	—	—	−0.441	—
		(−3.52)			(−4.01)	
T_I (−3)	—	—	—	—	—	—
T_I (−5)	−0.0414	—	—	−0.0238	—	—
	(−1.99)			(−0.95)		
ΔT_P (−1)	—	—	−0.317	—	—	−0.318
			(−2.24)			(−2.19)
ΔT_P (−2)	—	—	—	—	—	—
ΔT_P (−3)	—	—	—	—	—	—
ΔK_S (−1)	0.268	—	—	0.267	—	—
	(2.95)			(2.94)		
ΔK_S (−2)	0.109	—	—	0.140	—	—
	(1.24)			(1.50)		
T_NGN (−1)[a]	−0.0372	—	—	−0.0306	—	—
	(−3.31)			(−2.32)		
T_PPP (−1)[b]	—	—	—	−0.0372	0.253	−0.00415
				(−0.75)	(2.32)	(−0.96)

Note: See Table 10.1 for variable definitions. *t*-ratios are in parentheses.
[a] T_NGN = Neighboring country good news for Thailand.
[b] $T\_PPP = T\_S - T\_P$.

10.5.2 Contagion and Exchange Rates

In this section we discuss the results of incorporating the effect on own country exchange rates of neighboring country exchange rates and "news." To choose the vector autoregressive specification for the equation including neighboring country exchange rates, we used Hsiao's (1979a, 1979b) method described earlier. To choose the specification for the equation including news, we follow the Box and Jenkins (1970) identification procedure by correlating our neighboring country news dummy variables with the residuals of the models in Tables 10.3a, 10.4a, and 10.5a and drop the dummy variables that are insig-

Table 10.6. One-Period-Ahead Forecast Error
Comparison

Variables	A: Models without Contagion		B: Models with Contagion	
	Model 1	Model 2	Model 1	Model 2
K_S	0.0240	0.0197	0.0409	0.0546
K_I	0.0679	0.0637	0.0487	0.0486
K_P	0.0011	0.0011	0.0041	0.0042
M_S	0.0221	0.0210	0.0214	0.0221
M_I	0.0331	0.0363	0.0221	0.0237
M_P	0.0058	0.0059	0.0010	0.0012
T_S	0.0288	0.0268	0.0267	0.0250
T_I	0.2342	0.2605	0.0262	0.0273
T_P	0.0019	0.0018	0.0055	0.0056
ΔK_S	0.0240	0.0197	0.0409	0.0546
ΔK_I	0.0679	0.0637	0.0487	0.0486
ΔK_P	0.0011	0.0011	0.0041	0.0042
ΔM_S	0.0221	0.0210	0.0214	0.0221
ΔM_I	0.0331	0.0363	0.0221	0.0237
ΔM_P	0.0058	0.0059	0.0010	0.0012
ΔT_S	0.0288	0.0268	0.0267	0.0250
ΔT_I	0.2342	0.2605	0.0262	0.0273
ΔT_P	0.0019	0.0018	0.0055	0.0056

Note: Forecast errors are in terms of root mean square errors.

nificant.[12] This method is akin to examining the relationship between news and exchange rates, after holding fundamentals (interest rates) constant, as in previous research. In choosing our specification, we assumed that "news" was exogenous, so we also included contemporaneous (during the week) news. As it turned out, for all three countries, surprisingly, only the dummy variable representing lagged neighboring country good news was significant. Contemporaneous good or bad news or lagged bad news did not affect exchange rates. The results of the final specification without (Model 1) and with (Model 2) the imposition of the long-run PPP restrictions are reported in Tables 10.3b, 10.4b, and 10.5b

[12] Weekly neighboring country news dummy variables were constructed using the daily news reported and classified as "good" or "bad" in Baig and Goldfajn (1998). (We disregarded own country news.) Our estimation is at the weekly frequency. If any "good" news appeared during a certain week, then the "good" news dummy takes a value of one. If any "bad" news appeared during a certain week, then the "bad" news dummy takes a value of one.

Table 10.7. *H*-Period-Ahead Forecast Error
Comparison

Variables	A: Models without Contagion		B: Models with Contagion	
	Model 1	Model 2	Model 1	Model 2
K_S	0.1346	0.0907	0.0993	0.1390
K_I	0.3168	0.2460	0.0650	0.0827
K_P	0.0059	0.0047	0.0091	0.0068
M_S	0.0148	0.0319	0.0588	0.0473
M_I	0.0688	0.0973	0.0325	0.0372
M_P	0.0045	0.0045	0.0045	0.0052
T_S	0.0852	0.0661	0.0893	0.0733
T_I	0.4002	0.4422	0.0264	0.0631
T_P	0.0075	0.0066	0.0100	0.0116
ΔK_S	0.0332	0.0269	0.0291	0.0353
ΔK_I	0.0927	0.0770	0.0464	0.0473
ΔK_P	0.0014	0.0012	0.0045	0.0044
ΔM_S	0.0207	0.0207	0.0336	0.0229
ΔM_I	0.0327	0.0347	0.0207	0.0214
ΔM_P	0.0054	0.0055	0.0011	0.0012
ΔT_S	0.0284	0.0260	0.0273	0.0256
ΔT_I	0.1977	0.2009	0.0244	0.0280
ΔT_P	0.0017	0.0015	0.0057	0.0589

Note: Forecast errors are in terms of root mean square errors.

for Korea, Malaysia, and Thailand, respectively (models with contagion effects).

For all three countries, the responses of the own country exchange rate to the interest rate are basically unchanged from those depicted earlier. For Korea and Malaysia, the models including contagion effects give slightly higher short-run elasticities than the models excluding contagion effects. For Thailand, the current model gives slightly lower short-run elasticities.

With regard to the short-run impact of neighboring country exchange rates, a one percent appreciation of the won appreciates the ringgit by 0.34 percent, and the baht by about 0.38 percent, assuming no PPP. Assuming PPP, the impact of a one percent appreciation of the won on the ringgit and the baht are 0.35 percent and 0.41, respectively. For all three countries, the positive impacts on the domestic exchange rate of lagged neighboring country good news are highly significant.

Tables 10.6 and 10.7 (columns 3 and 4) present root mean square prediction errors of the one-period-ahead and deterministic forecasts of the changes and the levels of the spot exchange rate, the policy interest rate, and the price-level differential for the models with contagion effects. In general, the specifications including the contagion variables do not give a better fit than the specifications excluding the variables. This is somewhat surprising, since the contagion variables should capture to some extent the response of exchange rates to uncertainty. This could be because we only have a very limited number of observations for the news dummy. By splitting up the sample period in two, the number of observations available to estimate the news dummy coefficients is further reduced to only a small number.

10.6 CONCLUSIONS

In this chapter we have examined the relationships among the exchange rate, the policy interest rate, and the price-level differential in Korea, Malaysia, and Thailand during the Asian financial crisis and its aftermath. Both specifications with and without the long-run PPP restriction are estimated. The empirical results are supportive of the traditional view. We have not found any pervasive association between the rise in the policy interest rate and the depreciation of the exchange rate.

We have also examined the possible impact of contagion on exchange rates. We find that while Korean exchange rates influence the ringgit and the baht, the ringgit and the baht do not influence any other exchange rate. Furthermore, we find that the response of exchange rates to foreign "news" is asymmetric. "Bad" neighboring country news does not affect domestic exchange rates, but "good" news appreciates domestic exchange rates. The asymmetric relation could arise because during the crisis period the exchange rate overreacted and resulted in the undervaluation of crisis countries' currencies, hence leading to a negligible impact of further bad news.

Leamer and Leonard (1983) argued the following:

Researchers [are] given the task of identifying interesting families of alternative models and [are] expected to summarize the range of inferences which are implied by each of the families. When a range of inference is small enough to be useful and when the corresponding family of models is broad enough to be believable, we may conclude that these data yield useful information. When the range of inferences is too wide to be useful, and when the corresponding family of models is so narrow that it cannot credibly be reduced, then we must conclude that inferences from these data are too fragile to be useful.

In this sense, we may safely conclude that monetary tightening, and the consequent rise in interest rates, has a positive impact in stabilizing the exchange rate, at least in the short-run. Its long-run impact is less clear. If one believes in the long-run PPP relation, then the eventual impact of the interest rate change is almost nonexistent. If as indicated by the test statistics that long-run PPP does not hold, then raising the interest rate will have the impact of appreciating the nominal exchange rate in the long-run. However, the interest rate defense may not be the best policy option, since interest rates have to be kept high for a long time. The cost to the domestic economy of such a policy could be very high.

REFERENCES

Anderson, T.W. (1971). *The Statistical Analysis of Time Series*. New York: Wiley.

Baig, T. and I. Goldfajn (1998). "Financial Market Contagion in the Asian Crisis." IMF Working Paper, No. 98/155. Washington, D.C.

Bernanke, B. (1983). "Nonmonetary Effects of the Financial Crisis in the Propagation of the Great Depression," *American Economic Review* **73**:257–276.

Box, G. and G. Jenkins (1970). *Time Series Analysis Forecasting and Control*. San Francisco: Holden Day.

Dickey, D.A. and W.A. Fuller (1979). "Distribution of the Estimators for Autoregressive Time Series with a Unit Root," *Journal of the American Statistical Association* **74**:427–431.

Dornbusch, R. (1976). "Expectations and Exchange Rate Dynamics," *Journal of Political Economy* **84**:1161–1176.

Drazen, A. (1999). "Interest Rate Defense against Speculative Attack Under Asymmetric Information." Mimeo, University of Maryland.

Eichenbaum, M. and C. Evans (1995). "Some Empirical Evidence and the Effects of Monetary Policy Shocks on Exchange Rates," *Quarterly Journal of Economics* **110**:975–1010.

Engle, R.F. and C.W.J. Granger (1987). "Cointegration and Error Correction: Representation, Estimation and Testing," *Econometrica* **55**:251–276.

Feldstein, M. (1998). "Refocusing the IMF," *Foreign Affairs* **77**:20–33.

Fischer, S. (1998). "How the IMF Responded," *Finance and Development* **35**(2):2–5.

Forbes, K. and R. Rigobon (1998). "Contagion or Vulnerability." Mimeo, MIT–Sloan School of Management.

Frankel, J. and A. Rose (1995). "Empirical Research on Nominal Exchange Rates." In G. Grossman and Kenneth Rogoff, eds., *Handbook of International Economics*, Vol. 3. Amsterdam: North-Holland, pp. 1689–1729.

Friedman, Milton and Anna J. Schwartz (1991). "Alternative Approaches to Analyzing Economic Data, "*American Economic Review* **81**(1):39–49.

Froot, K. and K. Rogoff (1995). "Perspectives on PPP and Long-Run Real Exchange Rates." In K. Rogoff and G. Grossman, ed., *Handbook of International Economics*, Vol. 3. Amsterdam: North-Holland, pp. 1647–1688.

Furman, J. and J. Stiglitz (1998). "Economic Crisis: Evidence and Insights from East Asia," *Brookings Papers on Economic Activity*, No. 2:1–135.

Ghosh, A. and S. Phillips (1998). "Interest Rates, Stock Markets Prices, and Exchange Rates in East Asia." Mimeo, International Monetary Fund.

Goldfajn, I. and T. Baig (1998). "Monetary Policy in the Aftermath of Currency Crisis: The Case of Asia." IMF Working Paper No. 98/170. Washington, D.C.

Goldfajn, I. and P. Gupta (1999). "Does Monetary Policy Stabilize the Exchange Rate Following a Currency Crisis?" IMF Working Paper No. 99/42. Washington, D.C.

Granger, C.W.J. (1969). "Investigating Causal Relations by Econometric Models and Cross-Spectral Methods," *Econometrica* **37**:424–438.

Hsiao, C. (1979a). "Autoregressive Modelling of Canadian Money and Income Data," *Journal of the American Statistical Association* **74**:553–566.

——— (1979b). "Causality Tests in Econometrics," *Journal of Economic Dynamics and Control* **1**:321–346.

——— (1982a). "Autoregressive Modelling and Causal Ordering of Economic Variables," *Journal of Economic Dynamics and Control* **4**:243–259.

——— (1982b). "Time Series Modelling and Causal Ordering of Canadian Money, Income, and Interest Rate." In O.D. Anderson, ed., *Time Series Analysis: Theory and Practice*, Vol. 1. Amsterdam: North-Holland, pp. 671–698.

——— (1983). "Identification." In Z. Griliches and M. Intriligator, eds., *Handbook of Econometrics*, Vol. 1. Amersterdam: North-Holland, pp. 223–283.

——— (1997). "Cointegration and Dynamic Simultaneous Equations Models," *Econometrica* **65**:647–670.

——— (1998). "Identification and Dichotomization of Long- and Short-Run Relations of Cointegrated Vector Autoregressive Models." Mimeo, University of Southern California.

Hsiao, C. and H. Fujiki (1998). "Nonstationary Time Series Modeling versus Structural Equation Modeling – With an Application to Japanese Money Demand," Bank of Japan *Monetary and Economic Studies* **16**:57–79.

Hsiao, C. and B.H. Sun (1999). "To Pool or Not to Pool Panel Data." Mimeo.

Johansen, S. (1988). "Statistical Analysis of Cointegration Vectors," *Journal of Economic Dynamics and Control* **12**:231–254.

——— (1991). "Estimation and Hypothesis Testing of Cointegration Vectors in Gaussian Vector Autoregressive Models," *Econometrica* **59**:1551–1580.

Kaminsky, G. and C. Reinhart (1998). "On Crisis, Contagion, and Confusion," Mimeo, University of Maryland.

Kaminsky, G. and S. Schmukler (1998). "The Relationship between Interest Rates and Exchange Rates in Six Asian Countries." Mimeo, World Bank.

Kraay, A. (1998). "Do High Interest Rates Defend Currencies during Speculative Attacks." World Bank Policy Research Working Paper No. 2267. Washington, D.C.

Lahiri, A. and C. Vegh (1999). "Output Costs, BOP Crises, and Optimal Interest Rate Policy." Mimeo, University of California, Los Angeles.

Lau, L.J. (1999). "The East Asian Currency Risis: Causes, Effects, Lessons and Solutions." Mimeo, Stanford University.

Leamer, E. and H. Leonard (1983). "Reporting the Fragility of Regression Estimates," *Review of Economics and Statistics* **65**:306–317.

Lewis, K. (1995). "Puzzles in International Financial Markets." In K. Rogoff and G. Grossman, eds., *Handbook of International Economics*, Volume 3. Amsterdam: North-Holland, pp. 1913–1971.

Meese, R. and K. Rogoff (1983). "Empirical Exchange Rate Models of the Seventies: Do They Fit Out of Sample?" *Journal of International Economics* **14**:3–24.

Min, H. and J. McDonald (1999). "Does a Thin Foreign-Exchange Market Lead to Destabilizing Capital-Market Speculations in the Asian Crisis Countries?" Mimeo, World Bank.

Obstfeld, Maurice and Kenneth Rogoff (1996). *Foundations of International Macroeconomics*. Cambridge, MA: MIT Press.

Phillips, P.C.B. (1986). "Understanding Spurious Regressions in Econometrics." *Journal of Econometrics* **33**:311–340.

———(1987). "Time Series Regression with a Unit Root," *Econometrica* **55**:277–301.

———(1991). "Optimal Inference in Cointegrating Systems," *Econometrica* **59**:283–306.

———(1998). "Impulse Response and Forecast Error Variance Asymptotics in Nonstationary VARs," *Journal of Econometrics* **83**:21–56.

Radelet, S. and J. Sachs (1998). "The East Asian Financial Crisis: Diagnosis, Remedies, Prospects," *Brookings Papers on Economic Activity*, No. 1:1–74.

Schwarz, G. (1978). "Estimating the Dimension of a Model," *Annals of Statistics* **6**:461–464.

Tseng, W. and R. Corker (1991). "Financial Liberalization, Money Demand, and Monetary Policy in East Asian Countries." IMF Occasional Paper No. 84. Washington, D.C.

Zellner, Arnold (1962). "An Efficient Method of Estimating Seemingly Unrelated Regressions and Tests of Aggregation Bias," *Journal of the American Statistical Association* **57**:500–509.

Discussion

Interest Rate Stabilization of Exchange Rates and Contagion in the Asian Crisis Countries

Pierre-Richard Agénor

Dekle, Hsiao, and Wang (hereafter DHW) discuss two important issues in their chapter. The first is whether interest rates affected nominal exchange rates in postcrisis Asia, and in what direction; the second is whether "news" and exchange rate movements elsewhere had an impact on the behavior of domestic exchange rates in some of the crisis-stricken Asian countries. Due to space limitation, I will focus my discussion only on the empirical evidence that they attempt to provide on the first issue.[1]

As noted by the authors, the interest rate-exchange rate link has been discussed in a variety of other recent studies, including Ghosh and Phillips (1998), Goldfajn and Baig (1998), Goldfajn and Gupta (1999), Gould and Kamin (Chapter 11, this volume), Kraay (1998), Kaminsky and Schmukler (1998), and Furman and Stiglitz (1998). A review of this literature makes it clear that results are mixed and often not robust. Goldfajn and Baig (1998), for instance, used daily data and found no stable relationship between nominal interest rates and exchange rates. Gould and Kamin (Chapter 11, this volume), using weekly data and Granger-causality tests, were also unable to find any significant effect of interest rates on exchange rates.

Should the lack of robustness be surprising? In my view, not really. The short-run relationship between exchange rates and interest rates is well known to be unstable in "normal" times (Frankel and Rose, 1995); there is no reason to expect to find a stable relationship in the immediate aftermath of crisis episodes. A highly volatile environment is bound to make it more, not less, difficult to isolate a robust link between changes in policy instruments and forward-looking asset prices.

---

[1] DHW also present a theoretical analysis of the interest rate-exchange rate link. However, the value of this contribution is limited by the *ad hoc* nature of the experiment and the fact that their empirical analysis is not directed related to, or inspired by, the theoretical model.

More fundamentally, the lack of robustness may be related to the fact that most of the existing literature including the analysis of DHW suffers from severe methodological shortcomings. First, the frequency of the data used is quite often inadequate for estimation purposes. Studies based on monthly data (e.g., Goldfajn and Gupta, 1999) are likely to miss most of the action; speculative attacks (and policy responses aimed at fending them off) take place over periods of days, not weeks or months. Studies based on weekly data, as used by DHW, do not necessarily solve the problem. Second, it is not only the *level* of interest rates that affects the exchange rate; the *duration* of the hike may matter even more, as a result of signaling considerations and nonlinearities in expectations formation (see below). Almost all studies in this area [with the exception of Furman and Stiglitz (1998)] ignore this issue.

Third, most studies suffer from endogeneity and omitted-variable problems, and thus from potentially significant bias in estimated coefficients. Interest rates may be (and, in practice, are) changed in response to exchange market pressures; almost none of the studies listed above controls for that. Similarly, existing studies [except, again, for the chapter by Gould and Kamin (Chapter 11, this volume)] fail to control for changes in confidence and expectations. If an omitted factor (such as a loss of confidence by foreign investors) leads simultaneously to an increase in interest rates and a depreciation of the nominal exchange rate, the evidence of a perverse effect would have no *causal* implication regarding the relation between the two variables.

Finally, none of the existing studies pays any direct attention to credibility and reputational factors. It has been argued [see, for instance, Drazen (1999)] that the signaling effect of high interest rates (that is, their ability to convey information about policymakers' preferences) is a key argument in favor of the policy, and that the strength of this effect depends on the duration of the hike. An important insight of this literature is that high interest rates, particularly when maintained for a long period of time, may not strengthen reputation if adverse shocks are highly persistent. This makes it very important to account in regression models aimed at assessing the impact of interest rates for the perceived costs of signaling – such as lower output, higher bankruptcy rates, higher fiscal deficits, and increased financial fragility. The signaling argument suggests indeed the existence of possible nonlinearities in the link between interest rates and exchange rates. For instance, one may well argue that the strength of the relationship between interest rates and the exchange rate in Asia may have changed once the magnitude of the output losses associated with the crisis, and/or the potentially large fiscal costs associated with bank failures and financial sector restructuring, became apparent. One way of capturing these nonlinearities is to use interactive variables. An alternative approach would be to use rolling regression techniques and assess the sensitivity of the coefficient of interest rates to a measure of output losses and/or potential fiscal costs and ensuing tax liabilities (proxied, for example, by the share of nonperforming loans in total bank lending).

The DHW chapter suffers from most of the methodological shortcomings listed above. In addition, it also has problems of its own: most importantly, many of the *t*-ratios listed in Tables 10.3 to 10.5 are not significant at a 5 percent confidence level (and barely so at a 10 percent level), raising doubts about the validity of the authors' interpretations. In that regard, I find it hard to understand how the authors can claim to have identified "clearly that raising the interest rate has had the usual impact of appreciating the nominal exchange rate during the crisis period." On the contrary, I believe, we are still very far from being able to assess with any degree of confidence the direction in which interest rates affected the exchange rate, and by how much, in postcrisis Asia.

There is also much need to focus on a slightly different question, which is often lost in this debate: Even if high interest rates lead to an appreciation, how do we know if the hike was excessive or not? A possible avenue to address this issue would be to develop a testable model of credibility and reputation along the lines, for instance, of the Agénor and Masson model (1999), to account for the tradeoff between the cost of currency depreciation (e.g., the impact on inflation and the domestic-currency value of foreign-currency liabilities) and the cost of high interest rates (e.g., low output). The model could be solved for the probability of a weak government, as measured by the relative weight attached to the cost of high interest rates. A *credibility band* for interest rates could thus be derived, with a ceiling (floor) corresponding to a probability of a weak government close to zero (unity). Movements in actual interest rates outside the credibility band would indicate whether the policy was, in a sense, "excessive" or not.

REFERENCES

Agénor, Pierre-Richard, and Paul R. Masson (1999). "Credibility, Reputation, and the Mexican Peso Crisis," *Journal of Money, Credit, and Banking* **31**:70–84.
Drazen, Allan (1999). "Interest Rate Defense against Speculative Attack under Asymmetric Information." Mimeo, University of Maryland.
Frankel, Jeffrey, and Andrew Rose (1995). "Empirical Research on Nominal Exchange Rates." In S. Grossman and K. Rogoff, eds., *The Handbook of International Economics*, Vol. 3. Amsterdam: North-Holland, pp. 1689–1729.
Furman, Jason, and Joseph E. Stiglitz (1998). "Economic Crises: Evidence and Insights from East Asia," *Brookings Papers on Economic Activity*, No. 2:1–135.

Ghosh, Atish, and Steven Phillips (1998). "Interest Rates, Stock Market Prices and Exchange Rates in East Asia." Mimeo, International Monetary Fund, Washington, D.C.

Goldfajn, Ilan and Taimur Baig (1998). "Monetary Policy in the Aftermath of Currency Crises: The Case of Asia." IMF Working Paper No. 98/70. Washington, D.C.

Goldfajn, Ilan and Poonam Gupta (1999). "Does Tight Monetary Policy Stabilize the Exchange Rate Following a Crisis?" IMF Working Paper No. 99/42. Washington, D.C.

Kaminsky, Graciela and Sergio Schmukler (1998). "The Relationship Between Interest Rates and Exchange Rates in Six Asian Countries." Mimeo, the World Bank, Washington, D.C.

Kraay, Art (1998). "Do High Interest Rates Defend Currencies during Speculative Attacks?" World Bank Policy Research Paper No. 2267. Washington, D.C.

11

The Impact of Monetary Policy on Exchange Rates during Financial Crises

David Gould and Steven Kamin

11.1 INTRODUCTION

One of the most controversial issues that has emerged in the aftermath of the Asian financial crisis has been the appropriate response of monetary policy. Following the abandonment of exchange rate pegs, currencies depreciated rapidly in Thailand, Malaysia, Indonesia, Korea, and the Philippines. These depreciations appeared to be very adverse in their consequences, leading not only to somewhat higher inflation but also to banking sector distress and economic recession as falling currencies led to balance-sheet effects that exacerbated already existing financial sector problems. Consequently, some observers – and notably the IMF – have argued that a significant tightening of monetary policy was necessary in order to stabilize the exchange rate, restore confidence, and lay the groundwork for an eventual recovery of economic activity. Conversely, a substantial number of other economists contend that when balance-of-payments crises occur simultaneously with financial sector crises, as was the case in Asia, a tightening of monetary policy may be counterproductive. These "revisionists" argue that raising interest rates may further reduce investor confidence and lead to further weakening – not strengthening – of domestic currencies by reducing the ability of borrowers to repay loans and thereby weakening the banking system.

Roughly three years after the Asian financial crisis started, this debate remains unresolved. A key reason for this is that it is extremely difficult

The authors are Senior Economist, Institute of International Finance, and Assistant Director, International Finance Division, Federal Reserve Board of Governors. This chapter was written while David Gould was a Senior Economist and Policy Advisor at the Federal Reserve Bank of Dallas. Justin May and Trevor Dinmore provided superb research assistance on this project. The views expressed in this chapter do not necessarily reflect those of the Federal Reserve Board of Governors or the Federal Reserve System.

to use historical experience to identify the impact of monetary policy on the exchange rate. Generally, monetary authorities tighten policy during periods of strong downward pressure on the exchange rate and loosen policy as this pressure is alleviated. During the Asian financial crisis, collapses in currency values were associated with rising interest rates. Subsequently, exchange rate appreciations have been associated with falling interest rates. Although, at face value, it would seem that raising interest rates during the Asian crisis had the counterintuitive effect of depreciating the exchange rate, it would be inappropriate to place significant weight on this observation, given the potential endogeneity of both the interest rate and the exchange rate to other more fundamental factors. In consequence, the economics profession remains as divided as it ever was on the topic of appropriate monetary policy during crises.

In this chapter we first review the theoretical arguments and empirical evidence in support of the two sides of the controversy in greater detail. While this question has given rise to considerable polemics, there have been fewer objective discussions of the pros and cons of monetary tightening during financial crises.

We explore several new means of identifying the impact of interest rates on the value of floating exchange rates. Of the small body of empirical work that has emerged in the aftermath of the Asian crisis, much is subject to the problem discussed above – the endogeneity of both interest rates and exchange rates to other economic forces. Therefore, statistical analysis attempting to explain movements in the exchange rate using interest rate variables alone may be misleading, since during international financial crises, both the interest rate and the exchange rate are likely to be correlated with third factors not accounted for in the analysis.

Our conjecture is that, in the immediate aftermath of devaluation and financial crisis, one of the most important factors influencing the exchange rate is likely to be concerns about the country's ability to pay existing debt. Moreover, changes in the perceived ability to pay are likely to explain the movement in exchange rates more than concerns about interest rate differentials alone. Put another way, the sharp declines in currency values in the affected Asian economies in 1997 and 1998, and the consequent increases in interest rates, probably were motivated more by fears of default on debt than by concerns that domestic interest rates were not high enough to offset future inflation and depreciation. Therefore, if one could hold constant investor appraisals of country creditworthiness, it might then be possible to identify the independent impact of changes in interest rates on the exchange rate.

In this chapter we explore, among other factors, the use of spreads between the countries' dollar-denominated bond yields and U.S. Treasuries as proxies for perceived credit risk. Between July 1997 and July 1998, these yield spreads were reasonably well correlated (negatively) with changes in currency values, providing some support for the view that collapses in currency value may have been caused – at least in part – by mounting fears of default. Our hope is that by adding credit spreads to equations explaining the movements in exchange rates, it may then be possible to identify the independent impact of interest rates on exchange rates, holding all else constant. In our analysis we estimate equations of this sort using weekly data from the postdevaluation experiences of the affected Asian economies since mid-1997, as well as, for purposes of comparison, Mexico since 1995.

In addition to credit spreads, we also explore the use of several stock market variables – in particular, measures of aggregate stock and of bank stock returns – to control for investor expectations. Because stock market and bank stock returns are proxies for expectations of future profitability in the economy and of the banking sector, their movements may be as reflective of movements in investor perceptions of country risks as movements in credit spreads. Hence, adding stock market returns to our equations for the exchange rate may further reduce the correlation of domestic interest rates with omitted variables in the error term and thus further enhance our ability to identify independent impacts of interest rates on exchange rates.

Additionally, adding stock market prices to our equations allows us to explore a key facet of the revisionist hypothesis that a tightening of monetary policy may depreciate the exchange rate. In that hypothesis, monetary tightening leads to this perverse result because it threatens to further weaken the banking system, either indirectly by weakening the overall economy or directly by raising debt-service costs for bank loan recipients. If this hypothesis is correct, then adding measures of the stock market and of bank stocks as explanatory variables to our exchange-rate equations, and thereby holding constant investor perceptions of future profitability in the economy and of the banking sector, should increase the likelihood that increases in interest rates will be estimated to appreciate the exchange rate.

Finally, in addition to estimating equations for the exchange rate itself, we also estimate a broad array of Granger-causality tests among nearly all of the variables used in our analysis. These tests serve two purposes. First, they constitute yet another means of identifying the impact of monetary policy variables on the exchange rate. Second, they provide evidence on the suitability of other explanatory variables – including credit spreads and stock prices – as autonomous measures of investor risk appraisals.

The plan of the chapter is as follows. Section 11.2 reviews the arguments for both a positive and a negative effect of a tightening of monetary policy on the exchange value of the local currency, and it briefly surveys previous empirical work on this subject. Section 11.3 outlines the econometric strategy we have developed to identify the impact of monetary policy on exchange rates, while Section 11.4 describes our estimation results. Section 11.5 concludes.

11.2 MONETARY POLICY AND EXCHANGE RATES: ARGUMENTS AND EVIDENCE

11.2.1 Arguments

As the Asian crisis evolved, the official international community, and particularly the IMF, argued strongly that, in the aftermath of the floating of national currencies, currency depreciation should be constrained through a tightening of monetary policy. This recommendation was based on several rationales, some of them rooted in the experiences of financial crises and stabilizations in Latin American countries, others responding more directly to the experiences of the Asian countries themselves.

Monetary tightening was considered important for several reasons in the Latin American financial crises of the 1980s, as well as in Mexico in the mid-1990s. First, and most importantly, it could serve to convince private sector agents that monetary policy was under control, thereby acting to reduce inflationary expectations and prevent a vicious cycle of inflation and exchange rate depreciation. Second, by raising the attractiveness of domestic currency assets and thereby limiting exchange rate depreciation, it could accordingly limit tradable goods inflation and thus again prevent the development of an inflationary spiral. Finally, by reducing the level of aggregate demand, monetary tightening not only could reduce inflation, but also could help to cool down the economy, limit imports, improve the balance of payments, and hence improve investor confidence in the countries' prospects for external viability and debt repayment.

These considerations turned out, in retrospect, to be less relevant to the crisis Asian countries in 1997 and 1998 than they were to Latin America in the 1980s or even to Mexico in 1995. To begin with, while Asian exchange rate depreciations were expected to raise inflation rates somewhat, there were relatively few concerns that these depreciations would lead to hyperinflationary spirals of rising wages and falling currencies such as had occurred in Latin America. Asian economies had established reputations for relatively low inflation and prudent monetary policy; and only in Indonesia, where the exchange rate collapsed primarily for political reasons, was hyperinflation considered a genuine possibility. Moreover, only in Thailand was the economy considered by some observers to be overheated prior to the crisis; and even then, declines in output and asset prices were taking place by late 1996. Hence, the case for aggregate demand restraint in Asia was limited even at the outset of the crisis, and became more limited still as it became apparent that the economies of the region were moving into very deep recessions.

Notwithstanding these differences with Latin America, however, arguments still were made for the importance of tightening monetary policy in the Asian context. First, even if there was no need to contract aggregate demand, some contended that tightening monetary policy could play a useful role if it restrained the depreciation of exchange rates: The Asian currencies appeared to have declined by far more than was merited by equilibrium considerations alone, and their collapse had helped to roil financial markets and undermine confidence in the region.[1] Second, a major factor depressing activity and injuring the banking sector had been the effects of depreciating currencies on the balance sheets of borrowers in foreign currencies; therefore, supporting currencies was actually a way of helping to support the economy and the banking sector, even if pursued through tighter monetary policies. Finally, advocates of tighter monetary policy argued that raising domestic interest rates would support local currencies not only by making domestic-currency assets more attractive, but also by encouraging agents with external liabilities to attempt to reschedule these debts rather than finance repayments through borrowings in domestic credit markets; this would have the effect not only of reducing exchange rate depreciation, but also of strengthening the balance of payments by reducing runoffs of foreign liabilities.

Although these arguments are certainly plausible, the IMF's policy recommendations to the crisis Asian economies came under severe criticism as initial increases in interest rates failed to stabilize currencies, as the flow of domestic credit became sharply curtailed, and as these economies moved into very deep recessions. Critics of tighter monetary policy – as expressed most notably in Furman and Stiglitz (1998) and Radelet and Sachs (1998) – contended, among other things, that in the

---

[1] See International Monetary Fund (1998) for a useful discussion of the pros and cons of tightening monetary policy during financial crises, including the Asian crisis. The article also articulates the IMF case for a tightening of monetary policy in these circumstances.

midst of a financial crisis, tightening monetary policy might fail to support the currency and might even increase downward pressures on it. First, in the context of a run on the currency, the level of domestic interest rates required to compensate investors for extreme depreciation expectations might be so high as to be unsustainable and/or extremely injurious to the economy.[2] Second, in the context of what has been referred to as an "international bank run," with foreign investors determined to pull out of the region, domestic debtors may not have the option of rolling over their external obligations, even if they desire to. Finally, higher interest rates may increase debt-service burdens for firms, lower loan performance, add to pressures on the banking system, and thereby further raise prospects of financial collapse and external debt default, all of which would have the effect of further undermining investor confidence and thereby having a depressive effect on currency values.

On the face of it, both the proponents and critics of monetary tightening to stabilize the exchange rate make plausible arguments, and it is difficult on strictly *a priori* or theoretical grounds to ascertain which side of the issue carries the greater weight. Hence, this debate is more likely to be decided on the basis of actual experience and empirical evidence, a subject to which we now turn.

11.2.2 Evidence

Figure 11.1 presents the recent evolution of short-term nominal interest rates and the real exchange rate against the U.S. dollar for the five Asian crisis economies – Indonesia, Korea, Malaysia, the Philippines, and Thailand – as well for Mexico since the onset of its crisis at the end of 1994. In principle, if increases in domestic interest rates lead to appreciations of the exchange rate, then an inverse relationship should be observed between the interest rate and the exchange rate (portrayed as local currency per dollar) in these panels. In fact, as shown in Figure 11.1, in the neighborhood of a currency crisis, domestic interest rates and the local currency value of the dollar are more likely to be positively correlated than negatively correlated; this relationship is quite apparent for Korea, the Philippines, and Mexico and also applies to some extent in Indonesia, Malaysia, and Thailand.

---

[2] This point is underscored in Furman and Stiglitz (1998). For example, consider a situation in which the exchange rate is expected to depreciate by 10 percent against the dollar in the coming month. In order to induce an investor to hold domestic-currency assets (with no default risk), the domestic interest rate would have to be roughly 10 percentage points higher than U.S. interest rates on a monthly basis, but over 200 percentage points higher on an annual basis!

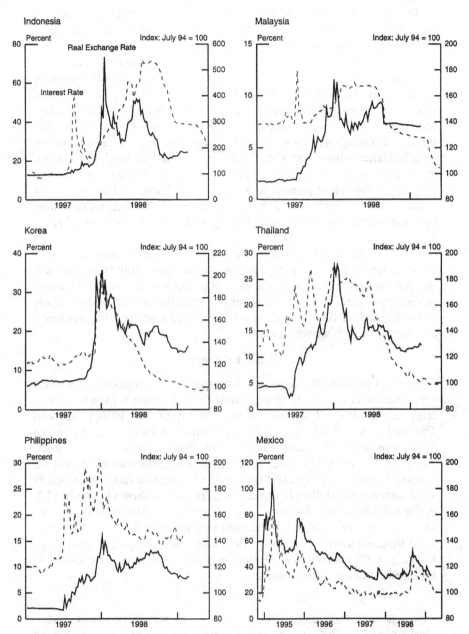

Figure 11.1. Interest rates and real exchange rates. Exchange rates are local currency per dollar.

While this positive relationship between the domestic interest rate and the exchange rate may be indicative of the perverse effects of monetary policy described by Radelet and Sachs (1998), Furman and Stiglitz (1998), and others, it most likely also reflects the fundamental endogeneity of domestic interest rates. The same factors that may cause a floating exchange rate to depreciate – expectations of future depreciation or default on debt – will also cause market interest rates to rise. Additionally, in cases where the monetary authority targets the short-term interest rate, declines in the value of the exchange rate may themselves prompt officials to raise interest rates.

This endogeneity of domestic interest rates with respect to depreciation expectations, default expectations, and/or recent movements in the exchange rate may obscure the *ceteris paribus* impact of interest rates on exchange rates, leading to a positive statistical correlation even if, all else equal, tightening monetary policy really does provide support to the local currency in the midst of the crisis. Recent efforts to statistically gauge the impact of domestic interest rates on exchange rates have not managed to fully address this endogeneity problem, and this could explain their relatively limited success in identifying a stable, statistically significant negative impact of domestic interest rates on the local currency value of the dollar.

Research on the effects of monetary policy on exchange rates in emerging market countries has generally taken two approaches. The first of these examines the time-series relationship between exchange rates and interest rates in one or more countries. Results here have been mixed. Goldfajn and Baig (1998) estimate a VAR with first-differenced, daily nominal interest rates and exchange rates in the five Asian crisis economies, and they find little impact of interest rates on exchange rates in either direction. Dekle, Hsiao, and Wang (Chapter 10, this volume) estimate VARs for Korea, Malaysia, and Thailand using weekly differences of nominal exchange rates, prices, and interest rates; they find that increases in interest rates generally appreciate the exchange rate, although the significance of this effect varies, depending upon the country and the specification of the equations estimated. Spicer and Goodhart (1999) examine the relationship between daily changes in interest rates, exchange rates, and stock prices for Brazil and Korea during their crisis periods. They find little evidence to suggest that increases in interest rates had a significant effect on the exchange rate or the stock market. They argue that this is evidence against the theory that monetary tightness during crises worsens the economic situation.

An alternative approach toward evaluating the impact of interest rates on exchange rates relies on looking at a large number of devaluation episodes and determining whether, in episodes where monetary policy was tightened, exchange rates were more likely to appreciate than in cases where monetary policy remained loose. Here, also, results have been mixed. Furman and Stiglitz (1998) look at cases where short-term nominal interest rates have been substantially elevated for short periods of time; and they find that, generally, these episodes are associated with exchange rate depreciation, not appreciation. Conversely, Goldfajn and Gupta (1999) studied a large number of episodes where real exchange rates had become highly depreciated relative to their long-term averages, and they assessed whether or not tighter monetary policy made it more likely that subsequent real appreciation would take place through nominal exchange rate appreciation rather than through higher inflation; they found that except in circumstances where financial sectors were under stress, tighter monetary policy – measured as concerted increases in real interest rates – did indeed lead to more nominal exchange rate appreciation.[3]

In sum, evidence on the impact of interest rates on exchange rates during financial crises has been decidedly nonrobust. This could reflect the fact that this impact varies considerably from situation to situation, depending upon any number of factors, so that identifying a robust relationship is very difficult. However, it may also be that the prior research has not succeeded in holding constant the factors affecting both interest rates and exchange rates, leading to omitted variable biases that in turn lead econometric results to be extremely unstable.

11.2.3 A Digression on Nominal and Real Interest Rates

An important issue in analyzing the impact of monetary policy on the exchange rate is how to gauge the stance of monetary policy. In principle, the *ex ante* real interest rate is the most appropriate measure of the tightness or looseness of monetary policy, but as inflation expectations generally are not observed directly, frequently the *ex post* real interest rate must be used instead. Unfortunately, while actual inflation may be a decent proxy for inflation expectations during normal periods, actual inflation may diverge considerably from inflation expectations during financial crises involving sharp depreciations of the exchange rate. Such depreciations may cause short bursts of inflation that cause real *ex post* interest rates to fall or even become negative tem-

---

[3] Kraay (1998) looks at factors determining whether or not defenses of a fixed peg against speculative attack succeed, and he concludes that tightening monetary policy does not increase the likelihood of a successful defense. It is not clear, however, whether these results, even if deemed correct for pegged exchange rate regimes, would apply to the impact of interest rates on exchange rates in floating exchange rate regimes.

porarily, even though nominal interest rates may have been raised substantially.

This problem may be seen quite readily in Figure 11.2, which compares short-term nominal interest rates with two measures of the *ex post* real interest rate: one deflated by inflation in the current month, and one deflated over a centered 13-week period. Particularly in the case of Korea and Mexico, even as nominal interest rates were hiked to very high levels, real interest rates fell below zero. Given the impact that high nominal interest rates have on the cash-flow position of corporate and household borrowers, it would seem unreasonable to describe the stance of monetary policy in these episodes as "stimulative."[4] Therefore, the results of studies that rely on the real interest rate as a measure of monetary stance may be misleading. In the work described below, we analyze separately the impacts of nominal interest rates and inflation on the exchange rate.

11.3 ECONOMETRIC IDENTIFICATION STRATEGY

In this section we discuss our strategy for addressing the endogeneity problem in domestic interest rates and thereby identifying the underlying relationship between exchange rates and interest rates during financial crises. We begin by presenting a simple theoretical framework, similar to that outlined in several previous papers on this topic, in order to clarify the discussion. We then outline our own econometric strategy.

11.3.1 Benchmark Theoretical Framework

The standard theory of uncovered interest rate arbitrage suggests that the real interest rate differential between two nations will be a function of the expected real depreciation of the exchange rate and any country risk premium associated with holding foreign currency denominated assets:

$$i_t - i_t^* = (E_{t+1}^e - E_t) + RP_t \qquad (1)$$

where i_t is the domestic real interest rate at time t, i_t^* is the foreign real interest rate at time t, E_{t+1}^e is the expected real exchange rate (local

---

[4] The case of Mexico in early 1995 is illustrative. Short-term interest rates rose close to 100 percent at certain points; and with much domestic bank debt either at floating rates or very short term, borrowers were hard-pressed to service their debt. The fact that CPI inflation was running even higher provided little short-term cash-flow relief, even if it did contribute to making the bank loans more repayable in the longer run. Moreover, because the inflation spike was concentrated in tradeable goods, many firms may have seen the nominal interest rates on their debt skyrocket even as the nominal value of their assets rose by far less.

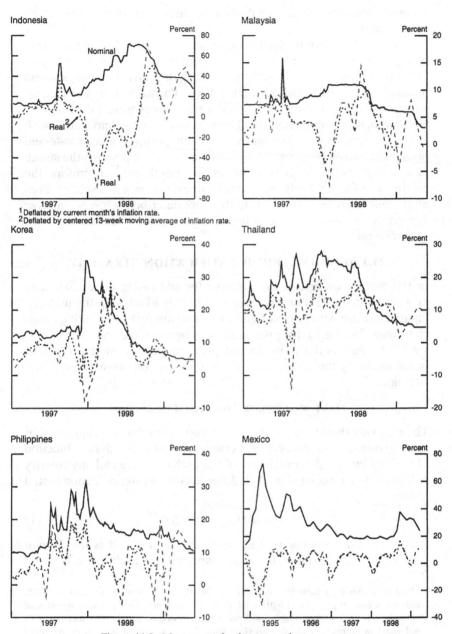

Figure 11.2. Movements in short-term interest rates.

currency per dollar) at time $t+1$, E_t is the real exchange rate at time t, and RP_t is the country risk premium at time t. This risk premium incorporates both compensation for exchange rate volatility and, perhaps more important, compensation for the risk of future default on domestic-currency liabilities.

Rearranging equation (1) and solving for E_t, we get

$$E_t = -(i_t - i_t^*) + E_{t+1}^e + RP_t \qquad (2)$$

Consequently, the standard uncovered interest rate arbitrage condition suggests that increases in real domestic rates relative to foreign rates will appreciate the current real exchange rate (lower E_t), while expected future depreciation and increases in the country risk premium will depreciate the current real exchange rate (raise E_t). Equation (2) forms the basis for most of the empirical analysis that has been conducted on this topic.

Recent arguments against the standard model suggest that raising domestic interest rates during a financial crisis can depreciate the exchange rate by increasing the probability of default of domestic borrowers and weakening the asset quality of domestic banks. Another way of describing this phenomenon is that the country risk premium, RP_t, and the expected future exchange rate, E_{t+1}^e, are endogenous and are adversely affected by increases in domestic interest rates.[5] In terms of our theoretical framework, this suggests that $E_{t+1}^e = f(i_t - i_t^*)$, $\partial E_{t+1}^e / \partial i_t > 0$ and $RP_t = g(i_t - i_t^*)$, $\partial RP_t / \partial i_t > 0$.

Most empirical work on this topic has, in a very broad sense, focused on estimating a variant of equation (2) – but without incorporating a measure of the risk premium or the expected future exchange rate, which are incorporated into the error term – and ascertaining whether the coefficient on the interest rate differential is positive or negative. However, as discussed above, the domestic interest rate i_t is likely to be endogenous with respect to both the risk premium RP and the expected future exchange rate E_{t+1}^e. Therefore, adverse events that raise the risk premium and expected future depreciation are likely to both boost interest rates

---

[5] While it is obvious why the risk premium should rise in the event of greater stress on the domestic financial sector – this raises the probability that banks and other borrowers will default on their liabilities – it is less obvious why the expected future exchange rate should depreciate under those conditions. In the very long term, the expected future exchange rate should be determined by the economy's equilibrium exchange rate, which in turn depends on trends in productivity and preferences. In the shorter term, however, the expected future exchange rate is likely to depend upon the economy's prospective balance-of-payments position. A bankrupt and defaulting financial sector will likely be associated with a cessation of net capital inflows, requiring a more depreciated real exchange rate as a result.

and depreciate the exchange rate, obscuring any supportive impact that a genuinely autonomous increase in interest rates – that is, a monetary policy *shock* – might have on the value of the local currency.

To a certain extent, time series analyses that focus on the effect of *lagged* interest rates on contemporaneous exchange rates may reduce the severity of the endogeneity problem, but they do not dispel it entirely. First, insofar as movements in the risk premium and the expected future exchange rate may be serially correlated, even the lagged interest rate may be correlated with the error term (which contains the risk premium and expected future exchange rate). Second, to the extent that much of the impact of the interest rate on the exchange rate may take place contemporaneously, relying upon lags of the interest rate as the measure of monetary policy may lead to a failure to measure the full impact of monetary policy moves on the exchange rate.

11.3.2 Empirical Strategy

In order to turn the benchmark model of exchange rate behavior into a testable model, our goal is to develop proxies for the expected future real exchange rate and the country risk premium, thereby taking them out of the error term in an estimated version of equation (2) and accordingly reducing or eliminating the extent of potential omitted variable bias.[6] The country risk premium is proxied by credit spreads of dollar-denominated government bonds over similar maturity U.S. treasuries.[7] These spreads are based on market assessments of the probability that governments will default on their external debt, and therefore they are likely to move closely with expectations that private institutions will default on their local-currency denominated liabilities.

Expected future real exchange rates are assumed to depend on the expectations of those factors that influence current real exchange rates (i.e., interest rate differentials and country risk premia). Optimally, weekly survey data of market expectations of future exchange rates would be the best proxy for expected real exchange rates. However, because these data are not readily available for the countries in our sample, we assume that expectations of future real exchange

---

[6] A more common approach to endogeneity problems is to use instrumental variables estimation to instrument for the endogenous explanatory variable. However, this would require finding instruments that are correlated with the interest rate and yet uncorrelated with the error term, that is, the risk premium and expected future exchange rate. Given that we can identify no such instrument, we have instead opted for the approach of controlling for as much of the risk premium and expected future exchange rate as possible, thereby (hopefully) shrinking the variability of the error term sufficiently to minimize endogeneity problems.

[7] See the Appendix 11A for a detailed description of the data and data sources.

rates depend on an adaptive expectations process of past values of interest rate differentials and country risk premia. Consequently, our empirical model includes lagged values of the dependent and independent variables.

The equations estimated take the form of unrestricted error-correction models for deviations of the real exchange rate from its cointegrating vector, shown in equation (2). The estimating equation is

$$\Delta E_t = \alpha_0 + \alpha_1 \sum_{j=1}^{2} \Delta E_{t-j} + \alpha_2 \sum_{j=0}^{2} \Delta INTDIFF_{t-j} + \alpha_3 \sum_{j=0}^{2} \Delta INFDIFF_{t-j}$$
$$+ \alpha_4 \sum_{j=0}^{2} \Delta SPREAD_{t-j} + \alpha_5 E_{t-1} + \alpha_6 INTDIFF_{t-1}$$
$$+ \alpha_7 INFDIFF_{t-1} + \alpha_8 SPREAD_{t-1} + \varepsilon \qquad (3)$$

where E_t is the log of the real bilateral exchange rate against the U.S. dollar, $INTDIFF_t$ is the domestic nominal interest rate differential against similar U.S. rates, $INFDIFF_t$ is the domestic inflation against U.S. inflation rates differential (based on a 13-week centered moving average of inflation rates),[8] and $SPREAD_t$ is the dollar-denominated credit spread for government-issued bonds against similar-maturity U.S. treasuries. The coefficients on the variables expressed in changes may be interpreted as representing the impact effect on the real exchange rate. The coefficients on the lagged levels of the explanatory variables in principle comprise the parameters in a cointegrating vector and hence represent longer-term effects; however, because these equations are estimated over only a year's worth of data, as discussed below, the permanence of these effects should not be overemphasized.

Finally, we explored using several versions of real stock returns – the log-change in the CPI-deflated index of stock prices – as additional proxies for investor perceptions of depreciation and default risk. In principle, measures of aggregate stock market performance and bank stock performance should represent good proxies for expectations of future economic activity and banking sector health, respectively. Expectations of future economic and banking sector viability, in turn, are likely to be well correlated with investor appraisals of the risk premium and the future expected exchange rate. Therefore, adding stock market variables to equation (3) should help to better control for omitted variables and

---

[8] In principle, the domestic nominal interest differentials and the inflation differentials could be combined to form a real interest rate differential. However, as discussed in Section 11.3.1, it is extremely uncertain what specification of actual inflation rates best captures the inflation expectations that are part of an *ex ante* real interest rate. Moreover, as will be shown below, the empirical results clearly fail to support a restriction tying the coefficients on the inflation differential to be equal in magnitude and opposite in value to those on the interest rate differential.

hence should enhance our ability to identify the impact of monetary policy shocks on the exchange rate.

Additionally, adding stock market variables to the analysis may help to test for the existence of a key channel in the linkage between interest rates and the exchange rate. The revisionist view that tighter monetary policy may actually depreciate the exchange rate depends upon the injurious effect of higher interest rates on economic activity, on corporate loan performance, and on the health of the banking sector. Therefore, if the revisionist view is correct, then when stock market proxies for expected economic and banking sector health are added as explanatory variables to equation (3), thereby holding constant the adverse expectational effects of a monetary tightening, it should be more likely that the coefficient on the nominal interest rate differential would adopt its conventionally expected negative sign.

11.4 ESTIMATION RESULTS

11.4.1 Data Sample

Analysis was performed on weekly data for the five countries most heavily affected by the Asian financial crisis: Indonesia, Korea, Malaysia, the Philippines, and Thailand. In addition, in order to get a sense of the generality of these results, we analyzed data for Mexico subsequent to its devaluation. More detailed descriptions of the data and their sources are provided in Appendix 11A.

The focus of analysis is on the behavior of exchange rates after they have floated and during a period of financial crisis. Therefore, the estimation samples begin at different points in time, depending upon when a country's currency was delinked from the dollar. For the Asian countries, the start of the sample period ranges from the week of July 4, 1997 in the case of Thailand to the week of August 15, 1997 in the case of Indonesia. Because Korea's exchange rate was never linked as tightly to the dollar as that of the other Asian countries, the point at which it started floating in earnest is less obviously delineated; accordingly, we have chosen the week of July 4, when the Thai baht was floated, as the starting date for the Korea regressions as well. The sample period for the Mexico regression starts in the week of December 23, 1994, shortly after the peso was floated on December 21.

All of the estimation samples extend through the week of July 31, 1998. This end date was chosen for two reasons. First, the focus of this analysis is the behavior of floating exchange rates during financial crises; by the end of July 1998, financial conditions had stabilized to a substantial degree in most of the crisis Asian economies. Second, following the

Russian devaluation and default in August 1998, credit spreads on emerging market bonds rose sharply throughout the world. Increases in spreads were not wholly indiscriminate; in Latin America, for example, they rose most in Brazil and Venezuela, which were indeed regarded as particularly vulnerable. However, the universal nature of the rise, along with the lack of precipitating events in many of the countries experiencing the rise, suggests that after July 1998 spreads may have been influenced more by generalized trends in investor liquidity and risk aversion than by country-specific risk factors per se.

In principle, it would be useful to compare the behavior of floating exchange rates during a financial crisis with their behavior during a noncrisis period. Unfortunately, the periods preceding the beginning of our estimation sample cannot be used for this purpose, since during these periods the nominal exchange rate was being pegged (or at least very tightly managed). Moreover, as noted above, much of the post-July 1998 period is contaminated by the aftereffects of the Russia crisis, when movements in credit spreads appear to have owed more to global factors than to changes in country-specific risks. In the future, however, as more noncrisis observations for Asian financial markets become available, a comparison of crisis and noncrisis exchange rate behavior should be possible.

11.4.2 Graphical Analysis

In order for credit spreads and stock prices to be useful instruments for identifying monetary policy shocks, these variables must be reasonably well correlated with the exchange rates in the countries under examination. Figure 11.3 presents data on the real exchange rate and credit spreads for the countries in our sample; the vertical line indicates the end of the sample period in July 1998. Up until that date, exchange rates and credit spreads were indeed reasonably well correlated among most of the Asian crisis countries; after that date, spreads moved up far more sharply than the exchange value of the dollar, probably reflecting the global factors discussed above. Interestingly, in Mexico, spreads and exchange rates are highly correlated both before and after the Russian devaluation.

Figures 11.4 and 11.5 present analogous data on exchange rates and centered 5-week moving averages of real stock returns for the entire economy and the banking sector, respectively. (Bank stock returns were not available for the Philippines.) They indicate that, like credit spreads, stock returns are to some extent correlated with real exchange rates, particularly during the period when the crisis was at its most severe.

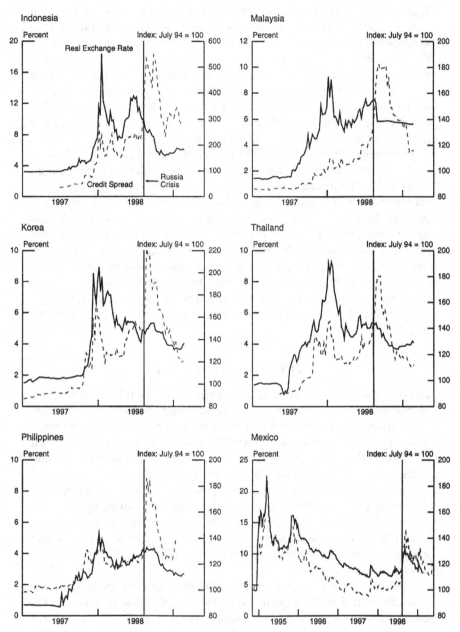

Figure 11.3. International credit spreads and real exchange rates. Exchange rates are local currency per dollar.

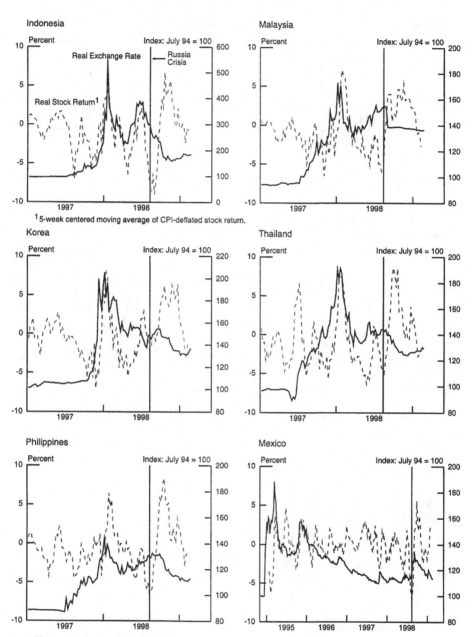

Figure 11.4. Real stock returns and real exchange rates. Exchange rates are local currency per dollar.

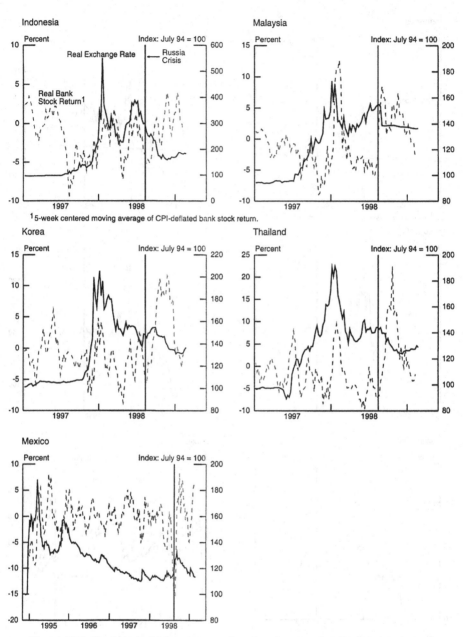

Figure 11.5. Real bank stock returns and real exchange rates. Exchange rates are local currency per dollar.

Table 11.1. Unit Root Tests: Augmented Dickey–Fuller Test Statistics

	Indonesia	Korea	Malaysia	Mexico	Philippines	Thailand
ΔE	−3.212	−3.303	−4.305	−7.152	−3.560	−4.067
$\Delta INTDIFF$	−4.861	−3.663	−6.532	−6.187	−5.739	−4.533
$\Delta INFDIFF$	−1.637	−1.242	−1.266	−2.162	−2.095	−1.489
$\Delta SPREAD$	−3.802	−3.979	−5.791	−8.985	−5.020	−4.149
$\Delta STKRET$	−6.908	−7.915	−8.225	−13.349	−7.181	−7.892
$\Delta(BSTKRET -$ $STKRET)$	−4.972	−4.293	−3.738	−7.841		−4.992
E	−1.664	−1.408	−1.094	−3.065	−1.839	−1.993
$INTDIFF$	−0.953	−1.645	−1.692	−1.972	−1.976	−2.768
$INFDIFF$	−1.134	−1.051	−1.053	−1.832	−0.509	−1.638
$SPREAD$	−1.277	−1.721	0.295	−2.187	−2.021	−1.835
$STKRET$	−4.228	−3.545	−4.115	−8.006	−4.331	−4.212
$BSTKRET -$ $STKRET$	−4.971	−4.293	−3.738	−7.841		−4.992
95% Critical value[a]	−2.919	−2.912	−2.912	−2.877	−2.915	−2.914
Period of observation	8/15/97 to 7/31/98	7/04/97 to 7/31/98	7/04/97 to 7/31/98	12/23/94 to 7/31/98	7/18/97 to 7/31/98	7/11/97 to 7/31/98

[a] MacKinnon critical value for rejection of the hypothesis of a unit root. The augmented Dickey–Fuller tests include two lags and a constant term.

11.4.3 Stationarity and Cointegration

Before describing the results of our error-correction regressions, we briefly summarize several of the statistical properties of our data. Table 11.1 presents the results of Dickey–Fuller tests applied to the levels and first differences of the variables used in our analysis. STKRET refers to real aggregate stock returns, and BSTKRET refers to real bank stock returns; because the difference between bank stock returns and aggregate stock returns is used as an explanatory variable in the error-correction regressions, it is this variable that we analyze in the Dickey–Fuller tests.

The results are broadly in line with our expectations. With the exception of the stock returns, the levels of the variables in our analysis generally do not appear to be stationary, while the first differences of these variables generally do appear to be stationary. The stock return variables clearly are stationary in all instances.

Table 11.2 presents the results of Johansen cointegration tests applied to three different sets of variables: (1) the benchmark model, which

Table 11.2. Johansen Cointegration Tests

	Indonesia	Korea	Malaysia	Mexico	Philippines	Thailand
Benchmark Model: $E = a*INTDIFF + b*INFDIFF + c*SPREAD$						
Maximum eigenvalue	0.4987	0.3861	0.3873	0.1833	0.3916	0.5458
Likelihood ratio test	43.76	34.94	41.56	61.96	49.45	59.71
95% Critical value[a]	39.89	39.89	39.89	39.89	39.89	39.89
Period of observation	8/15/97 to 7/31/98	7/04/97 to 7/31/98	7/04/97 to 7/31/98	12/23/94 to 7/31/98	7/18/97 to 7/31/98	7/11/97 to 7/31/98
Model: $E = a*INTDIFF + b*INFDIFF + c*SPREAD + d*STKRET$						
Maximum eigenvalue	0.6654	0.6792	0.4817	0.4199	0.5451	0.6991
Likelihood ratio test	85.56	89.90	79.94	158.88	91.01	97.64
95% Critical value[a]	59.46	59.46	59.46	59.46	59.46	59.46
Period of observation	8/15/97 to 7/31/98	7/04/97 to 7/31/98	7/04/97 to 7/31/98	12/23/94 to 7/31/98	7/18/97 to 7/31/98	7/11/97 to 7/31/98
Model: $E = a*INTDIFF + b*INFDIFF + c*SPREAD + d*STKRET +$ $e*(BSTKRET-STKRET)$						
Maximum eigenvalue	0.8100	0.6962	0.5951	0.4249		0.7208
Likelihood ratio test	149.79	121.23	117.45	235.43		153.56
95% Critical value[a]	82.49	82.49	82.49	82.49		82.49
Period of observation	8/15/97 to 7/31/98	7/04/97 to 7/31/98	7/04/97 to 7/31/98	12/23/94 to 7/31/98	7/18/97 to 7/31/98	7/11/97 to 7/31/98

[a] Null hypothesis is that there are no cointegrating vectors.

does not include stock returns; (2) the benchmark model plus aggregate stock returns; and (3) the benchmark model plus aggregate stock returns and the difference between aggregate and bank stock returns.[9] For

---

[9] This formulation was adopted to reduce the extent of multicollinearity between aggregate and banking sector stock returns.

the set of variables in the benchmark model, the tests – based on a comparison of the likelihood ratio with its 95 percent critical value – indicate the presence of at least one cointegrating vector for every country except Korea. For the expanded sets of variables, the tests indicate the presence of at least one cointegrating vector in every country, although this in part reflects the fact that the stock return variables themselves are stationary.

The Johansen tests provide strong *prima facie* evidence of significant linkages between real exchange rates, interest rates, credit spreads, inflation, and stock returns. The findings of cointegration also strongly support the error-correction specification for our estimated equations. On the other hand, they do not provide much sense of the direction of causality among the variables we are analyzing. Therefore, we turn now to a brief description of Granger-causality tests among the variables in the model.

11.4.4 Granger-Causality Tests

In addition to being well-correlated with real exchange rates, a second condition for credit spreads and stock prices to be a good proxy for autonomous movements in investor risk assessments is that they not be themselves influenced, at least contemporaneously, by feedbacks from exchange rates. To address this and a host of other issues involving inter-relationships among the different factors, Table 11.3 presents results of Granger-causality tests among all of the variables in the analysis. In these tests, differences in the "caused" variable were regressed on two lags of itself and of differences in the "causing" variable. Finding Granger causality consisted of using an *F*-test to reject the hypothesis that the coefficients on the "causing" variable were jointly equal to zero. A number of results stand out.

First, interest rates are found to significantly affect exchange rates in *none* of the six countries surveyed. This result does not rule out contemporaneous (i.e., within the same week) causality from interest rates to exchange rates, of course. This finding also is subject to some of the same endogeneity problems discussed above, although the use of lagged rather than contemporaneous interest rates to explain the exchange rate may ameliorate this problem to some degree. Nevertheless, this *prima facie* evidence seems to argue against the view that interest rates have any impact on exchange rates, in either direction.

Second, interest rates were found, with few exceptions, to not significantly Granger-cause credit spreads, aggregate stock prices, or bank stock prices. Hence, the revisionist view that a tightening of monetary policy leads to heightened concerns of future banking sector failures and defaults are not supported by these tests, although

Table 11.3. Granger-Causality Tests

	Indonesia	Korea	Malaysia	Mexico	Philippines	Thailand
$i \rightarrow$ spreads	0	0	0	−**	0	0
$i \leftarrow$ spreads	0	0	0	+***	0	0
$i \rightarrow$ ex-rate	0	0	0	0	0	0
$i \leftarrow$ ex-rate	0	+***	0	+***	0	0
$i \rightarrow$ stocks	0	0	0	0	0	0
$i \leftarrow$ stocks	0	−*	0	−**	0	−***
spread $\rightarrow$ stocks	0	0	0	0	−**	0
spread $\leftarrow$ stocks	0	−***	−**	−***	0	−***
ex-rates $\rightarrow$ spread	0	+**	0	0	0	+***
ex-rates $\leftarrow$ spread	+**	0	0	+**	0	0
ex-rates $\rightarrow$ stocks	+***	0	0	0	0	0
ex-rates $\leftarrow$ stocks	0	0	−*	−**	0	0
$i \rightarrow$ bank stocks	0	0	0	−*	0	0
$i \leftarrow$ bank stocks	0	−***	0	−***	0	−**
bank stocks $\rightarrow$ spread	0	−***	0	−**	0	−***
bank stocks $\leftarrow$ spread	0	0	0	0	0	−*
bank stocks $\rightarrow$ ex-rate	0	−***	−**	0	0	−*
bank stocks $\leftarrow$ ex-rate	0	0	0	−*	0	0
bank stocks $\rightarrow$ stocks	0	+**	0	−*	0	0
bank stocks $\leftarrow$ stocks	+*	0	0	+**	0	0

Note: * Significant at the 10 percent level. ** Significant at the 5 percent level. *** Significant at the 1 percent level. The regressions take the form: $y_t = \alpha_0 + \alpha_1 y_{t-1} + \alpha_2 y_{t-2} + \alpha_3 x_{t-1} + \alpha_4 x_{t-2} + \varepsilon$. Significance of the Granger-causality text is determined by an F-test of the null hypothesis that $\alpha_3 = 0$ and $\alpha_4 = 0$.

the same caveats as those mentioned in the previous paragraph still apply.

Third, exchange rates significantly Granger-cause credit spreads, aggregate stock prices, and bank stock prices in only a few instances. This suggests that these measures probably would not be themselves subject to endogeneity problems if used as explanatory variables in exchange rate equations, and hence, to the extent that they capture movements in the risk premium and expected future exchange rate, would serve to minimize endogeneity problems for the interest rate variable.

Fourth, credit spreads do not appear to be particularly influential, at least as measured by the Granger-causality tests. On the other hand, aggregate stock prices and bank stock prices appear to be relatively influential, significantly affecting interest rates, spreads, and exchange rates in numerous instances.

Finally, as a check on the reliability of the results, it should be noted that in most instances where Granger causality was identified, the sign

Table 11.4a. ECM Estimation: Benchmark Model (Dependent Variable: ΔE_t)

	Indonesia	Korea	Malaysia	Mexico	Philippines	Thailand
Constant	1.675	2.215	0.066	0.267	0.991	1.827
	(0.029)	(0.009)	(0.914)	(0.053)	(0.030)	(0.001)
$\Sigma_{j=1}^{2}\alpha_{1j}\Delta E_{t-j}$	−0.024	0.124	−0.534	−0.005	−0.264	0.475
	(0.225)	(0.485)	(0.111)	(0.223)	(0.344)	(0.053)
$\Sigma_{j=0}^{2}\alpha_{2j}\Delta INTDIFF_{t-j}$	0.003	−0.002	0.010	−0.001	0.004	0.004
	(0.332)	(0.626)	(0.640)	(0.005)	(0.289)	(0.493)
$\Sigma_{j=0}^{2}\alpha_{3j}\Delta INFDIFF_{t-j}$	−0.007	0.002	−0.201	−0.0005	−0.024	0.015
	(0.198)	(0.317)	(0.656)	(0.467)	(0.601)	(0.134)
$\Sigma_{j=0}^{2}\alpha_{4j}\Delta SPREAD_{t-j}$	0.041	0.034	−0.005	0.024	0.001	−0.029
	(0.000)	(0.004)	(0.989)	(0.000)	(0.002)	(0.069)
$\alpha_{5}E_{t-1}$	−0.352	−0.492	−0.0004	−0.058	−0.227	−0.415
	(0.035)	(0.009)	(0.996)	(0.051)	(0.036)	(0.001)
$\alpha_{6}INTDIFF_{t-1}$	−0.005	0.004	−0.011	−0.0002	0.0004	0.005
	(0.015)	(0.316)	(0.418)	(0.958)	(0.862)	(0.252)
$\alpha_{7}INFDIFF_{t-1}$	−0.001	0.004	−0.002	−0.0002	−0.0003	0.005
	(0.211)	(0.147)	(0.462)	(0.092)	(0.940)	(0.057)
$\alpha_{8}SPREAD_{t-1}$	0.096	0.045	0.004	0.003	0.031	0.043
	(0.002)	(0.029)	(0.868)	(0.011)	(0.038)	(0.012)
Period of observation	8/15/97	7/04/97	7/04/97	12/23/94	7/18/97	7/11/97
	to	to	to	to	to	to
	7/31/98	7/31/98	7/31/98	7/31/98	7/31/98	7/31/98
Observations	51	57	57	176	55	56
Adjusted R^2	0.65	0.31	0.03	0.58	0.32	0.14
Regression standard error	0.083	0.051	0.047	0.011	0.037	0.038
LM (significance level)[a]	0.933	0.792	0.518	0.633	0.892	0.850

Note: Significance levels are shown in parentheses.

[a] Lagrange multiplier test for autocorrelation of errors; null hypothesis is that there is no autocorrelation.

of the impact was in line with expectations. Hence, increases in credit spreads lead to higher interest rates, more depreciated exchange rates, and lower stock prices. Increases in stock prices (both aggregate and bank stocks) lead to lower interest rates, more appreciated exchange rates, and lower spreads.

11.4.5 Error-Correction Estimation Results

11.4.5.1 Benchmark Model

Table 11.4a presents the results of unrestricted OLS estimation of equation (3) for the six countries in our sample. For the lagged levels of the explanatory variables, their coefficients and (in parentheses) significance levels are presented[10]; for the explanatory variables that enter in difference form, the sums of the coefficients on the different lags of each variable are presented, along with their significance.[11] The following observations can be made about these results.

First, the coefficient on the lagged level of the real exchange rate, α_5, is appropriately negative and significantly different from zero for every country except Malaysia, suggesting that the error-correction specification used here is appropriate.[12] Put another way, econometric specifications based on first differences of the variables alone probably throw away useful information about the mean-reverting properties of the real exchange rate.

Second, the coefficients on the SPREAD term, both its lagged level and its first differences, are highly significant for every country except Malaysia. This is suggestive of a cointegrating relationship containing at least the real exchange rate and the spread; although with only a year's worth of data, one would not want to push that hypothesis too far. In any event, the results confirm the importance of the spread as a near-term determinant of exchange rate movements, consistent with both our hypothesis and with the visual evidence presented in Figure 11.3.

Third, inflation differentials fail to play much of a role in the determination of exchange rate movements among the countries in the sample; in no cases are the coefficients on either the level of this variable or its differences significant at the 5 percent level. In principle, increases in domestic inflation should lead to depreciation of the exchange rate, both because, for a given nominal interest rate, this lowers the real interest rate and because higher inflation may represent a signal that monetary policy is failing to stabilize the economy. In practice, inflation expectations are hard to measure and may be only loosely related to actual inflation outcomes over short periods of time, particularly because actual outcomes are observed only with a lag. Inflation among the Asian economies in the sample generally turned out to be lower than expected, with the possible exception of Indonesia. Even in Mexico, where inflationary impulses were much more apparent, the peak

---

[10] Specifically, the significance level is the probability that the coefficient might actually be equal to zero, given its estimated value and standard deviation.

[11] More precisely, for the explanatory variables entering in differences, the significance level is based on an F-test of the null hypothesis that the coefficients jointly are equal to zero.

[12] The phrase "statistically significant" is used in an impressionistic, rather than exact, sense in this context. Because the levels of the explanatory variables are not necessarily stationary, their standards errors may well be biased, leading to misleading inferences of significance in some cases.

of the financial crisis was reached in March 1995, before inflationary pass-through from the fall of the peso had a chance to fully manifest itself.

Finally, and most importantly, domestic interest rates do not appear to affect the exchange rate in a consistent manner. The coefficients on the lagged levels of the interest rate differential are negative in three countries – which would be consistent with conventional theory – and positive in three countries; the sum of the coefficients on the first differences are negative in two cases and positive in four. In the only two cases where results are significantly different from zero – the coefficient on the lagged level of the interest rate differential for Indonesia, and the coefficients on the first differences of the interest rate differential for Mexico – the sign of the effect is negative, consistent with the conventional view that raising domestic interest rates should appreciate the real exchange rate. Interestingly, Indonesia and Mexico also represent the cases where exchange rate depreciation led to significantly higher inflation, and one might expect that in those circumstances, raising interest rates might be more favorably regarded by the market than in cases where inflation and the credibility of monetary policy were not at issue. However, given the paucity of significant coefficients in our estimation results, it is not clear how much weight, if any, should be placed on these findings.

One reason for our failure to identify a more clear-cut impact of the interest rate differential on the exchange rate may be that there are too many parameters – many of them not statistically significant – being estimated in our equations; this is particularly a concern with the first differenced variables, since there generally are three lags (including the contemporaneous value) of each of them. To address this potential problem, we progressively reduced the number of parameters in the equations by deleting the least significant of the first-differenced explanatory variables from the models, re-estimating them, and proceeding in this fashion until only relatively significant parameters – usually in the neighborhood of the 5 percent level of significance – remained for the first-differenced variables in the equations; all of the lagged levels of the explanatory variables were retained.

The estimation results for these more parsimonious models are presented in Table 11.4b, which displays coefficient values and levels of significance for each of the coefficients in the equations. While some coefficients are now significant that were not in the unrestricted models, the basic findings are not much changed. With the exception of Malaysia, the coefficients on the lagged levels of the exchange rate and the spread remain highly significant and with the expected sign. Some coefficients on the inflation variables – both in levels and first differences – are now significant, but there is no consistency as to their sign. Finally, the

Table 11.4b. ECM Estimation: Parsimonious Benchmark Model
(Dependent Variable: ΔE_t)

	Indonesia	Korea	Malaysia	Mexico	Philippines	Thailand
Constant	2.723	1.787	0.244	0.317	0.948	1.731
	(0.000)	(0.001)	(0.516)	(0.017)	(0.015)	(0.001)
ΔE_{t-1}			−0.327		−0.278	
			(0.026)		(0.020)	
ΔE_{t-2}						0.341
						(0.015)
$\Delta INTDIFF_{t-0}$				0.002	0.004	
				(0.004)	(0.045)	
$\Delta INTDIFF_{t-1}$				−0.001		
				(0.008)		
$\Delta INTDIFF_{t-2}$		−0.006				
		(0.039)				
$\Delta INFDIFF_{t-0}$				−0.001		0.021
				(0.111)		(0.029)
$\Delta INFDIFF_{t-1}$		0.044				
		(0.012)				
$\Delta INFDIFF_{t-2}$		−0.039				
		(0.025)				
$\Delta SPREAD_{t-0}$	0.089	0.059		0.014	0.055	0.032
	(0.000)	(0.000)		(0.000)	(0.000)	(0.008)
$\Delta SPREAD_{t-1}$	−0.061				−0.036	−0.034
	(0.000)				(0.018)	(0.018)
$\Delta SPREAD_{t-2}$				0.006		−0.025
				(0.000)		(0.052)
$\alpha_5 E_{t-1}$	−0.591	−0.396	−0.048	−0.069	−0.214	−0.387
	(0.000)	(0.001)	(0.550)	(0.017)	(0.019)	(0.001)
$\alpha_6 INTDIFF_{t-1}$	−0.002	0.003	0.003	0.000	−0.000	0.002
	(0.055)	(0.306)	(0.631)	(0.926)	(0.891)	(0.387)
$\alpha_7 INFDIFF_{t-1}$	−0.001	0.004	−0.003	−0.000	−0.001	0.003
	(0.011)	(0.110)	(0.190)	(0.189)	(0.852)	(0.084)
$\alpha_8 SPREAD_{t-1}$	0.125	0.035	−0.001	0.003	0.026	0.043
	(0.000)	(0.013)	(0.931)	(0.011)	(0.023)	(0.002)
Period of observation	8/15/97	7/04/97	7/04/97	12/23/94	7/18/97	7/11/97
	to	to	to	to	to	to
	7/31/98	7/31/98	7/31/98	7/31/98	7/31/98	7/31/98
Observations	51	57	57	178	55	56
Adjusted R^2	0.626	0.380	0.096	0.647	0.361	0.165
Regression standard error	0.087	0.049	0.045	0.011	0.030	0.037
LM (significance level)[a]	0.451	0.659	0.575	0.724	0.927	0.987

Note: Significance levels are shown in parentheses.

[a] Lagrange multiplier test for autocorrelation of errors; null hypothesis is that there is no autocorrelation.

findings for the interest differential remain essentially unchanged; while a negative and significant coefficient on the second lag of the first-differenced interest rate differential is now indicated for Korea, there also is now a positive and significant contemporaneous value of the first-differenced interest rate differential for the Philippines.

11.4.5.2 Model with Aggregate Stock Returns

Table 11.5a presents the estimation results for the unrestricted model when the lagged level of stock returns – defined as the log change in a broad, price-deflated stock price index – and several lags of the first difference of stock returns are added to the model presented in Table 11.4a. As noted above, if higher interest rates lead to a depreciation of the exchange rate by raising concerns about future economic performance and debt repayment, as contended by some observers, then adding stock returns to the equations presented in Tables 11.4a and 11.4b, by holding these concerns constant, should lead to stronger estimates of a negative effect of interest rates on the local currency value of the dollar.

As indicated in Table 11.5a, the lagged level of stock returns is negative in five of the six cases, consistent with our expectations that improved expectations of economic performance lead to a stronger exchange rate, and is approximately significant in three of those cases. The sum of the lags on the first difference of stock returns also is significant in a number of cases, albeit with the wrong sign.

However, the addition of the stock return variables makes no appreciable difference to the estimated effect of the interest rate differential, either in levels or in first differences, on the real exchange rate. The same holds for the estimated effect of the interest rate differential in the parsimonious regression results presented in Table 11.5b.

11.4.5.3 Model with Both Aggregate and Bank Stock Returns

The story that tightening monetary policy leads to a depreciation of the exchange rate focuses most closely on the impact of higher interest rates on the health of the banking system. Therefore, in Table 11.6a we add to the model presented in Table 11.5a measures of the difference between aggregate stock returns and bank stock returns; this specification was chosen so as to include both aggregate and bank returns in the same model, while minimizing the extent of multicollinearity between them. Table 11.6b presents results for the parsimonious version of the model represented in Table 11.6a.

As a quick perusal of the tables will indicate, the addition of bank stock return variables makes little difference to the results, relative to either those shown in Tables 11.4a and 11.4b or those shown in Tables 11.5a and 11.5b.

Table 11.5a. ECM Estimation: Benchmark Model with Stock Return
(Dependent Variable: ΔE_t)

	Indonesia	Korea	Malaysia	Mexico	Philippines	Thailand
Constant	1.536	1.081	−0.180	0.251	0.718	1.899
	(0.070)	(0.132)	(0.724)	(0.072)	(0.119)	(0.004)
$\sum_{j=1}^{2}\alpha_{1j}\Delta E_{t-j}$	−0.006	−0.362	−0.622	0.023	−0.260	0.540
	(0.287)	(0.180)	(0.087)	(0.267)	(0.265)	(0.050)
$\sum_{j=0}^{2}\alpha_{2j}\Delta INTDIFF_{t-j}$	0.003	−0.001	0.007	−0.001	0.002	0.006
	(0.395)	(0.262)	(0.828)	(0.006)	(0.319)	(0.522)
$\sum_{j=0}^{2}\alpha_{3j}\Delta INFDIFF_{t-j}$	−0.006	0.025	0.014	−0.001	−0.021	0.017
	(0.091)	(0.102)	(0.654)	(0.572)	(0.698)	(0.725)
$\sum_{j=0}^{2}\alpha_{4j}\Delta SPREAD_{t-j}$	0.048	0.043	−0.090	0.022	−0.031	−0.020
	(0.000)	(0.129)	(0.397)	(0.000)	(0.034)	(0.026)
$\sum_{j=0}^{2}\alpha_{5j}\Delta STKRET_{t-j}$	0.296	0.512	0.264	−0.059	0.264	−0.312
	(0.845)	(0.000)	(0.000)	(0.393)	(0.123)	(0.449)
$\alpha_6 E_{t-1}$	−0.324	−0.245	0.043	−0.055	−0.175	−0.434
	(0.077)	(0.125)	(0.693)	(0.068)	(0.104)	(0.004)
$\alpha_7 INTDIFF_{t-1}$	−0.005	0.001	−0.005	0.0001	0.003	0.004
	(0.021)	(0.852)	(0.643)	(0.921)	(0.987)	(0.222)
$\alpha_8 INFDIFF_{t-1}$	−0.001	0.002	−0.001	−0.0003	0.001	0.006
	(0.324)	(0.293)	(0.761)	(0.055)	(0.752)	(0.045)
$\alpha_9 SPREAD_{t-1}$	0.089	0.030	−0.002	0.003	0.022	0.049
	(0.007)	(0.082)	(0.902)	(0.022)	(0.149)	(0.008)
$\alpha_{10} STKRET_{t-1}$	−0.290	−1.666	−1.148	−0.073	−0.459	0.081
	(0.724)	(0.000)	(0.001)	(0.270)	(0.079)	(0.723)
Period of observation	8/15/97	7/04/97	7/04/97	12/23/94	7/18/97	7/11/97
	to	to	to	to	to	to
	7/31/98	7/31/98	7/31/98	7/31/98	7/31/98	7/31/98
Observations	51	57	57	176	55	56
Adjusted R^2	0.63	0.55	0.32	0.58	0.36	0.19
Regression standard error	0.086	0.041	0.039	0.011	0.030	0.036
LM (significance level)[a]	0.902	0.575	0.809	0.836	0.846	0.694

Note: Significance levels are shown in parentheses.

[a] Lagrange multiplier test for autocorrelation of errors; null hypothesis is that there is no autocorrelation.

11.5 CONCLUSION

In this chapter we attempt to make a contribution to an important policy debate that has arisen in the aftermath of the Asian financial crisis: To what extent can a tightening of monetary policy prevent a depreciation of a floating exchange rate in the midst of a financial and balance-of-payment crisis? This debate is sufficiently balanced in theoretical terms

Table 11.5b. ECM Estimation: Parsimonious Benchmark Model with Stock Return (Dependent Variable: ΔE_t)

	Indonesia	Korea	Malaysia	Mexico	Philippines	Thailand
Constant	2.449	1.417	−0.095	0.257	0.949	0.635
	(0.000)	(0.002)	(0.776)	(0.049)	(0.016)	(0.117)
ΔE_{t-1}			−0.365		−0.271	
			(0.011)		(0.031)	
ΔE_{t-2}	0.214					0.269
	(0.032)					(0.043)
$\Delta INTDIFF_{t-0}$				0.001	0.004	
				(0.012)	(0.056)	
$\Delta INTDIFF_{t-1}$				−0.001		
				(0.010)		
$\Delta INTDIFF_{t-2}$		−0.008				
		(0.006)				
$\Delta INFDIFF_{t-0}$		0.019				
		(0.000)				
$\Delta INFDIFF_{t-1}$						
$\Delta INFDIFF_{t-2}$						
$\Delta SPREAD_{t-0}$	0.087			0.014	0.055	0.021
	(0.000)			(0.000)	(0.001)	(0.085)
$\Delta SPREAD_{t-1}$	−0.046	−0.034			−0.035	−0.015
	(0.006)	(0.010)			(0.034)	(0.212)
$\Delta SPREAD_{t-2}$				0.006		
				(0.000)		
$\Delta STKRET_{t-0}$		−0.568	−0.337			−0.240
		(0.000)	(0.000)			(0.016)
$\Delta STKRET_{t-1}$		0.544	0.218			
		(0.001)	(0.009)			
$\Delta STKRET_{t-2}$		0.196				
		(0.044)				
$\alpha_6 E_{t-1}$	−0.531	−0.319	0.022	−0.056	−0.213	−0.142
	(0.000)	(0.002)	(0.760)	(0.048)	(0.020)	(0.111)
$\alpha_7 INTDIFF_{t-1}$	−0.002	0.001	0.003	−0.000	−0.000	0.002
	(0.103)	(0.584)	(0.618)	(0.381)	(0.849)	(0.429)
$\alpha_8 INFDIFF_{t-1}$	−0.001	0.003	−0.001	−0.000	−0.001	0.000
	(0.124)	(0.063)	(0.562)	(0.595)	(0.832)	(0.804)
$\alpha_9 SPREAD_{t-1}$	0.107	0.036	−0.010	0.003	0.026	0.012
	(0.000)	(0.005)	(0.383)	(0.006)	(0.024)	(0.178)
$\alpha_{10} STKRET_{t-1}$	0.090	−1.47	−0.673	−0.025	0.020	−0.227
	(0.611)	(0.000)	(0.000)	(0.332)	(0.826)	(0.108)
Period of observation	8/15/97 to 7/31/98	7/4/97 to 7/31/98	7/4/97 to 7/31/98	12/23/94 to 7/31/98	7/18/97 to 7/31/98	7/11/97 to 7/31/98
Observations	51	57	57	178	55	56
Adjusted R^2	0.654	0.569	0.345	0.644	0.348	0.158
Regression standard error	0.083	0.041	0.038	0.012	0.030	0.037
LM (significance level)[a]	0.992	0.871	0.728	0.623	0.955	0.953

Note: Significance levels are shown in parentheses.

[a] Lagrange multiplier test for autocorrelation of errors; null hypothesis is that there is no autocorrelation.

Table 11.6a. ECM Estimation: Benchmark Model with Stock Return and Bank Stock Return (Dependent Variable: ΔE_t)

	Indonesia	Korea	Malaysia	Mexico	Thailand
Constant	1.295	1.484	−0.083	0.218	1.658
	(0.182)	(0.055)	(0.882)	(0.113)	(0.008)
$\sum_{j=1}^{2}\alpha_{1j}\Delta E_{t-j}$	−0.159	−0.242	−0.554	−0.001	0.183
	(0.216)	(0.373)	(0.205)	(0.086)	(0.604)
$\sum_{j=0}^{2}\alpha_{2j}\Delta INTDIFF_{t-j}$	−0.001	−0.002	0.005	−0.001	0.010
	(0.671)	(0.392)	(0.877)	(0.011)	(0.181)
$\sum_{j=0}^{2}\alpha_{3j}\Delta INFDIFF_{t-j}$	−0.006	0.020	0.010	−0.001	0.002
	(0.589)	(0.015)	(0.832)	(0.381)	(0.179)
$\sum_{j=0}^{2}\alpha_{4j}\Delta SPREAD_{t-j}$	0.041	0.013	−0.099	0.020	0.003
	(0.000)	(0.233)	(0.358)	(0.000)	(0.232)
$\sum_{j=0}^{2}\alpha_{5j}\Delta STKRET_{t-j}$	−0.102	0.351	0.213	0.012	−0.548
	(0.740)	(0.002)	(0.038)	(0.782)	(0.192)
$\sum_{j=0}^{2}\alpha_{6j}\Delta(BSTKRET - STKRET)_{t-j}$	−1.223	0.256	−0.192	−0.153	0.820
	(0.410)	(0.010)	(0.515)	(0.022)	(0.015)
$\alpha_{7}E_{t-1}$	−0.277	−0.334	0.021	−0.048	−0.369
	(0.193)	(0.053)	(0.862)	(0.109)	(0.009)
$\alpha_{8}INTDIFF_{t-1}$	−0.005	0.001	−0.002	−0.000	0.001
	(0.090)	(0.784)	(0.862)	(0.710)	(0.691)
$\alpha_{9}INFDIFF_{t-1}$	−0.001	0.004	−0.001	−0.000	0.006
	(0.311)	(0.105)	(0.725)	(0.112)	(0.018)
$\alpha_{10}SPREAD_{t-1}$	0.086	0.036	−0.002	0.003	0.030
	(0.042)	(0.042)	(0.901)	(0.010)	(0.097)
$\alpha_{11}STKRET_{t-1}$	−0.583	−1.284	−0.839	−0.085	0.460
	(0.513)	(0.004)	(0.068)	(0.197)	(0.061)
$\alpha_{12}(BSTKRET - STKRET)_{t-1}$	−0.406	−0.622	−0.362	0.042	−1.32
	(0.811)	(0.050)	(0.470)	(0.433)	(0.013)
Period of observation	8/15/97 to 7/31/98	7/4/97 to 7/31/98	7/4/97 to 7/31/98	12/23/94 to 7/31/98	7/11/97 to 7/31/98
Observations	51	57	57	176	56
Adjusted R^2	0.622	0.641	0.272	0.592	0.341
Regression standard error	0.087	0.037	0.040	0.011	0.033
LM (significance level)[a]	0.846	0.749	0.868	0.847	0.568

Note: Significance levels are shown in parentheses.

[a] Lagrange multiplier test for autocorrelation of errors; null hypothesis is that there is no autocorrelation.

Table 11.6b. ECM Estimation: Parsimonious Benchmark Model with Stock Return and Bank Stock Return (Dependent Variable: ΔE_t)

	Indonesia	Korea	Malaysia	Mexico	Thailand
Constant	1.396	1.797	0.046	0.229	1.193
	(0.006)	(0.000)	(0.888)	(0.072)	(0.005)
ΔE_{t-1}	−0.453		−0.416		
	(0.000)		(0.005)		
ΔE_{t-2}					
$\Delta INTDIFF_{t-0}$				0.001	0.010
				(0.003)	(0.010)
$\Delta INTDIFF_{t-1}$				−0.001	
				(0.006)	
$\Delta INTDIFF_{t-2}$		−0.006			
		(0.023)			
$\Delta INFDIFF_{t-0}$	−0.004	0.014			0.019
	(0.043)	(0.000)			(0.111)
$\Delta INFDIFF_{t-1}$					
$\Delta INFDIFF_{t-2}$					−0.024
					(0.021)
$\Delta SPREAD_{t-0}$	0.085	0.025		0.014	0.032
	(0.000)	(0.031)		(0.000)	(0.006)
$\Delta SPREAD_{t-1}$					
$\Delta SPREAD_{t-2}$				0.006	
				(0.000)	
$\Delta STKRET_{t-0}$		−0.445	−0.232		
		(0.000)	(0.013)		
$\Delta STKRET_{t-1}$		0.228			−0.206
		(0.018)			(0.029)
$\Delta STKRET_{t-2}$					
$\Delta(BSTKRET - STKRET)_{t-0}$	−0.770		−0.317		−0.297
	(0.006)		(0.037)		(0.016)
$\Delta(BSTKRET - STKRET)_{t-1}$		0.415		−0.071	0.633
		(0.000)		(0.002)	(0.000)
$\Delta(BSTKRET - STKRET)_{t-2}$					
$\alpha_7 E_{t-1}$	−0.299	−0.405	−0.009	−0.050	−0.259
	(0.007)	(0.000)	(0.896)	(0.070)	(0.006)
$\alpha_8 INTDIFF_{t-1}$	−0.003	0.004	0.006	−0.000	0.001
	(0.014)	(0.073)	(0.290)	(0.238)	(0.740)
$\alpha_9 INFDIFF_{t-1}$	−0.001	0.002	−0.002	−0.000	0.004
	(0.044)	(0.117)	(0.225)	(0.630)	(0.048)
$\alpha_{10} SPREAD_{t-1}$	0.078	0.039	−0.009	0.003	0.014
	(0.000)	(0.000)	(0.441)	(0.004)	(0.190)
$\alpha_{11} STKRET_{t-1}$	0.175	−0.921	−0.177	−0.021	0.440
	(0.355)	(0.000)	(0.257)	(0.425)	(0.003)

(continued)

Table 11.6b (*Continued*)

	Indonesia	Korea	Malaysia	Mexico	Thailand
$\alpha_{12}(BSTKRET - STKRET)_{t-1}$	−1.157	−0.472	−0.591	0.052	−1.130
	(0.011)	(0.002)	(0.005)	(0.124)	(0.000)
Period of observation	8/15/97	7/4/97	7/4/97	12/23/94	7/11/97
	to	to	to	to	to
	7/31/98	7/31/98	7/31/98	7/31/98	7/31/98
Observations	51	57	57	178	56
Adjusted R^2	0.660	0.664	0.345	0.661	0.415
Regression standard error	0.083	0.036	0.038	0.011	0.031
LM (significance level)[a]	0.827	0.589	0.159	0.468	0.546

Note: Significance levels are shown in parentheses.

[a] Lagrange multiplier test for autocorrelation of errors; null hypothesis is that there is no autocorrelation.

that it likely will only be settled on empirical grounds. However, a crucial obstacle to the empirical resolution of this issue is that while domestic interest rates may exert certain impacts on the exchange rate, these interest rates also are highly sensitive to the same factors that influence the exchange rate, especially investor perceptions of country risk. Therefore, prior attempts to assess the impact of interest rates on the exchange rate may have been adversely affected by endogeneity and omitted variable problems.

In our chapter we attempt to address these endogeneity problems by including dollar-denominated sovereign credit spreads – a measure of investor perceptions of country risk – in regression equations for the exchange rates of the Asian crisis economies. In principle, if increases in domestic interest rates really help support the exchange rate, this effect should have become apparent once this measure of investor perceptions was held constant in the equations. In fact, we find that credit spreads exerted a consistent and strongly significant impact on exchange rates for nearly all of the countries in our sample, consistent with our hypothesis that during financial crises, perceptions of country and credit risk become a major determinant of currency values. Nevertheless, even with credit spreads included as explanatory variables, we find little consistent evidence of an effect of interest rates on the exchange rate – either positive or negative – in our estimation results.

These findings are consistent with one of three different possibilities. First, it may be that there is no systematic effect of monetary policy on exchange rates, at least over the relatively limited time horizon – about a year's worth of weekly data – examined in our study. Second, it is possible that the inclusion of credit spreads, statistically significant as they are, nevertheless fails to correct the endogeneity of the domestic interest rate with respect to omitted variables. Finally, it may be the case that when monetary policy is tightened, the forces appreciating the exchange rate and depreciating the exchange rate are sufficiently well balanced that, on net, little systematic and identifiable change to the exchange rate actually occurs.

In order to assess these last two possibilities, we added to our benchmark regression model several measures of aggregate and banking-sector stock returns. These returns should reflect investor expectations of future prospects for the economy and the banking sector, and hence represent additional measures of investor assessments of country risk. Therefore, it is possible that the addition of stock returns could help to better identify the independent impact of monetary policy shocks on the exchange rate. Moreover, if a tightening of monetary policy tends to depress investor expectations and therefore depress the value of the local currency, holding stock returns constant should remove this effect from the estimated impact of interest rates on exchange rates. In consequence, compared with equations that do not include these stock returns, equations that include these returns as explanatory variables should be more likely to show a supportive effect of a monetary tightening on the exchange value of the local currency.

In fact, inclusion of stock market variables does little to change the minimal effect of interest rates on exchange rates estimated in our benchmark model. This finding would tend to diminish support for the view that, all else equal, monetary tightening undercuts the value of the exchange rate by depressing the economy or threatening the health of the banking sector. It also makes it less likely that the failure to identify consistent significant impacts of domestic interest rates on exchange rates reflects endogeneity problems, insofar as the combination of credit spreads and stock returns should in principle be adequate to control for movements in investor concerns about country risk and future depreciation.

We are therefore left with two possibilities. One is that monetary policy simply has no effect on the exchange rate. While one would not want to dismiss this possibility out of hand, it contradicts so much of the theory of international finance that to accept it would require rejecting nearly everything else we believe about the international financial system. Such a conclusion also fails to present any guidance for the conduct of monetary policy.

An alternative, and perhaps more likely, possibility is that monetary policy may indeed impact exchange rates in a systematic way, but only slowly and over relatively long time horizons, so that this impact would not be identified using weekly data over a relatively short one-year sample. In principle, of course, changes in monetary policy should have immediate effects on exchange rates and other asset prices in a free market with forward-looking investors. In practice, however, investors may have concerns that monetary policy actions might subsequently be reversed. It may take a sustained period of monetary tightness, for example, to establish the credibility of the central bank, convince market participants that the time is right to invest, and thereby strengthen the domestic currency. If this is the case, studies encompassing many financial crisis episodes, such as Furman and Stiglitz (1998) and Goldfajn and Gupta (1998), would be more likely to identify significant impacts of interest rates on exchange rates during financial crises.

Unfortunately, as noted earlier in this chapter, such studies have not, to date, provided any clear and consistent answers to the question of what impact monetary policy may have on the exchange rate. In the absence of such answers, what guidance is available to policymakers? The conclusion we draw, from both the theoretical arguments and the empirical results (or lack thereof), is that during financial crises, monetary policy should strive to be prudent, to establish credibility, and to avoid extremes of tightness or looseness. Such an approach would dictate maintaining positive real *ex post* interest rates, for example, but not necessarily over very short intervals, if temporary bursts of inflation would require unsustainably high nominal interest rates as a result. Such an approach would in general dictate discernible increases in nominal interest rates during financial crisis, if only to signal to the market that containing an inflation/depreciation spiral is a high priority of the monetary authority. At the same time, however, such an approach would argue against raising interest rates "through the roof" during a financial crisis, because that might well trigger concerns about the future viability of the banking system and the country's creditworthiness.

The definition of what constitutes an excessive increase in interest rates, of course, will vary from country to country. In postdevaluation Mexico (1995) and Brazil (1999), strong inflation expectations and the low credibility of monetary policy dictated extremely high interest rates. Conversely, in the Asian crisis countries, where inflation expectations were lower and the credibility of monetary policy higher, smaller increases in interest rates may have been required to support the stability of financial markets.

In conclusion, the impact of monetary policy on exchange rates during financial crises remains a very controversial and very important issue. Much more empirical work will be required if this issue is to be resolved.

Appendix 11A. Data Definitions and Sources

Variable	Description	Source
E	Weekly log real bilateral exchange rate relative to the U.S. dollar. Weekly domestic and foreign inflation rates are described below.	Authors' calculations from Bloomberg exchange rate data and country government CPI data.
$INTDIFF$	One-month domestic interest rate differential with respect to the one-month U.S. Treasury bill.	Data derived from: Indonesia: JIBOR 1-month rate. Korea: Seoul 15-day interbank rate. Malaysia: KLIBOR 1-month rate. Thailand: BIBOR 1-month rate. Mexico: 28-day CETES rate. Philippines: PHIBOR 1-month rate.
$INFDIFF$	Domestic inflation rate differential with respect to the U.S inflation rate. Weekly inflation rates were derived by distributing the monthly rate equally over the number of weeks in the month and then a 13-week rolling change was calculated. These data are at annual rates.	Authors' calculations from government data sources.
$SPREAD$	Government bonds spreads against similar maturity and coupon of U.S. government bond spreads.	Derived from Bloomberg data.
$STKRET$	Weekly total stock market return calculated as the log difference in the weekly total CPI-deflated stock market index.	Derived from Bloomberg data.
$BSTKRET-$ $STKRET$	Weekly bank stock index return minus weekly total stock market return.	Authors' calculations from Bloomberg stock market data.

REFERENCES

Dekle, R., C. Hsiao, and S. Wang (Chapter 10, this volume). "Interest Rate Stabilization of Exchange Rates and Contagion in the Asian Crisis Countries.

Furman, Jason and Joseph E. Stiglitz (1998). "Economic Crises: Evidence and Insights from East Asia." *Brookings Papers on Economic Activity*, No. 2:1–114.

Goldfajn, Ilan and Tamur Baig (1998). "Monetary Policy in the Aftermath of Currency Crises: The Case of Asia." IMF Working Paper No. 98/170. Washington, D.C.

Goldfajn, Ilan and Poonam Gupta (1999). "Does Monetary Policy Stabilize the Exchange Rate following a Currency Crisis?" Working Paper No. 99/42, International Monetary Fund. Washington, D.C.

International Monetary Fund (1998). "Box 2.3. The Role of Monetary Policy in Responding to Currency Crises." In *World Economic Outlook*, Washington, D.C., August.

Kraay, Aart (1998). "Do High Interest Rates Defend Currencies during Speculative Attacks?" Policy Research Working Paper No. 2267, World Bank. Washington, D.C.

Radelet, Steven and Jeffrey D. Sachs (1998). "The East Asian Financial Crisis: Diagnosis, Remedies, Prospects," *Brookings Papers on Economic Activity*, No. 1:1–74.

Spicer, John and Charles Goodhart (1999). "Monetary Policy's Effects during the Recent Financial Crises in Brazil and Korea." Mimeo, Bank of England.

Discussion

The Impact of Monetary Policy on Exchange Rates during Financial Crises

Henning Bohn

This chapter addresses an important topic, and it does so in a very appropriate way. The question how monetary policy affects exchange rates is essential for policy advice in any open economy, and it is absolutely crucial in a financial crisis. Different economic theories provide contradicting answers, however, creating a need for empirical evidence. The empirical focus of Gould and Kamin's chapter is therefore very appropriate. As usual with empirical work, I have concerns with how it is done and how it should be interpreted, but I like the chapter for what it does. It takes a good look at the data, as imperfect as they are, and it extracts some relevant lessons.

My comments focus on three issues: the motivation, the theoretical framework, and the empirical results.

MOTIVATION

The motivation of the chapter is excellent. The authors contrast two theories with radically different implications: "orthodox" (my label) and "revisionist" (their label). By orthodox theory I mean the textbook view that underlies the usual policy advice from the IMF and others: To limit or reverse a depreciation, the government should tighten monetary policy because this makes the domestic currency more attractive to international investors.[1] The revisionist objection is that in a crisis, tight money can be so harmful to the real economy that it reduces the demand for domestic currency, creates risk premiums, and therefore triggers further devaluations. The theoretical controversy suggests that the issue is empirical: What is the impact of tight monetary policy on the exchange rate?

---

[1] Usually, tight money is implemented by raising interest rates. I use the more fuzzy term "tight money" to describe the general thrust of policy without getting distracted by implementation issues (operating procedures) that may be country-specific.

Note that the chapter's title includes "during financial crises." This caveat is important because outside of crisis situations there is no serious controversy about the basic, qualitative effects of monetary policy. Orthodox theory deserves its name because it is correct under normal circumstances: The exchange rate is the relative price of national moneys. The domestic price levels are roughly proportional to the respective money supplies. Hence, tight money should normally generate an appreciation.[2] The critical question is whether or not different arguments apply during crises periods.

I suspect that this "crises-are-special" argument motivates the short sample period – just one year of crisis-time data per country. Otherwise, a longer sample would yield more precise estimates. My suggestion would be to do a test of the crises-are-special hypothesis – for example, by adding a control period of noncrisis data. Then one could determine if monetary policy is indeed working differently during crises than at other times.

THE THEORETICAL FRAMEWORK

My second set of comments is about the theoretical framework used for interpreting the empirical findings. This involves questions about (a) the longer-run context in which short-run policy decisions take place and (b) distinctions between different risk premiums and between exogenous and endogenous variables.

A long-run perspective is needed because international investors are presumably forward-looking and keenly interested in how the world will look like after the crisis. The expected end-of-crisis level of the exchange rate is probably more important for investors than any other variable. To see this, consider the decision problem of an international investor when a crisis occurs and the exchange rate has just depreciated by, say, 20 percent. (For example, recall the Mexican crisis in 1994.) The immediate question for investors is whether to sell or to hold on to their investments. If the 20 percent devaluation marks the end of the crisis, holding on is the right decision. But if the crisis gets worse and the exchange rate collapses, selling quickly is the only way to avoid heavy losses.

---

[2] In developed countries, most monetary policy debates are about the "details" omitted in this coarse quantity theoretic view. In the context of emerging markets and crises, however, the potential changes in money supplies, prices, and exchange rates are so huge that it is best to focus on getting the first-order magnitudes right and to worry about the details later. Quantity theory provides a good way to think about the first-order effects. Note that I use quantity theory without denying a role for interest rates. Interest rates may well be used as operating instruments to control the money supply.

The key question for investors *in a crisis* is therefore what determines the level of the exchange rate *after the crisis*. For this question, orthodox theory is again relevant. If the money supply, say, doubles during the crisis, domestic prices and the exchange rate will increase by about the same factor (eventually, even if prices are sticky in the short run), and investors will lose about half their investments. If the money supply triples or quintuples, the exchange rate will do the same, and investors will lose two-thirds or more. Hence, expectations about the future money supply are crucial for investment decisions. Other factors – say, temporary interest rate differentials – are likely small in comparison to the huge potential gains or losses from exchange rate changes.

From reading the introduction, it seems that Gould and Kamin are sympathetic to this view. They note that both the orthodox and the revisionist side claim that their respective policies are best to "restore confidence." So the dispute is fundamentally about which short-run policy is more likely to have a positive impact on investor expectations. Orthodox theory presumes that tight money in the short run will be interpreted by investors as a signal about tight money in the future. Then tight money builds confidence that the ultimate monetary expansion will be small. The revisionist view assumes that tight money signals the opposite: If monetary policy is too restrictive, the negative employment effects may undermine the political support for tight money so much that investors start to expect a policy reversal.[3] A further tightening would just reinforce investor concerns about a policy reversal. (For example, recall that in 1992, high interest rates failed to stop the speculative attacks on Sweden and the United Kingdom.)

Note that this interpretation of revisionism does not require a new economic model – no arguments about default risks, and so on. Revisionist policy advice may simply reflect a different view about the political implications of tight money in a crisis, not a disagreement about the economic effects.

This perspective provides a somewhat different interpretation of Gould and Kamin's theoretical framework (their Section 11.3.1). I would modify it as follows.

First, for theoretical purposes, we should distinguish money-market interest rates, which are endogenous and may include default risk, from the safe interest rate and from monetary controls. Let i_c be the monetary

---

[3] The idea of reverse-signaling should be familiar from Sargent and Wallace (1981). In their model, tight money signals more money growth in the future because of a fiscal policy that relies on monetization. Here, political problems relating to output and unemployment are perhaps more relevant than monetization, but the expectational argument is similar.

control (usually an interest rate, but not necessarily) and let $i_{nom} = i_{safe} + DP$ be a money market interest rate, which can be decomposed into a safe rate i_{safe} and a default premium DP. Monetary policy may affect both i_{safe} and (as emphasized by the revisionists) DP.

Second, uncovered interest rate parity calls for equal expected returns on domestic and foreign investments – that is, a match of expected depreciation and the interest rate differential between *safe* rates. Any mismatch would be interpreted as a currency risk premium CP, so that

$$i_{safe} - i^*_{safe} = E^e_{nom} - E_{nom} + CP \tag{1}$$

where E_{nom} and E^e_{nom} are the current and expected future exchange rates (nominal, in logs) and i^*_{safe} is the foreign safe interest rate. If one substitutes i_{nom} for the unobserved i_{safe} and assumes that the foreign nominal rate is a safe rate (e.g., $i^*_{safe} = i^*_{nom} = $ U.S. Treasury bill rate), one obtains

$$i_{nom} - i^*_{nom} = E^e_{nom} - E_{nom} + CP + DP \tag{2}$$

Note that equation (2) involves nominal variables, while Gould and Kamin work with real variables, that equation (2) includes two different risk premiums, and that neither E^e_{nom} nor the risk premiums are directly observable.

Gould and Kamin's equation (1) can be obtained from equation (2) above by subtracting the expected inflation differential $p^e - p^{e*}$ on both sides. This yields

$$(i_{nom} - p^e) - (i^*_{nom} - p^{e*}) = E^e_{real} - E_{real} + (CP + DP) \tag{3}$$

where E^e_{real} and E_{real} are the current and expected real exchange rates. Going from nominal to real variables strikes me as counterproductive, however, because equation (3) includes even more unobservables than equation (2).

In equation (2) above, we observe i_{nom}, i^*_{nom}, and E_{nom}. If we estimated a time-series model for E^e_{nom} (like Gould and Kamin's model for E^e_{real}), we could infer the total risk premium $CP + DP$. I have little confidence in such estimates, however, because average realized exchange rates over a short, one-year sample may be far from investors *ex-ante* expectations. Any "peso problem" would be interpreted as a risk premium. If one works with inflation-adjusted data, these problems become worse because errors in estimating expected inflation will further contaminate the measured risk premium.

Kamin and Gould use 13-week centered averages of actual inflation as a proxy for expected inflation. This approach is odd, because it uses information about future inflation that is unavailable to investors. If uncertainty about the postcrisis price level is a major source of uncertainty, as I have argued above, then assuming away this uncertainty assumes away much of the investors' decision problem.

What then is the impact of a change in the monetary control i_c on the current exchange rate? Equation (2) suggests four channels of influence, which are highlighted below:

$$i_{\text{safe}}(i_c) + DP(i_c) - i_{\text{nom}}^* = i_{\text{nom}}(i_c) - i_{\text{nom}}^*$$
$$= E_{\text{nom}}^e(i_c) - E_{\text{nom}} + DP(i_c) + CP(i_c) \qquad (4)$$

First, monetary policy (the control i_c) can raise i_{safe}, the domestic safe rate. This is a basic orthodox channel, saying that higher domestic interest rates produce an appreciation (reduce E_{nom}). Second, i_c may have an impact on the default premium DP. For given i_{safe}, this effect cancels out, however. Hence, linkages between tight money and domestic default risk cannot provide a foundation for revisionist claims. Third, monetary policy may have an impact on the currency premium CP. However, to identify this impact, one would have to distinguish it from an impact of i_c on the expected exchange rate itself; this is difficult.

Last but not least, i_c may affect the expected future exchange rate E_{nom}^e. As explained above, this effect may be huge and it can go in either direction, depending on how investors interpret the signal produced by a change in i_c. Gould and Kamin apparently associate the expected exchange rate effect with the revisionist view (i.e., they assume $dE^e/di > 0$). This association is part of the controversy, however. Orthodox theory would claim that tight money now signals tight money in the future and should therefore produce an appreciation ($dE^e/di < 0$). Overall, the combined impact of i_c on the exchange rate is ambiguous, which makes it an empirical question.

QUESTIONS ABOUT THE EMPIRICAL ANALYSIS

I am reluctant to complain too much about the empirics, because the empirical task is rather difficult and I applaud the attempt. Given the maintained hypothesis of crises being special, the number of observations is limited; and the analysis must rely on market interest rates to identify policy changes; that is, it uses i_{nom} as a proxy for the monetary control i_c. Still, I have three concerns.

First, why do the complicated inflation adjustments? I am particularly troubled by the centered averages used to proxy expected inflation, because the process uses advance information not available to agents at the time. In time-series regressions, such proxies may produce spurious lead–lag relationships.

Second, I wonder to what extent the analysis of lead–lag patterns and Granger causality is consistent with efficient markets. If monetary policy changes, all the relevant effects should be contemporaneous. Hence, I am not surprised about the lack of Granger causality. Similarly, I am not surprised about the lack of significant dynamic linkages in Tables 11.4a and 11.5a. Contemporaneous linkages unfortunately require more assumptions about causality. For future research, it would extremely valuable if one could find a policy indicator that one can plausibly treat as exogenous. If all else fails, perhaps a study of policy statements during crisis periods would help, say, along the lines of Romer and Romer (1989).

Third, what is country risk? In the chapter, country risk is proxied by the interest rate spreads between dollar-denominated Asian government bonds and U.S. government bonds. This spread captures a very different risk than the currency premium CP in equations (2)–(4), and it may be more correlated with the default risk DP than with CP. The use of stock market data, on the other hand, is an excellent idea, especially if the political support for tight money is important. A collapse of the stock market may be a good signal that tight money is not politically sustainable. Stock prices are volatile, however, so it is not surprising that the null hypothesis of no effect is difficult to reject.

Overall, my reading of the empirical findings is perhaps more positive than the authors conclusions. Yes, the results are largely negative as measured by statistical significance, but this is not surprising. After all, the sample period is short, and policy in the midst of a crisis is presumably volatile and erratic. Hence, short-term movements in short-term interest rates should not have much power to signal future monetary policy. They should not have a large impact on the exchange rate in either direction, unless accompanied by other signals suggesting that the changes are permanent. The data appear to be consistent with this intuition.

From this perspective, the chapter prepares the ground for the next big challenge: Suppose we agree that credibility is important and that interest rates changes have little effect in a crisis. Then what else can policymakers do to build investor confidence about monetary stability?

REFERENCES

Romer, Christina and David Romer (1989). "Does Monetary Policy Matter? A New Test in the Spirit of Friedman and Schwartz," *NBER Macroeconomics Annual, 1989* **4**:121–170.
Sargent Thomas and Neil Wallace (1981). "Some Unpleasant Monetarist Arithmetic," *Federal Reserve Bank of Minneapolis Quarterly Review* **5**:1–17.

12

Capital Controls during Financial Crises

The Cases of Malaysia and Thailand

Hali J. Edison and Carmen M. Reinhart

12.1 INTRODUCTION

In the 1990s, net capital inflows to developing countries grew substantially, particularly to those countries that had liberalized their capital accounts. As countries experienced surges in capital flows, the debate on how to manage these surges became a pressing policy topic. Capital controls, when they were discussed at all, were examined in the context of liberalizing restrictions on capital outflows, or in terms of which types of capital inflows should be taxed. However, with the most recent wave of financial market turbulence there has been a shift in the debate on capital controls. The types of controls that were contemplated or used during the recent crises were very different from the measures introduced during the inflow phase of the capital flow cycle (see Reinhart and Smith, 1998). These types of controls are applied mainly to outflows and are viewed as "last resort" measures as opposed to controls being applied to inflows which were interpreted as "prudential."

Controls on capital outflows have been advocated as a way of dealing with financial and currency crises. These controls can take a number of forms: restrictions on capital account transactions including taxes on funds remitted abroad, outright prohibition of funds' transfers, dual exchange rates, and outright prohibition of cross-border movement of funds.[1] The idea behind these measures is that they help slow down the

The authors wish to thank Vincent Reinhart for very helpful comments and suggestions. We also thank Gary Lee and Frank Warnock for providing us the U.S. Treasury International Capital Reports data and Rafael Romeu, Hayden Smith, and Michael Sharkey for excellent research assistance.

[1] The measures may also be more subtle. For instance, in early 1999, Brazil increased the share of a local financial firm's portfolio that must be held in domestic sovereign bonds (for details see Edison and Reinhart, 1999).

drainage of international reserves and capital outflows and give the authorities time to implement corrective policies. Paul Krugman (1998) has argued that countries facing major crisis might benefit from temporary imposition of controls on outflows, by giving the country the time to lower their domestic interest rates and put into place a pro-growth package.[2] Malaysia and, for a short while, Thailand followed this path in 1997–1999.

The initial reaction to the imposition of controls, especially for Malaysia, was quite negative. Subsequently, however, Malaysia seems to have fared reasonably well – although not as well as Korea, which did not introduce new restrictions on capital movements. Furthermore, institutional investors appear to have short memories, because Malaysia's controls do not seem to have reduced investors' appetite for returning to Malaysian capital markets once controls were eased. To quote a recent article on Malaysia:

Stocks of companies that were sold off two years ago and criticized for crony capitalist practices are being snapped up by foreign buyers at a fevered pace. Most companies have done little to address the flaws that foreign investors decried at the time. Almost all companies are under the same management as they were then.

Thomas Fuller, *International Herald Tribune, Paris*, January 18, 2000.

Not surprisingly, the use of such "market unfriendly" measures in times of stress is receiving considerable attention among academic and policy circles. The purpose of this study is to examine systematically two crisis-capital control episodes – Malaysia 1998–1999 and Thailand 1997 – in greater detail. We aim to assess the extent to which the capital controls were effective and successful in delivering some of the outcomes that motivated their inception in the first place.

For our case studies, we look at two types of data. First, we study monthly data. We focus on the movement of foreign exchange reserves and capital flows. In addition, we examine data from the United States International Capital Reports (TIC) to investigate how U.S. portfolio flows changed in the aftermath of controls. This data spans January 1988 to March 1999. Second, we examine daily data covering the period January 1996 through July 23, 1999 for key financial variables including: interest rates, equity market returns, exchange rate changes, domestic-foreign interest rate differentials, and bid–ask spreads on foreign exchange.

---

[2] For example, after the introduction of capital controls in Malaysia, other measures were introduced to stimulate the economy and reduce the burden of banks.

We employ a variety of empirical tests to attempt to examine the effectiveness of capital controls. For the monthly data, we test for differences in basic descriptive statistics in the capital control and no control periods. For the daily data, we also consider tests for the equality of moments and changes in persistence to address changes in behavior of key financial variables. In addition, we test for changes in cross-border volatility using GARCH tests for the effects of controls on volatility, as in Edwards (1998).

There are, of course, several limitations and concerns with the kind of analysis we undertake. First, results are episode-specific, not "stylized facts." Second, given that these kinds of controls are introduced during periods of turbulence, it is particularly difficult to separate what is attributable to the controls and what is due to the financial crisis per se. For instance, a generalized withdrawal from risk-taking (as what followed the Russia/LTCM episode in the fall of 1998) can have similar implications and outcomes as the introduction of capital controls (see Kaminsky and Reinhart, 2000). Namely, international flows dry up, spreads widen, volatility in asset markets increases, and so on. In addition, our empirical methodology assumes linearities in relationships, which may break down during periods of extreme market stress – an issue that is highlighted in multiple-equilibria crises models. These caveats apply especially to analysis of the daily data but also to the monthly data we consider as well.

With these caveats in mind, our key empirical findings are summarized below. First, the monthly data on foreign reserves and capital flows highlight some of the differences in the Malaysian and Thai experiences with capital controls. The monthly results suggest that in Malaysia, economic relationships changed, while in Thailand, things seemed to continue to get worse. For example, foreign exchange reserves continued to fall during the period of capital controls in Thailand, while they increased immediately following the imposition of controls in Malaysia.[3]

Second, we find that interest rates were less variable in both Malaysia and Thailand following the introduction of controls, but the level was lower only in Malaysia during the control period. Stock returns tended to be more variable following the introduction of capital controls – especially so in the case of Thailand – consistent with the view that more of the burden of adjustment falls on prices when the change in quantities is restricted. The exchange rate was more stable during the control period for Malaysia, while it was more variable for Thailand.

---

[3] As shown in Kaminsky, Lyons, and Schmukler (2000) and reproduced here, however, mutual fund flows to Malaysia turn sharply negative after the introduction of capital controls.

Third, as to the side effects of capital controls, we find that foreign exchange bid–ask spreads were uniformly wider and more variable during the control periods. Also, onshore–offshore interest rate spreads widened and become more volatile following the introduction of controls.

Fourth, our results suggest that there is little evidence that capital controls were effective in reducing volatility spillovers. In the case of Malaysia, the results suggested that capital controls dampened the spillover, but it did not eliminate the spillover, although this result was not robust across all model specifications.

The remainder of the paper is organized as follows. The next section discusses the reasons why countries might apply controls and also discusses the theoretical predictions of the effects of those controls. Section 12.3 describes the measures and their chronology in Malaysia and Thailand. The following two sections examine the effectiveness of capital controls, describing empirical tests performed, their outcomes, and their implications. First, we focus on monthly data, examining capital flows and other macroeconomic indicators. Then we consider daily data, assessing financial variables including interest rates, equity returns, and exchange rate changes. The final section discusses possible extensions and policy implications of the analysis.

12.2 THEORETICAL PREDICTIONS OF THE EFFECTS OF CONTROLS

In this section we first review some of the reasons most often voiced by policy makers for resorting to capital controls during periods of turbulence. Knowing what the stated expectations from the policy change are in the first place is essential to assess whether the policy was "effective" or "successful." Because many of these expectations are based on an implicit model, we then proceed to summarize the implications of capital controls for some of the variables of interest.

12.2.1 Reasons for Resorting to Capital Controls during Crisis Periods

The first line of defense by central banks dealing with speculative attacks on their currencies is usually to sell off their holdings of foreign exchange. However, central bank holdings of foreign exchange are often inadequate to support the currency; and even if the initial stock is high by international standards, recurring runs on the currency can quickly deplete the initial war chest. Not surprisingly, policymakers will often cite the need to stem the drain on foreign exchange reserves as a motivation for introducing capital controls during periods of extreme market stress.

Also central banks can (and often do) react to speculative pressures by raising interest rates, occasionally to prohibitively high levels. However, given the consequences of high interest rates on economic activity and debt servicing costs, this policy alternative is not particularly appealing either – especially if the pressures persist over an extended period and the domestic financial system is weak. Hence, capital controls are seen as a course of action that would enable the monetary authorities to maintain lower (and more stable) interest rates than would be the case under free capital mobility – especially if credibility has been lost. More generally, controls can (if they are effective) fulfill the authorities' desire to regain autonomy in monetary policy – without floating the exchange rate.

Because volatile international bond and equity portfolio flows are frequently viewed as a destabilizing force in asset markets and, more generally, in the financial system, another reason that is often cited for introducing controls is the desire to reduce the volatility in asset prices.

12.2.2 Theoretical Priors

The Mundellian trinity suggests that fixed (or quasi-fixed) exchange rates, independent monetary policy, and perfect capital mobility cannot be achieved simultaneously. Capital controls are a way of allowing the authorities to retain simultaneous control over the interest rate and the exchange rate. Capital controls may be particularly appealing when the authorities are reluctant to allow the exchange rate to float freely, which is the case in most emerging markets (EMs) (see Calvo and Reinhart, 1999). Fear of floating may arise for a variety of reasons, including the dollarization of liabilities – but for the purposes at hand, however, those reasons are not central to our analysis. The important point for our analysis is that controls introduce a systematic wedge between domestic and foreign interest rates. As uncovered interest rate parity breaks down, the domestic policy interest rate (from the vantage point of a small open economy) need not follow international interest rates.[4] In principle, variation in that wedge can be introduced by the authorities to influence the exchange rate systematically. One example of this is the theoretical model of Reinhart and Reinhart (1998), who trace out the effects of one of the simplest forms of capital controls – a reserve requirement. Depending on the degree of competition among financial intermediaries, Reinhart and Reinhart show that the wedge between foreign and

---

[4] Of course, imperfect asset substitutability and a time-varying risk premium are sufficient to explain a breakdown of uncovered interest parity – even in the absence of capital controls.

domestic interest rates induced by the reserve requirement influences the response of the exchange rate and the real economy to shocks.

The potential consequences of capital controls become even more pervasive in models that provide an important role for asset stocks in affecting an economy. The general mechanism at work is that, if the flow of capital is restricted in any way, then the burden of adjustment in asset markets falls more on prices. Calvo and Rodriguez (1979) first showed how sluggishness in the flow of international assets can generate overshooting of the exchange rate. Reinhart (2000) broadened that model by incorporating equity prices and introducing three different kinds of restrictions on capital flows. The implication in Reinhart's framework is that equity price volatility should increase with the imposition of controls. A shock to the desired portfolio allocation generally triggers adjustments to both asset quantities and prices. Capital controls shift more of that adjustment toward prices and, to the extent that they introduce interest rate wedges, may also alter the relationship between asset prices and the policy rate.

Edison and Reinhart (1999) provide details about the predictions of theory for a host of financial variables. Some of the key predictions are as follows:

- The declines in foreign exchange reserves and capital outflows should both either stop or reverse themselves.
- The level of domestic interest rates should decline as high interest rates are no longer necessary to prevent capital outflows. There should also be a decline in interest rate volatility.
- The implications of a decline in market liquidity – whether owing to a capital control or a generalized withdrawal from risk taking – are also straightforward. Bid–ask spreads in the market(s) where liquidity has diminished should widen and become more volatile.

12.3 THE CONTROL EPISODES

In this section we describe the timing and nature of the selected capital control episodes as well as some of the more relevant events surrounding the introduction and lifting of these measures.

12.3.1 The Policy Measures and Chronology of Events

The capital control episodes that we analyze are: Thailand (May 14, 1997–January 30, 1998) and Malaysia (September 1, 1998 to present). The chronology of the episodes and further details of the measures are summarized in Table 12.1. We briefly discuss these episodes below.

Table 12.1. A Chronology of Key Events

Episode and Country	Date	Key Events
Thailand, Asian crisis, 1997–1998	May 14, 1997	Bank of Thailand (BOT) introduces restrictions on capital account transactions.
	May 28	BOT limits outright forward transactions.
	June 2	BOT introduces additional measures to limit capital flows.
	June 10	Baht proceeds from sales of stocks required to be converted at the onshore exchange rate. Additional controls are introduced.
	June 18	The onshore–offshore interest rate differential hits a peak at 639 percent.
	July 2	BOT introduces a two-tier exchange rate. Thai baht is devalued.
	September 23	Additional controls on invisible and current account transactions are introduced.
	January 7, 1998	Proceeds on exports and invisible transactions and current account transfers must be surrendered after 7 days (instead of 15 days).
	January 30, 1998	BOT ends two-tier exchange rate.
	February 3, 1998	The stock market suffers its largest one-day decline (9.5 percent).
Malaysia, Asian crisis, 1997–1998	July 14, 1997	Interest rates peak.
	January 5, 1998	Ringgit suffers its largest daily decline (7.5 percent) against the dollar.
	September 1, 1998	Exchange controls introduced.
	September 2, 1998	Exchange rate is fixed.
	September 7, 1998	The stock market suffers its largest one-day decline (down 22 percent).
	February 4, 1999	Exchange controls modified. New rule introduced to replace one-year holding period rule for portfolio capital. Under the new rules, a declining scale of exit levies replaced the 12-month holding restriction on repatriation of portfolio capital.

Source: News and IMF reports.

In the face of speculative attacks, the Thai authorities imposed capital controls in May 1997. The goal of these controls was to stabilize the foreign exchange market as speculative pressure continued to mount. The Bank of Thailand was concerned that using an interest rate defense as a means to defend the baht would have adverse effects on economic activity and the banking system. The capital control measures put in place were aimed at closing the channels for speculation, creating a two-tiered currency market. This system was aimed at denying speculators access to funds. The measures they used were not as sweeping as those that Malaysia subsequently put in place. However, the controls initially seemed to work as offshore interest rates rose above the domestic rates. The baht was floated on July 2, 1997, and controls were left in place until January 30, 1998.

In September 1998 the Malaysian authorities imposed a number of administrative exchange and capital control measures aimed at containing ringgit speculation and the outflow of capital. The measures sought to increase monetary independence and insulate the economy from potential shocks from the global economy, such as Russia and LTCM. The Malaysian authorities were concerned that domestic interest rates would have to be kept unusually high for long periods of time, producing unhelpful effects on economic activity and the banking system.[5] Hence in September they closed all channels for the transfer of ringgit abroad and required repatriation of ringgit held abroad to Malaysia. In addition they blocked the repatriation of portfolio capital held by nonresidents for 12 months, and imposed restrictions on transfer of capital by residents. These controls were supported by additional measures to eliminate loopholes. On February 4, 1999, the 12-month holding restriction was replaced with a declining scale of exit levies.

There are two obvious differences between the Thai and Malaysian experience. The first difference is that Thailand was undergoing speculative attacks and tried to use capital controls as a defense mechanism. In contrast, Malaysia was not undergoing extreme speculative pressure when they applied their controls. The second difference is that the Malaysian controls were broad and attempted to eliminate all obvious loopholes. In contrast, the controls Thailand put into place, at least in hindsight, were not comprehensive enough to eliminate the speculative pressure on the baht.

---

[5] It is important to consider the highly leveraged condition of the Malaysian economy at this time, with bank loan to GDP ratios of about 160 percent.

12.4 THE EFFECTIVENESS OF CONTROLS: IMPACT ON CAPITAL FLOWS

In this section we attempt to describe broadly the economic situation prior to the application of capital controls and the subsequent developments, considering data on economic activity, foreign exchange reserves, interest rates, and exchange rates. In addition, we examine monthly capital flow data, using data from the U.S. International Capital Transaction Report; these data capture bilateral U.S. capital flows with Malaysia and Thailand. The data on mutual fund flows are taken from a broader study of the patterns and determinants of these flows by Kaminsky, Lyons, and Schmukler (2000).

12.4.1 Economic Performance

There are a limited number of tests that one can use to analyze the monthly data because there are too few observations during the period of controls in both cases. However, a quick look at some graphs and descriptive statistics illustrates the vast differences in the results that capital controls appear to have yielded in Malaysia and Thailand.

Figure 12.1 shows plots of data on industrial production, foreign exchange reserves, interest rates, and the exchange rate for Malaysia. After September 1998, industrial production increased more than 8 percent, despite dropping significantly after controls were initially applied. Foreign exchange reserves rose steadily from $20 billion in late August 1998 to $27 billion in April 1999. Interest rates fell to below precrisis levels: In 1997, interest rates averaged just over 7 percent; in June 1999 these same 1-month interest rates were slightly more than 3 percent. In addition, the exchange rate that had started depreciating in July 1997 was stabilized by the authorities, pegging the rate against the dollar. Taken by themselves, these facts suggest that the capital controls may have helped Malaysia insulate its economy. Yet, the behavior of interest rates and economic activity of the other crisis-hit countries, Korea and Thailand, suggests that these countries also experienced improved economic performance around the same time as Malaysia. It is not clear whether capital controls contributed to improving Malaysia's performance. At a minimum, this finding suggests that capital controls did not harm Malaysia, as some critics of the measures feared. However, as Figure 12.2 (taken from Kaminsky, Lyons, and Schmukler, 2000) suggests, in the month of September 1998 (labeled "After the Russian Crisis," which began on August 17, 1998) Malaysia posted record outflows among the countries in the sample, casting a lukewarm reading on the success of the controls.

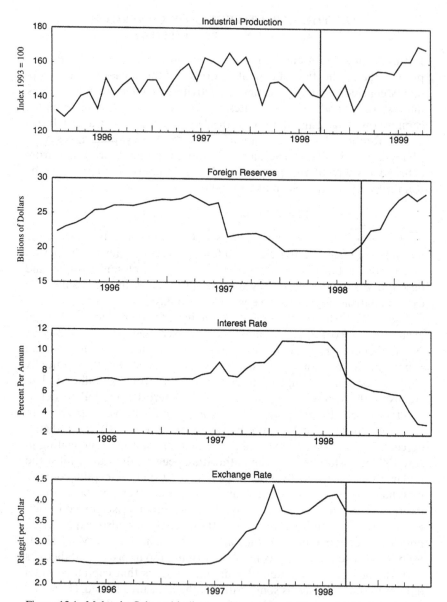

Figure 12.1. Malaysia: Selected indicators. (*Source*: Bank Negara Malaysia website.)

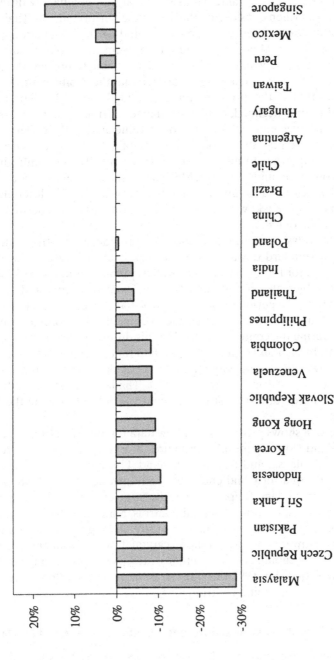

Figure 12.2. Mutual fund flows: Global spillovers. (*Source:* Kaminsky, Lyons, and Schmukler, 2000.) *Note:* The Russian crisis began August 1998. Mutual fund flows are the average net buying/selling (as percentage of the end of the preceding quarter holdings) in the two quarters following the outbreak of the crisis, relative to the sample average.

Figure 12.3 gives the same data for Thailand. A completely different story emerges when considering the economic performance of Thailand, following its use of capital controls. As noted earlier, Thailand applied capital controls in May 1997, hoping to prevent a full-blown currency crisis. In contrast to Malaysia, Thailand was not able to prevent the crisis and in fact some policymakers have argued that the capital controls may have exacerbated the problem for Thailand. Figure 12.3 shows that industrial output declined, foreign exchange reserves fell, interest rates rose, and the exchange rate lost half of its value against the dollar. These observations suggest that capital controls failed to stop the currency crisis. It is important to note, however, that while Thailand introduced the controls in the midst of crisis, Malaysia's controls were introduced at a time in which financial markets had begun to settle. This difference in timing may also be a key factor in explaining the difference between the two countries' outcomes.

The top rows of Tables 12.2 and 12.3 provide descriptive statistics (mean and standard deviations) for foreign exchange reserve levels in Malaysia and for foreign reserves as well as private capital flows in Thailand. The tables also report tests for the equality of first and second moments between period of capital control and free capital mobility. For Malaysia (Table 12.2) we find that the average level of foreign reserves is higher during the control episode, but this difference is not statistically significant. In Thailand (Table 12.3), we find that foreign reserves are, on average, lower during the capital controls period and that outflows are higher and more variable. The results for Thailand are statistically significant and are quite suggestive that controls did not insulate the Thai economy.

Figure 12.4 shows private capital flow data for Malaysia (upper panel) and Thailand (lower panel). Both figures are plotted in local currency: ringgit for Malaysia and baht for Thailand. Unfortunately, the data for Malaysia are quarterly and end with the fourth quarter of 1998, owing to long reporting lags. It appears that the large capital outflows stopped following the application of capital controls. Note that there was also a huge capital outflow the third quarter of 1997, owing to the general crisis in Asia. The lower panel, which shows capital flows for Thailand, suggests that Thailand's capital controls were not effective in preventing outflows of capital. From May 1997 through the crisis, capital outflows increased despite the use of capital controls.

12.4.2 Capital Flows to and from the United States: The TIC Data

In this section we employ a database on U.S. capital flows to and from Malaysia and Thailand, starting in January 1988 and ending in March

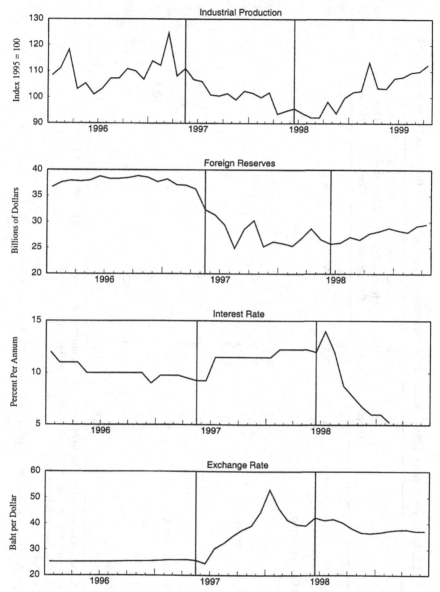

Figure 12.3. Thailand: Selected indicators. (*Source*: Bank of Thailand website.)

Table 12.2. Malaysia, January 1988 to March 1999: Descriptive Statistics for Monthly Data (in millions US $)

Variable	Mean, No Controls	Mean, Control Period	Equality of Means t-Test Probability	Standard Deviation, No Controls	Standard Deviation, Controls	Equality of Variance Test[a]
Foreign reserve level[b]	23.5	24.9	0.26	2.9	2.7	0.85
Private capital inflows	NA	NA	NA	NA	NA	NA
U.S. TIC Bilateral Capital Flows:						
Gross Flows						
All	2,144.5	508	0.05*	2,214.6	242.5	0.003*
All bonds	1,838.9	430.9	0.07**	2,054.3	212.2	0.03*
U.S. private and foreign bonds	142.3	49.1	0.29	227.4	49.5	0.23
Equity	327.8	124.3	0.1**	325.0	51.7	0.08**
Net Flows						
All	−58.8	99.2	0.3	393.2	234.8	0.9
All bonds	−45.9	74.0	0.4	395.2	193.4	0.9
U.S. private and foreign bonds	−37.5	−6.6	0.7	211.9	38.2	0.7
Equity	−17.5	19.4	0.2	66.4	62.7	0.4
Malaysian Equity Outflow						
Equity	155.1	71.9	0.2	159.4	56.3	0.08**
Malaysian Equity Inflow						
Equity	172.6	52.4	0.07**	172.1	11.5	0.19

Notes: Capital control period is September 1998 to March 1999; no-controls period is period prior to September 1998.
* denotes significant at 5 percent level and ** denotes significant at the 10 percent level.
[a] Reported test is based on Siegel–Tukey test.
[b] In billions of U.S. dollars.

Source: Bank Negara Malaysia, U.S. Treasury International Capital (TIC) Transaction Report.

Table 12.3. Thailand, January 1988 to March 1999: Descriptive Statistics for Monthly Capital Flow Data (in millions of U.S. dollars)

Variable	Mean, No Controls	Mean, Control Period	Equality in Means t-Test Probability	Standard Deviation, No Controls	Standard Deviation, Controls	Equality in Variance Test[a]
Foreign reserve level[b]	32.8	28.2	0.02*	5.3	2.8	0.5
Private capital inflows	11,907	−54,366	0.00*	36,776	71,554	0.01*
U.S. TIC Bilateral Capital Flows:						
Gross Flows						
All	1,629.4	3,243.9	0.00*	1,566.4	1,672.4	0.51
All bonds	1,577.2	3,133.8	0.00*	1,560.0	1,660.3	0.52
U.S. private and foreign bonds	11.1	25.7	0.00*	11.6	12.7	0.03*
Equity	55.7	111.5	0.09**	88.7	175.2	0.46
Net Flows						
All	476.9	585.6	0.66	711.3	884.9	0.00*
All bonds	490.3	672.4	0.47	717.6	891.8	0.00*
U.S. private and foreign bonds	1.3	−1.3	0.3	7.2	7.4	0.9
Equity	−12.4	−84.8	0.01*	79.7	161.8	0.41
Thailand Equity Outflow						
Equity	21.6	13.3	0.43	31.2	14.3	0.48
Thailand Equity Inflow						
Equity	34.0	98.2	0.03*	78.3	168.1	0.72

Notes: Capital control period is May 1997 to January 1998; no-controls period is January 1988 to April 1997 and February 1998 to March 1999.
* denotes significant at 5 percent level and ** denotes significant at the 10 percent level.
[a] Reported test is based on Siegel–Tukey test.
[b] In billions of U.S. dollars.

Source: Bank of Thailand, U.S. Treasury International Capital (TIC) Transaction Report.

441

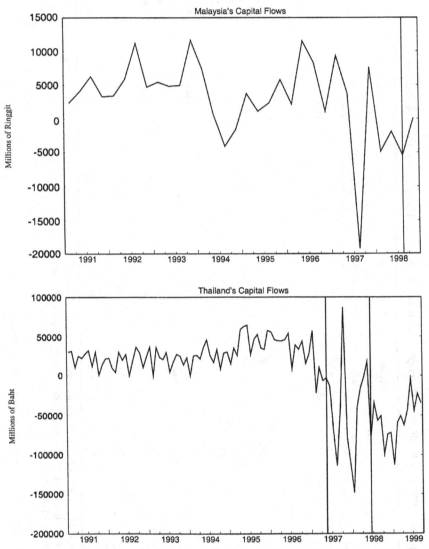

Figure 12.4. Capital flows for Malaysia and Thailand. (*Source*: Bank Negara Malaysia and Bank of Thailand websites.)

1999. The frequency of the data is monthly, and these times series were constructed using the International Capital Reports of the U.S. Treasury Department. We consider four broad categories of flows in the capital account: equity flows, U.S. private and foreign bond flows, all bond flows (including official U.S. flows), and total flows. We construct both gross and net flows. Many studies seem to use net measures for equity and gross measures for bond flows. Gross bond flow measures tend to be used to abstract from the effect of sterilization policy actions and other types of reserve operations.

Once again we employ descriptive statistics in analyzing the data. The lower panels of Tables 12.2 and 12.3 report the results for Malaysia and Thailand, respectively. In the case of Malaysia, controls in general do not seem to be associated with lower capital flows to/from the United States. There is some indication that gross bond flows and especially equity flows were lower during the period of capital controls, but most of the time this difference was not statistically significant. This result might arise in part because the data focus exclusively on flows to and from the United States, which was not heavily involved in Malaysia, and in part because the period prior to the employment of controls lead to a significant amount of capital outflow and volatility.

The results for Thailand are suggestive that, if anything, capital flows increased during the period of capital controls. For example, gross flows of all bonds nearly doubled during the control period. These flows rose on average from $1.5 billion to over $3 billion during the controls period. (It should be noted, however, that these data include official flows as a result of the intervention in the foreign exchange market by the Bank of Thailand.) Despite the fact that the numbers are not statistically significant, the results consistently show that the level and the variability of these flows increased during the control episode.

Overall, our examination of the monthly data suggests that the experiences of Malaysia and Thailand were quite different. In the next section we analyze their experiences further using daily financial data.

12.5 THE EFFECTIVENESS OF CONTROLS: EVIDENCE FROM DAILY FINANCIAL DATA

In this section we employ an eclectic variety of tests to examine whether the periods when capital controls are in place are different. First, we examine the movement of these data and look at changes in mean, variance, and persistence. We then turn our attention to testing for volatility spillovers.

12.5.1 Interest Rates, Stock Returns, and Exchange Rates during Control and Crisis Periods

In Section 12.2 we provided a sketch of what theory predicts as regards the behavior of selected key financial variables following the introduction of measures that curtail international capital movements. In this section we confront those predictions with the data from the recent episodes for Malaysia and Thailand. We examine the behavior of daily interest rates and changes in interest rates, stock returns, exchange rate changes, bid–ask spreads on foreign exchange, domestic–foreign interest rate differentials, and onshore–offshore interest rate differentials (where relevant).

For each of these time series we provide descriptive statistics (means and standard deviations) and test for the equality of first and second moments between the capital control and free capital mobility periods. A correlogram for the individual subperiods is also used to assess whether the persistence of shocks changes as a result of the change in policy. We compare the crisis and tranquil periods with the aim of assessing the extent to which observed changes in the key variables may be attributed to the crisis rather than the capital controls. Tables 12.4 and 12.5 report the results for each country.

In the case of Malaysia (Table 12.4), controls seem to be associated with the kind of changes one would expect *a priori* if the controls were effective. The interest rate declines, and its level becomes more stable and persistent. Domestic–foreign interest rate spreads become lower and less variable. This holds for the spreads based on three, six, and twelve months. Similarly, the exchange rate also becomes more stable (the ringgit was pegged to the U.S. dollar on September 2, 1998). However, as the burden of adjustment in asset markets falls more on prices than on quantities, equity prices become more volatile. Bid–ask spreads in the foreign exchange market widen and became more volatile, reflecting reduced market liquidity.

The upper panel of Figure 12.5 shows that bid–ask spreads are indeed more volatile, compared to spreads prior to the flotation of the Thai baht in July 1997. However, starting in July 1997, there was a sharp widening of spreads which continued to deteriorate until controls were applied. With the application of capital controls, the large increase in volatility brought on by the region's financial crisis diminished, but volatility remained above precrisis levels.

The results for the pre- and postcontrol comparisons for Thailand (Table 12.5) are somewhat different from those we saw for Malaysia. In both countries the volatility of interest rates declines during the control episode, but in Thailand the level of interest rates rises. While Thai domestic–foreign interest rate spreads widen, they do not become more volatile. As in Malaysia, stock returns tend to be more variable following the introduction of capital controls consistent with the view that more of the burdens of adjustment fall on prices when the change in

Table 12.4. Malaysia, January 1, 1996 to July 23, 1999: Descriptive Statistics for Daily Data

Variable	Mean, No Controls	Mean, Control Period	Equality of Means t-Test Probability	Standard Deviation, No Controls	Standard Deviation, Control Period	Equality of Variance Test[a]	Auto-correlation, No Controls	Auto-correlation, Control Period
Interest rate	8.328	5.720	0.000*	1.549	1.452	0.000*	0.935	0.956
Change in interest rate	0.121	−0.545	0.004*	0.386	0.140	0.157	0.212	0.219
Domestic–foreign interest rate spread: 3-month	3.192	1.473	0.000*	1.490	1.469	0.002*	0.912	0.934
Domestic–foreign interest rate spread: 6-month	3.163	1.491	0.000*	1.586	1.463	0.000*	0.914	0.940
Domestic–foreign interest rate spread: 12-month	3.045	1.541	0.000*	1.699	1.493	0.000*	0.925	0.942
Stock returns	−0.194	0.652	0.000*	2.089	3.385	0.000*	−0.080	0.133
Exchange rate changes	0.064	−0.011	0.405	1.241	0.166	0.000*	−0.011	0.049
Bid–ask spread	−0.006	−0.008	0.012*	0.015	0.006	0.000*	0.153	0.275

[a] Siegel–Tukey test is reported. Other test results are available from the authors upon request.

* denotes significant at 5 percent level.

Source: Bloomberg.

Table 12.5. Thailand, January 1, 1996 to July 23, 1999: Descriptive Statistics for Daily Data

Variable	Mean, No Controls	Mean, Control Period	Equality of Means t-Test Probability	Standard Deviation, No Controls	Standard Deviation, Control Period	Equality of Variance Test[a]	Auto-correlation, No Controls	Auto-correlation, Control Period
Interest rate	12.460	20.920	0.000*	5.779	3.829	0.000*	0.930	0.912
Change in interest rate	−0.0318	0.073	0.067**	0.600	0.818	0.000*	−0.061	0.202
Domestic–foreign interest rate spread: 1-month	7.704	15.941	0.000*	5.609	3.804	0.075**		
Stock returns	−0.114	0.019	0.510	2.153	2.923	0.000*	0.115	0.258
Exchange rate changes	−0.047	0.361	0.000*	0.828	2.623	0.000*	0.047	−0.123
Bid-ask spread	−0.074	−0.313	0.000*	0.111	0.978	0.033*	0.318	0.474
Onshore-offshore interest rate spreads								
Overnight	1.336	16.730	0.000*	4.878	85.488	0.000*	0.332	0.872
Weekly	3.978	17.004	0.000*	7.900	58.323	0.000*	0.725	0.882
One-month	4.381	11.633	0.000*	6.420	22.955	0.000*	0.806	0.869
Three-month	4.067	6.988	0.000*	4.923	6.937	0.021*	0.845	0.867
Six-month	3.655	5.097	0.035*	7.973	6.136	0.000*	0.158	0.850
Twelve-month	2.807	3.916	0.000*	2.978	3.752	0.000*	0.882	0.813

[a] Siegel–Tukey test is reported. Other test results are available from the authors upon request.

* denotes significant at 5 percent level, and ** denotes significant at 10 percent level.

Source: Bank of Thailand and Bloomberg.

446

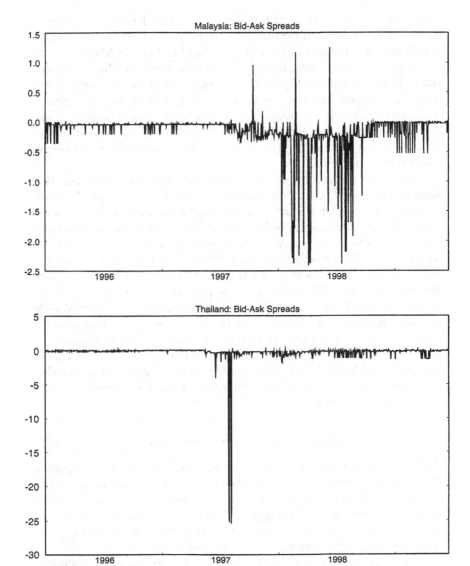

Figure 12.5. Bid–ask spreads for Malaysia and Thailand. (*Source*: Bloomberg.) *Note*: Daily bid–ask spread over midpoint spot rate (in percent).

quantities is restricted. We also see an increase in Thai exchange rate variability during the control period. Both Table 12.5 and the lower panel of Figure 12.5 show that the bid–ask spread in the foreign exchange market widens and that volatility increases after Thailand applied capital controls, similarly to what occurs in Malaysia.

Figure 12.6 plots Thai onshore–offshore interest rates at the one-month and three-month horizon. The onshore and offshore rates were for all practical purposes identical prior to May 1997. In May the Thai authorities imposed controls on capital transactions, shielding domestic interest rates. Initially, as Figure 12.6 shows, the controls effectively drove a wedge between onshore and offshore interest rates. The differential widened significantly and became more variable as controls squeezed liquidity in the offshore market. However, the segmentation of the market, especially after the baht floated, disappeared as the differential between the two rates narrowed.

Overall, the results between the two countries are quite different. The shared characteristics are: less variable interest rates, widening bid–ask spreads in the foreign exchange market, and more variable stock prices. Otherwise, the financial variables reacted differently in the two markets, with the reactions in Malaysia conforming more to those one would anticipate. In Edison and Reinhart (1999) we also consider the movement of these variables in South Korea and the Philippines to control for whether these differences arose in part as a result of the general turmoil created by the financial crisis and what might be associated with the introduction of capital controls. In general, we found that interest rate variability did not decline during the crisis period (it increased in Korea), equity price volatility was higher in both countries as the crisis unfolded, and for the Philippines market liquidity appeared to deteriorate during the crisis as bid–ask spreads on foreign exchange widened and became more volatile.[6]

12.5.2 Volatility and Capital Controls

The descriptive statistics discussed in Section 12.5.1 clearly suggested that there were important differences across regimes in second moments (i.e., variances) in for many of the financial variables analyzed. Furthermore, our theoretical priors suggested that there should be such differences. In this subsection, we focus on how capital controls and crises affect the volatility of interest rates and stock returns.

A related issue was examined in Edwards (1998). Using weekly interest rate data for Argentina, Chile, and Mexico, Edwards analyzed the consequences of the Mexican crisis for interest rate volatility in Argentina and Chile. The "Mexican spillover" dummies were statistically significant for Argentina, irrespective of the specification used, and uniformly insignificant for Chile. One possible interpretation of these

---

[6] These are unchanged for South Korea.

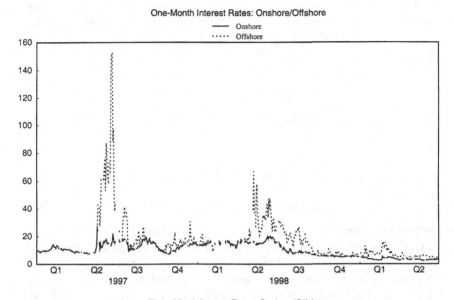

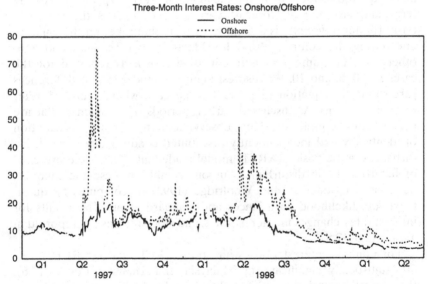

Figure 12.6. Thailand: Onshore and offshore interest rates. (*Source*: Bloomberg.)

results, he concluded, is that Chile's capital controls were effective in insulating Chile from the turmoil abroad.

In what follows, we will work with a variety of generalized autoregressive conditional heteroskedasticity (GARCH) models to examine whether there was an observed change in volatility during the capital controls episodes.[7] As before, we will contrast these results to the crisis episodes in the Philippines and South Korea where no controls were imposed during the crisis. We consider the following models:

$$r_t = \sum_{t=t-i}^{t-k} \beta_i r_{t-i} + \sum_{j=1}^{4} \gamma_j r_{jt}^* + \varepsilon_t$$

$$\sigma_{rt}^2 = \omega + dummy_c + \alpha\varepsilon_{t-1}^2 + \delta\sigma_{t-1}^2 \qquad (1)$$

and

$$\Delta r_t = \sum_{t=t-i}^{t-k} \beta_i \Delta r_{t-i} + \sum_{j=1}^{4} \gamma_j \Delta r_{jt}^* + \varepsilon_t$$

$$\sigma_{\Delta rt}^2 = \omega + dummy_c + \alpha\varepsilon_{t-1}^2 + \delta\sigma_{t-1}^2 \qquad (2)$$

where the domestic nominal interest rate is denoted by r_t, in equation (1), the foreign interest rates for the other four countries in the study are denoted by the r_{jt}^*, and the random shock is denoted by ε_t. In the variance equation, ω is the mean of the variance; the lag of the mean squared residual from the mean equation (i.e., ε_{t-1}^2) is the ARCH term, and last period's forecast variance (i.e., σ_{t-1}^2) is the GARCH term. The term $dummy_c$ is a dummy variable that takes on the value of one during the control period for Malaysia and Thailand and zero otherwise. The number of autoregressive lags, k, is reported for the cases $k = 0$, 5, and 10. We also estimate the model in first differences [Δr_t, shown in equation (2)] and for the case where r and r^* refer to equity returns. As discussed earlier, periods of turbulence that are part of our sample of daily observations render the assumption of identically and independently distributed conditionally normal disturbances in the basic GARCH model inadequate. Given the presence of heteroskedastic disturbances in our sample, we use the methods described in Bollersev and Woolridge (1992) to compute the quasi-maximum likelihood covariances and standard errors. The results for interest rates, changes in interest rates, and stock returns are reported in Tables 12.6–12.8.

For nominal interest rates, while both ARCH and GARCH terms are statistically significant in Malaysia and Thailand (Table 12.6), the capital control dummy variable is only significant for Malaysia – although this result is not robust across alternative lag specifications. In the case of Malaysia, the controls dummy variable has the anticipated negative sign, while in the case of Thailand the sign is positive,

---

[7] In all cases a GARCH (1, 1) model was estimated.

Table 12.6. Daily Interest Rate Variance Equation: Volatility Spillovers with and without Capital Controls

Country and Number of Autoregressive Lags Included	ARCH (1)	GARCH (1)	Controls Dummy
Malaysia			
0	0.503	0.559	−0.004
	(0.045)*	(0.000)*	(0.129)
5	1.464	0.117	−0.005
	(0.000)*	(0.060)**	(0.131)
10	1.442	0.136	−0.008
	(0.003)*	(0.037)*	(0.021)*
Thailand			
0	0.331	0.603	0.073
	(0.081)**	(0.000)*	(0.133)
5	0.342	0.582	0.074
	(0.062)**	(0.000)*	(0.109)
10	0.355	0.576	0.072
	(0.055)**	(0.000)*	(0.111)
Philippines			
0	0.099	0.697	−0.011
	(0.363)	(0.011)*	(0.506)
5	2.635	0.109	−0.045
	(0.002)*	(0.036)*	(0.243)
10	4.295	0.003	−0.046
	(0.001)*	(0.489)	(0.236)
South Korea			
0	0.347	0.046	0.007
	(0.018)*	(0.000)*	(0.860)
5	0.278	0.816	0.001
	(0.012)*	(0.000)*	(0.813)
10	0.275	0.816	0.001
	(0.014)*	(0.000)*	(0.775)

Notes: In all cases an ARCH (1) or a GARCH (1,1) model was estimated. Bollersev–Woolridge robust standard errors are used, with p-values reported in parentheses. The controls dummy variable takes on the value of one during the control period for Malaysia, and Thailand and zero otherwise. For the Philippines and South Korea the dummy variable takes on a value of one during the crisis period and zero otherwise.
* denotes significant at 5 percent level, and ** denotes significant at the 10 percent level.

Table 12.7. Daily Interest Rate Changes Variance Equation: Volatility Spillovers with and without Capital Controls

Country and Number of Autoregressive Lags Included	ARCH (1)	GARCH (1)	Controls Dummy
Malaysia			
0	0.465	0.583	−0.004
	(0.041)*	(0.000)*	(0.119)
5	0.543	0.495	−0.005
	(0.050)*	(0.000)*	(0.100)*
10	1.492	0.083	−0.009
	(0.001)*	(0.079)**	(0.025)*
Thailand			
0	0.316	0.601	0.078
	(0.090)**	(0.000)*	(0.136)
5	0.338	0.571	0.078
	(0.067)**	(0.000)*	(0.112)
10	0.345	0.577	0.072
	(0.058)**	(0.000)*	(0.111)
Philippines			
0	0.108	0.664	−0.013
	(0.400)	(0.078)**	(0.529)
5	0.100	0.666	−0.012
	(0.419)	(0.064)**	(0.524)
10	0.157	0.490	−0.002
	(0.292)	(0.073)**	(0.389)
South Korea			
0	0.350	0.804	−0.001
	(0.030)*	(0.000)*	(0.944)
5	0.323	0.815	−0.001
	(0.029)*	(0.000)*	(0.847)
10	0.327	0.808	−0.001
	(0.026)*	(0.000)*	(0.988)

Notes: In all cases an ARCH (1) or a GARCH (1,1) model was estimated. Bollersev–Wooldridge robust standard errors are used, with p-values reported in parentheses. The controls dummy variable takes on the value of one during the control period for Malaysia, and Thailand and zero otherwise. For the Philippines and South Korea the dummy variable takes on a value of one during the crisis period and zero otherwise.
* denotes significant at 5 percent level, and ** denotes significant at the 10 percent level.

Table 12.8. Daily Stock Returns Variance Equation: Volatility Spillovers with and without Capital Controls

Country and Number of Autoregressive Lags Included	ARCH (1)	GARCH (1)	Controls Dummy
Malaysia			
0	0.131	0.882	0.001
	(0.000)*	(0.000)*	(0.708)
5	0.129	0.884	0.001
	(0.000)*	(0.000)*	(0.738)
10	0.146	0.869	0.001
	(0.000)*	(0.000)*	(0.652)
Thailand			
0	0.140	0.818	0.002
	(0.000)*	(0.000)*	(0.082)**
5	0.148	0.805	0.002
	(0.067)**	(0.000)*	(0.072)**
10	0.137	0.828	0.002
	(0.000)*	(0.000)*	(0.079)**
Philippines			
0	0.184	0.781	0.001
	(0.000)*	(0.000)*	(0.071)**
5	0.198	0.766	0.001
	(0.000)*	(0.000)*	(0.082)**
10	0.216	0.742	0.001
	(0.000)*	(0.000)*	(0.056)**
South Korea			
0	0.086	0.910	0.001
	(0.000)*	(0.000)*	(0.156)
5	0.059	0.940	0.001
	(0.001)*	(0.000)*	(0.187)
10	0.061	0.938	0.001
	(0.001)*	(0.000)*	(0.199)

Notes: In all cases an ARCH (1) or a GARCH (1,1) model was estimated. Bollersev–Woolridge robust standard errors are used, with p-values reported in parentheses. The controls dummy variable takes on the value of one during the control period for Malaysia and Thailand and zero otherwise. For the Philippines and South Korea the dummy variable takes on a value of one during the crisis period and zero otherwise.
* denotes significant at 5 percent level, and ** denotes significant at the 10 percent level.

although not statistically significant. For the two countries that did not introduce capital controls, the crisis dummy variable is not statistically significant.

Turning next to the results for the first differences of interest rates (Table 12.7), we find the same pattern. Among the four countries we report, the dummy variable is only significant for Malaysia for most of the lag profiles used. For daily equity price returns, the control dummy is significant and positive for Thailand, indicating that the control period was associated with above-average volatility in the equity market (Table 12.8). However, it is difficult to attribute the increased volatility exclusively to the controls. Note that the crisis period in the Philippines (despite the absence of new capital account restrictions) was also associated with higher equity market volatility.

All in all, while the GARCH results do not point to across-the-board differences in volatility across capital account regimes, the three cases where the control dummies are significant (interest rates and interest rate changes in Malaysia and equity returns in Thailand) have the expected sign.

12.6 FINAL REMARKS

In this chapter we examined the recent application of capital controls in Malaysia and Thailand using monthly and daily data. First, we focused on monthly data considering broad changes in economic performance, foreign exchange reserves, and capital flows. Then we examined daily financial variables, focusing on changes in those key financial variables and testing for volatility spillovers.

The conclusion that emerges from our empirical work is that the controls used in Thailand did not appear to deliver much of what they were intended. By contrast, in the case of Malaysia, the controls did align more closely with the priors of what controls were intended to achieve – namely, greater interest rate and exchange rate stability and more policy autonomy – although initially, at least, these measures did not prevent mutual funds from exiting the country.

It should be noted that one cannot draw general policy conclusions from the results of this chapter because they are based on a scanty set of experiences. The results do suggest that the timing of capital controls and the types of controls that are applied might have something to do with the success of controls. One could speculate that Thailand's offshore banking center provided leakage and arbitrage opportunities that were absent in Malaysia. Further research on the effectiveness of capital controls should include more countries, classify the timing of controls, and differentiate between types of controls.

REFERENCES

Bollersev, Tim and Jeffrey M. Woolridge (1992). "Quasi-Maximum Likelihood Estimation and Inference in Dynamic Models with Time Varying Covariances," *Econometric Reviews* **11**:143–172.

Calvo, Guillermo A. and Carmen M. Reinhart (1999). "Fear of Floating." Mimeo, University of Maryland.

Calvo, Guillermo A. and Carlos A. Rodriguez (1979). "A Model of Exchange Rate Determination under Currency Substitution and Rational Expectations," *Journal of Political Economy* **85**(June):617–625.

Edison, Hali J. and Carmen M. Reinhart (1999). "Stopping Hot Money." Mimeo, Federal Reserve Board.

Edwards, Sebastian (1998). "Interest Rate Volatility, Contagion and Convergence: An Empirical Investigation of the Cases of Argentina, Chile, and Mexico," *Journal of Applied Economics* **1**(1):55–86.

Kaminsky, Graciela, Richard Lyons, and Sergio Schmukler (2000). "Economic Fragility, Liquidity and Risk: The Behavior of Mutual Funds during Crises." Mimeo, World Bank.

Kaminsky, Graciela and Carmen Reinhart (2000). "The Center and the Periphery: Tales of Financial Turmoil." Mimeo, University of Maryland.

Krugman, Paul (1998). "Saving Asia: It's Time to Get Radical," *Fortune*. **138**(5):74–80.

Reinhart, Carmen M. and Vincent R. Reinhart (1998), "Some Lessons for Policy Makers on the Mixed Blessing of Dealing with Capital Inflows." In M. Kahler, ed., *Financial Crises*. New York: Cornell University Press.

Reinhart, Carmen M. and Todd Smith (1998). "Too Much of a Good Thing: The Macroeconomic Effects of Taxing Capital Inflows." In R. Glick, ed., *Managing Capital Flows and Exchange Rates: Perspectives from the Pacific Basin*. New York: Cambridge University Press, pp. 436–464.

Reinhart, Vincent R. (2000). "How the Machinery of International Finance Runs with Sand in Its Wheels," *Review of International Economics* **8**(1):74–85.

Index

adverse selection: banks' loan portfolio choices, 197; in financial crises model, 215; related to foreign direct investment, 284–5; resulting from asymmetric information, 287–93

Allen, Franklin, 312

Argentina: Convertibility Plan (1991), 6; effect of Mexican peso crisis in, 6

Arifovic, Jasmina, 79n3

Asian countries: capital flow policies, 3; effect of crisis in, 18–19; exchange rate regimes (1980s, 1990s), 6; FDI flows during crisis, 283; growth in, 2; liberalization of capital account in, 3; post-crisis currency depreciation in, 384; post-crisis output growth, 28; post-crisis rejection of exchange rate pegs, 384; pre-crisis exchange rate pegs, 4; pre-crisis foreign borrowing, 21

Asian crisis: capital flows prior to and during, 4–5; currency depreciation, 347–8; difference from Latin American crisis, 387–8; differences in performances of firms during, 131–7; exchange rate-interest rate link during, 384–5; explanations for causes of, 9–12; interest rates raised, 347–8; phases and time frame of, 122–37; pre-crisis period and start of, 121–2; predicted

probability of bank and currency, 57–62

asset prices: cross-country correlation, 83–6; movements of, 86; volatility of, 83, 90

Baig, Taimur, 111–12, 113

balance of payments: Korean capital and current accounts (1970–96), 245–6; Mexican current account deficit (1994–5), 73; proposed capital account liberalization, 92

balance-of-payments crises: conditions for, 256; first-generation model of, 100. *See also* currency crises

Ball, Clifford A., 162

banks: advantages for domestic, 196; asset quality, 40–1; of creditor countries in uncertainty related to external debt, 178; financial intermediation in financial crises model, 205–7; foreign borrowing of Thai and Korean, 168–7; lending to emerging markets (1998), 91t; stock returns, 402, 411–12. *See also* banking sector; bank runs; borrowing, foreign; central banks; debt, external; foreign exchange reserves; lending, domestic

banks, Korea: asset growth (1990s), 264–5; assets denominated in foreign currencies (1987–98), 264–5; capital inflows with government guarantee, 257–71; declines in franchise values

457